THE CAMBRIDGE HANDBOOK OF ONE HEALTH AND THE LAW

This handbook is essential for legal scholars, policymakers, animal and public health professionals, and environmental advocates who want to understand and implement the One Health framework in governance and law. It explores how One Health – an approach integrating human, animal, and environmental health – can address some of the most pressing global challenges, including zoonotic diseases, biodiversity loss, climate change, and antimicrobial resistance.

Through detailed case studies, the book demonstrates how One Health is already embedded in legal and policy frameworks, evaluates its effectiveness, and offers practical guidance for improvement. It compares One Health with other interdisciplinary paradigms and existing legal frameworks, identifying valuable lessons and synergies.

The book concludes by mapping a transformative path forward, showing how One Health can be used to fundamentally reshape legal systems and their relationship with health and sustainability. This is an invaluable resource for anyone seeking innovative, equitable, and sustainable solutions to global health challenges.

KATIE WOOLASTON is a lawyer and researcher who works across the biodiversity–health nexus. Her previous award-winning book, *Ecological Vulnerability: The Law and Governance of Human–Wildlife Conflict*, was published by Cambridge University Press in 2022. She is Chair of the Technical Advisory Group for Nature4Health, and an executive editor for CUP's Research Directions: One Health.

JANE KOTZMANN is an Associate Professor at the School of Law, Deakin University. She has recently published collections entitled *The Legal Recognition of Animal Sentience* (2024, with Marcelo Rodriguez Ferrere) and *Animal Law in Australasia* (2025, with Joanna Kyriakakis). She has published articles in leading journals including the *Oxford Journal of Legal Studies, Sydney Law Review*, and *Columbia Journal of Environmental Law*.

The Cambridge Handbook of One Health and the Law

Existing Frameworks, Intersections and Future Pathways

Edited by

KATIE WOOLASTON

Green Governance Solutions, Griffith University

JANE KOTZMANN

Deakin University

CAMBRIDGE
UNIVERSITY PRESS

CAMBRIDGE
UNIVERSITY PRESS

Shaftesbury Road, Cambridge CB2 8EA, United Kingdom

One Liberty Plaza, 20th Floor, New York, NY 10006, USA

477 Williamstown Road, Port Melbourne, VIC 3207, Australia

314–321, 3rd Floor, Plot 3, Splendor Forum, Jasola District Centre, New Delhi – 110025, India

103 Penang Road, #05–06/07, Visioncrest Commercial, Singapore 238467

Cambridge University Press is part of Cambridge University Press & Assessment, a department of the University of Cambridge.

We share the University's mission to contribute to society through the pursuit of education, learning and research at the highest international levels of excellence.

www.cambridge.org
Information on this title: www.cambridge.org/9781009653718

DOI: 10.1017/9781009653732

When citing this work, please include a reference to the DOI 10.1017/9781009653732

First published 2025

Cover image: the_burtons / Moment / Getty Images

A catalogue record for this publication is available from the British Library

Library of Congress Cataloging-in-Publication Data
NAMES: Woolaston, Katie, 1983– editor. | Kotzmann, Jane, editor.
TITLE: The Cambridge handbook of One Health and the law : existing frameworks, intersections and future pathways / edited by Katie Woolaston, Green Governance Solutions, Griffith University, Jane Kotzmann, Deakin University.
DESCRIPTION: Cambridge, United Kingdom ; New York, NY : Cambridge University Press, 2025. | Includes bibliographical references and index.
IDENTIFIERS: LCCN 2025015676 | ISBN 9781009653718 (hardback) | ISBN 9781009653732 (ebook)
SUBJECTS: LCSH: One Health (Initiative) | Public health laws. | Public health laws – European Union countries. | Public health laws – South Africa. | Animal health – Law and legislation.
CLASSIFICATION: LCC K3570 .C36 2025 | DDC 344.03/21–dc23/eng/20250403
LC record available at https://lccn.loc.gov/2025015676

ISBN 978-1-009-65371-8 Hardback

Contents

Contributors

Kashish Aneja is a global health law and policy expert consulting for and leading initiatives in Asia at the O'Neill Institute for National and Global Health Law, Georgetown University. He serves as the co-secretariat, alongside the US Government, of the Procurement Negotiation & Management Sub-working Group of the GHSA Legal Preparedness Action Package. He is also a Spring 2025 Visiting Researcher at Harvard Law and a Visiting Scholar at Harvard Law School's Petrie-Flom Centre.

A practicing advocate at the Supreme Court of India and co-founder of the Society for Democratic Rights, Aneja is also on the WHO Roster of Consultants for Public Health Law and Policy. His work spans pandemic preparedness and response, global health security, NCDs risk-factor regulation, and evidence-based public health laws. He has advised international organizations like WHO, CEPI, and Gavi and governments in the Asia-Pacific. Aneja holds an LLM in Global Health Law from Georgetown University & the Graduate Institute, Geneva.

Maurizio Aragrande has a PhD in Agricultural Economics and is an Associate Professor of Agri-food Economics at the University of Bologna. His research is focused on agri-food systems and food supply chains, Animal Health Economics and One Health evaluation. He has completed evaluation studies on CAP (EU Commission, EU Parliament) and participated in various EU projects (H2020, Erasmus plus and Capacity Building, COST Actions).

Carmen Bullón Caro holds a law degree, a Masters in EU law, postgraduate studies in international trade and is completing her PhD on regulatory aspects of One Health. Following some years of work experience in public administration, she joined the FAO's Development Law Branch of the Legal Office in 2006. In her current position as Legal Officer she has provided legal assistance and advice to more than 70 countries on different areas related to One Health and sustainable agri-food production, including animal health, production and welfare, food safety and quality, plant protection and production and agriculture contracts, among others. She has publications in the areas of One Health, food safety and quality, organic agriculture, contract farming, and trade law.

Massimo Canali has a PhD in the Economics of Animal Production and is an Associate Professor of Agricultural Economics and Policy at the University of Bologna. He undertakes research on agri-food systems economics, animal health and One Health economics. He participates and plays leading roles in several European and national projects on these matters.

Elisa Cavallin is a postdoctoral researcher at Ghent University and a voluntary researcher at Hasselt University, currently working on the link between environment and health in international and EU law. She is a member of the Legal Working Group and of the Marine

Restoration Working Group of the Society for Ecological Restoration, European Chapter. She holds a Master's degree in Law, an LL.M. in International and European Law and a PhD in law. Her fields of work and interest include law and policy on environment and biodiversity, energy, agriculture, animal welfare and human health.

Francesca Coli is an international legal consultant at the FAO's Development Law Service and a member of the Sustainable Wildlife Management Programme's Legal Team. She specializes in legal analysis and research across various domains related to the One Health approach. She is also a postdoctoral researcher in agri-food and environmental law at the Sant'Anna School of Advanced Studies, where she completed her PhD with honours, writing her dissertation on implementing the One Health approach in the transition towards sustainable food systems. She also holds an LLM in Food Law and a Master's degree in Law.

Alison Durran is an associate at the O'Neill Institute's Center for Transformational Health Law. Her work focuses on the intersection of health, regulatory reform, and human rights, with a particular interest in how innovative legal frameworks can improve population health. Previously, she served as legal counsel and impact investment fellow at Grand Challenges Canada, advising on funding innovations in reproductive health, Indigenous health, and humanitarian innovation. She holds an M.P.H. from Yale University, a J.D. from the University of Toronto, and a B.A. in International Relations from the University of British Columbia.

Tony Gerrans lives in Cape Town South Africa, and has worked in government, private business and the not-for-profit sector, primarily in the agricultural and animal welfare fields. As a Principal Planner in the Restitution Research Directorate of the South African Department of Land Affairs, he was part of the team researching and advising the post-apartheid Commission on Restitution of Land Rights on the legal validity of land restitution claims filed by victims of South Africa's racially-based 'separate development' policy. He has also served as a trustee of the Humane Education Trust, the South African affiliate of Compassion in World Farming, and as legal advisor to and Chair of the Cape Animal Welfare Forum. He currently also chairs the South African Minister of Environment's Wildlife Wellbeing Forum.

Tony is now working with Humane World for Animals (formerly Humane Society International) as the Executive Director of African operations directing work across Africa in programs which protect wildlife, farmed animals, companion animals, animals used in testing, and those caught in disaster. He holds a Masters degree in Animal Law from Lewis & Clark Law School in Portland, Oregon, and has presented on animal law topics at events in the USA, across Africa and China. Tony was a 2021 Centre for Animal Law Studies Ambassador and a Visiting Fellow at the Animal Law and Policy Program at Harvard Law School in 2023.

Joshua Gilbert is a Worimi man who lives and works on country. Josh is the Assistant Director at the University of Technology's Centre for Indigenous People and Work and is completing his PhD at Charles Sturt University, focusing on the post-colonial involvement of Indigenous peoples in Western agricultural systems. He was recently recognised internationally for his work, announced in the inaugural 50 Next: People Shaping the Future of Gastronomy cohort. Josh is on the board for Indigenous Business Australia, the NSW Aboriginal Housing Office and the Australian Conservation Foundation, and is the Aboriginal Co-Chair of Reconciliation NSW.

Katherine Ginsbach is a senior associate with the Center for Transformational Health Law at the O'Neill Institute. Her primary research areas include pandemic preparedness and response legislation, global health governance, and disease surveillance. Her other areas of interest include Indigenous health law, and One Health with a specific focus on the Arctic Region.

Urias S. Goll is a legal, environmental, and natural resources practitioner. He holds a Bachelor's Degree in Biology (University of Liberia), a Master's Degree in Environmental

Economics and Management (University of York (England)), and a Bachelor of Law (LLB Hons) from the *Louis Arthur Grimes School of Law (University of Liberia)*. He has over 16 years of professional experience. During his career, he worked as the Deputy Executive Director of the Environmental Protection Agency (EPA) of Liberia, Deputy Chief of Party for the USAID Conservation Works Project, General Counsel for the Liberia Petroleum Regulatory Authority, and consultant on several programs for the UNDP and World Bank country offices. He currently serves as Lead Attorney for Extractives, Environmental, and Health law for the CMB Law Group, LLC, one of Liberia's reputable law firms. Cllr. Goll has lectured (part-time) on Environmental Law and Policy and Environmental Social Impact Assessment (ESIA) at the University of Liberia for the last 9 years.

Sam Halabi is a Professor at the Georgetown University School of Health and the Director of the Center for Transformational Health Law at Georgetown's O'Neill Institute for National and Global Health Law. His research explores One Health approaches to pandemic preparedness and prevention and with Kat Ginsbach, he leads the Global Health Security Agenda Legal Preparedness Action Package alongside the Ministry of Health of Argentina and the US Government. He is a member of the World Health Organization's Working Group on Regulatory Approaches to AI and Health. His research on the law of companies and corporations has been cited by both federal and state courts in the U.S.

Jane Kotzmann is an Associate Professor in the School of Law at Deakin University, cross-theme lead for animal and environmental protection with the Centre for Law as Protection at Deakin University, and Executive Committee member of the Australasian Animal Law Teachers' and Researchers' Association (AALTRA). Jane's research focuses on how laws can be strengthened to better protect animals, including through the recognition of animal rights. In 2024, the AALTRA Australian Animal Law Research Prize was awarded to Jane for her paper, 'Sentience and Intrinsic Worth as a Pluralist Foundation for Fundamental Animal Rights' published in the *Oxford Journal of Legal Studies*. Jane's article titled 'Recognising the Sentience of Animals in Law: A Justification and Framework for Australian States and Territories' published in the *Sydney Law Review* was given an Australian Legal Research Award in 2022 for Best Early Career Research Article. In 2024, Jane instituted units in animal law at Deakin University.

Claire Lajaunie is a researcher in environmental law and investigates the inter-linkages between biodiversity and health and their evolution due to global changes through the study on Global Environmental Law, governance and the associated ethical issues. She works for the French National Institute of Health and Medical Research at the LPED – Population-Environment-Development Laboratory in Marseille, France. She is also an Affiliate Researcher at the Strathclyde Centre for Environmental Law and Governance. Claire is in the roster of experts for the FAO as a Specialist of One Health. She is co-investigator on the One Ocean Hub and works on the One Health approach in relation to the ocean.

Bridget Lewis is an Associate Professor in the School of Law at Queensland University of Technology. Her research explores various issues at the intersection of the environment and human rights, including climate change, constitutional and regional environmental rights and intergenerational justice. Bridget's first book Environmental Human Rights and Climate Change: Current Status and Future Prospects (Springer, 2018) critically examines the concept of a human right to a healthy environment and its relevance to the climate crisis. Her recent research explores the human rights of future generations and children's climate litigation. Her next book, titled Environmental Rights for Future Generations, is published by Cambridge University Press in 2025.

Catherine Machalaba is a Planetary Health Scientist at The Nature Conservancy, working under the Human Dimensions Science Team. She serves on the One Health High-Level Expert Panel advising the Food and Agriculture Organization, United Nations Environment Programme, World Health Organization, and World Organisation for Animal Health in their collaborative work. She is also active in the American Public Health Association, IUCN's expert Commissions, and Future Earth. She holds a Masters in Public Health and a PhD in Environmental and Planetary Health Sciences. Catherine has served as a consultant to the World Bank's Agriculture, Health, and Environment global practices, interned with the Vermont Office of the Attorney General, and was a Principal Scientist at a One Health-focused organization, working closely with partners in Ghana and Liberia. Her work focuses on strengthening the environment sector role in One Health, including in protected and conserved areas.

Fiona McDonald is a Professor in the Faculty of Law at Te Herenga Waka/Victoria University of Wellington in Aotearoa/New Zealand. She is an Adjunct Associate Professor at the Department of Bioethics at Dalhousie University, Canada. Her area of expertise is in health law, focusing on the regulation of health systems.

Jack Nagy is the founder of Hello Bridges, a research and automation consultancy for non-profits and NGOs. He has previously worked as a regulatory compliance writer and analyst (LexisNexis) and as a tender and grant writing specialist (Bright Circle). Jack is currently completing his MBA at the Queensland University of Technology and recently completed a QUT x MIT collaboration project evaluating sustainability initiatives for the Brisbane 2032 Olympics.

Stefania Negri holds a PhD in International Law and is tenured Associate Professor of International Law (qualified as full professor by the Italian Ministry of University and Research) at the School of Law of the University of Salerno, where she teaches Public International Law and International Health and Environmental Law. Professor Negri is the current President of the European Association of Health Law; Director of the Jean Monnet Centre of Excellence "New Visions of the European Union's Role in Global Health"; Coordinator of th Jean Monnet Module "One Health: Global and EU Perspectives"; founder and director of the 'Observatory on Human Rights: Bioethics, Health, Environment'; member of the ILA Global Health Law Committee; co-founder of the Interest Group on International Health Law at the European Society of International Law; co-founder of the Interest Group on International and EU Health Law at the Italian Society of International Law. She was awarded by the European Commission a Jean Monnet Chair in European Health, Environmental and Food Safety Law (2016–2019), co-funded by the EU Erasmus Programme. In 2021, Professor Negri was appointed by the Italian Ministry of Health as a member of the Italian expert delegation at the Global Health Security Agenda (Action package on Legal preparedness). Her research interests focus on international and European health law, international and European environmental law, human rights and bioethics.

Rajesh K. Reddy directs the Animal Law Program at the Center for Animal Law Studies at Lewis & Clark Law School, where he also serves as an Assistant Professor of Law, teaching Animal Legal Philosophy, International Animal Law, and Emerging Topics in Animal Law, among others. Outside of Lewis & Clark, he sits on the boards of Minding Animals International and the International Coalition for Animal Protection.

Sam Roach is a Lecturer in the School of Law at the Queensland University of Technology. His research interests lie at the intersection of regulation and public health, with a particular focus on vaccination. A central theme of his work is the role of regulation in promoting individual capabilities to support public health objectives. His book, Vaccination and Inequality: The Capability to Choose (under contract with CUP), examines the relationship between inequality and vaccine hesitancy, exploring how regulation can help address this issue by empowering individuals to make informed health decisions.

Michelle Rourke is an Australian Research Council (ARC) Discovery Early Career Research Award (DECRA) Fellow at Griffith Law School, Griffith University. She spent ten years as a Scientific Officer in the Royal Australian Army Medical Corps where she researched mosquito-transmitted viruses of importance to the Australian Defence Force. She completed her doctoral studies in international law at Griffith University and as a Fulbright Scholar at the O'Neill Institute for National and Global Health Law at Georgetown University. Her PhD thesis examined how international access and benefit-sharing (ABS) laws under the United Nations' Convention on Biological Diversity and its Nagoya Protocol impact access to pathogen samples and associated information, including genetic sequence data. Michelle is a member of the Digital Sequence Information (DSI) Scientific Network, the Global Health Law Consortium and a non-resident Affiliate of the Center for Global Health Science and Security at Georgetown University.

Jeff Sebo is Associate Professor of Environmental Studies, Affiliated Professor of Bioethics, Medical Ethics, Philosophy, and Law, Director of the Center for Environmental and Animal Protection, Director of the Center for Mind, Ethics, and Policy, and Co-Director of the Wild Animal Welfare Program at New York University. His research focuses on animal minds, ethics, and policy; AI minds, ethics, and policy; and global health and climate ethics and policy. He is the author of *The Moral Circle* and *Saving Animals, Saving Ourselves* and co-author of *Chimpanzee Rights* and *Food, Animals, and the Environment*. He is also a board member at Minding Animals International, an advisory board member at the Insect Welfare Research Society, an advisor at Eleos AI, and a senior affiliate at the Institute for Law & AI. In 2024 *Vox* included him on its Future Perfect 50 list of "thinkers, innovators, and changemakers who are working to make the future a better place."

Cassandra Seery is an Associate Professor at the NIKERI Institute (formerly the Institute of Koorie Education) at Deakin University, having previously worked at the University of Melbourne and the Victorian Public Service. She currently serves as a member of the Victorian Government's Stolen Generations Independent Assessment Panel. #AlwaysWasAlwaysWillBe

Toni Sims has worked as a researcher, writer, and editor for a variety of academic and nonprofit institutions. She currently works as a researcher with the NYU Wild Animal Welfare and Mind, Ethics, and Policy programs. Previously, she worked as an editor at the Center for AI Safety, a research fellow at Longview Philanthropy, and the managing editor of *Social Theory and Practice*. She was also the director of research for Animal Charity Evaluators, where she led charity evaluations and managed two grant programs. Toni studied philosophy at NYU and received an MA in philosophy from Georgia State University.

Jessica C. Tselepy works in reconceptualising and reforming the treatment of non-human animals in both national legislation and international instruments. Jessica is completing her PhD at the University of Melbourne (Melbourne Law School). She has previously received the Animal Law Advocates Advanced Degree Scholarship to complete the LLM in Animal Law at Lewis & Clark Law School (Center for Animal Law Studies) in 2022/23. She has also completed a Juris Doctor at Bond University with First Class Distinction (specialising in International Law), and a Bachelor of Arts (International Relations and Psychology) at The University of Queensland. Jessica has worked on legal research projects for the Global Animal Law Association and the World Federation for Animals and conducted her practical legal training with the RSPCA Queensland Prosecutions Team.

Elien Verniers is a postdoctoral researcher at the law faculty of the University of Ghent (Belgium), where she teaches the course Animal & Law. Within the department of European,

Public and International Law, she is part of the Centre for Environmental Law. In October 2022 she obtained her doctoral degree with her PhD 'Towards new legal instruments for animal welfare'. During her academic career she received several awards such as the 2022 vdk-bank award on sustainable development, the 2022 Cambridge Centre for Animal Rights Law Essay award and the 2021 Young Legal researcher award.

Alisa E. White is the incoming LLM Teaching Fellow and Lecturer in Law in the Environmental Law and Policy Program at Stanford Law School (starting August 2025). She holds a JD from Yale Law School, a Masters of Environmental Science from Yale School of the Environment, and a BA from Dartmouth College. Her research focuses on climate change law, local land conservation, property and land use law, Indigenous land return, and animal law, among other topics. She is a co-founder of Law Students for Climate Accountability and previously served as a Legal Fellow at the Guarini Center on Environmental, Energy, and Land Use Law at New York University School of Law.

Katie Woolaston is an inter-disciplinary researcher and lawyer. She holds a Masters in Law (specialising in Human Rights & Social Justice) from the University of New South Wales, and a PhD in Environmental Law from Griffith University. Dr Woolaston's research is focused on international and domestic wildlife law and the regulation of the human-wildlife relationship. She is particularly interested in using the social sciences to resolve long-held and deeply-rooted attitudes and values that are contrary to conservation and embedding such processes in law and policy. Dr Woolaston's current research is focused on human-wildlife conflicts, and the integration of One Health approaches in wildlife trade and environmental policy in the wake of COVID-19. She was an expert on the Intergovernmental Science-Policy Platform on Biodiversity and Ecosystem Services (IPBES) panel concerning Biodiversity and Pandemics, and is on the Technical Advisory Group of the United Nations Environment Program's 'Nature4Health' Initiative. Her first book, titled 'Ecological Vulnerability: The Law and Governance of Human-Wildlife Relationships' was published by Cambridge University Press in 2022.

Helen Yu is an Associate Professor and the Associate Director of the Value-Based Health and Care Academy at the School of Management, Swansea University. Her research focuses on how the law can support the responsible development and sustainable implementation of new innovations to address societal challenges, particularly in the biomedical and healthcare fields. Helen holds a degree in neuroscience and practiced as an intellectual property lawyer and registered patent agent in Canada before pursuing an academic career.

Foreword

Our planet is amid some of the most complex environmental and development challenges in its history. As a conservation ecologist working with the United Nations Environment Programme, and previously with the United States Agency for International Development and the World Wildlife Fund, I have witnessed first-hand the multiple impacts of biodiversity loss, pollution, and climate change on the health of all species, including humans. For example, in Southern Africa the degradation of river basins, particularly the forested areas in upstream headwaters, has led to downstream die-offs of important species and contributed to disease in aquatic species consumed by humans, with human health and nutrition implications. These complex interactions of nature, animals, plants, and people, while not always easily understood, have important consequences for our ability to thrive on the one planet we all call home.

Many have come to recognise that human health is inextricably linked to the health of other animals and the planet. One Health is a policy approach based on recognition of this principle – that you cannot have healthy people in an unhealthy environment and that the health of humans, animals, and ecosystems are deeply intertwined. Addressing one aspect without considering the others will only lead to incomplete or unsustainable solutions.

One Health as a theory has existed since at least 2002, and probably much longer, but has taken on more prominence since the onset of COVID-19. It is being used as a premise in new international frameworks and agreements, including the Kunming–Montreal Global Biodiversity Framework and the International Agreement on Pandemic Prevention, Preparedness and Response currently under development, by multiple international organisations, and by various governments around the world. One Health offers various conceptual benefits, including governing for public health in a way that simultaneously protects the natural environments that we rely on. The practical benefits of One Health include the mobilisation of multiple governance sectors and the advancement of multidisciplinary collaboration. The potential of a One Health framework is immense. It could change the way we govern our own relationship with the natural world and could lead to health being considered as a matter of social justice.

The One Health framework, however, is still developing, and the limits of the approach as currently adopted continue to be revealed. For example, the framework, and its development and utilisation, still fall heavily within the realm of public and animal health and remain inherently anthropocentric. Wild animal, plant, and ecosystem perspectives are often neglected, particularly where multispecies communities are the centre of potential disease spread. In general, the many benefits of nature for health and well-being are overlooked in favour of a narrower focus on eradicating specific zoonotic diseases and antimicrobial resistance. Institutional silos and barriers between human, animal, and environmental disciplines persist. Additionally, and prominently for the purpose of this book, One Health has not been considered within a law and policy context on a broad scale. The need to better develop a legal, policy, and governance grounding for One Health was the subject of several plenary sessions at the recent 8th World One Health Congress (2024, Cape Town, South Africa), and was helpfully explored by some of the authors of this book in their panel on 'Science Policy Interface – One Health and the Law: Existing Frameworks, Intersections and Future Pathways'.

Considering this need, this book aims to give the theoretical paradigm of One Health a grounding in law and governance. It discusses how One Health may be institutionalised in a productive, just, and effective way, throughout governance and legal structures, to achieve a more holistic accounting of its purpose. The authors explore and analyse the ways that One Health is already embedded in law and policy; consider what One Health frameworks can learn from, and contribute to, other legal theories, concepts, and practice; and map a path forward for a One Health framework in law and policy.

Because the potential of a One Health approach is so great, the promise offered by this book is similarly important. It offers analysis and frameworks which, if implemented, would enable a better adoption of One Health, one that is truer to its holistic and systemic underlying principles. In this respect, I am grateful to the editors for putting together this work to further advance practical applications of a true One Health approach.

Doreen Robinson

Acknowledgements

The editors would like to thank each of the contributors to this volume for their thoughtful and engaging work; Tobias Ginsberg and Gemma Smith at Cambridge University Press for their patient and supportive guidance; and Aleesha Simoncini, Hayden Clift, and Sophie Farnsworth for their excellent research assistance.

Thanks also to the organisers of the 8th World One Health Congress for facilitating the panel discussion entitled 'Science Policy Interface – One Health and the Law: Existing Frameworks, Intersections and Future Pathways' involving contributors to this volume.

Table of Legislation

INTERNATIONAL TREATIES

DOMESTIC LEGISLATION

Australia

Chile

India

Liberia

Lithuania

Netherlands

South Africa

Tanzania

Abbreviations

4WL	four-way linking
ABS	access and benefit-sharing
ACB	ASEAN Centre for Biodiversity
ACCAHZ	ASEAN Coordinating Centre for Animal Health and Zoonoses
ACCHOs	Aboriginal Community Controlled Health Organisations
ACDC	Australian Centre for Disease Control
ACPHEED	ASEAN Centre for Public Health Emergencies and Emerging Diseases
AIPED	National Integrated Operational Program on Avian Influenza, Pandemic Preparedness and Emerging Infectious Diseases
AMA	American Medical Association
AMC	Autlán Mining Company
AMR	antimicrobial resistance
ANAW	Africa Network for Animal Welfare
APAP	agricultural policy action plan
ASEAN	Association of Southeast Asian Nations
ASFV	African swine fever virus
ATMPs	advanced therapy medical products
AU-IBAR	African Union Inter-African Bureau for Animal Resources
AVMA	American Veterinary Medical Association
CAP	common agricultural policy
CBD	Convention on Biological Diversity
CBTT	capacity building and technology transfer
CIC	International Council for Game and Wildlife Conservation
CITES	Convention on International Trade in Endangered Species of Fauna and Flora
CMS	Convention on the Conservation of Migratory Species of Wild Animals
CoH	Centre for One Health
COP	conference of the parties
CRC	Convention on the Rights of the Child
CRPD	Convention on the Rights of Persons with Disabilities
C-TAP	COVID-19 Health Technology Access Pool
DALRRD	Department of Agriculture, Land Reform and Rural Development
DFFE	Department of Forestry, Fisheries and the Environment

DOH	Department of Health
DSI	digital sequence information
EA	EcoHealth Alliance
EAFRD	European Agricultural Fund for Rural Development
EAGF	European Agricultural Guarantee Fund
ECDC	European Centre for Disease Prevention and Control
EEA	European Environment Agency
EFSA	European Food Safety Authority
EI	EcoHealth International
EIA	environmental impact assessment
EID	emerging infectious disease
EMA	European Medicines Agency
EPA	Environmental Protection Agency (of Liberia)
EPBC Act	Environment Protection and Biodiversity Conservation Act 1999 (Cth), Australia
EPML	Environmental Protection and Management Law of Liberia
ESIA	environmental and social impact assessment
FAO	Food and Agriculture Organization
FPIC	free, prior, and informed consent
FSC	Forest Stewardship Council
FVO	Food and Veterinary Office
GAEC	good agricultural and environmental practices
GAP	global action plan
GATT	General Agreement on Tariffs and Trade
GBF	Global Biodiversity Framework
GI	green infrastructure
GISN	Global Influenza Surveillance Network
GISRS	Global Influenza Surveillance and Response System
GSDR	Global Sustainable Development Report
HealthDEEP	Health, Disease Ecology, Environment, and Policy
HoPE-LVB	Health of People and Environment in the Lake Victoria Basin
HPAI	highly pathogenic avian influenza
HPED	highly pathogenic and emerging diseases
IAEH	International Association for Ecology and Health
IARDC	Indigenous Agricultural Research and Development Corporation
ICAP	International Coalition for Animal Protection
ICCPR	International Covenant on Civil and Political Rights
ICESCR	International Covenant on Economic, Social and Cultural Rights
IDRC	International Development Research Centre
IHR	International Health Regulations
ILM	indigenous land management
IMCAPI	Interministerial Conference on Animal and Pandemic Influenza
INB	intergovernmental negotiating body
IP	intellectual property
IPBES	Intergovernmental Science-Policy Platform on Biodiversity and Ecosystem Services
IPPC	International Plant Protection Convention

ITPGRFA	International Treaty on Plant Genetic Resources for Food and Agriculture
IUCN	International Union for Conservation of Nature
JIACRA	joint interagency antimicrobial consumption and resistance analysis
LMIC	low- and middle-income countries
LVB	Lake Victoria Basin
LVBC	Lake Victoria Basin Commission
MA	Millenium Ecosystem Assessment
M&E	monitoring and evaluation
MEAs	multilateral environmental agreements
MEFCC	Ministry of Environment, Forest and Climate Change
MERS-CoV	Middle East respiratory syndrome coronavirus
Mn	manganese
NACCHO	National Aboriginal Community Controlled Health Organisation
NAPs	national action plans
NBSAPs	national biodiversity strategies and action plans
NOHF	National One Health Forum
NRCP	National Rabies Control Program
OECMs	other effective area-based conservation measures
OFFLU	animal influenza network
OHEJP	One Health European Joint Programme
OHHLEP	One Health High-Level Expert Panel
OH JPA	Quadripartite One Health Joint Plan of Action
OHN	One Health networks
OHP	One Health Partnership for Zoonoses
OIE	Office international des épizooties, former name of the World Organisation for Animal Health (WOAH)
OPI	National Integrated Operational Program on Avian and Human Influenza
PABS	pathogen access and benefit-sharing
PCAs	protected and conserved areas
PHA	Planetary Health Alliance
PHE	planetary health equity
PIP	pandemic influenza preparedness
PPPR	pandemic prevention, preparedness, and response
PREZODE	preventing zoonotic disease emergence
RAPs	reconciliation action plans
R&D	research and development
RCZI	Roadmap to Combat Zoonoses in India
RRI	responsible research and innovation
SARS	severe acute respiratory syndrome
SDGs	Sustainable Development Goals
SMR	statutory management requirements
SPS	Sanitary and Phytosanitary Agreement
TrACSS	Quadripartite Global Database for Tracking Antimicrobial Resistance Country Self-Assessment Survey
UDAR	Universal Declaration of Animal Rights
UDAW	Universal Declaration on Animal Welfare
UN	United Nations

UNAPP	United Nations Animal Protection Programme
UNCAHP	United Nations Convention on Animal Health and Protection
UNCCD	United Nations Convention to Combat Desertification
UNDRIP	United Nations Declaration on the Rights of Indigenous Peoples
UNEA	United Nations Environment Assembly
UNEA-4	(Fourth) United Nations Environment Assembly
UNEA-5	(Fifth) United Nations Environment Assembly
UNEAPP	United Nations Environmental and Animal Protection Programme
UNEP	United Nations Environment Programme
UN ESCAP	United Nations Economic and Social Commission for Asia and the Pacific
UNESCO	United Nations Educational, Scientific and Cultural Organization
UNESCO-IOC	UNESCO Intergovernmental Oceanographic Commission
UNFCCC	United Nations Framework Convention on Climate Change
UNIDROIT	International Institute for the Unification of Private Law
UNODA	UN Office for Disarmament Affairs
USAID	US Agency for International Development
VBHC	value-based health and care
WASH	water, sanitation and hygiene
WCO	World Customs Organization
WCS	Wildlife Conservation Society
WFA	World Federation for Animals
WHA	World Health Assembly
WHC	Convention Concerning the Protection of the World Cultural and Natural Heritage
WHO	World Health Organization
WIPO	World Intellectual Property Organisation
WOAH	World Organisation for Animal Health
WTO	World Trade Organization
ZDU	Zoonotic Disease Unit

1

Introduction

Why One Health Needs to Engage with Law

Katie Woolaston and Jane Kotzmann

In an increasingly interconnected world, the health of humans, animals, and ecosystems must be viewed, not in isolation, but rather as an intricate web shaped by politics, anthropogenic systems, and relationships. This book is concerned with One Health, an approach that recognises this interconnectedness in seeking to optimise the health of humans, animals, and the environment. The central premise of this book is that because legal frameworks shape these interconnections, a deliberate engagement with legal frameworks is essential to realising the transformative potential of the One Health approach.

One Health as a theoretical framework has existed since at least 2002, but the values underlying the base concept have been around for millennia. Essentially, the framework promotes the interdependence of environmental, animal, and human health, and provides a method of collaboration between these areas to ensure all three areas are integrated into public health decision-making. With that said, it should be noted that Indigenous ways of knowing and being constitute the original and ultimate One Health framework (see Chapter 12), and traditional and local community forms of knowledge remain vital to the Western conceptualisation of One Health.

In modern history, the Western conceptualisation of One Health has been derived from 'One Medicine', a concept that emerged in the mid twentieth century and encouraged collaboration between human and animal medical professions.[1] The term 'One Medicine' was coined by parasitologist Calvin Schwabe to emphasise the connection between human and non-human health and the need for collaboration to prevent and respond to diseases impacting individuals across species.[2] The One Medicine approach evolved over time into more extensive and inclusive One Health frameworks,[3] which reach beyond consideration of zoonotic disease transmission to encompass ecological and environmental factors that influence health in humans and animals. Today, One Health has become a key focus of the global health agenda and underpins the work of the One Health Quadripartite, composed of the World Health Organization, the Food and Agriculture Organization of the United Nations (FAO), the United Nations Environment Programme, and the World Organisation for Animal Health, plus the One Health High-Level Expert Panel (OHHLEP), which advises these bodies on One Health issues.

1 Tracey A King, 'The One Medicine Concept: Its Emergence from History as a Systematic Approach to Re-Integrate Human and Veterinary Medicine' (2021) 5(5) *Emerging Topics in Life Sciences* 643, 643.

2 Centers for Disease Control and Prevention, 'One Health History'. Available at www.cdc.gov/one-health/about/one-health-history.html.

3 See Angela Cassidy, 'Humans, Other Animals and "One Health" in the Early Twenty-First Century' in Abigail Woods, Michael Bresalier, Angela Cassidy, and Rachel Mason Dentinger (eds.), *Animals and the Shaping of Modern Medicine: One Health and Its Histories* (Palgrave Macmillan 2018) 193, 198.

Broadly understood, One Health holds tremendous potential to help address numerous global challenges. Because of its initial developmental focus, One Health continues to centre largely on epidemiology and infectious disease surveillance. In this respect, around 70 per cent of all emerging infectious diseases are passed on to humans from non-human animals (known as spillover).[4] For example, the COVID-19 pandemic in 2020–2023 is widely accepted to have originated in bats. Moreover, the spread of disease is frequently aided by environmental changes, such as deforestation, intensification of agriculture, urbanisation, and climate change. Economic modelling and projections have suggested that investing in One Health for the purposes of disease control, as compared to business-as-usual approaches, could save between fifteen and thirty billion US dollars per year.[5] One Health is also recognised as having the potential to help address issues of antimicrobial resistance (AMR),[6] food safety and security,[7] biodiversity loss,[8] and climate change.[9]

Most recently, One Health was the central theoretical foundation to the Global Action Plan on Biodiversity and Health, agreed at the Convention on Biological Diversity's sixteenth conference of the parties in Cali, Colombia.[10] That document again reiterates the importance of considering law, policy, and governance mechanisms across the biodiversity to health nexus. Undoubtedly, it is becoming increasingly important for lawyers and policy-makers to consider the details, methods, and impacts of the One Health across disciplines and sectors.

1.1 DEFINING ONE HEALTH AND ONE HEALTH GOVERNANCE

As noted above, One Health can be understood in varying ways, both narrow and broad. In this collection, different authors have taken different approaches to their understanding and usage of the term. Many authors have adopted a One Health definition consistent with that of the OHHLEP. Pursuant to this definition:

> One Health is an integrated, unifying approach that aims to sustainably balance and optimize the health of people, animals, and ecosystems. It recognizes the health of humans, domestic and wild animals, plants, and the wider environment (including ecosystems) are closely linked and interdependent.
>
> The approach mobilizes multiple sectors, disciplines, and communities at varying levels of society to work together to foster well-being and tackle threats to health and ecosystems, while addressing the collective need for healthy food, water, energy, and air, taking action on climate change and contributing to sustainable development.[11]

[4] Joel Henrique Ellwanger and Jose Artur Bogo Chies, 'Zoonotic Spillover: Understanding Basic Aspects for Better Prevention' (2021) 44(1 Suppl 1) *Genetics and Molecular Biology* 1.

[5] World Bank, *People, Pathogens and Our Planet: The Economics of One Health* (World Bank 2012) 22–23.

[6] Maria Elena Velazquez-Meza, Miguel Galarde-López, Berta Carrillo-Quiróz, and Celia Mercedes Alpuche-Aranda, 'Antimicrobial Resistance: One Health Approach' (2022) 15(3) *Veterinary World* 743.

[7] Sara N Garcia, Bennie I Osburn, and Michele T Jay-Russell, 'One Health for Food Safety, Food Security, and Sustainable Food Production' (2020) 4(1) *Frontiers in Sustainable Food Systems* 1.

[8] Secretariat of the Convention on Biological Diversity, *Global Biodiversity Outlook* 5 (2020) 21. Available at: www.cbd.int/gbo5.

[9] OHHLEP, 'Climate Change and One Health' (2018) 365(11) *FEMS Microbiology Letters* 1.

[10] Katie Woolaston, Bridget Lewis, Ashley van Waardenberg, et al., 'Mapping Australian One Health Activities and Expertise' (2024) QUT Centre for Justice Briefing Paper.

[11] One Health High-Level Expert Panel (OHHLEP) et al., 'One Health: A New Definition for a Sustainable and Healthy Future' (2022) 18(6) *PLoS Pathogens* 1.

In relation to this definition, Francesca Coli, Maurizio Aragrande, and Massimo Canali (Chapter 6) assert that 'the definition enshrines the broadening of the scope of One Health and embraces it as a valuable approach to be applied across the board to global and national threats at the human–animal–ecosystem interface, but also to sustainability challenges'. Other authors have drawn upon a further expanded understanding of One Health. The editors are of the view that One Health definitions are limiting, and that the principles and values of One Health are more informative for a framework than a definition can be.

What is clear is that One Health is not a framework that is limited to the prevention of, and response to, zoonotic disease. The interlinkages between animal, environmental, and human health go far beyond this narrow focus. For example, mental health is linked to greenspace and engagement with nature,[12] and premature human deaths from air pollution are well documented.[13] Broader human–wildlife conflicts, such as crop-raiding, can lead to an increase in poverty, a driver of health issues.[14] This conflict, though, is increasing because of anthropogenic changes to ecosystems, a driver that is also instrumental in recent increases in zoonotic spillover.[15] Really, there are no limits to the number of issues that can and should be addressed with a One Health approach. What this means, and what you will see in this book, is that any discussion of One Health limited to disease surveillance, data sharing, and increasing laboratory capacity (as well as the other, more common usages of the phrase) are not representative of all that One Health is and all that it can be. *One Health has the potential to be a framework that fundamentally changes the way that humanity views and governs its relationship with the planet.*

This broader understanding of the *potential* of One Health is being increasingly recognised. The FAO Committee on Agriculture recently noted that '[o]perationalization efforts to date have often … focused on specific health-dominated agendas, e.g., AMR, zoonotic diseases, plant pests and agrochemical risk reduction'; however, One Health collaborative capacity permits 'linking in areas such as biodiversity, microbiome, clean water, soils and air, [and] can help with the promotion of efficient, inclusive, resilient and sustainable agrifood systems and healthy ecosystems'.[16] To realise this ambition, One Health must be embedded in legal, policy, and governance frameworks. In this respect, One Health governance refers to 'the establishment of structured mechanisms and processes that enable effective coordination, collaboration, and decision-making among diverse stakeholders'.[17]

1.2 LAW, POLICY, AND GOVERNANCE: OVERLOOKED ASPECTS OF ONE HEALTH FRAMEWORKS

While One Health, as a conceptual framework, has been around for decades, it has taken on more prominence since the onset of COVID-19. It is being used as a central premise in new international agreements, within multiple international organisations, and by various governments around the world. The One Health approach provides significant conceptual advantages,

[12] Jo Barton and Mike Rogerson, 'The Importance of Greenspace for Mental Health' (2017) 14(4) *BJPsych International* 79.

[13] Health Effects Institute, *State of Global Air/2024* (2024) 4.

[14] Wisdom Galley and Brandon P Anthony, 'Beyond Crop-Raiding: Unravelling the Broader Impacts of Human–Wildlife Conflict on Rural Communities' (2024) 74 *Environmental Management* 590.

[15] Christopher J Schell et al., 'The Evolutionary Consequences of Human–Wildlife Conflict in Cities' (2020) 14(1) *Evolutionary Applications* 178.

[16] FAO Committee on Agriculture, *One Health and Related Policy and Technical Guidance* (COAG/2022/7, 2022). Available at: nj006en.pdf.

[17] Darlington David Faijue et al., 'Constructing a One Health Governance Architecture: A Systematic Review and Analysis of Governance Mechanisms for One Health' (2024) 34(6) *European Journal of Public Health* 1086–1094, 1087.

enabling governance that prioritises public health while safeguarding the natural environments upon which we depend. Its practical benefits are equally compelling, encompassing coordination between diverse governance sectors and fostering multidisciplinary collaboration. By reimagining how we manage our relationship with the natural world, the One Health framework holds transformative potential, framing public health as an integral aspect of social justice. The One Health framework remains a work in progress, with its limitations becoming increasingly evident. For instance, its development and application are largely confined to the public health domain, rendering it predominantly anthropocentric. This focus often overlooks the perspectives of animals, especially in the context of multispecies communities that are central to potential disease transmission. Furthermore, and particularly relevant to this collection, the One Health approach has yet to be explored extensively within broader legal and policy contexts.

Increasingly, scholars are drawing attention to the fact that One Health as a conceptual framework is difficult to implement into existing governance structures.[18] While difficult, the task is not impossible, and One Health paradigms are already being used at different levels of governance and at different scales around the world. Indeed, the OHHLEP recently released a 'theory of change', suggesting that one pathway forward involves establishing a governance framework and models of One Health governance structures, legislation, and networks.[19] Additionally, a General Assembly resolution of 9 September 2024 recognises that AMR is one of the most urgent global health threats and development challenges of our time and notes that 'sustainable, efficient and accountable governance structures at local, national, regional and global levels are critical to an effective, coordinated and inclusive multisectoral response, including through a One Health approach'.[20]

There has, however, been very little attempt to engage in a practical discussion of how One Health may be institutionalised in a productive, just, and effective way, throughout governance and legal structures, to achieve a more holistic accounting of its purpose. A recent systematic review of governance mechanisms for One Health found that out of the 1,277 studies screened there were only nine eligible studies of One Health governance mechanisms according to stated criteria.[21] Instead, One Health as a concept remains under-utilised and continues to focus on single areas of scientific endeavour, such as disease surveillance, and medical and other responses to disease outbreak, such as the development and distribution of vaccines. While these dimensions are critical to the success of One Health frameworks, they do overshadow critical governance issues.

Many scientific contributions to the One Health literature continue to identify the need for 'multisectoral governance', but so far lawyers, and the legal discipline, have had very little to do with developing and embedding these approaches around the world.[22] For One Health to fully achieve its potential, legal and policy frameworks must be more fully incorporated, as they are fundamental to the creation of collaborative mechanisms, enforceable standards, coordinated responses, and long-term sustainability.

[18] See generally Mishal S Kahn et al., 'The Growth and Strategic Functioning of One Health Networks: A Systematic Analysis' (2018) 2(6) *Lancet Planet Health* 264.

[19] Osman Dar et al., *One Health Theory of Change* (OHHLEP 2018) 15–16.

[20] UNGA Res A/79/L.5 (30 September 2024) para 17.

[21] Although note this study had limited geographical scope: Faijue et al., 'Constructing a One Health Governance Architecture' 1088.

[22] See for example Hong Tham Pham and Minh-Hoang Tran, 'One Health: An Effective and Ethical Approach to Leptospirosis Control in Australia' (2022) 7(11) *Tropical Medicine and Infectious Disease* 1.

1.3 THE VALUE OF LAW IN PROGRESSING ONE HEALTH

It is not possible to have a holistic approach to solving a wicked problem like pandemics and emerging infectious diseases without considering law, policy, and governance. This is true for both the individual, disciplinary issues that arise under the One Health banner, such as wildlife surveillance, but also true for ensuring collaboration and coordination across disciplines and governance areas. In any single disciplinary context, laws and governance are crucial for creating coherent policies, enforcing compliance, and ensuring sustainable outcomes. Without embedding these things into law, we cannot guarantee that One Health projects will have institutional support and longevity and be able to be upscaled as needed.

Of course, in our globalised world, pandemics and infectious disease do not respect borders, nor do the drivers or spillover and other public-health-related issues such as climate change, pollution, and environmental destruction. International legal frameworks and treaties, such as the *International Health Regulations*, the *United Nations Framework Convention on Climate Change*, the *Sanitary and Phytosanitary Agreement*, and the *Convention on Biological Diversity*, amongst many others, provide platforms for countries to collaborate on addressing things like the drivers of disease spillover, disease surveillance, and response. Yet, without robust governance structures at the national level to enforce compliance with these agreements, the effectiveness of international coordination can be undermined, leading to gaps in One Health solutions.

It is noteworthy that governance has been used to evaluate One Health performance.[23] Various legal factors contribute to good governance, which in turn can significantly impact a country's ability to implement global health governance. Key indicators of a good governance system for One Health include the existence of the rule of law, transparency in decision-making, governance responsiveness to emergencies, a consensus-orientated approach to governance, equity and inclusiveness, efficiency and effectiveness.[24]

Legal aspects of One Health are not just complementary but foundational to the success of One Health initiatives and add to the value of the One Health approach. Ensuring cross-sectoral coordination across the many areas relevant to, and necessary for, appropriate One Health governance is crucial to long-term success. Engaging law appropriately is necessary to ensuring that legal tools provide an opportunity for the radical changes required for an expanded application of the One Health framework, instead of slowing the process down and delaying substantive action.[25]

1.4 ONE HEALTH GOVERNANCE BARRIERS

The barriers within the governance of One Health are much the same as the barriers and challenges within One Health itself. First, there is a lack of attention to what is often referred to as 'deep' or 'upstream' prevention, or, as the OHHLEP defines it, the 'ecological, meteorological and anthropogenic factors and activities that increase spillover risk'.[26] In governance practice, this results in a lack of engagement with environmental law practitioners and specific areas of

[23] Odel Y Li et al., 'The Approaching Pilot for One Health Governance Index' (2023) 12(16) *Infectious Diseases of Poverty* 1, 8.

[24] Ibid., 5.

[25] A Elnaiem et al., 'Global and Regional Governance of One Health and Implications for Global Health Security' (2023) 401(10377) *The Lancet* 688–704, 691.

[26] OHHLEP, 'Prevention of Zoonotic Spillover: From Relying on Response to Reducing the Risk at Source' (2023) 19(10) *PLOS Pathogens* 1, 3.

governance such as climate change, protected areas, land clearing, and agriculture. Indeed, recent research undertaken in Australia has shown that environmental law practitioners, non-governmental organisations and departments often do not consider One Health relevant to their work.[27]

In this book, we begin to address this barrier by engaging with environmental lawyers and others specifically working at the human–animal–environmental interface to address the drivers of spillover risk and reduce the likelihood of the need for preparedness and response. In Chapter 6, for example, Francesca Coli, Maurizio Aragrande, and Massimo Canali examine recent reforms to the European regulatory framework for sustainable agri-food systems to determine the extent to which they align with a One Health approach. In Chapter 14, Urias S. Goll and Catherine Machalaba examine how a One Health approach can increase the reach and usefulness of environmental laws and policies. By demonstrating the relevance of One Health to environmental law and governance, we hope to engage a wider set of practitioners who have traditionally been excluded from One Health collaborations and frameworks.

A further barrier to effective One Health governance is siloisation, which in this context refers to the tendency for people and institutions in One Health to work in isolation from each other. A similar problem occurs in law generally, where practitioners/firms focus on – for example – environmental law, *or* animal law, *or* health law, with little crossover or collaboration. In the One Health context, it remains an ongoing task to strengthen collaboration between sectors, breaking down institutional silos and facilitating joint strategy development.[28] For example, while antibiotics for human use are increasingly regulated, agri-vets reportedly sell antibiotics directly to farmers who may lack veterinary knowledge or understanding of AMR issues.[29] Nevertheless, the law is progressing through, for example, phrases such as 'integration' and 'mainstreaming', which promote consideration of issues across disciplines, sectors, and institutions.

One Health governance also faces a challenge in terms of a lack of legal and governance provision for monitoring, evaluation, and enforcement. This is also a challenge for One Health tools more generally.[30] In this collection, we seek to imagine how law and governance processes, rules, and systems could be improved with a One Health methodology and engagement with its core principles and values.

1.5 THE CONTRIBUTIONS IN THIS VOLUME

This collection is divided into three parts. Part I features five chapters that explore some ways in which One Health has been implemented in existing legal structures at global, regional, and national levels. In Chapter 2 Katherine Ginsbach, Kashish Aneja, Alison Durran, and Sam Halabi look at domestic and regional institutional collaborative frameworks dedicated to One Health implementation, including in Egypt, Viet Nam, Kenya, India, and the Arctic. This analysis highlights the opportunities and obstacles for future domestic policies seeking to implement One Health principles. By contrast, in Chapter 3 Elien Verniers focuses attention at the

[27] Woolaston et al., 'Mapping Australian One Health Activities and Expertise'.

[28] Nina Jamal et al., 'One Health, Breaking Institutional Silos and Achieving Health for All' available at https://sdgs.un.org/documents/jamal-one-health-breaking-institutional-siloes-and-achieving-health-all-52400.

[29] Fleming Fund, 'One Health: Breaking Down Silos and Driving the Fleming Fund Forward' (2023) available at www.flemingfund.org/publications/one-health-breaking-down-silos-and-driving-the-fleming-fund-forward/.

[30] Casey Barton Behravesh et al., 'An Integrated Inventory of One Health Tools: Mapping and Analysis of Globally Available Tools to Advance One Health' (2024) 3(1) *CABI One Health* 1.

global level and explores the synergies between One Health and the UN Animal Welfare Nexus Resolution.[31] Her analysis highlights the value of holistic and interdisciplinary approaches to tackle complex health challenges. In Chapter 4 Michelle Rourke considers the proposed pathogen access and benefit-sharing (PABS) system in the Pandemic Treaty negotiating documents from the perspective of its capacity to successfully implement One Health principles. Her analysis reveals that while One Health was intended to be a guiding principle for the Pandemic Treaty, this is not demonstrated in the current proposal for the PABS system.

Continuing the content in Part I of the collection, in Chapter 5 Claire Lajaunie demonstrates how conservation policies and environmental law have been instrumental in the development of the One Health approach. Her discussion reveals that, contrary to some understandings, One Health is not a new concept in environmental law. As noted above, in Chapter 6 Francesca Coli, Maurizio Aragrande, and Massimo Canali explore the degree to which One Health has effectively influenced EU legislation in relation to sustainable agri-food systems. They conclude that while significant progress has been made, the resulting framework lacks 'an organic and coherent approach'.

Part II of this collection shifts the focus to the relationships between contemporary legal structures – actual and proposed – and One Health. Chapter 7 is the first of five chapters in this part. In it, Bridget Lewis analyses the relationship between human rights and One Health and identifies ways in which human rights law might contribute to implementation of the One Health approach and its objectives. Her analysis suggests that while there are clear synergies between human rights and the human health aspect of One Health, the anthropocentric nature of human rights may give rise to incompatibilities between the two frameworks. In Chapter 8 Jane Kotzmann and Katie Woolaston seek to reconcile animal rights and One Health discourses, which may be conceived as incompatible. In doing so, they develop a One Health three-dimensional framework for moral concern, which could be used to identify moral significance in the human and non-human.

In Chapter 9 Elisa Cavallin focuses on the EU Deforestation-Free Products Regulation and considers how this regulation relates to One Health.[32] She makes the case that the regulation will improve ecosystems, which will in turn benefit humans and animals. In Chapter 10 Jessica C. Tselepy and Jack Nagy continue the theme of considering the relevance of environmental legal frameworks for One Health. They examine other leading interdisciplinary approaches to health problems – EcoHealth and Planetary Health – to determine what One Health can learn from these approaches. Chapter 11 is the final chapter in Part II and focuses on the experience of AMR. In it, Carmen Bullón and Stefania Negri consider the experience of AMR under a One Health approach that could be useful if applied to other complex health issues. They argue that the lessons learned in the experience of AMR should provide points of reference for other One Health issues.

Part III of this collection marks a shift to consideration of how One Health might be envisaged in future legal structures. It comprises seven chapters, which collectively explore a broad array of ways in which One Health might evolve and be relevant. Notably, as public health is a component of One Health, many of these chapters move beyond looking at One Health through a public health lens. In Chapter 12 Cassandra Seery and Joshua Gilbert examine ways to reconceptualise and reorientate One Health towards Indigenous understanding. Through their exploration of pre- and post-colonial Indigenous ways of being and doing in Australia, they

[31] Resolution on the animal welfare–environment–sustainable development nexus (7 March 2022) UNEP/EA5/RES.1.

[32] Regulation 2023/1115 of 31 May 2023.

make the case that Indigenous knowledges must be incorporated into One Health governance frameworks for them to succeed as integrated systems. While much attention has been devoted to drafts of the Pandemic Treaty, the failure to date to prohibit the types of animal use, confinement, and ill-treatment that are considered to have prompted the COVID-19 pandemic led to the drafting of a proposed Convention on Animal Protection (CAP). In Chapter 13, Rajesh K. Reddy – one of the co-drafters of the CAP – explores the promise the CAP holds in producing a One-Health-centered model.

As noted above, in Chapter 14 Urias S. Goll and Catherine Machalaba explore how a One Health approach can improve the reach and effectiveness of environmental law and policy. Their discussion reveals the many needs and opportunities for incorporation of One Health in this context and thus will be of great use for practitioners in this space. In Chapter 15 Jeff Sebo, Alisa E. White, and Toni Sims investigate the possibilities of the One Health concept providing a foundation for multispecies urban infrastructure. They argue that the animal welfare component of One Health should be included in local policy-making relating to institutional and infrastructural change. In Chapter 16 Helen Yu draws on the intellectual property framework 'responsible research and innovation' (RRI) and value-based health and care (VBHC) to develop an approach to innovation that could support the implementation of One Health principles.

The final two chapters in this collection look at, respectively, the potential implications of One Health for public health law and for rights to health and a protected environment. In Chapter 17 Sam Roach and Fiona McDonald argue that One Health approaches suggest that public health law must be reconceptualised to adequately address interdependencies between humans, animals, and the environment. In Chapter 18, the final chapter of the collection, Tony Gerrans explores two contexts in which One Health has been implemented in South Africa: the commercial farming of wildlife and intensive animal agriculture. This exploration enables him to advance suggestions as to how to more fully operationalise One Health principles.

We hope this collection is of interest and use to those involved in One Health now and in the future.

PART I

One Health in Existing Legal Structures

2

One Health Frameworks

Challenges and Opportunities for Country-Level Implementation

Katherine Ginsbach, Kashish Aneja, Alison Durran, and Sam Halabi

2.1 INTRODUCTION

One Health is an integrative and cooperative health initiative, with a multi-sectoral approach to attaining optimal health for people, animals, and the environment. Despite widespread agreement on the need for cross-sector collaboration to address interconnected health, animal, and environmental threats, the reality is that most responses remain confined within the separate silos of various departments. This chapter focuses on the legal instruments and policies that have been implemented across sectors at the international, regional, and country levels.

The benefits of implementing One Health to address issues including zoonotic and (re-)emerging infectious diseases, non-communicable diseases linked to environmental risk factors, anti-microbial resistance (AMR) and climate adaptation are clear. A comprehensive One Health approach, including tackling drivers of environmental degradation, preventing risks at source by prioritising upstream prevention, and investing in preparedness interventions, is essential to deliver health security.

One Health is an integrated, unifying approach to balance and optimise the health of people, animals, and ecosystems.[1] It uses the close, interdependent links among fields to create new surveillance and disease control methods. The COVID-19 pandemic put a spotlight on the need for a global framework for improved surveillance and a more holistic, integrated system that supports efforts at the regional, national, and local levels. Gaps in One Health knowledge, prevention, and integrated approaches were seen as key drivers of the pandemic. By addressing the linkages between human, animal, and environmental health, One Health can serve as a transformative approach to improved global health.[2] One Health applies to a range of issues, including AMR, zoonotic diseases, vector-borne diseases, food safety and foodborne diseases, and environmental health.[3]

To implement One Health, major structural changes are required to integrate the human, animal, and environmental health fields and support multi-sectoral communication, collaboration, coordination, and capacity strengthening.[4] Critical gaps in One Health implementation include: databases and resources to support information sharing and action in line with a One Health approach; identification and showcasing of best practices for One Health implementation;

[1] World Health Organization, 'One Health'. Available at www.who.int/health-topics/one-health#tab=tab_1.

[2] Ibid.

[3] Ibid.

[4] Ibid.

mapping of existing initiatives and capacities for One Health research and building the next generation One Health workforce; a model for an integrated One Health surveillance system; mechanisms for routine and emergency coordination with relevant stakeholders; a more complex understanding of the drivers of spillover of zoonotic diseases; a standardised approach for assessing the risks of spillover of pathogens between different animal populations and humans, and of the emergence of zoonotic diseases, including those arising in food systems; and methods for identifying and reducing spillover risks and the spread of zoonotic diseases in ways that minimise trade-offs and maximise co-benefits with other health and sustainable development objectives.[5]

2.2 INTERNATIONAL LEVEL ONE HEALTH FRAMEWORKS

At the international level, the One Health approach aims to overcome siloed ways of thinking among the various organisations and actors involved in the field. Its aim is to improve multilateral coordination of pandemic prevention, preparedness, and response. Data collection for disease surveillance is one area in particular need of such coordination. Current international legal agreements only partially address this area.[6] The International Health Regulations 2005 (IHR) is the main tool that prescribes the mechanism for reporting diseases to the World Health Organization (WHO). The IHR applies to an open list of diseases and plays a central role in the transparent exchange of data through the WHO Hub for Pandemic and Epidemic Intelligence.[7] The IHR, however, is a strictly anthropocentric tool of international law, requiring notification to the WHO when a disease spreads among humans.[8] To fill this gap, the World Organization for Animal Health (WOAH) has tools to promote animal health surveillance. The Terrestrial Animal Health Code and the Aquatic Animal Health Code have lists of diseases for which surveillance is a high priority. Designation of a disease of high priority, while not strictly anthropocentric, includes proven international spread of the pathogenic agent, at least one country has demonstrated infection or infestation in populations of susceptible animals, reliable means exist to identify cases, and natural transmission to humans has been proven or the disease has been shown to have a significant impact on the health of domestic animals or a significant impact on the health of wildlife, including direct economic losses and mortality.[9] Similarly, the Codex Alimentarius developed by the Food and Agriculture Organization of the United Nations (FAO) allows for monitoring practices in the food supply chain which might increase the risk of the spread of disease.

The WHO, WOAH, FAO, with the United Nations Environment Programme have formed a program of collaboration called 'the Quadripartite'. The purpose of the Quadripartite is to provide a formal and legal framework for the longstanding collaboration among the parties to further their shared goals and objectives in regard to the development and implementation of multi-sectoral approaches to complex health challenges at the animal–human–ecosystem interface, with particular emphasis on AMR. The objectives recognised in the Work Plan include: supporting the joint secretariat of the Interagency Coordination Group on AMR, established

[5] Ibid.
[6] Michael Bayerlein and Pedro A Villarreal, '"One Health" and Global Health Governance' (July 2023) *SWP Comment*. Available at: www.swp-berlin.org/publications/products/comments/2023C43_OneHealth_EN.pdf.
[7] Ibid.
[8] Ibid.
[9] World Organization for Animal Health, 'Chapter 1.2. Criteria for the inclusion of diseases, infections and infestations in the OIE List' in *Terrestrial Animal Health Code* (8 October 2022). Available at: www.OIE.org/fileadmin/Home/eng/Health_standards/tahc/current/chapitre_criteria_diseases.pdf.

by the political declaration adopted by the United Nations General Assembly in 2016 as well as continuing the coordinated implementation of the AMR Global Action Plan and respective global strategies of the parties; reinforcing of national and regional services in human health, animal health, and food safety through the assessment of these services; improving collaboration in foresight, risk assessment, preparedness, and response to emerging and neglected infectious diseases at the animal–human–ecosystems interface; addressing food safety challenges requiring a multi-sector approach in the context of reinforcing food security; adopting a common communication strategy in order to raise awareness and foster coordinated participation in forums of joint interest; and preparing a voluntary code of conduct to reinforce implementation of international standards on responsible and prudent use of anti-microbials.[10]

The framework of the Quadripartite will also contribute to reinforcing national and regional health systems and services.[11] The Quadripartite has released the One Health Joint Plan of Action that proposes a set of activities the four organisations can offer together to advance and sustainably scale up One Health: provide upstream policy and legislative advice and technical assistance to help set national targets and priorities across the sectors for the development and implementation of One Health legislation, initiatives, and programmes; take stock of existing cross-sectoral global and regional initiatives around One Health and identify and advise on synergies and overlaps, and support coordination; mobilise and make better use of resources across sectors, disciplines, and stakeholders. The Joint Action Plan is built around six interdependent action tracks that collectively contribute to achieving sustainable health and food systems, reducing global health threats, and improving ecosystem management. Each action track consists of a set of actions with specific activities, deliverables, and a timeline to achieve the objectives that have been laid out.[12] The six action tracks are: (1) enhancing One Health capacities to strengthen health systems; (2) reducing the risks of emerging and re-emerging zoonotic epidemics and pandemics; (3) controlling and eliminating endemic zoonotic, neglected tropical, and vector-borne diseases; (4) strengthening the assessment, management, and communication of food safety risks; (5) curbing the silent pandemic of AMR; and (6) integrating the environment into One Health.[13]

The Four-Way Linking (4WL) Framework is a collaborative effort between WHO, FAO, and WOAH, along with the joint network of expertise on avian influenza, and the Global Early Warning System to improve national, regional, and global qualitative risk assessments for animal and zoonotic influenza. This framework seeks to establish a national mechanism for routine, integrated, and qualitative assessments of virological and epidemiological influenza data from humans and animals. The aim of this framework is for decision-makers to use the information retrieved through the risk assessments to develop and implement new science-based

[10] Food and Agriculture Organization, World Health Organization for Animal Health, World Health Organization, and United Nations Environment Programme, 'Memorandum of Understanding between the Food and Agriculture Organization of the United Nations and the World Health Organization for Animal Health and the World Health Organization and the United Nations Environment Programme Regarding Cooperation to Combat Health Risks at the Animal-Human-Ecosystems Interface in the Context of the 'One Health' Approach and Including Antimicrobial Resistance', (29 April 2022). Available at: www.fao.org/3/cb9403en/cb9403en.pdf.

[11] World Health Organization, 'Quadripartite Memorandum of Understanding (MOU) Signed for a New Era of One Health Collaboration' (29 April 2022). Available at: www.who.int/news/item/29-04-2022-quadripartite-memorandum-of-understanding-(mou)-signed-for-a-new-era-of-one-health-collaboration.

[12] World Health Organisation, 'One Health Joint Plan of Action: Working Together for the Health of Humans, Animals, Plants and the Environment' (14 October 2022). Available at: https://reliefweb.int/report/world/one-health-joint-plan-action-2022-2026-working-together-health-humans-animals-plants-and-environment.

[13] Bayerlein and Villarreal, '"One Health" and Global Health Governance'.

measures for prioritising and managing the risks identified, and for evaluating the effects of the measures already in place.[14]

The current draft pandemic treaty (CA+) includes several provisions related to One Health implementation. Article 5 requires states to integrate measures that address the determinants of disease occurrence at the human–animal–environment interface into their national pandemic prevention plans, including climate change, land use change, wildlife trade, desertification, and AMR.[15] The draft treaty calls for enhanced synergies between multi-sectoral and transdisciplinary collaboration at the national level and cooperation at the international level, in order to identify, conduct risk assessments of, and share pathogens with, pandemic potential at the interface between human, animal, and environment ecosystems, while recognising their interdependence.[16]

At the international level, significant efforts are being made to integrate human and animal health through frameworks like the International Health Regulations, the Quadripartite, and the Four-Way Linking Framework, but there are still gaps in addressing all aspects of the One Health approach. With the current frameworks, there are gaps in surveillance mechanisms and reporting requirements, which can ultimately hinder effective responses to emerging health threats. While WOAH addresses animal health surveillance, the IHR primarily focuses on diseases that affect humans, overlooking the broader ecological context of disease transmission and framing One Health through an anthropocentric lens. There needs to be a more comprehensive approach to integrating environmental considerations into international frameworks. The formation of collaborations and integration of One Health into draft texts underscores the recognition of the interconnectedness of health across sectors and the need for coordinated action. The inclusion of One Health in the CA+ highlights the recognition of the importance of addressing the determinants of disease occurrence across human, animal, and environmental interfaces, but at the time of writing, those provisions are yet to be agreed on.[17] The treaty emphasises the need for multi-sectoral collaboration, risk assessments, and sharing of pathogen data at both the national and international levels to effectively address pandemic threats. Effective implementation of One Health requires sustained commitment, resource mobilisation, and global cooperation to protect animal, human, and environmental health.

2.3 REGIONAL ONE HEALTH FRAMEWORKS

2.3.1 *European Union*

Below the international level, regional organisations and entities can perform dual functions, serving as intermediaries between the global and national levels. These bodies can help member states in a vertical manner, by translating agreements and guidelines from the

[14] L Allal, H. Mahrous, A. Saad, et al., 'From Four-Way Linking to a One Health Platform in Egypt: Institutionalization of Multidisciplinary and Multi Sectoral One Health System' (2019) 38(1) *Revue scientifique et technique / Office international des épizooties*. Available at: https://doc.woah.org/dyn/portal/digidoc.xhtml?statelessToken=OhofrjOiIqsf9_1iKU7Cd5igbo7Jtlqk5eyfmLuP6o=&actionMethod=dyn%2Fportal%2Fdigidoc.xhtml%3AdownloadAttachment.openStateless.

[15] Bayerlein and Villarreal, '"One Health" and Global Health Governance'.

[16] World Health Organization, 'Bureau's Text of the WHO Convention, Agreement or Other International Instrument on Pandemic Prevention, Preparedness and Response (WHO CA+)' (2 June 2023) *A/INB/5/6*. Available at https://apps.who.int/gb/inb/pdf_files/inb5/A_INB5_6-en.pdf.

[17] At the time of writing this, Member States are currently deliberating the timing, format, and process to conclude the pandemic agreement. World Health Organization, 'WHO Member States Agree Way Forward to Conclude Pandemic Agreement' (28 May 2024). Available at: www.who.int/news/item/28-05-2024-who-member-states-agree-way-forward-to-conclude-pandemic-agreement.

global level to national policies and targets appropriate to their specific settings and mobilising resources to reach these goals. They can also assist horizontally by providing data and support to address cross-border policy challenges and supporting evidence-based coordination of these goals.

By way of example, the European Union (EU) plays an important role in taking the One Health approach from theory to practice by providing guidance to member states on how to tackle AMR and develop food safety policies.[18] The EU created the One Health European Joint Programme (OHEJP) in 2018, recognising that human health is tightly connected to the health of animals and the environment. The Joint Programme called for the study of infectious agents that can cross between species and the environment. The OHEJP has reinforced collaboration between institutes by enhancing transdisciplinary cooperation and integration of activities. The programme includes a landmark partnership between forty-three acclaimed food, veterinary, and medical laboratories and institutes across twenty-two member states in Europe, and also the Med-Vet-Net Association.[19] The OHEJP works to provide opportunities for the harmonisation of approaches, methodologies, databases, and procedures for the assessment and management of foodborne hazards, emerging threats, and AMR across Europe, to improve the quality and compatibility of information for decision-making. Two key instruments have facilitated the alignment of approaches: Joint Research Projects and Joint Integrative Projects. These projects have led to the development of a common strategic research agenda among partners, taking into account the related initiatives initiated by the international and European stakeholders.[20] Overall the approach improves the quality and compatibility of information taken from integrative research activities for decision- and policy-making.[21]

The OHEJP held its final meeting in September 2023. The programme created a unique EU consortium supporting and above all, implementing the One Health approach in food safety. The closing meeting focused on highlighting the research and training outcomes produced over more than five years in the foodborne zoonoses, AMR, and emerging threats domains, and the progress made for the sustainability of the OHEJP's outputs.[22] The OHEJP led the way for activities and outcomes related to food safety and created a structure for these approaches to be built upon for the sustainability and legacy of the OHEJP work. As a continuing collaboration of this work, the Med-Vet-Net Association will serve as a forum for all public organisations that took part in OHEJP.[23]

In June 2023, the Council of the European Union adopted a set of recommendations to strengthen action against AMR. The recommendation employs a 'One Health' approach to AMR, based on the fact that the health of humans, animals, and the environment is intrinsically

[18] European Centre for Disease Prevention and Control, 'The European Union Summary Report on Antimicrobial Resistance in Zoonotic and Indicator Bacteria from Humans Animals, and Food in 2021–2022' (2024) 22(2) *European Food Safety Authority*.

[19] One Health EJP, 'About'. Available at https://onehealthejp.eu/about.

[20] One Health EJP, 'Projects: Joint Research Projects (JRP), Joint Integrative Projects (JIP) and PhD Projects'. Available at https://onehealthejp.eu/projects. The Med-Vet-Net Association is a network of public and academic institutions in the medical/public health and food/veterinary domains, focused on combating zoonoses and antimicrobial resistance to support a healthy and sustainable food chain across Europe.

[21] Ibid.

[22] One Health EJP, 'The One Health European Joint Programme End' (2023) *ANSES*. Available at: www.anses.fr/en/end-ejp-one-health-2023.

[23] One Health EJP, 'Final Report September 2023' (30 September 2023). Available at: https://onehealthejp.eu/wp-content/uploads/2023/09/ohejp-final-report-september-2023.pdf.

linked and that AMR can only be overcome through joint efforts taken across all three areas.[24] The proposed measures in the recommendation include: (1) concrete targets to reduce anti-microbial use by 2030, including a 20 per cent reduction in total human consumption of antibiotics and a 50 per cent reduction in overall EU sales of anti-microbials used for farm animals and aquaculture; (2) strengthening of national action plans to help implement these targets and monitor the use of antibiotics at the national level, including indicators to assess progress; (3) better surveillance of AMR and anti-microbial consumption at all levels, including at hospitals and long-term care facilities; (4) efforts to improve the health and welfare of food-producing animals to decrease the spread of infectious diseases in farming and; (5) awareness-raising among the public and professionals working in the human health and veterinary sectors, including training for health professionals and communication campaigns.[25] While a 'recommendation' is not legally binding, these types of soft-law instruments can be used to set up political commitments or positions, invite members to take action, coordinate member states' actions, and make their views known.[26] This non-binding approach allows for flexibility and often more ambitious metrics as well as a higher acceptance in comparison to hard law.[27]

2.3.2 *Arctic Council*

The Arctic Council was formally established in 1996. It serves as the leading intergovernmental forum promoting cooperation, coordination, and interaction among the Arctic states, Arctic Indigenous peoples, and other Arctic inhabitants on common Arctic issues.[28] As defined in the Ottawa Declaration, the members of the Arctic Council are the eight states that have territories within the Arctic: Canada, the Kingdom of Denmark, Finland, Iceland, Norway, the Russian Federation, Sweden, and the United States.[29] Their national jurisdictions and international law govern the lands surrounding the Arctic Ocean and its waters. The Arctic Council is not an international organisation based on a legally binding instrument and it does not have the legal personality of an international organisation at the global level, which would enable it to develop legislation or conclude treaties with other subjects of international law.[30] The Council's activities are primarily conducted through six working groups, which regularly produce comprehensive environmental, ecological, and social assessments as well as policy guidance. The Council has been a forum for the negotiation of three important legally binding agreements among the eight Arctic states, but the Council only serves as a forum and does not and cannot implement or enforce its guidelines, assessments, or recommendations – that responsibility belongs to the individual Arctic states or international bodies.[31] With that in mind, the Council's Strategic

[24] Council of the European Union, 'Tackling Antimicrobial Resistance: Council Adopts Recommendation' (14 June 2023). Available at: www.consilium.europa.eu/en/press/press-releases/2023/06/13/tackling-antimicrobial-resistance-council-adopts-recommendation/.

[25] Ibid.

[26] European Union, 'Types of Legislation: Institutions, Law, Budget. European Union'. Available at: https://european union.europa.eu/institutions-law-budget/law/types-legislation_en.

[27] Guilia Bosi, 'Overcoming the "Soft vs Hard Law" Debate in the Development of New Global Health Instruments' (30 November 2021) *Opinio Juris*. Available at: http://opiniojuris.org/2021/11/30/overcoming-the-soft-vs-hard-law-debate-in-the-development-of-new-global-health-instruments/.

[28] The Arctic Council, 'About the Arctic Council' (2024). Available at: https://arctic-council.org/about/.

[29] Ibid.

[30] Natalia Loukavheva, 'The Arctic Council and "Law-Making"' (2020) 50 *The Northern Review* 109–135. Available at: https://thenorthernreview.ca/index.php/nr/article/download/861/859/1783.

[31] The Arctic Council, 'About the Arctic Council'.

Plan guides its work towards making the Arctic a 'region of peace, stability and constructive cooperation, that is a vibrant, prosperous, sustainable and secure home for all its inhabitants, including Indigenous Peoples, and where their rights and wellbeing are respected'.[32]

Tackling the health effects of climate change in a region warming at four times the global average rate requires a One Health approach and urgency.[33] Under the Arctic Council Sustainable Development Working Group, the 'One Arctic, One Health' project is designed to strengthen circumpolar knowledge and practice on disease outbreaks, natural disasters, and related phenomena, via a combination of knowledge sharing, tabletop exercises, and collaborative investigations. The goal is to establish One Health points of contact within each Arctic state and permanent participant organisation that can rapidly receive and process inquiries related to collaboration from other points of contact on an ongoing basis.[34] Under this working group, the Arctic Human Health Expert Group – a selection of health-focused specialists that provide guidance and expertise to the Sustainable Development Working Group – has provided contributions in the form of time and advice on priority One Health phenomena of interest, such as disease outbreaks and natural disasters. Some key successes include: (1) a circumpolar questionnaire on One Health awareness and practices; (2) tabletop exercises in the United States and Canada (the first Arctic Council exercises on health issues); (3) an international visitor leadership programme; (4) One Arctic, One Health research projects; and (5) a workshop focused on pathogens in thawing permafrost in 2019. The One Arctic, One Health project has not resulted in any legal outcomes, but the Arctic Council is able to help with harmonising domestic legislation in the Arctic states with soft-law activities having the ability to influence national processes.[35] As the Arctic Council plays a key role in generating scientific knowledge on the Arctic, it remains a vital voice for policy-making, contributing to the negotiations of the Stockholm Convention on Persistent Organic Pollutants (2002) and its subsequent implementation has served as a precedent for influencing global policy.[36] In this way, the Arctic Council remains crucial not only in shaping regional policies but also in influencing global health governance.

2.4 COUNTRY CASE STUDIES

While most international and regional entities operate within soft law and guidelines, at the country level, legislation is able to make concrete adoption of One Health policies and frameworks. We provide commentary on the national laws of Egypt, Vietnam, Kenya, and India as examples of country-level legal frameworks.

2.4.1 *Egypt*

Egypt has established a national One Health coordination mechanism. The coordination mechanism is a policy to guide actions and strategies within the government rather than a legally mandated requirement. The primary purpose of this mechanism is to provide a comprehensive, strategic approach to concurrent and future challenges facing public health and animal health, including environmental impacts. Through this work, its aim is to have the

[32] Ibid.
[33] Monica Medina, 'Virtual Welcome Remarks at the "One Arctic, One Health" Workshop' (9 November 2022) US Department of State. Available at: www.state.gov/virtual-welcome-remarks-at-the-one-arctic-one-health-workshop/.
[34] The Arctic Council, 'One Health Project' (2022). Available at: https://arctic-council.org/news/one-arctic-one-health/.
[35] The Arctic Council, 'Arctic Council Strategic Plan' (2024). Available at: https://arctic-council.org/explore/goals/.
[36] Loukavheva, 'The Arctic Council and "Law-Making"'.

public health, animal health, and environment sectors improve disease mitigation measures, develop stronger and more stable public and animal health services, promote effective national communication strategies, and improve One Health collaboration among all relevant sectors.[37]

The Four-Way Linking (4WL) Framework was initiated in Egypt in 2010. It has been approved by the Egyptian government but has not been formally institutionalised.[38] The WHO, FAO, and WOAH carried out a joint assessment mission to Egypt to identify key partners, national initiatives, current efforts, and existing operational tools and systems for the epidemiological and virological surveillance of influenza in both the human health and animal health sectors. The team assessed the existing systems of data collection, traceability, and exchange, as well as the reporting of influenza within the human and animal health sectors.[39] The mission identified major partners that should be included in a 4WL Framework, including epidemiology and laboratory departments in the Ministry of Health and Population and the Ministry of Agriculture and Land Reclamation. Through these actions, a 4WL Task Force was established with regulatory meetings conducted. The task force was the first technical One Health committee established in Egypt and the task force meetings have the dual purpose of data sharing and performing a risk assessment of the highly pathogenic avian influenza (HPAI) situation. The task force has expanded beyond influenza to include other emerging diseases, including Middle East Respiratory Syndrome Coronavirus (MERS-CoV) and other zoonotic diseases of importance in the country.[40]

In 2013, the 4WL expanded and transformed into the One Health Technical Advisory Group (OH-TAG) by facilitating collaborative work and coordination meetings among health practitioners from various government agencies to address HPAI and other emerging and re-emerging zoonotic diseases. During the period of 2013–2020, the Emergency Center for Transboundary Animal Diseases supported seven coordination meetings of the OH-TAG involving a total of 588 One Health practitioners. Those meetings resulted in facilitating and sustaining the data sharing and the joint conduct of situational assessments, establishing a task group responsible for the joint rapid assessment and joint outbreak investigation in emergency cases.[41]

In 2023, Egypt unveiled its new five-year nationwide strategic framework on One Health to sustainably promote the health of humans, animals, plants, and their shared environments. The strategic framework was co-created by Egypt's ministries of Higher Education and Scientific Research and Local Development, alongside the Egyptian Medicines Authority and the National Food Safety Authority. In partnership with the WHO, and FAO, Egypt's Health Minister launched the 'One Health National Strategic Framework (2023–2027)'. The technical document acts as a joint roadmap for the adoption of a One Health approach between the Ministries of Health and Population, Agriculture and Land Reclamation, and Environment in Egypt.

The five-year plan aims for joint action across sectors at all levels to achieve better health outcomes that can effectively contribute to preventing, predicting, and responding to global health threats in the wake of the COVID-19 pandemic.[42]

[37] L Allal et al., 'From Four-Way Linking to a One Health Platform in Egypt'.

[38] Ibid.

[39] Ibid.

[40] Ibid.

[41] Food and Agriculture Organization of the United Nations, 'Emergency Centre for Transboundary Animal Diseases (ECTAD) – Egypt' (2024). Available at: www.fao.org/egypt/ectad/en/.

[42] HealthCare Middle East & Africa, 'Egypt Lays Out Its New 5-Year One Health Strategic Plan to Promote a Multi-institutional Approach' (11 April 2023). Available at: www.healthcaremea.com/egypt-lays-out-its-new-5-year-one-health-strategic-plan-to-promote-a-multi-institutional-approach/.

2.4.2 *Vietnam*

Since 2003, Vietnam has experienced serious human and economic impacts from zoonotic emerging infectious diseases including SARS and avian influenza, as well as agricultural losses from livestock diseases estimated at over one billion US dollars.[43] Recognising this impact, since 2006 Vietnam has worked to enact effective high-level national coordination and international cooperation in response to emerging infectious diseases (EIDs) in humans and animals. The Partnership on Avian and Human Influenza with twenty-six national and international members, has supported national and international efforts within the framework of the National Integrated Operational Program on Avian and Human Influenza (OPI) 2006–2010, and the National Integrated Operational Program on Avian Influenza, Pandemic Preparedness and Emerging Infectious Diseases 2011–2015 (AIPED). The overall approach in Vietnam has progressively evolved from a single-disease focus towards long-term One Health capacity-building, preparedness, and prevention, encompassing multiple zoonotic EID threats, and incorporating human, livestock, wildlife, and environmental health aspects.[44]

In order to build on and expand the earlier efforts, Vietnam launched a One Health Partnership for Zoonoses (OHP) in March 2016. The partnership brings together national and international government and non-governmental One Health stakeholders under the leadership of the government of Vietnam. The partnership brings together national and international government and non-governmental One Health stakeholders under the leadership of the government of Vietnam, with the overall aim to enhance the capacity of Vietnam to address zoonotic infectious disease threats at the human–animal–ecosystem interface. Their work includes: establishing a sustainable and stable forum for policy dialogue, inter-sectoral and multi-disciplinary cooperation between government agencies and civil society partners in order to strengthen the protection and improvement of human, animal and wildlife health; provide recommendations to decisions makers on One Health policy, strategy, and research projects in Vietnam, strengthening institutional capacity for implementation of One Health in public health protection, as well as participation in policy advocacy activities; provide a framework for wide and timely information sharing and communication within national and international partners on One Health related issues, intensify community education, also facilitate engagement of community in One Health strategy planning and implementation and; enhance international operation for effective coordination and mobilisation of funding for One Health activities in Vietnam to facilitate and promote engagement of Vietnam in regional and global One Health effort.[45]

In early 2020, COVID-19 prompted the government to form a National Steering Committee for COVID-19 Prevention and Control, composed of twenty-three ministries and agencies. Multi-sector steering committees were also established at provincial and local levels. Together these sectors mobilised resources for tasks relevant to their technical function. In early 2021, Vietnam launched the second phase of OHP (2021–2025), which was signed by three ministries – the Ministry of Health, the Ministry of Agriculture and Rural Development, and the Ministry of Natural Resources and Environment – as well as twenty-eight national and international signatories, demonstrating Vietnam's ongoing commitment to One Health. Integrating One Health

43 Secretariat Office of the Vietnam One Health Partnership for Zoonoses, 'Overview of One Health in Viet Nam' (2024). Available at: https://onehealth.org.vn/overview.news.

44 Ibid.

45 Ibid.

principles into policy has allowed decisive and timely multi-sector action in controlling disease outbreaks in Vietnam.[46]

Vietnam's One Health Strategic Plan includes seven focus areas: (1) capacity-building to implement the One Health approach; (2) control of zoonotic diseases; (3) control of animal-originated pathogens; (4) control of zoonotic influenza virus with pandemic potential; (5) rabies control; (6) AMR control; and (7) control of other prioritised zoonotic diseases.

Within the One Health space, Vietnam has expanded its surveillance systems of zoonotic diseases that operate at various scales depending on their pandemic potential. Nearly 40 per cent of live bird markets have active avian influenza virus surveillance, commonly detecting H5N1, H5N6, and H9. Vietnam has also implemented a longitudinal influenza surveillance network that covers humans, livestock, and wildlife in three high-risk provinces. In 2005, the Vietnam Ministry of Health, supported by the WHO and the US Centers for Disease Control (CDC) initiated national influenza surveillance based on sentinel clinics linked to regional public health laboratories.[47] Outside of avian surveillance, the country has surveillance systems for severe acute respiratory infections focused on humans. The country has also invested in rabies prevention and control with strategies including rabies vaccination programmes, management of dog populations, post-exposure prophylaxis for persons bitten by rabies-suspect dogs, and communication activities to raise community awareness. The zoonoses that circulate within Vietnam have caused considerable health and economic losses in Vietnam, and for these reasons animal and human health sectors have been cooperating to address less salient diseases including anthrax, *Streptococcus suis*, and leptospirosis.[48]

Within the One Health area, food safety remains a key priority and major concern for the public and the government has deployed several programmes to control foodborne diseases.[49] Programmes that have been implemented include developing market-based approaches to improve hygienic practices at slaughterhouses and wet markets. There is a current focus on strengthening lab-based surveillance systems for *Escherichia coli*, *Salmonella* spp., and *Shigella* in Hanoi, Dong Thap, and Vung Tau provinces.

In addition to disease surveillance and food safety, a top priority of One Health remains antibiotic resistance. Vietnam was one of the first six countries in the Asia Pacific region to develop and implement national action plans for combating AMR in the human health sector, livestock production, and aquaculture. Notable actions include implementing a national AMR surveillance unit in 2016 and developing guidance for the use of antibiotics in hospitals, veterinary medicines, livestock feed, and veterinary prescriptions.[50]

Vietnam's One Health efforts are supported by existing structures including formal policies, informal policies, partnership frameworks, and international commitments, all of which were the product of several important starting conditions, namely growing awareness of One Health

[46] Hung Nguyen-Viet, Steven Lam, Houng Nguyen-Mai, et al., 'Decades of Emerging Infectious Disease, Food Safety, and Antimicrobial Resistance Response in Vietnam: The Role of One Health' (2022) 14 *One Health*. Available at: www.ncbi.nlm.nih.gov/pmc/articles/PMC8668232/#:~:text=Vietnam's%20first%20One%20Health%20Strategic,6)%20Antimicrobial%20resistance%20(AMR).

[47] Hien T Nguyen, N. Dharan, M. T.Q. Le, et al., 'National Influenza Surveillance in Vietnam, 2006–2007' (2009) 28(2) *Vaccine*. Available at: https://doi.org/10.1016/j.vaccine.2009.09.139.

[48] Hung Nguyen-Viet et al., 'Decades of Emerging Infectious Disease, Food Safety, and Antimicrobial Resistance Response in Vietnam'.

[49] Ibid.

[50] Ibid.

with the in-country history of inter-sectoral collaboration to address EIDs, government leadership, and donor funding for actions towards global health security.[51]

2.4.3 *Kenya*

Kenya adopted a One Health approach in 2006 by establishing a multi-sectoral committee aligned with global recommendations to coordinate preparedness efforts to prevent the spread of HPAI in the wake of the global spread of H5N1.[52] The aim of the creation of the coordinated framework between the public health and animal health sectors was to understand, prevent, and control re-emerging and endemic zoonotic diseases (we note the environmental sector is missing here).[53] In Africa, between 2012 and 2022, the number of outbreaks caused by zoonotic pathogens was 63 per cent higher than in the previous decade.[54] The implementation of One Health is critical as studies have shown that most camels in Kenya have antibodies against MERS-CoV but human infection in Africa remains rare. A One Health approach can help to give an early warning to identify and potentially prevent zoonotic outbreaks in human populations.[55]

In Kenya, livestock contributes over 5.5 per cent of the national gross domestic product, with about 60 per cent of all cattle, sheep, and goats found in arid and semi-arid areas. These areas overlap with approximately 10 million Kenyans who derive their livelihoods from livestock.[56] In 2004, the US CDC, in collaboration with the Kenya Medical Research Institute and the Kenyan Ministry of Health, established the Global Disease Detection Division at CDC Kenya to facilitate building diagnostic and epidemiologic capacity for epidemic-prone diseases and conducting public health research of global importance. From the Global Disease Detection Division, a One Health approach was identified as a key focus area for dedicated funding and personnel.[57]

The first challenge that the One Health framework faced was an outbreak of Rift Valley Fever in Eastern Africa. The outbreak was characterised by timely diagnosis and coordinated response that resulted in 700 suspected cases and ninety deaths; this is in comparison to the 1996–97 outbreak that resulted in 27,500 human infections and 170 deaths in North Eastern Kenya.[58] Part of the success of curtailing the 2006 outbreak is thought to be due to the increased efforts to build capacity for coordinated outbreak response and communication pathways within the Ministry of Health and Ministry of Agriculture, Livestock, and Fisheries. The coordination structure that was put in place for HPAI preparedness efforts and enhanced diagnostic capacities with improved research infrastructure resulted in collaborative One Health approaches among government departments.

The country used the successful collaborations from the 2006 RVF outbreak to expand and improve the approach for all potential zoonotic outbreaks but also to understand, prevent,

51 Ibid.

52 Peninah M Munyua, M. K. Njenga, E. M. Osoro, et al., 'Successes and Challenges of the One Health Approach in Kenya over the Last Decade' (2019) 19 *BMC Public Health* 465. Available at: https://doi.org/10.1186/s12889-019-6772-7.

53 Ibid.

54 Laura Salm-Reifferscheidt, 'One Health in Kenya' (2023) 401(10372) *The Lancet*. Available at: www.thelancet.com/journals/lancet/article/PIIS0140-6736(23)00088-0/fulltext.

55 Ibid.

56 Munyua et al., 'Successes and Challenges of the One Health Approach in Kenya over the Last Decade'.

57 Ibid.

58 Ibid.

and control endemic zoonotic disease.[59] One gap that was identified was the lack of a formal framework for systematic collaboration between government ministries and key stakeholders on the management of zoonotic disease outbreaks. Sustained advocacy resulted in the creation in 2012 of a formal collaborative framework between the public and animal health sectors with the formation of a national One Health coordinating office, the Zoonotic Disease Unit (ZDU).[60] Its key mandate is to act as a focal point of collaboration between the Ministry of Health and the Ministry of Agriculture, Livestock, and Fisheries; to establish structures and partnerships that promote the One Health approach; to enhance and build zoonotic epidemic and endemic disease surveillance; and to coordinate implementation of control measures and support public health research in Kenya. What resulted was the Kenyan One Health Strategic Plan (2012–2017), uniting efforts of ministries, professional disciplines, and non-governmental actors to address zoonotic, emerging, and re-emerging diseases.[61]

In 2013, the governance system in Kenya changed from a centralised to a devolved government of forty-seven counties, where the functions of public health and animal health reside in the county governments. This allowed One Health to expand to the sub-national level with country One Health units focused on initiating or enhancing communication platforms between the health and livestock sectors to improve surveillance reporting of zoonotic diseases, ensuring rapid joint investigation and response to zoonotic disease outbreaks to mitigate disease impact. By being able to share disease outbreak information across sectors and rapid joint outbreak response at the country level, it reduces the burden of spillover to humans who acquire zoonotic disease infections.[62]

Since then the development of the current plan, the One Health Strategic Plan for the Prevention and Control of Zoonotic Disease in Kenya (2021–2025) was informed by an end-evaluation of the 2012–2017 One Health Strategic Plan, with the ZDU hosting a stakeholder meeting to discuss the findings of the evaluation and guide the development of the new plan.[63] The current plan focuses on a stronger integration of ecosystem and environment expertise into the ZDU to improve the impact of the One Health approach, with stronger coordination between the ZDU and the Zoonoses Technical Working Group to work with committees on AMR and food safety.[64]

In addition to deploying county-level surveillance reporting mechanisms, the Kenyan Ministry of Health in 2004 launched Kenya's Field Epidemiology and Laboratory Training programme. This programme provides training in applied epidemiology and in 2006, after seeing the increased value of One Health, veterinarians were included in the training.

From training to surveillance mechanisms to building frameworks across partnerships, Kenya still faces challenges in the animal health sector, which is under-resourced in surveillance, reporting, and laboratory diagnosis. While there has been collaboration on animal and human health, the environmental health sector has not been fully incorporated to be compliant within the scope of One Health. This is found to be the result of having a separate government ministry that represents the environment sector.[65]

[59] Ibid.

[60] Ibid.

[61] Republic of Kenya Zoonotic Disease Unit, 'One Health Strategic Plan for the Prevention and Control of Zoonotic Diseases in Kenya (2021–2025)' (2021). Available at https://faolex.fao.org/docs/pdf/ken210718.pdf.

[62] Munyua et al., 'Successes and Challenges of the One Health Approach in Kenya over the Last Decade'.

[63] Republic of Kenya Zoonotic Disease Unit, 'One Health Strategic Plan for the Prevention and Control of Zoonotic Diseases in Kenya (2021–2025)'.

[64] Ibid.

[65] Munyua et al., 'Successes and Challenges of the One Health Approach in Kenya over the Last Decade'.

Kenya has worked to align their national One Health policies with international frameworks including the Sustainable Development Goals, the WHO International Health Regulations (2005), the WOAH Terrestrial and Aquatic Animal Health Code, the Global Health Security Agenda (2024), and the Sendai Framework for Disaster Risk Reduction (2015–2030). Within national-level documents, the One Health Strategic Plan conforms with the Kenyan Constitution (2010), as well as sectoral policies and strategies.[66] The One Health Strategic Plan is also supported by several laws that are relevant to the prevention and control of zoonotic diseases including the Animal Diseases Act,[67] the Meat Control Act,[68] the Public Health Act,[69] the Fisheries Act,[70] Kenya Veterinary Vaccines Production Institute Order,[71] and the Food, Drug, and Chemical Substances Act.[72]

Overall, Kenya has made a firm step in implementing a One Health approach since 2011 by establishing collaborative platforms and policy guidance among ministries that are responsible for human and animal health.

2.4.4 *India*

As early as 2008, India acknowledged the importance of the One Health concept by launching the 'Roadmap to Combat Zoonoses in India' initiative through the Union Ministry of Health and Family Welfare (MoHFW), the Union Ministry of Agriculture, and the Wildlife Institute of India.[73] This initiative stressed the importance of assessing the morbidity, mortality, and economic impact of zoonotic diseases and highlighted the benefits of adopting a One Health approach.

India's legal framework includes multiple laws regulated by various ministries that contribute to the One Health approach. Key among these are: the Wildlife (Protection) Act of 1972,[74] the Environment (Protection) Act of 1986,[75] the Biological Diversity Act of 2002,[76] and the Epidemic Diseases Act of 1897.[77]

66 Republic of Kenya Zoonotic Disease Unit, 'One Health Strategic Plan for the Prevention and Control of Zoonotic Diseases in Kenya (2021–2025)'.

67 National Council for Law Reporting, 'Chapter 364', in the Animal Disease Act (Kenya). Available at: https://kenyalaw.org/kl/fileadmin/pdfdownloads/Acts/AnimalDiseasesActCap364.pdf?_sm_au_=iVVjnD7RQ1QH5tqqKKQTWK37LBJkG.

68 Kenya Law, 'Chapter 356' in Meat Control Act (Kenya). Act No 5 of 2007. Available at http://kenyalaw.org:8181/exist/kenyalex/actview.xql?actid=CAP.%20356.

69 National Council for Law Reporting, 'Chapter 242' in Public Health Act 2012 (Kenya). Available at www.kenyalaw.org/kl/fileadmin/pdfdownloads/Acts/PublicHealthActCap242.pdf.

70 National Council for Law Reporting, 'Chapter 378' in the Fisheries Act 2012 (Kenya). Available at https://infotradekenya.go.ke/media/Fisheries%20Act%20CAP%20378.pdf.

71 'Kenya Veterinary Vaccines Production Institute Order 1990' Rev. 2012. (Kenya) in State Corporations Act. Available at https://faolex.fao.org/docs/pdf/ken128833.pdf.

72 National Council for Law Reporting, 'Chapter 254' in the Food, Drugs and Chemical Substances Act 1992 Rev. 2012 (Kenya). Available at https://infotradekenya.go.ke/media/Foods%20Drugs%20and%20Chemical%20Substances%20Act.pdf; Republic of Kenya Zoonotic Disease Unit, 'One Health Strategic Plan for the Prevention and Control of Zoonotic Diseases in Kenya (2021–2025)'.

73 Invest India Strategic Investment Research Unit (SIRU), 'One Health: The Evolving Paradigm to Boost India's Healthcare Infrastructure' (2021). Available at: www.investindia.gov.in/team-india-blogs/one-health-evolving-paradigm-boost-indias-healthcare-infrastructure.

74 The Wildlife (Protection) Act, No. 53 of 1972, modified in 1991 (India). Available at: www.animallaw.info/statute/wildlife-protection-act-1972.

75 The Environment (Protection) Act 1986, Act No. 29 of 1986 (India). Available at: www.indiacode.nic.in/bitstream/123456789/4316/1/ep_act_1986.pdf.

76 The Biological Diversity Act 2002, (India). Available at: https://jkforest.gov.in/assets/pdf/act/THE_BIOLOGICAL_DIVERSITY_ACT.pdf.

77 The Epidemic Diseases Act 1897 (India). Available at: www.indiacode.nic.in/bitstream/123456789/15942/1/epidemic_diseases_act%2C1897.pdf.

Apart from the statutes enacted by the Union and State legislatures, there are certain rules, regulations, and guidelines which cumulatively encompass and promote the concept of One Health:

(1) National Health Policy 2017, although zoonotic diseases have been mentioned only once in the context of rabies.[78]
(2) Environmental Impact Assessment Notification, 2006.[79]
(3) National Disaster Management Plan 2019, which addresses biological and public health emergencies and epidemics, noting that the increased interaction between humans and animals has increased the possibility of zoonotic diseases emerging in epidemic form.[80]
(4) National Disaster Management Guidelines for the Management of Biological Disasters 2008, which specifically observes the impact of human activities on the environment.[81]

The implementation of these laws and policies shows how intertwined they are with various strategies over time to enhance readiness for zoonotic disease outbreaks. This includes the creation of the Integrated Disease Surveillance Project aimed at improving surveillance efforts and response systems, as well as the establishment of a Department of Health Research under the Union MoHFW, tasked with offering technical assistance in the management and prevention of epidemics.[82]

Efforts are also underway in India to combat the resurgence of diseases.[83] The One Health intervention model of Odisha was successfully applied to eradicate human anthrax in a tribal district.[84] A cross-sectoral collaborative effort involving the community, animal, private, and non-governmental sectors was launched to engage communities in understanding dog behaviours.[85] In Tamil Nadu, a cost-effective, data-driven model was developed to tackle rabies.[86] To manage the Nipah virus outbreak in Kerala, a multi-disciplinary team from the National Centre for Disease Control was formed, comprising experts in zoonosis, epidemiology, respiratory medicine, emergency medicine, and animal husbandry. The recent severe outbreaks of ebola and Zika virus underscore the importance of well-prepared health systems in preventing global epidemics.[87]

78 Ministry of Health and Family Welfare Government of India, 'National Health Policy 2017' (2017). Available at: https://main.mohfw.gov.in/sites/default/files/9147562941489753121.pdf; and Ministry of Health and Family Welfare Government of India, 'Situation Analyses: Backdrop to the National Health Policy 2017' (2017). Available at: https://main.mohfw.gov.in/sites/default/files/71275472221489753307.pdf.

79 Ministry of Environment, Forest and Climate Change Government of India, 'EIA Notification, 2006 and Subsequent Amendments'. Available at: https://environmentclearance.nic.in/report/EIA_Notifications.aspx.

80 National Disaster Management Authority, *National Disaster Management Plan* (2019). Available at: https://covidlawlab.org/wp-content/uploads/2021/06/India_2019.11.01_Plan_National-Disaster-Management-Plan-2019_EN.pdf.

81 Ibid.

82 T Dikid, S K Jain, A Sharma, A Kumar, and J P Narain, 'Emerging & Re-emerging Infections in India: An Overview' (2013) 138(1) *The Indian Journal of Medical Research* 19–31. Available at: www.ncbi.nlm.nih.gov/pmc/articles/PMC3767269/.

83 Juhi Raut, A. Joshi, A. Mudey, et al., 'The Past, Present, and Future of One Health in India: A Narrative Review' (September 10, 2023) 15(9) *Cureus* e44992.

84 Debdutta Bhattacharya, J.S Kshatri, H.R. Choudhary, et al., 'One Health Approach for Elimination of Human Anthrax in a Tribal District of Odisha: Study Protocol' (2021) 16(5) *PLoS One* e0251041.

85 Vaishali Gautam, Pankaj Bhardwaj, Deepak Saxena, Nitesh Kumar, and Dileepan S, 'Multisectoral Approach to Achieve Canine Rabies Controlled Zone Using Intervention Mapping: Preliminary Results' (2020) 15(12) *PLoS One* e0242937.

86 Meagan C Fitzpatrick, H. A. Shah, A. Pandey, et al., 'One Health Approach to Cost-Effective Rabies Control in India' (2016) 113(51) *Proceedings of the National Academy of Sciences of the United States of America*.

87 Vijay K Chattu, Raman Kumar, Soosanna Kumary, Fnu Kajal, and Joseph K David, 'Nipah Virus Epidemic in Southern India and Emphasizing "One Health" Approach to Ensure Global Health Security' (2018) 7(2) *Journal of Family Medicine Primary Care*.

During the COVID-19 pandemic, India undertook a series of measures to bolster the One Health initiative, involving the rollout of diverse action plans, the launch of multiple projects that spanned different ministries, and the creation of new institutional structures. Although these efforts did not extend to enacting new laws, they encompassed a wide range of policies and infrastructural enhancements. This included the formulation and implementation of action plans and guidelines, the creation of new institutional entities and projects, and the development of new research facilities alongside the upgrading of existing ones.

2.4.5 *Action Plans and Guidelines*

In 2020, the Department-Related Parliamentary Standing Committee on Health and Family Welfare advocated for increased investment in health research and innovation, particularly to combat zoonotic diseases like COVID-19, and for the establishment of a One Health surveillance system equipped with an early warning system for microbial spillovers.[88] This recommendation was in response to the committee's concerns about insufficient funding for public health research.

In 2020, a collaborative document from the Department of Animal Husbandry and Dairying and the National Centre for Disease Control emphasised the importance of joint efforts in risk assessment, research, swift response, and monitoring of zoonotic diseases.[89] It proposed creating a standing committee on zoonoses, which would include representatives from the health, veterinary, environmental, and wildlife sectors.

The Union government introduced a National Action Plan on Climate Change and Human Health in 2021, featuring a detailed action plan on 'One Health for Climate Sensitive Zoonotic Diseases'.[90] This plan highlighted the necessity to identify climate-related factors that influence the prevalence of such diseases to tailor specific One Health strategies accordingly.

The 2021–2026 'National Human-Wildlife Conflict Mitigation Strategy and Action Plan of India', devised by the Ministry of Environment, Forest and Climate Change, stands out for not adopting a human-centric perspective on One Health. It integrates One Health frameworks and emphasises enhancing sample collection for research and establishing early warning systems for potential zoonotic diseases.[91]

2.4.6 *Institutional Bodies and Projects*

In October 2021, the Department of Biotechnology, under the Union Ministry of Science and Technology, initiated its inaugural 'One Health' project aimed at conducting surveillance of zoonotic and transboundary pathogens within India.[92] Later in 2021, the Department supported

88 Department-Related Parliamentary Standing Committee on Health and Family Welfare, 'One Hundred Twenty-Third Report on The Outbreak of Pandemic COVID-19 and Its Management' (2020). Available at: https://rajyasabha.nic.in/rsnew/Committee_site/Committee_File/ReportFile/14/142/123_2020_11_18.pdf.

89 Department of Animal Husbandry and Dairying & National Centre for Disease Control, 'One Health India, Multisectoral Collaboration' (2020). Available at: https://rr-asia.woah.org/wpcontent/uploads/2020/01/india-1.pdf.

90 Ministry of Health and Family Welfare, 'Dr. Harsh Vardhan Addresses the WHO High-Level Coalition on Health and Energy Platform of Action', Press release, (2021). Available at: https://pib.gov.in/PressReleasePage.aspx?PRID=1725863.

91 Ministry of Environment, Forest and Climate Change, 'National Human-Wildlife Conflict Mitigation Strategy and Action Plan of India 2021–26' (2021). Available at https://moef.gov.in/uploads/2022/01/National-Human-Wildlife-Conflict-Mitigation-Strategy-and-Action-Plan-of-India-2.pdf.

92 Ministry of Science and Technology, 'Country's First 'One Health' Consortium Launched by Department of Biotechnology, Post COVID-19', Press release, (2021). Available at www.pib.gov.in/PressReleasePage.aspx?PRID=1763772.

the creation of a substantial One Health Consortium involving twenty-seven entities, including hospitals, agricultural and veterinary institutions, medical research centres, and wildlife organisations. The consortium's goal is to foster interdisciplinary collaboration among professionals in animal, human, and wildlife health, although there has been no reported progress in this area yet.[93]

Furthermore, the Department of Health Research established a High-Level Inter-Ministerial Steering Committee in 2021, comprising representatives from various ministries and departments, tasked with formulating a One Health strategy for the nation.[94] Additionally, the announcement of a National Institute of One Health in 2022 marked a significant step towards addressing the emerging threats of zoonotic diseases through an integrated approach that encompasses human, animal, and environmental health.[95]

At the state level, initiatives have been rolled out to enhance One Health surveillance. The Department of Animal Husbandry and Dairying introduced pilot One Health programmes in Karnataka and Uttarakhand in June 2022, marking the beginning of efforts to establish a national One Health framework.[96] These programmes are designed to improve resource distribution at both national and state levels and to assist in developing mechanisms for early prediction and detection of health threats.

The Centre for One Health (CoH) at the National Centre for Disease Control, MoHFW, is working in coordination with all stakeholders to promote health and equity by undertaking activities necessary for the prevention and control of zoonotic diseases with the One Health approach. The centre implements the National Rabies Control Program, the National One Health Programme for Prevention and Control of Zoonoses, the Program for Prevention and Control of Leptospirosis, and the National Programme for Prevention and Control of Snakebite Envenoming.

2.5 LESSONS LEARNED

Countries can learn from these case studies to prioritise effective aspects when developing and implementing their own One Health frameworks. For example, key lessons learned include the establishment of coordinating mechanisms, legislative support, capacity-building, and international collaboration.

(1) Egypt established a national coordination mechanism and strategic framework for One Health, involving multiple ministries and international partners.
(2) Vietnam formed a multi-sectoral partnership (OHP), demonstrating effective inter-ministerial collaboration.
(3) Kenya established the ZDU to coordinate efforts between the health and agriculture sectors.
(4) India created institutional bodies like the CoH and initiative projects and action plans under various ministries.

[93] Ministry of Science and Technology, 'One Health Consortium', Press release, (2021). Available at https://pib.gov.in/PressReleasePage.aspx?PRID=1779757.

[94] Ministry of Environment, Forest and Climate Change, 'Notification S.O. 1247(E)' Indian Government (2021) Available at: http://environmentclearance.nic.in/writereaddata/EIA_Notifications/52_SO1240E_12032021.pdf.

[95] Ministry of Health and Family Welfare, 'Initiatives and Achievements 2022', Press release, (2022). Available at: https://pib.gov.in/PressReleasePage.aspx?PRID=1887285.

[96] K C Deepika, 'Karnataka among Two States to Host One Health Pilot with Focus on Zoonotic Diseases' (2022) *The Hindu*. Available at: www.thehindu.com/news/national/karnataka/karnataka-among-two-states-tohost-one-health-pilot-with-focus-on-zoonotic-diseases/article65533164.ece.

(5) India has a robust legal framework integrating health, environment, and wildlife laws supporting One Health initiatives.
(6) Vietnam and Kenya have invested in surveillance systems, training programmes, and infrastructure to enhance response capabilities.
(7) Egypt, Vietnam, and Kenya have engaged with international organisations like WHO, FAO, and WOAH for technical support and capacity-building.

From these case studies, countries can learn of areas to be more robust in when implementing a One Health approach, including:

(1) integrating the environmental sector (without full integration into a One Health framework, it can limit comprehensive ecosystem health management);
(2) strengthening resource allocation and sustainability in surveillance, reporting, and laboratory diagnosis within the animal health sector; and
(3) creating legally mandated national coordination mechanisms and legislation that supports One Health Frameworks, rather than policy-driven actions that can impact long-term sustainability.

In general, countries looking to implement One Health approaches should prioritise (1) policy and legislative frameworks by focusing on formalising One Health frameworks to ensure sustainable integration across sectors; (2) capacity-building and resource allocation, including investing in strengthening surveillance systems, laboratory capacity, and training programmes to enhance early detection and response to zoonotic diseases; (3) inter-sectoral collaboration between the health, agriculture, and environment sectors at the national and sub-national levels to address emerging health threats effectively; (4) international engagement by leveraging existing partnerships and creating new partnerships with international organisations and neighbouring countries to share best practices, resources, and expertise in One Health implementation; and (5) environmental health integration to include environmental health as a core component of One Health strategies to address ecosystem health and its impact on human and animal health.

Governments and stakeholders need to prioritise investment in One Health programmes to strengthen health systems and mitigate the impact of infectious diseases. By fostering collaboration, building capacity, strengthening laws and policies, and allocating resources, countries can better prepare for and respond to EIDs and other health threats. Investing in One Health initiatives with a strong legal or policy basis is not only essential for protecting public health but also for promoting sustainable development and global health security.

3

One Health and the UN Animal Welfare Nexus Resolution

A Milestone Step towards an Animal Welfare Revolution?

Elien Verniers

3.1 INTRODUCTION

The United Nations Environment Assembly's (UNEA) Resolution on the animal welfare–environment–sustainable development nexus (Nexus Resolution), adopted in March 2022 in Nairobi,[1] has interchangeably been called a 'landmark' and 'historic' resolution.[2] The UNEA stands at the forefront of global environmental governance, serving as a pivotal platform for addressing pressing environmental challenges. Against the backdrop of escalating concerns over biodiversity loss, climate change, and the interplay between human activities and ecosystem health, the UNEA has emerged as a crucial arena for advancing holistic approaches to sustainability. Central to this endeavour is the recognition of the intricate nexus between animal welfare, environmental conservation, and sustainable development. In response to mounting evidence linking the well-being of animals to ecosystem resilience and human welfare, the UNEA has embarked on a landmark initiative to foster synergies between these interconnected realms. The Nexus Resolution represents a watershed moment in global environmental governance, signalling a paradigm shift towards more inclusive and integrated approaches that prioritise the protection of animals as integral components of healthy ecosystems and sustainable development pathways.

The manner in which different aspects of One Health have been connected via the Nexus Resolution is intriguing. Animal welfare, sustainable development, 'One Health', and the environment have all been investigated separately but are now for the first time aggregated in a comprehensive resolution. This multifaceted and integrative approach may prove helpful to truly achieve 'harmony with nature'.[3]

This chapter examines why the Nexus Resolution constitutes a significant milestone, and provides insights into its context, content, and implementation status. The chapter delves into the implications of applying an anthropocentric approach to accommodate the interests of non-human animals. What can we expect from this pioneering resolution and how does it further the One Health legal framework? It is the first time that the UNEA has adopted a resolution

[1] United Nations Environment Assembly, 'Resolution on the Animal Welfare-Environment-Sustainable Development Nexus' (7 March 2022) UNEP/EA5/RES.1 (hereafter the UNEA Nexus Resolution).

[2] Eurogroup for Animals, 'Landmark Resolution Recognising Animal Welfare Adopted by UNEA' (2022). Available at: www.eurogroupforanimals.org/news/landmark-resolution-recognising-animal-welfare-adopted-unea; World Federation for Animals (WFA), 'Historic UN Resolution Recognizes Animal Welfare's Role in Sustainability' (2022). Available at: https://wfa.org/historic-un-resolution-recognizes-animal-welfares-role-in-sustainability/.

[3] See United Nations General Assembly (UNGA), 'Transforming Our World: The 2030 Agenda for Sustainable Development' (21 October 2015) A/RES/70/1 at 4/35, para 9.

with explicit and *inverbatim* reference to animal welfare, indicating that animal welfare is finally gathering momentum at the UN level. This chapter examines why this long-awaited breakthrough has the potential to ultimately enable harmony with nature, including human and non-human animals.

3.2 THE NEXUS RESOLUTION: CONTEXT AND CONTENT

3.2.1 *The Emergence: African Nations as Driving Force*

The adoption of the UNEA Nexus Resolution is rooted in the 2019 Africa Animal Welfare Conference.[4] The theme of this Conference was 'Animals, Environment and Sustainable Development in 21st Century Africa: An Interlinked Approach'. During this conference and under the organisation of both the Africa Network for Animal Welfare (ANAW) and the UN Environment Programme (UNEP) more than 270 participants from various African countries had the opportunity to discuss the outcomes of the fourth United Nations Environment Assembly (UNEA-4) and the expectations of fifth United Nations Environment Assembly (UNEA-5). One of the concluding statements was that 'Animal welfare issues have evolved into a topical issue of concern that merit global attention. It is clear that interaction between human society and the animal world are inextricably linked.'[5] Furthermore, the participants agreed to engage with the UNEP to 'consult and provide input to member states that would champion any proposal of a resolution to be adopted at UNEA-5 on animal welfare'.[6]

Following the deliberations at the 2019 Africa Animal Welfare Conference, ANAW, the African Union Inter-African Bureau for Animal Resources (AU-IBAR) and the World Federation for Animals (WFA) set up a steering committee in order to develop a first concept note for the resolution text.[7] In February 2021 the concept note was published and in March 2021 an accompanying fundraising campaign was launched.[8] The concept note provides valuable input and insights, which will be discussed in the next sections. One year later, as a result of the aforementioned collaboration and together with the pioneering core states of Burkina Faso, Democratic Republic of Congo, Ethiopia, Ghana, Islamic Republic of Pakistan, Senegal and South Sudan, the Nexus Resolution was adopted at the UNEA-5, which took place in Nairobi.

3.2.2 *The Content: Inger Andersen Needs to Deliver the First Nexus Report*

The Nexus Resolutions consists of a preamble of nine paragraphs and four substantive provisions. Although it seems rather small-scale to earn the title of being a milestone resolution, four strong provisions may be enough to spark an (animal welfare) revolution.

In general, the Nexus Resolution aims to map and gather information on a worldwide scale relating to the nexus between animal welfare, the environment, and sustainable development.

4 UNEP, 'The Africa Animal Welfare Conference 2019' (2019). Available at: www.unep.org/events/civil-society-events/africa-animal-welfare-conference-2019.

5 UNEP, 'Africa Animal Welfare Conference 2019'.

6 Ibid.

7 WFA, 'ANAW and WFA Lead Global Initiative for Adoption of UN Animal Welfare Resolution' (2021). Available at: https://wfa.org/wfa-anaw-resolution/.

8 Resolution for Animal Welfare, 'Concept Note: Animal Welfare-Environment-Sustainable Development Nexus' (2021). Available at: www.unep.org/events/civil-society-events/africa-animal-welfare-conference-2019#:~:text=The%203rd%20Africa%20Animal%20Welfare,for%20Animal%20Welfare%20(ANAW) (hereafter the 'Concept Note: Animal Welfare-Environment-Sustainable Development Nexus').

Consequently, Article 1 requires the UNEP Executive Director (a role undertaken by Inger Anderson at the time of writing) together with key partners such as the Food and Agriculture Organization of the United Nations (FAO), the World Health Organization (WHO) and the World Organization for Animal Health (WOAH), and the One Health High-Level Expert Panel to produce the first animal welfare nexus report. The remaining provisions require this report to: be peer-reviewed by UNEA member states (Article 2); intensive collaboration to take place between UNEP and the Tripartite Alliance (FAO-WHO-WOAH) in animal welfare related matters using a One Health approach (Article 3); and to present the first nexus report at the sixth session of the UN Environment Assembly (Article 4). UNEA 6 was held in February and March 2024 and failed to deliver the Nexus report. The latter is now expected at UNEA 7 in 2026.

The preamble of the final resolution included a topic which was absent in the initial draft provided by the Steering Committee: One Health. In this respect, the Nexus Resolution stipulates that 'animal welfare can contribute to addressing environmental challenges, promoting the One Health approach and achieving the Sustainable Development Goals' and that there exists an 'increasing need to address these [the health and welfare of animals, sustainable development, the environment and human health and well-being] connections through the One Health approach, among other holistic approaches'.[9] Instead of thus emphasising the COVID-19 pandemic, the focus of the narrative lies on One Health and what role it can play as a pragmatic, albeit holistic, approach.

In the body of both texts, we identify a similar pattern. One Health is again absent in the initial draft resolution but it is incorporated in Article 3 of the final resolution as well as in Article 1, insofar that it is requested that a close collaboration needs to be set up between the FAO, the WHO, the WOAH, and the One Health High-Level Expert Panel. Article 2 of the initial draft specifically targets member states and asks them to take responsibility for protecting animals and their habitats, but this has not been reiterated in the final resolution. The active participation of member states is, however, not completely removed as the adjusted Article 2 assigns the member states to peer review the report of Executive Director of UNEP.

3.3 EVALUATION: THE UNIQUENESS OF THE NEXUS RESOLUTION

The analysis above does not reveal any of the extraordinary provisions that we would expect from a historic or landmark resolution. Why is it nevertheless referred to in that way and how should we now evaluate it? This section of the chapter provides an in-depth analysis of six topics that need more explanation to gain insights into the uniqueness of the Nexus Resolution.

3.3.1 *The Global Animal Welfare Gap*

The uniqueness of this resolution pertains to mitigating the prominent animal welfare gap that currently exists in international law. At a national level, about two-thirds of the countries in the world have some sort of animal protection legislation in place and at the regional level the African Union and especially the European Union are establishing a strong animal welfare policy with accompanying enforceable legal instruments.[10] The Nexus Resolution was the first instance of an international resolution making explicit and *in verbatim* reference to animal

[9] Paragraphs 6–8 of the preamble of the UNEA Nexus Resolution.

[10] Anne Peters, 'Global Animal Law: What It Is and Why We Need It' (2016) 5(1) *Transnational Environmental Law* 9; Steven White, 'Into the Void: International Law and the Protection of Animal Welfare' (2013) 4(4) *Global Policy* 391.

welfare. The title ('5/1. Animal welfare-environment-sustainable development nexus') of the resolution clearly communicates animal welfare (not species protection or animal health, as is already acknowledged in other international laws) as a core topic.

3.3.2 *UN Institutionalisation*

Moreover, the uniqueness of the resolution also concerns endorsement of animal welfare within the United Nations context in particular. In the past, there have been attempts to address animal welfare in legal instruments at the international level. Examples of two soft law proposals are the Universal Declaration of Animal Rights (UDAR) and the Universal Declaration on Animal Welfare (UDAW). UDAR was presented at the Paris headquarters of the United Nations Educational, Scientific and Cultural Organization (UNESCO) in 1978, but was never formally adopted.[11] The World Society for the Protection of Animals (now World Animal Protection) also relentlessly tried for UDAW (first proclaimed at the Animals 2000 World Congress in London) to obtain official UN status but without any success.[12] More recently, a legally binding UN instrument has been proposed: a United Nations Convention on Animal Healths and Protection (UNCAHP).[13] The Global Animal Law Association (GAL) hope to have their framework convention adopted in 2029 by the United Nations General Assembly.[14] In addition, legal scholarship has also suggested UN institutionalisation of animal welfare through the creation of a new international organisation as part of the UN system.[15] Brels, for instance, put forward the idea of a United Nations Animal Protection Programme (UNAPP), analogous to UNEP, or alternatively the expansion of UNEP to United Nations Environmental and Animal Protection Programme (UNEAPP).[16] The concept note preceding the initial draft also reflects a similar way of thinking and is convinced that 'improving animal welfare must be fully incorporated into the UNEP Programme of Work in an integrated manner'.[17] Subsequently, the current UNEA Nexus Resolution may be the genesis for further UN institutionalisation. It is true that the inclusion of animal welfare may incur some costs (e.g. staff costs related to the recruitment of expertise in animal welfare).[18] It is nevertheless highly recommended to do so, as this would deliver significant social, environmental, and economic benefits in the long-term. The lack of animal welfare institutionalisation results in the absence of binding hard law that can tackle the extraterritorial and global nature of many animal abuses.[19]

11 Jean-Marc Neumann, 'The Universal Declaration of Animal Rights or the Creation of a New Equilibrium between Species' (2012) 19(1) *Animal Law Review* 91.

12 Miah Gibson, 'The Universal Declaration of Animal Welfare' (2011) 16(2) *Deakin Law Review* 539. Note that, as highlighted above, UDAW, in particular the phrase 'the ongoing effort by Member States to seek the adoption of a Universal Declaration on Animal welfare', was mentioned in the initial resolution draft but omitted in the final resolution.

13 Global Animal Law Association, 'UN Convention on Animal Health and Protection (UNCAHP)' (2018). Available at: www.uncahp.org/ (hereafter the UNCAHP). See also Elien Verniers and Sabine Brels, 'UNCAHP, One Health, and the Sustainable Development Goals' (2021) 24(1) *Journal of International Wildlife Law & Policy* 38.

14 Andrea Schapper and Cebuan Bliss, 'Transforming Our World? Strengthening Animal Rights and Animal Welfare at the United Nations' (2023) 37(3) *International Relations* 514, 519.

15 Ibid., 522; Anne Peters, *Animals in International Law* (Brill 2021) 568.

16 Sabine Brels, 'A Global Approach to Animal Protection' (2017) 20(1) *Journal of International Wildlife Law & Policy* 105, 122.

17 Concept Note: Animal Welfare-Environment-Sustainable Development Nexus, 2.

18 Ibid., 3–4.

19 Charlotte E Blattner, *Protecting Animals Within and Across Borders: Extraterritorial Jurisdiction and the Challenges of Globalization* (Oxford University Press 2019).

Current market mechanisms are failing to provide animal health and welfare as well as environmental protection with financial and economic value as they are not tradable and not restricted to tangible entities.[20] It is therefore the moral responsibility of the UN, as a universal global organisation that endorses an inclusive worldview of the environment, humans, and animals to not overlook animal welfare and its priceless worth.[21]

3.3.3 *Beyond the Environment–Animal Dichotomy*

There exists a long-lasting debate about whether concern for the environment is in tension with concern for (individual) animals.[22] In recent years, emphasis has increasingly been placed on the reconciliation between animal ethics and environmental ethics. After all, it has been argued that despite theoretical differences between environmentalism and animal ethics, there are multiple areas of convergence and instead of dividing each other, the fight against common enemies (e.g. abolishing factory farming as this is a major contributor to climate change) can instead provide mutual benefits.[23] This is, for instance, also the idea behind the compassionate conservation movement, whose central aim is to safeguard Earth's biological diversity while retaining a commitment to treating individuals with respect and concern for their well-being.[24] This Nexus Resolution appears to implicitly support that idea and displays animal welfare and environmental challenges as communicating vessels.

Paragraph 6 of the Nexus Resolution's preamble states 'Acknowledging that animal welfare can contribute to addressing environmental challenges'. The initially developed draft of the resolution specified that the 'unsustainable use of domestic and wild animals is a key driver of the triple environmental crises of biodiversity loss, climate change and pollution' (PDF available upon request).[25] The link between animal welfare and the environment is even more clearly described in paragraph 5 of the preamble of the initial draft: 'Keeping in mind that there is a nexus between animals and the environment whereby animals are an essential part of our ecosystems and that ecosystems are balanced by nature if allowed to self-regulate, and that detrimental impacts on animals or their habitats can harm nature and our natural environment in various ways.' The Nexus Resolution thus plays an important role in the further development of linking animal welfare and the environment, especially at the international level.

Previously, the reconciliation between attention for the environment and animals was limited to initiatives at the national level; predominantly Central and South American countries approached animal welfare as being part of environmental protection. In the Estrellita

[20] Richard van der Hoff and M N Anyango, 'Transforming Biodiversity Governance: Biodiversity Finance and Transformative Governance: The Limitations of Innovative Financial Instruments' in Ingrid Visseren-Hamakers and Marcel T J Kok (eds.), *Transforming Biodiversity Governance* (Cambridge University Press 2022).

[21] Antoine F Goetschel and Sabine Brels, 'Globally Protecting Animals at the UN: Why and How?' (2019) 45 *UN Observer* 193–225e.

[22] Catia Faria and Eze Paez, 'It's Splitsville: Why Animal Ethics and Environmental Ethics Are Incompatible' (2019) 63(8) *American Behavioral Scientist* 1047; Dale Jamieson, 'Animal Liberation Is an Environmental Ethic' (1998) 7(1) *Environmental Values* 41.

[23] Connor K Kianpour and Eze Paez, 'Red in Tooth and Claw No More: Animal Rights and the Permissibility to Redesign Nature' (2022) 31(2) *Environmental Values* 227.

[24] Anja Heister, 'The North American Model of Wildlife Conservation', in *Beyond the North American Model of Wildlife Conservation: From Lethal to Compassionate Conservation* (Springer, 2022) 216.

[25] Paragraph 6 of the preamble of the draft UNEA Nexus Resolution.

monkey case, for instance, the Ecuadorian Constitutional Court accepted the right to protect individual animals through the Rights of Nature.[26] Since 2008, Article 71 of the Ecuadorian Constitution recognises Nature or Pacha Mama as a rights holder and allows for standing to effectively enforce this provision. In 2022 the Ecuadorian Constitutional Court also accepted individual animals as subjects of rights protected by Article 71 of the Ecuadorian Constitution. The Court ruled that animal rights are 'a specific dimension – with their own particularities – of the rights of Nature' and clarified that 'Animal rights protect specific members of the animal kingdom who are therefore part of Nature.'[27] 'The conditions of their ecosystems, communities or habitats, also protected by the rights of Nature, necessarily affect them; just as the conditions of such individuals may eventually affect the systems in which they inhabit and their relationships.'[28] Constitutional environmental protection, especially in the context of Rights of Nature, offers an additional robust legal basis for also recognising the individual interests of animals. Similar to Ecuador where the (constitutional) Rights of Nature framework was used for advancing and acknowledging animal rights, Panama is attempting to follow and harness the new Rights of Nature Law as a legal means for animal rights groups to defend those rights.[29] In other Central and South American countries, it has been accepted that a constitutional obligation to protect the environment inherently also comprehends the constitutional obligation of animal protection.[30] For example, the Supreme Courts of Colombia and Costa Rica have ruled that the right to environmental protection not only protects fauna (wild animals) but also domestic animals.[31]

These examples demonstrate the increased attention to the nexus between animals and the environment and how they can tackle challenges together in legal discourse at the national level, with the Nexus Resolution paving the way for such recognition at the international level. Eventually, it could inspire the UN to rename UNEP into UNEAPP after all. By expressly underscoring the interlinkage between animal welfare and the environment, the Nexus Resolution not only elevates the debate on the animal–environment dichotomy to the global level, it also clearly chooses to focus on unity instead of on division. Furthermore, the Nexus Resolution explicitly mentions the report of the Secretary-General on harmony with nature.[32] In this report, Secretary-General Guterres affirmed that 'non-human animals are sentient beings, not mere property, and must be afforded respect and legal recognition'.[33] Taking into account the timeframe (July 2020), Guterres proposed to see COVID-19 and the process of

[26] Corte Constitucional del Ecuador, Case No. 253-20-JH, 2022 (Ecuador). See Macarena Montes Franceschini and Kristen Stilt, 'Estrellita the Woolly Monkey and the Ecuadorian Constitutional Court' (2023) 22(2) *ReVista (Cambridge)*. Available at: https://revista.drclas.harvard.edu/estrellita-the-wooly-monkey-and-the-ecuadorian-constitutional-court-animal-rights-through-the-rights-of-nature/.

[27] Corte Constitucional del Ecuador, Case No. 253-20-JH, 2022 (Ecuador), paras 83 and 91.

[28] Ibid., para 92.

[29] Nichola Daunton, 'Panama brings in new law granting nature the "right to exist"' (2022). Available at: www.euronews.com/green/2022/03/08/panama-brings-in-new-law-granting-nature-the-right-to-exist; Cooper Gegan, 'A New "Rights of Nature" Law in Panama Gives Rights to Sea Turtles' (2023). Available at: www.theinertia.com/environment/a-new-rights-of-nature-law-in-panama-gives-rights-to-sea-turtles/.

[30] Olivier Le Bot, 'Is It Useful to Have an Animal Protection in the Constitution' (2018) 15(1) *US-China Law Review* 58.

[31] Corte Constitucional República de Colombia, Case No. C-666-10 (30 August 2010), C-083-14 (12 February 2014) and C-095-16 (25 February 2016). See also Angie Vega, 'Colombia' (2023). Available at: www.animallaw.info/intro/colombia#:~:text=In%20decision%20SU016%20of%202020,and%20the%20right%20to%20freedom; and Sala Constitucional De La Corte Suprema De Justicia de San José (Costa Rica), Case No. 2016-13553 (21 September 2016). Available at: www.tse.go.cr/juris/electorales/SSC-13553-2016.html.

[32] Paragraph 3 of the preamble of the UNA Nexus Resolution.

[33] UNGA, 'Harmony with Nature: Report of the Secretary-General' (28 July 2020) A/75/266, 42.

recovery from COVID-19 as a unique opportunity and stepping stone for a global Earth-centred transition, in which the lives of all human and non-human species matter.[34] This is where the concept of One Health becomes pertinent.

3.3.4 *One Health*

Whereas the title of the resolution clearly emphasises the link between animal welfare, the environment, and sustainable development, this is not the case for One Health. Notwithstanding its absence, it nevertheless plays an important, albeit more disguised role that should not be overlooked. It may instead be considered the central linking pin and lens through which all three interrelated nexus concepts (animal welfare–environment–sustainable development) are shaped and approached. In this regard, the UNEA Nexus Resolution could, alternatively, have been titled 'Animal welfare–environment–sustainable development–one health nexus'. In some literature, animal welfare is even considered the basis of One Health.[35]

One Health has been defined as an approach aimed at tackling complex patterns of global change, in which the inextricable interconnection of humans, pets, livestock, and wildlife, along with their social and ecological environments, is evident. One Health solutions require integrated approaches to human and animal health and their respective social and environmental contexts.[36] The growing attention towards One Health after the onset of the COVID-19 pandemic suggests the approach has an anthropocentric impetus.[37] One Health itself is less anthropocentric than one might expect as the ultimate aim is arguably to have interspecies health equity, which implies the development of a framework for biocentric social justice.[38] So both human and non-human health needs to be achieved for interspecies flourishing.

One Health possesses at least three valuable features (integrative, inclusive, and transdisciplinary) that can enable a transformative change and potentially even an animal welfare revolution.[39] The first is its integrative functioning. One Health can be used to overcome silos and build bridges between disciplinary and organisational boundaries instead. It not only acknowledges the inextricable interconnection between human, animal, and environmental health but it also suggests that only united efforts will lead to success. In addition, One Health also sets in motion another integrative approach, that of One Welfare, which admittedly can be even more meaningful for the animal welfare discourse. Similar to One Health, One Welfare aims to develop a broader integrative and interlinked framework aligning the welfare of humans,

[34] Ibid., 94–95.

[35] E.g. Antoine F Goetschel, 'Animal Welfare as the Basis of One Health: A UN Convention on Animal Welfare, Health, and Protection Poses a Realistic Solution to Improved Animal Welfare and Human Health' (2024) 3(1) *CABI One Health* 1. See also Elisa Cavallin, 'Preventing Pandemics by Building Bridges in EU Policy and Law' (2021) 30(5) *European Energy and Environmental Law Review* 162, on how animal welfare and One Health can be linking pins for an adequate cross-cutting EU Policy and Law.

[36] Jakob Zinsstag, E Schelling, D Waltner-Toews, and M Tanner, 'From "One Medicine" to "One Health" and Systemic Approaches to Health and Well-Being' (2011) 101(3–4) *Preventive Veterinary Medicine* 148.

[37] Elien Verniers, 'International Law, Animal Health and Zoonosis: A Critical Analysis of EU Leadership' (2022) 10(2) *Global Journal of Animal Law* 1, 16.

[38] Hans Keune, Unnikrishnan Payyappallimana, Serge Morand, and Simon R Rüegg, 'One Health and Biodiversity' in Ingrid J Visseren-Hamakers and Marcel T J Kok (eds.), *Transforming Biodiversity Governance* (Cambridge University Press 2022) 104–105.

[39] Ibid., 108.

animals, and the environment.[40] The hard law proposal of UNCAHP incorporates both concepts in paragraph 7 of its preamble.[41]

Another example of an integrative approach, which has been mentioned in the previous section, is compassionate conservation. The compassionate conservation narrative strives for a more inclusive and relational form of nature conservation that questions mainstream conservation practice given concerns for individual wild animal welfare.[42] As with compassionate conservation, One Health also promotes inclusivity and transcends traditional health pluralism approaches.[43] As indicated above, the key to One Health as an overarching inclusive framework is the untapped potential to establish interspecies health equity. Finally, a last core element of One Health is its transdisciplinary dimension. One Health combines multiple knowledge angles and tries to bring together both different scientific disciplines and different societal perspectives.[44] This transdisciplinarity is crucial to enhance the practical relevance of the One Health discourse in the policy, science, and legislation interface and warrants increased mutual understanding.

In the Nexus Resolution, One Health appears on the one hand as a means and on the other hand as an end. As a means, One Health can be conceived as an integrative and transdisciplinary technique that uncovers the interlinkages between animal welfare, the environment, and sustainable development.[45] One Health as an end relates to the idea of obtaining or generating interspecies (health) equity; the inclusive facet of One Health. According to paragraph 6 of the preamble of the Nexus Resolution, animal welfare can contribute to promoting the One Health approach. A similar idea can be retrieved from the Animal Welfare Strategy for Africa in which One Health (also One Welfare) is one of the three core areas of focus.[46]

3.3.5 *SDGs*

In paragraph 6 of the resolution's preamble, it is specified that animal welfare can contribute to achieving the Sustainable Development Goals (SDGs). This statement can be framed in clarification of the animal welfare–sustainable development interlinkage. The relationship between animal welfare and sustainable development has been long ignored until recently. The first milestone pertains to the 2019 Global Sustainable Development Report (GSDR), which identified for the first (and only) time that animal welfare is a key issue missing in the 2030 Sustainable Development Agenda.[47] The 2019 GSDR articulates: 'The clear link between human health and well-being and animal welfare is increasingly being recognized in ethics- and rights-based

[40] Tristan J Colonius and Rosemary W Earley, 'One Welfare: A Call to Develop a Broader Framework of Thought and Action' (2013) 242(3) *Journal of the American Veterinary Medical Association* 309.

[41] Paragraph 7 of the preamble of UNCAHP: 'Considering the One Health and One Welfare concepts, acknowledging that global health and welfare of humans and animals are interdependent'.

[42] David Fraser, 'Toward a Synthesis of Conservation and Animal Welfare Science' (2010) 19(12) *Animal Welfare* 121.

[43] Keune et al., 'One Health and Biodiversity' 97.

[44] Ibid., 108.

[45] See paragraph 8 of the preamble of the UNEA Nexus Resolution, which has been reproduced in Article 3 of the UNEA Nexus Resolution: 'through the One Health approach'. See also Article 1 of the UNEA Nexus Resolution which points to the One Health High-Level Expert Panel as one of the relevant stakeholders that can inform and help the animal welfare–environment–sustainable development nexus.

[46] African Union Inter-African Bureau for Animal Resources, 'Animal Welfare Strategy for Africa (AWSA)', (2017). Available at: https://rr-africa.woah.org/wp-content/uploads/2019/05/awsa_executive_summary_layout_eng_2017.pdf at p. 6.

[47] Independent Group of Scientists appointed by the Secretary-General, 'Global Sustainable Development Report 2019: The Future is Now – Science for Achieving Sustainable Development' United Nations (2019) 117. Available at: https://sdgs.un.org/sites/default/files/2020-07/24797GSDR_report_2019.pdf.

frameworks. Strong governance should safeguard the well-being of both wildlife and domesticated animals with rules on animal welfare embedded in transnational trade.'[48] One would expect this message would be highlighted in the 2023 GSDR but remarkably this was not the case and animal welfare was missing altogether.[49] Notwithstanding this setback, the Nexus Resolution provided a new formal recognition of the animal welfare–sustainable development connection. Further, a recent UNGA resolution on agriculture development, food security, and nutrition made reference to the Nexus Resolution and emphasised that animal health and welfare can contribute to addressing challenges and achieving the Sustainable Development Goals.[50]

This relationship has already been proposed in legal scholarship.[51] Visseren-Hamakers, for example, discussed the creation of an 18th Sustainable Development Goal on animal health, welfare, and rights.[52] The animal welfare–sustainable development connection also received societal attention and support, which has been demonstrated in the framework of the Sustainable Development Goal consultation process when animal protection achieved the second highest score among several options for the seventeenth additional goal in the *My World 2015 Survey*.[53] In addition, several scientific studies have illuminated how animal welfare can positively impact the SDGs.[54] Although the Nexus Resolution only refers to animal welfare helping to achieve the SDGs, Keeling et al. revealed a mutually beneficial relationship between the SDGs and animal welfare.[55] The Swedish study discovered that on average the impact of achieving an SDG was slightly better at leading to improved animal welfare than the impact of improving animal welfare on achieving the SDG. However, the researchers mitigated this finding as they noticed that this result was not consistent across all SDGs and concluded that overall the mean score displayed an undeniable co-benefit.

3.3.6 *Animal Welfare Science*

The scientific value of animal welfare in the Nexus Resolution is twofold. On the one hand, the Nexus Resolution already confirms that there is a strong body of science supporting

48 Ibid, 117.

49 Independent Group of Scientists appointed by the Secretary-General, 'Global Sustainable Development Report 2023: Times of Crisis, Times of Change: Science for Accelerating Transformations to Sustainable Development' United Nations (2023). Available at: https://sdgs.un.org/sites/default/files/2023-09/FINAL%20GSDR%202023-Digital%20-110923_1.pdf.

50 UNGA, 'Resolution on Agriculture Development, Food Security and Nutrition' (15 November 2023) UNGA/A/C.2/78/L.65, 27. Note that this same paragraph also acknowledged the importance of One Health as a holistic approach which can deliver multiple benefits to the health and well-being of people, animals, plants, and ecosystems.

51 Livia Boscardin and Leonie Bossert, 'Sustainable Development and Nonhuman Animals: Why Anthropocentric Concepts of Sustainability Are Outdated and Need to Be Extended' in S Meisch, et al. (eds.), *Ethics of Science in the Research for Sustainable Development* (Nomos, 2015) 1–15; Elien Verniers, 'Bringing Animal Welfare under the Umbrella of Sustainable Development: A Legal Analysis' (2021) 30(3) *Review of European, Comparative & International Environmental Law* 349.

52 Ingrid J Visseren-Hamakers, 'The 18th Sustainable Development Goal' (2020) 3 *Earth System Governance* 100047.

53 Felix Dodds, Ambassador David Donoghue, and Jimena Leiva Roesch, *Negotiating the Sustainable Development Goals: A Transformational Agenda for an Insecure World* (Routledge, 2017) 51.

54 For a study linking better animal welfare conditions to positive impacts on several SDGs (establishing correlations with ten out of seventeen SDGs), see Eurogroup for Animals, 'Policy Brief Animal Welfare, Trade and Sustainable Development Goals' (2019), 7–15. Available at: www.eurogroupforanimals.org/files/eurogroupforanimals/2021-12/E4A-SDG-and-AW_Report_03-2019-screen.pdf. For an article elaborating on the importance of animal welfare with regard to SDG 2 (Zero Hunger) and SDG 12 (Responsible Consumption and Production), see NGO Major Group, 'Position Paper High Level Political Forum 2021' (2021), 10, 22. Available at: www.ngomg.org/reports.

55 Linda Keeling, Håkan Tunón, Gabriela Olmos, et al., 'Animal Welfare and the United Nations Sustainable Development Goals' (2019) 6 *Frontiers in Veterinary Science* 336.

animal welfare.[56] On the other hand, the underlying idea behind the Nexus Resolution is to create and request interdisciplinary scientific analysis on animal welfare as well as sustainable development, the environment, and One Health. As One Health is inherently evidence-based, the evidence obtained in the framework of animal welfare science can equally inform One Health approaches. A good alignment of scientific parameters with law and policy may potentially allow for the transformation of the current soft law approach to a hard law instrument. The expected report will either provide a firm scientific basis to build on or an incremental jumping-off point for the next steps in future policy. In this regard, the concept note also pays attention to the scientific nature of the added value of the initiative: 'The consideration of animal welfare within UNEP's policy mandate would help to broaden and enrich its science-policy base, leading to better-informed and more effective policymaking and programme development. It will also help with the achievement of many SDGs and the prevention of future pandemics.'[57]

3.4 IMPLEMENTATION UPDATES: SLOW AND STEADY WINS THE RACE?

As mentioned above, to date no Nexus Resolution Report has been submitted. Consequently, the UNEP Director now has two more years to complete an effective report (in addition and in response to an initial scoping study). An explanation for not meeting the deadline can be found in the slow start of the Nexus Resolution. During UNEA 5 the animal welfare nexus resolution was not the only resolution adopted. In total 14 resolutions were adopted, including resolutions on sustainable nitrogen management,[58] future global environment outlook,[59] and a circular economy.[60] While UNEP prioritised the implementation of some UNEA 5 headline resolutions, such as Resolution 8 on the creation of a science-policy panel regarding the management of chemicals and waste,[61] and Resolution 14 on an international legally binding instrument to end plastic pollution,[62] the Nexus Resolution was not considered such a priority.[63] The implementation roadmap and indicative budget remains unclear and the process has so far not been transparent.

However, in July 2023, Major Groups and Stakeholders Consultations were held in Rabat (Morocco) as a preparatory event on the way to UNEA 6 which also included a progress overview on the UNEA 5 resolutions.[64] This meeting shed light on the (lack of) implementation of

[56] Paragraph 9 of the preamble of the UNEA Nexus Resolution.
[57] Concept Note: Animal Welfare-Environment-Sustainable Development Nexus, 3.
[58] UNEA, 'Resolution on Sustainable Nitrogen Management' (7 March 2022) UNEP/EA5/RES.2.
[59] UNEA, 'Resolution on the Future of the Global Environment Outlook' (7 March 2022) UNEP/EA5/RES.3.
[60] UNEA, 'Resolution on Enhancing Circular Economy as a Contribution to Achieving Sustainable Consumption and Production' (7 March 2022) UNEP/EA5/RES.11.
[61] UNEA, 'Resolution on a Science-Policy Panel to Contribute Further to the Sound Management of Chemicals and Waste and to Prevent Pollution' (7 March 2022) UNEP/EA5/RES.8.
[62] UNEA, 'Resolution on End Plastic Pollution: Towards an International Legally Binding Instrument' (7 March 2022) UNEP/EA5/RES.14.
[63] WFA, 'The Animal Welfare Nexus Resolution – Current State of Play' (2023). Available at: https://wfa.org/the-animal-welfare-nexus-resolution-current-state-of-play/.
[64] UNEP, 'Major Groups and Stakeholders Consultations – 2023' (2023). Available at: www.unep.org/events/civil-society-events/major-groups-and-stakeholders-consultations-2023; UNEP, 'Progress Report on UNEA 5 Resolutions' (2023). Available at: https://wedocs.unep.org/bitstream/handle/20.500.11822/42929/Progress%20of%20UNEA%205%20Resolutions.pdf?sequence=1&isAllowed=y.

the Nexus Resolution.[65] It was communicated that some administrative actions had been taken, including high-level meetings between UNEP and WOAH, which confirmed the shared interest to work together to implement the Nexus Resolution, as well as the recruitment processes for facilitation and coordination roles. Resource mobilisation has also been considered. With these actions, the first hurdles appear to have been overcome and substance may have been given to Articles 1 and 3 of the Nexus Resolution. However, Article 2 (requiring the submission of the report for peer review by member states), as well as Article 4 (requiring presentation of the findings of the developed report at UNEA 6), have not been accomplished within the deadline of UNEA 6.[66]

It is too early to speculate on what might be expected in terms of national implementation or what laws might be developed in response to the Nexus Report. Nevertheless, the mere adoption of the Nexus Resolution has triggered scholarship to delve deeper into the quest of animal welfare and sustainable development issues, both at the international and regional levels.[67] Notwithstanding the not-so-timely implementation proceedings, there also exists a proactive attitude with a group of member states as well as with NGOs. For example, following the one-year anniversary of the Nexus Resolution, the World Federation for Animals drafted a vision paper on the Nexus and the Nexus report process.[68] In tandem, the pioneering core states behind the Nexus Resolution together with ANAW and AU-IBAR created the group of Friends of the Nexus Resolution comprised (in November 2023) of 31 member states.[69] The Friends of the Resolution is an open-ended working group of member states who meet with various international organisations (WHO, WOAH, World Bank, UNEP, FAO) to keep the pressure high for the development of the Nexus report.

Although no full report has been presented so far, currently a scoping study has been published which ultimately needs to support the drafters of the full nexus report as it puts forward existing resources and knowledge regarding the animal welfare–environment–sustainable development nexus.[70] In the scoping study, it is repeatedly highlighted that the study is not meant to provide a report on the animal welfare–environment–sustainable development nexus, but should rather be conceived as an overview of useful sources and approaches that should be considered, and further developed when the full report is being established, which will require further multi-disciplinary scientific, practical and ethical expertise and research.[71] In the opinion of WFA 'a process that includes iterative consultation and analysis in preparing the report is

[65] UNEP, 'UNEA 5/1 Resolution: Animal Welfare-Environment–Sustainable Development Nexus' (2023). Available at: https://wedocs.unep.org/bitstream/handle/20.500.11822/42928/Updates%20on%20UNEA%20Res5-1-%20thirds%20meeting%20of%20FoR%20working%20group-Abdelkader%20-%20%20Morocco%202023.pdf?sequence=1&isAllowed=y.

[66] Note, however, that 'UNEP/EA.6/5 on the Progress in the Implementation of Resolution 5/1 on the Animal Welfare–Environment–Sustainable Development Nexus' mentions that an information session with member states was planned in early 2024. Available at: https://docs.un.org/en/UNEP/EA.6/5.

[67] Wolf Gordon Clifton, 'Sustainability Policy and the Stage of Divine Play: Hindu Philosophy at the Nexus of Animal Welfare, Environment, and Sustainable Development' (2023) 13(2) *Journal of Animal Ethics* 169; Schapper and Bliss, 'Transforming Our World'.

[68] WFA, 'Unveiling the Nexus: The Interdependence of Animal Welfare, Environment & Sustainable Development' (2023). Available at: www.wellbeingintlstudiesrepository.org/es_nexus/2/.

[69] Friends of the Resolution on Animal Welfare, Environment, and Sustainable Development Nexus, 'Statement on Behalf of the Friends of the Resolution on Animal Welfare, Environment, and Sustainable Development Nexus at the 10th United Nations Environment Program Annual Sub-Committee Meeting 23/4 November 2023' (2023). Available at: https://wedocs.unep.org/bitstream/handle/20.500.11822/44181/AG1_Friends.pdf.

[70] Janice H Cox, 'Animal Welfare-Environment-Sustainable Development Nexus: Scoping Study' (2023). Available at: www.wellbeingintlstudiesrepository.org/es_nexus/3/.

[71] Ibid., 4, 15.

essential for developing a strong report and for ownership and acceptance of its findings by the UN system and Member States'.[72] With the additional two years to finalise an effective Nexus Report, it can be expected that slow and steady will win the race.

3.5 CONCLUSION

In March 2022 the 'world's parliament on the environment' (UNEA) adopted at its fifth session a revolutionary resolution on the animal welfare–environment–sustainable development nexus. Several African nations were an important catalyst for this milestone resolution. It was the first time that animal welfare was explicitly recognised at the international level by the United Nations. As discussed throughout this chapter, the institutionalising of animal welfare by the UN as well as extending the scope of One Health to consider animal welfare can play a pivotal role in mitigating the existing global animal welfare gap. The UN's support of animal welfare in this way is commendable; however, this is counterbalanced by the soft law nature of the Nexus Resolution. Another disadvantage is the lack of strong language and substantive provisions as only a mere commitment to establish a Nexus Report is established. Apart from preparing a report, it is yet to be seen whether concrete measures will be developed to strengthen the animal welfare–environmen–sustainable development nexus. Not meeting the deadline of UNEA 6 is also a setback that should not be underestimated, as these deadlines will be crucial to integrate animal welfare in efforts to tackle the triple environmental crises.

At first sight, One Health seems redundant within the Nexus Resolution, but this chapter has demonstrated the opposite when delving deeper into both the preamble and provisions of the Nexus Resolution. Due to COVID-19 the attention given to the One Health framework has increased exponentially. This chapter has argued that the integrative, inclusive, and transdisciplinary dimensions of the One Health framework are essential for the animal welfare–environment–sustainable development nexus. The increased attention directed towards One Health was coupled with a rise in scientific research and expertise, one of the principal aims of the Nexus Resolution. More than the intention to produce a report, the primary idea is to collect and disseminate information from experts on animal welfare in general and the nexus in particular. This can then be used as a building block for specific actions and next steps.

As a revolutionary document, the Nexus Resolution possesses plenty of (untapped) potential and has the ability to ensure change within the discipline of animal welfare. However, the extent of this change will depend on the effective implementation of the resolution which, as this chapter has demonstrated, has been delayed. The engagement of both NGOs and member states willing to fully participate, embody and embrace the animal welfare revolution has been perhaps the most encouraging aspect of the Nexus Resolution development and adoption, and it is this engagement that will ensure the Resolution does not remain a theoretical document only.

[72] WFA, 'The Animal Welfare Nexus Resolution – Current State of Play'.

4

One Health and Pathogen Sharing

What's Missing in the Pandemic Treaty's Proposed Pathogen Access and Benefit-Sharing (PABS) System?

Michelle Rourke

4.1 INTRODUCTION: PATHOGEN ACCESS AND BENEFIT-SHARING IN THE PANDEMIC TREATY NEGOTIATIONS

The public health response to the COVID-19 pandemic demonstrated the importance of physical SARS-CoV-2 samples for the development and validation of diagnostic tests and vaccines. Genetic sequence data associated with those physical samples were used to monitor the spread of the virus around the globe and the emergence of new variants of concern. For more than a decade, the World Health Organisation (WHO), along with other United Nations (UN) bodies, has recognised the sovereign rights of states over their pathogen samples and their right to regulate such samples as they deem appropriate.[1] Most countries shared their SARS-CoV-2 samples with the international scientific community, and the associated genetic sequence data was regularly published on publicly accessible databases.[2] Throughout the pandemic, however, there was an ongoing concern that countries would start to restrict access to these vital resources,[3] in accordance with their sovereign rights under international law.

In December 2021, two years into the COVID-19 pandemic, a Special Session of the World Health Assembly (WHA) agreed to 'draft and negotiate a WHO convention, agreement or other international instrument on pandemic prevention, preparedness and response' (referred to by some as the 'Pandemic Treaty') under the Constitution of the World Health Organisation 1948.[4] The original plan was for an Intergovernmental Negotiating Body (INB) to present a consensus text for the Pandemic Treaty by the Seventy-seventh WHA in May 2024. The INB process to negotiate a new Pandemic Treaty was occurring in parallel with the negotiations to amend the

[1] See Michelle Rourke, 'Restricting Access to Pathogen Samples and Epidemiological Data: A Not-So-Brief History of "Viral Sovereignty" and the Mark It Left on the World' in Mark Eccleston-Turner and Iain Brassington (eds.), *Infectious Diseases in the New Millennium* (Springer Nature 2020) 167–191.

[2] Hassan Salem and Martin Kaltenpoth, 'The Nagoya Protocol and Its Implications for Microbiology' (2023) 8(12) *Nature Microbiology* 2234, 2236. 'The recent COVID-19 pandemic has dramatically illustrated how important the rapid international exchange of samples and the public release of sequence data was for the timely development of diagnostic tests and vaccines. This exchange, however, happened on a voluntary basis, with provider countries renouncing their right to negotiate ABS terms on viral samples in favour of a rapid international effort to combat the disease' (citations omitted).

[3] Michelle Rourke, Mark Eccleston-Turner, Alexandra Phelan, and Lawrence Gostin, 'Policy Opportunities to Enhance Sharing for Pandemic Research' (2020) 368(6492) *Science* 716.

[4] World Health Assembly, 'The World Together: Establishment of an Intergovernmental Negotiating Body to Strengthen Pandemic Prevention, Preparedness and Response' (1 December 2021) SSA2(5). Available at: https://apps.who.int/gb/ebwha/pdf_files/WHASSA2/SSA2(5)-en.pdf.

text of the International Health Regulations 2005, with considerable crossover in scope between the two agreements. At the Seventy-seventh WHA, member states adopted the amendments to the International Health Regulations 2005,[5] but could not come to a consensus on the text of the Pandemic Treaty. Instead, the INB presented a draft text 'reflecting progress up to Friday 24 May' 2024,[6] and the mandate of the INB was extended with a requirement to submit the outcome of this additional negotiation period to the Seventy-eighth WHA in May 2025 (or earlier if possible).[7]

Article 12 of the draft text outlines a pathogen surveillance system: the 'WHO Pathogen Access and Benefit-Sharing System (WHO PABS System)' to ensure rapid access to pathogen samples and associated genetic sequence data, and the fair and equitable sharing of related pandemic products, such as vaccines, diagnostics, and therapeutics.[8] Access and benefit-sharing (ABS) has been a core component of each (publicly available) iteration of the draft Pandemic Treaty.[9] The PABS System, as currently proposed, would require parties to share samples of pathogens with pandemic potential,[10] (PABS Materials) with WHO-authorised laboratories.[11] A 'pathogen with pandemic potential' is defined by the draft text as 'any pathogen that has been identified to infect a human and that is novel' with the 'potential to cause a public health emergency of international concern or pandemic emergency'.[12] The parties to the Pandemic Treaty would also be required to upload the genetic sequence of such pathogens to a relevant sequence database.[13] The WHO PABS System could then forward on PABS Materials to third-party recipients, such as pharmaceutical companies, for use in the development and manufacture of various pandemic-related products (e.g. diagnostics, medicines, vaccines) under the terms of a yet-to-be-negotiated legally-binding contract.[14] The contract forms a private agreement between the WHO and the third-party recipient of PABS Materials, which would require the recipient

[5] World Health Assembly, 'Strengthening Preparedness for and Response to Public Health Emergencies through Targeted Amendments to the International Health Regulations (2005)' (1 June 2024) WHA77/17. Available at: https://apps.who.int/gb/ebwha/pdf_files/WHA77/A77_R17-en.pdf.

[6] World Health Assembly, 'Intergovernmental Negotiating Body to Draft and Negotiate a WHO Convention, Agreement or Other International Instrument on Pandemic Prevention, Preparedness and Response. Report by the Director-General' (27 May 2024) A77/10. Available at: https://apps.who.int/gb/ebwha/pdf_files/WHA77/A77_10-en.pdf.

[7] World Health Assembly, 'Intergovernmental Negotiating Body to Draft and Negotiate a WHO Convention, Agreement or other International Instrument on Pandemic Prevention, Preparedness and Response' (1 June 2024) WHA77(20). Available at: https://apps.who.int/gb/ebwha/pdf_files/WHA77/A77_(20)-en.pdf.

[8] WHO, 'Intergovernmental Negotiating Body', A77/10, Annex, Art. 12. Note that this language had not been agreed by the negotiators. Available at: https://apps.who.int/gb/ebwha/pdf_files/WHA77/A77_10-en.pdf.

[9] See WHO, 'Draft Annotated Outline of a WHO Convention, Agreement or Other International Instrument on Pandemic Prevention, Preparedness and Response' (14 June 2022) A/INB/1/12, available at: https://apps.who.int/gb/inb/pdf_files/inb1/A_INB1_12-en.pdf; WHO, 'Working Draft, Presented on the Basis of Progress Achieved, for the Consideration of the Intergovernmental Negotiating Body at its Second Meeting' (13 July 2022) A/INB/2/3, available at: https://apps.who.int/gb/inb/pdf_files/inb2/A_INB2_3-en.pdf; WHO, 'Conceptual Zero Draft for the Consideration of the Intergovernmental Negotiating Body at its Third Meeting' (25 November 2022) A/INB/3/3, available at: https://apps.who.int/gb/inb/pdf_files/inb3/A_INB3_3-en.pdf; WHO, 'Zero Draft of the WHO CA+ for the Consideration of the Intergovernmental Negotiating Body at its Fourth Meeting' (1 February 2023) A/INB/4/3, available at: https://apps.who.int/gb/inb/pdf_files/inb4/A_INB4_3-en.pdf; WHO, 'Bureau's Text of the WHO Convention, Agreement or Other International Instrument on Pandemic Prevention, Preparedness and Response (WHO CA+)' (2 June 2023) A/INB/5/6, available at: https://apps.who.int/gb/inb/pdf_files/inb4/A_INB4_3-en.pdf; WHO, 'Proposal for Negotiating Text of the WHO Pandemic Agreement' (30 October 2023) A/INB/7/3, available at: https://apps.who.int/gb/inb/pdf_files/inb7/A_INB7_3-en.pdf.

[10] WHO, 'Intergovernmental Negotiating Body', A77/10, Annex, Art. 1(c). Available at: https://apps.who.int/gb/ebwha/pdf_files/WHA77/A77_10-en.pdf.

[11] Ibid., Annex, Art. 12(4)(a). Previous drafts noted that this should occur 'at all times, both during and between pandemics'. See WHO, 'Proposal for Negotiating Text', Art. 12(3)(b).

[12] WHO, 'Intergovernmental Negotiating Body', A77/10, Annex, Art. 1(f).

[13] Ibid., Annex, Art. 12(4)(a).

[14] Ibid., Annex, Art. 12(4)(b).

to make contributions to the PABS System. This could be in the form of monetary benefits (e.g. annual monetary contributions to the WHO)[15] or non-monetary benefits according to the nature and capabilities of the recipient (e.g. shared royalties, diagnostic kits, or vaccine doses)[16] that the WHO will allocate to WHO Member States during a pandemic 'on the basis of public health risk and need'.[17]

This is a proposed multilateral ABS system with providers and users of PABS Materials engaging the WHO as a middleman. In short, the PABS System outlined in the Pandemic Treaty is designed to create obligations for member states to share their pathogen samples and associated genetic sequence data with the WHO. The WHO will then share the samples with third parties who can use the samples and associated data to generate pandemic-related products. Contracts will be signed between the WHO and the third parties to ensure that a portion of those products (or other benefits) will be contributed to the PABS System for the WHO to distribute to member states on the basis of public health risks and needs.

Another recurring feature through each of the Pandemic Treaty drafts is the concept of One Health. In the negotiating text presented to the WHA in May 2024, Article 5 asks parties to 'promote a One Health approach for pandemic prevention, preparedness and response … that is coherent, integrated, coordinated and collaborative among all relevant organizations, sectors and actors'.[18] In a previous iteration of the Pandemic Treaty's draft text, there is even a provision connecting the PABS System to the One Health concept:

> The Parties shall promote and enhance synergies between multisectoral and transdisciplinary collaboration at the national level and cooperation at the international level, in order to identify and conduct risk assessments at the interface between human, animal and environment ecosystems, while recognizing their interdependence, and with applicable sharing of the benefits, per the terms of Article 12 [Access and Benefit-Sharing] herein.[19]

The inclusion of the One Health principle since the very beginning of the INB's deliberations, and its explicit connection to the PABS System in some iterations of the negotiating texts, makes the fact that the scope of the proposed PABS System is limited to *human* pathogens with pandemic potential so utterly baffling. This is not an oversight: the earliest publicly available draft of the Pandemic Treaty also contains a version of the PABS System that only covers human pathogens.[20] The baffling part is that the majority of emerging infectious disease outbreaks in humans originate in animals.[21] By only including human samples, the PABS System is arbitrarily limiting itself to detecting pathogens that have already spilled over into

15 Ibid., Annex, Art. 12(4)(b)(iii).
16 Ibid., Annex, Art. 12(4)(b).
17 Ibid., Annex, Art. 12(4)(b) (i and ii).
18 Ibid., Annex, Art. 5(1).
19 WHO, 'Proposal for Negotiating Text', Art. 5(2).
20 WHO, 'Draft Annotated Outline', Part VIII: 'This part could address pandemic-related access and benefit sharing, such as proposals to build upon existing mechanisms in the global health access and benefit-sharing arena, i.e. proposals aimed at addressing all emerging and novel pathogens of human pandemic potential by adopting the mechanisms and/or principles contained in existing (Global Influenza Surveillance and Response System and Pandemic Influenza Preparedness Framework) or previous (Global Action Plan for Influenza vaccine manufacturing capacity) influenza-related systems'.
21 Kelley Lee, 'The Global Governance of Emerging Zoonotic Diseases: Challenges and Proposed Reforms', Council on Foreign Relations Global Health Program: Workshop Policy Paper (13 February 2023): www.cfr.org/report/global-governance-emerging-zoonotic-diseases. Also, 'EID (Emerging Infectious Disease) events are dominated by zoonoses (60.3% of EIDs): the majority of these (71.8%) originate in wildlife (example, severe acute respiratory virus, Ebola virus), and are increasing significantly over time'; Kate Jones, Nikkita Patel, Marc Levy et al., 'Global Trends in Emerging Infectious Diseases' (2008) 451 *Nature* 990, 990.

humans *from* animals. It fails to consider that it might be possible (and desirable) to detect animal pathogens before a spillover event takes place. Any international system for pathogen ABS that does not include animal and environmental samples is destined to fall short of any mission to prevent epidemics and pandemics, will likely become outdated very quickly, and it certainly cannot be said to be incorporating the One Health principle.

This chapter will examine how the PABS System outlined in the Pandemic Treaty could be improved if it genuinely applied the One Health principle to policies on accessing pathogen samples and associated genetic sequence data for use in research and development (R&D),[22] and the fair and equitable sharing of benefits associated with that use. It will start by providing a brief background on the origins of the ABS concept from environmental law. It will then demonstrate how the PABS System has relied on the WHO's Pandemic Influenza Preparedness Framework (PIP Framework, 2011) as a model for pathogen ABS, replicating not only its strengths but also its weaknesses. The remainder of the chapter will analyse how there are clear synergies between One Health and the original intent of the ABS concept, and how the thoughtful application of the One Health framework could result in a more robust and effective multilateral pathogen ABS system, both now and into the future.

4.2 BACKGROUND: WHAT IS ABS AND WHY IS IT IN THE PANDEMIC TREATY?

4.2.1 *The Convention on Biological Diversity*

Access and Benefit-Sharing is a policy mechanism that was developed for the United Nations Environment Programme's (UNEP's) Convention on Biological Diversity (CBD) 1992. This binding treaty has 196 contracting parties (with the notable exception of the United States of America) and has three key objectives: '[1] the conservation of biological diversity, [2] the sustainable use of its components and [3] the fair and equitable sharing of the benefits arising out of the utilization of genetic resources'.[23] The third objective is elaborated in Article 15 of the CBD. It recognises that countries have sovereign rights over their genetic resources and that they can regulate access through national legislation.[24] It further states that potential users of genetic resources in R&D must obtain the prior informed consent of the provider country,[25] and that access and use must be on mutually agreed terms,[26] which can include the sharing of associated benefits (be they monetary or non-monetary benefits).[27] This is the policy mechanism abbreviated as ABS. It was devised to ensure provider countries could obtain a share of the benefits associated with R&D on their sovereign genetic resources, to put towards achieving the environmental conservation and sustainable development objectives of the CBD.[28]

[22] Note that in the ABS policy space, the term 'Digital Sequence Information' (DSI) is being used to refer to 'genetic sequence data' and potentially other types of data. A precise definition for DSI has not yet been determined by the Conference of the Parties to the CBD. See Conference of the Parties to the Convention on Biological Diversity, 'Decision Adopted by the Conference of the Parties to the Convention on Biological Diversity: 15/9 Digital Sequence Information on Genetic Resources' (19 December 2022) CBD/COP/DEC/15/9, 2, available at: www.cbd.int/doc/decisions/cop-15/cop-15-dec-09-en.pdf.

[23] Convention on Biological Diversity (1992) Art. 1 (hereafter 'CBD'), available at: www.cbd.int/doc/legal/cbd-en.pdf.

[24] Ibid., Art. 15(1).

[25] Ibid., Art. 15(5).

[26] Ibid., Art. 15(4).

[27] Ibid., Art. 15(7).

[28] It is important to remember that environmental conservation is just one of three objectives of the CBD, and that the fair and equitable sharing of benefits is an objective of the CBD in its own right and not just as a mechanism to deliver the other two objectives (environmental conservation and sustainable development).

The ABS mechanism in the CBD applies to 'genetic resources', which are defined as 'genetic material … of plant, animal, microbial, or other origin' embodying 'actual or potential value'.[29] Despite the scope of the term 'genetic resources' specifically including microbes, pathogenic microbes were not initially considered an obvious inclusion within the scope of the CBD, particularly in light of its status as an environmental conservation treaty.[30] Pathogens are not the sort of biodiversity people think to conserve. Rather, 'the strategy is to contain and ultimately eradicate' them.[31] But by the time the Conference of the Parties (COP) to the CBD convened in 2010 to adopt the Nagoya Protocol on Access to Genetic Resources and the Fair and Equitable Sharing of Benefits Arising from their Utilization to the Convention on Biological Diversity (Nagoya Protocol), international discussions under the auspices of the WHO had made it clear that pathogens are indeed genetic resources that are within the scope of the CBD's ABS provisions.[32] This 'means that the country from which a virus sample was isolated has the sovereign authority to determine how and by whom that sample is utilized',[33] and that prior informed consent and mutually agreed terms need to be negotiated on a case-by-case basis, bilaterally between the provider party and the user party. Prior to this, pathogen samples had largely been shared without regard to ABS laws.

The Nagoya Protocol created further ABS requirements for users of Traditional Knowledge associated with genetic resources held by Indigenous peoples and local communities.[34] It also recognised that multilateral ABS models may be more appropriate for certain types of genetic resources,[35] and stated that specialised (multilateral) international ABS instruments could be created for specific sets of genetic resources and could bypass the default ABS mechanism, so long as the new instrument was consistent with the objectives of the CBD and Nagoya Protocol.[36]

The Nagoya Protocol also identifies a 'special consideration' related to pathogens, stating that parties should ensure expeditious ABS in 'cases of present or imminent emergencies that threaten or damage human, animal or plant health, as determined nationally

[29] CBD, Art. 2. Note that the CBD was originally intended to cover human genetic resources but these were excluded from the scope of the treaty after adoption. See Sachin Chaturvedi, Sara Crager, Miltos Ladikas, Vasantha Muthuswami, Yeyang Su, and Huanming Yang, 'Promoting an Inclusive Approach to Benefit Sharing: Expanding the Scope of the CBD?' in Doris Schroeder and Julie Lucas Cook (eds.), *Benefit Sharing: From Biodiversity to Human Genetics* (Springer 2013) 153–177.

[30] Pathogens are a major component of biodiversity and play a vital role in healthy ecosystems (including keeping pest population sizes in check). For these reasons, pathogens are also used in synthetic biology applications for biocontrol and other biotechnological developments.

[31] David Fidler, 'Influenza Virus Samples, International Law, and Global Health Diplomacy' (2008) 14(1) *Emerging Infectious Diseases* 88.

[32] See Section 4.2.2 herein. A more detailed history of how pathogens came to be recognised as 'genetic resources' under the remit of the CBD and Nagoya Protocol can be found in Rourke, 'Restricting Access to Pathogen Samples and Epidemiological Data'.

[33] Sally Mueni Katee and Christian Keambou Tiambo, 'Discussing the Drawbacks of the Implementation of Access and Benefit Sharing of the Nagoya Protocol Following the COVID-19 Pandemic' (2021) 9 *Frontiers in Public Health* 639581, 2.

[34] Nagoya Protocol 2010, Arts 7 and 12, available at: www.cbd.int/abs/doc/protocol/nagoya-protocol-en.pdf.

[35] Such as in situations where the country of origin is not known or the genetic resource is endemic to multiple territories ('transboundary situations'). Ibid., Art. 10.

[36] 'This Protocol is the instrument for the implementation of the access and benefit-sharing provisions of the Convention. Where a specialized international access and benefit-sharing instrument applies that is consistent with, and does not run counter to the objectives of the Convention and this Protocol, this Protocol does not apply for the Party or Parties to the specialized instrument in respect of the specific genetic resource covered by and for the purpose of the specialized instrument'. Ibid., Art. 4(4).

or internationally'.[37] This special consideration for expeditious ABS during health emergencies was adopted 'as a weak and perhaps hasty solution' to (at the time) the new problem of pathogens technically falling within the scope of the international ABS regime.[38] This provision of the Nagoya Protocol strengthened the argument that pathogens were indeed sovereign genetic resources under the CBD and Nagoya Protocol and were therefore subject to the same ABS rules as other genetic resources.

4.2.2 *The WHO's PIP Framework*

The WHO negotiations that, in part, led to the special consideration for health emergencies in the Nagoya Protocol were precipitated by the actions of Indonesia in 2006/2007. Simply put, countries around the world (including Indonesia) had been sending their influenza virus samples to the WHO's Global Influenza Surveillance Network (GISN) without formal conditions since the Network's inception in the 1950s. After the adoption of the CBD, the transfer of virus samples to the GISN continued without regard to ABS laws. During an intense outbreak of H5N1 avian influenza, Indonesia decided they would no longer send their sovereign genetic resources (influenza viruses) to the WHO's GISN unless they could obtain a fair share of the benefits that are generated from the use of their virus samples, namely vaccines.[39] This attracted a great deal of criticism at the time, and even now the exercise of 'viral sovereignty' is viewed as a 'desire to gatekeep important biological specimens' with potentially disastrous consequences.[40] But this misses the larger point about distributional equity that Indonesia was making at the time.

The open sharing of influenza viruses, most often originating in low and middle-income countries, directly led to the accrual of specific benefits (like vaccine doses and profits) to high-income countries. Therefore, the provision of these genetic resources (influenza viruses) to the WHO was not apolitical.[41] What high-income countries and the WHO's GISN treated as global public goods and what they considered private goods was entirely political.[42] Life-saving medicines, which require R&D, specialised personnel, laboratory and distribution infrastructures, were considered private goods (belonging to pharmaceutical companies) while pathogen samples, which require clinical and/or laboratory space, equipment, specialised personnel and other resources to collect (and can sometimes even cost lives), were considered a public good. As the technology currently stands, the pathogen samples themselves form an essential input

[37] 'In the development and implementation of its access and benefit-sharing legislation or regulatory requirements, each Party shall: … (b) Pay due regard to cases of present or imminent emergencies that threaten or damage human, animal or plant health, as determined nationally or internationally. Parties may take into consideration the need for expeditious access to genetic resources and expeditious fair and equitable sharing of benefits arising out of the use of such genetic resources, including access to affordable treatments by those in need, especially in developing countries'. Ibid., Art. 8(b).

[38] Maria Serena Beato and Valentina Veneroso, 'The Nagoya Protocol on Access and Benefit Sharing: The Neglected Issue of Animal Health' (2023) 14 *Frontiers in Microbiology* 1124120, 2.

[39] This has been called 'viral sovereignty'. For a fuller accounting of this event in context, see Rourke, 'Restricting Access to Pathogen Samples and Epidemiological Data'.

[40] Rana Sulieman, Lawrence N. Anyanwu, Vicky Cardenas, Mohamed Moussif, Ebere Okereke, and Oyeronke Oyebanji, 'International Legal Issues of National Sovereignty and Authority Impacting Global Health Security' in Scott J N McNabb, Affan T Shaikh, Carol J Haley (eds.), *Modernizing Global Health Security to Prevent, Detect, and Respond* (Academic Press, 2024) 71–85, 78 https://doi.org/10.1016/B978-0-323-90945-7.00015-4.

[41] See Natalie Porter, *Viral Economies: Bird Flu Experiments in Vietnam* (University of Chicago Press, 2019), chapter 5.

[42] Ibid.

to the value chain that generates privatised profits for pharmaceutical companies. So, part of the point is: why does an essential raw material with undeniable use value not also have a market value?

This situation was basically replicating the old colonial relations between the Global North and the Global South, where the Global South 'had been reduced to being providers of raw materials and consumers of manufactured goods produced in Europe and the United States'.[43] Even when pathogens are used for non-commercial purposes (epidemiological studies or academic research) the benefits often accrue to scientists in high-income countries (in the form of publications, professional recognition, and enhanced opportunities), not to those people in low and middle-income countries for whom the costs of collecting the pathogen samples were often considerable. Thus, we see how Open Science, open data and open access to samples, while often claiming to benefit *all* of humanity, does not benefit all alike. Scientists and companies in high-income countries are better positioned to take advantage of this openness to capture (privatise) the benefits of public goods. This action by Indonesia, supported by other low and middle-income countries, meant that pathogens were finally recognised as genetic resources under the CBD and were therefore subject to domestic ABS rules.

In 2011, Member States of the WHO adopted the PIP Framework which, in line with the CBD, recognised the sovereign rights of states over their genetic resources and created ABS provisions that would guide the transfer of influenza viruses through the GISN, now renamed the WHO's Global Influenza Surveillance and Response System (GISRS). As the PIP Framework only applies to influenza viruses with human pandemic potential, this means that every other human pathogen (including seasonal influenza viruses) remains under the remit of the CBD and Nagoya Protocol's ABS framework, which defaults to bilateral ABS agreements if a multilateral ABS arrangement is not already in place.

The WHO's 2016 Review of the PIP Framework stated that 'The PIP Framework is a foundational model of reciprocity for global public health that could be applied to other pathogens',[44] but it also warned that while the principles of ABS could be applied to other pathogens, 'using the PIP Framework as a template is likely to present significant implementational and operational challenges'.[45] This is the seed of the idea for the PABS System that was proposed during the Pandemic Treaty negotiations, which borrows heavily from the PIP Framework as a template.[46]

[43] Vijay Prashad, *The Darker Nations: A People's History of the Third World* (The New Press 2022), 44. Note that Prashad states that the 'spatial metaphor' of the Global North and the Global South 'ignores the mature class hierarchies' that exist in both the Global North and Global South countries (277).

[44] World Health Organization, 'Report of the 2016 PIP Framework Review Group' (2016) Annex 1 EB140/16 38, available at: https://apps.who.int/gb/ebwha/pdf_files/EB140/B140_16-en.pdf.

[45] Ibid., 37. Most notably, the PIP Framework was built around an existing WHO-affiliated global laboratory network that already shared influenza viruses (GISN), and that included the active participation of pharmaceutical companies (and other users). The PIP Framework simply formalised the international transfers of viruses that were already occurring. There is no such WHO-affiliated infrastructure for the transfer of all human pathogens with pandemic potential that could be similarly formalised for the swift deployment of a global pathogen ABS system.

[46] One very concerning aspect of calling the PIP Framework a success in terms of benefit-sharing is that it has never been tested during an influenza pandemic (the most recent influenza pandemic was declared in 2009 and the PIP Framework was adopted in 2011). Therefore, the triggering event that initiates the sharing of vaccines and other tangible benefits through the PIP Framework has not occurred during the lifetime of the agreement.

4.3 THE PABS SYSTEM: REPEATING THE MISTAKES OF THE PIP FRAMEWORK

The PIP Framework limits its scope to 'the sharing of H_5N_1 and other influenza viruses with *human* pandemic potential'.[47] Influenza viruses are notorious for infecting mammals and birds, particularly pigs and chickens, and for readily spreading via direct contact with an infected animal or indirect contact with contaminated environments. Influenza viruses can spread vast distances in wild bird populations, and highly pathogenic avian influenza viruses are known to frequently spill over into human hosts.[48]

The animal influenza network, OFFLU,[49] is run in partnership between the World Organisation for Animal Health (WOAH) and the Food and Agriculture Organization (FAO) of the UN. It runs in parallel with the WHO's Global Influenza Surveillance and Response System (GISRS). The two networks exchange information, but the samples themselves stay within their own networks. The samples that countries provide to GISRS are shared under the ABS terms outlined in the PIP Framework, but animal influenza viruses are shared without regard to this multilateral benefit-sharing arrangement. This means that for the purposes of ABS, influenza viruses from animal hosts remain under the remit of the CBD and Nagoya Protocol, which favour bilateral ABS agreements between provider and user parties on a case-by-case basis.

Not only does treating animal samples separately from human samples fragment the ABS legal landscape, it also provides opportunities for users to avoid their benefit-sharing obligations by obtaining similar samples outside of the defined ABS terms of the multilateral system. It also creates an artificial distinction between influenza host species (remembering that humans are part of the animal kingdom, and are not that different from other influenza hosts, at least not from the perspective of the virus). Having separate ABS rules for the influenza viruses depending on whether they were isolated from human or animal hosts erects categorical barriers where the whole idea of the One Health concept is to remove such barriers and deal with health threats more holistically.

Despite being urged to take a more critical look at the PIP Framework,[50] and to learn from its mistakes,[51] the PABS System proposed in the Pandemic Treaty negotiations has copied many of

47 Emphasis added. World Health Organization, 'Pandemic Influenza Preparedness Framework for the Sharing of Influenza Viruses and Access to Vaccines and Other Benefits' (24 May 2011), 2nd Edition, Art. 2(i) (hereafter the 'PIP Framework'). To be clear, the PIP Framework applies to 'PIP biological materials' which it defines as 'human clinical specimens, virus isolates of wild type human H_5N_1 and other influenza viruses with human pandemic potential; and modified viruses prepared from H_5N_1 and/or other influenza viruses with human pandemic potential developed by WHO GISRS laboratories' (Art. 4.1). Available at: https://iris.who.int/bitstream/handle/10665/341850/9789240024854-eng.pdf.

48 Priya Venkatesan, 'Avian influenza spillover into mammals' (2023) 7 *The Lancet Microbe* e492. Available at https://doi.org/10.1016/S2666-5247(23)00173-8.

49 The name OFFLU came from the first letters of the OIE (Office International des Epizooties, the former name of WOAH) and FAO, plus the contraction 'flu'.

50 Mueni Katee and Keambou Tiambo, 'Discussing the Drawbacks of the Implementation of Access and Benefit Sharing of the Nagoya Protocol Following the COVID-19 Pandemic', 8.

51 Adam Kamradt-Scott and Kelley Lee, 'The 2011 Pandemic Influenza Preparedness Framework: Global Health Secured or a Missed Opportunity?' (2011) 59 *Political Studies* 831; Mark Eccleston-Turner, 'The Pandemic Influenza Preparedness Framework: A Viable Procurement Option for Developing States?' (2017) 17(4) *Medical Law International* 227; Michelle Rourke, 'Access by Design, Benefits If Convenient: A Closer Look at the Pandemic Influenza Preparedness Framework's Standard Material Transfer Agreements', (2019) 97 *The Milbank Quarterly* 91; Abbie-Rose Hampton, 'Pathogen Dematerialization and the ABS Loophole' (2023) 10(1) *Journal of Law and the Biosciences* 1.

them. Limiting the scope of the PABS System to pathogens with *human* pandemic potential is just one such mistake that indicates that the One Health concept has not been seriously considered or applied for pathogen ABS under the Pandemic Treaty.

4.4 A HIGHER AUTHORITY: INCLUDING THE REST OF THE ONE HEALTH QUADRIPARTITE

Given the PIP Framework was adopted in 2011, and the 'Memorandum of Understanding [MoU] between the FAO, WOAH and WHO (Tripartite) Regarding Cooperation to Combat Health Risks at the Animal-Human-Ecosystem Interface in the Context of the One Health Approach and Including Antimicrobial Resistance' was not signed until 2018,[52] it is perhaps somewhat understandable that the WHO did not deem it necessary to take a One Health approach to the PIP Framework.[53] But by the time the international community was dealing with COVID-19, it was abundantly clear that the international regulation of pathogen samples and associated data could not and should not be confined to the WHO. All aspects of human health are intertwined with animal and environmental health, and the management of pathogens at the international level is no different.

Pathogen ABS is an issue that cuts across multiple UN bodies. For instance, the management of veterinary pathogens falls within the remit of the WOAH and agriculturally relevant pathogens are within the remit of WOAH as well as the FAO. The United Nations Environment Programme (UNEP) is responsible for the CBD and its subsidiary agreements that create international rules for the transfer of sovereign genetic resources (including human, plant, and animal pathogens). In 2022, the Tripartite was expanded to become the Quadripartite with the inclusion of UNEP.[54] But there are additional (perhaps unexpected) UN bodies that play a role in the management of pathogen samples and associated data.[55] As the CBD and Nagoya Protocol also prescribe rules for the transfer of Traditional Knowledge associated with genetic resources, pathogen ABS can involve Indigenous peoples and local communities as stakeholders in the transfer of pathogen-associated Traditional Knowledge.[56]

[52] 'Memorandum of Understanding Between the United Nations Food and Agriculture Organization, World Organisation for Animal Health, and the World Health Organization Regarding Cooperation to Combat Health Risks at the Animal-Human-Ecosystem Interface in the Context of the One Health Approach and Including Antimicrobial Resistance' (30 May 2018). Available at: https://web.archive.org/web/20220308023910/https://www.who.int/zoonoses/MoU-Tripartite-May-2018.pdf.

[53] Having said that, the FAO/OIE/WHO Tripartite Concept Note was released a year before the PIP Framework was adopted and as H5N1 avian influenza was at the centre of the 2006/2007 dispute about viral sovereignty and virus ABS, the link with animals was clear from the beginning. WHO, 'The FAO-OIE-WHO Collaboration: A Tripartite Concept Note' (28 September 2010). Available at www.who.int/publications/m/item/the-fao-oie-who-collaboration.

[54] 'Memorandum of Understanding Between the Food and Agriculture Organization of the United Nations and the World Organisation for Animal Health and the World Health Organization and the United Nations Environment Programme Regarding Cooperation to Combat Health Risks at the Animal-Human-Ecosystems Interface in the Context of the "One Health" Approach and Including Antimicrobial Resistance' (17 March 2022). Available at www.fao.org/3/cb9403en/cb9403en.pdf.

[55] There are other international bodies and forums that regulate dealings with pathogens that demonstrate how complex the issue of international pathogen sharing can be. For instance, commercially relevant pathogens and pathogen-related technologies are likely to come under the remit of the World Trade Organisation, World Customs Organisation and the World Intellectual Property Organisation. Pathogens that have the potential to be used in bioterror or biowarfare fall under the UN Office for Disarmament Affairs and are covered by the Biological and Toxin Weapons Convention 1972. The WHO and its member states are yet to grapple with these complexities.

[56] See Michelle Rourke, 'When Knowledge Goes Viral: Assessing the Possibility of Virus-Related Traditional Knowledge for Access and Benefit-Sharing' (2018) 21 *Journal of World Intellectual Property* 356.

Therefore, the United Nations Declaration on the Rights of Indigenous Peoples 2007 (UNDRIP) will also be relevant.[57]

Focusing only on human pathogens does not adequately account for the very complexity that the One Health concept aims to address. For instance, African Swine Fever Virus (ASFV) was first reported in domestic pig populations in China in 2018, devastating the Chinese pork industry.[58] Researchers have speculated that this left consumers looking for alternative sources of protein:

> While it is unclear how disruption to pork markets may have affected activity at wildlife markets, the convergence of circumstances outlined here, with first the incursion of ASF virus into China followed closely with the first detection of SARS-CoV-2 virus, suggest that acceleration of COVID-19 cases due to severe disruption of the Chinese pork market is plausible, possibly through increased congregation of vendors and consumers at the markets.[59]

The complexities are compounded by the fact that COVID-19 has likely impacted the spread of ASFV.[60] The COVID-19 pandemic created a huge demand for diagnostic laboratory reagents, straining the ability of veterinary laboratories to monitor the distribution of ASFV.[61] This is just one example of two pathogens that have potentially had a mutual impact on the spread of each other. The fact is, however, that the proposed PABS System takes none of this complexity into account. As discussed, it is modelled on the PIP Framework and has been designed with COVID-19 in mind. Therefore, it is focused on dealing with airborne threats from highly contagious respiratory pathogens and does not seem to have considered how pathogens with alternative transmission routes (e.g. foodborne illnesses), pathogens with multiple animal reservoirs, or issues like antimicrobial resistance might factor in.

If the PABS System were to take a genuine One Health approach, it would need the active involvement of at least the other Quadripartite members in addition to the WHO: that means the FAO, WOAH, and UNEP should be closely involved in this process as well. Another approach might be to place the PABS System under the higher authority of the UN General Assembly,[62] which would have greater coordination powers across *all* elements of the UN (not just the Quadripartite, but other agencies like the World Intellectual Property Organisation). Stefania Negri and Mark Eccleston-Turner go even further:

> Ultimately, a bolder proposal to advance cooperation under the One Health approach could be the establishment of an UN-OneHealth, following the example of other specific UN-led interagency collaboration mechanisms existing in the field of environmental protection – namely UN-Oceans, UN-Water and UN-Energy – or in the field of public health, like UNAIDS.

[57] See Section 4.5 herein.

[58] 'With Chinese citizens consuming 28% of the global meat production, China has emerged as the primary pork-producing country, with half of the world's pigs – upward of 700 million head per year – being raised in China'. Claire Tucker, Anna Fagre, George Wittemyer, Tracy Webb, Edward Okoth Abworo, and Sue VandeWoude, 'Parallel Pandemics Illustrate the Need for One Health Solutions' (2021) 12 *Frontiers in Microbiology* 2.

[59] Ibid.

[60] 'Indeed, the COVID-19 pandemic could have affected several aspects of the ASFV entry pathways into ASF free countries. Since December 2019, ASF has been continued spreading into new areas due to the diffusive nature of the virus. This further spread could have been facilitated by the difficulties in animal diseases prevention and control due to the COVID-19 lockdown' (citations omitted). Angela Fanelli, Olga Muñoz, Luca Mantegazza, Marco De Nardi, and Ilaria Capua, 'Is the COVID-19 Pandemic Impacting on the Risk of African Swine Fever Virus (ASFV) Introduction into the United States? A Short-Term Assessment of the Risk Factors' (2022) 69 *Transboundary and Emerging Diseases* e505, e506.

[61] Ibid., e506.

[62] Elliot Hannon, Layth Hanbali, Susanna Lehtimaki, and Nina Schwalbe, 'Why We Still Need a Pandemic Treaty' (2022) 10 *The Lancet* e1232, e1232.

> As already noted elsewhere, UNAIDS in particular presents relevant characteristics facilitating multisectoral, interinstitutional and multi-stakeholder cooperation, notably an institutionally independent interagency coordination mechanism, with a structure including a dedicated intergovernmental forum, and a separate body for participating agencies to operationalise policy decisions.[63]

4.5 TAKING TRADITIONAL KNOWLEDGE INTO ACCOUNT

As a concept, One Health is an acknowledgement that '[p]rediction, prevention, mitigation, and restoration phases of [emerging infectious disease] outbreaks require consideration of cultural, political, industrial, economic, nutritional, and psychological components of complex, overlapping societies and habitats',[64] and there is a growing recognition of the importance of non-Western ways of knowing about these elements.[65] The CBD recognises the importance of Traditional Knowledge in environmental conservation and sustainable development, and encourages parties to seek the 'approval and involvement of the holders of such knowledge' and for the users of traditional 'knowledge, innovations and practices' to share benefits in a fair and equitable way.[66] The Nagoya Protocol goes further in requiring users of Traditional Knowledge associated with genetic resources to obtain prior informed consent and come to mutually agreed terms before using the Traditional Knowledge belonging to Indigenous peoples and local communities. Given that Traditional Knowledge is an integral part of the international ABS regime, it is astonishing that Traditional Knowledge has not been included in any of the INB's negotiating documents of the Pandemic Treaty, particularly when the INB intends for the PABS System to be formally recognised under the Nagoya Protocol. Indeed, it is not even clear that this issue has been considered at all.

Mark Eccleston-Turner and I have previously suggested that traditional burial practices associated with the spread of Ebola virus during the West African epidemic in 2014,[67] and traditional pig or poultry farming practices that could provide insights about influenza virus emergence, transmission, and virulence would certainly fit the definition of Traditional Knowledge associated with human pathogens.[68] If the PABS System were to take a One Health approach to 'detect and prevent health threats at the animal and human interface',[69] then the scope of Traditional Knowledge associated with pathogens is likely to be quite broad and include things like the distribution of bat populations over time, various geographical considerations impacting pathogen

[63] Stefania Negri and Mark Eccleston-Turner, 'One Health and Pathogen Sharing: Filling the Gap in the International Health Regulations to Strengthen Global Pandemic Preparedness and Response' (2022) 12 *International Organizations Law Review* 188, 210.

[64] Tucker et al., 'Parallel Pandemics Illustrate the Need for One Health Solutions', 4.

[65] See, for example, Alex Tasker and Ian Scoones, 'High Reliability Knowledge Networks: Responding to Animal Diseases in a Pastoral Area of Northern Kenya' (2022) 58(5) *The Journal of Development Studies* 968.

[66] 'Each Contracting Party shall, as far as possible and as appropriate … Subject to its national legislation, respect, preserve and maintain knowledge, innovations and practices of indigenous and local communities embodying traditional lifestyles relevant for the conservation and sustainable use of biological diversity and promote their wider application with the approval and involvement of the holders of such knowledge, innovations and practices and encourage the equitable sharing of the benefits arising from the utilization of such knowledge, innovations and practices' CBD, Art. 8(j).

[67] Michelle Rourke and Mark Eccleston-Turner, 'The Pandemic Influenza Preparedness Framework as a "Specialized International Access and Benefit-Sharing Instrument" Under the Nagoya Protocol' (2021) 72(3) *Norther Ireland Legal Quarterly* 411, 427.

[68] Rourke, 'When Knowledge Goes Viral', 365.

[69] WHO, 'Proposal for negotiating text', Preamble, para. 8.

distribution, seasonal weather patterns, livestock management (e.g. herding routes, food and water sources), the identification of sick animals, and various cultural practices (e.g. meat preparation). In the above example about ASFV, researchers noted that feeding pigs 'kitchen waste (including both raw and cooked pork)' and pig population density were both major factors in the transmission of the virus.[70] Such information could also be deemed 'knowledge, innovations and practices' within the scope of the CBD and Nagoya Protocol. If the PABS System of the Pandemic Treaty is to be recognised as a specialised international ABS instrument within the meaning of Article 4(4) of the Nagoya Protocol,[71] then it cannot simply disregard one of the major components of the Nagoya Protocol: the fair and equitable sharing of benefits arising from the utilisation of Traditional Knowledge associated with genetic resources.

4.6 DEEP PREVENTION OR SPILLOVER DETECTION?

The rapid international sharing of pathogen samples and associated genetic sequence data plays a vital role in epidemic and pandemic prevention. Ginevra Le Moli makes a distinction between two types of prevention: preventing the spillover of disease from animals to humans (which Le Moli calls 'spillover prevention' or 'deep prevention') and preventing the spread of diseases across international borders (disease containment).[72] Le Moli points out that the global health law architecture, since the International Sanitary Conferences in the mid nineteenth century, through to the most modern version of the International Health Regulations 2005, is primarily concerned with disease containment rather than preventing the spillover from animal species occurring in the first place.[73]

With its scope limited to just human pathogens, it is clear that the proposed PABS System is not at all focused on deep/spillover prevention. Le Moli states that the historical focus on containment was perhaps justifiable when containment was all that could reasonably be achieved, but that the science has evolved to the point where deep prevention is possible: where the inclusion of metagenomic approaches used to analyse environmental samples,[74] for example, could help form a more holistic appreciation of disease threats in both animals and humans. And yet, the proposed PABS System in the Pandemic Treaty still appears to be 'trapped within a prior framing of the problem',[75] perpetuating the structural bias of containment within the UN system while deploying One Health rhetoric.

Many new political, policy, and scientific initiatives have sprung up in the wake of the COVID-19 pandemic, but 'there is a persistent gap between pledges to advance integrated action, often

[70] Tucker et al., 'Parallel Pandemics Illustrate the Need for One Health Solutions', 2.

[71] Note that it is not yet clear what international body has the authority to have a specialised international ABS instrument recognised under the Nagoya Protocol, but it is likely that it is the Meeting of the Parties to the Nagoya Protocol (i.e. the WHO does not have the authority to recognise the PABS System under the Pandemic Treaty as a specialised international ABS instrument). See Convention on Biological Diversity, 'Study into Criteria to Identify a Specialized International Access and Benefit-Sharing Instrument, and a Possible Process for Its Recognition: Note by The Executive Secretary' (29 May 2018) CBD/SBI/2/INF/17, available at: www.cbd.int/doc/c/9376/a644/1bed20a1837af8e3d1edc5f9/sbi-02-inf-17-en.pdf; and further analysis in Rourke and Eccleston-Turner, 'The Pandemic Influenza Preparedness Framework'.

[72] Ginevra Le Moli, 'The Containment Bias of the WHO International Health Regulations' (2023) *British Yearbook of International Law* 5. Available at https://doi.org/10.1093/bybil/brad001. This distinction is also referred to as 'primary prevention' (spillover prevention) and 'secondary prevention' (containment). See Lee, 'The Global Governance of Emerging Zoonotic Diseases', 2.

[73] Le Moli, 'The Containment Bias of the WHO International Health Regulations', 8.

[74] Chelsea Liang et al., 'Managing the Transition to Widespread Metagenomic Monitoring: Policy Considerations for Future Biosurveillance' (2023) 21(1) *Health Security* 34.

[75] Le Moli, 'The Containment Bias of the WHO International Health Regulations', 25.

under the One Health banner, and effective implementation'.[76] Nithin Ramakrishnan recently analysed three One Health policy initiatives within the UN system, demonstrating that the One Health concept is steadily morphing into an agenda for bio-surveillance, particularly surveillance of the Global South.[77] Ramakrishnan states that:

> Such a skewed application of the One Health approach is problematic for a twofold reason. It serves the interests of industrialized countries, potentially favouring them in gaining further access and control over the world's biological resources or genetic diversity. Secondly, it diverts attention from high income countries' differentiated responsibilities when it comes to addressing global warming or loss of biodiversity as drivers of zoonotic spillovers through One Health approach.[78]

Indeed, the PIP Framework also falls into this trap. While not explicitly a One Health initiative, the PIP Framework is dealing with a zoonotic disease, only it does so solely from a human perspective.[79] The sharing of tangible benefits under the PIP Framework (such as pandemic vaccine doses and diagnostic kits) is triggered when there is an influenza pandemic. The only ongoing benefit-sharing that occurs under the PIP Framework is in the form of Partnership Contributions: voluntary payments from pharmaceutical companies totalling US$28 million per year.[80] The vast majority of this money goes towards enhancing laboratory and surveillance capacity,[81] with the specific aim of aiding countries to share their influenza samples with the WHO's GISRS network and report influenza data.[82] Furthermore, an analysis of the SMTAs used in the PIP Framework indicated that the sharing of influenza virus samples is basically mandatory for participating labs, while the provision of tangible benefits from pharmaceutical companies is not guaranteed.[83] This all adds up to the perception that 'the only actionable objectives [of many UN One Health initiatives] ultimately come down to surveillance and rapid (continuous) data sharing activities about biological materials, grossly disregarding the link between such sharing of these resources and benefits sharing'.[84]

In the Pandemic Treaty negotiations, the proposed PABS System (in its current form) recycles many of the same problems of the PIP Framework. Its focus is on obtaining access to human pathogens, seemingly without regard to the One Health approach that is also contained

[76] Lee, 'The Global Governance of Emerging Zoonotic Diseases', 3.

[77] Nithin Ramakrishnan, 'Bio-surveillance as One Health: A Critique of Recent Definitions and Policy Initiatives' (2023) 66 *Development* 1. Available at https://doi.org/10.1057/s41301-023-00396-x.

[78] Ibid., 2.

[79] To be clear, I am referring to the PIP Framework here (i.e. the ABS framework), not the GISRS (the network of influenza laboratories).

[80] World Health Organization, 'Pandemic Influenza Preparedness (PIP) Framework: Partnership Contribution (PC) Preparedness High-Level Implementation Plan II 2018–2023' (revised version, 2021) WHO/WHE/IHM/PIP/2018.1 Rev.1, 3. Available at: https://iris.who.int/bitstream/handle/10665/260538/WHO-WHE-IHM-PIP-2018.1-eng.pdf.

[81] See World Health Organization, 'Pandemic Influenza Preparedness (PIP) Framework: Partnership Contribution (PC) Preparedness High-Level Implementation Plan II 2018–2023' (revised version, 2021) WHO/WHE/IHM/PIP/2018.1 Rev.1, Annex 2: Budget, 52. Note that for some reason, the PIP Framework's Partnership Contribution (PC) Preparedness High-Level Implementation Plan combines Output 1 (L&S: Laboratory and Surveillance Capacity Building) and Output 6 (IPPP: National Pandemic Influenza Preparedness and Response Plans) in the High-Level Budget for 2018–2023, seemingly because IPPP was once part of L&S (6). However, this makes it impossible to tell how these funds are apportioned based on this publicly available document.

[82] Ibid., 65–66. 'In the name of global health and prevention, countries from the Global South are then induced to expand their investments in surveillance – a somewhat new and perplexing conditionality'. Ramakrishnan, 'Bio-surveillance as One Health', 4.

[83] Rourke, 'Access by Design, Benefits If Convenient'; Hampton, 'Pathogen Dematerialization and the ABS Loophole'.

[84] Ramakrishnan, 'Bio-surveillance as One Health', 7. Note that Ramakrishnan is referring specifically to the Pandemic Treaty draft in this quote.

in the Pandemic Treaty draft, and where reciprocal benefits are far from guaranteed.[85] This makes the PABS System seem fundamentally extractive; an effort to 'modernize the intrinsically neo-colonial character of international health law' that allows high-income countries to collect samples from low- and middle-income countries and turning low- and middle-income countries into the early warning system for high-income countries.[86]

On the topic of benefits, the PABS System focuses on the delivery of 'pandemic-related products' (such as vaccines, medications, personal protective equipment, etc.), meaning a pandemic will need to be declared before such benefits are made available to countries with the greatest need. On the other hand, benefits could be shared during inter-pandemic times to enhance deep prevention (spillover prevention). This means that countries would not have to wait for a pandemic before they can access benefits from a PABS System they have had to consistently contribute to during inter-pandemic periods. Deep prevention benefits could be channelled into initiatives that reduce deforestation, intensive agricultural practices (including antibiotic overuse), and destructive mining practices. They could be used to increase biodiversity, clean up polluted waterways and diversify land use. Such initiatives tackle the primary drivers of infectious disease emergence and align well with the CBD's key objectives of environmental conservation and sustainable development. Put simply, the sharing of benefits for deep prevention activities is more in line with the One Health concept, and it could mean that countries see tangible benefits *before* the outbreak of an emerging infectious disease that can reduce the risk of the disease emerging in the first place.

4.7 CONCLUSION: WHAT COULD A ONE HEALTH APPROACH ACHIEVE?

The proposed PABS System, like the rest of the Pandemic Treaty, suffered from a rush to meet impossibly tight deadlines. The international ABS regime under the CBD and Nagoya Protocol is complex (and is getting more complicated still with the negotiation of a new multilateral approach to the sharing of benefits arising from the use of Digital Sequence Information under the newly-adopted Post-2020 Global Biodiversity Framework).[87] The members of the INB were tasked with negotiating and drafting an entirely new international instrument for pandemic prevention, preparedness, and response, and pathogen ABS was just one component within that mandate. This means the complexities of the existing system for ABS have not been adequately factored into the design of the PABS System, despite the INB intending for it to be recognised as a specialised international ABS instrument under the Nagoya Protocol. Furthermore, the One Health approach was supposed to be a guiding principle of the Pandemic Treaty from the beginning, but this is not evidenced in the current proposal for the PABS System.

A genuine attempt at incorporating a One Health approach in the PABS System would mean that its scope incorporates animal pathogens and potentially environmental samples, that the WHO would (at the very least) include the other members of the One Health Quadripartite in the design of the PABS System, and would ensure they were also involved in the eventual

85 See Abbie-Rose Hampton, Mark Eccleston-Turner, Michelle Rourke, and Stephanie Switzer, '"Equity" in the Pandemic Treaty: The False Hope of "Access and Benefit-Sharing"' 72(4) (2023) *International and Comparative Law Quarterly* 1.

86 Ramakrishnan, 'Bio-surveillance as One Health', 7.

87 Conference of the Parties to the Convention on Biological Diversity, 'Decision 15/9: Digital Sequence Information on Genetic Resources' (19 December 2022) CBD/COP/DEC/15/9 3. Available at: www.cbd.int/doc/decisions/cop-15/cop-15-dec-09-en.pdf.

implementation and operation of the System. A better understanding of the finer points of ABS and its connection to the One Health approach would mean that a One Health PABS System accounts for Traditional Knowledge held by Indigenous peoples and local communities for knowledge associated with pathogenic genetic resources. Finally, a PABS System that made a genuine effort at applying the One Health approach to pandemic prevention would aim for *deep* prevention. That is, it would make an effort to channel benefits into meeting the key objectives of the CBD: environmental sustainability and sustainable development, particularly in low- and middle-income countries. This would increase the likelihood that countries would get access to benefits early (as it is not guaranteed that they will receive any benefits during a pandemic) and it would reduce the chance that a pathogen will spill over from animal populations into humans in the first place.

5

The Environmental Law Arena and the Development of the One Health Approach

Addressing the Threats to the Health of the Planet

Claire Lajaunie

5.1 INTRODUCTION

The need to implement the One Health approach to facilitate collaboration on human, animal, environmental, and climate health challenges has been highlighted in the Declaration on Climate and Health endorsed by global leaders on the first Health Day at the 28th United Nations Climate Change Conference of the Parties (COP) in December 2023.[1] It is one of numerous examples of the recent significance given to the One Health approach in the international arena, especially since the COVID-19 pandemic.

The development of modern international environmental law dates to the end of the 1960s with a growing scientific concern for the quality of the environment.[2] The 1968 UNESCO Biosphere Conference was the first intergovernmental conference to consider both human and health ecology (scientific field that seeks to contribute to our understanding of health problems at the interfaces between humans, wild and domestic animals, and their environments) from a scientific point of view. Thus, it has had a leading role in addressing health issues related to ecological diversity on a global scale.[3] It insists on the need for integrated, planned, multidisciplinary policy action for the use and conservation of natural resources within the framework of international cooperation. The conference was organised by UNESCO, with the active participation of the United Nations, the Food and Agriculture Organization (FAO) and the World Health Organization (WHO), and in cooperation with the International Biological Programme and the World Conservation Union which became the International Union for Conservation of Nature (IUCN).[4]

The UNESCO Conference led to the first international conference to make the environment a major issue, the United Nations Conference on the Human Environment,[5] also known as the Stockholm Conference, held in 1972. The conference aimed to respond to 'the need for intensified action at the national, regional and international level in order to limit and, where possible, eliminate the impairment of the human environment and in order to protect and

1 COP28 Presidency, World Health Organization, 'COP28 UAE Declaration on Climate and Health', Dubai, 2 December 2023. Available at: www.who.int/publications/m/item/cop28-uae-declaration-on-climate-and-health.

2 Alexandre Charles Kiss, *Introduction to International Environmental Law* (UNITAR 2005).

3 Serge Morand and Claire Lajaunie, *Biodiversity and Health: Linking Life, Ecosystems and Societies* (Elsevier 2017), 173.

4 Malcolm Hadley, 'A Practical Ecology: The Man and the Biosphere (MAB) Programme' in Patrick Petitjean, Vladimir Zharov, Gisbert Glaser, et al. (eds.), *Sixty Years of Science at UNESCO 1945–2005* (UNESCO 2005) 260–261.

5 United Nations Conference on the Human Environment, Stockholm, Sweden, 5–16 June 1972. Available at: https://docs.un.org/en/A/CONF.48/INF.5/rev.1.

improve the natural surroundings in the interest of man'.[6] The conference, which constitutes a landmark in the development of international environmental law, considered the quality of the environment in relation to human health. In the aftermath of the Stockholm Conference, the United Nations Environment Programme (UNEP) was created to coordinate the activities of the United Nations in the field of the environment. It has played a decisive catalytic role in the development of international environmental law.

Subsequent international conferences such as the United Nations Conference on Environment and Development (1992) and the World Summit on Sustainable Development (2002) have seen the refining of international environmental law principles first with a focus on global environmental issues and then on the links between environment and development.[7] The World Health Organisation developed a Global Strategy on Health and the Environment (1993),[8] focusing on human health while the UNEP, particularly through the multilateral environmental agreements linked to biodiversity, insists on the protection of the environment and biodiversity and its effect on health.[9] The trajectories of reflection on the link between health and the environment evolved in parallel in the disciplines relating to health (animal health or human health) on the one hand and conservation and environmental law on the other hand. Both did not officially converge until very recently.

Since the COVID-19 pandemic, the One Health approach is often presented as a new concept in environmental law while, since its official inception in 2004, its use has been associated with veterinary medicine and human health. The aim of this chapter is to show the role of conservation policies and environmental law in the development of the One Health approach.

It is important to come back to the recent origins of the One Health approach to identify the role, barely analysed, of the environmental law arena in the development and adoption of the concept by international organisations.

In this chapter we will show how the development of the One Health approach has been historically favoured by environmental law, acknowledging the interactions between health and biodiversity. We will detail how it has spread into the multilateral environmental agreements linked to biodiversity conservation and how the environmental protection arena has evolved quite independently from the health sector in implementing the One Health approach. The specific role of One Health in relation to the ocean and marine biodiversity will be highlighted. We will conclude with examples of One Health implementation related to environmental law, with particular reference to Southeast Asia.

5.2 FROM THE 2004 MANHATTAN SYMPOSIUM: THE INTERNATIONAL ENVIRONMENTAL LAW PERSPECTIVE ON ONE HEALTH

The acknowledgement of the close interlinkages between health and the environment is not new although it is still difficult to put them into practice in scientific settings or

6 United Nations General Assembly, 'Resolution on Problems of the Human Environment' (entered into force 3 December 1968). Available at: https://docs.un.org/en/A/RES/2398(XXIII).

7 United Nations Conference on Environment and Development, Rio de Janeiro, Brazil, 3–14 June 1992; World Summit on Sustainable Development, Johannesburg, South Africa, 26 August–4 September 2002. Available at: https://docs.un.org/en/A/RES/44/228.

8 World Health Assembly, Resolution 45.31 Health and Environment (May 1992) §4, al. 1; WHO Global Strategy for Health and Environment (1993). Available at: https://iris.who.int/bitstream/handle/10665/175841/WHA45_R31_eng.pdf.

9 The Preamble of the Convention on Biological Diversity states 'Aware that conservation and sustainable use of biological diversity is of critical importance for meeting the food, health and other needs of the growing world population'. Available at: www.cbd.int/convention/text.

political decision-making.[10] Concerning animal health, for instance, the areas of wildlife conservation and veterinary medicine and livestock were working separately,[11] until only two decades ago. In 2001, the Wildlife Disease Association and the Society for Tropical Veterinary Medicine held a scientific meeting to address the issue of diseases transmitted between domestic and wild animals. At that meeting, the conservation and veterinary medicine scientists insisted on the fact that the recognition of animal health sciences as a whole by donors and project funders is crucial to the design and management of sustainable wildlife-based or livestock-based programmes. They recognised the necessity to work together to build synergies and to encourage projects that foster integrative approaches to livestock production, food security, human health, economic growth, democracy and governance, biodiversity conservation, and natural resource management.[12] They adopted the Pilanesberg resolution, which notably acknowledged the need to develop joint activities that require expertise in domestic animal health and wildlife health.[13] The resolution emphasises that the sustainable management of livestock as well as the conservation of wildlife require ground-level stewardship.

In 2004, The Wildlife Conservation Society (WCS) organised a symposium on the current and potential movements of diseases among human, domestic animal, and wildlife populations with health experts (veterinary medicine, human health, conservation) and with representatives from the WHO, the FAO, the United States Centers for Disease Control and Prevention and the IUCN Commission on Environmental Law.[14] It is interesting to reflect on the presence of the Commission on Environmental Law providing a legal perspective during that symposium which officially minted the term One Health (in the expression 'One World, One Health'). Professor Kheng-Lian Koh, the representative of the commission, demonstrated how the One Health approach led to novel legal issues that had more questions than answers. She specifically highlighted the contradictions between conservation policies and the precautionary principle, used as a one-time approach as a risk management method resulting in the culling of animals. She emphasised the interest of using the ecosystem approach as a holistic view on these issues. She referred to the international environmental agreements such as the CITES to address the circulation of zoonotic diseases at the interface between human, domestic animals, and wildlife and highlighted the need for regional cooperation. The meeting resulted in the adoption of the Manhattan Principles, which promote the integration of biodiversity conservation aspects into decision making (principle 6), culling measures (principle 8), or the collaboration between different sectors (principle 10).[15]

Months later a follow-up workshop was hosted in Bangkok by the Thai Ministry of Public Health that aimed to go 'Beyond Zoonoses', with a focus on the policy implications of the threat of emerging diseases. That meeting gathered speakers from different organisations and disciplines, including various representatives of the environmental law arena such as the IUCN Commission on Environmental Law; the IUCN Commission on Environmental, Economic

10 Morand and Lajaunie, *Biodiversity and Health*, 12–14.

11 William B Karesh, Steven A. Osofsky, Tonie E. Rocke, and Paul L. Barrows, 'Joining Forces to Improve Our World' (2002) 16(5) *Conservation Biology* 1432.

12 Wildlife Disease Association and the Society for Tropical Veterinary Medicine, 'Pilaneberg Resolution 2001', Pilanesberg, South Africa (22–27 July 2001). Available at: www.wcs-ahead.org/pilanesberg.html.

13 William B Karesh et al., 'Joining Forces to Improve Our World'.

14 World Conservation Society, Symposium One World, 'One Health: Building Interdisciplinary Bridges to Health in a Globalized World', September 2004. Available at: www.oneworldonehealth.org/sept2004/owoh_sept04.html.

15 The Twelve Manhattan Principles, 'One World, One Health', www.oneworldonehealth.org/.

and Social Policy; the International Institute for Sustainable Development; the Centre for Environmental Legal Studies of Pace University School of Law; and the Asia-Pacific Centre for Environmental Law at the National University of Singapore. The IUCN advocated for building capacity within national and global institutions responsible for public health and animal health to analyse and address issues at the nexus between human, domestic animal, and wildlife health.[16]

The questioning about the integration of the One Health approach into international environmental law took a specific path in relation to international events related to the environment and health. The ecosystem approach highlighted during the Manhattan Symposium and put forward by the Convention on Biodiversity in 2000 has a 'strategy for the integrated management of land, water and living resources that promotes conservation and sustainable use in an equitable way' and by the IUCN.[17]

The objective of the Millenium Ecosystem Assessment (MA), launched in 2000, was to assess the consequences of ecosystem change for human well-being. In the Health synthesis of the MA published in 2005, the WHO states that 'ecosystems are essential to human well-being and especially to human health'.[18] The WHO distinguishes two strategies to address the health consequences of ecosystems change 'One–preferable in principle–is to prevent, limit or manage the environmental damage. The other is to make adaptive changes that will protect individuals and populations from the adverse consequences of ecosystem change.'[19] It entails cross-sectoral policies, institutions, and investments on local, national, regional, and global scales.

The promotion of the ecosystem approach, then of the ecosystem health associated with human health led to the acknowledgement of the One Health approach in the international conventions linked to the protection of biodiversity.

5.3 INTERNATIONAL AGREEMENTS ON BIODIVERSITY CONSERVATION: THE ONE HEALTH APPROACH IN INTERNATIONAL ENVIRONMENTAL LAW

The ecosystem approach is the primary framework for action under the Convention on Biological Diversity (CBD).[20] It is mentioned in the elaboration and implementation of the various thematic and cross-cutting programmes of work and in the guidelines regarding these programmes.[21]

[16] IUCN World Conservation Congress, 'Resolution 3.011 Addressing the Linkages between Conservation, Human and Animal Health, and Security', Bangkok, Thailand, 17–25 November 2004. Available at: https://portals.iucn.org/library/sites/library/files/resrecfiles/WCC_2004_RES_11_EN.pdf.

[17] Convention on Biological Diversity, COP5, Decision V/6 Ecosystem approach, Nairobi, Kenya, 15–26 May 2000, available at: www.cbd.int/doc/meetings/esa/ecosys-01/other/ecosys-01-dec-cop-05-06-en.pdf; Richard D Smith and Edward Maltby, *Using the Ecosystem Approach to Implement the Convention on Biological Diversity: Key Issues and Case Studies* (IUCN 2003) 118.

[18] WHO, *Millenium Ecosystem Assessment. Ecosystems and Human Well–Being: Biodiversity Synthesis* (Island Press 2005).

[19] WHO, *Millenium Ecosystem Assessment. Ecosystems and Human Well–Being.*

[20] UNEP, Convention on Biological Diversity, Rio de Janeiro, Brazil, 5 June 1992. Available at: www.cbd.int.

[21] 'The ecosystem approach is based on the application of appropriate scientific methodologies focused on levels of biological organization, which encompass the essential structure, processes, functions and interactions among organisms and their environment. It also recognises that humans, with their cultural diversity, are an integral component of many ecosystems': Secretariat of the Convention on Biological Diversity, *The Ecosystem Approach: CBD Guidelines* (Secretariat of the Convention on Biological Diversity 2004), 50.

In a previous analysis,[22] we examined thoroughly how the notion of health then the One Health approach historically emerged in international conventions related to biodiversity in the CBD – the Convention on the Conservation of Migratory Species of Wild Animals (1979);[23] the Convention on International Trade in Endangered Species of Wild Fauna and Flora (1973);[24] and the Convention on Wetlands (also known as Ramsar Convention, 1971)[25] – through the study of the text of the conventions themselves and of all the resolutions or decisions adopted during all the COPs (Conference of the Parties, the decision-making body of the Conventions from the first COP to 2014).[26] In this chapter, we refer to that work and select the explicit references made to the One Health approach to present how they emerged.

After various SARS and avian influenza episodes and in accordance with the WHO International Health Regulations (2005), initiatives were developed to improve international awareness and cooperation to prevent infectious disease pandemics. The Convention on Migratory Species, in cooperation with the Agreement on the Conservation of African Eurasian Migratory Waterbirds (AEWA), created the Scientific Task Force on Avian Influenza and Wild Birds to integrate migratory species and other environmental considerations into the international efforts to combat Highly Pathogenic Avian Influenza.[27]

The promotion of cooperation between all relevant international instruments and processes to enhance policy coherence is one of the objectives of the Strategic Plan of the CBD (2002–2010). Liaison groups for cooperation between multilateral environmental agreements – the Joint Liaison Group between the Rio conventions (2001) (i.e. the CBD),[28] the United Nations Framework Convention on Climate Change (UNFCCC), the United Nations Convention to Combat Desertification (UNCCD), and the Biodiversity Liaison Group between the seven biodiversity-related conventions (2004)[29] – have been created to foster the synergies and

[22] Claire Lajaunie and Pierre Mazzega, 'One Health and Biodiversity Conventions: The Emergence of Health Issues in Biodiversity Conventions' (2016) 8 *IUCN Academy of Environmental Law eJournal* 105.

[23] Convention on the Conservation of Migratory Species of Wild Animals, Bonn, Germany, 23 June 1979, in force 1 November 1983. Available at: www.cms.int.

[24] Convention on International Trade in Endangered Species of Wild Fauna and Flora, Washington, United States, 3 March 1973, into force 1 July 1975. Available at: www.cites.org.

[25] Convention on Wetlands of International Importance Especially as Waterfowl Habitat, Ramsar, Iran, 2 February 1971, into force 21 December 1975. Available at: www.ramsar.org.

[26] Lajaunie and Mazzega, 'One Health and Biodiversity Conventions', 105–121.

[27] It gathered representatives from UNEP, CMS, AEWA, Ramsar, BirdLife International, the International Council for Game and Wildlife Conservation (CIC), Wetlands International, the Wildlife Conservation Society, and the Zoological Society of London, with the UN Food and Agriculture Organization (FAO), WHO, and the World Organization for Animal Health (OIE) participating as observers.

[28] Convention on Biological Diversity, COP 6 Decision VI/20 Cooperation with other organisations, initiatives, and conventions, The Hague, Netherlands, 7–19 April 2002. In 2001, the Subsidiary Body for Scientific and Technological Advice of the UNFCCC welcomed an oral report provided by the secretariat relating to the work of a joint liaison group between the secretariats of the UNFCCC, the CBD, and the CCD, and the information provided by the representatives of the CBD and UNCCD secretariats. See UNFCCC/SBSTA/2001/L.14 Cooperation with relevant international organisations, Marrakesh, Morocco, 29 October–6 November 2001, available at: https://unfccc.int/documents/2462. In August 2001, the Conventions established a Joint Liaison Group as an informal forum for exchanging information, exploring opportunities for synergistic activities and increasing coordination.

[29] The Biodiversity Liaison Group links the secretariats of the seven biodiversity-related conventions: the Convention on Biological Diversity (CBD); the Convention on International Trade in Endangered Species of Fauna and Flora (CITES); the Convention on the Conservation of Migratory Species of Wild Animals (CMS); the Ramsar Convention on Wetlands (Ramsar); the UNESCO Convention Concerning the Protection of the World Cultural and Natural Heritage; the International Treaty on Plant Genetic Resources for Food and Agriculture; and the International Plant Protection Convention. See Mandate for Establishing the Liaison Group of Biodiversity-related Conventions was Set Out by the Parties to the CBD, in decision VII/26 (paragraphs 1 and 2), available at: www.cbd.int/decision/cop/default.shtml?id=7763.

avoid duplication of the decisions. Thus, the Scientific Task Force coordinated by the CMS Secretariat welcomed the CBD in 2006.[30]

The synergies between conventions are expressed by mutual references in the diverse COP decisions, shared knowledge, and a common focus. In 2008, the CMS adopted a resolution to respond to the challenges of emerging and reemerging diseases in migratory species.[31] This resolution is of importance as it calls for the creation of a Scientific Task Force on Wildlife Disease with a broader focus than the Task Force on Avian Influenza and Wild Birds created in 2006.

This resolution contains the first explicit reference to One Health as it requests the FAO to integrate 'disease and management issues that can be brought to the attention of the Scientific Task Force on Wildlife Disease' into the One Health approach.[32] It also refers to the outcomes of the COP 10 of the Ramsar Conference on the theme of 'Healthy Wetlands, Healthy People' held earlier in 2008, which stressed the functional linkages between the role that wetlands play in providing ecosystem services for the support of both human and wildlife populations; and that aquatic waterbirds and other migratory species can be valuable indicators of ecosystem health.[33]

In 2008, the Strategic Framework for Reducing Risks of Infectious Diseases, drafted by the FAO, Office International des Epizooties (OIE) (now known as the World Organisation for Animal Health (WOAH)), UNICEF, UN System Influenza Coordination, World Bank, and the WHO was launched.[34]

In 2011, the CMS adopted a resolution on wildlife and migratory species, acknowledging the increasing progress of the One Health approach as a multidisciplinary way of addressing emerging infectious diseases and noting that the concept had been endorsed by several international organisations.[35] This resolution renamed the Task Force on Wildlife Disease to the 'Scientific Task Force on Wildlife and Ecosystem Health' to 'reflect more comprehensively the One Health approach to integrating wildlife, livestock, human and ecosystem health issues'. The CITES Secretariat was invited by the Secretariat of the CMS to become a core affiliate of the Scientific Task Force.

Later, the Ramsar COP XI, in 2012, adopted a resolution acknowledging the One Health and the EcoHealth movements (already supported by many organisations),[36] as they 'place disease dynamics in the broader contexts of sustainable agriculture, socio-economic development, environment protection and sustainability, and the complex patterns of global change'.[37] The same year, the Animal Committee of the CITES adopted the term of reference of the Scientific Task Force on Wildlife and Ecosystem Health, which states:

[30] In 2007, the FAO became a full member of the task force and contributed to its coordination.

[31] Convention on the Conservation of Migratory Species of Wild Animals, 'COP9 Resolution 9.8, Responding to the Challenge of Emerging and Re-emerging Diseases in Migratory Species, including Highly Pathogenic Avian Influenza H5n1', Rome, Italy, 1–5 December 2008.

[32] It refers to 'One World, One Health', the expression used during the Manhattan Symposium, 2004.

[33] See Ramsar convention, Resolution X.3 The Changwon Declaration on human well-being and wetlands, Changwon, Republic of Korea, 28 October to 4 November 2008 www.ramsar.org/sites/default/files/documents/pdf/res/key_res_x_03_e.pdf.

[34] FAO, OIE, WHO, UN System Influenza Coordination, UNICEF, and the World Bank, 'Contributing to One World, One Health. A Strategic Framework for Reducing Risks of Infectious Diseases at the Animal-Human-Ecosystems Interface' (14 October 2008).

[35] CMS, 'COP10, Resolution 10.22 Wildlife Disease and Migratory Species', Bergen, Norway, 20–25 November 2011. Available at: www.cms.int/sites/default/files/document/10_22_diseases_e_0_0.pdf.

[36] Ramsar, 'COP11, Resolution 11.12 Wetlands and Health: Taking an Ecosystem Approach', Bucharest, Romania, 6–13 July 2012. Available at: www.ramsar.org/sites/default/files/documents/pdf/cop11/res/cop11-res12-e.pdf.

[37] Ibid.

> It has become clear that while the emergence of pathogens is highly complex in nature, it can be traced back to ecosystem changes associated with an expanding human population, food insecurity, and unsustainable use of natural resources resulting in biodiversity loss and changes to ecosystem functioning … The health of all species including wildlife, livestock, humans, and plant life are negatively impacted by decreased availability of ecosystem services.[38]

Thus, the vision of the Task Force expressed in this document was to achieve better health for ecosystems, wildlife, livestock, and people by promoting an integrated scientific approach within the 'One Health' framework.

In 2013, the Committee on Science and Technology of the UNCCD recognised that One Health as 'an integrated approach in managing health risks through an interdisciplinary interface for human, animal and environmental health care – can be a powerful tool to successfully cope with the drivers and consequences of desertification'.[39] The same year, the CBD and the OIE signed a cooperation agreement in fields of mutual interest such as the conservation and sustainable use of biodiversity, improvement of animal health and welfare, and the promotion of the 'One Health' approach to manage the risks presented by animal diseases and zoonoses at the animal–human–ecosystem interface.[40]

During the following COP of the CBD in 2014, two resolutions acknowledged the One Health approach: one on bushmeat and sustainable wildlife management and the other on biodiversity and human health,[41] which considered One Health as 'an integrated approach consistent with the ecosystem approach (decision V/6) that integrates the complex relationships between humans, microorganisms, animals, plants, agriculture, wildlife and the environment'.[42]

In another work, drawing an analogy to epidemiology, we studied the transmission, circulation, and persistence of health issues in the CBD, CMS, and CITES Conventions and in the resolutions or decisions of their COPs. The analysis, using text-mining, shows how these terms are diffusing in the conventions and in the resolutions of their COPs over time through a network induced by their transmission between texts. The CBD plays a central role as a source of terms related to health and the environment.[43]

Since 2014, each Conference of the Party of the CBD has adopted a resolution on biodiversity and health refining the value of the One Health approach. The acknowledgement of this approach started with a reflection on how to tackle the spread of zoonotic diseases like avian influenza and SARS. It appeared necessary to consider zoonotic, wildlife diseases and finally the health of all species in relation to biodiversity in general or to specific ecosystems such as wetlands or deserts.

38 CITES, Animals Committee, 'Relationship between Wildlife Trade and Wildlife Diseases', 26th Meeting, AC26 Doc. 23 (Rev. 1), Annex Terms of Reference, Geneva (Switzerland), 15–20 March 2012 and Dublin (Ireland), 22–24 March 2012. Available at: www.cites.org/sites/default/files/eng/com/ac/26/E26-23.pdf.

39 UNCCD COP11, Committee on Science and Technology, Final outcome of the UNCCD 2nd Scientific Conference, COP (11)/CST/INF.3/Corr.1, §29, Windhoek, Namibia, 17–20 September 2013. Available at: www.unccd.int/sites/default/files/sessions/documents/ICCD_COP11_CST_INF.3/cstinf3eng.pdf.

40 Cooperation Agreement between the Secretariat of the Convention on Biological Diversity and the World Organisation for Animal Health (OIE), 15 February 2013. Available at: www.woah.org/app/uploads/2021/03/cbd-accord-ang.pdf.

41 CBD COP12, Decision 12.18 Sustainable Use of Biodiversity: Bushmeat and Sustainable Wildlife Management and CBD COP 12 Decision 12.21 Biodiversity and Human Health, Pyeongchang, Republic of Korea, 6–17 October 2014.

42 Ibid.

43 Claire Lajaunie and Pierre Mazzega, 'Transmission, circulation et persistance des enjeux de santé dans les conventions internationales liées à la Biodiversité et Conventions de Rio' in Sandrine Maljean-Dubois (ed), *Numero Special Diffusion de normes et circulations d'acteurs dans la gouvernance internationale de l'environnement* (Confluence des Droits 1, DICE Editions 2017) 61–80.

5.4 FROM SOUTHEAST ASIA TO THE INTERNATIONAL ARENA

The Southeast Asian region, the epicentre of the emergence of several infectious diseases, has established foregoing and favourable ingredients to the One Health approach. Since the 1980s, the Association of Southeast Asian Nations (ASEAN) considered health as an essential part of the socio-economic development of the region and aimed for a coordinated action of its member states in the public health sector.[44] In 1993, following the WHO Global Strategy on Health and the Environment, the two regional offices of the WHO adopted a Regional Strategy on Health and the Environment.[45] The Strategy of the Southeast Asia Regional Office states that environmental interventions may contribute to enhancing health and that a holistic approach of health, environment, and development in accordance with the Rio Declaration (1992) is needed. Together with hygiene, sanitation, water supply, and the environmental health aspects of water resources, the regional priorities integrate infectious disease risks (waterborne, vector-borne, or foodborne diseases). Building on successful experiences and initiatives related to health and the environment,[46] the region played a leading role in the international adoption of this approach.[47] In this section, this chapter presents the main decisive steps towards the adoption of the One Health approach in Southeast Asia, in association with international organisations.

The Asia Pacific Strategy for Emerging Diseases was first launched in 2005 to support member states in meeting the obligations of the International Health Regulations (2005).[48] It is a common strategic action framework for member states of the WHO Southeast Asia and Western Pacific regions and their partners. It aims to strengthen regional and national core capacities to effectively prepare for and respond to threats posed by emerging infectious diseases and other public health emergencies.

At the Interministerial Conference on Animal and Pandemic Influenza in Hanoi in 2010, the states and international agencies gathered to develop a coordinated response to pandemic risks (in particular avian influenza) and to control infectious diseases.[49] They formally decided to operate a One Health approach. Noticing a deficit of regional coordination within the ASEAN, the European Commission developed a programme to improve regional coordination regarding highly pathogenic and emerging diseases.[50] This programme, called Highly Pathogenic and Emerging Diseases (HPED) targeted a global response to avian flu by adopting the One Health approach. In a workshop gathering the various partners of the programme in Bangkok in 2011, one relevant agenda item was the variety of definitions and

[44] Claire Lajaunie and Pierre Mazzega, 'Organization Networks as Information Integration System: Case Study on Environment and Health in Southeast Asia' (2016) 5 *ACSIJ Adv Computer Science* 28–39.

[45] WHO SEARO, *Regional Strategic Plan for Health and Environment for the WHO Southeast Asia Region* (New Delhi: WHO SEARO, 1993).

[46] Lajaunie and Mazzega, 'Organization Networks as Information Integration System: Case Study on Environment and Health in Southeast Asia', 28.

[47] Claire Lajaunie and Serge Morand, 'L'approche One Health: l'Asie du Sud Est comme lieu privilégié de sa mise en œuvre' in Gabriel Facal et Jérôme Samuel (eds.), *L'Asie du Sud-Est 2022: bilan, enjeux et perspectives* (Bangkok, Thailand: Institut de recherche sur l'Asie du Sud-Est contemporaine, 2023) 33–47.

[48] WHO WPRO, *Asia Pacific Strategy for Emerging Diseases* (WHO WPRO, 2005) 50.

[49] Interministerial Conference on Animal and Pandemic Influenza (IMCAPI) 'Animal and Pandemic Influenza: The Way Forward' hosted by the Government of Vietnam, in coordination with the European Union and the United States of America, with the support of the UN System Influenza Coordination and international organisations, Hanoi, Vietnam, 19–21 April 2010.

[50] European Commission, *Outcome and Impact Assessment of the Global Response to the Avian Influenza Crisis 2005–2010* (Luxembourg: Publications Office of the European Union, 2010) 29.

perceptions of the One Health approach and the difficulties regarding its notably trans-sectoral implementation.[51]

Thailand plays a key role in promoting the One Health approach among the ASEAN member states, and in the region, notably through the network of the Southeast Asian One Health Universities Network. That regional network, created in 2011, is based in Chiang Mai (Thailand) and gathers more than ninety-five universities in seven Southeast Asia countries (Cambodia, Indonesia, Malaysia, Myanmar, Philippines, Thailand and Vietnam) and six universities in Taiwan, an associated member state.[52] The aim of this network is to improve One Health manpower capacity by leveraging education to train the next generation of One Health professionals in using a systems approach to problem solving that considers all aspects of the human–animal–ecosystem interface. Thailand hosts numerous regional offices of international organisations (including UNEP, WOAH, WHO, FAO, UNDP, UNESCO, UN Habitat, and UN ESCAP) which facilitates the dialogue between the regional level and international organisations.

In 2008, the health ministers of the ASEAN member states of China, Japan, and South Korea (ASEAN+3) met in Manila with the common goal to improve the sanitary conditions in the region and committed to adopt the One Health approach for the prevention and control of emerging infectious diseases and to consider the adverse impacts of trade liberalisation.[53] In a Declaration on Animal Health and Zoonoses, the ministers of Agriculture and Forestry of the ASEAN gathered in Phnom Penh (Cambodia) and declared their commitment to advance the One Health approach and support existing collaborative frameworks on animal and public health governance at global, regional, and national levels to address vulnerabilities associated with zoonotic diseases.[54]

These examples show the acknowledgement of the One Health approach in the definition of regional policies. In 2017, the Chief of States and government of the ASEAN decided to combat antimicrobial resistance through the One Health approach (ASEAN Leaders' Declaration on Antimicrobial Resistance, 2017),[55] with the elaboration of a Global Action Plan to be implemented by the member states through comprehensive multisectoral responsibility and governance; inclusive mechanisms to actively engage the participation of relevant stakeholders; and defined objectives and goals that are aligned with the ASEAN Global Action Plan. The ASEAN Strategic Framework to Combat Antimicrobial Resistance through the One Health Approach (2019–2030) states its mission: 'to formulate and implement an ASEAN regional action plan adopting the One Health Approach in combating AMR through the comprehensive multisectoral and multidisciplinary engagement and participation of all

[51] HPED networking event, 2011, 'Linking the Actors of the EU-Asia Regional One Health Programme', Workshop Report, Bangkok, 18–19 January 2011, 42–43.

[52] SEAOHUN, 'The 1st One Health International Conference in Taiwan', 7 October 2019. Available at: www.seaohun.org/single-post/the-1st-one-health-international-conference-in-taiwan.

[53] Joint Statement of the Third ASEAN Plus Three Health Ministers Meeting, 'Trade Liberalisation: Its Adverse Impact on our Borderless Health Problems', Manila, 10 October 2008. Available at: www.asean.org/joint-statement-of-the-third-asean-plus-three-health-ministers-meeting-manila/.

[54] Thirty-Second Meeting of the ASEAN Ministers on Agriculture and Forestry (32nd AMAF), 'ASEAN Ministerial Statement on ASEAN Cooperation on Animal Health and Zoonoses: Avian Influenza and Beyond', Phnom Penh, 23 October 2010. Available at: www.asean.org/the-thirty-second-meeting-of-the-asean-minsters-on-agriculture-and-forestry-32nd-amaf-phnom-penh-23-october-2010/.

[55] ASEAN Head of States and Government of the Member States, 'ASEAN Leaders' Declaration on Antimicrobial Resistance (AMR), Combating AMR through One Health Approach, Manila', 13 November 2017. See Chapter 16. Available at: www.asean.org/wp-content/uploads/2017/11/3.-ADOPTION_2017_ALD-on-AMR_Endorsed-13th-AHMM.pdf.

governments and stakeholders'. It details activities in four main sectors: human, animal and agriculture, food safety, and environment.[56] Among the strategic objectives, objective 5 is 'to conduct research to support the implementation of the ASEAN Strategic Plan to Combat AMR through One Health approach',[57] materialised by the provision of a platform for the ASEAN member states to share and disseminate existing research on AMR (e.g. websites, research fora, conferences, publications). Objective 6 is 'to ensure adequate and sustainable resource management and mobilisation, as appropriate at national or regional levels, for the implementation of the regional AMR activities',[58] which aims to foster international collaboration and partnerships, as well as benchmarking, in the sharing of technical expertise and experience in the ASEAN network.

As an example of implementation of these obligations in the sphere of environmental law, in 2020, the ASEAN Centre for Biodiversity (ACB),[59] in collaboration with the Vietnam Ministry of Natural Resources and Environment, the ASEAN Secretariat, the WOAH, and the WCS organised a webinar with a focus on wildlife conservation and animal health linkage to zoonotic diseases spread and prevention as well as preparedness for the future with a One Health approach.[60] The purpose of this meeting is to inform the ASEAN sectoral bodies and the relevant stakeholders of issues and efforts relating to the links between animal and human health, especially in the areas of livestock production, wildlife habitat protection, wildlife trade, zoonotic and emerging infectious diseases; it is also to inform the public on these issues and to highlight the efforts of ASEAN and its member states as well as organisations working in the region.

The ASEAN Coordinating Centre for Animal Health and Zoonoses (ACCAHZ) was created in 2016 to provide a framework of cooperation and coordination among ASEAN Member States to prevent, control, and eradicate transboundary animal diseases and zoonoses in ASEAN and to contribute towards food security and safety, animal and human health, poverty alleviation, and the well-being and livelihood of the people of ASEAN. To complete its actions, in 2020, leaders of all the ASEAN countries decided on the creation of the ASEAN Centre for Public Health Emergencies and Emerging Diseases (ACPHEED) in Bangkok.[61]

At the regional level, the dynamic of networks launched in a more-or-less formal way to respond to health or environmental issues and associated numerous actors to create a flexible network of organisations that favour the implementation of the One Health approach with the constant development of intersectoral work at the ASEAN level and a dialogue with international organisations.[62]

56 Asean Health Ministers, 'ASEAN Strategic Framework to Combat Antimicrobial Resistance through One Health Approach [2019–2030]'. Available at: www.asean.org/wp-content/uploads/2021/10/Agd-6.2.b_ASEAN-Strategic-Framework-to-Combat-AMR_Adopted-by-AHMM.pdf.

57 Ibid.

58 Ibid.

59 The ACB is an intergovernmental organisation that facilitates cooperation and coordination among the ten ASEAN Member States and with regional and international organisations on the conservation and sustainable use of biological diversity.

60 ASEAN Centre for Biodiversity, 'Wildlife Conservation and Zoonotic Diseases: Halting Species Loss and Tackling Public Health in the ASEA', Webinar, 19 November 2020. Available at: https://asean.chm-cbd.net/wildlife-conservation-and-zoonotic-diseases-halting-species-loss-and-tackling-public-health-asean.

61 37th ASEAN Summit (chaired by Vietnam), ASEAN Strategic Framework for Public Health Emergencies, II, § 5, November 2020.

62 Pierre Mazzega and Claire Lajaunie, 'Modelling Organisation Networks Collaborating on Health and Environment within ASEAN' in Rebecca S Martinez (ed.), *Complex Systems: Theory and Applications* (NOVA Publ. Hauppauge 2017), Chap. 5, 117–148.

5.5 THE INTERNATIONAL DEFINITION OF ONE HEALTH AND ITS ENVIRONMENTAL DIMENSION

The FAO, the WHO, and the WOAH (formerly OIE), also known as the Tripartite, have developed joint strategies and guidelines based on the One Health approach from 2006; however, at that time, the environmental side was not formally represented.

5.5.1 *International Definition of One Health*

The creation of a One Health High-Level Expert Panel (OHHLEP) was officially announced by the French and German Foreign Ministers and the leadership of the WHO, the WOAH, the FAO, and the UNEP at the Paris Peace Forum on 12 November 2020.[63] In May 2021, the OHHLEP was launched with 26 selected key international experts selected by the Tripartite plus UNEP.[64] OHHLEP is a One Health advisory group created to provide the Quadripartite with evidence-based scientific and policy advice to address the challenges raised at the animal–human–environment interface using the One Health approach. The first task of OHHLEP has been to develop a comprehensive definition of One Health, promoting a clear understanding across sectors and areas of expertise.

There is now an international and common definition of One Health:

> **One Health** is an integrated, unifying approach that aims to sustainably balance and optimise the health of people, animals, and ecosystems. It recognises the health of humans, domestic and wild animals, plants, and the wider environment (including ecosystems) are closely linked and interdependent.
>
> The approach mobilises multiple sectors, disciplines, and communities at varying levels of society to work together to foster well-being and tackle threats to health and ecosystems, while addressing the collective need for healthy food, water, energy, and air, taking action on climate change and contributing to sustainable development.[65]

5.5.2 *The Acknowledgement of the Right to a Healthy Environment*

UNEP joined the Tripartite in 2022 and the same year the United Nations General Assembly recognised the right to a clean, healthy, and sustainable environment.[66] This resolution followed the acknowledgement of this right by the United Nations Human Rights Council in October 2021.[67] It affirms that the promotion of the human right to a clean, healthy, and sustainable environment requires the full implementation of the multilateral environmental agreements under the principles of international environmental law. This right is related to other rights and existing international law.

[63] Following a proposal by the French and German governments. Cf. Thomas C Mettenleiter et al., 'The One Health High-Level Expert Panel (OHHLEP)' (2023) 5 *One Health Outlook* 1–8.

[64] UNEP joined the Tripartite in May 2021 and in March 2022 the four international agencies signed a Memorandum of Understanding which provides a legal and formal framework to tackle the challenges at the human, animal, plant, and ecosystem interface using a more integrated and coordinated approach constituting the Quadripartite.

[65] One Health High-Level Expert Panel, Wiku B Adisasmito, Salama Almuhairi, Casey Barton Behravesh, et al., 'One Health: A New Definition for a Sustainable and Healthy Future' (2022) 18 *PLoS Pathogens* e1010537.

[66] United Nations General Assembly, Resolution A/RES/76/300, The Human Right to a Clean, Healthy and Sustainable Environment, July 2022. See Chapter 7.

[67] United Nations Human Rights Council, Resolution 48/13 48/13, The Human Right to a Clean, Healthy and Sustainable Environment, October 2021.

Let us recall that in a 2017 report, the United Nations Special Rapporteur J. H. Knox concluded that biodiversity is necessary for ecosystem services that support the full enjoyment of a wide range of human rights, including the rights to life, health, food, water, and culture. In order to protect human rights, states have a general obligation to protect ecosystems and biodiversity.[68]

Thus in 2022 the United Nations Environment Assembly 'Strengthening Actions for Nature to Achieve the Sustainable Development Goals' requests the Executive Director of the United Nations Environment Programme and the Quadripartite to support member states and members of specialised agencies, upon their request, in assessing the environmental dimension of health.[69]

The Quadripartite One Health Joint Plan of Action (OH JPA) contains a specific action track aiming at integrating the environment into One Health.[70] Acknowledging the fact that every form of environmental degradation has direct or indirect negative consequences for human and animal health, the Action Plan details activities (associated to deliverables and a timeline) under four main actions in relation to the main objective of this action track: 'Protect and restore biodiversity, prevent the degradation of ecosystems and the wider environment to jointly support the health of people, animals, plants and ecosystems, underpinning sustainable development'.[71] The OH JPA is guided by the Theory of Change developed by OHHLEP which defines the pathways of change and high-level actions. While the right to a healthy environment can constitute a way to strengthen the implementation of the One Health approach into environmental law, two pathways of the Theory of Change should be considered jointly in order to promote sound One Health environmental law and policies. The first pathway refers to actions related to policy development, political will, and regulatory frameworks, and the third pathway targets actions related to strengthening the scientific evidence base. A strong scientific basis is crucial to develop efficient environmental law and policies that can be monitored thanks to quantitative indicators in addition to qualitative criteria.

5.5.3 *One Health and the Need to Improve the Science Policy Dialogue: The Example of One Health and the Ocean*

The OH JPA highlights that many negative consequences of human activities are 'compounded by climate change, which only multiplies these threats, exacerbating their impact and undermining the resilience of environmental and ecological systems'.[72] During a side event of the UNFCC COP26,[73] we presented a textual analysis of the UNESCO Intergovernmental

[68] J. H. Knox, 'Report of the Special Rapporteur on the Issue of Human Rights Obligations Relating to the Enjoyment of a Safe, Clean, Healthy and Sustainable Environment', A/HRC/34/49, January 2017, 21.

[69] UNEP, UNEA, Resolution 5.6 Biodiversity and Health, March 2022, § 4.

[70] Action Track 6.

[71] Action 6.1. Protect, restore and prevent the degradation of ecosystems and the wider environment; Action 6.2. Mainstream the health of the environment and ecosystems into the One Health approach; Action 6.3. Integrate environmental knowledge, data and evidence into One Health decision-making; Action 6.4. Create an interoperable One Health academic and in-service training programme for environmental, medical, agricultural and veterinary sector professionals. In FAO, UNEP, WHO, and WOAH. 2022. One Health Joint Plan of Action (2022–2026). Working together for the health of humans, animals, plants, and the environment. Rome.

[72] Ibid., 3.

[73] Claire Lajaunie and Pierre Mazzega, 'Connecting the One Health Approach to the Ocean-Climate Nexus', One Ocean Hub, 23 November 2021. Available at: https://oneoceanhub.org/connecting-the-one-health-approach-to-the-ocean-climate-nexus/.

Oceanographic Commission (IOC) document of the UN Ocean Decade.[74] For the IOC, the Ocean Decade was an 'opportunity to engage the ocean science community in achieving the Sustainable Development Goals'. The document mentions ocean health and evokes major themes that can be related to ocean health as seen through environmental, ecosystemic, and bio-physical lenses. However, no mention is made of the One Health approach. The United Nations Decade of Ocean Science for Sustainable Development (2021–2030) aims at the development of good science to ensure the conservation of the ocean, the sustainability of its uses, and the protection of ocean health. Nevertheless, there is no common understanding of what 'ocean health' could encompass under the Decade, and definitions in the literature differ, depending on the scientific discipline concerned.[75]

We analysed the metadata of 4,886 scientific papers mentioning One Health (over the period from January 2004 to April 2021) found in the Web of Science. Only twenty-four of them mention at least one of the seventy-six expressions of the UN Decade directly related to the ocean,[76] such as the 'blue economy', 'marine conservation', 'marine pollution', 'ocean acidification', 'ocean literacy', 'marine and coastal environment', or 'coastal communities'. In contrast, 4,377 One Health articles contain at least one of the 148 keywords of the UN Decade that relate to the field of governance. Thus, very little research is yet devoted to the links between ocean science and the interconnection between human, animal health, and health of the marine environment. The potential contributions of the One Health approach in marine resources management and use, particularly biological and genetic resources, also seem to be relatively poorly identified and explored. Conversely, the UN Decade document does not integrate a One Health perspective into the initiatives it promotes. While the UN Decade and One Health can easily find a common area of action through the establishment of multi-level governance, marine sciences in connection with human, animal and marine ecosystem health are not yet in a position to nourish this governance with a body of knowledge that could inform public action. The Ocean Decade is expected to help strengthen the development and implementation of science-based solutions, but the ongoing scientific research on the ocean is barely in line with the challenges identified by the Ocean Decade. While the goal of the Ocean Decade is to protect ocean health, there is no common scientific definition of ocean health.

In 2022, during the Fifth Asia-Pacific Day for the Ocean organised by the UN ESCAP, during the dialogue on ocean and climate change, we presented on how the One Health approach is an integrated approach that should be extended to the ocean in accordance with the roadmap given by the OHHLEP.[77] We presented the first results of the Session on One Health and the ocean during the Science Summit UNGA77, drawing attention to the following:[78] the lack of interlinkages between norms and policies from different sectors; the lack of a global standard for microplastic collection, and lack of consistency among norms and sectors involved; the need to have the best available ocean science observation, data, and services to meet the Sustainable

[74] UNESCO-IOC, *The Science We Need for the Ocean We Want: The United Nations Decade of Ocean Science for Sustainable Development (2021–2030)* (Paris: UNESCO, 2020).

[75] Lajaunie and Mazzega, 'Connecting the One Health Approach to the Ocean-Climate Nexus'.

[76] Note that the word 'ocean' is one of these expressions.

[77] Claire Lajaunie and Pierre Mazzega, 'Presentation One Health, the Ocean and Climate Change, Fifth Asia-Pacific Day for the Ocean', 30 November 2022: cf. UN ESCAP, 'Fifth Asia-Pacific Day for the Ocean', Meeting Report (Bangkok: UN ESCAP, UNDP, UNEP, 2022).

[78] 'Session One Health and the Ocean, from the Coast to the Deep Sea', Science Summit at the United Nations General Assembly (UNGA77) convened by Claire Lajaunie, 19 September 2021. Available at: https://ssunga77.sched.com/event/14WL4/ref-19044-one-health-and-the-ocean-from-the-coast-to-the-deep-sea-convened-by-claire-lajaunie.

Development Goal (SDG) targets; the role of ocean policies that focus on intersectorality in facilitating the implementation of the One Health approach, such as policies in the Pacific; and a potential opportunity after COVID-19 to shift from an implicit to an explicit use of the One Health approach. We insisted on the need to strengthen dialogue between science and policy in order to structure a coherent set of actions for One Health.

5.6 CONCLUSION

As we have seen, Southeast Asia and more broadly the Asia-Pacific region already largely contributed to the adoption of the One Health approach at the international level and engaged in its implementation at the regional level.[79] The ASEAN-UN Comprehensive Partnership is significant in the collective efforts in addressing global and regional concerns and ASEAN recognised the instrumental role of the UN in ensuring multilateral approaches and solutions to global challenges in close collaboration with regional organisations.[80] In May 2023, the ASEAN leaders adopted a Declaration on the One Health Initiative: they decided to establish a One Health Network to strengthen multisectoral collaboration and coordination of the One Health Initiative among ASEAN member states and to develop an ASEAN One Health Joint Plan of Action to improve regional and national capacity and capabilities with targets that are tangible, measurable, and time-bound, that calls for a stronger cross-sectoral collaboration between the relevant sectors involved in human, animal, plant, and environmental health, as well as food safety among the ASEAN member states. In August of the same year, the ASEAN Environmental Rights Working Group convened its first meeting in Bangkok, chaired by the Representative of Thailand to the ASEAN Intergovernmental Commission on Human Rights. This working group committed to developing a framework in line with the internationally recognised norms and standards on the rights to a safe, clean, healthy, and sustainable environment, taking into consideration national circumstances and domestic laws of the member states.

The cross-sectoral collaboration should also include the findings of a long-standing collaborative research between scientists, communities, and local administrations. The targets to be included into a One Health National Plan of Action should result from co-designed research involving the local actors. This kind of research is developed by the new international research laboratory, HealthDEEP (Health, Disease Ecology, Environment, and Policy), under the supervision of the CNRS together with Kasetsart University and Mahidol University (Bangkok, Thailand), well positioned to coordinate large interdisciplinary projects involving French institutions and other research networks and universities in Asia and within the PREZODE initiative.[81] The Social–Ecological Observatory of Health and Biodiversity of Saen Thong,[82] located in Nan Province, is one of the two observatories of HealthDEEP. The different projects conducted in Saen Thong brought a substantial set of qualitative and quantitative data to be used by various scientific fields (anthropology, sociology, medicine,

[79] UN ESCAP, *Accelerating One Health in Asia and the Pacific. Policy Brief* (Bangkok: UN ESCAP, 2022).

[80] Chairman's Statement of the 12th ASEAN-United Nations Summit, 'ASEAN A.C.T: Addressing Challenges Together', Phnom Penh, Cambodia, 11 November 2022. Available at: www.asean.org/wp-content/uploads/2022/11/7.-Final-CS-12th-ASEAN-UN-Summit.pdf.

[81] Serge Morand and Claire Lajaunie, 'Biodiversity and Covid-19: A Report and a Long Road Ahead to Avoid a Next Pandemic' (2021) 4(7) *One Earth*, 920–923.

[82] Kittipong Chaisiri et al., 'A Social-Ecological and One Health Observatory: Ten Years of Collaborative Studies in Saen Thong (Nan, Thailand)', *CABI One Health Cases* (2023).

ecology, molecular genetics, geography, law) and by the stakeholders (local administration, primary care unit). The local empirical knowledge is considered in order to guide research while Thailand International Cooperation Agency (TICA) provide support for projects involving foreign experts.[83]

Thanks to a broad partnership with research institutions and international organisations in the region, collaborative grounded research can contribute to a better understanding of environmental issues in the One Health community and improve the science-policy dialogue locally, regionally, and globally.

[83] HealthDEEP and its French researchers benefit from this recognition through the 'Innovative Animal Health Project' granted by TICA.

6

Like Mixing Oil and Water

Integrating One Health into the EU's Common Agricultural Policy

Francesca Coli, Maurizio Aragrande, and Massimo Canali

6.1 INTRODUCTION

The evolution of the narrative of the One Health conceptual framework, culminating in the new comprehensive definition provided by the One Health High-Level Expert Panel, has finally recognised the importance of applying a holistic understanding of health in the agri-food sustainability discourse.[1] Indeed, the definition enshrines the broadening of the scope of One Health and embraces it as a valuable approach to be applied across the board to global and national threats at the human–animal–ecosystem interface, but also to sustainability challenges. These explicitly include the 'collective need for … safe and nutritious food'; that is, the need to ensure food safety and food security, both of which lie at the heart of the transition to sustainable agri-food systems.[2]

Although it is still considered a 'novelty' to refer to One Health in relation to agri-food systems, it is certainly not unexpected. The expansion of the One Health concept over the past decade can be seen as a top-down trend, established as the interaction between the major global

While the idea of this chapter, its structure, and the concluding discussion (Section 6.5) are the result of a joint effort by the authors, Sections 6.1, 6.2, and part of Section 6.3 are attributed to Francesca Coli.

[1] 'One Health is an integrated, unifying approach that aims to sustainably balance and optimize the health of people, animals, and ecosystems. It recognizes the health of humans, domestic and wild animals, plants, and the wider environment (including ecosystems) are closely linked and interdependent. The approach mobilizes multiple sectors, disciplines, and communities at varying levels of society to work together to foster well-being and tackle threats to health and ecosystems, while addressing the collective need for clean water, energy and air, safe and nutritious food, taking action on climate change and contributing to sustainable development'. See One Health High-Level Expert Panel (OHHLEP) and others, 'One Health: A New Definition for a Sustainable and Healthy Future' (2022) 18(e1010537) *PLOS Pathogens*. On One Health and the agri-food sustainability discourse see Sara N. Garcia, Bennie I. Osburn, and Michele T. Jay-Russell, 'One Health for Food Safety, Food Security, and Sustainable Food Production' (2020) 4 *Frontiers in Sustainable Food Systems*; G. M. Bron, J. J. Siebenga, and L. O. Fresco, 'In the Age of Pandemics, Connecting Food Systems and Health: A Global One Health Approach' in J. von Braun, K. Afsana, L. O. Fresco, and M. H. A. Hassan (eds.), *Science and Innovations for Food Systems Transformation* (Springer, 2023); FAO, 'One Health in Agrifood System Transformation Fund' (2022); Y. Devos, E. Bray, S. Bronzwaer, B. Gallani, and B. Url, 'Advancing Food Safety: Strategic Recommendations from the "ONE – Health, Environment & Society – Conference 2022"' (2022) 20 *EFSA Journal* e201101; Francesca Coli, 'L'approccio One Health' (2022) 3 *Rivista di Diritto Agrario* 489–513.

[2] The Committee on World Food Security defines sustainable food systems as 'food systems that enable food safety, food security and nutrition for current and future generations in accordance with the three dimensions (economic, social, and environmental) of sustainable development. Sustainable food systems must be inclusive, equitable and resilient'. See Committee on World Food Security (CFS), 'The CFS Voluntary Guidelines on Food Systems and Nutrition (VGFSyN)' (FAO, 2021).

agencies involved in human, animal, and environmental health and agriculture intensified with regard to pandemic risk preparedness and prevention.

This has been achieved in particular by placing One Health at the centre of antimicrobial resistance (AMR) policy at global, regional, and national levels.[3] In the European Union, as mentioned in Chapter 11, the European Commission had already outlined a holistic One Health approach for its 2011–2016 Action Plan on AMR.[4] When the European Commission relaunched the plan in 2017, it was titled 'A European One Health Action Plan against AMR'.[5] The latter proposed a robust agenda of legislative reforms aimed at making the EU a 'best practice region' for antimicrobial use in agriculture, which would progressively subject the use of antibiotics in European livestock farming to strict controls and significant restrictions, leading to relevant adjustments in livestock farming practices as early as the end of the past decade.[6]

The One Health–AMR nexus has thus paved the way for a gradual broadening of the scope of One Health. As the FAO recently noted, 'to date, efforts at operationalizing One Health have often … focused on specific health-dominated agendas, e.g., AMR, zoonotic diseases, plant pests and agrochemical risk reduction'; however, One Health collaborative capacity 'also allows linking in areas such as biodiversity, microbiome, clean water, soils and air, can help with the promotion of efficient, inclusive, resilient and sustainable agri-food systems and healthy ecosystems'.[7]

Indeed, it is not surprising that a holistic and systemic approach to health has begun to be seen as valuable in promoting sustainable agricultural production and the resilience of ecosystems and agri-food systems, as well as addressing inequalities within agri-food supply chains. Agriculture, as part of the food supply system, has a key role to play in improving public health in the holistic sense of One Health. The interplay between agriculture and health is determined by systemic and interrelated relationships, which, in a very simplified way, are driven by food production, the use of natural resources and industrial inputs.

Food production determines food security and food safety, both of which in turn influence human health and individual and social development. Food production also affects and

[3] The World Health Assembly Resolution of May 2015, approving the Global Action Plan against AMR, recognised that 'the main impact of AMR is on human health, but that both the contributing factors and the consequences, including economic ones, go beyond health, and that there is a need for a coherent, comprehensive and integrated approach at global, regional and national levels, in a "One Health" approach and beyond, involving different actors and sectors such as human and veterinary medicine, agriculture, finance, environment and consumers', and requested to the WHO Director General 'to strengthen the tripartite collaboration between FAO, OIE and WHO for combating AMR in the spirit of the "One Health" approach'. See WHO, 'Global action plan on antimicrobial resistance', in *Sixty-eight World Health Assembly. Resolutions and Decisions Annexes*, WHA68/2015/REC/1, Geneva, 18–26 May 2015, available at: https://iris.who.int/bitstream/handle/10665/253469/A68_R1_REC1-en.pdf?sequence=1&isAllowed=y and UN General Assembly, *Political Declaration of the High-level Meeting of the General Assembly on Antimicrobial Resistance* (September 2016) 22 (A/71/L2) available at: A/71/L2: https://digitallibrary.un.org/record/842813?v=pdf.

[4] European Commission, 'Action Plan Against the Rising Threats from Antimicrobial Resistance' in *Communication from the Commission to the European Parliament and Council* (2011) 748 final, available at: https://eur-lex.europa.eu/legal-content/EN/TXT/PDF/?uri=CELEX:52011DC0748.

[5] European Commission, 'A European One Health Action Plan against Antimicrobial Resistance (AMR)' (2017) 339 final, 1–24, available at: https://eur-lex.europa.eu/legal-content/EN/TXT/PDF/?uri=CELEX:52017DC0339.

[6] In 2020, the use of antibiotics in European farms had decreased by more than 45 per cent compared to 2010 levels. In 2022, the decline exceeded 55 per cent. See EMA, 'Sales of Veterinary Antimicrobial Agents in 31 European Countries in 2022 –Trends from 2010 to 2022 – 13th ESVAC Report' (Amsterdam: European Medicines Agency, 2020).

[7] Food and Agriculture Organisation, 'COAG/2022/7 – One Health and Related Policy and Technical Guidance' (2022) *Committee on Agriculture* 1–8.

shapes territorial conditions that can, directly and indirectly, benefit several elements of health and well-being (e.g. air and soil health, recreation in the natural environment). Moreover, intensive livestock production raises animal welfare concerns, influences disease dynamics and can lead to the misuse of antibiotics for disease prevention and growth promotion, contributing to AMR. Agricultural production then clearly involves the use of various types of natural resources (including animals and insects, energy from fossil and renewable sources, soil, and water), their transformation and, to some extent, their degradation. Indeed, in their quest for efficiency and competitiveness, farm activities can affect soil health and biodiversity, leading to ecosystem depletion and unhealthy environments. Furthermore, the use of pesticides or other chemicals, if not well managed, can affect animal and plant health, and thus human health, including food consumption. Lastly, the use of inputs (including technological ones) may affect the way natural resources are used to guarantee food security and food safety, determining the sustainability of agricultural practices and the long-term health of ecosystems.

Despite this background and the evolutionary path dictated by international governance on the importance of integrating One Health into the agri-food agenda, there are still few studies that address this issue from a legal perspective, in particular through the analysis of agri-food laws and policies. The originality of this chapter lies in its aim to help fill this gap by examining the extent to which the European regulatory framework for sustainable agri-food systems has recently been reformed in line with a One Health approach.

Such an analysis is justified by the conviction that agri-food systems are precisely one of the 'new' regulatory areas in which the implementation of One Health should be tested and promoted. Indeed, we believe that the transition to sustainable agriculture and food is one of the most critical challenges of our time and one of the most complex issues that would benefit from a holistic approach to the human–animal–ecosystem interface.

The discussion is structured as follows: Section 6.2 places One Health in the broader context of the European Green Deal (Green Deal),[8] the main overarching policy shaping EU action from 2019, and the Farm to Fork Strategy,[9] the policy document stemming from the Green Deal that launched the EU's transition to sustainable agri-food systems. Section 6.3 introduces the Common Agricultural Policy (CAP), which is the main legal instrument regulating the EU agricultural sector, as well as the broader regulatory tool for the agricultural industry that has existed in the world for over sixty years. Section 6.4 then examines the legislative framework of the recently adopted CAP 2023–2027 to assess whether it is effectively inspired by the One Health approach. Finally, the conclusion summarises the main findings of the research.

6.2 ONE HEALTH, THE EUROPEAN GREEN DEAL, AND THE FARM TO FORK STRATEGY: A CONCEPTUAL ALIGNMENT

Before the COVID-19 pandemic and the gradual implementation of the EU Green Deal (see below), One Health was considered in the European regulatory framework first as an

[8] European Commission, 'The European Green Deal' in *Communication from the Commission to the European Parliament, the European Council, the Council, the European Economic and Social Committee and the Committee of the Regions* (2019) 640 final.

[9] European Commission, 'A Farm to Fork Strategy for a Fair, Healthy and Environmentally-Friendly Food System 2020' in *Communication from the Commission to the European Parliament, the Enropean Council, the Council, the European Economic and Social Committee and the Committee of the Regions* (2020) 381 final.

international initiative to be supported and then as an internal policy tool to fight AMR.[10] This picture is also supported by the analysis of the few Regulations (i.e. sources of law) published between 2016 and 2018 that mention One Health: they address One Health in the context of AMR, leading to reforms of animal health and veterinary medicines legislation that set new standards for animal health management and the use of medicines on farms, significantly improving the framework for animal production in terms of biosecurity and reducing the use of antibiotics in the EU.[11]

In December 2019, the newly appointed European Commission President published the Green Deal, a policy project that aims to transform the EU into a 'fair and prosperous society, with a modern, resource-efficient and competitive economy where there are no net emissions of greenhouse gases in 2050 and where economic growth is decoupled from resource use'.[12] It was presented as a response to multiple climate-related challenges and as an integral part of the implementation of the UN 2030 Agenda for Sustainable Development.[13]

Formally, the Green Deal is a Communication from the European Commission; that is, a forward-looking policy document that describes the vision of the EU executive. As such, it is an administrative soft law measure with the external function of showing where the EU wants to go and by what means. It is accompanied by a detailed roadmap (annexed to the Communication) of all the implementing measures to be adopted over the next five to ten years. These implementing measures include legislative proposals (e.g. the European Climate Law, which had already entered into force in July 2021),[14] action plans (e.g. the A New Circular Economy Action Plan),[15] strategies (e.g. the Farm to Fork Strategy and the Biodiversity Strategy),[16] programmes (e.g. the Fit for 55),[17] and the revision of existing legislation (e.g. in the area of land use, energy efficiency, and renewable sources of energy).

The following subsections briefly introduce both the Green Deal (Section 6.2.1) and the Farm to Fork Strategy (Section 6.2.2), as these are the main policy documents influencing EU action on sustainability in general (through the Green Deal) and on agri-food systems in

[10] The first time we encounter the term 'One Health' is in COM (2010) 0128, which referred to 'the concept of one world, one health', clearly alluding to the international context of the Manhattan Principles. The following year, the first action plan on AMR of the European Commission referred to it as an 'initiative', emphasising only the link between human and veterinary medicine (COM (2011) 748 final). Since 2017, with the publication of the One Health Action Plan against AMR (which also includes the first-ever definition of One Health at EU level), One Health has become a European regulatory instrument, making it a de facto principle or approach for public decision-makers when dealing with antimicrobial resistance issues (COM (2017) 339 final).

[11] Regulation (EU) 2016/429 of 9 March 2016 on transmissible animal diseases ('Animal Health Law'), OJ 2016 No. L 84, 31 March 2016; Regulation (EU) 2019/4 of 11 December 2018 on the manufacture, placing on the market and use of medicated feed, OJ 2019 No. L 4, 7 January 2019; Regulation (EU) 2019/6 of 11 December 2018 on veterinary medical products, the manufacture, placing on the market and use of medicated feed, OJ 2019 No. L 4, 7 January 2019 are case in point. They referred to One Health emphasising the intersection of animal and human health in the context of AMR.

[12] European Commission, 'The European Green Deal', COM(2019) 640 final, Brussels, 11 December 2019.

[13] UN General Assembly, 'The 2030 Agenda for Sustainable Development Seventieth session' (21 October 2015) A/RES/70/1.

[14] Regulation (EU) 2021/111 of 30 June 2021 on establishing the framework for achieving climate neutrality ('European Climate Law'), OJ 2021 No. L243, 9 July 2021.

[15] The European Economic and Social Committee and the Committee off the Regions, 'A New Circular Economy Action Plan for a Cleaner and More Competitive Europe' in *Communication from the Commission to the European Parliament* (2020) 98 final.

[16] European Commission, 'EU Biodiversity Strategy 2030 – Bringing Nature Back into our Lives 2020' (2020) 380 final.

[17] European Commission, 'Fit for 55: Delivering the EU's 2030 Climate Target on the Way to Climate Neutrality' in *Communication from the Commission to the European Parliament, the Council, the European Economic and Social Committee and the Committee of the Regions Empty* (2021) 550 final.

particular (through the Farm to Fork Strategy). The aim is to set the scene by illustrating the general regulatory context of the CAP and to briefly examine whether it takes One Health into account.

6.2.1 *The European Green Deal*

Given its ambition to transform EU society, the Green Deal is not just about environmental protection. Rather, it sets out the EU's growth strategy in the face of climate, economic, and social challenges, seeking to balance different interests to make the EU a climate-neutral economy by 2050. This means achieving a state of zero net greenhouse gas emissions and decoupling economic growth from resource use. As such, it is a wide-ranging, cross-sectoral regulatory project that aims to provide 'a political vision of the future of Europe rather than merely an emergency response to a new dimension of the crisis'.[18]

In this respect, the Green Deal has been recognised as a promising tool for achieving major improvements in public health while reducing growing health risks from several perspectives, including climate change, globalisation, and food and agriculture.[19] In fact, its regulatory scope includes the need to ensure environmental health, which underpins the commitment to protect biodiversity, restore ecosystems, and provide healthy and sustainable diets.

Health considerations have been an integral part of the Green Deal initiative since its inception, but primarily as a derivative of various green and sustainable policy objectives rather than as a stand-alone priority. In addition, a holistic understanding of health issues was not included in the original Green Deal Communication, which only refers to health in rather specific contexts.[20]

However, in parallel with the implementation of the Green Deal, the landscape changed significantly due to the emergence of the COVID-19 pandemic. In fact, while the Green Deal Communication was published in December 2019, meaning just before the outbreak of the pandemic, its implementing measures started to be published in 2020, when the pandemic had already spread globally. As a result, the Green Deal implementing measures gradually incorporated health considerations into their content.

The Farm to Fork Strategy,[21] the Biodiversity Strategy,[22] the EU strategy on Adaptation to Climate Change,[23] and the Zero Pollution Action Plan,[24] published between 2020 and 2021, illustrate this evolution. Indeed, in contrast to the Green Deal Communication, these implementing tools explicitly recognised the interconnectedness of human, animal, and

[18] Edoardo Chiti, 'Managing the Ecological Transition of the EU: The European Green Deal as a Regulatory Process' (2022) 59 *Common Market Law Review* 19, 8.

[19] Andy Haines and Pauline Scheelbeek, 'European Green Deal: A Major Opportunity for Health Improvement' (2020) 395 *The Lancet* 1327.

[20] European Commission, 'The European Green Deal'. Reference is made to: page 2, which mentions the need to 'protect the health and well-being of citizens from environment-related risks and impact'; page 10, which mentions that 'the price of transport must reflect the impact it has on the environment and on health'; page 12, which mentions the commitment of the Farm to Fork Strategy 'to stimulate sustainable food consumption and promote affordable healthy food for all'.

[21] European Commission, 'A Farm to Fork Strategy for a Fair, Healthy and Environmentally-Friendly Food System' (2020) 381 final.

[22] European Commision, 'EU Biodiversity Strategy 2030'.

[23] European Commission, 'Forging a Climate-Resilient Europe – the new EU Strategy on Adaptation to Climate Change' (2021) 82 final.

[24] European Commission, 'Pathway to a Healthy Planet for All – EU Action Plan: Towards Zero Pollution for Air, Water and Soil' in *Communication from the Commission to the European Parliament, the Council, the European Economic and Social Committee and the Committee of the Regions* (2021) 400 final.

environmental health, with specific reference to the One Health approach. It is therefore clear that the outbreak has facilitated an unprecedented convergence of environmental and health objectives, fostering a symbiotic relationship to move the EU towards greater sustainability and improved public health.[25]

Within this context, a new understanding of One Health began to emerge in the EU policy and legislative landscape. It started to be mentioned more frequently in policy documents and to be framed beyond AMR, including in the broader context of sustainability. Moreover, and most importantly, One Health appeared to be increasingly included in Regulations, to the extent that it took the form not only of a policy instrument but also of a legal one. By way of example only, the EU4Health Regulation,[26] published in 2021, provides the first EU legal definition of One Health in its Article 2(5),[27] and gives it the function of a kind of organisational legal guideline in the implementation of its general and specific objectives, which must be 'pursue[d] … in keeping with the One Health approach' (Articles 3 and 4).[28] In addition, the Reinforced EMA Regulation,[29] as well as the recent Regulation on cross-border health threats,[30] and the Regulation on the European Centre for Disease Prevention and Control (ECDC),[31] take One Health into account in both their recitals and articles. In particular, they have strengthened the link between One Health and the need to preserve the natural ecosystem, protect biodiversity, and enhance cooperation in responding to health threats.

The pattern observed in the EU legal and policy landscape is therefore fairly straightforward: One Health is penetrating more and more binding legal instruments, expanding its scope and becoming an approach or a principle to be – at least – invoked by EU legislators when regulating areas with an impact on (public) health. This paradigm shift occurred during the

25 By way of example, see page 2 of European Commission 'A Farm to Fork Strategy': 'The COVID-19 pandemic has underlined the importance of a robust and resilient food system that functions in all circumstances, and is capable of ensuring access to a sufficient supply of affordable food for citizens. It has also made us acutely aware of the interrelations between our health, ecosystems, supply chains, consumption patterns and planetary boundaries. It is clear that we need to do much more to keep ourselves and the planet healthy'. See page 1 of the Biodiversity Strategy: 'Healthy and resilient societies depend on giving nature the space it needs. The recent COVID-19 pandemic makes the need to protect and restore nature all the more urgent. The pandemic is raising awareness of the links between our own health and the health of ecosystems. It is demonstrating the need for sustainable supply chains and consumption patterns that do not exceed planetary boundaries. This reflects the fact that the risk of emergence and spread of infectious diseases increases as nature is destroyed. Protecting and restoring biodiversity and well-functioning ecosystems is therefore key to boost our resilience and prevent the emergence and spread of future diseases'; page 3 'Adopted in the heart of the COVID-19 pandemic, this strategy will also be a central element of the EU's recovery plan. It will be crucial to prevent and build resilience to future zoonosis outbreaks and to provide immediate business and investment opportunities for restoring the EU's economy'; page 12 'The recent lockdowns due to the COVID-19 pandemic have shown us the value of green urban spaces for our physical and mental wellbeing. While protection of some urban green spaces has increased, green spaces often lose out in the competition for land as the share of the population living in urban areas continues to rise.'

26 Regulation (EU) 2021/522 of 24 March 2021 on establishing a Programme for the Union's action in the field of Health ('EU4Health Programme') for the period 2021–2027, OJ 2021 No. L. 107, 26 March 2021.

27 'One Health approach' means a multisectoral approach which recognises that human health is connected to animal health and to the environment, and that actions to tackle threats to health must take into account those three dimensions'. Consider that it is a comprehensive definition which considers animal and environmental health as equally connected to human health. In addition, it broadly refers to health threats, and not only AMR.

28 See Francesca Coli and Hanna Schebesta, 'One Health in the EU: The Next Future?' (2023) 8 *European Papers – A Journal on Law and Integration* 310–312.

29 Regulation (EU) 2022/123 of 25 January 2022 on a reinforced role for the European Medicines Agency in crisis preparedness and management for medical products and medical devices, OJ 2022 No. L. 20, 31 January 2022.

30 Regulation (EU) 2022/2371 of 23 November 2022 on serious cross-border threats to health and repealing Decision No. 1082/2013/EU, OJ 2022 No. L 314, 6 December 2022.

31 Regulation (EU) 2022/2370 of 23 November 2022 on establishing a European centre for disease prevention and control, OJ 2022 No. L 314, 6 December 2022.

implementation of the Green Deal, with the result that One Health has started to be invoked in regulatory instruments aimed at addressing sustainability challenges (e.g. climate change, resilient nature, and pollution, to name but a few). However, the implications and consequences of this pattern are still uncertain: this sudden momentum for One Health in the (EU) legal sphere is still in its infancy and its normative and legal significance is not known yet. Based on these premises, the following analysis focuses on a specific aspect of the transition initiated by the Green Deal: that of sustainable agriculture within the broader framework of agri-food systems.

6.2.2 *The Farm to Fork Strategy*

The European Green Deal aims, among other objectives, to create a fair, healthy, and environmentally friendly agri-food system under the premise that 'European food is famous for being safe, nutritious and of high quality. It should now also become the global standard for sustainability.'[32]

The first is the Farm to Fork Strategy, the Green Deal policy document dedicated to the transition to sustainable agri-food systems. The second is the new CAP 2023-2027, which has a legally binding nature that makes the analysis from a One Health perspective even more compelling (see next section).

The Farm to Fork Strategy is a European Commission Communication with specific targets to ensure sustainable food production, processing, distribution, and consumption, including the prevention of food waste and losses.[33] The regulatory measures to implement the targets are listed in the Annex to the Farm to Fork Strategy and consist of 27 actions,[34] including revisions of existing legislation, new codes (e.g. the Code of Conduct on Responsible Food Business and Marketing Practices),[35] and legislative proposals. The potential impact of implementing the Farm to Fork Strategy on the EU's agri-food regulatory framework is majestic for two main reasons. First, it targets the European food system rather than a specific food chain or individual components of the food system; and second, it addresses sustainability rather than food safety or security, which have been the objectives of European agri-food legislation since its inception.

In terms of what is of most interest to this chapter, the Strategy generally refers to the concept of health in taking a holistic approach to the food system. It does so by recognising the 'inextricable links between healthy people, healthy societies and a healthy planet' and the need to move towards healthy diets and to improve and protect public health. However, beyond these general references, One Health was not given a clear role. The Farm to Fork Strategy did make explicit reference to One Health, but only in the context of the target to reduce sales of antimicrobials for livestock and aquaculture by 50 per cent by 2030. In addition, the ongoing

[32] European Commission, 'A Farm to Fork Strategy for a Fair, Healthy and Environmentally-Friendly Food System'.

[33] These targets include: (1) reducing the overall use and risk of chemical pesticides by 50 per cent and the use of more hazardous pesticides by 50 per cent by 2030; (2) reducing nutrient losses by at least 50 per cent while ensuring that soil fertility is not degraded; (3) reducing the use of fertilisers by at least 20 per cent by 2030; (4) a 50 per cent reduction in total EU sales of antimicrobials for livestock and aquaculture by 2030; (5) a target of at least 25 per cent of the EU's agricultural land under organic farming by 2030 and a significant increase in organic aquaculture; and (6) accelerating the roll-out of high-speed broadband internet in rural areas to reach the target of 100 per cent access by 2025.

[34] European Commission, 'Final ANNEX to A Farm to Fork Strategy for a Fair, Healthy and Environmentally Friendly Food System' (Draft Action Plan) (2020) 381. Available at: https://eur-lex.europa.eu/resource.html?uri=cellar:ea0f9f73-9ab2-11ea-9d2d-01aa75ed71a1.0001.02/DOC_2&format=PDF.

[35] EU Code of Conduct on Responsible Food Business and Marketing Practices, a common aspirational path towards sustainable food systems of June 2021, available at https://food.ec.europa.eu/document/download/08709964-ef08-4332-a899-a456bdf0bff5_en?filename=f2f_sfpd_coc_final_en.pdf.

implementation of the twenty-seven actions is threatened by several factors, including the geo-political crises that have hit the world in recent years, raising concerns about food security and the stability of international trade. This situation has led to a significant setback in the adoption of several of the Strategy's implementing measures, which could have been crucial for the implementation of One Health within the EU's agri-food legislative framework.

By way of example only, the European Commission adopted on 22 June a proposal for a new Regulation on the Sustainable Use of Plant Protection Products,[36] including EU-wide targets to reduce the use and risks of chemical pesticides by 50 per cent by 2030. The proposal, as part of the Farm to Fork Strategy, aimed to reduce the environmental footprint of the EU food system and thus bring the existing rules on the sustainable use of pesticides (e.g. Directive 2009/128/EC) in line with the ambitions set out in the EU Green Deal.[37] On 27 March 2024, the Commission withdrew the proposal as no agreement was in sight given the European Parliament's rejection of the proposal and the lack of progress in the Council. The same happened with the Commission's commitment to a general review of animal welfare legislation, with proposals expected by the end of 2023. So far, the Commission has only adopted a proposal to revise the regulation on the protection of animals during transport and a proposal for a new regulation on the welfare and traceability of dogs and cats, excluding, for example, the long-awaited proposal for new legislation on animal welfare labelling.[38] Given the extreme relevance of both pesticide and animal welfare legislation to One Health, these setbacks could indeed be seen as missed opportunities to reform part of the EU regulatory framework for sustainable agri-food systems in line with a holistic approach to human, animal, and ecosystem health.

6.3 THE CAP 2023–2027 IN A NUTSHELL

As mentioned above, the second regulatory front with the ambition to transform EU agri-food systems is the Common Agricultural Policy. It is one of the most important EU regulatory tools, the first in terms of expenditure since the establishment of the European Economic Community in 1957 and accounting for 32.3 per cent of the current EU multiannual budget for 2021–2027.[39] Indeed, while the food sustainability agenda of the Farm to Fork Strategy represents the new frontier of the EU's agri-food regulatory framework, the CAP is one of the Union's oldest pillars, supporting European agriculture and rural areas and helping to ensure food security for the European population for more than sixty years.

Articles 38–47 of the 1957 Treaty of Rome, now Articles 39–44 of the Treaty on the Functioning of the European Union (TFEU), provide the legal basis for the CAP. In particular, Article 39 TFEU lists the objectives of the CAP: (1) to increase agricultural productivity by promoting technical progress and by ensuring the rational development of agricultural production and

[36] European Commission, 'Proposal for a Regulation on the Sustainable Use of Plant Protection Products and Amending Regulation (EU) 2021/2115' (2022) 305 final.

[37] Directive 2009/128/EC of 21 October 2009 establishing a framework for Community action to achieve the sustainable use of pesticides, OJ 2009 No. L 309/71, 24 November 2009.

[38] European Commission, 'Proposal for a Regulation on the Protection of Animals during Transport and Related Operations, Amending Council Regulation (EC) No. 1255/97 and repealing Council Regulation (EC) No. 1/2005' (2023) 770 final; European Commission, 'Proposal for a Regulation on the Welfare of Dogs and Cats and their Traceability' (2023) 769 final.

[39] €378.3 billion out of a total EU budget of €1,210.9 billion, excluding the additional €806.9 billion of the Next Generation EU special fund for recovery from the COVID-19 crisis. See European Commission, *The EU's 2021–2027 long-term Budget and Next Generation EU, Facts and Figures* (Luxembourg: Publications Office of the EU, 2021). KV-02-21-232-EN-N. ISBN 978-92-76-30627-6, 73.

the optimum utilisation of the factors of production, in particular, labour; (2) to ensure a fair standard of living for the agricultural community, in particular by increasing the individual earnings of persons engaged in agriculture; (3) to stabilise markets; (4) to assure the availability of supplies; and (5) to ensure that supplies reach consumers at reasonable prices.

Although the objectives have remained the same, the features and mechanisms within the CAP have changed significantly since it was first adopted in 1962.[40] In particular, over time, direct payments to farmers have become increasingly conditional on compliance with agri-environmental good practices and animal welfare standards. This approach justifies direct payments as a form of remuneration for environmental services and other positive externalities that farmers provide to society by supporting food security and local food traditions, biodiversity, ecosystems, landscape, and employment in rural areas, as well as contributing to the conservation of European cultural identities.[41]

Indeed, while the CAP has not historically been a policy instrument designed to address health issues directly, it is increasingly incorporating within its scope considerations that appear to lie at the human–animal–ecosystem interface, while maintaining the original objectives set out in the Treaty of Rome and thus continuing to pursue the competitiveness of farms, and the promotion of employment, growth, and local development.[42] This leads to many trade-offs that the legislator is struggling to manage. Indeed, the previous CAP 2014–2020 has been heavily criticised over the years concerning the success of its environmental commitments, even by the European Court of Auditors' Special Report 21/2017, which highlighted that the environmentally friendly practices did not contribute to significant climate and environmental results.[43] In the same vein, the European Court of Auditors' Special Report 16/2021 sought to determine whether the CAP 2014–2020 promoted climate change mitigation strategies that could have reduced greenhouse gas emissions from agriculture between 2014 and 2020. It found that the

[40] Before 1992, the Common Market Organizations (CMOs) provided European farmers with strong income support based on guaranteed minimum prices, tariff protections, and export subsidies for key products such as wheat, milk, and beef. In 1992 the CAP underwent the so-called MacSharry reform, which significantly dismantled the European guaranteed prices system allowing agriculture to be integrated into the global General Agreement on Tariffs and Trade (GATT). The decrease in prices was balanced by the introduction of compensatory payments, shifting the burden of support from consumers to taxpayers. Since 2000, a new Rural Development Policy (also called the 2nd Pillar of the CAP) has begun to co-finance farm investments and infrastructure improvements for agriculture and rural areas. A major reform known as 'Fischler reform' was then carried out in 2003. Under this new CAP, direct payments, hitherto still partially coupled (i.e. linked to cultivated areas and heads of livestock), were consolidated into the Single Farm Payment. This payment was distributed over 'eligible hectares' instead of being linked to cropland. From that moment on, the European Commission has considered that decoupling between support and farm production has become 'complete', and the right to receive the direct payments is not lost even if production ceases on eligible areas.

[41] European Commission, 'The CAP Towards 2020: Meeting the Food, Natural Resources and Territorial Challenges of the Future' (2010) 672 final.

[42] It is worth remembering, however, that in the second half of the 1980s, the European Court of Justice legitimised the exclusive use of the agricultural procedure (Article 37 TEC, later Article 43 TFEU) to legislate on food health and hygiene rules, thus turning the legal basis of the CAP into a tool for adopting measures affecting public health. This happened mainly because there is no specific provision in the Treaty to regulate food and its safety. Indeed, The Court has held in a number of rulings that Article 37 (ex 43) EC is a proper legal basis for health protection measures in the field of agri-food law, as these form part of the common agricultural policy: Case 68/86 *UK v. Council (Hormones in Beef)* [1988] ECR 855; Case C-131/87 *Commission v. Council (Animal glands and organs)* [1989] ECR 3743; Case C-331/88 *R v. Minister of Agriculture, Fisheries and Food and Secretary of State for Health, ex parte Fedesa and others* [1990] ECR I-4023; Case C-180/96 *UK v. Commission (BSE)* [1998] ECR I-2265; Case C-269/97 *Commission v. Council (Beef Labelling)*. See also Tamara K. Hervey and Jean V. McHale, *Health Law and the European Union* (Cambridge University Press, 2004).

[43] European Court of Auditors, 'Special Report N°21/2017: Greening: A More Complex Income Support Scheme, Not Yet Environmentally Effective' (2017). Available at: www.eca.europa.eu/en/Pages/DocItem.aspx?did=44179.

€100 billions of CAP funds allocated to climate action between 2014 and 2020 'had little impact on agricultural emissions, which have not changed significantly since 2010'.[44]

The new CAP 2023–2027, clearly influenced by both the EU Green Deal and its strategies, including the Farm to Fork Strategy, has been presented as a key instrument to drive the transition towards sustainable agri-food systems in the EU, introducing innovative tools to contribute to climate change mitigation and adaptation, carbon sequestration, efficient management of natural resources, reduction of chemical dependency, halting and reversing biodiversity loss, enhancing ecosystem services, and preserving habitats and landscapes. Given its ambition and relevance in the EU regulatory space, the next section looks in detail at the legal framework of the new CAP 2023–2027 to explore the extent to which it incorporates a One Health perspective.

6.4 THE REGULATORY FRAMEWORK OF THE CAP 2023–2027 IN THE LIGHT OF ONE HEALTH

In December 2021, the agreement to reform the CAP was formally adopted. In particular, the new legislation, which entered into force in January 2023, aims to ensure a sustainable future for Europe's farmers and has been presented as a key tool to achieve the ambitions of the Farm to Fork Strategy, contributing to the Green Deal objectives of environmental, social, and economic sustainability.

Regulations 2021/2115,[45] 2021/2116,[46] and 2021/2117 constitute the legal framework of the CAP and give practical expression to its general thrust.[47] In particular, Regulation 2021/2115 is most relevant to the content of this research, as it sets out rules for the general and specific objectives to be pursued by the new CAP and aims to steer individual and societal behaviour towards what society considers to be positive health externalities. With this in mind, we will go through the provisions of the above-mentioned Regulation to understand how and to what extent they are consistent with the One Health approach.

6.4.1 *Regulation 2021/2115: Objectives, Implementing Measures, and Rural Development*

The Regulation lays down 'rules on support for strategic plans to be drawn up by Member States under the common agricultural policy (CAP Strategic Plans) and financed by the European Agricultural Guarantee Fund (EAGF) and by the European Agricultural Fund for Rural Development (EAFRD)' replacing the former Regulation 1305/2013 and Regulation

[44] European Court of Auditors, 'Special Report 16/2021: Common Agricultural Policy and Climate_ Half of EU Climate Spending but Farm Emissions Are Not Decreasing' (2021) available at: www.eca.europa.eu/Lists/ECADocuments/SR21_16/SR_CAP-and-Climate_EN.pdf.

[45] Regulation (EU) 2021/2115 of 2 December 2021 on establishing rules on support for strategic plans to be drawn up by member states under the common agricultural policy (CAP Strategic Plans) and financed by the European Agricultural Guarantee Fund (EAGF) and by the European Agricultural Fund for Rural Development (EAFRD) and repealing Regulations (EU) No. 1305/2013 and (EU) No. 1307/2013, OJ 2021 No. L 435, 6 December 2021.

[46] Regulation (EU) 2021/2116 of 2 December 2021 on the financing, management and monitoring of the common agricultural policy and repealing Regulation (EU) No. 1306/2013, OJ 2021 No. L 435, 6 December 2021.

[47] Regulation (EU) 2021/2117 of 2 December 2021 on establishing a common organisation of the markets in agricultural products, (EU) No. 1151/2012 on quality schemes for agricultural products and foodstuff, (EU) No. 251/2014 on the definition, description, presentation, labelling, and the protection of geographical indications of aromatised wine products and (EU) No. 228/2013 laying down specific measures for agriculture in the outermost regions of the Union, OJ 2021 No. L 435, 6 December 2021.

1307/2013. The reference to the EU funds reflects the basic, historical distinction between typical CAP objectives, respectively related to the Common Market Organization (CMO, financed by EAGF) and the so-called structural objectives (Rural development, financed by EAFRD). As mentioned, the new CAP introduces a delivery model based on a decentralised approach where member states propose a CAP Strategic Plan for the use of the financial resources made available. This is one of the main regulatory innovations of the new CAP, as it gives to the member states the responsibility to 'set targets, specify conditions for interventions and allocate financial resources, according to the specific objectives and identified needs' (Article 1(c); the conditions to be set out in the CAP Strategic Plans are better specified in Article 4). These are thus prepared through a specific internal assessment and identification of national and regional needs concerning CAP objectives. In this new mechanism, the European Commission has a co-management role together with the member states and carries out an ex-post and ex-ante assessment of the CAP Strategic Plans. According to Recital 122 of the Regulation, 'When assessing the proposed CAP Strategic Plans, the Commission should assess the consistency and contribution of the proposed CAP Strategic Plans to the Union's environmental and climate legislation and commitments and, in particular, to the Union targets for 2030 set out in the Commission communication of 20 May 2020 entitled "Farm to Fork Strategy"'.

6.4.2 *Objectives*

The general objectives of the Regulation are set out in Article 5,[48] which includes two main directions for action, namely environmental protection and climate change mitigation (point (a)) and food security (point (b)), both consistent with a One Health approach. Article 6 (Specific Objectives) articulates the specific objectives derived from the general ones, which clearly reflect the Green Deal and Farm to Fork Strategy.[49]

Among these specific objectives, point (1) is relevant to our purpose as it introduces the need to respond to societal demands for health, safe food, animal welfare, and AMR. Others reflect the One Health approach, taking into account the contribution of the environment to health (point (4) on tackling climate change and its causes; point (5) on reducing

[48] Article 5: '(a) to foster a smart, competitive, resilient and diversified agricultural sector ensuring long-term food security; (b) to support and strengthen environmental protection, including biodiversity, and climate action and to contribute to achieving the environmental and climate-related objectives of the Union, including its commitments under the Paris Agreement; (c) to strengthen the socio-economic fabric of rural areas'.

[49] The specific objectives are as follows: (1) to support viable farm income and resilience of the agricultural sector across the Union in order to enhance long-term food security and agricultural diversity as well as to ensure the economic sustainability of agricultural production in the Union; (2) to enhance market orientation and increase farm competitiveness both in the short and long term, including greater focus on research, technology and digitalisation; (3) to improve the farmers' position in the value chain; (4) to contribute to climate change mitigation and adaptation, including by reducing greenhouse gas emissions and enhancing carbon sequestration, as well as to promote sustainable energy; (5) to foster sustainable development and efficient management of natural resources such as water, soil and air, including by reducing chemical dependency; (6) to contribute to halting and reversing biodiversity loss, enhance ecosystem services and preserve habitats and landscapes; (7) to attract and sustain young farmers and new farmers and facilitate sustainable business development in rural areas; (8) to promote employment, growth, gender equality, including the participation of women in farming, social inclusion and local development in rural areas, including the circular bio-economy and sustainable forestry; and (9) to improve the response of Union agriculture to societal demands on food and health, including high-quality, safe, and nutritious food produced in a sustainable way, to reduce food waste, as well as to improve animal welfare and to combat antimicrobial resistance.

chemical dependency) and the need to halt and reverse biodiversity losses and enhance ecosystems (point (6)).[50]

Under Article 9, member states design their measures following good agricultural and environmental practices (GAECs) and the statutory management requirements (SMRs), both of which create the so-called increased/enhanced conditionality (extending the environmental commitments linked to the receipt of direct payments). In particular, the SMRs are a set of rules coming from thirteen existing EU Directives and Regulations on public, animal and plant health, animal welfare, and the environment.[51] They apply to all farmers, whether or not they receive support under the CAP and as such do not have an impact on the 'sustainability direction' of the CAP.[52] On the contrary, the GAECs are a set of nine specific conditions and practices that apply only to farmers receiving support under the CAP and that farmers must respect to receive the payments.[53] More specifically, according to Article 12, the main areas of intervention of the GAEC are:

(1) climate and environment (climate change mitigation and adaptation, water control, soil protection and quality, biodiversity and landscape conservation and quality);
(2) public health and plant health (food safety, management of plant protection products, marketing rules, use of pesticides); and
(3) animal welfare.

Farmers violating the 'increased/enhanced conditionality' will have their EU support reduced and may face other penalties. Annex III of the Regulation describes in detail the technical provisions relating to the GAEC and SMRs.

Finally, Article 14 introduces the 'social conditionality'; that is, the general rules on the respect of working and employment conditions. It provides that farmers and other beneficiaries receiving direct payments or annual payments shall comply with the requirements relating to the applicable working and employment conditions or the employer's obligations arising from certain legal acts (in particular, Annex IV refers to the measures to encourage

[50] See C. Romanelli, H. D. Cooper, and B. F. de Souza Dias 'The Integration of Biodiversity into One Health' (2014) 33(2) *Revue scientifique et technique / Office international des épizooties* 487–496 (DOI: 10.20506/rst.33.2.2291): 'because of the complexity of interactions among the components of biodiversity at various tropical levels (including parasites and symbionts), and across ecosystems at various scales (from the planetary-scale biomes to human-microbial interactions), positive, negative and neutral links are quite likely to occur simultaneously', p. 492.

[51] These rules come from several pieces of EU legislation, which include Regulation (EU) No. 178/2002 of 28 January 2002 on laying down the general principles and requirements of food law, establishing the European Food Safety Authority and laying down procedures in matters of food safety, OJ 2002 No. L 31, 1 January 2002; Council Directive 96/22/EC of 29 April 1996 concerning the prohibition on the use in stockfarming of certain substances having a hormonal or thyrostatic action and of B-agonists, OJ 1996 No. L 125, 23 May 1006; Regulation (EC) 1107/2009 of 21 October 2009 concerning the placing of plant protection products on the market and repealing Council Directives 79/117/EEC and 91/414/EEC, OJ 2009 No. L 309, 24 November 2009; Directive 2009/128/EC of 21 October 2009 establishing a framework for Community action to achieve the sustainable use of pesticides, OJ 2009 No. L 309, 24 November 2009; Directive 2000/60/EC of 23 October 2000 on establishing a framework for Community action in the field of water policy, OJ 2000 No. L 327, 22 December 2000; Directive 2009/147/EC of 30 November 2009 on the conservation of wild birds, OJ 2010 No. L. 20, 26 January 2010. Annex III of Regulation 2021/2115 sets out the following SMR main issues: SMR 1–2 'Water'; SMR 3–4 'Biodiversity and Landscape (Protection and Quality)'; SMR 5–6 'Food Safety'; SMR 7–8 'Plant Protection Products'; SMR 9-11 'Animal Welfare'.

[52] E. Mezzacapo, 'Mind the Gap: Assessing Member States' Implementation of Farm to Farm-to-Fork Targets within the 2023–2027 Common Agricultural Policy' (2024) 15(2) *The EU European Journal of Risk Regulation* 265–279.

[53] Annex III of Regulation 2021/2115 sets out the following GAEC main issues: GAEC 1–3 'Climate Change (Mitigation of and Adaptation to)'; GAEC 4 'Water'; GAEC 5–7 'Soil (Protection and Quality)'; GAEC 8-9 'Biodiversity and Landscape (Protection and Quality)'.

improvements in safety and health of workers;[54] and minimum safety and health requirements for use of work equipment by workers).[55]

6.4.3 *Implementation Measures*

The GAEC and social conditionality are mandatory as they are part of the CAP National Strategic Plans and entitle farmers to a payment per hectare of land in return for implementing them. As mentioned, this mechanism makes farmers' access to direct payments conditional on their compliance with the sustainability standards, both environmental and social, set out in Articles 12–14. Payments (or direct payments) are incentives designed to compensate farmers for the implementation of rules to achieve the objectives of the CAP, including climate, environmental, and animal welfare requirements (Article 16).[56] These payments are decoupled, in the sense that they are not linked to production in any way. Coupled payments (i.e. payments linked to production)[57] are also provided (point 3) for selected products and under certain circumstances listed in Article 33.[58]

Additional provisions, in the form of a direct decoupled payment, are foreseen for farmers participating in 'eco-schemes', as provided for in Article 31. These are voluntary climate, environmental, and animal welfare schemes that provide an additional payment on top of direct payments conditional on GAEC standards, SMRs, and social conditionality. They are voluntary for farmers, while it is mandatory for member states to allocate 25 per cent of the direct payment envelope and to draw up the list of eco-schemes they wish to propose to their farmers. Article 31 lists seven areas of intervention (essentially mirroring Article 6 and the areas of the GAEC) and stipulates that eco-schemes should cover at least two of these areas to qualify for direct payments.[59]

6.4.4 *Rural Development*

Article 69 sets out provisions for rural development including 'environmental, climate-related and other management commitments' (point (a)) and 'natural or other area-specific constraints' (point (b)). Following the same eco-scheme approach, payments (i.e. contributions to investments in this case) are granted to farmers who (1) go beyond the relevant statutory management requirements and GAEC standards; and (2) go beyond the relevant minimum requirements for the use of fertilisers and plant protection products or animal welfare, as well as other relevant mandatory requirements established by national and Union law.

[54] Council Directive of 12 June 1989, on the introduction of measures to encourage improvements in the safety and health of workers at work, OJ 1989 No. L 183/1, 29 June 1989.

[55] Directive of 16 September 2009 concerning the minimum safety and health requirements for the use of work equipment by workers at work, OJ 2009 No. L 260/5, 3 October 2009.

[56] Direct decoupled payments also concur to the sustainability objective (point 2(a) and 2(b)) including young farmers (point 2(c)).

[57] See previous section.

[58] Special provisions are also foreseen for cotton, fruits and vegetable, olive, hop, bees, wine (Articles 36–68).

[59] These practices must necessarily include at least two areas of the main climate and biodiversity objectives. These objectives are gathered in the following categories: (1) climate change mitigation; (2) climate change adaptation; (3) water quality; (4) soil quality; (5) biodiversity; (6) pesticide use reductions; and (7) animal welfare and antimicrobial resistance. The European Commission list of potential agricultural practices that eco-schemes could support is available at: https://agriculture.ec.europa.eu/system/files/2021-01/factsheet-agri-practices-under-ecoscheme_en_0.pdf.

6.4.4.1 *Regulation 2021/2115 versus One Health*

Regulation 2021/2115 provides for a wide range of measures that may affect the relationship between the environment, human health, and animal health. In this context, the management of agricultural practices to reduce their impact on the environment and conserve biodiversity is of great importance. On the other side, animal health is given less consideration. However, animal welfare is targeted by specific measures (Animal Welfare Area, SRM 8, 9, 10) and AMR is often mentioned, but little is said about biosecurity in livestock farming.[60] Biosecurity measures are the technical means to reduce disease contamination on and between farms, which can prevent the misuse or abuse of antimicrobials and AMR in animals, humans, and the environment. Furthermore, the relationship between animal welfare and disease transmission can be critical and conflicting (e.g. free-range systems improve animal welfare but expose animals to contamination risks through contact with wildlife).

This Regulation also provides the legal basis for the already mentioned eco-schemes, which support the income of farmers undertaking specific commitments to sustainability voluntarily. The eco-schemes' framework includes measures to preserve water quality, reduce the use of pesticides, improve animal welfare, and combat antimicrobial resistance. In terms of implementation mechanisms, all the above-mentioned provisions are subject to compliance under penalty of law. Indeed, regarding environmental conditionality (Articles 12–13), the new CAP mentions non-compliance with European legislation on the environment, public health, plant health, and animal welfare as grounds for administrative sanctions in the granting of direct payments. Under social conditionality, set out in Article 14, sanctions will also be applied for non-compliance with national and international standards on workers' conditions, which include standards on health and safety at work.

From a One Health perspective this approach might be criticised (One Health is recommended to be participatory, based on consensus and information).[61] On the other hand, the provisions on farm advisory services (Article 15), which are intended to help farmers achieve the objectives of the Regulation, seem to mitigate this criticism. Article 15(4)(c) also refers to the fact that the farm advisory services shall be adapted to the various types of production and farms, covering also 'farm practices preventing the development of antimicrobial resistance as set out in the Commission communication of 29 June 2017 entitled "A European One Health Action Plan against Antimicrobial Resistance"'. Lastly, the EU gives the member states the responsibility to draw up CAP National Strategic Plans, which may lead to different national interpretations, including the possibility of neglecting implementation to some extent, thus reducing the effectiveness of the overall policy.

6.5 AGRICULTURE AND ONE HEALTH: COMPATIBILITY IN THE EU

This chapter aimed to examine the role of One Health in the main new EU policies dealing with the transition to sustainable agri-food systems and to determine whether One Health is

[60] In particular, biosecurity is mentioned in Article 47 (point 1(vi), together with animal health and welfare) among the list of actions that member states can choose in their strategic plans to go beyond the 'minimum requirements established under Union and national law' (Article 46, point e/iii). Biosecurity is also mentioned in Annex I among the output indicators ('O.18 Number of livestock units (LU) benefitting from support for animal welfare, health or increased biosecurity measures') of the environmental, climate-related and other management commitments (Article 70) of the rural development actions.

[61] Simon R. Rüegg, Liza R. Nielsen, Sandra C. Buttigieg, et al., 'A Systems Approach to Evaluate One Health Initiatives' (2018) 5 *Frontiers in Veterinary Science* 23.

effectively guiding the future of EU legislation in this area. It shows that although One Health has undoubtedly gained new legitimacy in the EU legislative landscape following the COVID-19 pandemic and the progressive implementation of the Green Deal, it is still not at the centre of the EU action to ensure more sustainable and healthier agri-food systems.

First, the Farm to Fork Strategy makes only a tentative reference to One Health in the context of AMR. However, the Strategy contains important elements that could allow for a broader and more consistent use of One Health in the various implementation measures envisaged in the Action Plan. For example, the Strategy refers to the need to make European food systems more sustainable, fair, healthy, and equitable. It also explicitly adopts a holistic and all-encompassing approach to the drivers and outcomes of food systems, which should clearly include threats at the human–animal–ecosystem interface. This means that while One Health is not the driver of the transition to food sustainability, its implementation would certainly be consistent with existing policy goals on food sustainability. Of course, much will depend on the ambition of the EU legislator in implementing the Strategy.

As far as the CAP is concerned, we have tried to assess the 'One Health-ness' of Regulation 2021/2115, even though One Health is not one of its explicit objectives. This exercise was considered relevant in the light of the new understanding and scope of One Health promoted by international global governance, which includes the commitment to 'mainstream One Health across agri-food systems and integrate the One Health approach in agricultural production'.[62] Indeed, activities related to agricultural production and food systems, in general, are at the intersection of the different dimensions of One Health: valuing this comprehensive perspective could lead to better public health outcomes (for humans, animals, and ecosystems). To be successful, this integration should go beyond mere formal recognition (even in policy or legal documents) of the links between the three dimensions of One Health: rather, it should be implemented through mechanisms of coordination, communication, knowledge and information sharing, policy coherence, strong dialogue at the science-policy interface, and participatory processes, to name but a few.

What emerges from the analysis is that Regulation 2021/2115 represents a significant step forward on previous EU reforms (which, it must be said, have probably never been assessed from a One Health perspective). However, it is difficult to assess the balance of pros and cons. In general, the new CAP contains provisions at the nexus of agriculture, animal health and welfare, public health, and environmental health. However, it fails to systematise these efforts and bring the various elements together in a holistic perspective. The outcome is a list of provisions that attempt to bring elements at the human–animal–environment interface within the traditional scope and objectives of legislation regulating agricultural activities. The resulting framework is therefore not fully satisfactory from a One Health perspective, as it lacks an organic and coherent approach that identifies its internal and external relationships and the various trade-offs. Regarding the latter, the conflicts arising within the CAP between the pursuit of sustainability objectives (especially environmental) and those of productivity and competitiveness in the name of food security (often still understood as mere food production) should certainly be mentioned.[63] In fact, these conflicts are hardly addressed by the legislation, which since the 1992 reform has tried to move in both directions, but not always in an integrated way.

[62] Food and Agriculture Organisation, 'COAG/2022/7 – One Health and Related Policy and Technical Guidance', available at: https://openknowledge.fao.org/server/api/core/bitstreams/5dec68ca-db4e-4fac-9585-36409e61c115/content.

[63] Mariagrazia Alabrese, 'Food Security: Different Systems, Different Notions' (2019) 11 *Perspectives on Federalism* 1.

On this issue, the CAP has always been widely criticised,[64] including, as mentioned above, by the European Court of Auditors,[65] for allegedly failing to deliver on its environmental ambitions. As far as the new CAP 2023–2027 is concerned, scientists have already predicted that it will not produce any significant progress in terms of climate change and the environment.[66] It seems though, that there are no best practice examples that can replace the CAP at this time, given CAP has long been one of the most attentive agricultural policies to the issue of environmental sustainability,[67] considering the economic and territorial dimensions of the EU, and that even small prosperous countries that are considered models of virtuous agricultural policies, even better than the CAP, are by no means exempt from the same kind of criticism.[68]

Recent developments in European animal welfare policy have suffered from a similar contradiction between what was announced and what was delivered. Indeed, there has been great disappointment that the European Commission has only managed to produce a legislative proposal on animal transport and has failed to implement the reforms promised in the Farm to Fork strategy on slaughter, captive animals, and labelling.[69] However, these failures should be seen in a context that recognises that the development of European legislation on these issues has been well-advanced since the 1990s (even in comparison with other countries in the world)[70] and that it is inevitable that decision-makers, when faced with complex issues in a period of major change (cultural, social, economic, environmental, ethical), may arrive at contradictory and not always satisfactory results.

In this evolving scenario, One Health should not be invoked as a 'buzzword', but rather as a tool to help first identify these conflicts through a holistic vision and then manage them through specific provisions that help to balance and find compromise solutions (again through coordination, communication, data sharing, and multidisciplinarity).[71] To do this in a

[64] G. Pe'er, A. Bonn, H. Bruelheide, et al., 'Action Needed for the EU Common Agricultural Policy to Address Sustainability Challenges' (2020) 2(2) *People and Nature* 305–316. Available at: https://doi.org/10.1002/pan3.10080.

[65] European Court of Auditors, 'Special Report 16/2021'.

[66] H. Guyomard, C. Détang-Dessendre, P. Dupraz, et al., 'How the Green Architecture of the 2023–2027 Common Agricultural Policy Could Have Been Greener' (2023)52 *Ambio* 1327–1338. Available at: https://doi.org/10.1007/s13280-023-01861-0.

[67] D. Wuepper, I. Wiebecke, L. Meier, et al., 'Agri-environmental Policies from 1960 to 2022' (2024) 5(4) *Nature Food* 323–331. Available at: https://doi.org/10.1038/s43016-024-00945-8.

[68] S. Mann and A. Kaiser, 'Why Is Agricultural Policy Not More Environmentally Ambitious? Comparing Failed Attempts in Switzerland' (2023) 11(100096) *Resources, Environment and Sustainability*. Available at: https://doi.org/10.1016/j.resenv.2022.100096.

[69] Eurogroup for Animals, 'Democratic Failure: European Commission Backtracks on its Commitments for Animals in Work Programme' (2023) Press Release. Available at: www.eurogroupforanimals.org/news/democratic-failure-european-commission-backtracks-its-commitments-animals-work-programme.

[70] S. Hild and L. Schweitzer (eds.), *Animal Welfare: From Science to Law*, (*La Fondation Droit Animal, Éthique et Sciences (LFDA)* 2019), 194; World Animal Protection, 'Animal Protection Index Website' (2024). Available at: https://api.worldanimalprotection.org.

[71] The expansion of the One Health concept has gone well beyond the idea of an approach aimed at improving the efficiency of institutions responsible for human, animal, and environmental public health based on scientific interdisciplinarity and sectoral trans-disciplinarity. In the view of One Health theorists, it should incorporate goals such as social and environmental justice, diversity, equity, and inclusiveness: 'Indigenous peoples and representatives of local communities, and traditionally generated knowledge, must be included. These systems of knowledge can then be braided together with mainstream science to comprise a holistic framework for decision-making … The spectrum of considered worldviews must also expand to authentically integrate the expanded scope and approach into action and sustainable impact' (E. L. Mumford, et al. (2023), 'Evolution and Expansion of the One Health Approach to Promote Sustainable and Resilient Health and Well-Being: A Call to Action', *Frontiers in Public Health*, 10, 1056459. Available at: doi:10.3389/fpubh.2022.1056459). See also T. Lang, D. Barling, and M. Caraher, *Food Policy: Integrating Health, Environment and Society* (Oxford (UK): Oxford University Press, 2009). Available at: doi:10.1093/acprof:oso/9780198567882.001.0001.

legislative text, it is necessary to clarify the legal dimension of One Health. For the time being, in the new CAP, One Health is neither a principle inspiring its content nor an approach for its implementing measures.

Regulation 2021/2115 could even be considered an 'old' instrument when seen in the context of the speed with which the One Health conceptual framework has been developed in the last two years, also within the legal order. The legal entry points for One Health in legislation, in general, and in agri-food legislation, in particular, still need to be defined: nevertheless, this paradigm shift will likely happen soon and the new CAP contains provisions that could be placed in this direction. In conclusion, it seems promising to assess the improvement of the EU legal framework for agri-food systems along the roadmap of the process, which is accompanied by clear and critical social conflicts between different visions of what agriculture should be.

PART II

One Health and Contemporary Legal Structures

7

Human Rights and One Health

Mutual Benefits or Irreconcilable Differences?

Bridget Lewis

7.1 INTRODUCTION

The relationship between One Health and human rights is both symbiotic and antagonistic. The objectives of One Health align with human rights to the extent that they advance specific rights, particularly the rights to life, health, and an adequate standard of living. One Health also promotes human dignity, the foundation of human rights, by improving environmental conditions and addressing threats to health that impact people's lives. Yet the inherent anthropocentrism of human rights sits uneasily with the tripartite balance of One Health's commitment to human, animal, and environmental health. The growing field of environmental human rights may offer some way forward for resolving this tension and advancing the legal framework for One Health.

Early environmental human rights jurisprudence positioned the environment as a precondition for the enjoyment of human rights. Human rights courts found that violations had occurred where environmental conditions directly affected specific human rights for particular people.[1] However, they did not accept that environmental degradation generally was a human rights issue and gave almost no consideration to animal or wildlife health.[2] More recently, the right to a clean, healthy, and sustainable environment has been recognised more widely as a standalone right, expanding the potential for human rights objectives to include protection of environmental health, and perhaps also animal health. However, it remains to be seen whether the framing of a healthy environment as a *human* right will be able to enhance One Health in a meaningful way, as its inherent anthropocentrism remains at odds with One Health's more balanced tripartite approach.

This chapter will explore the relationship between human rights and One Health and consider the contribution that human rights law might make to the implementation of a One Health

[1] For example, in *Lopez Ostra v. Spain* (1994), the European Court of Human Rights found that the noise, smell, and fumes from a waste treatment plant close to the applicant's home was a breach of the right to privacy and home under Article 8 of the European Convention on Human Rights. More recently, in *Solyanik v. Russia* (2022), contamination of land and water from a cemetery close to the applicant's house constituted a breach of Article 8. In the Inter-American Commission and Court of Human Rights, environmental degradation like logging and mining has been held to be a breach of Indigenous peoples' right to property and to use their traditional lands, see e.g. *Maya Indigenous Community of Toledo Case* (Commission, 2004); *Case of the Saramaka People v. Suriname* (2007).

[2] By comparison, in *Kyrtatos v. Greece* (2003), the European Court of Human Rights held that there is no right to a good environment as such and found that the impact of urban development on ecosystems was not a breach of human rights.

approach and the realisation of its objectives. It argues that the One Health and human rights can be mutually beneficial, but that this effect is largely limited to the human health pillar of One Health. When it comes to advancing environmental and especially animal health, human rights have less to offer and may in fact create barriers to a truly integrated approach. However, there are ways that this relationship could potentially be improved, and on balance there is more to be gained than lost from an open dialogue between human rights and One Health.

The chapter begins by providing a brief overview of human rights law and the specific rights that align most closely with One Health. This section also includes a short history of environmental rights, critiquing the way that the environment has typically been framed as being instrumental to human rights through a process known as the 'greening' of human rights. Section 7.3 then explores the benefits that human rights and One Health might offer to one another. Section 7.4 moves on to elaborate on the tensions between One Health and human rights, focusing on the anthropocentrism of human rights and considering the extent to which this is relieved by the right to a healthy environment. The chapter concludes by outlining some areas of potential for capitalising on the mutually beneficial aspects of the relationship and mitigating the anthropocentrism of human rights in a way that better promotes the triple objectives of One Health.

7.2 A BRIEF OVERVIEW OF HUMAN RIGHTS

Human rights have both moral and legal dimensions. As a concept within political philosophy, human rights encompass the basic rights and freedoms that citizens are entitled to claim from their government. There exist different theoretical explanations for why human rights exist, and over time there have been debates about which things should properly be considered to be human rights.[3] Yet, despite these differences, all versions of human rights theory agree that human rights are possessed by all people, without discrimination, and that they give rise to duties that sit with the state, other individuals, or both.

In human rights theory and law, different rights are understood to have positive and negative dimensions that affect the way that obligations are framed in relation to each right. Positive obligations require governments to take some action in order to assure the enjoyment of the right; for example, by building schools to deliver the right to education. Negative obligations, by contrast, constrain government action; for example, by prohibiting torture or unreasonable limits on free speech.

In most countries, human rights are protected by law, either in constitutions, legislation, or judicial decisions. Here too there are many variations, often influenced by the specific political, cultural, or religious traditions of the state, its colonial past, or other historical experiences. For some countries, the national human rights instrument emerged following a revolution or independence movement; for example, those in France and America. In more recent times, however, domestic human rights laws have been strongly influenced by international and regional human rights treaties.

This chapter will focus on human rights as they are articulated in these international and regional treaties. This is done for several reasons. First, they are the most widely accepted set of human rights and have been implemented in the domestic laws of many countries, providing a set of common norms that are well understood. Second, countries that have signed and ratified human rights treaties are legally bound to comply with them under international law, making them a strong set of standards that are supported by various enforcement processes. Third, the

[3] See the discussion in Section 7.4 for more detail on the theoretical bases for human rights.

international human rights treaties adopted under the auspices of the United Nations represent a framework that underpins the work of many UN agencies across different fields of endeavour, including those involved with One Health.[4] That being said, while most of the discussion here refers to international and regional human rights treaties, many of the comments made are broadly applicable to any human rights laws.

7.2.1 *International Human Rights Framework*

The United Nations human rights system consists of nine core treaties, which build on the foundational human rights instrument, the Universal Declaration of Human Rights.[5] Two principal treaties are the International Covenant on Civil and Political Rights (ICCPR)[6] and the International Covenant on Economic, Social and Cultural Rights (ICESCR).[7] Alongside these general instruments are several more specific treaties that focus either on particular human rights issues (for example the Convention Against Torture)[8] or on protecting particular vulnerable groups (for example the Convention on the Rights of the Child (CRC)[9] and the Convention on the Rights of Persons with Disabilities).[10] Typically, these human rights treaties are supported by a dedicated committee of experts that monitors states' performance of their obligations, raises issues of concern, and provides guidance on what actions they should take. In some cases, these committees are also empowered to hear complaints from individuals who allege that their rights have been violated. For example, the Human Rights Committee can hear complaints about alleged violations of the ICCPR, while the Committee on the Rights of the Child accepts complaints from children about breaches of the CRC. The ability of the human rights committee to hear a complaint will depend on the respondent state having agreed to be subject to the committee's jurisdiction, and the applicant is usually required to have exhausted all options for a resolution within the domestic legal system.[11]

Human rights treaties are also in place in several regional areas, such as the European Convention for the Protection of Human Rights and Fundamental Freedoms (ECHR), the American Convention on Human Rights, and the African Charter on Human and Peoples' Rights.[12] The regional human rights systems usually have a court or commission (sometimes both) that

[4] For example, the Constitution of the World Health Organization recognises that 'the enjoyment of the highest attainable standard of health is one of the fundamental rights of every human being without distinction of race, religion, political belief, economic or social condition.' *Constitution of the World Health Organization* 1946 preamble.

[5] Universal Declaration of Human Rights, United Nations General Assembly Resolution 217 (III) A, Paris, entered into force on 10 December 1948.

[6] International Covenant on Civil and Political Rights 1966, United Nations General Assembly Resolution 2200A (XXI), New York City, 16 December 1966, entered into force on 23 March 1976.

[7] International Covenant on Economic, Social and Cultural Rights 1966, United Nations General Assembly Resolution 2200A (XXI), 16 December 1966, entered into force on 3 January 1976.

[8] Convention against Torture and Other Cruel, Inhuman or Degrading Treatment or Punishment 1984, United Nations General Assembly Resolution 39/46, 10 December 1984, entered into force on 26 June 1987.

[9] Convention on the Rights of the Child 1989, United Nations General Assembly Resolution 44/25, 20 November 1989, entered into force on 2 September 1990.

[10] Convention on the Rights of Persons with Disabilities 2006, United Nations General Assembly Resolution A/RES/61/106, 12 December 2006, entered into force on 3 May 2008.

[11] First Optional Protocol to the International Covenant on Civil and Political Rights 1966, United Nations General Assembly Resolution 2200A (XXI), 16 December 1966, Articles 1, 2, and 5; Optional Protocol to the Convention on the Rights of the Child on a Communications Procedure 2011, United Nations General Assembly Resolution A/RES/66/138, 19 December 2011, entered into force on14 April 2014, Articles 1, 7(e).

[12] European Convention for the Protection of Human Rights and Fundamental Freedoms 1950, Italy, 4 November 1950, entered into force on 3 September 1953; African Charter on Human and Peoples' Rights 1986, 27 June 1981, entered into force on 21 October 1986 ILM 58 (1982).

has jurisdiction to hear complaints against states; for example, the European Court of Human Rights and the Inter-American Court of Human Rights.[13]

7.2.2 *Rights Most Relevant to One Health*

One Health has been defined by the One Health High-Level Expert Panel (OHHLEP) as 'an integrated, unifying approach that aims to sustainably balance and optimize the health of people, animals, and ecosystems. It recognizes the health of humans, domestic and wild animals, plants, and the wider environment (including ecosystems) are closely linked and inter-dependent.'[14]

When discussing the relations between human rights and One Health, several specific human rights are immediately obvious as being relevant. These include the right to health, the right to an adequate standard of living, and the right to life. However, the list of rights that could be useful for achieving a One Health approach is broader than it might first appear.

The natural starting point for this discussion is the right to health. This is protected in international human rights law in Article 12 of the ICESCR. This is not a right to be *healthy*, but rather a right to the 'highest attainable standard of health'.[15] The Committee on Economic, Social and Cultural Rights (CESCR) has explained that this is a relative standard, judged with regard to a person's own circumstances and the available resources of the state.[16] It includes both freedoms – for example, to make choices about one's own sexual and reproductive health – and entitlements, including access to quality health services, treatments, and medicines.[17] It also encompasses the full range of factors that contribute to a person's standard of health, such as food, water, housing, sanitation, education, and safe working conditions.[18]

The Committee has also acknowledged that enjoyment of the right to health depends on a healthy environment, recognising that environmental conditions like clean air, water, and soil are essential to a wide range of health outcomes, while a poor or polluted environment can have significant health ramifications.[19] For children, the right to health guaranteed in Article 24 of the CRC explicitly mentions the need to address environmental contamination.[20] The African Charter recognises the right of all people to environmental conditions that are favourable to their environment,[21] alongside the right to the best attainable state of physical and mental health.[22] The latter has been applied in cases of environmental pollution.[23] However, while the right to health has been interpreted by courts and committees to include the environmental determinants of health, in most international and regional treaties there is no explicit mention of the environment.

[13] European Convention for the Protection of Human Rights and Fundamental Freedoms, Article 34; African Charter on Human and People's Rights 1986, Article 55.
[14] One Health High Level Expert Panel, 'Definition of One Health'.
[15] International Covenant on Economic, Social and Cultural Rights 1966, Article 12.
[16] Committee on Economic Social and Cultural Rights, 'General Comment No. 14: The Right to the Highest Attainable Standard of Health' (2000) 14.
[17] Ibid., 8.
[18] Ibid., 14.
[19] Committee on Economic Social and Cultural Rights, 'General Comment No. 14', 4, 11, and 15.
[20] Convention on the Rights of the Child, Article 24(2)(c).
[21] African Charter on Human and Peoples' Rights, Article 24.
[22] Ibid., Article 16.
[23] *Social and Economic Rights Action Center and the Center for Economic and Social Rights v. Nigeria* [2002] African Commission on Human and Peoples' Rights No 155/96.

An important feature of human rights law is the understanding that all rights are interdependent. The CESCR has explained this in relation to the right to health:

> The right to health is closely related to and dependent upon the realization of other human rights … including the rights to food, housing, work, education, human dignity, life, non-discrimination, equality, the prohibition against torture, privacy, access to information, and the freedoms of association, assembly and movement.[24]

The right to an adequate standard of living is protected under Article 11 of the ICESCR. This provision guarantees 'adequate food, clothing and housing, and the continuous improvement of living standards'.[25] The CESCR has expanded on the content of this right in several General Comments relating to food, water, and housing.[26] In this work, it has explained the importance of governments adopting appropriate environmental policies to ensure the availability of safe and adequate food, housing, and water.[27] It has also stressed the need to ensure that natural water resources are protected from contamination and managed in a way that addresses their potential as a habitat for disease vectors, noting the links between the right to water specifically and the right to health.[28]

The right to water is included in other human rights treaties, including the CRC, which guarantees to all children the right to safe drinking water as a component of the right to health in Article 24. The Convention on the Elimination of All Forms of Discrimination Against Women (CEDAW) refers to water in relation to the provision of adequate living standards for all women.[29] Wherever environmental degradation affects the availability of clean and secure water, the right to an adequate standard of living will be impacted, with potential also to impinge upon the right to health and, where serious enough, even the right to life.

The right to life is protected in the ICCPR, along with all regional human rights instruments.[30] It includes both positive and negative components. In a negative sense, it operates as a prohibition against killing (at least arbitrarily; in some states, capital punishment is still permitted provided adequate legal processes are followed). In a positive sense, states are obliged to protect people against threats to life and provide the essential conditions for life.[31] The UN Human Rights Committee, which adjudicates on alleged breaches of the ICCPR, has recognised that environmental conditions can constitute a breach of the right to life where they are serious enough.[32]

There are other rights that are also connected to human well-being, and these too have a role to play in relation to One Health. They include the right to social security, protected under the ICESCR, which provides an essential economic safety net that can help to avoid negative impacts

[24] Committee on Economic Social and Cultural Rights, 'General Comment No. 14', 3.

[25] International Covenant on Economic, Social and Cultural Rights, Article 11.

[26] Committee on Economic Social and Cultural Rights, 'General Comment No. 12: The Right to Adequate Food', Article 11 (1999); 'General Comment No. 4: The Right to Adequate Housing', 7; Committee on Economic Social and Cultural Rights, 'General Comment No. 15: The Right to Water' (2003).

[27] Committee on Economic Social and Cultural Rights, 'General Comment No. 12', 14.

[28] Committee on Economic Social and Cultural Rights, 'General Comment No. 15', 8.

[29] Convention on the Elimination of All Forms of Discrimination against Women 1979, United Nations General Assembly, 18 December 1979, entered into force on 3 September 1981, Article 14.2(h).

[30] International Covenant on Economic, Social and Cultural Rights, Article 6; European Convention for the Protection of Human Rights and Fundamental Freedoms, Article 2; African Charter on Human and Peoples' Rights, Article 4; American Convention on Human Rights, Article 4.

[31] Human Rights Committee, 'General Comment No. 36: Article 6 (the Right to Life)' (30 October 2018).

[32] *Port Hope Environmental Group v. Canada* [1984] Human Rights Committee Communication No. 67/1980; *Ioane Teitiota v. New Zealand* [2019] Human Rights Committee Communication No 2728/2016.

on health.[33] Freedom from cruel, inhuman or degrading treatment or punishment is also an important right for promoting human health, as it prohibits any treatment of a person that could harm either their physical or mental well-being.[34] The rights to equality before the law and to be free from discrimination are found in various forms across international human rights law.[35] In the context of health, these are important rights for ensuring that all people can access health services and the necessary conditions for a healthy life regardless of race, religion, gender, sex, or any other factor.

When it comes to designing and implementing One Health policies, several other specific human rights may also be relevant. For example, under Article 13 of the ICESCR, states are required to realise the right to education, which 'shall be directed to the full development of the human personality and the sense of its dignity, and shall strengthen the respect for human rights and fundamental freedoms'.[36] Education plays a critical role in developing One Health thinking. As Villanueva-Cabezas et al. have argued, achieving the sort of transdisciplinary, planetary-level understanding necessary to advance One Health requires early and holistic education.[37] While their work focused on undergraduate-level university training, there is arguably a role for secondary and even primary education to help embed long-lasting knowledges and practices in support of One Health.

Another relevant right is freedom of information, guaranteed under the ICCPR.[38] This protects the right of all people to access information in different forms and is an important component of ensuring transparency and accountability in the implementation of laws and policy. Its relevance to One Health-based policies can be seen in the fact that accurate, timely, and accessible information about health problems is necessary for public education and understanding. Not only does this enhance the effectiveness of response strategies but it also helps ensure that policy responses are viewed as legitimate by those who are affected by them.

The right to freedom of movement might also be relevant to One Health-based policies, especially those that are intended to respond to pandemics or other major health issues.[39] Freedom of opinion, expression and protest will also have a role to play in balancing state responses to public criticism of such policies.[40] These freedoms can be limited under human rights law, but only where these are necessary and proportionate to protecting other human rights or to addressing issues of public health and safety.[41]

The relevance of these civil and political rights to One Health can be seen in some of the legal disputes that arose during the COVID-19 pandemic. Human rights law was used as the basis

[33] Committee on Economic Social and Cultural Rights, 'General Comment No. 19: The Right to Social Security (Art. 9 of the Covenant)'.

[34] Human Rights Committee, 'General Comment No. 20: Article 7 (Prohibition of Torture, or Other Cruel, Inhuman or Degrading Treatment or Punishment)' (1992); Convention against Torture and Other Cruel, Inhuman or Degrading Treatment or Punishment.

[35] International Covenant on Economic, Social and Cultural, Articles 2 and 26; International Convention on the Elimination of All Forms of Racial Discrimination 1965, United Nations General Assembly Resolution 2106 (XX), 21 December 1965, entered into force on 4 January 1969; Convention on the Elimination of All Forms of Discrimination against Women.

[36] International Covenant on Economic, Social and Cultural, Article 13(1).

[37] Juan Pablo Villanueva-Cabezas, Kenneth D. Winkel, Patricia T. Campbell, Anke Wiethoelter, and Caitlin Pfeiffer, 'One Health Education Should Be Early, Inclusive, and Holistic' (2022) 6(3) *The Lancet Planetary Health* e188; Juan Pablo Villanueva-Cabezas, Arjun Rajkhowa, and Angus J. D. Campbell, 'One Health Needs a Vision beyond Zoonoses' (2020) 67(6) *Transboundary and Emerging Diseases* 2271.

[38] International Covenant on Civil and Political Rights, Article 19(2).

[39] Ibid., Article 12.

[40] Ibid., Articles 18, 19, and 21.

[41] Ibid., Articles 12(3) and 19(3).

to challenge lock-downs,[42] travel restrictions,[43] border closures,[44] vaccine mandates,[45] access to vaccines,[46] and regulation of misinformation.[47] In many cases the need to safeguard public health and safety was viewed as a legitimate justification for the limitation of human rights, but courts have been clear that even then restrictions must be enacted via law, must remain reasonable, and should be the least restrictive means of protecting public health and safety.[48]

Taken together, these various human rights help to advance the objectives and practice of One Health, while also providing important standards and safeguards for the implementation of One Health policies.

7.2.3 *The 'Greening' of Human Rights*

As identified above, some of the rights within international human rights law are defined to include an environmental dimension, for instance children's right to health. Others have been interpreted by courts and committees to include environmental preconditions. Over the past couple of decades, the role of the environment in supporting the enjoyment of human rights generally has been increasingly recognised. This process has been referred to as the 'greening' of human rights.[49]

In its early days, this approach framed environmental conditions as being instrumental to the enjoyment of human rights. For example, in several cases, courts and committees have found that air, water, or soil pollution constituted an unlawful interference with the enjoyment of human rights.[50] Other cases held that logging, mining or other environmental destruction could represent a breach of rights to property, subsistence, health and even the right to life, especially for Indigenous peoples.[51] More recently, human rights bodies have begun recognising climate change as a potential violation of human rights.[52]

42 *De Beer and Others v. Minister of Cooperative Governance* [2020] High Court of South Africa (Gauteng Division, Pretoria) 21542/2020.

43 *Charles Mwenda v. Inspector General of Police, National Police Service & 2 others* [2021] eKLR High Court of Kenya Petition 8 of 2020.

44 *Grounded Kiwis Group Inc v. Minister of Health* [2022] NZHC 832.

45 *BST Holdings, LLC v. Occupational Safety & Health Admin* [2021] United States Court of Appeals, Fifth Circuit No. 21-60845.

46 *Supreme Court of Justice of Costa Rica (Constitutional Chamber), Case No. 02924 – 2022* [2022] Costa Rica, Supreme Court of Justice Constitutional Chamber, 9 February 2022, No. 02924 – 2022 02924 – 2022.

47 *District of Columbia v. Meta Platforms* [2022] Superior Court of the District of Columbia (Civil Division) 2021 CA 004450 2.

48 For a full range of caselaw, see Faculty of Law, University of Trento, 'Covid-19 Litigation: Open-Access Case Law Database', *Covid-19 Litigation*. Available at: www.covid19litigation.org/.

49 See for example Alan Boyle, 'Human Rights and the Environment: Where Next?' (2012) 23(3) *European Journal of International Law* 613; Clive Miller, 'The Greening of Human Rights' (1998) 30(6) *Environment and Planning A: Economy and Space* 954; John H. Knox, 'Greening Human Rights', *openDemocracy* (14 July 2015). Available at: www.opendemocracy.net/en/openglobalrights-openpage/greening-human-rights/.

50 *Lopez Ostra v. Spain* [1994] Eur Court HR 16798/90; *Guerra v. Italy* [1998] Eur Court HR App No 14967/89; *Fadeyeva v. Russia* [2005] Eur Court HR App No 55723/00; *Tatar v. Romania* [2009] Eur Court HR 67021/01; *Saramaka People v. Suriname (Preliminary Objections, Merits, Reparations, and Costs)* (28 November 2007); *Port Hope Environmental Group v. Canada*.

51 *Mayagna (Sumo) Awas Tingni Community v. Nicaragua (Merits, Reparations and Costs)* (Inter-American Court of Human Rights, 31 August 2001); *Saramaka People v. Suriname (Preliminary Objections, Merits, Reparations, and Costs); Comunidad Yanomami Caso N° 7615 Resolución N° 12/85 [ENG]; Case of the Sawhoyamaxa Indigenous Community v. Paraguay (Merits, Reparations and Costs)* [2006] Inter-American Court of Human Rights Petition No. 0322/2001.

52 *Sacchi et al v. Argentina* [2021] Committee on the Rights of the Child Communication No. 104/2019; *Ioane Teitiota v. New Zealand; Daniel Billy and others v. Australia (Torres Strait Islanders Petition)* [2022] Human Rights Committee

While these cases recognised the environmental preconditions for the enjoyment of human rights, courts were clear that there was no human right to a good environment per se. For environmental harm to constitute a breach of human rights it needed to result in an actual or imminent interference with human rights.[53] In other words, it was *people* who were protected through human rights law, not the environment. What is more, human rights complaints cannot usually be based on a general concern for the environment. Instead, specific people need to be identified as the 'victims' of environmental harm.[54] And because victimhood is based on experiencing actual or imminent harm, human rights law is ill-equipped to deal with long-term environmental risks.[55]

The 'greening' of human rights has therefore been monodirectional and instrumental, built on an understanding that the environment is necessary for human well-being but is otherwise not the concern of human rights law. Some domestic jurisdictions have recognised a legal right to a healthy environment but as will be discussed below, in most cases this is still understood in rather anthropocentric terms.

As a result of this process of greening human rights, we now have a field of human rights known as 'environmental rights'.[56] The evolution of environmental rights shows the extent to which human rights can advance environmental health and, by extension, helps us to understand the ways human rights can support One Health. The potential for a mutually beneficial relationship between human rights and One Health will be explored in more detail in the next section.

7.3 SYNERGY BETWEEN HUMAN RIGHTS AND ONE HEALTH

This section outlines the extent to which One Health and human rights are mutually supportive. As will be explained, this is mostly limited to the 'human health' pillar of One Health, as this has a significant substantive overlap with several human rights.

7.3.1 *One Health Supports Human Rights*

Because One Health aims to advance human health as one of its objectives, it naturally has benefits for fulfilling health-related human rights. Pursuing a One Health approach to health policy and regulation will help to ensure respect for and protection of human rights, particularly

Communication No. 3624/2019; *Cláudia Duarte Agostinho and others v. Portugal and 32 Other States* (European Court of Human Rights, App No. 29371/20); Inter-American Court of Human Rights, *Environment and Human Rights: Advisory Opinion OC-23/17 of November 15, 2017 Requested by the Republic of Colombia* (official summary issued by the Inter-American Court, 15 November 2017). Available at: www.corteidh.or.cr/docs/opiniones/resumen_seriea_23_eng.pdf.

[53] *EW et al v. The Netherlands* [1993] UN Doc. CCPR/C/47/D/429/1990 (1993) Human Rights Committee Communication No. 429/1990; *Balmer-Schafroth and others v. Switzerland* [1996] Eur Court HR App No 22110/93; *Ioane Teitiota v. New Zealand*.

[54] *Andersen v. Denmark* [2010] Human Rights Committee Communication No. 1868/2009; *SC and GP v. Italy* [2019] Committee on Economic, Social and Cultural Rights Communication No. 22/2017.

[55] See for example, *Ioane Teitiota v. New Zealand* [2019] Human Rights Committee Communication No. 2728/2016; Bridget Lewis, 'Protecting Environmental Human Rights for Future Generations' in Walter F. Baber and James May (eds.), *Environmental Human Rights in the Anthropocene: Concepts, Contexts, and Challenges* (Cambridge University Press, 2023). Available at: www.cambridge.org/core/books/environmental-human-rights-in-the-anthropocene/A9B9003BCCE93051C516945B06425F2F.

[56] Bridget Lewis, *Environmental Human Rights and Climate Change: Current Status and Future Prospects* (Springer, 2018); Bridget Lewis, 'Environmental Rights or a Right to the Environment? Exploring the Nexus between Human Rights and Environmental Protection' (2012) 8 *Macquarie Journal of Comparative and International Environmental Law* 36.

the rights to health, life, and an adequate standard of living (discussed above). For example, addressing the causes and spread of zoonotic diseases through environmental and animal health policies minimises public health risks that might undermine the right to the highest attainable standard of health.

One Health's contribution to environmental health and animal health is also positive for human rights because environmental conditions are critical to the enjoyment of many human rights. A good example of this can be seen in the connection between the environment and wildlife and the rights of many Indigenous peoples. Human rights case law has shown that where the environment is damaged, for example through the impacts of climate change, the rights of Indigenous people to practice and pass on their culture can be breached, along with their right to property over their traditional lands.[57] One Health-based policies that protect the environment and the species that live within it can help to protect these rights.

7.3.2 *Human Rights Support One Health*

Because of the thematic alignment of human rights with (at least) the human health pillar of One Health, the advancement of human rights will also likely help to support and promote the objectives of One Health. For example, many activities designed to address poverty and provide clean water, nutritious food, adequate housing, and essential healthcare will naturally promote the human health pillar of One Health. Beyond this alignment of purposes, human rights also support One Health through the framework of laws and principles on which modern human rights are built. This can provide valuable legal scaffolding to One Health policies. A key feature of this legal framework is the tripartite set of obligations that states take on; namely, the duties to respect, protect, and fulfil human rights. What is required by each level of duty will vary according to the specific right in question and, in some circumstances, the capacity of the state to perform its obligations.

The first level of obligation is the duty to respect human rights. This is a negative duty that requires states to refrain from actions that would interfere with human rights.[58] It is particularly relevant for civil and political rights like the right to freedom from torture or cruel and inhuman treatment or punishment, and states are expected to take immediate measures to ensure these things do not occur.[59] The next level up is the duty to protect human rights. This requires that states enact laws and adopt measures that will protect people from rights violations caused by private actors, such as corporations.[60] The third and most demanding level of obligation is the duty to fulfil human rights. This requires that states take positive steps to ensure all people can enjoy their human rights.[61] The duty to fulfil is typically more onerous for economic, social, and cultural rights, as these can require greater investment of resources to be fully realised.

[57] For example, *Daniel Billy and Others v. Australia (Torres Strait Islanders Petition)*; *Case of the Sawhoyamaxa Indigenous Community v. Paraguay (Merits, Reparations and Costs)*; *Mayagna (Sumo) Awas Tingni Community v. Nicaragua (Merits, Reparations and Costs)*; Stacey Lee, 'Sacchi v. Argentina: Fighting for Indigenous Children's Climate Rights', *UCLA Law Review* (27 March 2020). Available at: www.uclalawreview.org/sacchi-v-argentina-fighting-for-indigenous-childrens-climate-rights/.

[58] Ryan Goodman, Henry J. Steiner, and Philip Alston, *International Human Rights in Context*. 3rd ed. (Oxford University Press, 2007) 187.

[59] International Covenant on Civil and Political Rights, Article 2.

[60] Manfred Nowak, *U.N. Covenant on Civil and Political Rights: CCPR Commentary*. 2nd rev. ed. (N.P. Engel, 2005) 37–39.

[61] Goodman, Steiner and Alston, 'International Human Rights in Context', 118.

Human rights law also provides a progressive scaffolding that could be used to achieve One Health goals. For many human rights, the standard of obligation on states is one of progressive realisation, having regard to their capabilities and resources. This is the approach taken to most economic, social, and cultural rights, like the right to health and the right to an adequate standard of living.[62] Significantly for the operationalisation of One Health, these rights are intended to be achieved through international cooperation and assistance. This expectation is potentially useful for implementing One Health policies on a global scale and aligns with our understanding of the interconnectedness of natural systems. Together, these standards of obligation potentially promote state investment in One Health both domestically and internationally, as well as an approach which is geared towards ambitious targets achieved progressively over time.

The interdependence of human rights noted above also aligns with the integrated approach envisaged by One Health and promotes a way of thinking about diverse objectives that recognises their close connections. Human rights law also provides principles for balancing objectives when they compete with one another. There are some human rights that are viewed as being 'non-derogable', meaning that no violation of them could ever be permitted. They include, for example, freedom from torture and slavery. Other rights can be validly restricted where doing so is necessary to achieve some legitimate aim, including the protection of other rights. The limitation must be proportionate, however, and should represent the least restrictive option available. These requirements of necessity and proportionality could help inform a One Health response in circumstances where the objectives of animal, human, and environmental health conflict, or where One Health conflicts with other social or economic objectives.

Human rights also provide important standards and safeguards that could apply to the design and implementation of One Health-based policies. These include rights relating to freedom of information, expression, and movement; Indigenous rights to self-determination, land, and culture; and rights to a fair trial and equality before the law. These rights can help to ensure that policies which, for example, prohibit certain uses of land in the name of One Health do not have disproportionately harmful collateral effects on human rights.

One area that has been identified as requiring more work in the One Health space is gender.[63] A commitment to human rights, particularly women's rights, equality, and non-discrimination, could help to fill this gap. For example, this could occur by helping to focus attention on the different ways that women and girls are at risk of and experience infectious diseases and the factors that contribute to their vulnerability. For instance, a human rights-based approach helps to identify inequalities in distribution of work and economic power within communities that often leave women exposed to environmental health risks.[64]

A human rights-based approach can better ensure that adequate work is done to address health issues that specifically affect women, girls, and non-binary people. It can also promote an

[62] International Covenant on Economic, Social and Cultural Rights, Article 2.

[63] Julie Garnier, Sara Savic, Elena Boriani, Brigitte Bagnol, Barbara Häsler, and Richard Kock, 'Helping to Heal Nature and Ourselves through Human-Rights-Based and Gender-Responsive One Health' (2020) 2(1) *One Health Outlook* 22; Julie Garnier et al., 'Mainstreaming Gender-Responsive One Health: Now Is the Time' (2022) 10 *Frontiers in Public Health* 10:845866; Claudia Cataldo, Maria Bellenghi, Roberta Masella, and Luca Busani, 'One Health Challenges and Actions: Integration of Gender Considerations to Reduce Risks at the Human-Animal-Environmental Interface' (2023) 16 *One Health* 100530.

[64] M O'Leary et al., A Gender-Transformative Framework for Nutrition: Advancing Nutrition and Gender Equality Together (2020); Esther Onyango and Rowena Maguire, 'Gendered Exposure, Vulnerability, and Response: Malaria Risk in a Changing Climate in Western Kenya' (2022) 4 *Frontiers in Climate*.

intersectional approach to health that acknowledges the connected factors across gender, race, religion, socio-economic status, and other dimensions that impact on health. Further, attention to human rights can help improve representation of women throughout law and policy-making areas, including at the highest levels of government and institutions.

The extent to which these gains can be realised is limited by the tension that exists between the multidimensional focus of One Health and the fundamental anthropocentrism of human rights. This will be examined in the following section.

7.4 TENSIONS BETWEEN HUMAN RIGHTS AND ONE HEALTH

As discussed above, there are clear overlaps between the content and objectives of human rights and One Health, which mean that they can be mutually supportive in their implementation. Further, the legal framework of human rights could provide important reinforcement for One Health strategies, while also ensuring that those policies adhere to minimum standards of human rights protections. However, these mutual benefits are most obvious in relation to the human health pillar of One Health and are less assured in relation to environmental and animal health. Perhaps more significantly, the inherent anthropocentrism in *human* rights may not sit comfortably with the more balanced approach of One Health, in which human well-being is intended to be integrated with environmental and animal health in a more equal partnership. At its worst, there is potential for human rights to frustrate One Health efforts by prioritising human concerns over those of nature and other species.

7.4.1 *Anthropocentrism*

Human rights are, by definition, anthropocentric. The theoretical foundations of human rights are heterogeneous, with modern human rights law being traceable back to various philosophical traditions. But while there are variations, these theories are rooted in inherent human value, dignity, interests, or some combination of these. Human rights are generally considered to be things that are necessary for humans to live a life of dignity or to fulfil their interests.

For example, modern human rights law draws heavily on natural rights theory.[65] This theory is based on the work of Western philosophers like Thomas Hobbes and John Locke, and posits that human rights are the entitlements that each human can claim based on their inherent human dignity. An alternative explanation is found in interest theories of rights, which view human rights as those things that are fundamentally in the human interest and weighty enough to impose an obligation on others.[66] Interest theory has been used by scholars like Feinberg to argue for recognition of the rights of animals as well, though these would not presently be considered to fall within the scope of 'human' rights.[67] Animal rights theorists like Saskia Stucki have argued for recognition of animals as rights-holders, based on their sentience or 'self-hood'

[65] See John Finnis, *Natural Law and Natural Rights* (Oxford University Press, 2011); Philip Alston, 'Making Space for New Human Rights: The Case of the Right to Development' (1988) 1 *Harvard Human Rights Year Book* 3.

[66] See Joseph Raz, *The Morality of Freedom* (Oxford University Press, 1988).

[67] Joel Feinberg, 'The Rights of Animals and Future Generations', Conference paper – presented to the Fourth Annual Conference in Philosophy at the University of Georgia (18 February 1971). Published in William Blackstone (ed.) *Philosophy and Environmental Crisis* (University of Georgia Press 1974) 43–68; see also Saskia Stucki, 'Towards a Theory of Legal Animal Rights: Simple and Fundamental Rights' (2020) 40(3) *Oxford Journal of Legal Studies* 533; Saskia Stucki, *One Rights: Human and Animal Rights in the Anthropocene* (Springer International Publishing, 2023).

and their inherent value. In this way, animal rights are framed in similar language to human rights: animals have rights by virtue of their being animals.[68] However, this is a novel approach and is not yet commonplace among human rights thinking, and especially not within human rights law.

Whichever philosophical version of human rights we adopt, it is hard to escape the centrality of the 'human', either as the locus of inherent dignity giving rise to rights or the subject whose interests we seek to protect. As a result, attempts to include the environment within the scope of human rights have traditionally framed the environment as being instrumental to human well-being, as is evident in the 'greening' of human rights, described above. In terms of achieving One Health's environmental and animal health objectives, while this approach acknowledges some interconnectedness between humans and the natural world, it positions human health as the end, and animal/environmental health as merely means. Human health therefore takes priority, and animal and environmental issues are only relevant to human rights to the extent that they advance or impact on human well-being.

The issue of pandemic prevention provides some illustrations of how a human rights approach might complicate One Health efforts. Zoonotic spillover is a key risk factor for pandemics, which can occur where human activity moves into new areas of the environment, exposing people to zoonoses. For example, encroachment into and logging of forests for timber or to clear land for agriculture increases the risk of zoonosis, but also promises important economic benefits to communities.[69] Hunting of animals for food or commerce is another area of risk for zoonotic spillover, but again may be seen as an important activity for subsistence.[70] To the extent that these activities support livelihoods or provide a means of subsistence, they could be seen as important for the fulfilment of human rights. Policies that seek to regulate or prohibit them could consequently face allegations that they breach human rights. Once a pandemic begins, human rights to freedom of movement and opinion might be viewed as constraining potential response efforts. Alternatively, a government seeking to avoid international pandemic prevention expectations might use the language of human rights to justify its position.

While there is clearly potential for human rights to frustrate One Health efforts by prioritising human interests over those of other animals or the environment, the significance of this shouldn't be overstated. Human rights law has tools for dealing with competing interests and will permit the limitation of some rights where doing so is necessary and proportionate to achieving another legitimate aim. It is not the case that human rights will always be trumps. Furthermore, when it comes to activities that are environmentally harmful or hazardous, supporting the full enjoyment of human rights like the right to an adequate standard of living can reduce the need for people to rely on those practices for their livelihoods. Nonetheless, there has always been an inevitable anthropocentrism in human rights and a sense that the environment is valuable because of its usefulness for humans, rather than valuable in its own right. This understanding is fundamentally different from the more evenly weighted approach of One Health.

68 Saskia Stucki, 'Towards a Theory of Legal Animal Rights', 533.

69 Serge Morand and Claire Lajaunie, 'Outbreaks of Vector-Borne and Zoonotic Diseases Are Associated with Changes in Forest Cover and Oil Palm Expansion at Global Scale' (2021) 8 *Frontiers in Veterinary Science* 661063.

70 Charlotte Milbank and Bhaskar Vira, 'Wildmeat Consumption and Zoonotic Spillover: Contextualising Disease Emergence and Policy Responses' (2022) 6(5) *The Lancet Planetary Health* e439; Lucy O. Keatts et al., 'Implications of Zoonoses from Hunting and Use of Wildlife in North American Arctic and Boreal Biomes: Pandemic Potential, Monitoring, and Mitigation' (2021) 9 *Frontiers in Public Health*.

7.4.2 The Right to a Healthy Environment

More recently, there has been a shift towards greater recognition of the right to a healthy environment, which could potentially open the way for a more ecocentric approach that is more closely aligned with the tripartite framing of One Health.[71]

In 2022, the United Nations General Assembly adopted a resolution recognising that 'all people have the right to a clean, healthy and sustainable environment'.[72] The resolution was widely supported, with over 160 states voting in favour.[73] It followed the adoption of a similarly worded resolution by the Human Rights Council the previous year.[74] The resolutions call on states to 'scale up efforts' to guarantee the right to a healthy environment (as it is commonly abbreviated), though this request is not legally binding. Indeed, the non-legally binding status of the resolutions may partly explain the strong positive reception from UN member states, who might have been more circumspect had there been legal duties involved.

The resolutions were adopted against the backdrop of considerable recognition of similar rights within domestic jurisdictions and regional human rights systems. A recent study found that over 130 countries recognise some form of enforceable environmental right.[75] Of these, eighty-four national constitutions included an explicit right to a healthy environment.[76] Some have argued that this provides evidence that the right exists as part of customary international law, though this is by no means settled.[77]

Across these domestic jurisdictions, there is still considerable diversity in terms of how environmental rights are defined and, consequently, how well they might align with the three dimensions of One Health. Some rights have a more ecocentric approach, protecting the rights of animals, natural features like rivers or forests, or even the whole of nature.[78]

71 For analysis of the concept of a right to a healthy environment, see John H. Knox and Ramin Pejan (eds.), *The Human Right to a Healthy Environment* (Cambridge University Press, 2018); John H. Knox, 'Constructing the Human Right to a Healthy Environment' (2020) 16(1) *Annual Review of Law and Social Science* 79; David Boyd, John Knox, and Marc Limon, *The Time Is Now: The Case for Universal Recognition of the Right to a Safe, Clean, Healthy and Sustainable Environment* (Universal Rights Group, 2021).

72 United Nations General Assembly, 'Resolution 76/300: The Human Right to a Clean, Healthy and Sustainable Environment'.

73 UN Press, 'With 161 Votes in Favour, 8 Abstentions, General Assembly Adopts Landmark Resolution Recognizing Clean, Healthy, Sustainable Environment as Human Right' (28 July 2022). Available at: https://press.un.org/en/2022/ga12437.doc.htm.

74 United Nations Human Rights Council, 'Resolution 48/13: The Human Right to a Clean, Healthy and Sustainable Environment'. Available at: https://documents-dds-ny.un.org/doc/UNDOC/GEN/G21/289/50/PDF/G2128950.pdf?OpenElement.

75 James R. May, 'The Case for Environmental Rights: Recognition, Implementation and Outcomes' (2021) 42(3) *Cardozo Law Review* 983.

76 For example, the constitutions of Colombia, Nicaragua, and Slovenia guarantee the right to live in a healthy environment, while the constitutions of Costa Rica, Mozambique, and Portugal protect the right to a healthy and ecologically balanced environment.

77 César Rodríguez-Garavito, 'A Human Right to a Healthy Environment?: Moral, Legal, and Empirical Considerations' in John H. Knox and Ramin Pejan (eds.), *The Human Right to a Healthy Environment* (Cambridge University Press, 2018) 155; Rebecca M. Bratspies, 'Reasoning Up: Environmental Rights as Customary International Law' in John H. Knox and Ramin Pejan (eds.), *The Human Right to a Healthy Environment* (Cambridge University Press, 2018) 122; Sumudu Atapattu, 'The Right to a Healthy Life or the Right to Die Polluted: The Emergence of a Human Right to a Healthy Environment under International Law' (2002) 16(1) *Tulane Environmental Law Journal* 65; John Lee, 'The Underlying Legal Theory to Support a Well-Defined Human Right to a Healthy Environment as a Principle of Customary International Law' (2000) 25 *Columbia Journal of Environmental Law* 283; Lewis, 'Environmental Rights or a Right to the Environment?' 40–43; Lewis, *Environmental Human Rights and Climate Changes*, 86–89 and 139–140.

78 For example, Ecuador. Countries like Bhutan, Lithuania, and Uzbekistan impose obligations on the government to protect flora and fauna, though they do not explicitly recognise the rights of nature.

Some constitutions protect people's right to an ecologically balanced or sustainable environment.[79] Many constitutions guarantee a clean, safe, or unpolluted environment,[80] suggesting a more anthropocentric, instrumental understanding of the relationship between nature and humans. This diversity and ambiguity make it hard to pin down the content of environmental rights and their corresponding duties. Even the term 'healthy environment' is open to various meanings and could refer to an environment that is healthy in its own right or merely healthy for humans.

The recent UN resolutions indicate that the international human rights community is starting to recognise the more subtle interconnections between the environment and humans, and the fact that environmental degradation could be a violation of human rights, even where no direct impact on human lives is evident. However, this approach is still one of recognising the *human* right to a healthy environment. Equivalent discussions on animal or environmental rights are underdeveloped or lacking at the international level.[81] As a result, despite all these advances, the right to a healthy environment is unlikely ever to truly overcome the anthropocentrism inherent in human rights.

7.5 CONCLUSION AND POSSIBLE WAYS FORWARD

Looking at the current state of play within human rights, particularly environmental human rights, a few things seem clear about the relationship between human rights and One Health. Firstly, human rights are clearly relevant to the human health dimension of One Health. The substantive overlap between One Health and the right to health in particular, but also rights to adequate food, shelter, water, employment, and education, suggests that efforts to promote human well-being through a One Health approach will inevitably help to achieve some human rights objectives as well. Similarly, a human rights-based approach to health-related issues will likely be well-suited to achieving the human dimension of One Health. The legal framework of human rights law also provides some potentially useful standards and processes to help provide structure and authority to One Health activities in the human health domain.

The environmental and animal health dimensions of One Health are more difficult to reconcile with human rights, however. While there has been considerable progress on the recognition of environmental rights, and particularly the right to a healthy environment, these remain framed as *human* rights to an environment of a particular quality. Even where the right is defined in terms of ecological balance or sustainability, this almost always is justified because of its importance to humans. This goes some way to acknowledging the interdependence of humans, animals, and nature, but without affording rights to the non-human parties in the relationship, the prioritisation of the human remains inescapable.

The anthropocentrism of human rights will likely remain at odds with One Health's tripartite approach, which aims for a much greater equilibrium between human, animal, and environmental health. At its worst, this may even hamper efforts to implement a One Health approach, as detrimental human rights impacts may be given more weight than beneficial environmental or animal outcomes where these are in conflict. However, a commitment to the fulfilment of

79 For example, Brazil.

80 For example, Ethiopia, Togo, Chile, Ukraine.

81 There is a campaign for a Convention on Animal Health and Protection, but this has yet to be endorsed by the United Nations. See 'UN Convention on Animal Health and Protection'. Available at: www.uncahp.org/. See also Chapter 13 of this book.

human rights can lessen this by reducing the need for people to rely on environmentally harmful activities to provide for their livelihoods.

Bringing these points together, there are some lessons we can learn and steps we could take to enhance the mutually supportive relationship between One Health and human rights while mitigating the tensions. To begin with, One Health policies should be informed by human rights, particularly best practices for the right to health. This will help minimise any incompatibility.

Work on the right to a healthy environment should continue to find ways to promote a more integrated, ecocentric approach. In doing this, One Health can help to grow the understanding of the many and varied ways in which humans, animals, and the environment are interdependent. Ultimately this could lead to legal recognition that environmental degradation breaches human rights, even without a direct impact on human lives.

One Health policies can benefit from the standards and safeguards provided by human rights law, as well as from the widespread recognition and adoption of human rights around the world. However, we need to recognise that human rights alone will not achieve One Health. It would be counterproductive and inappropriate to reduce One Health to a human rights project or to put too great an emphasis on human rights. Instead, the synergies between the two frameworks should be understood so that they can be capitalised upon, while at the same time allowing them to diverge where it is necessary to do so.

8

Animal Rights and One Health

Locating Animal Intrinsic Worth in the One Health Paradigm

Jane Kotzmann and Katie Woolaston

8.1 INTRODUCTION

Our contemporary time period is now often referred to as the Anthropocene, a term which denotes that human activity has become the central influence on the planetary environment.[1] Human influence in this respect is a pressing issue because much of human activity is detrimental to Earth's climate and environment. Human activities including animal agriculture, deforestation, and burning of fossil fuels contribute to global environmental challenges including climate change, biodiversity loss, and ocean acidification.[2] If these activities continue at their current pace, the Earth will quickly become uninhabitable for humans and many other animals.

Various legal and policy changes have and continue to be explored as potential solutions to the critical situation of life on Earth. Animal rights discourse, while predating much of this environmental concern, has been proposed as a means by which detrimental human impact on the environment can be mitigated.[3] While various proposals for legal animal rights exist, they commonly focus on the inherent worth of individual animals and the consequent need to recognise animals as legal rights holders.[4] Although figures vary, livestock produces approximately 15 per cent of total global greenhouse gas emissions and contributes significantly to deforestation, biodiversity loss, and environmental pollution.[5] Recognition of animals as legal

Many thanks to Aleesha Simoncini, Hayden Clift, and Sophie Farnsworth for their excellent research assistance that informed this chapter.

[1] Chen Ly, 'Has Human Activity Put Earth into a New Epoch?' (2023) 260(3471) *New Scientist* 15.

[2] See, for example, L. Godden and J. Peel, *Environmental Law: Scientific, Policy and Regulatory Dimensions* (Oxford University Press, 2010) 290; Sverker C. Jagers, Simon Matti, Anne-Sophie Crépin, et al., 'Societal Causes of, and Responses to, Ocean Acidification' (2019) 48 *Ambio* 816–830; Shanna McCormack, 'Climate Change and Animal Agriculture: Federal Actions Protect the Biggest Contributors from the Disasters they Cause' (2021) 51(3) *Environmental Law* 745–769; European Commission, 'Causes of Climate Change'. Available at: https://climate.ec.europa.eu/climate-change/causes-climate-change_en.

[3] See, for example, Carter Dillard, 'Environmentalism as a Form of Animal Rights' (Animal Legal Defense Fund). Available at: https://aldf.org/article/environmentalism-as-a-form-of-animal-rights/; Saskia Stucki, 'Ethical and Practical Arguments for Animal Rights' (22 May 2024) *Politics and Rights Review*. Available at: https://politicsrights.com/ethical-practical-arguments-animal-rights/.

[4] Saskia Stucki and Visa Kurki, 'Animal Rights' in M. Sellers and S. Kirste (eds.), *Encyclopedia of the Philosophy of Law and Social Philosophy* (Springer, 2020) 98; Tom Regan, 'The Case for Animal Rights' in P. Singer (ed.), *In Defense of Animals* (Basil Blackwell, 1985) 21; Jane Kotzmann, 'Sentience and Intrinsic Worth as a Pluralist Foundation for Fundamental Animal Rights' (2023) 43(2) *Oxford Journal of Legal Studies* 405.

[5] Food and Agriculture Organization of the United Nations, 'Tackling Climate Change Through Livestock: A Global Assessment of Emissions and Mitigation Opportunities' (Report, 2013) xii, 1–2; Food System Impacts on Biodiversity Loss, 19; and Energy, Environment and Resources Programme, 'Food System Impacts on Biodiversity Loss; Three

rights holders would, by most accounts, require the cessation of intensive animal agriculture.[6] It would also improve legal protections for other animals with beneficial consequences for habitat protection and biodiversity.[7]

One Health, which refers to a 'collaborative, multisectoral and transdisciplinary approach',[8] with the aim of optimising the health of people, animals, and the environment,[9] has also been promoted as a policy solution to issues of the Anthropocene. While at its inception One Health was largely focused on public health, contemporary literature has advocated for a broadening of One Health, to extend moral consideration to non-human animals,[10] and concern beyond health to encompass welfare and rights.[11] One Health recognises the interconnectedness of human, animal, and environmental health,[12] thus an approach underpinned by One Health principles should be more likely to limit human activities that are detrimental to the environment.

Animal rights and One Health discourses hold significant promise as potential legal and policy means to combat human activity that is destructive to the environment. While they may appear complementary, however, closer analysis reveals some fundamental tensions between their foundational commitments. Animal rights are premised on the inherent worth of individual animals, which accordingly should not be used – in Kantian terms – as a means to others' ends.[13] One Health, in contrast, appears to be focused on the overall health of groups of people, animals, or ecosystems (in other words, on global health or planetary health), at least in practice.[14] Where individual interests of humans or animals conflict with group interests, One Health will prioritise the group. In essence, animal rights are underpinned by deontological philosophy, while One Health is utilitarian in nature.

To reconcile these promising theories, this chapter seeks to locate a recognition of animal intrinsic worth within the One Health paradigm. In pursuing this objective, it seeks to conceive of animal rights as compatible with and as part of a broader One Health paradigm. In this respect, it draws on literature from compassionate conservation, multispecies justice, and rights of nature that have grappled with similar issues. To ensure the viability and utility of such a conception for legal and policy practice, the chapter explores the theoretical implications of such an approach for contemporary societies and their common uses of animals.

The second part of this chapter commences with an exploration of the ethical foundations of One Health and animal rights to highlight and describe the apparent philosophical tensions between them. In the third part of this chapter, we put forward a way of conceiving of animal rights and One Health as complementary, by developing a three-layered value framework.[15]

Levers for Food System Transformation in Support of Nature' (Research paper, 3 February 2021) 2–3, 10. Available at: www.unep.org/resources/publication/food-system-impacts-biodiversity-loss.

6 See, for example, Gary L. Francione, 'The Abolition of Animal Exploitation' in Gary L. Francione and Robert Garner (eds.), *The Animal Rights Debate: Abolition or Regulation?* (Columbia University Press, 2010) 1; Sue Donaldson and Will Kymlicka, *Zoopolis: A Political Theory of Animal Rights* (Oxford University Press, 2011) 49, 76–77.

7 Donaldson, 'Zoopolis', 160; Andrea Schapper and Cebuan Bliss, 'Transforming our World? Strengthening Animal Rights and Animal Welfare at the United Nations' (2023) 37(3) *International Relations* 514, 529.

8 See www.cdc.gov/onehealth/about/?CDC_AAref_Val=https://www.cdc.gov/onehealth/basics/index.html.

9 Ibid., see also www.who.int/health-topics/one-health#tab=tab_1.

10 Simon Coghlan, Benjamin John Coghlan, Anthony Capon, and Peter Singer, 'A Bolder One Health: Expanding the Moral Circle to Optimize Health for All' (2021) 3(1) *One Health Outlook* 21.

11 Laurie Sellars, Kimberly Bernotas, and Jeff Sebo, 'One Health, COVID-19, and a Right to Health for Human and Nonhuman Animals' (2021) 23(2) *Health and Human Rights Journal* 35, 36.

12 See 'One Health'. Available at: www.who.int/health-topics/one-health#tab=tab_1.

13 Regan, 'The Case for Animal Rights', 21.

14 See Chapter 11.

15 Eva Bernet Kempers, 'Do Rights of Nature Include Animal Rights?' (Helsinki Animal Law Blog, 4 May 2023). Available at: https://blogs.helsinki.fi/animallawblogseries/2023/05/04/do-rights-of-nature-include-animal-rights/.

We explore the interpretive implications of this value framework for law and governance in the final part of the chapter.

8.2 ONE HEALTH AND ANIMAL RIGHTS: CONFLICTING PRINCIPLES?

8.2.1 *Ethical Foundations of One Health*

The ethical foundations of One Health are highly contested. A key problem is that the framework has multiple definitions/interpretations that are polysemic and can have different ethical and normative consequences. Notwithstanding, some argue that One Health does not have its own ethical framework and does not need one as it relies on existing ethics and principles.[16] Others argue that One Health can benefit from its own ethical framework,[17] or that it is a requirement for sound implementation.[18]

While there are some near-universal agreed ethical principles within the framework (collaboration, interdisciplinarity, justice, and/or equity)[19] a key ongoing debate centres on whether the framework is intended to be anthropocentric, ecocentric, or something else.[20] While the foundational premise is that public health, environmental health, and animal health are inherently interconnected and should be governed as such, the question remains as to whether environmental and animal health are managed for the benefit of public health, or because of their intrinsic value.

The recent definition of One Health, published by the One Health High-Level Expert Panel (OHHLEP), encourages equal consideration of animal, environmental, and human health, at least at face value: 'One Health is an integrated, unifying approach that aims to sustainably balance and optimize the health of people, animals, and ecosystems. It recognizes the health of humans, domestic and wild animals, plants, and the wider environment (including ecosystems) are closely linked and interdependent.'[21] Similarly, the Berlin Principles adapted in 2019, authored by another group of world-leading One Health experts, and updating the 2004 Manhattan Principles, include increased reliance on biodiversity conservation as a means of adhering to a One Health framework.[22] They also include other principles of equity and justice inherent in the One Health approach.

What we see in the practice of One Health, however, is a very different ethical framework than that which is called for in the literature. At the ground level, One Health remains a public health framework, and so the ideology of the framework remains stuck within that paradigm.

[16] Marcel Verweij and Bernice Bovenkerk, 'Ethical Promises and Pitfalls of OneHealth'. Available at: https://academic.oup.com/phe/article-abstract/9/1/1/2362819.

[17] Jane Johnson and Chris Degeling, 'Does One Health Require a Novel Ethical Framework?' (2019) 45(4) *Journal of Medical Ethics* 239.

[18] Felicitas Selter and Sabine Salloch, 'Whose Health and Which Health? Two Theoretical Flaws in the One Health Paradigm' (2023) 37(7) *Bioethics* 674.

[19] Chris Degeling, Jane Johnson, Ian Kerridge, et al., 'Implementing a One Health Approach to Emerging Infectious Disease: Reflections on the Socio-Political, Ethical and Legal Dimensions' (2015) 15 *BMC Public Health* 4; One Health High-Level Expert Panel (OHHLEP), Wiku B. Adisasmito, Salama Almuhairi, et al., 'One Health: A New Definition for a Sustainable and Healthy Future' (2022) 18(6) *PLOS Pathogens* e1010537; Kim Gruetzmacher, William B Karesh, John H. Amuasi, et al, 'The Berlin Principles on One Health – Bridging Global Health and Conservation' (2021) 764 *Science of The Total Environment* 142919.

[20] See, for example, Vittorio A. Sironi, Silvia Inglese, and Andrea Lavazza, 'The "One Health" Approach in the Face of Covid-19: How Radical Should It Be?' (2022) 17(3) *Philosophy, Ethics and Humanities in Medicine* 3.

[21] One Health High-Level Expert Panel (OHHLEP) 'One Health', 2–4.

[22] Gruetzmacher, 'The Berlin Principles on One Health', 3.

This dichotomy between the operationalisation and theory of One Health has also been noted by ethicists. Sironi calls the two approaches the 'prudent' and the 'radical' approach, with the former representing a forward step for human health and the latter a true epistemological and ethical change, including proper integration of animal value into human societal systems.[23] Beever and Morar distinguish between the 'moderate' and 'strong' approaches, with the former prioritising multidisciplinary collaboration and interconnectivity, and the latter focusing on interdisciplinarity and interdependence.[24] The term 'interdependence' implies symbiosis, where each sphere of health takes care of the other. Each of these distinctions bears weight, but not necessarily across each and every iteration of One Health.

This primary debate has very practical implications for how One Health is operationalised. By way of example, managing animals with disease depends very much on the value we place on individual animals, conservation, and public health. Ultimately though, it is generally agreed that the ethics of One Health both in theory and practice remain anthropocentric, despite its promising foundations. Diller and Williamson argue this is because it is premised on the individually focused bioethics,[25] and Coghlan argues that One Health has yet to expand its circle of moral concern.[26] Yet even the anthropocentric theory of One Health is not without critique. Lysaght argues that there is an absence of justice, although Johnson and Degeling argue that justice is a developing principle of the framework. Ramakrishnan, and Laine and Morand, argue that the historical coloniality of public health systems has embedded neocoloniality into the framework, and its operationalisation by international organisations.[27] Indeed, Ramakrishnan goes further to say that the One Health framework is 'nothing but a vehicle enabling the incorporation of bio-surveillance obligations'.[28] This is certainly also arguable given the current OHHLEP Theory of Change, where One Health still appears to be primarily focused on animal disease surveillance.[29]

This approach has very real implications for animal rights and welfare. If we view One Health as a way to conduct bio-surveillance, we are only focusing on the detection of the disease and not on the factors that cause the disease or its spread to people. For example, we would focus only on the detection of Hendra in flying foxes, and not protect the natural habitats in forests that feed them and prevent them feeding in human residential areas.[30] The implications for flying foxes can be dire, as feeding in human areas can lead to net entanglement and lethal management where they can be viewed as 'pests'.[31]

[23] Vittorio A. Sironi, Silvia Inglese, and Andrea Lavazza, 'The "One Health" Approach in the Face of Covid-19: How Radical Should It Be?' (2022) 17(1) *Philosophy, Ethics, and Humanities in Medicine* 3.

[24] Jonathan Beever and Nicolae Morar, 'The Epistemic and Ethical Onus of "One Health"' (2019) 33(1) *Bioethics* 185.

[25] Elena R Diller and Laura Williamson, 'Supporting One Health for Pandemic Prevention: The Need for Ethical Innovation' (2023) 20(3) *Journal of Bioethical Inquiry* 345.

[26] Simon Coghlan, Benjamin John Coghlan, Anthony Capon, and Peter Singer, 'A Bolder One Health: Expanding the Moral Circle to Optimize Health for All' (2021) 3(1) *One Health Outlook* 21.

[27] Nicolas Lainé and Serge Morand, 'Linking Humans, Their Animals, and the Environment Again: A Decolonized and More-than-Human Approach to "One Health"' (2020) 27 *Parasite* 55; Nithin Ramakrishnan, 'Bio-Surveillance as One Health: A Critique of Recent Definitions and Policy Initiatives' (2023) 66(3) *Development* 215; Tamra Lysaght, Benjamin Capps, Michele Bailey, et al., 'Justice Is the Missing Link in One Health: Results of a Mixed Methods Study in an Urban City State' (2017) 12(1) *PLoS One*, 2.

[28] Ramakrishnan, 'Bio-Surveillance as One Health' 215.

[29] OHHLEP, *One Health Theory of Change* (2023). Available at: https://cdn.who.int/media/docs/default-source/one-health/ohhlep/ohhlep–one-health-theory-of-chance.pdf?sfvrsn=f0a46f49_6&download=true.

[30] For more on the need to protect feeding habitat, see Peggy Eby, Alison J Peel, Andrew Hoegh, et al., 'Pathogen Spillover Driven by Rapid Changes in Bat Ecology' (2023) 613(7943) *Nature* 340.

[31] See for example the Australian 'flying fox case', *Booth v. Bosworth* (2001) 114 FCR 39.

What we can see is that the ethical foundations of One Health are important in determining the scope of One Health, whether that be One Health as bio-surveillance, a public health framework, or something beyond that considers animals rights and/or welfare, as well as the rights and welfare of nature more generally. The ethical foundations are also vital for providing guidance on resolving the conflicts that are inevitable between the three areas of the framework that we outline below.

Over the remainder of this chapter, we consider One Health frameworks as if they were an embodiment of an expanded ideology advocated for in much of the ethical literature. We ask: if One Health was a true representation of the interdependence of animal, environmental, and human health, how do animal rights fit in? This itself is an interesting question that does not fit the standard debate about the ethical foundations of One Health, because the main competing paradigms are anthropocentrism and ecocentrism, neither of which prioritises animals outside their value as a species. Instead, ecocentrism is based on the ethical framework of ecological holism, espoused by Aldo Leopold and his utilitarian concept of conservation: that what is good for the ecosystem is good for the whole.[32] This form of ecocentrism allows the dismissal of individual interests if they are detrimental to a hubristic form of 'the whole'.[33]

Animal interests seem even further removed from a One Health ethical framework, except to the extent that animal disease can cause human health impacts. In practice, animal welfare is considered relevant in managing disease through, for example, the administration of antibiotics and other preventative medicine in agricultural animals. The question of whether intensive and industrial animal agriculture is problematic from the perspective of the animal is not seen as relevant. Coghlan and others argue that One Health operations work within the parameters set by industrial agriculture, through biosecurity laws and policies, and monitoring pathogens. They state that a bolder One Health ethic would recognise that the benefits of industrial agriculture do not outweigh the harm done to the billions of individual animals subject to its operations, in addition to the environmental damage caused as a result of the industry.[34] Even further removed from the ethical debate are wild animals, although there has recently been some interest in the welfare of wild animals sold in live animal markets.[35]

So, One Health ethics have the potential to promote ecocentricity, but what can we learn regarding the inclusion of animal rights? And how do we fit all three paradigms into One Health law and governance? Philosophy and ethics already have much to offer on how to expand our circle of moral concern to animals, and this is the topic of the following section.

8.2.2 *Ethical Foundations of Animal Rights*

Traditional ideas about morality focused on the way humans treat other humans. As Deborah Cao, Katrina Sharman, and Steven White identify, this conception of morality was 'human-centred and human-exclusive'.[36] According to Cartesian philosophy, for example, other

[32] Aldo Leopold, 'A Sand County Almanac. 1949' [1970] *New York: Ballantine*. Available at: https://jdyeakel.github.io/teaching/ecology/papers/Leopold_Excerpts.pdf.

[33] For more on this see Katie Woolaston, *Ecological Vulnerability; The Law and Governance of Human-Wildlife Conflict* (Cambridge University Press, 2022), chapter 2.

[34] Coghlan, 'A Bolder One Health'.

[35] See, for example, Clifford Warwick and Catrina Steedman, 'Wildlife-Pet Markets in a One-Health Context' (2021) 7(1) *International Journal of One Health* 42; Amanda Whitfort, 'COVID-19 and Wildlife Farming in China: Legislating to Protect Wild Animal Health and Welfare in the Wake of a Global Pandemic' (2021) 33(1) *Journal of Environmental Law* 57.

[36] Deborah Cao, Katrina Sharman, and Steven White, *Animal Law in Australia*, 3rd ed. (Lawbook Co, 2023).

animals are unfeeling automata that 'eat without pleasure, cry without pain, grow without knowing it; they desire nothing, fear nothing, know nothing'.[37] As a result, even vivisection could be considered morally justifiable.[38] Similarly, while Immanuel Kant expressly rejected the Cartesian view of animals as automata,[39] he claimed that humans only have indirect duties in relation to animals, on the basis that mistreating animals would harm human moral character.[40]

In contrast, contemporary animal rights discourse ascribes moral status to other animals.[41] Prominent scholars that argue for animal moral rights,[42] including Tom Regan and Christine Korsgaard, base their arguments on a conception of other animals as living beings, many of whom have capacities for positive and negative feelings, who have inherent value. According to American philosopher Tom Regan, animals' inherent worth stems from their individual subjective experience of life. He states, 'the basic similarity is simply this: we are each of us [human and animal] the experiencing subject of a life, a conscious creature having an individual welfare that has importance to us whatever our usefulness to others'.[43] Importantly, this value is not dependent on how useful animals are to others; they are not merely a means to human ends, but must – as Korsgaard argues – be treated as 'ends in themselves'.[44] From a moral standpoint, this places limits on how human should treat animals, because to treat animals in a way that fails to respect their inherent value is immoral and infringes their individual moral rights.[45] From an animal rights perspective then, animals possess equal inherent value to humans, and are part of our moral community whose interests require human consideration.

While many animal rights scholars employ deontological theory in their arguments, they reject Kant's emphasis on rationality and autonomy as the foundation for individual rights and his conclusion that humans only owe indirect duties to animals. In this respect, Regan points out that many animals, such as non-human primates, share the cognitive characteristics that are claimed to give rise to human moral rights and should therefore share those rights.[46] On the other hand, many humans, including infants and persons experiencing severe mental disability, do not have these mental capacities and yet are recognised moral rights holders.[47] If rationality and autonomy are the foundations for moral rights, these positions are untenable.

37 Nicolas Malebranche, *Euvres completes*, ed. G. Rodis-Lewis (Paris: J. Vrin, 1958–70), II, 394. The philosophy is named after the seventeenth-century philosopher Rene Descartes; however, the extent to which he held such views is disputed: see Peter Harrison, 'Descartes on Animals' (1992) 42 *Philosophy Quarterly* 219.

38 See Leonora C. Rosenfield, *Beast-Machine to Man-Machine: Animal Soul in French Letters from Descartes to La Mettrie* (New York: Oxford University Press, 1941), 54.

39 Steve Naragon, 'Kant on Descartes and the Brutes' (1990) 81(1) *Kant-Studien* 1–23.

40 I. Kant, Louis Infield (Translator), and Lewis White Beck (Foreword), *Lectures on Ethics* (New York: Harper & Row Publishers, 1963) 239; Lucy Allais and John J. Callanan, 'Introduction: Kant and Other Animals: An Overview' in John J Callanan and Lucy Allais (eds.), *Kant and Animals* (Oxford University Press, 2020) 10–11.

41 This section focuses on animal moral rights rather than legal rights, as legal rights are not essential to the adoption of a One Health approach that recognises and respects animals. In this respect, moral rights are 'an entitlement which confers moral libertiesi on those who have them to do certain things, and the moral constraint on others to abstain from interference': Raymond Wacks, *Animal Lives Matter: The Continuing Quest for Justice* (Routledge, 2024) 54.

42 In contrast with animal legal rights, which are often informed by conceptions of animal moral rights.

43 Tom Regan, 'The Case for Animal Rights', 22.

44 Christine M. Korsgaard, *Fellow Creatures: Our Obligations to the Other Animals* (Oxford: Oxford University Press, 2018).

45 Tom Regan, 'The Case for Animal Rights' 21.

46 Ibid., 155.

47 Ibid., 154–155.

Animal rights scholars suggest alternatives to rationality and autonomy as the foundation for individual moral rights. For Regan, the defining characteristic that gives rise to moral rights is being a 'subject of a life'.[48] Similarly, Korsgaard argues that 'all creatures who are capable of feeling pleasure and pain' have moral standing.[49] For some scholars, their theories in this respect serve to provide the foundation for both human and animal moral rights.[50]

The practical consequence of animal moral rights theories for One Health is that animal moral rights cannot be overridden solely on the basis that there might be an overall benefit to people and/or animals.[51] In contemporary public health practice, for example, the risk of an infectious disease spreading from animals to humans is often used to justify culling the diseased animals and those with whom they have been in contact.[52] This approach would be unacceptable if proposed in relation to humans, because humans are considered to have inherent value and moral rights. Similarly, if animals are considered to have inherent value and moral rights, their interests would need to be fully considered before deciding how best to respond to the disease threat.

8.2.3 *Apparent Philosophical Conflict between One Health and Animal Rights*

The philosophical conflict arising within the One Health framework is clear from competing 'limbs' of the framework itself; those being environmental, animal, and human health. The philosophical tension here arises from the focus on the macro (conceived holistically as nature as a whole, or the Earth, or conceived systemically as groups of people, other species or ecosystems),[53] versus a focus on the micro (individuals of all species). Although interdependence is a core principle of One Health, there are, and always will be, circumstances where two or more of these limbs conflict. For example, conservation can impact on human wellbeing when communities are forced to relocate from their traditional lands (known as 'conservation displacement').[54] Individual animals can be killed or relocated if they are viewed as not belonging to a particular ecosystem. Animals can also be killed and mistreated to provide sustenance for human health.[55]

This tension between working towards the optimisation of the wellbeing of a collective versus seeking to protect the individual from pain and suffering can also be seen in the two most prominent approaches to animal advocacy; welfarist and rights approaches. Early supporters of animals, for example, included English philosopher Jeremy Bentham, who based his regard for

48 Ibid., 248–250.

49 Korsgaard, 'Fellow Creatures', 155.

50 See for example, Tom Regan, 'The Case for Animal Rights'.

51 See Tom Regan, *The Case for Animal Rights* (Berkeley: University of California Press, 1983) 240–250.

52 W. A. Geering, M. L. Penrith, and D. Nyakahuma, 'FAO Manual on Procedures for Disease Eradication by Stamping Out.' (2001) 12 *Manual on Procedures for Disease Eradication by Stamping Out*, Foreword. Available at: www.fao.org/3/y0660e/y0660e.htm; Maria Vang Johansen and Mary-Lou Penrith, 'Has Culling Been Properly Assessed as a Valid and Justified Control Intervention Measure for *Zoonotic Diseases?*' (2009) 3(10) *PLOS Neglected Tropical Diseases* e541.

53 See Eva Bernet Kempers, 'Do Rights of Nature Include Animal Rights?' (Helsinki Animal Law Blog, 4 May 2023). Available at: https://blogs.helsinki.fi/animallawblogseries/2023/05/04/do-rights-of-nature-include-animal-rights/.

54 Daniel Brockington and James Igoe, 'Eviction for Conservation: A Global Overview' (2006) 4(3) *Conservation and Society* 424.

55 Although we note that animal meat is not vital for a healthy diet in many Western societies where options are unlimited, this is often not the case in many communities in the Global South. See generally Callum Brockett and Katie Woolaston, 'Environmental Justice in the Post Covid-19 Regulation of Wildlife Trade and Markets' (2022) 13(2) *Journal of Human Rights and the Environment* 371–398.

other animals on their ability to feel.[56] Bentham's concern with minimising pain and suffering underpinned his utilitarian ethic, reflecting a theory of morality that seeks to maximise happiness and minimise suffering for the *greatest possible number* of individuals.[57] Determining the morality of conduct under this approach involves a calculation of all the pleasure and pain that will result from the conduct. This focus on aggregate pleasure, however, can be used to justify practices like experimenting on animals that will cause immense individual suffering. In contrast, animal rights advocates like Regan focus on the inherent worth of the *individual* and argue for individual rights that cannot be outweighed by aggregate consequences.[58]

Thus, the apparent conflict between animal rights and One Health has echoes both in similar debates of the past and in contemporary conceptualisations of One Health itself. While this makes resolving the apparent conflict challenging, it also means that developing an approach that reconciles the conflict need not require 'reinventing the wheel'. In the next Part, we look at how similar conflicts have been addressed in compassionate conservation, multi-species justice, and rights of nature literature to develop a conception of animal rights as compatible with and as part of a broader One Health paradigm.

8.3 THE INDIVIDUAL IN ONE HEALTH

One Health is, appropriately, the internationally adopted approach to managing public health.[59] As Degeling et al. identify in the context of responses to emerging infectious diseases, implementing One Health in an integrated and well-thought-out manner necessitates identifying some agreement over what constitutes the public interest and an awareness of the values that support it.[60] Here, we contend that animal wellbeing is one of these values and should inform any conception of the public interest. In this respect, there is a clear public acceptance of a greater need for animal welfare, at least in modern liberal democracies. For example, a survey conducted in 2023 by BehaviourWorks Australia identified that '9 in 10 Australians agree that animal welfare should be protected by the government through legislation'.[61] A survey undertaken in 2018 found that the Australian public has developed a 'fundamental … belief that animals are entitled to the protection of relevant rights and freedoms, closely aligning with activist sentiment'.[62]

Ample evidence also exists at the international level for the public acceptance of a greater need for animal welfare. Legal provisions recognising animals as sentient and as having intrinsic worth have proliferated and can be located in jurisdictions as diverse as the European Union,[63]

56 Jeremy Bentham famously stated, 'The question is not, "Can they reason?" nor, "Can they talk?" but Can they suffer? Introduction to the Principles of Morals and Legislation' in B. J. H. Burns and H. L. A. Hart (eds.), *The Collected Works of Jeremy Bentham* (Oxford University Press, 1789, published in print in 1970), 283.

57 Bentham's approach is broadly adopted by Peter Singer, who argues for preference utilitarianism, which 'judges actions, not by their tendency to maximise pleasure or minimise pain, but by the extent to which they accord with the preferences of any being affected by the action or its consequences': P. Singer, *Writings on an Ethical Life* (London: Fourth Estate Publishers (Harper Collins), 2001), 133.

58 R. Sandoe and R. Crisp, 'Ethics' in M. Appleby and B. Hughes (eds.), *Animal Welfare*, (CAB International 1997) 10.

59 See FAO, UNEP, WHO, and WOAH. *One Health Joint Plan of Action (2022–2026)*. (Rome 2022) Available at: https://doi.org/10.4060/cc2289en.

60 Degeling, 'Implementing a One Health Approach to Emerging Infectious Disease', 5.

61 Alexander Saeri and Emily Grundy, 'Australian Animal Welfare Survey 2023 Summary Report' (Research Report, 2023) 2, 13, 15. https://osf.io/download/b694p/.

62 Futureye, 'Commodity or Sentient Being? Australia's Shifting Mindset on Farm Animal Welfare' (Research Report, 2018) 4. www.sheepcentral.com/wp-content/uploads/2019/05/190129-Commodity-or-Sentient-Being-Australias-Shifting-Mindset-on-Farm-Animal-Welfare-v.-7.0.pdf.

63 Protocol annexed to the Treaty of the European Community – Protocol on Protection and Welfare of Animals [1997] OJ C340/110.

Tanzania,[64] Chile,[65] the Netherlands,[66] Lithuania,[67] and Spain.[68] More broadly, in 2022, the United Nations' resolution on the animal welfare environment–sustainable development nexus[69] recognised the key linkages between humans, animals, and environmental wellbeing, and thus accepted that considering animal interests is critical for the realisation of many of the sustainable development goals. Accordingly, the resolution encourages states to consider these key linkages in developing public policy. This public support for increased animal welfare points to the need to conceive of One Health as an approach that encompasses animal well-being, which experience and scholarly literature demonstrates is most likely to be achieved through recognition of animal rights.[70]

8.4 APPROACHES IN COMPASSIONATE CONSERVATION, MULTISPECIES JUSTICE, AND RIGHTS OF NATURE

There are several existing ethical theories that could be used to inform a conception of One Health as encompassing animal rights, thus expanding the circle of moral concern for a One Health ethical theory. In this section, we explore the way scholars in compassionate conservation, multispecies justice and rights of nature have approached this challenge.

8.4.1 *Compassionate Conservation*

The theory of compassionate conservation seeks to mitigate the inherent conflict between the macro ecosystem and micro individual when making conservation decisions. It is premised on the ethical position that 'all actions taken to protect biodiversity should be guided by compassion for all sentient beings'.[71] The theory argues against an either/or approach to conservation and individual animal welfare and instead posits that there are win-win solutions where both can be prioritised.[72] It is specifically contrasted against the apparent subordination of animals in traditional wildlife conservation practices that results from humans believing they have authority over decisions concerning animals and labelling certain animals problematic, thereby ignoring their sentience.[73]

Despite protestations from traditional conservationists, compassionate conservation expands the scope of concern to give conservation a more holistic perspective. It seeks to be inclusive

64 Animal Welfare Act 2008 (TZ), Sections 3 and 4(b)(i).
65 Ley 20.380, 2009 (CL), Article 2.
66 Wet dieren 2011 (Animals Act) (NL), Article 1.3.
67 Gyvūnų Gerovės Ir Apsaugos Įstatymas (Law on Welfare and protection of Animals) No. XI-2271, Valstybės Žinios, 20 October 2012 No. 122-6216 (LT) (2012), Article 1(a).
68 Civil Code of Catalonia (Ley de 2006), Article 511-1 (3). For further examples, see Jane Kotzmann, 'Sentience Recognition as a Means for Moving beyond Animal Welfare to Animal Rights' in Jane Kotzmann and M. B. Rodriguez Ferrere (eds.), *The Legal Recognition of Animal Sentience: Principles, Approaches and Applications* (Hart Publishing, 2024) 63–78, 68–69.
69 UNEP/EA.5/Res.1.
70 Jane Kotzmann and Nicholas Pendergrast, 'Animal Rights: Time to Start Unpacking What Rights and for Whom' (2019) 46(1) *Mitchell Hamline Law Review* 157, 160.
71 Arian D. Wallach, Chelsea Batavia, Marc Bekoff et al., 'Recognizing Animal Personhood in Compassionate Conservation' (2020) 34(5) *Conservation Biology* 1097, 1097.
72 Arian D. Wallach, Marc Bekoff, Chelsea Batavia, Michael Paul Nelson, Daniel Ramp, 'Summoning Compassion to Address the Challenges of Conservation' (2018) 32(6) *Conservation Biology* 1255.
73 Émilie Edelblutte, Roopa Krithivasan, and Matthew Nassif Hayek, 'Animal Agency in Wildlife Conservation and Management' (2022) 37(1) *Conservation Biology* 1, 7.

not only of different philosophical thought, but of animals and their intrinsic worth.[74] An additional major premise of compassionate conservation is that animal agency, and the effects of that agency on ecosystems and other species, is not systematically investigated in conservation research. This idea of agency is established by animals' intelligence, sentience, social structures, and how they influence ecosystems and human–wildlife spaces.[75] A study conducted by Wallach and others that researched Australia's migrant vertebrate species provides insight into the value that a compassionate conservation approach can add.[76] By adopting a more inclusive approach in their research, specifically an approach that does not solely focus on nativism, they were able to find that migrant species in Australia can act as safeguards for threatened native species.[77] Even in areas where there are increasing levels of extinction, migrant species have the potential to improve local species richness.

Like compassionate conservation, One Health has been limited by anthropocentric notions of the human–animal relationship. Animal agency is not considered within the One Health research paradigm. If, however, we extended the approach taken in compassionate conservation research to the One Health space, we may be able to move past understanding wildlife and animals as 'problematic' in terms of pandemic potential. In this respect, there is some evidence that increased biodiversity leads to less transmission of microbes from animals to people under certain circumstances; however, this research is limited.[78] It seems the traditional method of conservation research continues to impact One Health research in more than one way.

8.4.2 *Multispecies Justice*

The idea that humans exist within nature and are interdependent with other living things, embedded in the concept of One Health, is also central to multispecies justice theory. This theory operates to extend environmental justice theory through the inclusion of non-human animals, species, and ecosystems.[79] This theoretical extension results in an amalgamation of environmental, ecological, and social justice that embraces non-human animals. From a multispecies justice perspective, considering different beings' subjective experiences of life is critical to multispecies flourishing. A more comprehensive understanding of multispecies justice theory can be seen in Indigenous approaches, whereby respect for all things is required, as 'disrespect to any part is disrespect to everything'.[80] Aboriginal and Torres Strait Islanders, for example, would ensure that waterholes were kept clear, which maintained water supply for animals and thus contributed to their survival.[81] This approach clearly aligns with the Indigenous Australians' law requiring care for country.[82]

74 Arian D. Wallach et al., 'When All Life Counts in Conservation' (2019) 34(4) *Conservation Biology* 997, 1004; Edelblutte, 'Animal Agency in Wildlife Conservation and Management', 1, 9.
75 Edelblutte, 'Animal Agency in Wildlife Conservation and Management', 1, 3.
76 Wallach, 'When All Life Counts in Conservation', 1002.
77 Ibid., 1004.
78 IPBES Workshop Report on Biodiversity and Pandemics, 11.
79 Thom van Dooren and Deborah Bird Rose, 'Lively Ethography: Storying Animist Worlds' (2016) 8(1) *Environmental Humanities* 77, 82; Krithika Srinivasan and Rajesh Kasturirangan, 'Political Ecology, Development, and Human Exceptionalism' (2016) 75 *Geoforum* 125, 126.
80 Danielle Celermajer, David Schlosberg, Lauren Rickards et al, 'Multispecies Justice: Theories, Challenges, and a Research Agenda for Environmental Politics' (2021) 30(1-2) *Environmental Politics* 119, 129.
81 Kerrin O'Dea, 'Traditional Diet and Food Preferences of Australian Aboriginal Hunter-Gatherers' (1991) 334(1270) *Philosophical Transactions: Biological Sciences* 233, 235.
82 Bill Gammage, *The Biggest Estate on Earth: How Aborigines Made Australia* (Allen & Unwin 2011) 2.

A key issue that arises in the application of multispecies justice theory is how to address conflicts of rights and justice that are more prolific in the context of an expanded circle of moral concern.[83] Nevertheless, there is evidence that individual rights and justice concepts can coexist, at least in some situations. An argument may be made, for example, that justice for sentient animals requires humans not to eat them. However, research is clear as to the human health benefits of a vegetarian diet, thus prohibiting the consumption of animals where plant-based foods are readily available may also work in favour of human justice.[84] Moreover, such an approach would potentially benefit not only animal and human justice, but also environmental justice, as plant-based foods are more environmentally friendly than animal food products. In this respect, Poore and Nemecek's study demonstrated that a global transition to predominantly plant-based diets would result in a reduction in deforestation of 76 per cent and a decrease of 49 per cent in greenhouse gas emissions from food production.[85]

8.4.3 *Rights of Nature*

Rights of nature refers to the conception of nature itself as a subject of rights. The importance of this conception lies in its contrast with traditional views of nature as human property that can be exploited.[86] In broad terms, while rights of nature 'have both multiple histories and multiple meanings',[87] it 'propounds the inherent value of Nature, independent of its extractive value for humans, and seeks to give Nature a voice in decision-making structures'.[88] In this respect, nature is taken to include the holistic conception of nature as a whole, and also nature as specific places (for example, the Whanganui river in New Zealand, or the Mar Menor lagoon in Spain).[89]

While nature would seemingly include animals, it is unclear whether rights of nature encompass animal rights. To understand rights of nature in this way would raise a similar issue to that which arises in compassionate conservation and multispecies justice: how should conflicts between the interests of nature/ecosystems and the interests of individual animals be resolved? Nevertheless, some courts have interpreted holistic forms of rights of nature as inclusive of individual animals. For example, in 2022 the Constitutional Court of Ecuador heard a case in which the release of a woolly monkey named Estrellita from a zoo was sought.[90] Estrellita had been transferred from her home of 18 years to the zoo on the basis that keeping a wild animal is banned in Ecuador. The Court held that '[w]ithin the levels of ecological organization, an

83 Danielle Celermajer, 'Multispecies justice'.

84 Elizabeth Cripps, 'Saving the Polar Bear, Saving the World: Can the Capabilities Approach do Justice to Humans, Animals and Ecosystems?' (2010) 16 *Res Publica* 1, 6; Christine J Winter, 'Introduction: What's the Value of Multispecies Justice?' (2022) 31(2) *Environmental Politics* 251, 252.

85 J. Poore and T. Nemecek, 'Reducing Food's Environmental Impacts through Producers and Consumers' (2018) 360(6392) *Science* 987, 991.

86 See Becca Blease, 'The Rights of Nature' (July/August 2024) 345(8) *Resurgence & Ecologist* 8.

87 Mihnea Tănăsescu, *Understanding the Rights of Nature: A Critical Introduction* [transcript] (New Ecology, 2022) 15.

88 See Blease, 'The Rights of Nature', 9.

89 Tănăsescu, 'Understanding the Rights of Nature', 47–71; Javier Tous, 'Book Review: Understanding the Rights of Nature: A Critical Introduction and The Politics of Rights of Nature: Strategies for Building a More Sustainable Future' (2022) 11(2) *Transnational Environmental Law* 441, 442.

90 Corte Constitucional del Ecuador [Constitutional Court of Ecuador], *Rights of Nature and Animals as Subject of Rights, 'Estrellita Monkey' Case*, No. 253-20-JH/22, 27 January 2022; 'A Landmark Ruling for Animal Rights in Ecuador', *Nonhuman Rights* (Blog Post, 23 March 2022). Available at: www.nonhumanrights.org/blog/landmark-ruling-animal-rights-ecuador/; 'Historic Milestone in Ecuador: Constitutional Court Recognizes Individual Animals as Subjects of Rights Protected by the Rights of Nature', *World Lawyers' Pledge on Climate Action* (8 May 2022). Available at: https://lawyersclimatepledge.org/historic-milestone-in-ecuador-constitutional-court-recognizes-individual-animals-as-subjects-of-rights-protected-by-the-rights-of-nature/.

animal is a basic unit of ecological organization, and being an element of Nature, it is protected by the rights of Nature and enjoys an inherent individual value',[91] thus finding that non-human animals can have legal rights.

To reconcile this apparent '[p]hilosophical animosity', legal scholar Eva Bernet Kempers proposes understanding rights of nature as a 'three-dimensional concept'.[92] In this theory, she distinguishes between the holistic, systemic, and individualistic (sentient and non-sentient) dimensions of nature. Bringing the individual and collective into the same conceptual understanding of rights can help to resolve rights conflicts. Bernet Kempers provides some examples in this respect: while animal rights may outweigh plant rights, they also need to be understood in the context of the health of species or ecosystems of which they are a part. This may mean that an endangered plant's rights could prevail over the rights of a non-native animal whose activities present a risk to the ecosystem. Bernet Kempers notes that while this approach reconciles the apparent philosophical incongruity between individual and collective rights, it also risks 'naturalizing' rights, meaning it risks strengthening the natural state in which stronger beings can exploit weaker ones.

8.5 CONCEIVING OF ONE HEALTH AS A THREE-DIMENSIONAL FRAMEWORK FOR MORAL CONCERN

Traditionally, One Health has been conceived of as involving three interconnected aspects: environmental, human, and animal health.[93] As discussed above, however, this approach raises questions as to the philosophical value of each of these limbs within the One Health approach. Building on the expanded ideology described in Part 8.2 above, and Bernet Kempers' notion of rights of nature as including animal rights,[94] we propose that our understanding of One Health be supplemented with a three-dimensional concept for moral concern that embraces individual animal rights (the 'framework'). In this framework, while nature encompasses humans, other animals, and the environment, it can also be reconceived to better understand tensions between the interests of individuals and collectives. In this respect, the Court in the *Estrellita* case helpfully sets out the six levels of ecological organisation into which nature may be categorised:

(1) the individual or organism;
(2) populations of the same species living in a particular area;
(3) communities of different species living in an ecosystem;
(4) ecosystems or sets of biological communities in a particular area;
(5) 'The biome or biotic area, which constitutes all those biogeographical zones into which the biosphere is divided, which are characterized by having common climates and biotic components (animals, vegetation, etc)'; and
(6) nature or the Earth.[95]

For our purposes and building on Bernet Kempers' theory, this categorisation can be consolidated into three dimensions: individuals, groups, and nature or the whole. To account for the

[91] See www.animallaw.info/case/253-20-jh22-case-estrellita.
[92] Eva Bernet Kempers, 'Do Rights of Nature Include Animal Rights?' (Helsinki Animal Law Blog, 4 May 2023). Available at: https://blogs.helsinki.fi/animallawblogseries/2023/05/04/do-rights-of-nature-include-animal-rights/.
[93] See, for example: www.unep.org/news-and-stories/statements/joint-tripartite-and-unep-statement-definition-one-health.
[94] Eva Bernet Kempers, 'Do Rights of Nature Include Animal Rights?'.
[95] Corte Constitucional del Ecuador [Constitutional Court of Ecuador], *Rights of Nature and Animals as Subject of Rights, 'Estrellita Monkey' Case*, No. 253-20-JH/22, 27 January 2022, fn 68, 23.

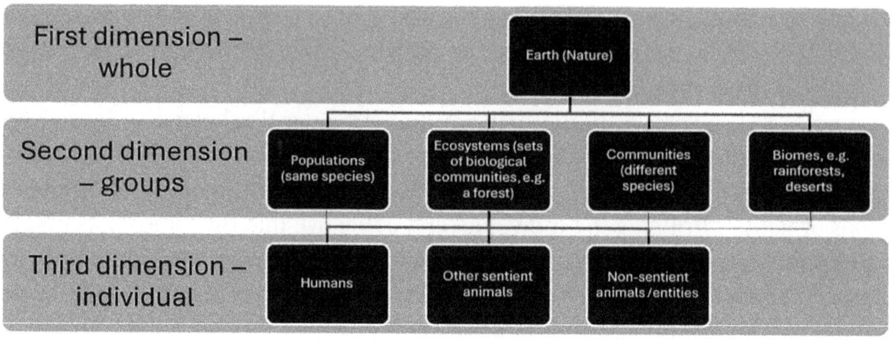

FIGURE 8.1 Proposed One Health three-dimensional framework for moral concern

nature of human rights and animal rights as being those rights founded on individual sentience and intrinsic value,[96] we can further categorise individuals (and to some degree the groups in which they exist) into sentient and non-sentient beings/entities. The resulting framework, adapted from Bernet Kempers' diagram and drawing on the Constitutional Court of Ecuador's framework for ecological organisation, is depicted in Figure 8.1.

In this framework, value is ascribed to the holistic dimension of the Earth, or nature; the group dimensions of populations, communities, ecosystems, and biomes; and the individual dimensions of humans, other sentient animals, and non-sentient animals or entities. As Bernet Kempers observes, '[t]he different dimensions are interdependent: individual entities always exist as embedded in larger networks of collectives and ecosystems, which again exist in the context of the planet (or "nature")'.[97] This interconnectedness and interdependence resonates with key principles of One Health and emphasises the need to recognise the inherent value of all dimensions.

This framework can assist in determining how to address conflicts between the interests of humans, other animals, and the environment when taking a One Health approach. Where there is a conflict of interests, a proportional approach should be taken that balances the relevant interests. Individual sentience merits recognition of a particular kind of interest in contrast with non-sentient entities or collectives, and this should be accounted for in this proportional approach.[98] The approach should include identification of potential risks to different dimensions, consideration of the source or cause of the risk (conceived broadly), consideration of the potential impact and likelihood of occurrence of the risks, and potentialities for prevention and mitigation of risks.[99] Such an approach brings together aspects of the literature discussed above. Like Bernet Kempers' framework for Rights of Nature, this framework brings different notions of rights together into one theory. Like compassionate conservation, resolutions within this framework will cease viewing animals as inherently problematic because all dimensions and

[96] See generally Jane Kotzmann, 'Sentience and Intrinsic Worth as a Pluralist Foundation for Fundamental Animal Rights' (2023) 43(2) *Oxford Journal of Legal Studies* 405.

[97] Eva Bernet Kempers, 'Do Rights of Nature Include Animal Rights?'. Understanding individuals as existing within these frameworks and relations is helpful in addressing critiques regarding the excessive individuality of human rights: See David Hollenbach, 'A Relational Understanding of Human Rights: Human Dignity in Social Solidarity' (2022) 71(7) *Emory Law Journal* 1487, 1488–1493.

[98] Contemporary international law seeks to protect individual human interests through human rights that are limited in some circumstances, although some rights are considered non-derogable. Animal rights may be protected in a similar way. See generally Teraya Koji, 'Emerging Hierarchy in International Human Rights and Beyond: From the Perspective of Non-derogable Rights' (2001) 12(5) *European Journal of International Law* 917.

[99] Note this approach is inspired to some degree by the risk management principles set out in AS/NZS ISO 31000:2018 Risk Management – Principles and Guidelines.

individuals are recognised as having inherent value and conflict resolution will favour win-win solutions. Like multispecies justice, determinations regarding rights conflicts should be based on broader perspectives of justice.

In her conceptualisation, Bernet Kempers identifies a risk of 'naturalizing' rights. We propose that a proper understanding of sentience as sometimes including the capacity to make moral choices operates to negate this risk. Within this framework, humans and other sentient animals are part of nature. As an aspect of their sentience, humans and some other species also have the capacity to make moral choices,[100] which may include choosing to protect others from harm or not to cause pain and suffering to others. While exploitation of weaker species is certainly a part of the state of nature, making moral choices not to exploit others in this way may also be considered part of the state of nature. This framework embraces human moral choice, which should be factored into determinations regarding conflicts between interests. It is incumbent on humans to try and make moral choices appropriately. In the next part of this chapter, we discuss how this framework can be integrated into law and policy, focusing on the context of zoonotic disease transmission.

8.6 IMPLEMENTATION OF THE FRAMEWORK IN LAW AND POLICY RELATING TO ZOONOTIC DISEASE TRANSMISSION

To envisage how the framework might broaden current One Health approaches to better account for the moral value of animals and the environment, we will consider legal and policy approaches to zoonotic disease transmission, focusing particularly on intensive animal agriculture. Zoonotic disease transmission is a primary context in which the adoption of a One Health approach is advocated.[101] First, to establish common legal and policy approaches to zoonotic disease transmission, we establish some of the key features of zoonotic disease regulation in the systems of Australia, the United States, and China. These countries are among the biggest producers of farmed animal products globally.[102] We then examine how the framework could supplement these common legal and policy approaches to better account for the moral value of animals and the environment.

8.6.1 *Common Legal and Policy Approaches to Zoonotic Disease Transmission*

Most contemporary legal systems are underpinned by anthropocentrism, which is reflected in the legal status of animals as human property.[103] In anthropocentric legal systems, humans are at the centre of legal concern and other animals' interests merit only indirect consideration, when

[100] James William Yeates states that 'Animal sentience is therefore an aspect or part of nature: specifically, it is a capacity of components of nature': 'Sentience, Harmony and the Value of Nature' (2023) 13(38) *Animals* 29. See also Frans de Waal and Stephen A. Sherblom, 'Bottom-Up Morality: The Basis of Human Morality in Our Primate Nature' (2018) 47(2) *Journal of Moral Education* 248.

[101] Delia Grace Randolph, Johannes Refisch, Susan MacMillan et al., *Preventing the Next Pandemic: Zoonotic Diseases and How to Break the Chain of Transmission* (United Nations Environment Programme Report, 6 July 2020) 15–17; Joost van Herten, Bernice Bovenkerk, and Marcel Verweij, 'One Health as a Moral Dilemma: Towards a Socially Responsible Zoonotic Disease Control' (2019) 66(1) *Zoonoses Public Health* 26. Available at: https://doi.org/10.1111/zph.12536.

[102] See https://ruminants.ceva.pro/beef-producing-countries and www.worldatlas.com/articles/largest-meat-producing-nations-in-the-world.html.

[103] Peter D. Burdon, 'Earth Jurisprudence and the Project of Earth Democracy' in Peter Burdon and Michelle Maloney (eds.), *Wild Law: In Practice* (Taylor & Francis, 2014) 19–20; Alex Bruce, *Animal Law in Australia: An Integrated Approach*, 2nd ed. (LexisNexis Butterworths 2018) 77.

they align with human interests.[104] Intensive animal agriculture can be considered an expression of anthropocentrism, as it utilises farming methods that sacrifice animal welfare concerns in order to maximise production and efficiency.[105] Legal regulation of zoonotic disease transmission in the context of intensive animal agriculture in Australia, the United States, and China is reflective of anthropocentric attitudes. In each of these countries, animals are legally categorised as property,[106] and intensive animal agriculture practices are widely employed.[107]

A common approach to ensuring animal welfare in animal agriculture (and more broadly) is to enact legislation that restricts property owners' rights in relation to their animals. Restrictions might include requirements such as, for example, space allowances for chickens.[108] Australia,[109] the United States,[110] and China,[111] all have laws that regulate what farmers can do in relation to their animals. Where, however, the interests of animals and productivity concerns misalign, commercial interests are likely to prevail. This is demonstrated through the broad failure of intensive farming systems to allow animals to engage in natural behaviours, like sows' preference for nesting.[112] While safeguarding animal welfare in animal farming should help to prevent zoonotic disease transmission, restrictions on intensive farming are generally insufficient to manage the risk of transmission in these contexts, as evidenced by zoonotic disease outbreaks linked to intensive farming methods.[113]

Approaches to regulation for the prevention of zoonotic disease transmission focus primarily on controlling disease rather than addressing 'the structural drivers of emergence and transmission'.[114] One common approach is to use surveillance to identify emergent zoonotic diseases. Surveillance includes gathering and interpreting health data. Systems are intended to identify emerging diseases early to limit outbreaks.[115] Surveillance is ordinarily undertaken at different

[104] Jane Kotzmann and Gisela Nip, 'Bringing Animal Protection Legislation into Line with Its Purported Purposes: A Proposal for Equality amongst Non-Human Animals' (2020) 37(2) *Pace Environmental Law Review* 247, 250.

[105] Rachel Carey, Christine Parker, and Gyorgy Scrinis, 'How Free Is Sow Stall Free? Incremental Regulatory Reform and Industry Co-optation of Activism' (2020) 42(3) *Law and Policy* 284, 289. Available at: https://doi.org/10.1111/lapo.12154.

[106] In relation to Australia this is the case under common law and statute; see for example, Alex Bruce, *Animal Law in Australia: An Integrated Approach*, 2nd ed. (LexisNexis Butterworths 2018) 77; *Competition and Consumer Act 2010* (Cth) Section 4, where 'goods' are defined to include animals as well as ships, aircraft, and other vehicles.

[107] K. Sharman, 'Farm Animals and Welfare Law: An Unhappy Union' in P. Sankoff, S. White, and C. Black (eds.), *Animal Law in Australasia*, 2nd ed. (Federation Press, 2013) 61–83. Available at: https://vaci.voiceless.org.au/countries/australia/; https://vaci.voiceless.org.au/countries/china/; and https://vaci.voiceless.org.au/countries/united-states/. Jay P. Graham, Jessica H Leibler, Lance B Price, et al, 'The Animal-Human Interface and Infectious Disease in Industrial Food Animal Production: Rethinking Biosecurity and Biocontainment' (2008) 123 *Public Health Reports* 282, 283.

[108] See Primary Industries Standing Committee, *Model Code of Practice for the Welfare of Animals: Domestic Poultry*, 4th ed. (CSIRO Publishing 2002) 17 [12.5] 25–6 app 1.

[109] See https://api.worldanimalprotection.org/country/australia.

[110] See https://api.worldanimalprotection.org/country/usa.

[111] See https://api.worldanimalprotection.org/country/china.

[112] Jed Goodfellow, 'Animal Welfare Regulation in the Australian Agricultural Sector: A Legitimacy Maximising Analysis' (PhD Thesis, Macquarie University, September 2015) 85. Caveat for ACT prohibitions.

[113] For example, Nipah virus, the 1997 Bird flu ('H5N1') and 2009 Swine flu ('H1N1'). For discussion see Jane Kotzmann and Morgan Stonebridge, 'Considering Zoonotic Disease Risk in Australia: An Analysis of the Adequacy of Intensive Animal Agriculture Regulation' (2022) 45(3) *UNSW Law Journal* 1220, 1227–1228.

[114] Degeling, 'Implementing a One Health Approach to Emerging Infectious Disease', 4. See also, P. Daszak, J Amuasi, CG das Neves, et al., *IPBES Workshop on Biodiversity and Pandemics* (Report, 2020) 29. Available at: https://doi.org/10.5281/zenodo.4147317.

[115] Animal and Plant Health Inspection Service – US Department of Agriculture, 'APHIS' American Rescue Plan (ARP) Surveillance Program: Strategic Framework' (2022). Available at: www.aphis.usda.gov/publications/aphis_general/arp-strategic-framework.pdf. Also see https://perma.cc/5NPX-RMJ4 at 1.

levels; for example, in Australia at national and state or territory levels.[116] In Australia, surveillance is supported by the National Health Security Act 2007 (Cth) and responsibilities are shared by the Australian Government Department of Health, the Communicable Diseases Network Australia, and OzFoodNet.[117] In the United States, federal responsibilities for surveillance activities are shared by the federal Commissioner of Food and Drugs, the Director of the Centers for Disease Control and Prevention (including the National Center for Emerging and Zoonotic Infectious Diseases), and the Secretary of Agriculture (including the Animal and Plant Health Inspection Service).[118] Nevertheless, states have the primary role in surveillance, and there is a strong focus on surveillance in states with high levels of animal agriculture.[119] In China, human health and veterinary departments are responsible for monitoring zoonotic diseases,[120] and the Law of Prevention and Treatment of Infectious Diseases governs infectious diseases divided into three classes.[121]

Another common method to prevent the spread of zoonotic disease is biosecurity. This refers to procedures implemented to stop zoonotic disease from being introduced and spread amongst intensively farmed animals.[122] In these contexts, visiting wildlife are often responsible for the introduction of disease.[123] In Australia, biosecurity procedures are driven by industry.[124] In the United States, biosafety, biosecurity, and bio-surveillance are key activities implemented to reduce the risk of zoonotic disease spillover.[125] Biosecurity is also an important tool for prevention of zoonotic disease spread in China.[126] Nevertheless, significant obstacles exist to

[116] I. Johnson, A. Hansen, and P. Bi, 'The Challenges of Implementing an Integrated One Health Surveillance System in Australia' (2018) 65(1) *Zoonoses and Public Health* 229, 230. Available at: https://doi.org/10.1111/zph.12433.

[117] Department of Health and Aged Care, 'Communicable Diseases Network Australia (CDNA)', *Australian Government* (12 July 2022). Available at: www1.health.gov.au/internet/main/publishing.nsf/Content/cda-cdna-index.htm; 'OzFoodNet: Enhancing Surveillance for Foodborne Disease in Australia', *Australian Government Department of Health* (30 September 2020). Available at: www1.health.gov.au/internet/main/publishing.nsf/Content/cdna-ozfoodnet.htm.

[118] 7 U.S.C § 8319; 2157 U.S.C. § 8310(a); *Our Partners*, National Center for Emerging and Zoonotic Infections Diseases (NCEZID), Centers for Disease Control and Prevention (CDC). Available at: https://perma.cc/P4GZ-EED4; *National Center for Emerging and Zoonotic Infectious Diseases (NCEZID)*, Centers for Disease Control and Prevention (CDC), www.cdc.gov/ncezid/index.html [https://perma.cc/7BY6-82CA].

[119] For discussion, see Jane Kotzmann and Morgan Stonebridge, 'Preventing Another Pandemic: How Changing the Legal Paradigm Governing Intensive Animal Agriculture Will Reduce the Risk of Future Zoonoses' (2022) 47(2) *Columbia Journal of Environmental Law* 457, 491–492.

[120] Hongying Li, Yufei Chen, Catherine C Machalaba, et al., 'Wild Animal and Zoonotic Disease Risk management and Regulation in China: Examining Gaps and One Health Opportunities in Scope, Mandates, and Monitoring Systems' (2021) 13 *One Health* 4.

[121] Law of The People's Republic of China on Prevention and Treatment of Infectious Diseases (2013 Amendment). Available at: bit.ly/4jSciHx.

[122] Jane Kotzmann and Morgan Stonebridge, 'Considering Zoonotic Disease Risk in Australia: An Analysis of the Adequacy of Intensive Animal Agriculture Regulation' (2022) 45(3) *UNSW Law Journal* 1220, 1235. See also World Organisation for Animal Health, Office of Innovation and Entrepreneurship. Terrestrial animal health code glossary 2018. [cited 1 November 2021]. Available at: www.oie.int/fileadmin/Home/eng/Health_standards/tahc/2018/en_glossaire.htm.

[123] Bryony A. Jones, Delia Grace, Richard Kock, et al., 'Zoonosis Emergence Linked to Agricultural Intensification and Environmental Change' (2013) 110(21) *Proceedings of the National Academy of Sciences* 8399, 8401. Available at: https://doi.org/10.1073/pnas.1208059110.

[124] J. W. Aleri and M. Laurence, 'A Description of Biosecurity Practices among Selected Dairy Framers across Australia' (2020) 60(14) *Animal Production Science* 1711. Available at: https://doi.org/10.1071/AN19340.

[125] National Biodefense Strategy and Implementation Plan for Countering Biological Threats, Enhancing Pandemic Preparedness, and Achieving Global Health Security (October 2022). Available at: www.whitehouse.gov/wp-content/uploads/2022/10/National-Biodefense-Strategy-and-Implementation-Plan-Final.pdf.

[126] Zinjie Wei, Wanlong Lin, and David A. Hennessy, 'Biosecurity and Disease Management in China's Animal Agriculture Sector' (2015) 54 *Food Policy* 52.

implementing effective biosecurity measures in intensive agricultural facilities. In particular, the scale and intensity of industrialised agriculture generate different and higher disease risks.[127]

Where the spread of zoonotic disease cannot be controlled through surveillance and biosecurity measures, the common approach is to mandate animal culling.[128] Culling refers to killing diseased or at-risk agricultural animals to stop the spread of disease.[129] In Australia, the Australian Veterinary Emergency Plan outlines the policies that should be followed where an emergency animal disease is present, including policies requiring killing and disposal of diseased and at-risk animals.[130] The policy requires that 'a high standard of euthanasia and respect for the animals is an essential consideration during an EAD response'[131] where a large number of animals may need to be quickly 'destroy[ed]'.[132] In the US, zoonotic disease regulation provides for depopulation or culling, where a disease is identified in an animal population.[133] The American Veterinary Medical Association provides rules for undertaking mass culling. These include requirements as to appropriate methods.[134] States also have regulations in place in relation to culling.[135] In China, compulsory culling is required in relation to farmed animals that are infected by specified diseases.[136]

8.6.2 *Integrating the Three-Dimensional Framework for Moral Concern*

The framework serves to highlight that humans are not the only stakeholder of moral concern in decisions relating to zoonotic disease transmission. Not only are humans, animals, and the environment interconnected – as acknowledged by the One Health approach – but they also all have moral value (individually and collectively) beyond their economic usefulness to humans. While all three limbs may be impacted by the negative consequences of zoonotic disease spillover in the context of intensive animal agriculture, under current legal and policy frameworks animals disproportionately suffer the worst consequences. Negative impacts for animals include loss of habitat to facilitate animal agriculture, poor welfare for farmed animals, infection, and potential culling (or death).

[127] Marco Liverani, Jeff Waage, Tony Barnett, et al., 'Understanding and Managing Zoonotic Risk in the New Livestock Industries' (2013) 121(8) *Environmental Health Perspectives* 873, 874. Available at: https://doi.org/10.1289/ehp.1206001; J. Otte, D. Roland-Holst, D. Pfeiffer, et al., *Industrial Livestock Production and Global Health Risks* (Research Report, June 2007) 6–10. For discussion see Jane Kotzmann and Morgan Stonebridge, 'Considering Zoonotic Disease Risk in Australia: An Analysis of the Adequacy of Intensive Animal Agriculture Regulation' (2022) 45(3) *UNSW Law Journal* 1220, 1235–1237.

[128] J. Van Herten and B. Bovenkerk, 'The Precautionary Principle in Zoonotic Disease Control' (2021) 14(2) *Public Health Ethics* 180, 181; Chris Degeling, Zohar Lederman, and Melanie Rock, 'Culling and the Common Good: Re-evaluating Harms and Benefits Under the One Health Paradigm' (2016) 9(3) *Public Health Ethics* 244, 244.

[129] Royal Society of Prevention of Cruelty to Animals, 'What Is Mass Euthanasia?', *RSPCA Knowledge Base* (31 May 2022). Available at: https://kb.rspca.org.au/knowledge-base/what-is-mass-euthanasia/.

[130] Animal Health Australia, 'Australian Veterinary Emergency Plan Operational Manual: Disposal' (Manual, Version 5.0, 2021) 95.

[131] Animal Health Australia, 'Australian Veterinary Emergency Plan Operational Manual: Destruction of Animals' (Manual, Version 3.2, 2015) 9 ('Destruction of Animals').

[132] Ibid.

[133] See US Department of Agriculture, Emergency Response Procedures – Depopulation and Disposal (2015). Available at: www.aphis.usda.gov/animal_health/downloads/animal_diseases/ai/ERDepopDisposal.pdf.

[134] 232AM. Veterinary Medical Association, 'AVMA Guidelines for the Euthanasia of Animals' (2020) ed. 111. Available at: www.avma.org/resources-tools/avma-policies/avma-guidelines-euthanasia-animals.

[135] See e.g. IOWA CODE §163.2 (2021).

[136] Xinjie Wei, Wanlong Lin, and David A. Hennessy, 'Biosecurity and Disease Management in China's Animal Agriculture Sector' (2015) 54 *Food Policy* 52, 59.

Changing the paradigm to acknowledge that humans, animals, and the environment are all of moral concern prompts a greater focus on tackling the structural drivers of zoonotic disease. This is because preventing initial spillover will minimise negative consequences for humans, animals, and the environment. The United Nations has identified seven key anthropogenic drivers of zoonotic disease spillover, which include an increasing demand for animal protein and unsustainable agricultural intensification.[137] Law and policy should be directed towards minimising these drivers. In this context, this would mean implementing laws and policies to reduce demand for animal protein and to shift towards a 'de-intensification' of animal agriculture.

In terms of the demand for animal protein, in high-income countries where alternatives to animal proteins are widely available and affordable, policies should encourage consumption of alternative proteins such as pulses rather than animal proteins. Policies could include, for example, removal of subsidies to intensive animal agriculture producers, restrictions or bans on advertising animal products, education initiatives to highlight the benefits of more plant-centric diets and restrictions on inclusion of animal proteins in publicly provided food (e.g. in publicly funded universities, prisons, and the public service). In low and middle-income countries where there are challenges in the availability of alternative proteins, policies should be directed towards increasing availability. Notably, while there is increasing demand for animal protein, 'the long-term trend for pulses is of sustained consumption levels'.[138] Law and policy should be directed towards reversing these trends. In relation to 'de-intensifying' animal agriculture, legislators need to increase regulation of agricultural operations. Measures could include removing subsidies, use of competition laws to de-concentrate industry, prohibiting additional intensive agricultural farms, requiring intensive animal agricultural operations to internalise the true costs of production including environmental, animal, and human health and welfare costs, removing animal welfare exemptions for farmed animals, and strengthening regulations.[139]

Where a zoonotic disease has emerged, the framework can be drawn upon to modify or at least prompt deep consideration of regulatory responses. Traditional approaches to control zoonotic diseases outbreaks include the culling of livestock and wildlife to limit their movement and their potential interaction with humans and other animals.[140] However, as Degeling, Lederman, and Rock explain, these approaches are founded on a harm principle that excludes the interests of other animals.[141] If we judge the appropriateness of regulatory responses on the basis of consequences for the collective (humans and other animals, groups, and the Earth) different conclusions may be drawn. For example, Lederman, Magalhães-Sant'Ana, and Chuan Voo explain how the use of vaccine baits would be more effective in controlling rabies than culling, which remains a mainstream method of disease control.[142] As a minimum threshold, clear scientific, social, and ethical justification should be required in relation to any decision to cull.[143]

137 Delia Grace Randolph et al., 'Preventing the Next Pandemic: Zoonotic Diseases and How to Break the Chain of Transmission' (United Nations Environment Programme Report, 6 July 2020) 15.

138 Ibid.

139 For detailed discussion see Lindsay Walton and Kristen King Jaiven, 'Regulating CAFOs for the Well-Being of Farm Animals, Consumers, and the Environment' (2020) 50(6) *Environmental Law Reporter* 10485.

140 Chris Degeling, Zohar Lederman, and Melanie Rock, 'Culling and the Common Good: Re-evaluating Harms and Benefits Under the One Health *Paradigm'* (2016) 9(3) *Public Health Ethics* 244, 245.

141 Ibid., 244, 245.

142 Zohar Lederman, Manuel Magalhaes-Sant'Ana, and Teck Chuan Voo, 'Stamping Out Animal Culling: From Anthropocentrism to One Health Ethics' (2021) 34 *Journal of Agricultural and Environmental Ethics* 3.

143 Lederman, 'Stamping Out Animal Culling', 10.

8.7 CONCLUSION

While One Health is internationally recognised as the optimum approach to the prevention and control of zoonotic disease transmission, in practice it remains confined to anthropocentric considerations of moral value. In this respect, while One Health recognises the interconnectedness of people, animals, and the environment, it does not approach them as having equal moral worth. Instead, as is the case with traditional approaches to public health, humans are considered superior, and where conflict between interests occurs, it is the interests of humans that prevail.

A deeper understanding of One Health, however, mandates that humans are not and should not be the only actors considered to have moral worth.[144] As Degeling et al. state, '[t]o be both ethical and effective, [One Health] approaches might require us to understand health as a universal good that is necessarily shared between species'.[145] Moreover, to provide a real policy solution to issues of the Anthropocene, One Health must be understood as an expanded ideology in the manner expounded in much of the ethical literature. To further develop this broader understanding of One Health, and to reconcile it with animal rights theory, which also provides a promising pathway towards mitigating the detrimental impact of humans on the Earth, this chapter has sought to demonstrate how a broader conception of One Health can, and should, be conceived of as inclusive of animal rights.

The One Health Three-Dimensional Framework for Moral Concern developed in this chapter is designed to be used as a tool to identify moral relevance in the human and non-human. In ascribing value to the Earth, to groups, and to individuals (human and non-human), the framework recognises interconnectedness and interdependence and emphasises the inherent value of all dimensions. The framework also understands animal rights as compatible with and part of the broader One Health paradigm and can help to determine how to address conflicts between the interests of humans, other animals, and the environment when adopting a One Health approach.

In developing the framework, this chapter has established a method by which to locate recognition of animal inherent worth within the One Health paradigm. Discussion of the potential implementation of this approach in the context of zoonotic disease prevention and control has assisted in demonstrating the theoretical implications of the approach for contemporary societies and their common uses of animals.

[144] Ibid., 6.

[145] Degeling, 'Culling and the Common Good', 244–251.

9

The One Health Approach and the Tackling of Drivers of Environmental Degradation

The Case of the EU Deforestation-Free Products Regulation

Elisa Cavallin

9.1 INTRODUCTION

Forests cover about 30 per cent of the global land area and host about 80 per cent of its biodiversity.[1] They provide important ecosystem services, including subsistence and income to 25 per cent of the world's population, clean air, water flow regulation, carbon sequestration, habitats for species,[2] and disease regulation and control.[3]

However, forests are also seriously under threat due to deforestation and forest degradation.[4] The Food and Agriculture Organisation (FAO) estimates that 420 million hectares of forests (10 per cent of the remaining global forests), corresponding to an area larger than the European Union (EU), were lost between 1990 and 2020.[5] The FAO reports also noted increasing disturbances in relation to forest ecosystem health and observed that 10 per cent of forests are considered to be severely fragmented.[6]

The causes behind such loss and fragmentation are traced back to the expansion of land used for agriculture (about 80 per cent of global deforestation), but also – to a lesser extent – urban expansion, infrastructure development, and mining, with differences in relation to the location,

1 European Commission, 'Stepping up EU Action to Protect and Restore the World's Forests' COM (2019) 352 final, 23 July 2019.

2 Ibid.

3 See, e.g.: J. A. Foley, G. P. Asner, M. H. Costa, et al., 'Amazonia Revealed: Forest Degradation and Loss of Ecosystem Goods and Services in the Amazon Basin' (2007) 5 *Frontiers in Ecology and the Environment* 1–25; S. Morand and C. Lajaunie, 'Outbreaks of Vector-Borne and Zoonotic Diseases are Associated with Changes in Forest Cover and Oil Palm Expansion at Global Scale' (2021) 8 *Frontiers in Veterinary Science* 230; E. Karjalainen, T. Sarjala, and H. Raitio, 'Promoting Human Health through Forests: Overview and Major Challenges' (2010) 15(1) *Environmental Health Preventive Medicine* 1–8.

4 European Commission, 'Factsheet – Protecting and Restoring the World's Forests: Stepping up EU Action to Halt Deforestation and Forest Degradation', Available at: https://commission.europa.eu/publications/eu-communication-2019-stepping-eu-action-protect-and-restore-worlds-forests_en.

5 Regulation (EU) 2023/1115 of the European Parliament and of the Council of 31 May 2023 on the Making Available on the Union Market and the Export from the Union of Certain Commodities and Products Associated with Deforestation and Forest Degradation and Repealing Regulation (EU) No. 995/2010 (2023) OJ L 150/206. Recital 2.

6 FAO – Food and Agriculture Organisation and UNEP – United Nations Environment Programme, 'The State of the World's Forests 2020. Forests, Biodiversity and People' (Rome: FAO and UNEP, 2020). Available at: www.fao.org/documents/card/en/c/ca8642en; K. Bougas, V. Cherrier, L. Constantine, et al., 'Service Contract on EU Policy on Forest Products and Deforestation. Task 3 – Impact Assessment on Demand-side Measures to Address Deforestation – Final report' (Report for DG Environment – European Commission, Brussels, Belgium, Wood, Trinomics, Ricardo, WUR, Tyrsky, 2021). Available at: https://circabc.europa.eu/ui/group/34861680-e799-4d7c-bbad-da83c45da458/library/5d098237-8bab-48a6-a6c8-2a907d80c791/details?download=true.

and between regions and within continents.[7] Additionally, the drivers of deforestation and forest degradation are not limited to the forestry sector itself, as there are also matters of weak land tenure regime, weak government and legal enforcement and protection of Indigenous rights and broader human rights, climate change, democracy and political freedoms, consumption levels of the commodities, dependence on feed imports, and agricultural and other policies.[8]

In terms of the One Health framework, this loss comes with significant consequences for people, wildlife, and the environment, such as increased opportunities for contact between people and wildlife and related disease emergence and spread, human diseases linked to environmental degradation, loss of habitats, increase of greenhouse gas (GHG) emissions, and other effects.[9]

To mitigate this loss, legislation can assist in three key ways. First, legislation can contribute to ecosystem and species protection,[10] as well as restoration.[11] Second, legislation can regulate the interface between nature and other policy fields (agriculture and food production, climate, and energy).[12] Third, legislation can regulate the value chains and supply chains. The term 'supply chain' has been defined as 'a dynamic process that includes the continuous flow of materials, funds, and information across multiple functional areas within and between chain members'.[13] In simpler terms, supply chains refer to the sequence of linked processes and stages involved in product production, movement, distribution, and sale.[14] As such, 'greening' supply chains of products and materials represents a way in which nature loss and degradation can be prevented.

In recent years, the EU has initiated action on this third pathway and adopted the 'Deforestation-free Products Regulation' (The Regulation).[15] The Regulation contains rules on the placing and making available on the Union market and the export of certain products that contain, have been fed, or have been made with certain commodities (cattle, cocoa, coffee, oil palm, rubber, soya, and wood),[16] thus 'targeting' the EU consumption of these products, which accounts for a non-negligible amount of the global share of deforestation and forest

[7] European Commission, 'Factsheet – Protecting and Restoring the World's Forests: Stepping up EU Action to Halt Deforestation and Forest Degradation'; FAO – Food and Agriculture Organisation and UNEP – United Nations Environment Programme, *The State of the World's Forests 2020. Forests, Biodiversity and People*.

[8] European Parliament, 'Report with Recommendations to the Commission on an EU Legal Framework to Halt and Reverse EU-driven Global Deforestation' (2020/2006(INL)) (2020). Available at: www.europarl.europa.eu/doceo/document/A-9-2020-0179_EN.html; Bougas, 'Service Contract on EU Policy on Forest Products and Deforestation'.

[9] E.g: Peter Daszak, C. das Neves, J. Amuasi, et al., 'Workshop Report on Biodiversity and Pandemics of the Intergovernmental Platform on Biodiversity and Ecosystem Services' (Intergovernmental Platform on Biodiversity and Ecosystem Services – IPBES, 2020). Available at: www.ipbes.net/events/ipbes-workshop-biodiversity-and-pandemics; C. J. P. Colfer, D. Sheil, and M. Kishi, *Forests and Human Health: Assessing the Evidence* (Center for International Forestry Research, 2006); Karjalainen 'Promoting Human Health through Forests'.

[10] In the EU, this is done through the so-called Nature Directives: Council Directive 92/43/EEC of 21 May 1992 on the Conservation of Natural Habitats and of Wild Fauna and Flora (1992) OJ L206/7; Directive 2009/147/EC of the European Parliament and of the Council of 30 November 2009 on the Conservation of Wild Birds (2009) OJ L20/7.

[11] In the EU, a Nature Restoration Law has just been adopted. The agreed text: Council of the European Union, 'Interinstitutional Agreement or Provisional Deal on the Proposal for Regulation of the European Parliament and of the Council on Nature Restoration' Interinstitutional File: 2022/0195(COD) (2023). Available at: https://data.consilium.europa.eu/doc/document/ST-15907-2023-INIT/en/pdf. Retrievable at: www.consilium.europa.eu/en/press/press-releases/2023/11/09/nature-restoration-council-and-parliament-reach-agreement-on-new-rules-to-restore-and-preserve-degraded-habitats-in-the-eu/.

[12] In the EU, this is pursued (with varying results) with different instruments: among others, the agricultural policy, legislative measures on land use and land use change and forestry, and renewables.

[13] Payman Ahi and Cory Searcy, 'A Comparative Literature Analysis of Definitions for Green and Sustainable Supply Chain Management' (2013) 52 *Journal of Cleaner Production* 329.

[14] Karl Montevirgen, 'Supply Chain Management: From Raw Materials to Retail' (*Encyclopedia Britannica | Britannica*, n.d.). Available at: www.britannica.com/money/what-is-supply-chain-management.

[15] Regulation 2023/1115 of 31 May 2023, Deforestation-free Products Regulation.

[16] Ibid., Article 1.

degradation.[17] Indeed, the Regulation aims to minimise the contribution of the EU to deforestation and forest degradation that might accompany these products if there is a lack of a proper due diligence system in place. A second connected aim of the Regulation is to reduce the EU's contribution to GHG emissions and biodiversity loss.[18]

If this is an environmental instrument that touches on the supply chain of certain products with clear due diligence obligations in relation to these products, what does the Regulation have to do with health and the One Health approach? What are some elements of interest from a One Health point of view?

In the quest to find answers to the above questions, this chapter is structured as follows.

In Section 9.2, the systemic importance of forests and the interlinkages between forests and health will be illustrated. Section 9.3 will consider the relevance of environmental protection for disease prevention in the context of the One Health Approach. These two sections combined will provide the basis for Section 9.4, where the (hidden) health dimension of the Regulation and the Regulation itself will be explored. Section 9.5 will present a discussion on the themes covered and conclusions.

9.2 FORESTS AND HEALTH

Land use and land use change emissions (including deforestation) are among the biggest drivers of climate change, exerting a sizeable impact as the second most significant cause of climate change after fossil fuels.[19] In fact, forest harvesting and conversion to agricultural land release a substantial part of the carbon stored in biomass and soil.[20] In addition, forests act as carbon sinks and deforestation and forest degradation reduce the carbon-absorbing capacity of forests.[21] The contribution of deforestation and forest degradation to climate change is so substantial that estimates indicate that forest and natural ecosystem protection could potentially contribute to 16–30 per cent of climate change mitigation needs,[22] to meet the targets of the Paris Agreement.[23]

Deforestation and forest degradation also cause loss of species, habitat loss, habitat fragmentation, and a consequent decreased capability of species to adapt to climate change and other pressures and stressors.[24] Population decline and/or local extinction of such species and a different biodiversity composition in these spaces may also have a domino effect on other

[17] Dieter Cuypers, T. Geerken, L. Gorissen, et al., 'The Impact of EU Consumption on Deforestation: Comprehensive Analysis of the Impact of EU Consumption on Deforestation' (Study funded by the European Commission, DG ENV Contract N° 070307/2010/577031/ETU/E2 and carried out by VITO, the IIASA, CICERO, 2013). Available at: https://pure.iiasa.ac.at/14868/1/1.%20Report%20analysis%20of%20impact.pdf.

[18] Regulation 2023/1115 of 31 May 2023, Deforestation-free Products Regulation, Article 1.

[19] European Commission, 'Factsheet – Protecting and Restoring the World's Forests: Stepping up EU Action to Halt Deforestation and Forest Degradation'. See also data from: P. R. Shukla, J. Skea, E. Calvo Buendia, et al., 'Climate Change and Land: An IPCC Special Report on Climate Change, Desertification, Land Degradation, Sustainable Land Management, Food Security, and Greenhouse Gas Fluxes in Terrestrial Ecosystems '(IPCC, 2019). Available at: www.ipcc.ch/site/assets/uploads/sites/4/2020/08/200730-IPCCJ7230-SRCCL-Complete-BOOK-HRES.pdf.

[20] Bougas, 'Service Contract on EU Policy on Forest Products and Deforestation'.

[21] Ibid.

[22] See, e.g.: S. Roe, C. Streck, M. Obersteiner, et al., 'Contribution of the Land Sector to a 1.5 C World' (2019) 9 *Nature Climate Change* 817; B. W. Griscom, J. Adams, P. W. Ellis, et al., 'Natural Climate Solutions' (2017) 114(11645) *Proceedings of the National Academy of Sciences* 44. As considered in Bougas, 'Service Contract on EU Policy on Forest Products and Deforestation'.

[23] Paris Agreement. Adopted on 12 December 2015; entered into force on 4 November 2016. Paris, Conference of the Parties, Twenty-first session (United Nations Framework Convention on Climate Change, 2015).

[24] Bougas, 'Service Contract on EU Policy on Forest Products and Deforestation'.

species due to, e.g. food-web interactions and other ecosystem processes, with further potential future effects.[25]

Finally, wider environmental degradation is often brought about by deforestation forest degradation, and land use change, namely water quality issues (e.g. linked to decreased soil filtration with possible effects on access to clean drinking water),[26] soil quality (e.g. erosion, which also may lead to an impacted capacity of rivers and dams and increased runoff),[27] and air quality (this might be especially true where deforestation is conducted through slash and burn techniques or where we have spontaneous fires).[28]

The environmental issues connected to deforestation and forest degradation discussed above are notably woven together and, both singularly and cumulatively, have implications for animal and human health.

First, climate change and biodiversity loss have, on their own, been linked to a possible increase in disease emergence and spread.[29] Along with a more 'obvious' variation in temperature and climate, climate change causes the environmental conditions of habitats to change. A spatial rearrangement or shifting of habitats and species might also occur, depending on the internal species traits and external drivers of change: this would be, essentially, a 'relocation' of species out of certain areas and into other areas, in line with the shifting of habitats.[30] For example, climate change has already been linked to a change in the distribution of tick-borne pathogens.[31] This 'movement' could allow for changes in species composition and represent a suitable opportunity for new contact between species and between species and pathogens, potentially facilitating a disease spillover event (where disease spreads from non-human species to humans).[32] Additionally, climate change has been associated with increased health events due to higher temperatures.[33]

[25] K. Norris, 'Ecology: The Tropical Deforestation Debt' (2016) 26 *Current Biology* 16. R770. I. M. Rosa, M. J. Smith, O. R. Wearn, D. Purves, and R. M. Ewers, 'The Environmental Legacy of Modern Tropical Deforestation' (2016) 26(16) *Current Biology* 2161; Bougas, 'Service Contract on EU Policy on Forest Products and Deforestation'.

[26] A. M. Mapulanga and H. Naito, 'Effect of Deforestation on Access to Clean Drinking Water' (2019) 116(17) *Proceedings of the National Academy of Sciences* 8249. As considered in Bougas, 'Service Contract on EU Policy on Forest Products and Deforestation'.

[27] See: W. Huang, M. Zong, Z. Fan, et al., 'Determining the Impacts of Deforestation and Corn Cultivation on Soil Quality in Tropical Acidic Red Soils Using a Soil Quality Index' (2021) 125 *Ecological Indicators* 107580; E. Amoakwah, M. A. Rahman, KA. Nketia, R. Djouaka, N. O. Didenko, and K. R. Islam, 'Impact of Deforestation and Subsequent Land-use Change on Soil Quality' (2021) 10(2) *Eurasian Journal of Soil Science* 150.

[28] See: C. Reddington, E. W. Butt, D. A. Ridley, et al., 'Air Quality and Human Health Improvements from Reductions in Deforestation-related Fire in Brazil' (2015) 8(10) *Nature Geoscience* 768; E. W. Butt, L. Conibear, C. Knote, and D. V. Spracklen, 'Large Air Quality and Public Health Impacts due to Amazonian Deforestation Fires in 2019' (2021) 5(7) *GeoHealth* e2021GH000429.

[29] This will not happen in all cases, but in many cases: B. Slenning, 'Global Climate Change and Implications for Disease Emergence' (2010) 47(1) *Veterinary Pathology* 28. See, also: A. El-Sayed and M. Kamel, 'Climatic Changes and Their Role in Emergence and Re-emergence of Diseases' (2020) 27 *Environmental Science and Pollution Research* 22336; D. S. Schmeller, F. Courchamp, and G. Killeen, 'Biodiversity Loss, Emerging Pathogens and Human Health Risks' (2020) 29 *Biodiversity and Conservation* 3095; J. N. Mills, 'Biodiversity Loss and Emerging Infectious Disease: An Example from the Rodent-Borne Hemorrhagic Fevers' (2006) 7(1) *Biodiversity* 9.

[30] See, e.g.: I.-C. Chen, J. K. Hill, R. Ohlemüller, D. B. Roy, and C. D. Thomas, 'Rapid Range Shifts of Species Associated with High Levels of Climate Warming' (2011) 333 *Science* 6045.

[31] Daszak, 'Workshop Report on Biodiversity and Pandemics of the Intergovernmental Platform on Biodiversity and Ecosystem Services'.

[32] C. J. Carlson, G. F. Albery, C. Merow, et al., 'Climate Change Increases Cross-Species Viral Transmission Risk' (2022) 607(7919) *Nature* 555. For an overview on research progress and gaps and for a predictive framework, see: S. Altizer, R. S. Ostfeld, P. T. Johnson, S. Kutz, and C. D. Harvell, 'Climate Change and Infectious Diseases: from Evidence to a Predictive Framework' (2013) 341(6145) *Science* 514.

[33] A. Kazmierczak, R. Lowe, K. R. van Daalen, K. Johnson, S. Dasgupta, and E. Robinson, 'Climate Change as a Threat to Health and Well-being in Europe: Focus on Heat and Infectious Diseases' (EEA Report No 07/2022, European Environment Agency, 2022).

As for the importance of biodiversity for health,[34] it has been hypothesised, for example, that a reduction of animal populations and biodiversity might result in the loss of the 'dilution effect' or 'wasted transmission' between (non-specific) hosts and (zoonotic) pathogen spread.[35] This hypothesis suggests that biodiverse communities limit the spread of diseases through several mechanisms,[36] essentially 'diverting' free-living parasites from suitable hosts (i.e. completely unsuitable hosts: decoy effect; or low competency hosts: alternative hosts).[37] Biodiversity is also an interesting 'tool' for the production of medicines,[38] meaning that biodiversity loss might be detrimental to their research and development, impairing the finding of disease cures or the use of better alternative ingredients for pharmaceuticals.[39]

Second, there may be a causal link between deforestation and forest degradation, contact with, and trade of wildlife and virus emergence and spread.[40] This may be due to increased contact between humans and wildlife, causing viruses to cross barriers between species and may, eventually, lead to increased chances of a spillover event of a pathogen (with epidemic or pandemic potential) in cases of deforestation and forest degradation.[41] Regarding the degree of risks related to disease spread, habitat fragmentation is particularly problematic (besides the potential biodiversity loss associated with it) because the length of the perimeter of the forest edge where humans and livestock may more likely come into contact with wildlife increases.[42] Deforestation may also involve the creation of roads with potential consequences for disease emergence and transmission, such as via increased access and/or increased hunting behaviour.[43]

Naturally, these aspects are not only relevant to human health. The route or direction of the transmission of the disease might not be a 'one-way street' as certain diseases can also be transmitted to (wild) animals by humans, thus adding another problematic dimension to the issue at

[34] For a broad overview transcending forest biodiversity, see: S. Prakash, C. Estreguil, A. Neuville, E. Chinchio, and M. Baccaro, 'Biodiversity and Health – A Knowledge Synthesis and Analysis of the Complex Connections between Biodiversity and Health Highlighting the Relevant EU Policies Projects and Initiatives.' (2023). Available at: https://publications.jrc.ec.europa.eu/repository/handle/JRC134740.

[35] See e.g.: Jessica Scott, 'Proposed Integrated Control of Zoonotic Plasmodium Knowlesi in Southeast Asia using Themes of One Health' (2020) 5(4) *Tropical Medicine and Infectious Disease* 175.

[36] For example, through the regulation of populations of susceptible hosts or interference with parasite transmission.

[37] See, e.g.: David J. Civitello, J. Cohen, H. Fatima, et al., 'Biodiversity Inhibits Parasites: Broad Evidence for the Dilution Effect' (2015) 112(28) *Proceedings of the National Academy of Sciences* 8667; Serge Morand, S. Jittapalapong, Y. Supputtamongkol, M. T. Abdullah, and T. B. Huan, 'Infectious Diseases and Their Outbreaks in Asia-Pacific: Biodiversity and Its Regulation Loss Matter' (2014) 9(2) *PloS one* e90032; P. T. J. Johnson and D. W. Thieltges, 'Diversity, Decoys and the Dilution Effect: How Ecological Communities Affect Disease Risk' (2010) 213(6) *Journal of Experimental Biology* 961.It should be noted that, in matters of dilution effect, studies have also reported a highly heterogeneous relationship between host biodiversity and disease, leading to heterogeneous effects. See: Daniel J. Salkeld, Kerry A. Padgett, and James Holland Jones, 'A Meta-Analysis Suggesting that the Relationship between Biodiversity and Risk of Zoonotic Pathogen Transmission is Idiosyncratic' (2013) 16(5) *Ecology Letters* 679.

[38] See, e.g.: G. M. Cragg and D. J. Newman, 'Biodiversity: A Continuing Source of Novel Drug Leads' (2005) 77(1) *Pure and Applied Chemistry* 7.

[39] See, e.g.: Y. Linhares, A. Kaganski, C. Agyare, et al., 'Biodiversity: The Overlooked Source of Human Health' (2023) 29(3) *Trends in Molecular Medicine* 173.

[40] See, among others: J. H. Ellwanger, B. Kulmann-Leal, V. L. Kaminski, et al., 'Beyond Diversity Loss and Climate Change: Impacts of Amazon Deforestation on Infectious Diseases and Public Health' (2020) 92(1) *Anais da Academia Brasileira de Ciências*.

[41] A. P. Dobson, S. L. Pimm, L. Hannah, et al., 'Ecology and Economics for Pandemic Prevention' (2020) 369(6502) *Science* 379; J. H. Ellwanger and J. A. B. Chies, 'Zoonotic Spillover: Understanding Basic Aspects for Better Prevention' (2021) 44(1) *Genetics and Molecular Biology* 1; M. C. Rulli, M. Santini, D. T. S. Hayman, and P. D'Odorico, 'The Nexus between Forest Fragmentation in Africa and Ebola Virus Disease Outbreaks' (2017) 7(1) *Scientific Reports* 41613.

[42] Dobson, 'Ecology and Economics for Pandemic Prevention'.

[43] N. D. Wolfe, M. N. Eitel, J. Gockowski, et al., 'Deforestation, Hunting and the Ecology of Microbial Emergence' (2000) 1 *Global Change and Human Health* 10.

hand: potential added biodiversity (and economic) loss among infected (domesticated or wild) animal populations.[44]

Finally, looking beyond infectious diseases, there may be health consequences due to increased heat (for both humans and animals) and mental health issues associated with deforestation,[45] but also the potential for other diseases linked to environmental degradation, such as the already mentioned air quality, soil quality, and water quality issues.[46]

Given the above, tackling deforestation and forest degradation and broader forest protection measures could be considered as having broader health implications and representing a strategy for disease prevention, and of benefit to human and animal health, and not just climate and biodiversity protection measures.

9.3 THE RELEVANCE OF ENVIRONMENTAL PROTECTION FOR DISEASE PREVENTION IN THE ONE HEALTH APPROACH

The One Health approach is an approach based on collaboration, multidisciplinarity, and multisectorality, founded on the notion that human health, animal, and environmental health are interdependent.[47] The approach should contribute to and inform the design and implementation of programmes, policies, legislation, and research and support the collaboration and communication between sectors and disciplines. The ultimate goal is to achieve better public health outcomes.[48] If one were to schematically represent One Health, the approach would appear as having different nexuses, which could be considered singularly (the human–animal nexus, the human–environment nexus, and the animal–environment nexus) or together (the human–animal–environment nexus).[49] Because the approach involves so many interfaces and

[44] E.g.: J. H. Epstein and J. T. Price, 'The Significant but Understudied Impact of Pathogen Transmission from Humans to Animals' (2009) 76(5) *Mount Sinai Journal of Medicine: A Journal of Translational and Personalized Medicine* 448; C. C. Tan, S. D. Lam, D. Richard, et al., 'Transmission of SARS-CoV-2 from Humans to Animals and Potential Host Adaptation' (2022) 13(1) *Nature Communications* 2988; L. Fernández-Bastit, J. Vergara-Alert, and J. Segalés, 'Transmission of Severe Acute Respiratory Syndrome Coronavirus 2 from Humans to Animals: Is There a Risk of Novel Reservoirs?' (2023) 63 *Current Opinion in Virology* 101365; M. Marrana, 'Chapter 3 – Epidemiology of Disease through the Interactions between Humans, Domestic Animals, and Wildlife' in Joana C. Prata, Ana Isabel Ribeiro and Teresa Rocha-Santos (eds.), *One Health* (Academic Press 2022).

[45] For more information on the links between forests and health, see: C. Beatty, M. Stevenson, P. Pacheco, A. Terrana, M. Folse, and A. Cody, 'The Vitality of Forests: Illustrating the Evidence Connecting Forests and Human Health' (World Wildlife Fund – WWF, 2022). Available at: www.worldwildlife.org/publications/the-vitality-of-forests-illustrating-the-evidence-connecting-forests-and-human-health. On forests and heat, see: J. Palmer, 'No Escape from the Heat: The Cost of Deforestation on Human and Animal Health' (2022) 72(11) *BioScience* 1037. For a broad overview on forest and health, see, also: C. J. P. Colfer, D. Sheil, and M. Kishi, *Forests and Human Health: Assessing the Evidence* (Center for International Forestry Research, 2006). Also see Karjalainen 'Promoting Human Health through Forests'.

[46] Bougas, 'Service Contract on EU Policy on Forest Products and Deforestation'.

[47] On this, see also: Ronald M. Atlas, 'One Health: Its Origins and Future' in J. Mackenzie, M. Jeggo, P. Daszak, and J. Richt (eds.), *One Health: The Human-Animal-Environment Interfaces in Emerging Infectious Diseases Current Topics in Microbiology and Immunology*, vol. 365 (Springer, 2012); John S. Mackenzie and Martyn Jeggo, 'The One Health Approach – Why Is It So Important?' (2019) 4(2) *Tropical Medicine and Infectious Disease* 88.

[48] World Health Organisation – WHO, 'One Health' (2017). Available at: www.who.int/news-room/q-a-detail/one-health; World Organisation for Animal Health – OIE, 'One Health "at a Glance"' (n.d.). Available at: www.oie.int/en/for-the-media/onehealth/; World Health Organisation – WHO, 'Tripartite (FAO, OIE, WHO) and UNEP support OHHLEP's definition of "One Health"' (n.d.). Available at: www.who.int/news/item/01-12-2021-tripartite-and-unep-support-ohhlep-s-definition-of-one-health.

[49] See, e.g.: Centers for Diseases Control and Prevention, 'One Health Basics' (n.d.). Available at: www.cdc.gov/onehealth/basics/index.html#:~:text=One%20Health%20is%20a%20collaborative,plants%2C%20and%20their%20shared%20environment. World Health Organisation – WHO, 'One Health'.

elements, it can be an excellent tool in the pursuit of more effective measures and actions for problems that involve a systems approach.

Given that each of these nexuses forms part of the One Health approach, strategies tackling even one of its elements could be regarded as a factual operationalisation of the approach, perhaps even when the connection is not explicitly considered. Indeed, a One Health approach also implies the need to reduce human pressure on the environment, which could be seen as a medical intervention in itself, and calls for better integration of environmental and wildlife issues to address challenges related to disease spillover.[50]

In particular, given that the origins and roots of diseases can often be found in ecological systems and their management, integrating ecological approaches along with the more 'traditional' biomedical approaches would make for a comprehensive and balanced disease prevention strategy.[51] In this sense, ecological countermeasures (strategic conservation and restoration of nature and, hence, the mitigation of risks for at-risk humans) can prevent spillovers and protect human and animal health, with the added benefit of addressing climate change and biodiversity loss.[52] In the optic of disease prevention in relation to ecological approaches, the focus would be on maintaining habitat integrity, heterogeneity, and connectivity to prevent new interfaces enabling disease emergence and spread.[53] From a legal standpoint, this would translate into establishing measures with protective, conservation, and restoration goals, which, if sufficiently ambitious and well implemented, could have positive One Health implications from a prevention angle.

That said, pandemic and disease policy discussions generally focus more on enhancing preparedness and response.[54] It has also been noted that the environmental sector is often forgotten or left to the sidelines in national and global strategies for pandemic preparedness and mitigation,[55] and that current health security priorities and planning neglect the significant role of environmental factors in pandemic and disease prevention.[56]

Tentative steps to further include the environmental element or environmental protection as a prevention measure have been attempted in the draft of the World Health

[50] 'One Health: A Call for Ecological Equity' (2023) 401(10372) *Lancet* 169.

[51] Raina K. Plowright, A. N. Ahmed, T. Coulson, et al., 'Ecological Countermeasures to Prevent Pathogen Spillover and Subsequent Pandemics' (2024) 15(1) *Nature Communications* 2577. Along these lines, see also: Daszak, 'Workshop Report on Biodiversity and Pandemics of the Intergovernmental Platform on Biodiversity and Ecosystem Services'; A. S. Bernstein, A. W. Ando, T. Loch-Temzelides, et al., 'The Costs and Benefits of Primary Prevention of Zoonotic Pandemics' (2022) 8(5) *Science Advances*; United Nations Environment Programme and International Livestock Research Institute, 'Preventing the Next Pandemic: Zoonotic Diseases and how to Break the Chain of Transmission' (2020). Available at: www.unep.org/resources/report/preventing-future-zoonotic-disease-outbreaks-protecting-environment-animals-and; M. N. Hayek, 'The Infectious Disease Trap of Animal Agriculture' (2022) 8(44) *Science Advances*.

[52] Plowright et al., 'Ecological Countermeasures'.

[53] Ibid.

[54] Neil M. Vora, L. Hannah, S. Lieberman, M. M. Vale, R. K. Plowright, and A. S. Bernstein, 'Want to Prevent Pandemics? Stop Spillovers' (2022) 605(7910) *Nature* 419; Pallavi A. Kache, S. Cook, N. Sizer, L. Hannah, and N. M. Vora, 'Urgent Need for Integrated Pandemic Policies on Pathogen Spillover' (2021) 5(10) *The Lancet Planetary Health* e668. As considered in: Plowright, 'Ecological Countermeasures to Prevent Pathogen Spillover and Subsequent Pandemics'.

[55] See, e.g, Kache, 'Urgent Need for Integrated Pandemic Policies on Pathogen Spillover'. S. H. Olson, A. E. Fine, M. Pruvot, L. O. Keatts, and C. Walzer, 'Ground Zero for Pandemic Prevention: Reinforcing Environmental Sector Integration' (2023) 8(10) *BMJ Global Health*.

[56] Catherine Machalaba, M. Uhart, M. Ryser-Degiorgis, and W. B. Karesh, 'Gaps in Health Security Related to Wildlife and Environment Affecting Pandemic Prevention and Preparedness, 2007–2020' (2021) 99(5) *Bulletin of the World Health Organization* 342; Olson, 'Ground Zero for Pandemic Prevention'.

Organisation's Pandemic Treaty (yet to be adopted at the time of writing).[57] Article 4, dedicated to pandemic prevention, recognises that certain factors increase the risk of pandemics (i.e. environmental, climatic, social, anthropogenic, and economic factors), and places importance in their identification and in their consideration in the development and implementation of relevant policies, strategies, and measures at the international, regional, and national levels. Additionally, Article 5, where the One Health approach is further addressed after its definition in Article 1, expresses the commitment of the parties to identify and address the drivers of pandemics and the emergence and re-emergence of diseases at the interface between humans, animals, and the environment by introducing and integrating interventions into relevant pandemic plans.[58]

Lastly, Article 3 includes the best available science and evidence as the basis for public health decisions for pandemic prevention among the principles guiding the parties:[59] theoretically, this could also include science advocating for area-based measures or other types of protective measures to maintain the integrity and coherence of habitats.[60]

The above considerations denote that the inclusion of environmental considerations and environmental law measures in the fight against diseases in a One Health fashion is not as straightforward as one might expect; they do not mean to convey that overlaps do not exist in current legislation. Indeed, in the EU, a notable example of the integration of environmental and health considerations under one text is the Waste Framework Directive, where both environmental and human health protection have a prominent role.[61]

Additionally, it should be noted that environmental law instruments have, at almost all times, developed independently from human health considerations.[62] This could be valid for the EU Nature Directives and for the Regulation on Deforestation-Free Products on forestry supply chains, which may nonetheless indirectly contribute to health objectives.

9.4 REGULATION 2023/1115 ON DEFORESTATION-FREE PRODUCTS: A REGULATION WITH A (HIDDEN) HEALTH DIMENSION?

9.4.1 *Preliminary Observations*

The Regulation is part of a broader set of actions meant to address deforestation and forest degradation delineated in the European Green Deal:[63] the Biodiversity Strategy,[64] the Forest Strategy,[65]

57 Proposal for the WHO Pandemic Agreement (A/INB/9/3 Rev.1 – 22 April 2024) Resumed Ninth Meeting of the Intergovernmental Negotiating Body to Draft and Negotiate a WHO Convention, Agreement or Other International Instrument on Pandemic Prevention, Preparedness and Response, Provisional Agenda Item 2.

58 Ibid.

59 Ibid.

60 It should be noted that these provisions have yet to be agreed at the time of writing.

61 Directive 2008/98/EC of the European Parliament and of the Council of 19 November 2008 on Waste and Repealing Certain Directives (2008) OJ L312/3. Articles 1 and 13.

62 For more on this see Chapter 5.

63 European Commission, 'The European Green Deal' (Communication) COM (2019) 640 final, 11 December 2019. Available at: https://eur-lex.europa.eu/legal-content/EN/TXT/?qid=1576150542719&uri=COM%3A2019%3A640%3AFIN.

64 European Commission, 'EU Biodiversity Strategy for 2030. Bringing Nature Back into our Lives' (Communication) COM (2020) 380 final, 20 May 2020. Available at: https://eur-lex.europa.eu/legal-content/EN/TXT/?uri=celex%3A52020DC0380.

65 European Commission, 'New EU Forest Strategy for 2030 – To Improve the Quantity and Quality of EU Forests' (n.d.). Available at: https://environment.ec.europa.eu/strategy/forest-strategy_en.

the Farm to Fork Strategy,[66] and the Commission's Communication on stepping up EU action to protect and restore the world forests.[67] Together with the provisional agreement on the Nature Restoration Law concluded at the end of 2023 and its adoption in 2024 (which also covers forest ecosystems in the EU),[68] the Deforestation-free Products Regulation represents a significant step forward in the protection of the environment – forests in particular – both in the EU and in third countries.

The Regulation requires that the products it covers (products that contain, have been fed, or have been made with certain commodities, i.e. cattle, cocoa, coffee, oil palm, rubber, soya, and wood) are 'deforestation-free'. This marks a bold difference from the EU Timber Regulation,[69] which only focused on the legal provenance of timber products and which is repealed by this new Regulation. Indeed, a significant part of ongoing deforestation is legal according to the laws of the country of production,[70] meaning that focusing only on the legality element has not been entirely effective.[71] The Regulation is meant to fill these gaps to minimise the connected risk of lowered environmental standards to obtain market access.[72]

9.4.2 *The (Hidden) Link with the One Health Approach*

The Regulation is, quite clearly, an environmental measure. Yet, it also has links to human and animal health. Indeed, addressing the link between land and health should be considered as belonging to a wider One Health strategy for disease emergence and spread, an environment-targeted operationalisation of the One Health approach as an integrated approach.[73]

As observed above, measures on nature and forest protection, conservation, and restoration, if sufficiently ambitious, may have positive One Health implications. Most notably, efforts to keep forests intact in the EU and outside the EU constitute an expression of the One Health approach in the form of preventative action. Targeting value chains and supply chains connected to deforestation and forest degradation, which is what the Regulation is set out to accomplish from the European Union's side, may be considered one of these preventative actions.

The relevance of the Regulation and its measures would be higher in relation to the comprehensive nexus connecting humans, animals, and the environment, but it is also noticeable with

66 European Commission, 'A Farm to Fork Strategy for a Fair, Healthy and Environmentally-friendly Food System' (Communication) COM (2020) 381 final, 20 May 2020. Available at: https://eur-lex.europa.eu/legal-content/EN/TXT/?uri=celex:52020DC0381.

67 European Commission, 'Stepping up EU Action to Protect and Restore the World's Forests'.

68 Council of the European Union, 'Interinstitutional Agreement or Provisional Deal on the Proposal for Regulation of the European Parliament and of the Council on Nature Restoration'.

69 Regulation (EU) 995/2010 of the European Parliament and of the Council of 20 October 2010 Laying Down the Obligations of Operators who Place Timber and Timber Products on the Market (2010) OJ L295/23.

70 See: C.Dummett, A. Blundell, K. Canby, M. Wolosin, and E. Bodnar, *Illicit Harvest, Complicit Goods: The State of Illegal Deforestation for Agriculture* (Forest Policy Trade and Finance Initiative Report, 2021) 3.

71 European Commission, 'Commission Staff Working Document – Fitness Check on Regulation (EU) No 995/2010 of the European Parliament and of the Council of 20 October 2010 Laying Down the Obligations of Operators who Place Timber and Timber Products on the Market (the EU Timber Regulation) and on Regulation (EC) No 2173/2005 of 20 December 2005 on the Establishment of a FLEGT Licensing Scheme for Imports of Timber into the European Community (FLEGT Regulation)' SWD(2021) 328 final, 17 November 2021.

72 See: Regulation 2023/1115 of 31 May 2023, Deforestation-free Products Regulation. Recital 34.

73 See, e.g.: United Nations Convention to Combat Desertification, 'Supporting the Global Response to the COVID-19 Pandemic: Land-based Solutions for Healthy People and a Healthy Planet' (2020). Available at: www.unccd.int/sites/default/files/documents/2020-06/1498_UNCCD_%20Covid_%20layout-low%20res-1.pdf.

respect to the individual nexuses of the One Health approach, especially the animal–environmental and environmental–human health nexuses.

That said, the protection of human and animal health in keeping with a One Health approach is not among the goals of the Regulation (Article 1). Preambular 20 of the Regulation, recalling the importance of measures against deforestation and forest degradation for achieving the Sustainable Development Goals (SDGs), does state that the Regulation should contribute to meeting the goals of SDG 3 – good health and well-being – among others,[74] but this is not reflected in the Articles and Article 1 in particular, which only expressly considers the link of deforestation and forest degradation with climate change and biodiversity.

Considering the above, it can be wondered how effective the Regulation could be in tackling deforestation and forest degradation, and thus be instrumental from a One Health perspective.

While it is true that most commodities may be consumed at the local or regional level, it is crucial to account for the relevance of imports and exports. The EU consumption of products such as palm oil, cattle, soy, cocoa, coffee, timber, and rubber, also in their processed forms, accounts for 10 per cent of the global share of deforestation and forest degradation when considering the total final consumption (which is, then, deforestation embodied in the consumption).[75] In this sense, tackling these commodities through Union policy intervention could bring the highest benefits for the unit value of trade,[76] and demand-side action seemed to hold the most substantial potential to deliver the EU's commitments and ensure increased sustainability in supply practices:[77] indeed, the more significant the EU consumption and, thus, intra and extra EU imports, the larger the leverage can be expected from EU action targeting deforestation and forest degradation.[78]

Further, from the list of commodities covered (wood, cattle, cocoa, coffee, palm oil, rubber, and soya), it can immediately be noted how this instrument could be interesting to consider from a One Health perspective. First, forest activities and forest work, which could be associated with any commodity linked to deforestation, are among the epidemiological risk factors for certain zoonotic diseases,[79] and a higher risk of deforestation for different commodities would likely be carried onto the epidemiological risk. A second relevant matter is the possibility of detrimental practices in the cultivation of these commodities. For example, palm oil plantations not only involve deforestation and biodiversity loss,[80] but are also linked to respiratory illnesses and pollution.[81] Third, and this specifically concerns the rearing of cattle, not only would deforestation be carried out to make space for cattle with all the environmental

74 Regulation 2023/1115 of 31 May 2023, Deforestation-free Products Regulation. Recital 20.

75 Cuypers, 'The Impact of EU Consumption on Deforestation'. See, also: European Commission, 'Stepping up EU Action to Protect and Restore the World's Forests'.

76 Regulation 2023/1115 of 31 May 2023, Deforestation-free Products Regulation. Recital 38.

77 European Commission, 'Commission Staff Working Document – Accompanying the Document "Stepping up EU Action to Protect and Restore the World's Forests"' SWD (2019) 307 final, 23 July 2019. Available at: https://commission.europa.eu/system/files/2019-07/communication-eu-action-protect-restore-forests_swd_en.pdf.

78 See: Bougas, 'Service Contract on EU Policy on Forest Products and Deforestation'.

79 E.g: A. Y. Vittor, B. Armien, P. Gonzalez, et al., 'Epidemiology of Emergent Madariaga Encephalitis in a Region with Endemic Venezuelan Equine Encephalitis: Initial Host Studies and Human Cross-sectional Study in Darien, Panama' (2016) 10(4) *PLoS Neglected Tropical Diseases* e0004554; A. Erhart et al., 'Epidemiology of Forest Malaria in Central Vietnam: A Large Scale Cross-sectional Survey' (2005) 4(1) *Malaria Journal* 1.

80 V. Vijay, S. L. Pimm, C. N. Jenkins, and S. J. Smith, 'The Impacts of Oil Palm on Recent Deforestation and Biodiversity Loss' (2016) 11(7) *PloS one* e0159668.

81 S. Kadandale, R. Marten, and R. Smith, 'The Palm Oil Industry and Noncommunicable Diseases' (2019) 97(2) *Bulletin of the World Health Organization* 118.

issues that this would entail, but cattle rearing in deforested land could lead to increased contacts between wildlife or disease vectors, farm animals, and humans.[82]

Finally, the Regulation covers the supply chain of the concerned products deriving from these commodities (imports and exports), meaning that it can be considered as having some extraterritorial (extra-EU) effects, potentially making the Regulation a measure of global interest.[83] Indeed, the responsibility in relation to ensuring deforestation-free or forest degradation-free supply chains is placed on EU-based companies, but the impact of complying with the due diligence requirements is likely to be felt also in third countries.[84]

What is more, the Regulation may encourage non-EU countries to take (similar) protective measures, which could be beneficial for forests and, in turn, for human and animal health: while the Regulation does not create obligations for non-EU countries (it does so only for operators and traders, EU member states, and competent authorities), it introduces facilitations for the tasks of companies under this Regulation if non-EU countries have undertaken actions to enhance deforestation-free supply chains and reinforce traceability systems on commodities.[85]

9.4.3 *Structural Elements of the Regulation Having Relevance from a One Health Perspective*

9.4.3.1 *Matters of Scope and Definitions*

With the scope of the Regulation, the concepts to consider are those of 'relevant commodities' (wood, cattle, cocoa, coffee, palm oil, rubber, and soya)[86] and of 'relevant products' ('products listed in Annex I that contain, have been fed with or have been made using relevant commodities').[87]

It is essential to note that the Regulation only applies to the 'relevant products'. Cumulatively with the concept of relevant commodities, the notion of 'relevant products' helps more precisely identify the scope and the reach of the Regulation. However, it also *limits* its scope: with a list of defined products, there may be significant gaps concerning products that are not included in Annex I, and that contain, have been made, or have been fed with the relevant commodities.[88] This could limit the effectiveness of the Regulation in tackling deforestation phenomena.

Further, one of the most important definitions in this Regulation is the definition of 'forest'. This definition is crucial for the scope of the legal act because the Regulation is built around the additional (and also critical) concepts of 'deforestation' and 'forest degradation', which can only occur in what is considered a 'forest' by the law. The definition of 'forest' in

[82] See, e.g.: D. I. Ortiz, M. Piche-Ovares, L. M. Romero-Vega, J. Wagman, and A. Troyo, 'The Impact of Deforestation, Urbanization, and Changing Land Use Patterns on the Ecology of Mosquito and Tick-borne Diseases in Central America' (2022) 13(1) *Insects* 20.

[83] It should be noted that an analysis on the compatibility with World Trade Organisation rules is not within the scope of this contribution but is an important element for the viability and operability of this Regulation.

[84] See: European Commission, 'Implementation of the EU Deforestation Regulation – Traceability' (n.d.). Available at: https://green-business.ec.europa.eu/implementation-eu-deforestation-regulation/traceability_en.

[85] See: ibid., More in Section 9.4.3 herein.

[86] Regulation 2023/1115 of 31 May 2023, Deforestation-free Products Regulation. Article 2(1).

[87] Regulation 2023/1115 of 31 May 2023, Deforestation-free Products Regulation. Article 2(2).

[88] To be noted: the list might be amended to include additional products following a Commission assessment. Ibid., Article 34(3).

the Regulation[89] mirrors the FAO definition of forest.[90] This was a conscious choice as it was considered (particularly by the EU Council)[91] that the definitions in the Regulation should be built on internationally agreed concepts.[92] Accordingly, 'forest' in the Regulation is defined as: 'land spanning more than 0,5 hectares with trees higher than 5 metres and a canopy cover of more than 10 per cent, or trees able to reach those thresholds in situ, excluding land that is predominantly under agricultural or urban land use'.[93]

Given that the Regulation is built around the concept of 'forest', other ecosystems that are not 'forest', which could also be interesting to protect from a One Health perspective, are not covered by the Regulation. Forests are not the only ecosystems impacted by economic activities, and forest protection should not lead to the conversion or degradation of other natural ecosystems.[94] With this in mind, the possibility of extending the scope beyond forests was embedded in the law,[95] particularly with regard to land with high carbon stocks and with high biodiversity value, such as grassland, peatlands, and wetlands[96] (with the potential challenges from a One Health point of view),[97] as these are also increasingly under pressure from conversion and degradation due to commodity production for the EU market.[98]

Two other crucial definitions are those of 'deforestation' and 'forest degradation', which also carry the scope of the Regulation: the legal act is dedicated to market access and the export of deforestation-free products, and being 'deforestation-free' is one of the criteria for market access and export.[99]

The Regulation defines 'deforestation' as 'the conversion of forest to agricultural use, whether human-induced or not',[100] where 'agricultural use' is 'the use of land for the purpose of agriculture, including for agricultural plantations and set-aside agricultural areas, and for rearing livestock'.[101] It should be noted that 'deforestation' only includes situations of forest clearance for subsequent agricultural use, be it plant or animal agriculture, thus leaving out other important types of deforestation such as deforestation for infrastructure,[102] which is a relevant aspect for

[89] Ibid.

[90] See: P. Holmgren and R. Davis, 'FRA 2000. On Definitions of Forest and Forest Change' (Food and Agriculture Organization – FAO, Forestry Department. Working Paper 33, Rome, 2000). Note that the FAO definition of forest was criticised: Rainforest Movement et al., 'Open Letter from Various NGOs to FAO on the Occasion of the International Day of Forests 2014' (2014). Available at: www.wrm.org.uy/all-campaigns/open-letter-to-fao-on-the-occasion-of-the-international-day-of-forests-2014.

[91] Council of the European Union, 'Council General Approach – Draft Regulation of the European Parliament and of the Council on the Making Available on the Union Market as well as Export from the Union of Certain Commodities and Products Associated with Deforestation and Forest Degradation and Repealing Regulation (EU) No. 995/2010 – General approach' (2022). Point no. 12.

[92] Regulation 2023/1115 of 31 May 2023, Deforestation-free Products Regulation. See Recital 44.

[93] Ibid., Article 2(4).

[94] Regulation 2023/1115 of 31 May 2023, Deforestation-free Products Regulation. See Recital 82.

[95] Ibid., Articles 31(1) and (2).

[96] Ibid.

[97] In particular, the management of wetlands represents an interesting challenge in relation to disease control. On this, see: P. E. R. Dale and J. M. Knight, 'Wetlands and Mosquitoes: A Review' (2008) 16 *Wetlands Ecology and Management* 255. See also: C. M. Finlayson and P. Horwitz, 'Wetlands as Settings for Human Health – The Benefits and the Paradox' in C. Max Finlayson, Pierre Horwitz and Philip M. Weinstein (eds.), *Wetlands and Human Health* (Springer, 2015).

[98] Regulation 2023/1115 of 31 May 2023, Deforestation-free Products Regulation, Recital 82.

[99] Regulation 2023/1115 of 31 May 2023, Deforestation-free Products Regulation. Article 3(a).

[100] Ibid., Article 2(3).

[101] Ibid., Article 2(5).

[102] See also the analysis of: B. G. Da Silva and P.-N. Milcamps, 'The Regulation on Deforestation-Free Products: When the EU Takes on Deforestation's Corrupted Roots' (2023) 32(6) *European Energy and Environmental Law Review* 293–310.

health considerations. With regard to this definition, questions arise in the case of deforestation aimed at timber harvesting not followed by conversion to agricultural or other use, as this does not seem to be included in the realm of situations covered by the definition of deforestation or forest degradation.

The definition of 'forest degradation' covers structural changes to forest cover in the form of specific forms of conversion: 'conversion of (a) primary forests or naturally regenerating forests into plantation forests or into other wooded land; or (b) primary forests into planted forests'.[103]

There is no definition of what *degradation* is beyond the indicated types of conversion. The justification for this specific choice is that it would make it possible to act quickly and in a manner that is instantly measurable and verifiable. This would be, at least, the initial definition, potentially subject to future expansion in the revision of the text.[104] While these reasons have some merit, opting for such a definition might lead to other types of degradation not being covered, such as timber harvesting not followed by conversion. That said, the door was left open (with careful wording) for reconsidering the definition of 'forest degradation', taking into account progress made in international discussions and forest diversity worldwide, after an in-depth analysis has been conducted regarding that process.[105]

9.4.3.2 *Requirements for 'Access' to, or Export from, the EU Market*

The commodities and products covered by the Regulation must meet certain requirements to be placed or made available on the EU market or exported from the EU.

The requirements are cumulatively indicated in Article 3: such products and commodities (1) must be deforestation-free, (2) must be produced following the relevant legislation of the country of production, and (3) must be covered by a due diligence statement.[106]

The status of 'deforestation-free', which also relies on the definitions above, indicates that only certain products can be considered 'deforestation-free' within the meaning of the Regulation: deforestation-free products are those that have not caused deforestation *or* forest degradation.[107] In principle, any commodity originating from a situation of deforestation or conversion to a plantation or planted forest is regarded as *not* deforestation-free, affecting the possibility of placing or making it available on the EU market or exporting it, as per Article 3.

This makes for a particularly interesting element from both environmental protection and a One Health perspective as it provides incisiveness to the Regulation by identifying clear and important consequences and, thus, potentially discouraging types of practices linked to deforestation and forest degradation worldwide.

The criterion of the legality of production relies necessarily on the definition of 'relevant legislation of the country of production'. Interestingly, the definition includes not only land-use rights, environmental protection, and forest-related rules (e.g. forest management and biodiversity conservation) but also the rights of third parties; labour rights and human rights protected under international law; the principle of free, prior, and informed consent; and tax,

[103] Regulation 2023/1115 of 31 May 2023, Deforestation-free Products Regulation. Article 2(7).

[104] Council of the European Union, 'Council General Approach – Draft Regulation of the European Parliament and of the Council on the Making Available on the Union Market as well as Export from the Union of Certain Commodities and Products Associated with Deforestation and Forest Degradation and Repealing Regulation (EU) No. 995/2010 – General approach'. Point no. 13.

[105] Regulation 2023/1115 of 31 May 2023, Deforestation-free Products Regulation. Articles 34(6) and Recital 44.

[106] Regulation 2023/1115 of 31 May 2023, Deforestation-free Products Regulation. Article 3.

[107] Ibid., Article 2(13).

anti-corruption, trade, and customs regulations.[108] While some criticisms can be formulated,[109] this broad definition of relevant legislation also makes the Regulation more incisive, with clear consequences.

The third criterion is related to the presence of a due diligence statement, entailing a due diligence process that operators have to carry out for all relevant products supplied by each supplier.[110] The due diligence system is a mechanism to ensure that the criteria of Article 3 (a) and (b) are complied with. Unless a simplified form of due diligence can be performed,[111] the 'standard' due diligence system foresees robust requirements in terms of: (1) mandatory information and proof;[112] (2) a robust risk assessment system to guarantee that there is no or only negligible risk that the products are not in line with Article 3;[113] and (3) a system of risk mitigation for those cases where the risk assessment has revealed that there is a risk or a non-negligible risk of non-compliance with the requirements in Article 3.[114]

These due diligence rules present a comprehensive due diligence system that should be effective in 'ferreting out' non-deforestation-free and illegal products or commodities along the supply chain and indirectly contributing to the protection of the environment in the country of origin, thus strengthening the environmental–animal–human health nexus of the One Health framework.[115]

9.4.3.3 *Three-Tier System Regarding the Assessment of Countries*

The three-tier system is envisaged in Article 29; it involves the assessment and classification of countries or parts of countries into three risk categories following an assessment: high-risk, low-risk, and standard-risk, respectively qualifying countries or parts of thereof where there is a corresponding risk of having relevant products not complying with the deforestation-free criterion (Article 3(a)).[116] The assessment needs to be based on certain criteria[117] but may also consider additional criteria, such as information submitted by NGOs and other parties (e.g. Indigenous people), and transparency (or lack thereof) of the country concerned.[118]

Such classification as low- or high-risk countries determines certain consequences. For example, products or commodities produced in low-risk countries enjoy certain facilitations, the most important of which is simplified due diligence.[119]

The classification of countries according to a risk assessment is an interesting feature of the Regulation. If properly and objectively carried out, it could help modulate the efforts concerning the risks identified in the assessment and recognise the most problematic situations concerning deforestation and forest degradation, potentially generating positive environmental

108 Ibid., Article 2(40).
109 Da Silva, 'The Regulation on Deforestation-Free Products'.
110 Regulation 2023/1115 of 31 May 2023, Deforestation-free Products Regulation. Article 8.
111 Ibid., Article 13.
112 Ibid., Article 9.
113 Ibid., Article 10.
114 Ibid., Article 11.
115 For a more detailed analysis, see: Da Silva, 'The Regulation on Deforestation-Free Products'. For an analysis of the initial Proposal (some elements were maintained in the final text), see: Client Earth, 'The Proposed EU Law on Deforestation-Free Products. What is in the European Commission's Proposal and what is Left Out?' (2021). Available at: www.clientearth.org/media/sbjhtw3c/eu-deforestation-proposal_main-elements-and-omissions_dec21.pdf.
116 Regulation 2023/1115 of 31 May 2023, Deforestation-free Products Regulation, Article 29(1).
117 Ibid., Article 29(3).
118 Ibid., Article 29(4).
119 Ibid., Article 13(1).

outcomes and positive effects on implementation and enforcement. This classification might also help steer consumption to safer (as in lower-risk) supply chains in low-risk countries due to the simplified due diligence required, and it might encourage higher-risk countries to take action against deforestation and forest degradation, with related health-connected outcomes. At the same time, aggregated assessments might overlook risks in key sourcing areas and risks associated with a specific supply chain.[120] With this in mind, the simplified due diligence as per Article 13 is, perhaps, too simplified as it represents quite a 'dispensation' from important provisions, warranting consideration of whether some form of risk assessment and risk mitigation should still be required.

9.5 DISCUSSION AND CONCLUSIONS: THE REGULATION AS PART OF A ONE HEALTH STRATEGIC APPROACH?

This chapter has highlighted the systemic importance of forests for the climate, the environment, and biodiversity and the specific value of forests for health, particularly in their role in disease regulation and of the interlinkages between climate change, environmental problems, biodiversity loss, and disease emergence and spread. This suggests that forest protection and care and avoiding deforestation and forest degradation should be a significant element of One Health-based preventative solutions.

The Deforestation-free Products Regulation inserts itself among the EU measures to counteract deforestation and forest degradation in the EU and abroad. The Regulation is bound to affect the supply chain of several products. While it might create additional burdens along the supply chains, it will be instrumental in ensuring that commodity and product production does not come at the price of deforestation and forest degradation.

The Regulation is a well-rounded text; it pays attention to many aspects related to forest commodities and their supply chain, deforestation, and forest degradation. It addresses not only the issue of the illegality of harvesting but also includes a more qualitative assessment with respect to deforestation and forest degradation with the central concept of 'deforestation-free'. Admittedly, the definitions of forest, deforestation, and forest degradation could be more in line with scientific concepts, and the Regulation could be extended to cover more commodities, products, and different ecosystems. However, overall, the final result seems sufficiently tight and ambitious. Additionally, it should be noted that the Regulation also foresees several types of obligations on the EU member states or competent authorities on checks, controls, and reporting obligations,[121] which are instrumental for the effective implementation and enforcement of the Regulation.

The Regulation is not meant to address human and animal health but 'only' to respond to the climate and biodiversity crises. However, without expressly saying so in its objectives, it can be appreciated how the Regulation promotes healthier and more intact ecosystems, likely with worldwide effects, and can work to mitigate climate change and biodiversity loss, all elements linked to the potential for better health outcomes for people and animals. The relatively high ambition of the text and its 'tightness' (potentially not allowing for many loopholes) can be sufficient to reap certain benefits from a health perspective, including by steering and encouraging the adoption of forest-friendly practices and modes of agriculture which reduce deforestation. The Regulation's incisiveness in relation to its implementation and enforcement is

[120] See: Client Earth, 'The Proposed EU Law on Deforestation-Free Products.'

[121] Regulation 2023/1115 of 31 May 2023, Deforestation-free Products Regulation, Article 16.

also an element of value for human and animal health, in addition to its obvious relevance for environmental health. In this perspective, the Regulation could serve as a way to kickstart the process of better forest care and protection outside the EU, complement the EU framework on nature protection and potentially contribute to disease prevention, especially if considered together with other vital measures (e.g. disease surveillance, public health measures) in true One Health fashion.

10

One Health among Many

What Can One Health Learn from EcoHealth and Planetary Health Projects to Encourage Legal Reform?

Jessica C. Tselepy and Jack Nagy

10.1 INTRODUCTION

In the pursuit of more meaningful legal integration, the One Health practitioner can greatly benefit by learning from the unique accomplishments of their interdisciplinary neighbours. Amid a thriving global interest in interdisciplinarity, now is an apt moment to critically examine what *applications* of interdisciplinarity beyond One Health have been most effective and what *lessons* can be drawn from these applications. This chapter examines three leading interdisciplinary approaches to health problems: One Health, EcoHealth, and Planetary Health. We focus on lessons that One Health practitioners can learn from projects that have implemented EcoHealth and Planetary Health approaches to address health problems effectively and achieve legal reform in Mexico, Uganda, Ecuador, and Sri Lanka. We argue that by prioritising community engagement and limiting project scope creep, One Health practitioners can both deliver better health outcomes and create more conducive conditions for legal reform to occur.

10.2 OVERVIEW OF THE HEALTH FRAMEWORKS

10.2.1 *Historical Development*

10.2.1.1 *One Health*

Current usage of the term 'One Health' can be most closely traced back to the 'One Medicine' concept coined by Calvin Schwabe in 1984 in his textbook *Veterinary Medicine and Human Health*.[1] This concept acknowledged the connection between the health of humans, animals, and ecosystems, and recognised that human and veterinary medicine could contribute to each other.[2] One Health perspectives have also been tied to writings ranging from the ancient world,[3]

1 J. S. Mackenzie, M. McKinnon, and M. Jeggo (eds.), *One Health: From Concept to Practice. Confronting Emerging Zoonoses: The One Health Paradigm*. 3rd ed. (2014) 163–189, citing C. W. Schwabe, *Veterinary Medicine and Human Health* (Baltimore: Williams and Wilkins 1984).

2 J. Zinsstag, E. Schelling, D. Waltner-Toews, and M. Tanner, 'From "One Medicine" to "One Health" and Systemic Approaches to Health and Well-being' (2011) 101(3–4) *Preventive Veterinary Medicine* 148–156 at 151.

3 Such as Charlotte Berg, who linked the One Health perspective to King Ashoka's (ca. 304 BCE to 232 BCE) Fourteen Rock Edicts. See H. Lerner and C. Berg, 'The Concept of Health in One Health and Some Practical Implications for Research and Education: What Is One Health?' (2015) 5(1) *Infection Ecology & Epidemiology* 1.

to the Enlightenment.[4] However, these associations primarily relate to the fact that medicine and health interventions do not always seek to exclusively benefit humans. Present-day uses of the term 'One Health' additionally emphasise wide interdisciplinary collaboration,[5] and certainly the use of the 'One Health' phrase specifically is comparatively modern.

Around the introduction of Schwabe's 'One Medicine' terminology, similar acknowledgements of interconnection grew within the veterinary field. In 2004, health experts gathered for a Wildlife Conservation Society (WCS) symposium and developed the Manhattan Principles, which highlight links between human, animal, and wildlife health as essential.[6] By 2007, the American Veterinary Medical Association (AVMA) and American Medical Association (AMA) had both adopted the phrase 'One Health' for their own initiatives.[7] The term increased in popularity leading up to the early–mid 2000s, and developed primarily within both an American context and a medical and veterinary context. This inceptive context continues to pervade One Health articles advocating for or applying the One Health concept: 23.5 per cent of the articles (between 2015–2021) analysed by Byomkesh et al. focused on veterinary medicine and another 19.1 per cent focused on public health.[8]

Although the 'One Health' framework has now become widely accepted and deployed by major international organisations – such as through the creation of the One Health High-Level Expert Panel (OHHLEP),[9] to advising the Food and Agriculture Organization (FAO), United Nations Environment Programme (UNEP), World Health Organization (WHO), and World Organisation for Animal Health (WOAH)[10] – the field retains many of its medicinal roots and perspectives. Additionally, One Health's grounding in public health has directed it towards top-down governance, planning, and surveillance strategies; bottom-up approaches (that is, 'grassroots' projects or emergent behaviours) may remain comparatively innovative within the One Health paradigm.[11]

10.2.1.2 *EcoHealth*

The term 'EcoHealth' was often used in co-occurring but not distinct or synonymous ways before concrete attempts were made to clarify its meaning. Lebel (2003) notably marked the emergence and consolidation of EcoHealth as 'an historical step', presenting it as an ecosystem-focused approach to health arising out of an appropriation of 'ecological knowledge

[4] See, for instance: When founding the first veterinary school in Lyon, France in 1761, Claude Bourgelat emphasised the importance of comparative biopathology in Samantha E. J. Gibbs and E. Paul J. Gibbs, 'The Historical, Present, and Future Role of Veterinarians in One Health' in J. Mackenzie, M. Jeggo, P. Daszak, and J. Richt (eds). *One Health: The Human-Animal-Environment Interfaces in Emerging Infectious Diseases: The Concept and Examples of a One Health Approach* (2013) 31–47, 33, citing W. R. Waters, M. V. Palmer, B. M. Buddle, et al. 'Bovine Tuberculosis Vaccine Research: Historical Perspectives and Recent Advances' (2012) 30(16) *Vaccine* 2611–2622.

[5] E. P. J. Gibbs, 'The Evolution of One Health: A Decade of Progress and Challenges for the Future' (2014) 174(4) *Veterinary Record* 85–91, at 85.

[6] Robert A. Cook, William B. Karesh, and Steven A. Osofsky, 'The Manhattan Principles' (WCS, 2021). Available at: https://oneworldonehealth.wcs.org/About-Us/Mission/The-Manhattan-Principles.aspx.

[7] Ibid.

[8] Talukder Byomkesh, Nilanjana Ganguli, Eunice Choi, Mohammadali Tofighi, Gary W. vanloon, and James Orbinski, 'Exploring the Nexus: Comparing and Aligning Planetary Health, One Health, and EcoHealth' (2024) 6 *Global Transitions* 66–75, at 70–71.

[9] World Health Organisation, 'One Health: Questions and Answers' (2017). Available at: www.who.int/news-room/questions-and-answers/item/one-health.

[10] The implications of this focus may be subject to subsequent review but are beyond the purview of this piece.

[11] C. Dos, S. Ribeiro, L. H. M. van de Burgwal, and B. J. Regeer, 'Overcoming Challenges for Designing and Implementing the One Health Approach: A Systematic Review of the Literature' (2019) 18(7) *One Health* 100085.

and methodology by the prescriptive sector of the social science' in the post-1950s period.[12] By the 1990s, even the (previously narrowly focused) veterinary field was specifically considering the role of ecosystems in its approach,[13] suggesting that EcoHealth perspectives evolved concurrently with One Health perspectives in that domain. The establishment of Canada's International Development Research Centre (IDRC) in 1996 represented one of the earliest milestones of a 'deliberately transdisciplinary approach' being used in a distinctively EcoHealth way and is now one of the foremost EcoHealth organisations in the world.[14]

By 2012, in Kunming, China, 105 persons from 38 countries attended the fourth biennial conference of the International Association for Ecology and Health (IAEH),[15] which included a workshop on 'ways to increase demand for EcoHealth-type research and practice', including a further attempt to clarify and define the EcoHealth approach.[16] By 2016, EcoHealth International (EI) was established 'building on the legacy of the International Association of Ecology and Health (founded in 2006)' and ostensibly overtaking its work.[17] In practice, EcoHealth appears to place the greatest emphasis on ecosystem disruptions and ecological knowledge.[18]

10.2.1.3 *Planetary Health*

Planetary Health is a relative newcomer to the field of interdisciplinary approaches to the global health scene. Formally conceived by the Rockefeller-Foundation-Lancet Commission in 2014, Planetary Health was preliminarily described as an 'attitude towards life and a philosophy for living [that] emphasises people, not diseases, and equity, not the creation of unjust societies'.[19] The Commission first met in Italy in 2014, and claimed to represent a 'diverse group of global experts in environmental health, medicine, biodiversity, and ecology'.[20]

Today, Planetary Health collaboration, research, and activism is primarily co-ordinated by the Planetary Health Alliance (PHA). The PHA has grown to a consortium of over 400 organisations from 60+ countries around the world and continues to cite the Commission report as the basis of its work.[21] By the time of Planetary Health's introduction, both One Health and EcoHealth had become widely known and consolidated paradigms, though academic interest in Planetary Health rose noticeably during 2019–2020.[22] Although the Commission's report explicitly mentions these two frameworks and encourages unity with them, it also seems to

[12] J. Lebel, 'Health: An Ecosystem Approach; The Issue, Case Studies, Lessons and Recommendations' (Ottawa: International Development Research Centre, 2003), vii.

[13] D. Waltner-Toews, 'Eco-Health: A Primer for Veterinarians' (2009) 50(5) *The Canadian Veterinary Journal* 519.

[14] Ibid., xii.

[15] Established by the IDRC in 2006. See E. Mi, E. Mi, and M. Jeggo, 'Where to Now for One Health and Ecohealth?' (2016) 13(1) *EcoHealth* at 12–17.

[16] J. Saint-Charles, J. Webb, A. Sanchez, H. Mallee, B. van Wendel de Joode, and H. Nguyen-Viet, 'EcoHealth as a Field: Looking Forward' (2014) 11 *EcoHealth* 300–307 at 301.

[17] EcoHealth International (2018) Home. Available at: www.EcoHealthinternational.org/.

[18] For instance, the top 'fundamental questions' for EcoHealth as listed by Byomkesh et al. were 'How do ecosystem changes and disruptions affect human health?' and 'How can traditional ecological knowledge be integrated with scientific research to inform EcoHealth interventions?': Talukder Byomkesh, 'Exploring the Nexus', 72.

[19] R. Horton, R. Beaglehole, R. Bonita, J. Raeburn, M. McKee, and S. Wall, 'From Public to Planetary Health: A Manifesto' (2014) 383(9920) *The Lancet* 847.

[20] R. Horton and S. Lo, 'Planetary Health: A New Science for Exceptional Action' (2015) 386(10007) *The Lancet* 1921–1922 at 1922.

[21] Planetary Health Alliance: About Us. Available at: www.planetaryhealthalliance.org/about-the-pha.

[22] Byomkesh et al. posit that this interest may have stemmed from the pandemic. See Talukder Byomkesh, 'Exploring the Nexus', 70.

have felt the burden of proving the need for yet another interdisciplinary approach; accordingly, it has taken more obvious steps to mark its conceptual distinction from the three frameworks considered.[23]

10.2.2 *Conceptual Comparisons*

10.2.2.1 *EcoHealth*

One Health and EcoHealth are similar in concept and scope, and major EcoHealth organisations often view their approach as complementary with (or even intrinsically dependent on) the One Health framework. The EcoHealth Alliance (EA), when operational, had professed to 'practice a One Health approach, incorporating the needs of humans, animals, and the environment in all dimensions of our work'.[24] Similarly, EI states that they 'collaborate with members of One Health and Planetary Health initiatives around the world'.[25]

Where there are foundational differences between One Health and EcoHealth, they seem likely to fade with increased interdisciplinary and inter-framework collaboration. For example, One Health may have drawn more from molecular- and micro-biological domains than EcoHealth, while EcoHealth gave greater emphasis to anthropological and rural/urban planning knowledge.[26] This gulf seems mostly a byproduct of their respective historical developments (rather than a genuine conceptual barrier between the two) and may disappear with time.

Broad similarities in concept and contributing expertise, however, do not guarantee that both frameworks will be implemented identically in practice. While both One Health and EcoHealth acknowledge and value the concept of ecosystem health in theory, it is difficult not to wonder if the active choice of the prefix 'Eco' (in 'EcoHealth') suggests a greater *felt* concern for ecosystem-centred health, analysis, and solutions. The One Health framework has often been criticised for gravitating towards human needs and outcomes, and is often viewed primarily as a public health framework;[27] an important caveat being One Health's historical involvement in animal treatment and prevention of zoonoses.

The EcoHealth system additionally placed 'participation' as one of its three original methodological pillars,[28] (although these have subsequently been expanded to six)[29] and continues to place a particularly high degree of emphasis on community engagement (among other forms of participation) and understanding of local context.[30] We shall return to both of these themes of emphasis on participation and ecosystem matters later.

[23] Notably by prioritising the importance of human health, but additionally the role of humans in creating environmental issues impacting human health. For instance, the top 'fundamental questions' for Planetary Health as listed by Byomkesh et al. were 'How do changes in earth systems affect human health?' and 'What are the fundamental drivers of environmental change and their impact on health?'. Ibid. 72.

[24] EcoHealth Alliance, 'Fiscal Year 2021 Annual Report' (2021). Available at: www.ecohealthalliance.org/wp-content/uploads/2023/03/FY2021-Annual-Report.pdf.

[25] EcoHealth International, 'Home' (2018). Available at: www.ecohealthinternational.org/.

[26] H. Lerner and C. Berg, 'A Comparison of Three Holistic Approaches to Health: One Health, Ecohealth, and Planetary Health' (2017) 4 *Frontiers in Veterinary Science* 163–166.

[27] See, generally, Jane Kotzmann and Morgan Stonebridge, 'Considering Zoonotic Disease Risk in Australia: An Analysis of the Adequacy of the Intensive Animal Agriculture Regulation' (2022) 45 *UNSWLJ* 1220. A. Davis and J. Sharp, 'Rethinking One Health: Emergent Human, Animal and Environmental Assemblages' (2020) 258 *Social Science & Medicine* 1.

[28] J. Lebel, 'EcoHealth and the Development World' (2004) 1 *EcoHealth* 325–326.

[29] Dominique F. Charron (ed.), 'EcoHealth Research in Practice: Innovative Applications of an Ecosystem Approach to Health' in *EcoHealth Research in Practice* (New York: Springer, 2011) 255–271.

[30] Talukder Byomkesh, 'Exploring the Nexus', 73.

10.2.2.2 *Planetary Health*

Compared to EcoHealth and even One Health, the Planetary Health approach is 'clearly anthropocentric and focuses primarily on human health'.[31] Although Planetary Health does take ecosystem and animal health into consideration (and climate change in particular), it does so almost *exclusively* with respect to their value and/or threat to humans and civilization. While the PHA expanded their goals in 2021 to also consider human effects on 'all life on Earth', the language used by the PHA and planetary health researchers is still skewed heavily towards human health. Similarly, although the One Health framework has been criticised for anthropocentrism (as above), its grounding in veterinary science and zoonoses *has*, at least, propagated a consideration of animal health (and related terms like 'wildlife', 'cattle', and 'poultry') heavily through related literature; a focus on animal welfare that Planetary Health research lacks in comparison.[32] While both frameworks have a tendency to put humans first, this tendency is more *central* to Planetary Health's early conception.

This anthropocentrism, however, cuts both ways. Where Planetary Health researchers are primarily interested in environmental factors that may harm human health, they are equally intensely focused on potential human catalysts behind those environmental factors. Myers (2006) suggests that at least six dimensions of human activity – climate disruption, pollution, destruction of biodiversity, biogeochemical interference, land use, and inducement of resource scarcity – trickle down into 'every dimension of our health and wellbeing' under a Planetary Health model.[33]

Planetary Health also focuses on empowering communities to create a planet that 'nourishes and sustains the diversity of life with which we coexist and depend' and highlights 'collective action at every level of society'.[34] The Commission characterises those citizens they seek to include in solution-building as having been 'often marginalised by prevailing sociopolitical systems and who are most susceptible to disruptions in natural systems'.[35] Of the three frameworks considered here, Planetary Health perhaps assigns the greatest recognition of the role of institutional and governance failures (as a consequence of 'prevailing sociopolitical systems').

This approach is thus somewhat divergent from both One Health and EcoHealth in emphasising 'governance challenges' as one of their three categories of challenges.[36] The Commission describes this challenge as including 'how governments and institutions delay recognition and responses to threats, especially when faced with uncertainties, pooled common resources, and time lags between actions and effect'.[37] Likewise, the Commission stresses the importance of economic reform strategies, describing Planetary Health as an 'unprecedented opportunity for advocacy of global and national reforms of taxes and subsidies for many sectors of the economy'.[38]

[31] H. Lerner, 'A Comparison of Three Holistic Approaches to Health', 6.

[32] Rafael Ruiz de Castañeda, Jennifer Villersa, Carlos A. Faerron Guzmánc, et al., 'One Health and Planetary Health Research: Leveraging Differences to Grow Together' (2023) 7(2) *The Lancet Planetary Health* e109–e111 at e109.

[33] S. Myers, 'Planetary Health: Protecting Human Health on a Rapidly Changing Planet' (2006) 390(10114) *The Lancet* 2860–2868.

[34] R. Horton, R. Beaglehole, R. Bonita, J. Raeburn, M. McKee, and S. Wall, 'From Public to Planetary Health: A Manifesto' (2014) 383(9920) *The Lancet* 847.

[35] Sarah Whitmee, Andy Haines, Chris Beyrer, et al., 'Safeguarding Human Health in the Anthropocene Epoch: Report of The Rockefeller Foundation–Lancet Commission on Planetary Health' (2015) 386(10007) *The Lancet* 1973–2028 at 2017.

[36] The other two being 'imagination' and 'research and information' challenges.

[37] Whitmee, 'Safeguarding Human Health in the Anthropocene Epoch', 1973.

[38] Ibid.

TABLE 10.1 *Key Differentiating Elements between the One Health, Eco Health and Planetary Health Frameworks*

Framework	Key Differentiating Elements
One Health	• Aims to improve the health of humans, animals, and the environment. • Primarily grounded in veterinary, medical, and public health sciences (despite growing interdisciplinarity). • Broadly considers 'health' as a specific property that an individual human or animal may possess.[39] • Projects and initiatives are generally top-down and reactive to health issues; particularly zoonoses, epidemics, etc.
Eco Health	• Aims to improve the health of humans, animals, and the environment. • Primarily grounded in veterinary, medical, ecological, anthropological, and community planning sciences. • Conceives of 'health' equally as an individual attribute and an aggregate property of (eco)systems.[40] • Likely bias towards ecosystem-focused perspectives and solutions. • Likely bias towards participatory approaches, particularly emphasising community engagement.
Planetary Health	• Aims to improve the health of humans as its primary goal (considering animal and ecosystem health, but through an anthropocentric lens). • Primarily grounded in climate, agricultural, and ecological sciences. • Likely bias towards root cause analysis and identifying human impacts on the environment that later harm humans. • Likely bias towards participatory approaches; particularly emphasising legal, institutional, and governance roadblocks to long-term solutions.

In this way, the Planetary Health approach is inherently political in a way that One Health and EcoHealth are not. Where the other two approaches typically view community engagement as a means of achieving better outcomes within individual health projects, Planetary Health is the most forthright (right from its initial conception via manifesto) about the inextricability of legal and institutional reform from health outcomes; importing perhaps a wider view of project efficacy than the other two approaches.

10.2.3 *Key Differentiating Elements*

As interdisciplinary frameworks undergoing constant evolution, each of our three approaches lack 'any generally, centrally agreed definitions, and are sometimes handled as almost synonymous, sometimes as overlapping and sometimes as quite distinctly separate'.[41] However, strictly for the purposes of this chapter, let us establish some key differentiating elements of each approach below, with an emphasis on conceptual differences that (although necessarily reductionist) will serve as useful premises for the remainder of this chapter's analysis. These elements can be found in Table 10.1.

39 Ibid.
40 Ibid.
41 Lerner, 'A Comparison of Three Holistic Approaches to Health', 163–166.

10.3 PATHWAYS TO LEGAL REFORM

10.3.1 *Direct Legal Reform*

If we seek to discover what One Health can learn from other health frameworks (in the context of seeking the institutionalisation of One Health into legal and governance structures), we must begin by answering two questions. First, what is the current status of these health frameworks in law and governance? Second, what is their *desired* status?

Let us begin with the current legal status of these health frameworks. As outlined elsewhere in this book, explicit recognition of the One Health approach in binding federal or international law is comparatively limited.[42] Although One Health has clearly formed the basis of many international collaborations and policy guidelines – and is now championed in several United Nations resolutions – it is difficult to determine the extent of any direct causal role that One Health has played in effecting permanent legislative change. Where legal instruments are implicitly compatible with a One Health approach, it typically remains an open question as to how concretely One Health informed that legal instrument's development (as opposed to being developed or popularised in tandem).

EcoHealth and Planetary Health currently possess even more limited, if any, overt recognition in federal or international legislation. This is naturally to be expected, given their relative youth as formalised frameworks, but similarly makes it difficult to assess their direct impact on legislative and governance structures. Assessments of international law from EcoHealth and Planetary Health perspectives tend to regard the landscape as 'fragmented' and 'weak',[43] suggesting that the authors do not perceive the legal instruments considered as strongly aligned with EcoHealth or Planetary Health aspirations.

Let us secondly address the question of how these approaches *aim* to achieve legal reform. From a One Health perspective, this debate is still very much alive and this book will serve an important role in assessing potential routes forward. While Planetary Health explicitly aims to address legal and governance challenges and has broadly aligned with a rights-based approach to international environmental law,[44] the movement has yet to directly notch a victory in 'hard law' (i.e. binding legislation) or completely reconcile its anthropocentric roots with the potential rights of nature. And where EcoHealth practitioners consider their ability to influence policy, they consider primarily indirect mechanisms such as producing effective research to pass on to policymakers.[45]

If One Health, EcoHealth, and Planetary Health so far have had ambiguous or limited success in achieving direct legal reform, and their aspirations for high-level integration into legal and governance structures continue to mature, what, then, can these approaches learn from each other? And how can they work together in overcoming legal and governance roadblocks in a way that does not privilege one of these approaches above the other (potentially hindering their ability to collaborate and co-evolve at the implementation level)?

42 H. De Pooter, G. L. Burci, P. A. Villarreal, A. Berman, M. M. Mbengue, and D. Yeow, 'White Paper 22 – One Health' (2022) Association de droit International/International Law Association.

43 Eric Ip, 'An Emergent Planetary Health Law' (2023) 72(4) *International & Comparative Law Quarterly* 1047–1067 at 1053, citing L. O. Gostin, *Global Health Law* (Harvard University Press, 2014) 59; James Wingard, Sofija Belajcic, Manohar Samal, et. al. (2020) *Wildlife Trade, Pandemics and the Law: Fighting This Year's Virus with Last Year's Law*. Legal Atlas, LLC.

44 Ip, 'An Emergent Planetary Health Law', 1056.

45 Charron, 'EcoHealth Research in Practice'.

EcoHealth and Planetary Health may have already stumbled upon the answer: legal reform does not only follow top-down consolidation of ideas and philosophies, but also often *reflects* bottom-up approaches that have already achieved success. It is this indirect approach to legal reform that we turn to now.

10.3.2 *Indirect Legal Reform*

This chapter recognises the value of a practical approach to legal reform. By more effectively delivering health outcomes to people, animals, and ecosystems in need, all three health frameworks dramatically increase the odds that supporting legal and institutional reforms will follow. We will examine several EcoHealth and Planetary Health case studies to assess both *why* the projects in question were successful, and *how* subsequent legal reforms emerged. By showing that effective health initiatives frequently precede related legal reforms, this chapter argues that a two-way causal link between the two likely exists; just as modernised legal structures could enable more effective health projects (a link that we will not explore in this chapter), so too can effective health projects lay the foundations for better legal structures to arise. These lessons can then inform One Health practitioners in seeking better health outcomes and effective reform of their own.

Such a bottom-up approach to legal reform recognises that substantial progress can still be made to improve health outcomes even within existing legal paradigms at national or international levels. Few countries strictly *need* a radically new legal conception of health or ecology to achieve better outcomes; for many problems, the solution can be as simple (in theory) as getting a local council to take a matter more seriously and finally implement basic but important regulations.

None of this is to imply that One Health practitioners can or should simply go about their business and rely on legal progress to occur purely incidentally to health work. Rather, this chapter suggests that One Health practitioners can consciously pursue methodologies that are conducive to legal reform through their projects even without a rigid preconception or expectation of what that reform may entail. Several projects that we will examine pursued methodologies, such as extensive community empowerment, which were conducive to subsequent legal or policy reform efforts. Engaging the public and relevant stakeholders in law reform processes habitually creates 'strengthened democracy, more inclusive democracy, and efficacious law'.[46]

Legal instruments do not need to *explicitly* or *entirely* adopt a One Health approach in order to align with it more closely. Indeed, as any legal system 'is continually engaged in carrying out the self-reproduction (autopoiesis) of the overall social system as well as its own',[47] those seeking to reform the system are bound to reflect and respect the social context within which each system functions. While attempts to homogenise the One Health framework for ease of practice (such as pushes towards a Global One Health Index weighting of factors)[48] are admirable, a globally uniform approach to seeking legal reform may be unnecessary to make tangible progress.

46 Natalina Nheu, 'By the People, For the People? Community Participation in Law Reform' (2010) 6 *Law and Justice Foundation* 269.
47 Niklas Luhmann, 'Law as a Social System' (1988) 83 *Northwestern University Law Review* 136–138.
48 Xiao-Xi Zhang, Jing-Shu Liu, Le-Fei Han et al., 'Towards a Global One Health Index: A Potential Assessment Tool for One Health Performance' (2022) 11(1) *Infect Dis Poverty* 57.

We are now equipped to dive into our EcoHealth and Planetary Health case studies. This chapter will organise them as supporting evidence under two theses, both of which are oriented towards actionable suggestions for One Health practitioners to work towards better health outcomes and improved odds of compatible legal reform. One Health projects should:

(1) prioritise community engagement – and equip project stakeholders with the tools and confidence to pursue subsequent legislative change; and
(2) limit project scope creep – especially in situations where the full scope of One Health's framework risks becoming cumbersome

10.4 CASE STUDY ANALYSIS

10.4.1 *Lesson #1: Prioritise Community Engagement*

In our earlier table of key differentiating elements (Table 10.1), 'community engagement' was flagged as a distinct virtue of both the EcoHealth and Planetary Health frameworks. How can this be so, when there are many instances of One Health recognising the importance of community engagement and even elevating it as a 'pillar' of the approach?[49]

The rationale for this distinction lies in practice, rather than in theory. A 2018 systematic analysis of One Health Networks (OHNs) found that 'activities such as communication and collaboration, data and information sharing, and human resource capacity building were reported by OHNs far more often than were other activities, such as community engagement and education or implementation research'.[50] Moreover, the discrepancy is not a mild one: the analysis found that engagement with local populations to help adapt interventions to more specific socio-cultural contexts was 'being done by less than 15% of OHNs'.[51] While certain OHNs do perform exceptional community outreach, they are so far the minority.[52] This discrepancy remains despite more recent attempts to by One Health institutions to recognise the importance of community engagement;[53] One Health research (from 2015–2021) demonstrated a 'a gap between advocacy and implementation, indicating a need for closer coordination'.[54]

This discrepancy is easily understood in the context of One Health's empirical roots and rise to popularity. One Health draws primarily from scientific fields that are notoriously difficult to communicate as local knowledge: a rural village has little chance of independently formulating and producing a technical veterinary drug. Similarly, as a health approach geared particularly to the outbreak and spread of disease, One Health projects have likely uncovered

[49] Paul Gwakisa, Janeth George, Calvin Sindato, et al. 'Pillars for Successful Operationalization of One Health as an Ecosystem Approach: Experience from a Human-animal Interface in the Maasai Steppe in Tanzania' (2023) 5(11) *One Health Outlook*.

[50] Mishal S. Khan, Peregrine Rothman-Ostrow, Julia Spencer, et al., 'The Growth and Strategic Functioning of One Health Networks: A Systematic Analysis' (2018) 2(6) *The Lancet Planetary Health* e264–e273.

[51] Ibid.

[52] We acknowledge that the OHHLEP has since released a technical document ('One Health Theory of Change') that includes as one of its main 'Pathways' the need to prioritise 'Actions related to implementation of One Health including scaling up of capacity development, *community engagement* and mobilization for action, multisectoral coordination, collaboration and communication, and equitable integration of sectors' (at 16) (emphasis added). However, the release of this more institutionalised policy position, while encouraging, does not counter the historical failure of OHNs in this regard, especially considering that OHNs are not always clearly motivated in their project implementation by the OHHLEP. See OHHLEP, 'One Health Theory of Change' (2022) at www.who.int/publications/m/item/one-health-theory-of-change.

[53] See ibid.

[54] Talukder Byomkesh, 'Exploring the Nexus', 74.

greater attention and funding when addressing 'outbreak narratives' rather than fundamental and structural drivers like intensification of animal agriculture;[55] biasing the approach further towards reactive, top-down responses less likely to require long-term community engagement.

This chapter will present several EcoHealth and Planetary Health case studies that successfully prioritised community engagement. They did so not only in a manner that contributed to desired health outcomes but also facilitated future legal reform and recognition.

10.4.1.1 *Manganese Mining in Mexico*

One of the largest Manganese (Mn) deposits in the world is found in the tiny region of Molango, Mexico. With a population of barely 12,000 people,[56] the local economy is dominated by mining operations conducted by the Autlán Mining Company (AMC). In a now-archetypal dilemma for similar regions, these mining operations bring much-needed revenue to the local population while simultaneously damaging their health. Public complaints in the 1980s led the Hidalgo state government to commission a study into health risks in the area, which predictably uncovered elevated Mn concentrations in blood and associated neurobehavioural deficits.[57] These results were shared with various authorities and the AMC, catalysing a more comprehensive study and project (built on an EcoHealth framework) to begin in 2001.[58]

An ongoing focus of this project was multistakeholder consultation. Meetings and workshops were held with community representatives (among others) throughout the study, from project planning to dissemination of results. One key discovery of this study was that AMC's manganese emissions were very likely responsible for developmental delays in children. Documenting this link and providing the community with those results better equips the people of Molango to advocate for their health going forward.

After a decade of focused work in the region, the EcoHealth team saw tangible reward for their efforts: the AMC (in conjunction with the state government) launched an Environmental Improvement Program including community support programs, pavement of transited areas, and acquisition of new dust collectors and an emissions-reducing ball mill.[59] Additionally, although immediate legislative progress proved difficult due to close governance links between the AMC and municipal councils,[60] as well as a perception among municipal officers that they did not have the authority to act,[61] local health officials 'clearly recognized that mining pollution affected the health-illness pattern' of residents.[62]

In September 2022, members of the local Ixcotla community blockaded a highway in a move to pressure the AMC to help fund community needs, including private medical insurance for

[55] Jane Kotzmann and Morgan Stonebridge, 'Considering Zoonotic Disease Risk in Australia: An Analysis of the Adequacy of the Intensive Animal Agriculture Regulation' (2022) 45 *UNSWLJ* 1220.

[56] Gobierno de Mexico, 'Molango de Escamilla'. Available at: www.economia.gob.mx/datamexico/en/profile/geo/molango-de-escamilla.

[57] H. Riojas-Rodriguez and S. Rodriguez-Dozal, 'An Ecosystem Study of Manganese Mining in Molango, Mexico' (2012) 1 *Ecohealth Research in Practice* 87–96.

[58] Ibid.

[59] M. Catalán-Vázquez, H. Riojas-Rodríguez, M. Cortez-Lugo, S. L. Rodríguez-Dozal, D. Hernández-Bonilla, and B. E. Pelcastre-Villafuerte, 'Social Representations of Mining Activity after an Environmental Improvement Program in the Manganese District of Molango, in Mexico, and Their Implications for Risk Management' (2019) 62(10) *Journal of Environmental Planning and Management* 1714–1735.

[60] Gobierno de Mexico, 'Molango de Escamilla'. Available at: www.economia.gob.mx/datamexico/en/profile/geo/molango-de-escamilla.

[61] Catalan-Vazquez, 'Social Representations of Mining Activity After an Environmental Improvement Program in the Manganese District of Molango, in Mexico', 1714–1735.

[62] Ibid.

each inhabitant.[63] This effort paid off, and the Hidalgo state government facilitated negotiations that led the AMC to invest a further US$715,600 into development programs for the region.[64] Almost half a century after locals had to pressure the state government to even *investigate* the health effects of AMC's mining operations, their sustained commitment has enabled them to sit down at a negotiating table with that same government completely independently of any facilitating structure.

Mexico is also making progress at a federal level. The Mexican Congress introduced Mining Reform legislation in 2023, broadly cracking down on exploitative mining. The regulations establish 'contamination with dangerous repercussions for the ecosystem or for public health' as a rationale for cancellation of mining concessions,[65] include 'revised and expanded indigenous public consultation rules and processes',[66] and require concession holders to pay at least 5 per cent of net profits to affected indigenous communities.[67] Stricter environmental regulations were by no means guaranteed by the election of a broadly left-wing President (Andrés Manuel López Obrador), either; indeed, his administration allocated 35 per cent less funding to its environmental department than his predecessor.[68] In other words, the focus on environmental regulation that explicitly mandated community consultation was not a 'given' simply by virtue of the government's general position on a left–right political continuum.

Can the EcoHealth framework take full credit for the regulatory triumphs of the Obrador administration or the bold action of the Ixcotla peoples? No. But it must be acknowledged that a decade of community-inclusive health work in the region likely better equipped that community with strong arguments and data to lobby for their interests with the AMC and Hidalgo state government. Similarly, widespread projects of this nature can give policymakers both the popular support and understanding they need to pass more effective legislation.

10.4.1.2 *Mangrove Conservation in Sri Lanka*

Mangroves and their biomes (*mangals*) are vital to the health of the Sri Lankan population through a wide range of mechanisms. They support coastal fisheries that provide income and healthy proteins rich in iodine, vitamin D, and omega-3 fats. Their root systems dampen sea surges and protect the over 90 per cent of Sri Lanka's coast considered vulnerable to tsunamis.[69] Their leaves and bark are widespread in traditional medicines that are known to exhibit effective antibacterial properties.[70] The Seacology-Sudeesa Sri Lanka Mangrove Conservation Project has made enormous strides in protecting these valuable habitats. As a member of the

63 K. Dilge, 'Minera Autlán Reaches an Agreement to Stop Blockade' (2022) *Mexico Business News*. Available at: https://mexicobusiness.news/mining/news/minera-autlan-reaches-agreement-stop-blockade.

64 F. Mares, 'Minera Autlán to Invest a Further US$700,000 In Social Programs' (2022) *Mexico Business News*. Available at: https://mexicobusiness.news/mining/news/minera-autlan-invest-further-us700000-social-programs.

65 A. Lieja, 'Mining Reform in Mexico: Principal Amendments, Effect, and Implications for Foreign Investors' (2023) *Jones Day*. Available at: www.jonesday.com/en/insights/2023/06/mining-reform-in-mexico-amendments-and-impact.

66 D. Trevedan and H. Gonzalez, 'Major Overhaul to Mexico's Mining Regulation' (2023) *Norton Rose Fulbright*. Available at: www.nortonrosefulbright.com/en/knowledge/publications/04715af1/major-overhaul-to-mexicos-mining-regulation.

67 Ibid.

68 D. Shailer, 'More Parks, Less Money: Advocates Say Mexico's New Budget Doesn't Add Up for Natural Protected Areas' (2023) *Associated Press*, https://apnews.com/article/mexico-budget-environment-park-protection-funding-6d26b85334069269362b5686344cf92b.

69 Behara Satyanarayana, Tom Van der Stocken, Guillaume Rans, et al. 'Island-wide Coastal Vulnerability Assessment of Sri Lanka Reveals that Sand Dunes, Planted Trees and Natural Vegetation may Play a Role as Potential Barriers Against Ocean Surges' (2023) 12 *Global Ecology and Conservation* 144–157.

70 P. D. Abeysinghe 'Antibacterial Activity of some Medicinal Mangroves against Antibiotic Resistant Pathogenic Bacteria' (2010) 72(2) *Indian Journal of Pharmaceutical Sciences* 167–172.

Planetary Health Alliance,[71] Seacology operates projects across the world to protect threatened island ecosystems. They paired with Sudeesa (an already existing local federation of small-scale fishing and farming community organisations) in 2001 to help educate community and government stakeholders about the financial and (human) health benefits of intact mangroves;[72] a people-focused lens that remains core to the Planetary Health approach.

Remarkably, the Seacology-Sudeesa project demonstrated both the ambition to seek national legal reform in Sri Lanka and the patience to pursue it through often indirect channels. While initiative leads always knew they ultimately sought country-wide legal protections, the project began more humbly by scaling Sudeesa's grassroots activism across other coastal communities.[73] These activities involved direct education on mangrove conservation, but also included business training, replanting programs, and microloan support for local women.[74]

By prioritising local community engagement in this way, Sudeesa has become 'a bridge between community perspective and government policy', able to inform the government about how the community is feeling. A government official from Sri Lanka's Ministry of Mahaweli Development and Environment acknowledged that 'the Seacology-Sudeesa project is the most direct way the ministry receives input from the community'.[75]

Similarly, the project developed unprecedented support from the government (which had previously disregarded environmental assessments and advice) specifically *because* the project 'never [tried] to interfere politically'.[76] This blossoming of both community education and government goodwill soon made a real impact at the governance level; when locals reported mangrove destruction, officials listened, and even the Navy became involved in replanting projects.[77]

In 2015, the project finally accomplished the national legal reform it had sought all along. Seacology, Sudeesa, and the national government signed a tripartite Memorandum of Understanding (MoU), with Sri Lanka becoming 'the first nation in history to make a pledge to preserve and replant all of its mangrove forests'.[78] Sudeesa's trajectory from a local alliance of fisherfolk to a federal-level policy leader is a clear demonstration of the accomplishments that may be gained through grassroots activism.

How did Sudeesa achieve these considerable successes? Certainly not by fighting bureaucratic inertia head-on; community members have remarked that 'top-down management hasn't done anything in places like Chilaw Lagoon',[79] and prior laws attempting to address the issue of illegal logging of mangroves did not achieve sustainable protection. Rather, the Seacology-Sudeesa project focused on community empowerment on its own merits, and slowly but steadily broke down trust barriers through emergent interactions. When the political climate was finally ready for legal reform, the project found strong and trusting communities willing to help lobby for change, and a government at last willing to listen.

[71] Planetary Health Alliance Members. Available at: www.planetaryhealthalliance.org/pha-members-sz.

[72] H. Duff, C. Faerron Guzmán, A. Almada, C. Golden, and S. Myers, *Planetary Health Case Studies: An Anthology of Solutions* (Planetary Health Alliance 2020).

[73] Ibid., 440.

[74] Ibid., 442.

[75] Ibid., 447.

[76] Ibid., 446–447.

[77] Ibid.

[78] United Nations Framework Convention on Climate Change website. Available at: https://unfccc.int/climate-action/momentum-for-change/planetary-health/sri-lanka-mangrove-conservation-project.

[79] Duff, *Planetary Health Case Studies*, 446.

10.4.1.3 *Pesticide Regulation in Ecuador*

The 'once fertile' slopes of the Ecuadorian Andes have been transformed by modern agricultural practices, and not for the better.[80] Widespread use of hazardous pesticides, primarily chosen for their lower cost and perceived efficacy, have led to declining production and increased reports of related neurotoxicity and poisonings.[81]

The Ecosalud I and II projects, built on an EcoHealth approach and funded by Canada's International Development Research Centre (IDRC),[82] worked to 'tackle the complex drivers of inappropriate use of highly hazardous pesticides' in the Carchi, Chimborazo, and Tungurahua regions.[83] Ecosalud I showed that 'community-based educational activities (for example, farmer-field schools, women's groups, school activities, and radio spots)' could improve understanding of pesticide uses. Ecosalud II expanded the geographic reach of this work and collaborated with agronomists from partner institutions (such as the International Potato Center) to continue delivering community health interventions.[84]

A particular feature of Ecosalud II was the creation of 'potato platforms': social spaces that brought together a wide range of community and authority figures to discuss issues related to potato farming every month.[85] Community consultations (including through these potato platforms) uncovered an important lesson: pesticides and their harms were often *already* important issues to local farmers, but they did not know how to apply related concepts in practice.

This community-driven lesson helped the Ecosalud II team make a lasting impact on local governance: the Ministry of Health would soon adopt the project's information, training, tools, and even trainees, while one municipality even formed an entirely new Department for Agricultural Production and Development. Ultimately, continued pressure by Ecosalud and related networks led to the national cancellation of registration of type Ia and Ib pesticides;[86] showcasing again that health projects that *begin* with a community outreach focus can often later transform into effective channels for legal reform activism.

Of additional interest is the project's development of a Charter of Farmer's Rights ('Charter') related to pesticide use in Ecuador. This Charter was not a fundamentally new legal instrument, but rather a reframing of the United Nations FAO's existing Code of Conduct on the Distribution and Use of Pesticides ('Code'). By reformulating the Code to inform the community more clearly about what they could and should expect from pesticide manufacturers, Ecosalud II aimed to 'transform the Code into a tool for community decision-making around–rather than technocratic management of–pesticide use'.[87] The Charter was subsequently recognised by the National Council of Citizen Participation as an important tool for farmers.[88]

80 F. A. Orozco and D. C. Cole, 'Tackling Challenges to Farmers: Health and Agro-ecosystem Sustainability in Highland Ecuador' (2012) 1 *Ecohealth Research in Practice* 47–58.

81 Ibid., 47.

82 D. C. Cole, C. C Crissman, and F. A. Orozco, 'Canada's International Development Research Centre's Eco-Health Projects with Latin Americans' (2006) 97(6) *Canadian Journal of Public Health* I8–I14.

83 Orozco, 'Tackling Challenges to Farmers', 48.

84 F. A. Orozco, Donald C. Cole, Selahadin Ibrahim, and Susitha Wanigaratne, 'Health Promotion Outcomes Associated with a Community-based Program to Reduce Pesticide-related Risks among Small Farm Households' (2011) 26(4) *Health Promotion International* 432–446.

85 Orozco, 'Tackling Challenges to Farmers', 49.

86 Orozco, 'Tackling Challenges to Farmers', 56.

87 F. A. Orozco, Donald C. Cole, Greg Forbes, Jürgen Kroschel, Susitha Wanigaratne, and Denis Arica, 'Monitoring Adherence to the International Code of Conduct Highly Hazardous Pesticides in Central Andean Agriculture and Farmers' Rights to Health' (2009) 15(3) *International Journal of Occupational and Environmental Health* 255–68.

88 Orozco, 'Tackling Challenges to Farmers', 53.

There is an important distinction to be made here: this EcoHealth project did not attempt to shoehorn a rights-based approach into Ecuadorian law as a legal philosophy preferred by the project team (or even EcoHealth itself as a framework). Rather, Ecosalud II succeeded because consistent community engagement helped the project team discover that a rights-based reinterpretation would be easier to understand and apply for the people who needed it most. A decade later, as Ecuador still struggles to implement pesticide regulations that are accessible and relevant to small farmers,[89] these community-centric approaches to legal reform are more desperately needed than ever.

10.4.2 *Lesson #2: Limit Project Scope Creep*

One Health's determination to expand beyond its original veterinary and medicinal roots often left the framework in nebulous conceptual territory. As one public health practitioner put it, 'we need to work a bit harder on defining what One Health actually is'.[90] In 2022, the OHHELP published an updated definition of the framework, along with a Theory of Change and outcome targets. These high-level objectives state that One Health aims to 'sustainably balance and optimize the health of people, animals, and ecosystems', recognises the 'intrinsic value of all living things', and values 'equity between sectors and disciplines', while retaining One Health's historical duties (from its medicinal and veterinary roots) such as identification and treatment of zoonoses.[91]

While it now seems settled that One Health *aspires* to be much more than a public health framework for doctors and veterinarians, the OHHELP's language persistently frames One Health as a kind of panacea; potentially applicable to anybody, anywhere, working on anything related to the health of any other thing. All three frameworks considered here are broad umbrellas in nature, but arguably One Health most of all.

This approach has its virtues: openness to a wide range of definitions and implementations makes room for interdisciplinarity, and One Health's ubiquity has facilitated adoption by several United Nations bodies. However, this approach also risks 'suboptimal strategic planning, coordination, and stakeholder engagement' and has made 'determining what would constitute improvements … challenging'.[92] One Health initiatives can be bogged down at the emphasised 'collaboration' phase, and begin to work against their own values.[93] For instance, Degeling et al. (2017) note that 'lack of evidence about how different sectors understand One Health, their roles and responsibilities, and how they pursue their priorities, could limit collaboration and its benefits.'[94]

This challenge may be surmountable with time and sufficient communication, but these are luxuries that not all health projects can afford. Sparsely staffed or funded projects often

89 E. Mollocana-Lara and F. Gonzales, 'Control of Pesticides in Ecuador: An Underrated Problem?' (2020) 5(3) *Revista Bionatura* 1257–1263.

90 I. Johnson, A. Hansen, and P. Bi, 'The Challenges of Implementing an Integrated One Health Surveillance System in Australia' (2018) 65(1) *Zoonoses and Public Health* e229–e236.

91 See n 12 (OHHLEP, W. B. Adisasmito, S. Almuhairi, et al., 'One Health: A New Definition for a Sustainable and Healthy Future' (2022) 18(6) *PLoS Pathogens* e1010537). See also n 52 (OHHLEP, 'One Health Theory of Change' (2022) at www.who.int/publications/m/item/one-health-theory-of-change).

92 Mishal S. Khan 'The Growth and Strategic Functioning of One Health Networks', e70–e271.

93 Byomkesh et al. found that the greatest emphases of One Health are on 'collaboration across multiple disciplines', rather than on a substantive subject matter like its neighbours (i.e. 'ecosystem and community well-being' for EcoHealth, and 'sustainability' for Planetary Health). Talukder Byomkesh, 'Exploring the Nexus', 72 (table 4).

94 Chris Degeling, Jane Johnson, Michael Ward, Andrew Wilson, and Gwendolyn Gilbert, 'A Delphi Survey and Analysis of Expert Perspectives on One Health in Australia' (2017) 14 *EcoHealth* 783–792.

only have the resourcing to operate for a few years and are often situated in developing nations with language barriers to overcome and scarcely any nearby OHNs. Expectations for these One Health practitioners to carefully consider and communicate an increasingly far-reaching framework may take valuable time away from the fieldwork that counts most.

This chapter will present EcoHealth and Planetary Health projects that – although still complex at the implementation level – benefitted from a high level of clarity. By choosing their objectives carefully, these projects delivered stronger health outcomes to the communities affected and helped catalyse future legal reform.

10.4.2.1 *Family Planning in Uganda*

Nestled in the heart of the African Great Lakes region and framed by mountain ranges to the east and west, Uganda continues a near-silent struggle against an equally quiet epidemic: population growth. From 2015–2020, the nation held the sixth-highest population growth rate in the world, at a staggering 3.2 per cent annually;[95] approximately the equivalent of 1 in 17 adults having a child each year.[96]

This growth is at once causal and symptomatic of a range of health impacts. Poor rates of contraception use have skyrocketed both birth and disease rates, and the extra mouths to feed sparked a chain of environmental impacts from the depletion of local fish stocks in the Lake Victoria Basin (LVB) to increasing deforestation for both fuel and profit.[97]

Since 2012, Pathfinder International has applied a Planetary Health approach to addressing this issue through the Health of People and Environment in the Lake Victoria Basin (HoPE-LVB) project. The three major arms of the project relate to sexual health and sanitation, family planning education, and sustainable use of the environment; a broad suite of objectives, but without One Health or EcoHealth's prioritisation of animal/ecosystem health as their own intrinsic goods.[98]

The project's scope faced further pressure as HoPE-LVB got underway. Sono Aibe, Senior Program Advisor at Pathfinder found that '[t]here definitely was pushback [as] people thought [PHE] would be a mission creep … They envisioned us having to work with environmental groups, share resources, and learn about conservation terminology and monitoring indicators. There was this whole anxiety around going into a completely non-health sector'.[99]

While this did not deter HoPE-LVB from continuing their work, it is clear that the team gradually learned to be selective about how they would operate. Planetary Health Alliance advocate Hilary Duff notes that the project 'prefers to build the capacity of existing community groups' rather than entirely new facilities to expand contraceptive delivery.[100] Similarly, although HoPE-LVB frames itself as a 'rights-based approach', it also seems to realise that gender-related rights

95 Global population data. *United Nations Department of Economic and Social Affairs – Population Division*. Available at: https://population.un.org/wpp/Download/Standard/Population/.

96 Around 55 per cent of Uganda's population is aged 15 years or older: 3.2 per cent population growth per year implies that for each 100 people (55 of whom are 15+), 3.2 new births will occur; or around 1 birth for every 17th person aged 15+.

97 H. Duff, C. Faerron Guzmán, A. Almada, C. Golden, and S. Myers, 'Family Planning for People and Planet' (2020) *Planetary Health Case Studies: An Anthology of Solutions* 363–401.

98 Pathfinder's framing of environmental impacts almost always ties them back to harms to humans 'such as high maternal mortality rates and poor sexual and reproductive health outcomes'. Pathfinder International. 'Scaling-Up the Population, Health, And Environment Approach in the Lake Victoria Basin: A Review of the Results from Phases I And II of the HoPE-LVB Project' (2018) *Hope-LVB Project Report.*

99 Duff, 'Family Planning for People and Planet', 380.

100 Ibid., 388.

advocacy can be tricky when engaging with faith-based or public organisations, and instead deploys a more inclusive framing around improving health and livelihoods.[101] The Pathfinder team identified what it could and could not accomplish, and adapted its framework and philosophy to that context.

This approach has worked to deliver strong health outcomes: over a third of nearby residents (especially women and those currently in sexual relationships) now have 'good' knowledge of family planning methods.[102] A US Agency for International Development (USAID) study found that even after the planned closure of the HoPE-LVB project in 2019, communities 'have sustained many HoPE-LVB model household practices–for example, tree planting, awareness of modern contraception, improved sanitation, kitchen gardens, fruit cultivation, use of energy-efficient stoves, encouraging girls' education, and promoting sustainable fishing practices'.[103]

Over time, HoPE-LVB also became a major architect of policy and legal reform. In earlier years, the project took small steps, such as involving county officials in activities and creating district-level steering committees.[104] In 2015, HoPE-LVB signed an agreement with the Lake Victoria Basin Commission (LVBC), which in turn advocates for change to Ministers. Doreen Othero, Regional Programme Coordinator at the LVBC, believes that without crucial evidence from the HoPE-LVB project, 'we would not have convinced our ministers' to make policy changes.[105]

Today, Pathfinder's (Planetary Health Equity) PHE framework is integrated into virtually every level of Ugandan policy, including the Vision 2030 national development plan.[106] What began as a regional project tightly focused on sexual and reproductive health has become a federal framework underpinning a far wider range of activities, demonstrating that piecemeal institutionalisation of frameworks like Planetary Health or PHE can be just as viable as seeking adoption all at once.

10.4.2.2 *Gold Mining in Ecuador*

Precious metals are graded by the proportion of that metal within the surrounding ore. A commercially viable gold mine might possess just 4 grams of gold in every 1,000 kilograms; each speck being literally a 'one in a million' find. But nestled in the Puyango river basin of Ecuador, beneath forested towns like Zaruma and Portovelo, lie hidden gold veins yielding as much as 180 grams per ton; a treasure rich enough that many risk life and limb to extract it.[107] Gold miners in the region have created tunnels and caverns so fragile that sinkholes have swallowed up homes,[108] often built in secret and with minimal precaution.

Another symptom of local artisanal gold mining is pollution of the Puyango river itself: both from the toxic chemicals used to extract gold from the ore, and from other potentially harmful metals (like mercury and lead) that are naturally found in soils but are being disturbed and

[101] Ibid., 389.

[102] A. Nanvubya, Rhoda K. Wanyenze, Teddy Nakaweesa, et al. 'Correlates of Knowledge of Family Planning among People Living in Fishing Communities of Lake Victoria, Uganda' (2020) 20 *BMC Public Health* 1642.

[103] USAID and Johns Hopkins Center for Communication Programs, 'What happened to the HoPE-LVB project post-closure?' (2022). Available at: https://peopleplanetconnect.org/wp-content/uploads/2020/12/Brief-PHELakeVictoria_v3-digital.pdf.

[104] Duff, 'Family Planning for People and Planet', 398–401.

[105] Ibid.

[106] USAID and Johns Hopkins Center for Communication Programs, 'What happened to the HoPE-LVB project post-closure?'.

[107] Peter Millard and Stephan Kueffner, 'The Sinking Gold Town' (2022) *Bloomberg News*. Available at: www.bloomberg.com/features/2022-illegal-gold-mining-sinkhole-zaruma-ecuador.

[108] Ibid.

swept into the river at a heightened scale.[109] Locals always knew the river was contaminated, but the exact contaminants and their direct causes and effects were unknown.

EcoHealth-aligned research teams conducted several studies in the region to address this knowledge gap. They uncovered a range of culprits: high cyanide concentrations immediately downstream of mining activities, mercury exposure even further down (potentially inversely correlated with the cyanide concentration), and lead overexposure virtually everywhere.[110] These harms were indicated by a range of forms of evidence, including neurobehavioural test results from adult and children.

Curiously, lead levels in fish were moderate, suggesting that mining activities may not be the only cause of the issue, and researchers subsequently discovered that 84 per cent of local families were using kitchenware thought to have a high concentration of lead.[111] By approaching the problem through an ecosystem-based approach (instead of simply offering remedies for sicknesses caused by the contamination), researchers were able to identify where ecosystem exposure alone could not explain a health outcome, and inform *both* miners and non-miners of other practical actions they could take to reduce their risk. Similar complexities were discovered relating to the interaction between cyanide and mercury methylation in the river.[112]

At this point, a project lead could be forgiven for radically widening the scope of the endeavour: perhaps spearheading kitchenware replacement across the region; seeking additional schooling resources in towns suffering most from contamination; or aiming to create alternative employment for local miners. A wide range of problems *seems* to enable and even demand a wide range of solutions.

Wisely, however, the EcoHealth team continued to focus on the water contamination issue as their primary concern. The researchers helped inform new municipal bylaws around the dumping of effluents in rivers, convinced mining organisations to adopt new pollution-control strategies, and persuaded *canton* (province subdivision) committees to develop related environmental and health management plans;[113] they even created a new municipal authority to handle related issues.[114] And shortly after Ecuador passed a ban on mercury use in the sector in 2015, mercury levels in the urine of miners in the region finally began to drop.[115] While illegal and unchecked gold mining continues to pose problems in the Puyango river basin, it is clear that ongoing, focused river contamination assessment projects will be necessary to provide evidentiary support for further reform.

10.5 CONCLUSION

One Health, EcoHealth, and Planetary Health are ultimately more alike than they are dissimilar. Each framework recognises the importance and interlinkage of human, animal, and ecosystem health, and has committed to interdisciplinary and interframework cooperation to achieve

109 O. Betancourt, Ramiro Barriga, Jean Remy Davée Guimarães, Edwin Cueva, and Sebastián Betancourt, 'Impacts on Environmental Health of Small-Scale Gold Mining in Ecuador' in *Ecohealth Research in Practice* (2012) 119–130.

110 Betancourt, 'Impacts on Environmental Health of Small-Scale Gold Mining in Ecuador', 119–130.

111 Ibid.

112 Ibid.

113 Ibid.

114 Lisa Waldick, 'Mining, Contamination, and Health in Ecuador' (2011) *International Development Research Centre (IDRC)*. Available at: https://idrc-crdi.ca/en/stories/mining-contamination-and-health-ecuador.

115 Paul Schutzmeier, Ursula Berger, and Stephan Bose-O'Reilly, 'Gold Mining in Ecuador: A Cross-Sectional Assessment of Mercury in Urine and Medical Symptoms in Miners from Portovelo/Zaruma' (2016) 14(1) *International Journal of Environmental Research and Public Health* 34.

these goals. Borne of this cooperation is a new, shared challenge: how can each framework (or perhaps a coming merger of the three) continue to expand in scope and flexibility *without* losing the requisite clarity to support institutional reform? What will it mean to integrate One Health more tightly into law, even as it evolves to become an eclectic theory of health for all life, all practitioners, and all levels of governance?

The problem may well be a Gordian knot: an intractable problem best cut through by other means. What will matter to sick miners from Molango to Zaruma, and what will matter to the potato farmers of the Andes or to new mothers on the shores of Lake Victoria, is not what name a governance body goes by, or whether it pays heed to 'This Health' or 'That Health' as a conceptual framework; rather, what matters will simply be *their health*, and the health of the world around them. EcoHealth and Planetary Health have demonstrated that simply focusing on successful implementation of projects from the bottom up, and letting legal reform organically *follow* as it may (though not without effort!), is a viable way to effect institutional change in line with the principles of their framework. In the end, the most vital actors in the journey towards One Health's implementation into governance structures may not be lawyers or politicians or bureaucrats, but the practitioners on the ground doing the work that matters most.

11

Drawing from AMR Experience for Better Prevention, Preparedness, and Response to Complex Health Threats under a One Health Approach

Carmen Bullón Caro and Stefania Negri

11.1 INTRODUCTION

Antimicrobial resistance (AMR) is the ability of microorganisms to resist the action of antimicrobials – including antibiotics, antivirals, antifungals, and antiparasitics – to which they were initially sensitive. While this phenomenon occurs naturally through genetic changes in pathogens, the overuse and misuse of antimicrobials, combined with their uncontrolled release into the environment, have accelerated the evolutionary process of microbes, making them more adept at developing drug resistance. The World Health Organization (WHO) considers this unnatural development of AMR as one of the top ten global public health and development threats.[1] The estimated impact of AMR suggests a global toll of 10 million human deaths annually by 2050 and a cumulative cost of US$100 trillion if urgent measures are not taken.[2] Consequently, AMR is often referred to as 'the silent pandemic'.

As a global public good, safeguarding antimicrobials and mitigating the threat of AMR are the responsibilities of all countries and people.[3] Due to its complexity, AMR also requires coordinated efforts across various sectors, including human health, animal and plant health and production, and environmental protection, in line with the One Health approach. Overuses and misuses have been reported – both in the human healthcare sector and in animal and plant production – that require attention.[4] These include the excessive use of antimicrobials for non-therapeutic purposes, such as for growth promotion, as well as the availability of substandard and counterfeited antimicrobials that facilitate sub-therapeutic doses that are not effective and exacerbate further resistance development.[5] Unregulated discharges from hospitals, farms, and

The Authors appreciate the comments provided by Juan Lubroth, Katie Woolaston, Jane Kotzmann, Elien Verniers, Elisa Cavallin, Francesca Coli, and Maurizio Aragrande.

1 'Ten Threats to Global Health in 2019'. Available at: www.who.int/news-room/spotlight/ten-threats-to-global-health-in-2019.

2 Jim O'Neill, 'Tackling Drug-Resistant Infections Globally. Final Report and Recommendations' (2016). Available at: https://amr-review.org/sites/default/files/160518_Final%20paper_with%20cover.pdf; See also, Interagency Coordination Group on Antimicrobial Resistance (IACG). 'No Time to Wait: Securing the Future from Drug-resistant Infections. Report to the Secretary-General of the United Nations' (2019) Available at: www.who.int/docs/default-source/documents/no-time-to-wait-securing-the-future-from-drug-resistant-infections-en.pdf.

3 Ponnu Padiyara, Hajime Inoue, and Marc Sprenger, 'Global Governance Mechanisms to Address Antimicrobial Resistance' (2018) 11 *Infectious Diseases: Research and Treatment* 1178633718767887.

4 O'Neill, 'Tackling Drug-resistant Infections Globally'; Interagency Coordination Group on Antimicrobial Resistance (IACG), 'No time to wait'.

5 Interagency Coordination Group on Antimicrobial Resistance (IACG), 'No time to wait', 4.

pharmaceutical companies that include antimicrobial-contaminated waste and other residues have transformed the environment into a reservoir for resistant bacteria and other pathogens.[6] The need for coordinated and collective multisectoral action has prompted the recognition of AMR as the 'quintessential' One Health challenge.[7]

From a governance standpoint, a One Health approach to AMR underscores the need for multisectoral policy and regulatory responses that promote joint interventions. Policies and legal frameworks must create an environment where institutions and stakeholders work collaboratively and are accountable for contributing to common goals. International collaboration is essential for addressing AMR, as it knows no borders. Countries must ensure multisectoral coordination at the national, regional, and global levels, along with consistency between domestic policies and international trade. In this context, identifying regulatory areas and strategies to curb AMR serves as the first step in driving this action. Innovative governance mechanisms should be established to facilitate the transition from coordination to collaboration and, ultimately, to integrated actions.

This chapter's objective is to derive lessons from the global, regional, and national governance of AMR under a One Health approach that may be successfully applied to other complex health challenges, with a focus on policies, institutional frameworks, and relevant legal aspects. The global governance of AMR will be described, along with governance challenges and regulatory solutions at the national level. The chapter proposes the regulatory framework of the European Union on AMR as a case study to conclude with concrete insights on AMR governance and regulation that can be applicable to other areas demanding a One Health response.

11.2 THE IMPORTANCE OF GOVERNANCE IN ADDRESSING AMR

There is broad consensus that appropriate governance structures are instrumental to addressing AMR. By Resolution WHA68.7 the World Health Assembly adopted the Global Action Plan (GAP) for AMR and urged WHO member states to develop National Action Plans (NAPs) in line with the GAP and international standards, while addressing national and local governance arrangements.[8] The GAP called upon member states to set up effective and enforceable regulation and governance for antimicrobial use.

Institutional fragmentation, scattered responsibilities and poor coordination are broadly recognised as drawbacks for the comprehensive, sustainable, and effective implementation of AMR objectives.[9] Dame Sally Davis, former Chief Medical Officer of the UK, has been quoted to affirm 'the biggest problem of AMR is not the science, it is the governance'.[10] As a multifaceted problem, AMR requires inter/intra-institutional coordination to be addressed. Studies have shown that a fragmented institutional structure makes coherent action in deal-

[6] United Nations Environment Programme, *Bracing for Superbugs: Strengthening Environmental Action in the One Health Response to Antimicrobial Resistance* (Geneva, 2023) 10, 14.

[7] T. P. Robinson, D. P. Bu, J. Carrique-Mas, E. M. Fèvre, M. Gilbert, and D. Grace, 'Antibiotic Resistance Is the Quintessential One Health Issue' (2016) 110(7) *Transactions of the Royal Society of Tropical Medicine and Hygiene* 377–380.

[8] Resolution WHA68.7, 'Global Action Plan on Antimicrobial Resistance', 26 May 2015, paras 1–2 and Annex 3, para. 49.

[9] Jon Pierre, Daniel Carelli, and Guy Peters, 'The Four Worlds of Politics and Administration in the EU: How Institutional Arrangements Shape the Struggle against Antimicrobial Resistance' (2023) 31(12) *Journal of European Public Policy* 4088–4115.

[10] Ibid.

ing with issues such as AMR more difficult. Socioeconomic analysis has revealed correlations between strong governance and lower levels of AMR.[11] The sectors involved in AMR governance pursue different objectives and often lack understanding and communication of each others' objectives and regulation, hindering collaboration and challenging the implementation of joint solutions.[12] Even in the absence of explicit conflict, the traditional separation between human, animal health, and the environment creates specific challenges for institutional coordination,[13] as does the fact that each of these areas is governed by different legal frameworks based on different international legal instruments and principles of international law. Finally, the fact that stakeholders are typically aligned with specific ministries and that resources differ greatly among sectors indicates serious barriers to coordinated or integrated governance. At the global level, Rogers Van Katwyk has highlighted that past attempts to tackle AMR have failed because stewardship regimes have been too narrow in national or sectoral scope, and policy responses too fragmented, pointing out the need for more structured and comprehensive AMR governance responses.[14]

Under a One Health approach, AMR governance must encompass all relevant sectors under a framework of equity and transdisciplinarity. A framework of equity would require specific administrative structures and financial mechanisms that do not prioritise one sector over another, ensuring equal roles and responsibilities under a framework of shared accountability.

A systems approach to AMR governance would emphasise network-centric approaches that encourage relationship building among organisations, systems organisation to improve organisational structures and functions, and the flow of knowledge and data across institutions. Systems have been defined as a set of different elements so connected and interrelated as to perform a unique function not performable by the elements alone.[15] Systems thinking facilitates understanding of complex and wicked problems and is particularly useful in relation to areas such as health and food systems where contexts are often changing,[16] and interventions may yield unexpected results.[17] By promoting systems-based transdisciplinarity, members representing different fields work together to develop shared conceptual and methodological frameworks that not only integrate but transcend their respective perspectives.[18]

[11] Peter Collingnon, Prema-chandra Athukorala, Sanjaya Senanayake, and Fahad Khan, 'Antimicrobial Resistance: The Major Contribution of Poor Governance and Corruption to This Growing Problem' (2015) 3(e0116746) *PLoSONE* 10. Available at: https://doi.org/10.1371/journal.pone.0116746. See also Andrea Maugeri, Martina Barchitta, Federico Puglisi, and Antonella Agodi, 'Socio-Economic, Governance and Health Indicators Shaping Antimicrobial Resistance: An Ecological Analysis of 30 European Countries' (2023) 19(1) *Global Health* 12.

[12] Arne Ruckert, Patrick Fafard, Suzanne Hindmarch, et al., 'Governing Antimicrobial Resistance: A Narrative Review of Global Governance Mechanisms' (2020) 41(4) *Journal of Public Health Policy* 515–528.

[13] D. Wallinga, G. Rayner, and T. Lang, 'Antimicrobial Resistance and Biological Governance: Explanations for Policy Failure' (2015) 129(10) *Public Health* 1314–25. See also Pita Spruijt and Arthur C. Petersen, 'Multilevel Governance of Antimicrobial Resistance Risks: A Literature Review' (2015) 25(8) *Journal of Risk Research* 945–958.

[14] Susan Rogers Van Katwyk, Alberto Giubilini, Class Kirchhelle, et al., 'Exploring Models for an International Legal Agreement on the Global Antimicrobial Commons: Lessons from Climate Agreements' (2023) 31 *Health Care Anal* 25–46. Available at: https://doi-org.fao.idm.oclc.org/10.1007/s10728-019-00389-3.

[15] Eberhardt Rechtin and Mark W. Maier, 'The Art of Systems Architecting' in Annette J. Krygiely (ed.), *Behind the Wizard's Curtain. An Integration Environment for a System of Systems.* (Cooperative Research Program (CCRP), US Library of Congress 1999). Available at: www.dodccrp.org/files/Krygiel_Wizards.pdf.

[16] Ross Arnold and Jon Wade, 'A Definition of Systems Thinking: A Systems Approach' (2015) 44 *Procedia Computer Science* 669–678.

[17] Kevin Queenan, Julie Garnier, Liza Rosenbaum Nielsen, et al., 'Roadmap to a One Health Agenda' (2017) *CABI Reviews* 1–17. Available at: https://doi.org/10.1079/PAVSNNR201712014.

[18] Scott J. Leischow, Allan Best, William M. Trochim, et al., 'Systems Thinking to Improve the Public's Health' (2008) 35(2 Suppl) *American Journal of Preventive Medicine* S196–203.

11.3 GLOBAL GOVERNANCE OF AMR

11.3.1 *Evolution of AMR Global Governance*

To date, global action to address AMR has mostly relied on soft law instruments and political declarations led by different intergovernmental organisations. In 2011, the Food and Agriculture Organization (FAO), the World Health Organization (WHO), and the World Animal Health Organization (WOAH) recognised the significance of AMR as one of the three topics that require multisectoral collaboration to advance the One Health approach, alongside rabies and zoonotic influenza.[19]

Following Resolution WHA68.7,[20] 2015 was a crucial year for AMR, with the adoption of the GAP, the launching of the Global Antimicrobial Resistance and Use Surveillance System (GLASS),[21] and the establishment of the UK Fleming Fund to fight AMR. In May 2016 the landmark AMR report 'Tackling Drug-resistant Infections Globally' by Jim O'Neill was published. Commissioned by the UK government and the Wellcome Trust, this report illustrated the economic and social risks resulting from AMR and offered concrete actions to address the global AMR challenge.[22]

At the 71st Session of the United Nations General Assembly (hereinafter General Assembly) in September 2016, the High-level meeting on AMR adopted a Political Declaration on antimicrobial resistance included in Resolution 73/1. This Resolution emphasised the relevance of the One Health approach, recognising the interconnection between the animal, human, and environmental dimensions in combating AMR. It also called for the engagement of relevant government sectors in developing and implementing multisectoral national action plans, policies, and regulations, tailored to each country's context and legal system. With this declaration, countries committed to developing multisectoral One Health national action plans for AMR and ensuring their implementation through appropriate regulatory frameworks. The Declaration also called for the establishment of an 'Ad hoc inter-agency coordination group' to provide practical guidance for sustained global AMR action. As a follow-up to this Political Declaration, the different intergovernmental organisations working on matters relevant to AMR joined forces within the Interagency Coordination Group on Antimicrobial Resistance (hereinafter Interagency Coordination Group) to identify shared solutions.

In its 2019 report, the Interagency Coordination Group on AMR resulting from this UN General Assembly Resolution proposed the creation of a One Health Global Leadership Group on Antimicrobial Resistance, supported by a Joint Secretariat managed by FAO, WHO, and WOAH (at the time, OIE).[23] Additionally, the Interagency Coordination Group recommended the establishment of an Independent Panel on Evidence for Action against Antimicrobial Resistance for action against AMR in a One Health context.[24]

[19] Food and Agriculture Organization of the United Nations (FAO), The World Organisation for Animal Health, and the World Health Organization (WHO), 'High Level Technical Meeting to Address Health Risks at the Human-Animal-Ecosystems interface' (Mexico City, 2011). Available at: www.fao.org/4/i3119e/i3119e.pdf.

[20] Resolution WHA68.7, 'Global Action Plan on Antimicrobial Resistance', 26 May 2015. Available at: https://iris.who.int/bitstream/handle/10665/193736/9789241509763_eng.pdf?sequence=1

[21] See at www.who.int/initiatives/glass.

[22] O'Neill J, Tackling drug-resistant infections globally: Final report and recommendations (Review on Antimicrobial Resistance, Wellcome Trust & HM Government, May 2016) https://amr-review.org/sites/default/files/160518_Final%20paper_with%20cover.pdf

[23] IACG, 'No Time to Wait: Securing the Future from Drug-resistant Infections'. Report to the Secretary-General of the United Nations, p. 21, recommendation E2. Available at: www.who.int/publications/i/item/no-time-to-wait-securing-the-future-from-drug-resistant-infections.

[24] Ibid., recommendation E3.

In response to the mandates from UN General Assembly and the Interagency Coordination Group, FAO, WHO and WOAH signed a Memorandum of Understanding (MoU) in 2018,[25] which was later expanded to include UNEP in 2022, creating a quadripartite framework (the Quadripartite).[26] The MoU provides a legal and formal framework for the four organisations to enhance integrated and coordinated efforts at the human, animal, plant, and ecosystem interface to reinforce national and regional health systems and services. AMR is precisely one of the major areas of cooperation.

Over time, these partner organisations have created governance structures for AMR, including a Joint Secretariat with rotating chairmanship, an Executive Committee composed of the Directors-General, and a Senior Management Group. They have also developed mechanisms to enhance consultation and coordination, including cooperation among technical experts, the organisation of annual executive coordination meetings, and the appointment of liaison officers at the global level. Under the quadripartite framework, the Quadripartite Joint Secretariat on AMR supports global, regional, and national AMR initiatives. This includes the development of a Joint Strategy on AMR, facilitating effective policy and legislative responses to AMR in countries.[27]

Established in November 2020, the Global Leaders Group on AMR (hereinafter Global Leaders Group) is composed of heads of state, regulators, and high-level public and private experts, including the principals of the Quadripartite. It collaborates with public and private stakeholders globally to prioritise AMR on international and national agendas. The Global Leaders Group has published several statements and guidance on topics such as AMR in food systems.[28] It has also advocated for AMR's inclusion in the Pandemics Treaty and the organisation of a UN General Assembly High-level meeting in 2024.

The AMR Multi-Stakeholder Partnership Platform (the Platform) serves as a neutral forum for discussion among the various sectors relevant to AMR, fostering coordinated actions and facilitating engagement among governments, academia, civil society, the private sector, and intergovernmental organisations. It also serves as space for developing specific coordinated joint actions through members-driven action groups. The Platform was launched on 15 November 2023.

Furthermore, AMR has been a recurrent topic in G7 and G20 ministers' declarations. G20 ministers have addressed AMR in their declarations since 2016 (Hangzou Summit) and including the 2017 Hamburg Summit, the G20 Action Plan on AMR approved in Buenos Aires in 2018, and the Bali Summit in 2022, in which ministers committed to embracing a multi-sectoral One Health approach to AMR. In August 2023, G20 Health Ministers recalled their commitment to 'tackle AMR comprehensively following the One Health approach' and indicated multi-sectoral governance and coordination as a necessary step. Also, G7 Ministers have consistently addressed AMR in their declarations since 2014 (Brussels summit declaration), and

[25] 'Memorandum of Understanding between the United Nations Food and Agriculture Organization and the World Organization for Animal Health and the World Health Organization Regarding Cooperation to Combat Health Risks at the Animal-Human-Ecosystem Interface in the Context of the One Health Approach and Including Antimicrobial Resistance' (30 May 2018). Available at: www.who.int/zoonoses/MoU-Tripartite-May-2018.pdf.

[26] 'Memorandum of Understanding between the Food and Agriculture Organization of the United Nations and the World Organization for Animal Health and the World Health Organization and the United Nations Environment Programme Regarding Cooperation to Combat Health at the Animal-Human-Ecosystem Interface in the Context of the "One Health" Approach and Including Antimicrobial Resistance' (17 March 2022). Available at: www.fao.org/3/cb9403en/cb9403en.pdf.

[27] Jorge Pinto Ferreira, Daniela Battaglia, Alejandro Dorado García, et al., 'Achieving Antimicrobial Stewardship on the Global Scale: Challenges and Opportunities' (2022) 10(8) *Microorganisms* 1599.

[28] Global Leaders Group, 'A Pocket Guide for Ministers across Sectors' (2022). Available at: www.amrleaders.org/docs/librariesprovider20/default-document-library/a6-pocket-guide_final.pdf?sfvrsn=797cf4cb_5&download=true.

more substantially in the Leader's declarations of 2015, 2016, 2018 (recalling the One Health approach), 2021, and 2022.

At the time of writing this chapter, countries were preparing for a forthcoming UN General Assembly High-Level meeting on AMR scheduled for September 2024.

In summary, the global governance of AMR has been spearheaded by intergovernmental organisations such as the UN and the Quadripartite. The UN General Assembly played a pivotal role by issuing landmark Resolutions that laid the groundwork for subsequent intergovernmental efforts. The resulting governance framework incorporated various components, including policy-makers represented by the Global Leaders Group, scientific expertise to be facilitated by the forthcoming Independent Panel of Experts, and stakeholders' participation through the AMR Multistakeholders platform. This structure fosters multidisciplinary and multilevel knowledge exchange, political involvement, and widespread public participation; three fundamental elements consistent with the principles of One Health.

11.3.2 *International Law Instruments Applicable to AMR*

Besides the legal instruments and policy structures mentioned earlier, the multifaceted nature of issues pertinent to AMR spans across various international instruments. These instruments play a crucial role in shaping the global governance of AMR.[29]

For instance, the International Health Regulations (IHR) provide a framework for cooperation among countries to prevent, protect against, control, and respond to the international spread of diseases, including those related to AMR. Some scholars have suggested that the emergence and spread of AMR bacteria,[30] especially those for which there is no suitable treatment, may constitute a public health emergency of international concern under the terms of the International Health Regulations. Under these circumstances, countries would be required to notify the WHO under Article 6 of the IHR.[31] Under this view, applying the IHR to AMR could serve to strengthen global AMR surveillance and response, and to contain AMR. This opinion, however, is debatable to the extent that AMR does not meet the definitional requirements of a Public Health Emergency of International Concern.[32] Moreover, relying on a possible declaration of a Public Health Emergency of International Concern to address AMR globally would not put sufficient emphasis on the need for 'deep prevention' to effectively address the AMR 'silent pandemic'.[33]

[29] Van Katwyk, 'Exploring Models for an International Legal Agreement on the Global Antimicrobial Commons', 25–46.

[30] Didier Wernli, Thomas Haustein, John Conly, et al., 'A Call for Action: The Application of The International Health Regulations to the Global Threat of Antimicrobial Resistance' (2011) 8(4) *PLoS Medicine* e1001022.

[31] It is noteworthy that the proposals for amendment of the IHR submitted by WHO member states and some regional integration organisations, currently under consideration of the Working Group on Amendments to the International Health Regulations (2005), do not include any new provision incorporating the One Health approach. A stronger collaboration between the WHO and the other partners from the Quadripartite is only foreseen in a proposal advanced by India for revision of Article 6, where it is added that if the notification received by WHO involves the competency of FAO, WOAH, or UNEP, these entities should be immediately notified. All relevant information on the revision process are available at www.who.int/teams/ihr/working-group-on-amendments-to-the-international-health-regulations-(2005).

[32] According to Article 1 IHR, a PHEIC is a 'an extraordinary event which is determined, as provided in these Regulations: (i) to constitute a public health risk to other States through the international spread of disease and (ii) to potentially require a coordinated international response'.

[33] On the concept of 'deep prevention' see J. Vinuales, S. Moon, G. Le Moli, and G. L. Burci, 'A Global Pandemic Treaty Should Aim for Deep Prevention' (2021) 397(10287) *The Lancet* 1791–1792; G. Le Moli, J. E. Viñuales, G. L. Burci, A. Strobeyko, and S. Moon, 'The Deep Prevention of Future Pandemics through a One Health Approach:

Beyond the IHR, several agreements under the World Trade Organization apply to AMR. The Agreement on Sanitary and Phytosanitary Measures (SPS Agreement) would be applicable for countries approving import restrictions to detect and stop the entrance of animals or animal products potentially contaminated with antimicrobial residues or resistant pathogens. In this respect, several international reference standards have approved detailed and granular guidance on antimicrobial use and AMR.[34] Quality standards for antimicrobials could also be influenced by the Agreement on Technical Barriers to Trade (TBT Agreement).

Similarly, access and availability of safe and effective antimicrobials are influenced by the intellectual property rights provisions in the Trade-Related Aspects of Intellectual Property Rights Agreement (TRIPS Agreement), which may have an impact on the equitable access to antimicrobials in all countries if the flexibilities granted under TRIPS are not taken into consideration.[35] Other potentially relevant international agreements include the International Convention on the Harmonized Commodity Description and Coding System concerning customs procedures.[36]

The international trade of antimicrobials could be protected by the UN Convention of Contracts for the International Sale of Goods and, although soft law, the 2016 Principles of International Commercial Contracts of the International Institute for the Unification of Private Law (UNIDROIT). The UN Convention against Transnational Organized Crime could be also applicable to networks that trade in substandard, illegal, or counterfeit medicines, as long as they meet the definition of transnational crime. Finally, the illegal trade of animals, including wildlife, which could constitute an important avenue for the transmission of resistant pathogens across countries, is also influenced by the Convention on International Trade of Endangered Species of Wild Flora and Fauna (CITES).

The global governance of AMR is further shaped by international reference standards and guidance documents. The Quadripartite publication 'International Instruments on the Use of Antimicrobials across the Human, Animal and Plant Sectors' identifies key international guidance documents that may support the development of AMR policies and regulation across sectors.[37] In addition to different guidance documents published by the WHO, these standards include the updated Codex Alimentarius Code of Practice to Minimize and Contain Foodborne AMR,[38] the Guidelines for Risk Analysis of Foodborne AMR,[39] and the Guidelines on Integrated Monitoring and Surveillance of Foodborne AMR.[40] They also include the AMR-specific standards and articles introduced by the WOAH into the Terrestrial and the Aquatic Animal Health Codes,[41] which are periodically updated. These standards guide countries to apply a One Health approach to AMR governance and regulation and, while they are not

What Role for a Pandemic Instrument?' (2022) *Global Health Centre Policy Brief*. Retrieved from https://hdl.handle.net/1887/3561531.

34 See, among others, the standards approved by the Codex Alimentarius Commission in www.fao.org/fao-who-codexalimentarius/thematic-areas/antimicrobial-resistance/en/.

35 Joanna Hanefeld, Mishal Khan, Goran Tomson, and Richard Smith, 'Trade Is Central to Achieving the Sustainable Development Goals: A Case Study of Antimicrobial Resistance' (2017) 358 *BMJ* j3505.

36 Van Katwyk, 'Exploring Models for an International Legal Agreement on the Global Antimicrobial Commons' 25–46.

37 FAO, OIE, and WHO, 'International Instruments on the Use of Antimicrobials across the Human, Animal and Plant Sectors' (2019). Available at: www.who.int/publications/i/item/9789240013964 (last accessed on 22 October 2023).

38 Codex Alimentarius, 'Code of Practice to Contain Foodborne Antimicrobial Resistance' (CXC 61-2005).

39 'Guidelines for Risk Analysis of Foodborne Antimicrobial Resistance' (CXG 77-2011).

40 'Guidelines on Integrated Monitoring and Surveillance of Foodborne AMR' (CXG 94-2021).

41 See www.woah.org/en/what-we-do/standards/codes-and-manuals/.

legally binding in nature, the fact that both Codex and WOAH are nominated as reference international setting bodies in the SPS Agreement gives them a relevant regulatory role.

These international agreements and standards shape the regulatory framework for AMR at both the international and national levels. Conducting a mapping exercise of international obligations and the division of roles and functions at the national level helps identify the key actors and areas requiring coordination. Similarly, in the context of One Health, multisectoral governance mechanisms must consider existing international obligations across various sectors. This includes sectors such as health, agriculture, environment, trade, and intellectual property. Strengthening collaboration across these sectors is essential for addressing the complex challenges posed by One Health comprehensively.

11.3.3 *From Soft Law to a Binding Global Framework for AMR*

Global opinion has long debated the best international law instrument to address AMR. Some scholars advocate for flexible soft law instruments or a mix of binding and non-binding models.[42] These models propose progressively introducing new norms that create political momentum, fostering voluntary compliance and adaptive governance models,[43] and granting AMR the flexibility that is needed for every area based on science and uncertainty. Other academics signal the limitations of soft law and propose a legally binding instrument that anchors concrete binding obligations and provides for accountability mechanisms.[44] The Paris Agreement has been proposed as a model to develop a binding AMR instrument given the similarities between climate change and AMR and the challenges to be overcome.[45] Any successful legal intervention must strive for a balance between access, conservation, and innovation.[46] Measures must span across the human health, animal, agriculture, and environmental sectors and aim to preserve the efficacy of antimicrobials to achieve intergenerational justice, ensuring wins for present and future generations.[47] In summary, the adoption of a One Health approach to regulating AMR at a global level is imperative. This approach ensures that AMR regulation aligns with principles of multisectoriality, equity across sectors and disciplines, and stakeholder participation.

The COVID-19 pandemic strongly influenced the discussions on a potential global level response to AMR, connecting this to the more specific topic of pandemic prevention, preparedness, and response (PPPR). The devastating impact of the pandemic placed pandemic prevention high on the international agenda and the possibility of crystalizing AMR as a silent pandemic within an international treaty gained scholarly support.[48] At the time of writing this

[42] Padiyara, 'Global Governance Mechanisms to Address Antimicrobial Resistance'; Arne Ruckert, Patrick Fafard, Suzanne Hindmarch, et al., 'Governing Antimicrobial Resistance: A Narrative Review of Global Governance Mechanisms' (2020) 41(4) *Journal of Public Health Policy* 515–528; Ruckert, 'Governing antimicrobial resistance: a narrative review of global governance mechanisms'.

[43] Rubin, Olivier. 'The Glocalization of Antimicrobial Stewardship' (2019) 15 *Global Health* 54. Available at: https://doi.org/10.1186/s12992-019-0498-2.

[44] Padiyara, 'Global Governance Mechanisms to Address Antimicrobial Resistance'; Connor Rochford, Devi Sridhar, Ngaire Woods, et al., 'Global Governance of Antimicrobial Resistance' (2018) 391(10134) *The Lancet* 1976–1978. Available at: https://doi.org/10.1016/S0140-6736(18)31117-6.

[45] Van Katwyk, 'Exploring Models for an International Legal Agreement on the Global Antimicrobial Commons' 25–46.

[46] Ibid.

[47] Ibid.

[48] See, among others, Andrea M. Caceres, Kshitji K. Singh, T. Minssen, S. R. Van Katwyk, and S. J. Hoffman, 'Using the International Pandemic Instrument to Revitalize the Innovation Ecosystem for Antimicrobial R&D' (2022) 50(S2) *Journal of Law, Medicine & Ethics* 47–54.

chapter, the negotiations for the drafting of a Pandemic Agreement by the Intergovernmental Negotiation Body have been further prolonged after the missed opportunity of reaching consensus at the 77th session of the World Health Assembly. That said, different countries, international and non-governmental organisations have strongly advocated for AMR to be considered as a silent pandemic. A strong recognition of AMR as part of the Agreement would offer an excellent opportunity to consolidate soft law rules that have been broadly accepted by countries. It would recognise the mandate of the Conference of Parties to develop intergovernmental and consensus-based implementation guidance and to negotiate complementary binding (including an additional protocol) or non-binding more granular instruments on AMR.[49]

11.4 AMR GOVERNANCE AND REGULATION AT THE NATIONAL AND REGIONAL LEVELS

11.4.1 *Trends in the Development and Implementation of the GAP and NAPs*

Both the Global Action Plan for AMR and the Interagency Coordination Group report recommended that countries establish multisectoral coordination mechanisms for AMR governance and approve multisectoral National Action Plans (NAPs) to consolidate their policy objectives. Over the past years, many countries have advanced in establishing both. In 2023,[50] among the 175 countries responding to the Quadripartite Global Database for Tracking Antimicrobial Resistance Country Self-Assessment Survey (TraCSS), only eighteen declared not to have a multisectoral governance or coordination mechanism. A total of ninety-two countries reported having a formalised and functional multisectoral coordination mechanism, with thirty-five out of those countries utilizing these structures to implement integrated approaches to NAP implementation. This represents significant progress from the 2017 data, where forty-one countries declared lacking a multisectoral coordination mechanism, and only thirty-one reported having formal and functioning structures.

Regarding NAPs, a comparison between the TrACCS results of 2017 and 2023 under the topic 'Country Progress with Development of a NAP' reveals an observable increase in the number of countries incorporating a costed and budgeted operational plan and/or financial provisions for implementation.[51] Despite TrACSS being a voluntary self-assessment mechanism, the data indicates a positive shift towards more formalised governance structures such as joint work and integrated approaches. This positive movement is gradually followed by effective implementation, as reflected in financial allocations. This positive trend alleviates the pessimism regarding the implementation (or the lack thereof) of NAPs.[52] In 2018, FAO, WHO, and WOAH affirmed that despite countries declaring firm commitment, many countries had not implemented NAPs or aligned their domestic policies with global recommendations.[53] Empirical analysis also revealed that, following an initial momentum for NAP development

[49] Arne Ruckert, S. Lake, and Susan Rogers Van Katwyk, 'Developing a Protocol on Antimicrobial Resistance through WHO's Pandemic Treaty Will Protect Lives in Future Pandemics' (2024) 20(1) *Global Health* 10.

[50] See TrACCS. Available at: https://amrcountryprogress.org/#/visualization-view.

[51] Ibid.

[52] Mohan P. Joshi, Chifumbe Chintu, Mirfin Mpundu, et al., 'Multidisciplinary and Multisectoral Coalitions as Catalysts for Action against Antimicrobial Resistance: Implementation Experiences at National and Regional Levels' (2018) 13(12) *Global Public Health* 1781–1795.

[53] FAO, OIE, WHO. Monitoring Global Progress on Addressing Antimicrobial Resistance. 2018. Available at: https://iris.who.int/bitstream/handle/10665/273128/9789241514422-eng.pdf?sequence=1.

and the establishment of multisectoral structures, collaborations were challenging to sustain due to reliance on voluntary partnerships.[54]

The term 'isomorfic mimicry' was introduced to the AMR landscape to explain the differences between the content of the NAPs and their actual implementation.[55] This phenomenon elucidates why low and middle-income countries tended to develop NAPs following the recommendations of the GAP but were unable to implement them due to financial constraints, as well as institutional and political challenges. In 2022, the WHO published an 'Implementation Handbook for National Action Plans on Antimicrobial Resistance in the Human Health Sector' targeting national and subnational stakeholders working on AMR to help them 'guide and accelerate sustainable implementation' of NAPs-AMR.[56] This document includes concrete steps to set up a multisectoral governance mechanism promoting broad multisectoral engagement under the coordination of a higher-level authority.

TrACCS data allows for the conclusion that multisectoral AMR governance mechanisms have broadly been established with dissimilar success and standing challenges. However, informal mechanisms have shown signs of tiredness and weak accountability, compromising their long-term sustainability. Countries are facing challenges to setting up integrated mechanisms, such as integrated surveillance programs in the absence of a concrete framework for accountability and data sharing.

11.4.2 *Elements and Principles of AMR National Governance and the Role of Legislation*

Numerous authors have debated the best regulatory approach to establish a multisectoral governance mechanism for AMR at the national level. Some argue for flexible governance mechanisms to avoid the pitfalls of over-regulation. Rubin proposed a nuanced approach combining binding and non-binding instruments at multiple levels, emphasizing 'glocalisation', where global guidance adapts thoughtfully to local capacities and needs.[57] This chapter argues that national AMR governance should be based on horizontal and decentralised collaboration reflecting the principle of subsidiarity, by ensuring that global recommendations are adjusted to national regulatory and enforcement capacities and needs.[58] Birgand et al. suggested an AMR national governance model combining top-down power with 'network governance'.[59] In this decentralised approach, the central level shapes policies, and the local level, including beneficiaries and the private sector, defines bottom-up implementation mechanisms,

[54] Alvin Q. Chua, Monica Verma, Li Yang Hsu, and Helena Legido-Quigley, 'An Analysis of National Action Plans on Antimicrobial Resistance in Southeast Asia Using a Governance Framework Approach' (2021) 7 *Lancet Regional Health Western Pacific* 100084.

[55] Louise Munkholm and Olivier Rubin, 'The Global Governance of Antimicrobial Resistance: A Cross-Country Study of Alignment between the Global Action Plan and National Action Plans' (2020) 16 *Global Health* 109. Available at: https://doi.org/10.1186/s12992-020-00639-3. Olivier Rubin and Louise Munkholm, 'Isomorphic Dynamics in National Action Plans on Antimicrobial Resistance' (2022) 42(2) *Public Administration & Development* 142–153.

[56] World Health Organization, 'WHO Implementation Handbook for National Action Plans on Antimicrobial Resistance: Guidance for the Human Health Sector' (2022). Available at: www.who.int/publications/i/item/9789240041981.

[57] Rubin, 'The Glocalization of Antimicrobial Stewardship'.

[58] Ibid.

[59] Gabriel Birgand, Enrique Castro-Sánchez, Sonja Hansen, et al., 'Comparison of Governance Approaches for the Control of Antimicrobial Resistance: Analysis of Three European Countries' (2018) 7 *Antimicrobial Resistance Infection Control* 28.

enhancing democratisation and collaboration. Spruijt and Petersen advocated for flexible governance arrangements for scientific areas marked by constant evolution, uncertainty, and adaptiveness.[60]

However, flexible legal solutions must be coupled with clear roles and mandates and a functional accountability framework. In some legal systems, establishing a new interministerial group may require novel legislation that clarifies roles and responsibilities, introduces financial or reporting obligations, and sets up sustainable mechanisms for stakeholders' participation. Such legislation can facilitate the transition from coordination to collaboration and integration, enabling joint interventions. The challenge is to ensure that legislation fosters an enabling environment, preserving its flexibility while building trust among all members, including the private sector.

Anderson, Schulze, and Cassini proposed a governance framework for AMR based on three core governance pillars:[61] policy, implementation, and monitoring and evaluation (M&E). Suggested indicators for policy include: multisectoral coordination, accountability, equity, transparency, and sustainability, among others. These indicators represent important foundational principles for the functioning of a multisectoral governance mechanism. Crucial for the implementation of AMR NAPs, *accountability* demands binding obligations for coordinating authorities and ensuring enforcement. This ties closely to sustainability, as accountability mechanisms influence long-term institutional engagement beyond the political momentum. *Equity* among countries and populations introduces a human rights dimension, ensuring equitable access to antimicrobials and sanitary care, particularly for vulnerable groups. This aligns with the One Health principle of equity,[62] emphasizing accessibility and affordability of healthcare for all, and considering gender and socio-economic factors affecting AMR exposure.

In addition to the proposed principles of accountability and equity, an effective AMR governance structure should embody the principles of good governance, solidarity, and subsidiarity.[63] A well-established principle in public international law, *solidarity* safeguards human dignity amidst the reality of our shared vulnerabilities to the challenge of antimicrobial effectiveness reduction, an issue demanding integrated management. *Subsidiarity* directs the management to commence at the local level, acknowledging local communities' better understanding of their specific AMR challenges.

For effective *multisectoriality* under the equity principle, all relevant ministries should be involved in AMR management. The Global Leaders Group 'Pocket Guide for Ministers across Sectors' identifies as potentially relevant for AMR governance not only the ministries of health, agriculture, and the environment, but also the ministries in charge of finance, industry, education, research, and innovation.[64] Depending on a country's constitutional structure, decentralised and local authorities might be directly responsible for certain elements of AMR

[60] Pita Spruijt and Arthur Petersen, 'Multilevel Governance of Antimicrobial Resistance Risks: A Literature Review' (2020) 25 *Journal of Risk Research* 1–14.

[61] Michael Anderson, Kai Schulze, Alessandro Cassini, Diamantis Plachouras, and Elias Mossialos, 'A Governance Framework for Development and Assessment of National Action Plans on Antimicrobial Resistance' (2019) 19(11) *Lancet Infectious Diseases* e371–e384.

[62] See the principles of One Health enunciated by OHHLEP in One Health High-Level Expert Panel (OHHLEP). 'One Health: A New Definition for a Sustainable and Healthy Future' (2022) 18(6) *PLoS Pathogens* e1010537. Available at: https://doi.org/10.1371/journal.ppat.1010537.

[63] Thana Campos-Rudinsky, 'A Principled Account of AMR Global Governance Solidarity, Subsidiarity, and Stewardship' (2023) 31 *Health Care Analysis* 1–6.

[64] Global Leaders Group, 'Pocket Guide for Ministers across Sectors' (2022). Available at: www.amrleaders.org/resources/m/item/pocket-guide.

management and deserve recognition of their roles and mandate. Collaborating with the diversity of actors that are part of the private sector (from the pharmaceutical industry to farmers) is also vital, as they can contribute significantly to NAP development and implementation and to AMR effective regulation, through co-regulation and self-regulation strategies.

A rapid check of national legislation using AMRLex,[65] a FAO-based repository of AMR relevant policies and legislation in the food and agriculture sectors, reveals that, while most countries have adopted policies, strategies, or national action plans for AMR (155 are included in the WHO NAP Library), only a few have translated these commitments into specific legislation. Most of these instruments establish multisectoral governance mechanisms and define their composition and functions. Typically led by the Ministries of Health, these bodies vary widely in composition, with Ministries of Health, Agriculture, and Environment often included, alongside a diverse array of other entities, as exemplified by the national committees established in Guinea and Algeria.[66] There are exceptions to this trend where members have a shared responsibility to lead coordination. For instance, in Ecuador's Comité Nacional de Prevención y Control de la Resistencia Antimicrobiana,[67] the Presidency alternates among members. The Executive Order issued by the President of the United States of America of 2014 provides another interesting example, by establishing a multisectoral task force and a Presidential Advisory Council.[68] This global, albeit partial, overview emphasises the diverse strategies nations employ in translating AMR objectives into legislative action and highlights the importance of learning from innovative approaches across different jurisdictions.

11.4.3 *The Role of Sector-Specific Legislation*

In addition to a multisectoral governance mechanism backed by appropriate legislation, a conducive legal framework for AMR should encompass sector-specific laws that not only incorporate international guidance and best practices but also promote collaboration and coordination across various sectors and foster effective compliance and enforcement.

Sector-specific legislation is instrumental in shaping the availability and access to antimicrobials. It can introduce antimicrobial use requirements for products entering the food supply chain and regulate the disposal and release of antimicrobials into the environment. Jeleff's empirical research underscores the need for a shift from non-binding to legally binding obligations, particularly in antimicrobial stewardship programs and consumption surveillance in hospitals.[69] Legally binding individual responsibilities, as suggested by Munkholm and Rubin,[70] can enhance implementation and enforcement. Hoffman, Bakshi and Van Katwyk argue that

65 See https://amr-lex.fao.org/.

66 Guinea – Arrêté A/2021/1238/MS/SGG portant Création, Organisation, Composition et Fonctionnement du Comité National de Pilotage de la Lutte Contre la Résistance aux Antimicrobiens. Available at: https://faolex.fao.org/docs/pdf/gui219519.pdf; Algeria – Décret exécutif n° 17–310 du 4 Safar 1439 correspondant au 24 octobre 2017 portant création, missions, organisation et fonctionnement du comité national multisectoriel de lutte contre la résistance aux antimicrobiens. Available at: https://faolex.fao.org/docs/pdf/Alg172305.pdf.

67 Ecuador – Acuerdo Interinstitucional N° 1-2020 – Crea el Comité Nacional de Prevención y Control de la Resistencia Antimicrobiana. Available at: https://faolex.fao.org/docs/pdf/ecu196277.pdf.

68 United States of America, 'Executive Order – Combating Antibiotic-Resistant Bacteria'. Available at: https://faolex.fao.org/docs/pdf/usa176919.pdf.

69 Maren Jeleff, Christian Haddad, and Ruth Kutalek, 'Between Superimposition and Local Initiatives: Making Sense of 'implementation gaps' as a Governance Problem of Antimicrobial Resistance' (2023) 4 *SSM – Qualitative Research in Health* 100332. Available at: https://doi.org/10.1016/j.ssmqr.2023.100332.

70 Munkholm and Rubin, 'The Global Governance of Antimicrobial Resistance'.

effective AMR strategies must extend beyond individual behaviour change and incorporate institutional-level action.[71]

Relevant legal sectors for AMR include, among others, public health, animal health, food safety laws, and laws regulating the environment, waste, and pollution control. These sectors have traditionally been regulated in silos, with one sector usually regulated under specific legislation implemented by one Minister. While it is probably neither possible nor desirable to fully eliminate these silos, sector-specific legislation should incorporate appropriate mechanisms to enable multisectoral coordination across them.

The Quadripartite One Health Legislative Assessment Tool for AMR, launched in November 2023, warns against the risks of horizontal cross-sectoral AMR legal instruments that regulate fragments of different sectors. The Tool proposes a combination of horizontal AMR legislation addressing multisectoral issues, such as multisectoral governance, coupled with legal responses to be addressed in sector-specific laws.[72]

As results from this section, implementation of AMR under a One Health approach demands national mechanisms for coordination, collaboration, or integration of policies and strategies of common interest. While these mechanisms can take various shapes, it is important that they are accompanied by a substantive accountability mechanism that facilitates their long-term sustainability. Legislation can serve to provide legal basis to these mechanisms. This legislation should co-exist with sector-specific legal instruments incorporating international guidance into national law. Sector-specific legislation should preserve its internal consistency avoiding fragmentation. The solution is not to merge laws for AMR but to ensure that all sector-specific laws include the appropriate cross-references to work harmoniously, contributing to common goals.

11.5 CASE STUDY: THE EU REGULATORY FRAMEWORK FOR AMR

In 2022 the European Commission and its member states identified AMR as one of their top three priority health threats.[73] This recognition underscores the EU's strong commitment to combating AMR. Since the early years of the twenty-first century, the EU has been at the forefront, championing an active regulatory agenda targeting AMR and acting as a catalyst for global efforts.

While the EU's regulatory experience in tackling AMR is specific to its constitutional structure and division of powers between the regional and national levels, it provides an interesting model that integrates overarching cross-sectoral instruments with sector-specific legal reforms. Furthermore, it demonstrates a gradual and holistic incorporation of a One Health approach to multisectoral coordination that began with the health and agriculture sectors, and progressively integrated environment. This final stage aligns with the adoption of ambitious EU environmental initiatives exemplified by the European Green Deal.[74]

The EU is supported by several scientific agencies whose competences are particularly relevant to AMR, and more in general, to the implementation of the One Health approach. The European Food Safety Authority (EFSA), the European Medicines Agency (EMA), and the

[71] Stephen J. Hoffman, Reema Bakshi, and Susan Rogers Van Katwyk, 'How Law Can Help Solve the Collective Action Problem of Antimicrobial Resistance' (2019) 33(7) *Bioethics* 798–804.

[72] See www.qjsamr.org/technical-work/one-health-legislative-assessment-tool-on-amr. See also Ambra Gobena, Carmen Bullon, and Teemu Viinikainen, 'Regulatory Frameworks to Address Antimicrobial Resistance in the Food and Agriculture Sectors' (2024) *FAO Legislative Study* 122.

[73] HERA Factsheet, 'HEALTH UNION: Identifying Top 3 Priority Health Threats' (8 July 2022). Available at: https://health.ec.europa.eu/publications/hera-factsheet-health-union-identifying-top-3-priority-health-threats_en.

[74] 'Communication from the Commission to the European Parliament, the Council, the European Economic and Social Committee and the Committee of the Regions The European Green Deal' COM/2019/640 final (2019).

European Centre for Disease Prevention and Control (ECDC) work together in the development of Joint Interagency Antimicrobial Consumption and Resistance Analysis (JIACRA). The European Environment Agency (EEA) also has a preeminent and increasing role.[75]

Against this background, this section presents a non-comprehensive overview of the various regulatory initiatives pursued by the EU to tackle AMR. While this model may not be directly applicable at the national level, its clear sectoral approach to AMR interventions, coupled with targeted cross-sectoral actions and robust financial support, positions the EU as an instructive case study.

11.5.1 *Public Health Regulation in the European Union*

The EU's approach to public health has been shaped by its distinctive constitutional framework, regulatory nature, and its historical emphasis on internal market development.[76] The delineation of competencies between the EU and its member states is meticulously outlined in its foundational treaties. These treaties have evolved over the years from an initial focus on the establishment of an internal market, to increased integration in areas of common interest. The Treaty of Lisbon of 2007 recognised public health as a shared competency between the EU institutions and the member states, unlike policies such as the agricultural policy, where sovereignty is largely transferred to the EU institutions. This acknowledgment underscores the EU's commitment to a collaborative approach in addressing health challenges, achieving a nuanced balance between central coordination and member state autonomy.

EU member states have traditionally hesitated to transfer sovereignty powers in public health from the state to the EU level.[77] This reluctance is attributed, in part, to the significance of the health budget and the nature of health systems, which gain legitimacy through a direct political process.[78] For these reasons, despite the heightened attention to health policies prompted by the COVID-19 pandemic, with both global and EU health policies experiencing expansion, scholars caution that this focus might be ephemeral, drawing parallels with historical trends in the field.[79]

Before 1992, references to public health were primarily associated with the establishment of the internal market and were regulated as exceptions to free trade arrangements, echoing international trade law and the SPS agreement.[80] The Cassis de Dijon case at the European Court of Justice exemplifies this, confirming that countries can only impose restrictions on the free movement of goods under certain exceptions, including the protection of public health and the defence of consumers.[81]

[75] It is noteworthy that, in November 2023, the five European Agencies relevant to One Health published the document 'Cross-Agency Knowledge for One Health Action', which includes references to AMR. Available at: www.efsa.europa.eu/sites/default/files/2023-11/one-health-2023-joint-statement.pdf.

[76] Scott Greer and Holly Jarman, 'What Is EU Public Health and Why? Explaining the Scope and Organization of Public Health in the European Union' (2021) 46(1) *Journal of Health Politics, Policy Law* 23–47.

[77] Eleanor Brooks and Anniek de Ruijter, 'Towards More Comprehensive Health Law and Policy Research' (2021) 16 *Health Economics, Policy, and Law* 104–110.

[78] Brooks and de Ruijter, 'Towards more comprehensive health law and policy research'.

[79] Eleanor Brooks, Anniek de Ruijter, and Scott Greer, 'Covid19 and European Union Health Policy: From Crisis to Collective Action' in Vanhercke, Spasova, and Fronteddu (eds.) *Social Policy in the European Union: State of Play 2020* (ETUI aibsl, Brussels, 2020) 220. Available at: www.etui.org/sites/default/files/2020-12/Social%20policy%20in%20the%20European%20Union%20state%20of%20play%202020-web.pdf.

[80] Anniek de Ruijter, *EU Health Law and Policy: The Expansion of EU Power in Public Health and Health Care* (Oxford University Press, 2019). Cited in Scott Greer and Holly Jarman, 'What Is EU Public Health and Why? Explaining the Scope and Organization of Public Health in the European Union' (2021) 46(1) *Journal of Health Politics, Policy and Law*.

[81] Judgment of the Court of Justice of 20 February 1979, *Rewe-Zentral AG v. Bundesmonopolverwaltung für Branntwein*. Case 120/78. Available at: https://eur-lex.europa.eu/legal-content/EN/TXT/?uri=CELEX%3A61978CJ0120.

Following the Maastricht Treaty in 1992, and more prominently with the revisions of the EU foundational treaties in Amsterdam (1997), Nice (2002), and finally in Lisbon (2007), the EU progressively gained the capacity to intervene in public health. Article 168 of the Lisbon Treaty recognises a high level of health protection as a core objective and principle for all EU policies and activities with EU action, complementing national policies and fostering cooperation between member states. The EU acquired the ability to initiate the establishment of common guidance and conduct periodic monitoring and evaluation (Article 168.2). Under this article, the regulatory capacity of the European Parliament and the Council over health matters is limited to the quality and safety of human tissues, veterinary, and phytosanitary fields, and the quality and safety of medicinal products and devices. Additionally, the EU Parliament and the Council may approve incentives to protect and improve human health (Article 168.4), with the Council empowered to adopt recommendations upon the Commission's proposal (Article 168.5).

This background is essential to understand the evolution of AMR regulation in the EU. To dig into this topic, this section identifies some of the key elements of the EU regulatory framework for antimicrobial resistance, emphasizing its character as a shared policy marked by diverse and dissimilar responses across the EU member states. The intention is not to provide an exhaustive account of the very prolific legislative production and accompanying initiatives of the EU, but to show growth and evolution in the development of a robust AMR regulatory framework under a One Health approach.

11.5.2 *EU Cross-Sectoral AMR Regulatory Instruments*

The EU institutions have led the way in developing policies and regulatory frameworks to address antimicrobial resistance. The first Community Strategy to combat AMR was approved in 2001,[82] alongside Council Recommendations regarding the prudent use of antimicrobial agents in human medicine.[83] Framed by the above-mentioned constitutional division of powers and responsibilities, the regulatory framework for AMR primarily comprises soft law instruments, including Council recommendations and Conclusions, the Commission Action Plan on AMR, and the monitoring reports approved by the Commission and its specialised agencies on AMR, AMR surveillance and other specific AMR aspects of cross-cutting nature. These soft law instruments have influenced the revision and update of various sector-specific AMR-relevant legislation across various domains such as food and veterinary controls, veterinary medicines, feed, waste, wastewater, and soon, the authorisation of pharmaceuticals for human use.

Early documents, such as the Community Action Plan 2001 and the Council Recommendations and Conclusions of 2001, 2002,[84] and 2008,[85] focused on both the human and animal sectors, addressing aspects related to the coordinated management of medicines, antimicrobial stewardship, and the development of new medicines.[86] The slightly later second Commission Action Plan of 2011 and the Council Conclusions of 22 June 2012 introduce references to the One Health approach emphasizing the intersection between the human and

[82] Communication from the Commission on a Community Strategy Against Antimicrobial Resistance, COM/2001/0333 final Volume I, 26 June 2001.

[83] Council Recommendation of 15 November 2001 on the Prudent Use of Antimicrobial Agents in Human Medicine, OJ L 34, 5 February 2002, 13.

[84] Council Recommendation (2002/77/EC) on the Prudent Use of Antimicrobial Agents in Human Medicine.

[85] Council Conclusions on Antimicrobial Resistance (10 June 2008). Available at: www.consilium.europa.eu/uedocs/cms_data/docs/pressdata/en/lsa/101035.pdf.

[86] Council Conclusions of 23 November 2009 on Innovative Incentives for Effective Antibiotic, OJ C 302 (12 December 2009) 10.

the veterinary sectors.[87] One Health is also expressly mentioned in the European Parliament Resolutions on AMR adopted in May,[88] and October 2011,[89] 2012,[90] and 2015.[91]

However, it was in 2017, with the introduction of the last EU One Health Action Plan Against AMR (the 2017 AMR Action Plan) that the role of the environment was highlighted, and thus better encompassing the overarching One Health approach to the AMR issue and challenges.[92] EU actions under the plan aimed at focusing on the areas with the highest added value for member states such as promoting the prudent use of antimicrobials, enhancing cross-sectorial work, improving infection prevention, consolidating surveillance of AMR and antimicrobial consumption, and reporting.

In the same vein, the 2023 Council Recommendations on stepping EU actions to combat AMR under a One Health approach[93] encourages member states to implement One Health Action Plans for coordinated AMR response involving all sectors, including the environment, to ensure their full implementation. The recommendations further suggest concrete and measurable targets to reduce antimicrobial use, which consider national situations. Similarly, the European Parliament resolution of 1 June 2023 on EU action to combat AMR adopts a One Health approach and encourages members to foster multisectoral and sustainable AMR coordination and integrated surveillance addressing the environmental sector.[94]

The Commission's overview report of member states' One Health National Action Plans against AMR of November 2022 showed that while most member states have enacted NAPs under a One Health approach,[95] these Action Plans varied considerably in terms of implementation, with measures related to the environment often missing. Furthermore, weaknesses in the areas of financing, monitoring, control, and evaluation were identified that could compromise the long-term sustainability of the NAPs.

11.5.3 *Sector-Specific Legislation*

In addition to the aforementioned cross-cutting AMR legal soft law instruments, the EU has undergone a comprehensive revision of sector-specific legislation across key legal areas crucial for AMR. This revision encompasses the regulation of antimicrobials, measures to prevent the contamination of food and the environment with antimicrobials, and initiatives related to disease prevention and animal welfare that minimise the need for antimicrobials.

[87] Council Conclusions of 22 June 2012 on the Impact of Antimicrobial Resistance in the Human Health Sector and in the Veterinary Sector – a 'One Health' Perspective, OJ C, C/211, 18.07.2012, p. 2, CELEX. Available at: https://eur-lex.europa.eu/legal-content/EN/TXT/?uri=CELEX:52012XG0718(01).

[88] European Parliament Resolution of 12 May 2011 on Antibiotic Resistance. Available at: www.europarl.europa.eu/doceo/document/TA-7-2011-0238_EN.html.

[89] European Parliament Resolution of 27 October 2011 on the Public Health Threat of Antimicrobial Resistance. Available at: www.europarl.europa.eu/doceo/document/TA-7-2011-0473_EN.html.

[90] European Parliament Resolution of 11 December 2012 on the Microbial Challenge – Rising Threats from Antimicrobial Resistance (2012/2041(INI)). Available at: www.europarl.europa.eu/doceo/document/TA-7-2012-0483_EN.html.

[91] European Parliament Resolution of 13 September 2018 on a European One Health Action Plan against Antimicrobial Resistance (AMR) (2017/2254(INI)). Available at: www.europarl.europa.eu/doceo/document/TA-8-2018-0354_EN.html.

[92] Commission's Communication of 29 June 2017 'A European One Health Action Plan against AMR' (the '2017 AMR Action Plan'). Available at: https://health.ec.europa.eu/system/files/2020-01/amr_2017_action-plan_0.pdf.

[93] See https://ec.europa.eu/commission/presscorner/detail/en/IP_23_1843.

[94] European Parliament Resolution on EU Action to Combat Antimicrobial Resistance. 2023/2703(RSP).

[95] Overview report: Member States' One Health National Action Plans against Antimicrobial Resistance (17 November 2022). Available at: https://health.ec.europa.eu/publications/overview-report-member-states-one-health-national-action-plans-against-antimicrobial-resistance_en.

11.5.3.1 *Regulation of Antimicrobials*

A robust legal framework for medicines and medical devices is in place to protect the access, safety, and quality of these products.[96] It covers the whole life cycle, from authorisation to recall and surveillance, as well as monitoring, control, and disposal.

11.5.3.2 *Human Medicines*

In the realm of human medicines, the need for addressing AMR and the demand for new antimicrobials are at the basis of the Commission's proposed legislative package to revise the EU pharmaceutical legislation.[97] Comprising proposals for a Regulation,[98] and a Directive,[99] this package seeks to reform the current system governing the development, authorisation, and distribution of medicines. Its objectives include improving accessibility, affordability, and availability while addressing the environmental impact of medicine production and the presence of antimicrobials in the environment under a One Health approach. The proposed legislation aims to provide incentives for innovation and research to facilitate the development of new antimicrobials. Furthermore, in alignment with the 2017 AMR Action Plan, the Commission has adopted EU Guidelines for the prudent use of antimicrobials in human health.[100]

11.5.3.3 *Veterinary Medicines*

AMR considerations have played a pivotal role in the revision of the EU Regulation 2019/6 on veterinary medicinal products.[101] This regulation encompasses all stages of the veterinary medicine life cycle, including stewardship and use, access, pharmacovigilance, and control. It emphasises that veterinary medicines must be used for therapeutic purposes rather than for prophylaxis. The implementation of this regulation involves various delegated regulations, including those governing data collection on the volume of sales and use of antimicrobial medicinal products in animals.[102] Additionally, it serves as the foundation for Commission delegated Regulation (2021/1760) that establishes the criteria to reserve certain antimicrobials for the treatment of human infections only.[103] Finally, in the implementation of this Regulation,

96 See https://health.ec.europa.eu/medicinal-products/legal-framework-governing-medicinal-products-human-use-eu_en. See also the proposals for the revision of pharmaceutical legislation in https://health.ec.europa.eu/medicinal-products/pharmaceutical-strategy-europe/reform-eu-pharmaceutical-legislation_en.

97 See https://ec.europa.eu/commission/presscorner/detail/en/IP_23_1843.

98 Proposal for a Regulation of the European Parliament and of the Council laying down Union procedures for the authorisation and supervision of medicinal products for human use and establishing rules governing the European Medicines Agency, amending Regulation (EC) No. 1394/2007 and Regulation (EU) No. 536/2014 and repealing Regulation (EC) No. 726/2004, Regulation (EC) No. 141/2000 and Regulation (EC) No. 1901/2006 COM/2023/193 final.

99 Proposal for a Directive of the European Parliament and of the Council on the Union Code relating to medicinal products for human use, and repealing Directive 2001/83/EC and Directive 2009/35/EC. COM/2023/192 final.

100 Commission notice – EU Guidelines for the prudent use of antimicrobials in human health. C/2017/4326 OJ C 212 (1 July 2017).

101 Regulation (EU) 2019/6 of the European Parliament and of the Council of 11 December 2018 on veterinary medicinal products and repealing Directive 2001/82/EC (1) and in particular Article 37(4) thereof. OJL4/43 (7 January 2019).

102 Commission Delegated Regulation (EU) 2021/578 of 29 January 2021 supplementing Regulation (EU) 2019/6 of the European Parliament and of the Council with regard to requirements for the collection of data on the volume of sales and on the use of antimicrobial medicinal products in animals OJ L 123, 9.4.2021, 7–20. Also, Commission Implementing Regulation (EU) 2022/209 of 16 February 2022 establishing the format of the data to be collected and reported in order to determine the volume of sales and the use of antimicrobial medicinal products in animals in accordance with Regulation (EU) 2019/6 of the European Parliament and of the Council OJ L 35 (17 February 2022).

103 Commission Delegated Regulation (EU) 2021/1760 of 26 May 2021 supplementing Regulation (EU) 2019/6 of the European Parliament and the Council by establishing the criteria for the designation of antimicrobials to be reserved for the treatment of certain infections in humans. C/2021/3552 OJ L 353 (6 October 2021).

the EU introduced a common logo that must appear on websites offering veterinary medicines for sale at a distance.[104]

Regulation 2019/6 consolidates an evolution that was initiated with the prohibition of antibiotic growth promoters in 2003,[105] the 2015 EU Guidelines on the prudent use of antimicrobials in animal health,[106] and the revised rules for the packaging and labelling of veterinary medicinal products in 2022.[107] Additionally, in 2019, and as part of the implementation of the 2017 AMR Action Plan, Regulation 2019/4 introduced revised rules on the manufacture, authorisation, and use of medicated feed, including rules on the prescription and safe disposal of unused or expired products.[108]

11.5.3.4 *Food Safety*

AMR has also influenced the regulation of food production and controls in Europe. The EU's 2020 Farm to Fork Strategy incorporates specific AMR objectives, including a reduction by 50 per cent in the sales of antimicrobials for farmed animals and in aquaculture.[109] Furthermore, Regulation 2017/625 on official controls on food and feed, animal health and welfare, plant health and plant protection products, includes several references to antimicrobial resistance. Finally, the establishment of maximum residue limits for pharmacologically active substances in food of animal origin is regulated through Regulation 470/2009.[110]

11.5.3.5 *Integrated Surveillance*

Compliance with food and veterinary legislation falls under the oversight of the Food and Veterinary Office (FVO), a division of the Directorate General for Health and Food Safety with a dedicated focus on Commission controls. The FVO conducts targeted audits on antimicrobial resistance and the findings are presented in various reports available in the FVO website.[111] These reports delve into One Health antimicrobial resistance policies and regulation and evaluate key aspects such as multisectoral coordination mechanisms, NAP, environmental monitoring, antimicrobial use, and laboratory capacity. The audits provide useful insight into the effectiveness of policies and serve as mechanism for the implementation and enforcement of the legislation.

[104] Commission Implementing Regulation (EU) 2021/1904 of 29 October 2021 adopting the design of a common logo for the retail of veterinary medicinal products at a distance OJ L 387 (3 November 2021).

[105] Regulation (EC) No. 1831/2003 of the European Parliament and of the Council of 22 September 2003 on additives for use in animal nutrition prohibiting the use of antibiotic growth promoters OJ L 268 (18 October 2003) 29.

[106] Commission notice – EU Guidelines for the prudent use of antimicrobials in animal health. C/2015/4326 OJ C 299/7 (11 September 2015).

[107] Regulation (EU) 2022/839 of the European Parliament and of the Council of 30 May 2022 laying down transitional rules for the packaging and labelling of veterinary medicinal products authorised or registered in accordance with Directive 2001/82/EC or Regulation (EC) No 726/2004 OJ L 148 (31 May 2022) 6–7.

[108] Regulation (EU) 2019/4 of the European Parliament and of the Council of 11 December 2018 on the manufacture, placing on the market and use of medicated feed, amending Regulation (EC) No. 183/2005 of the European Parliament and of the Council and repealing Council Directive 90/167/EEC OJ L 4 (7 January 2019) 1–23.

[109] Communication from the Commission to the European Parliament, the Council, the European Economic and Social Committee and the Committee of the Regions A Farm to Fork Strategy for a fair, healthy, and environmentally friendly food system. COM/2020/381 final (20 May 2020).

[110] Regulation (EC) No. 470/2009 of the European Parliament and of the Council of 6 May 2009 laying down Community procedures for the establishment of residue limits of pharmacologically active substances in foodstuffs of animal origin, repealing Council Regulation (EEC) No. 2377/90 and amending Directive 2001/82/EC of the European Parliament and of the Council and Regulation (EC) No. 726/2004 of the European Parliament and of the Council OJ L 152 (16 June 2009).

[111] See https://ec.europa.eu/food/audits-analysis/audit-report.

Additionally, in the early twenty-first century, the EU established an integrated framework to facilitate cross-border controls relevant to the identification and control of AMR bacteria. Directive 2003/99/EC on the monitoring of zoonoses and zoonotic agents incorporates antimicrobial resistance monitoring related to zoonoses within its scope.[112] This Directive mandates member states to ensure the comprehensive collection, analysis, and publication of data concerning the occurrence of antimicrobial resistance-related zoonoses. Similarly, Regulation (EU) 2022/2371 addressing serious cross-border threats to health encompasses the collection of comparable and compatible data and information on AMR within the context of national prevention, preparedness, and response plans.[113]

11.5.3.6 *Environmental Protection*

The 2017 EU AMR Action Plan recognises the environment as one of the important pillars to address AMR, emphasizing the need for an EU strategic approach to pharmaceuticals in the environment. The plan highlights the need to revise key directives, including the Urban Waste Water Treatment Directive and the Water Framework Directive to understand the occurrence and spread of antimicrobials in the environment.[114]

In 2019, the Commission published a Communication outlining a Strategic Approach to Pharmaceuticals in the Environment.[115] This document identified six action areas covering all stages of the pharmaceutical life cycle, from production to disposal and waste management. This Communication aligns with the later EU Action Plan 'Towards a Zero Pollution for Air, Water, and Soil' adopted by the Commission in 2021 and approved as part of the European Green Deal.[116] This includes a zero pollution vision for 2050 and key targets to reduce pollution by 2030, including the reduction by 50 per cent in the use of antimicrobials in farm animals and aquaculture.

In 2022 the Commission put forth two directives on water and wastewater.[117] Both Directives include several references to AMR and introduce new mechanisms to collect AMR data in water and wastewater. Lastly, it is worth noting the Commission proposal on nature restoration,[118] which expressly mentions One Health and pollution from pharmaceuticals.

112 Directive 2003/99/EC of the European Parliament and of the Council of 17 November 2003 on the monitoring of zoonoses and zoonotic agents, amending Council Decision 90/424/EEC and repealing Council Directive 92/117/EEC OJ L 325 (12 December 2003) 31–40. This Directive is complemented by the Commission implementing decisions on the monitoring and reporting of AMR, including the Commission Implementing Decision (EU) 2020/1729 of 17 November 2020 on the monitoring and reporting of antimicrobial resistance in zoonotic and commensal bacteria and repealing Implementing Decision 2013/652/EU OJ L 387 (19 November 2020) 8–21.

113 Regulation (EU) 2022/2371 of the European Parliament and of the Council of 23 November 2022 on serious cross-border threats to health and repealing Decision No. 1082/2013/EU [2022] OJ L 314/26 (6 December 2022).

114 Directive 2000/60/EC of the European Parliament and of the Council of 23 October 2000 establishing a framework for Community action in the field of water policy OJ L 327 (22 December 2000).

115 Communication from the Commission to the European Parliament, the Council and the European Economic and Social Committee, European Union Strategic Approach to Pharmaceuticals in the Environment. COM (2019) 128 final.

116 Communication from the Commission to the European Parliament, the Council and the European Economic and Social Committee, and the Committee of the Regions Pathway to a Healthy Planet for All EU Action Plan: 'Towards Zero Pollution for Air, Water and Soil'. COM/2021/400 final/.

117 Proposal for a Directive of the European Parliament and of the Council amending Directive 2000/60/EC establishing a framework for Community action in the field of water policy; Directive 2006/118/EC on the protection of groundwater against pollution and deterioration; and Directive 2008/105/EC on environmental quality standards in the field of water policy. COM (2022) 540 final (26 October 2022). Also, Proposal for a Directive of the European Parliament and of the Council concerning urban wastewater treatment (recast). COM/2022/541 final (26 October 2022).

118 Proposal for a Regulation of the European Parliament and of the Council on nature restoration. COM/2022/304 final (22 June 2022).

11.5.3.7 *Prevention*

As an integral aspect of AMR prevention and control, the EU has implemented new legislation aimed at enhancing animal health and resilience to disease threats, thereby reducing the reliance on antimicrobials. Regulation (EU) 2016/429 on transmissible animal diseases ('Animal Health Law') incorporates several references to antimicrobial resistance.[119] This regulation sets up the basis to regulate AMR surveillance in veterinary medicine,[120] facilitating the listing of diseases when the disease agent has developed resistance to treatment posing a danger to human or animal health.[121] It also includes resistance as part of the capacity development requirements for operators and animal health professionals,[122] and their awareness-raising responsibilities.[123]

11.5.3.8 *Financing*

Beyond common harmonisation rules, encompassing common objectives and obligations, the EU regulatory framework for AMR includes several financial mechanisms that contribute to the deployment of various incentives to tackle antimicrobial resistance. Among these instruments, the Common Agriculture Policy plays a significant role by providing financial incentives to enhance animal welfare,[124] improve biosecurity in farms, and promote organic farming and eco-schemes, thereby reducing the reliance on antimicrobials and implementing control mechanisms to prevent environmental pollution. The EU4Health programme (2021–2027)[125] includes AMR as one of its key areas of action. Similarly, the Horizon Europe programme for research and innovation provides funding for research and development in AMR.[126]

In conclusion, the EU has played a pioneering role in the regulation of AMR across its 27 members. The structure of the EU regulatory framework effectively combines cross-cutting and sector-specific legal instruments, establishing a holistic and comprehensive coordination framework. Instead of creating overarching AMR legislation leading to legal fragmentation, the EU regulatory spans various sectors, highlighting a One Health approach that recognises the interconnectedness of human, animal, and environmental health. The implementation of this framework is supported by specific monitoring and control mechanisms, involving data collection, sharing, and direct oversight through dedicated audits. Sustainability is further promoted through financial mechanisms encouraging the implementation of good practices, innovation, research, and development. The participatory approach to law-making, involving extensive

[119] Regulation (EU) 2016/429 of the European Parliament and of the Council of 9 March 2016 on transmissible animal diseases and amending and repealing certain acts in the area of animal health ('Animal Health Law'). OJ L 153 (3 May 2021).

[120] Policy brief: European Antimicrobial Resistance Surveillance Network in Veterinary Medicine (EARS-VET). Available at: https://eu-jamrai.eu/wp-content/uploads/2021/02/201116_EUJAMRAI_policy-brief_WP7_EARS-Vet.pdf.

[121] Regulation (EU) 2016/429. Article 5.3(b)(ii).

[122] Ibid., Article 11.1.(e).

[123] Ibid., Article 12.1.(c)(iv).

[124] Regulation (EU) 2021/2115 of the European Parliament and of the Council of 2 December 2021 establishing rules on support for strategic plans to be drawn up by member states under the common agricultural policy (CAP Strategic Plans) and financed by the European Agricultural Guarantee Fund (EAGF) and by the (EAFRD) and repealing Regulations (EU) No. 1305/2013 and (EU) No. 1307/2013. OJ L 435 (6 December 2021).

[125] Regulation (EU) 2021/522 of the European Parliament and of the Council of 24 March 2021 establishing a Programme for the Union's action in the field of health ('EU4Health Programme') for the period 2021–2027, and repealing Regulation (EU) No. 282/2014. OJ L 107 (26 March 2021).

[126] Regulation (EU) 2021/695 of the European Parliament and of the Council of 28 April 2021 establishing *Horizon Europe* – the Framework Programme for Research and Innovation, laying down its rules for participation and dissemination, and repealing Regulations (EU) No. 1290/2013 and (EU) No. 1291/2013 OJ L 170 (12 May 2021).

consultations with stakeholders and bottom-up development, facilitates consensus building and fosters effective behavioural change.

However, the challenge lies in ensuring sustainable implementation at the country level, where EU countries exhibit varying levels of compliance with EU *acquis*. This diversity in implementation and compliance underscores the need for concerted efforts to enhance uniformity and effectiveness across member states.

11.6 INSIGHTS FROM AMR GOVERNANCE THAT MIGHT BE FURTHER APPLICABLE TO OTHER COMPLEX HEALTH THREATS UNDER THE ONE HEALTH APPROACH

This chapter aims to derive insights from the global, regional, and national governance and regulation of AMR, as detailed in the preceding sections. These lessons are intended to provide a broader applicability beyond AMR, to other areas benefiting from a One Health approach.[127]

In this section, One Health is understood as an approach dedicated to providing a collaborative and integrated response to health-related topics that demands a multisectoral and multidisciplinary perspective encompassing human, animal, and environmental factors. As defined by OHHLEP, this approach should embody the principles of equity across sectors, maintaining sociological equilibrium, fostering inclusivity and parity, stewardship in resources management, and embracing transdisciplinarity.[128]

AMR governance provides an excellent example of the implementation of the One Health approach and One Health principles in practice. International governance and regulation of AMR have solidified over the years, gaining broad recognition at the UN General Assembly and through collaborative efforts by the Quadripartite and other Intergovernmental Organisations. The GAP for AMR served as a pivotal milestone, offering countries a structured governance model with concrete sector-specific objectives, necessitating a combination of cross-sectoral and sector-specific efforts. The Interagency Coordination Group contributed to a transparent, comprehensive, and inclusive process, paving the way to a solid international governance framework. This might further consolidate within the Pandemics Agreement.

At the national level, AMR regulation demands a combination of cross-sectoral coordination mechanisms and sector-specific legislation to enable multisectoral coordination and the incorporation of international guidance into sectoral laws. Multisectoral and multidisciplinary mechanisms should facilitate equitable involvement and leadership capacity for all sectors to avoid perpetuating existing power dynamics. All relevant stakeholders should have the opportunity to voice their concerns and see their rights represented with particular attention to Indigenous Peoples, local communities, and vulnerable populations. Equity across sectors and parity among stakeholders, combined with transparency and access to information, facilitate stewardship of natural resources and a renewed attention to all species and living organisms in socioecological equilibrium. An enabling regulatory framework, with a clear delineation

[127] See for example, the proposals advanced by Negri and Eccleston-Turner concerning the application of the AMR pilot experience to the prevention of and response to zoonoses with pandemic potential, in Stefania Negri and Mark Eccleston-Turner, 'One Health and Pathogen Sharing: Filling the Gap in the International Health Regulations to Strengthen Global Pandemic Preparedness and Response' (2022) 19(1) *International Organizations Law Review* 188–214 (Special Issue 'Reforming the International Health Regulations' with guest editors Gian Luca Burci, Lisa Forman, and Steven J. Hoffman).

[128] One Health High-Level Expert Panel (OHHLEP), 'One Health: A New Definition for a Sustainable and Healthy Future'.

of roles and responsibilities, would provide these multisectoral mechanisms with a structure, solidifying shared obligations for data sharing and reporting. Legislation may further facilitate the introduction of a common accountability framework and joint indicators, securing participation rights for all stakeholders and financial resources.

The experience of AMR further underscores the potential role of legislation in facilitating data sharing for integrated surveillance. Integrated data management encompasses obligations for data collection and reporting, interoperability, protection, exchange, and joint analysis among institutions, alongside rules governing the publication and access to data, and the right to information. Caution must be paid when engaging the private sector in data generation to avoid overriding data, reporting obligations, and imposing unnecessary burdens, particularly on smallholders.[129] In cases where data involve the collection of genetic or biological information, an appropriate mechanism for benefit sharing must be in place, ensuring that communities or countries producing such data have the right to enjoy the benefits generated.

Beyond the coordination mechanism, every specific sector should adhere to the principles of equity, sociopolitical parity, and socioecological equilibrium in their sector-specific interventions. In the context of One Health collaboration, every sector must ensure that sector-specific legislation pays attention to its potential impact on the environment, biodiversity, animal health and welfare, plant health, and human health and wellbeing. Sector-specific policies and legislation should facilitate the stewardship of common public goods. Similar to antimicrobials, stewardship should guarantee the sustainable management of other public goods and natural resources, particularly in situations of shared rights over such resources.

The main research argument of this chapter is that the elements discussed could apply to other complex global health challenges that require a One Health approach. These challenges include the management of complex zoonoses such as rabies and avian influenza, but also broader areas such as sustainable wildlife management, a multisectoral response to pollution control, climate change or agri-food systems transformation.

Introducing a One Health approach will indeed vary across the different topics, depending on their objectives, stakeholders involved, and areas of focus. Nevertheless, drawing from the analysis of AMR, several principles can be extrapolated and applied, with necessary adjustments, to regulate other topics within a One Health framework.

At the international level, effective implementation requires political commitment, scientific expertise, and inclusive stakeholder engagement to integrate a One Health approach comprehensively. This entails fostering collaboration across sectors, disciplines, and nations to address complex health challenges holistically. At the national and regional levels, establishing robust multistakeholder mechanisms is crucial for promoting multisectoral coordination and integration. Such mechanisms should be underpinned by comprehensive and multisectoral frameworks, ensuring clear delineation of roles and responsibilities for each stakeholder. Legislation can support these frameworks by introducing long-term accountability mechanisms.

Additionally, it is imperative for countries to enact separate sector-specific legislation for each relevant area, aligning with international standards and best practices, thereby facilitating the incorporation of global guidelines into national regulatory frameworks and preventing legal fragmentation. Strengthening the regulatory landscape does not entail the consolidation or

[129] Si Ruishi, Yumeng Yao, Xin Liu, Qian Lu, and Mingyue Liu, 'Role of Risk Perception and Government Regulation in Reducing Over-Utilization of Veterinary Antibiotics: Evidence from Hog Farmers of China' (2022) 15 *One Health* 100448. Maria Paula and David Demeritt, 'Paperwork and the Decoupling of Audit and Animal Welfare: The Challenges of Materiality for Better Regulation' (2017) 35 *Environment and Planning C: Politics and Space* 169–190.

merging of different legal instruments, but their harmonisation. Laws that have traditionally operated in isolation must incorporate provisions for cross-referencing and cross-fertilisation, thereby facilitating coordinated action across diverse sectors. By integrating complementary laws and regulations, nations can optimise their regulatory frameworks to effectively address complex health challenges under the One Health approach.

In conclusion, AMR is a complex intersectoral challenge requiring a One Health approach. Led by the Quadripartite, the development of an AMR governance framework has rapidly evolved, resulting in consolidated and new structures at the national, regional, and global levels. The lessons learnt in the governance and regulation of AMR serve as insightful references in structuring the path forward for other One Health issues and their governance and regulation in other areas of priority for global/planetary health. By embracing the One Health principles of equity, socioecological equilibrium, transdisciplinarity, sociopolitical parity, and stewardship within national institutional and regulatory frameworks, a balance can be achieved that fosters an equilibrium among the health of humans, animals, plant, and the environment.

PART III

One Health and Future Legal Structures

12

Reorienting One Health Governance towards Indigenous Understanding

A Need for the Prioritisation of Indigenous Knowledges

Cassandra Seery and Joshua Gilbert

12.1 INTRODUCTION

One Health approaches seek to recognise the complex inter-relatedness and interdependence between Country, animals and peoples, an approach that Indigenous peoples have been refining for millennia.[1] It is through this lens that First Nations people share insights such as, 'when Country's sick, we are sick' and a feeling of Country as *Mother*, noting the rich relationship between land and people. As One Health frameworks seek to transform from responding to incidents to being proactive in the prevention of future events, Indigenous Knowledges and wisdom will be integral to this transformation. Critically, Indigenous Knowledges should be placed at the centre of this movement, ensuring Indigenous leadership and self-determination permeates each aspect of future One Health models.

Indigenous Knowledges and their evolution across pre- and post-colonial Australia provide a demonstrated understanding and application of practices beyond One Health. Despite being most impacted by the failures of adopting interdisciplinary One Health approaches, particularly during colonisation, Indigenous Knowledges provide critical methodologies and governance structures to implement and understand the relationship between people, animals, and Country. Most recently, this was demonstrated during the COVID-19 pandemic whereby Indigenous peoples developed their own public health strategies to complement broader health directions. This included, but was not limited to, locking down communities and self-mobilising to obtain resources, even despite direct opposition from police.[2]

There are a range of national and international agreements that inform how Indigenous rights and Knowledges should be applied in a One Health context. The United Nations Declaration on the Rights of Indigenous Peoples (UNDRIP),[3] for example, notes the right to the improvement of Indigenous health. Particular inclusion within UNDRIP are the rights that note Indigenous self-determination in relation to the active involvement in the development and determination of health programs, for access to healthcare services more

[1] Please note, the terms 'Indigenous', 'First Nations', and 'Aboriginal and Torres Strait Islander' are used interchangeably throughout this paper to refer to Aboriginal and/or Torres Strait Islander peoples in Australia.

[2] See, for example, S. Rubinsztein-Dunlop, 'NSW Police Deputy Commissioner Opposed COVID Plan to Lock Down Remote Aboriginal Communities', 12 November 2021. Available at: www.abc.net.au/news/2021-11-12/nsw-police-opposed-covid-plan-to-protect-aboriginal-communities/100606756.

[3] United Nations Declaration on the Rights of Indigenous Peoples, GA Res 61/295, UN Doc A/RES/61/295 (2 October 2007, adopted 13 September 2007).

broadly and the continuance of traditional health practices. Despite Australia endorsing UNDRIP in 2009, the Australian Human Rights Commission have remained critical over the implementation of these rights in Australian legislation,[4] and this impacts government approaches to collaboration and partnership with Indigenous communities and organisations. Australia has also ratified the Convention on Biological Diversity (CBD), which recognises the ecological knowledge of Indigenous peoples and the importance but not the requirement of free, prior, and informed consent in the application of such Knowledges. It also requires signatories to respect, preserve, and maintain Indigenous peoples' ecological knowledge and practices in relation to conservation and sustainable use of biological diversity.[5] Australia is also a signatory to the Nagoya Protocol on Access to Genetic Resources and the Fair and Equitable Sharing of Benefits Arising from their Utilization (Nagoya),[6] a global agreement that implements the access and benefit-sharing obligations of the CBD and extends the requirements (from the CBD) of Prior Informed Consent and Mutually Agreed Terms to Traditional Knowledge. The protocol creates a framework that ensures the fair and equitable sharing of benefits that arise from the use of genetic resources.[7] Yet again, the national implementation of the CBD and Nagoya Protocols are yet to influence practice for all Indigenous peoples across Australia.

Indigenous peoples have always seen this Country through connections, with an alignment between land, animals, and people demonstrated through embodiment and reflections in ceremonial dancing, for example, and trust between nations that we will all enact our role of protecting and caring for our individual countries. As such, One Health strategies should be developed and implemented in parallel with the UNDRIP, CBD, and Nagoya principles, particularly given the strong Caring for Country alignment and the vast connection that Indigenous peoples have with the various countries across Australia.

This chapter explores methods to reconceptualise and reorientate One Health understanding within Australia by aspiring to precolonial Indigenous ways of being and doing. Importantly, it also draws upon the post-colonial involvement and learnings of Indigenous peoples in Australia, integrating through self-determination or forced into modern economies and society. It is underpinned by the Indigenist research paradigm as articulated by Lester-Irabinna Rigney that places lived experience, 'ideas, traditions, dreams, interest, aspirations, and struggles' of First Nations individuals and communities at the centre of research to 'serve and inform the Indigenous struggle for self-determination'.[8] The experiences, Knowledges and perspectives of First Nations peoples cannot be understood without centring and prioritising Indigenous voices. Consequently, this contribution is designed to place Indigenous understandings and priorities at its centre.

4 See, for example, Australian Human Rights Commission. 'Implementing UNDRIP', 2021. Available at: https://humanrights.gov.au/sites/default/files/2020-10/implementing_undrip_-_australias_third_upr_2021.pdf.

5 Convention on Biological Diversity; 2020 Independent Review of the Environment Protection and Biodiversity Conservation Act 1999 (Cth), 58. Aichi Biodiversity Targets agreed under the CBD include a specific target (Target 18) that 'by 2020, the traditional knowledge, innovations and practices of Indigenous and local communities relevant for the conservation and sustainable use of biodiversity, and their customary use of biological resources, are respected, subject to national legislation and relevant international obligations, and fully integrated and reflected in the implementation of the Convention with the full and effective participation of Indigenous and local communities, at all relevant levels'.

6 But is yet to ratify the protocol.

7 The Protocol; 2020 Independent Review of the Environment Protection and Biodiversity Conservation Act 1999 (Cth), 58–9.

8 Lester-Irabinna Rigney, 'Internationalisation of an Indigenous Anticolonial Cultural Critique of Research Methodologies: A Guide to Indigenist Research Methodology and Its Principles' (1999) 14 *Wicazo Sa Review* 109–110.

12.2 PRE-COLONISATION AND IMPACT OF COLONISATION

Aboriginal and Torres Strait Islander peoples, Australia's Indigenous peoples, lived sustainably across Australia from time immemorial. Complex relationships and structures were developed, with each of the over 260 nations having developed a variety of languages and lifestyle systems synonymous with the landscapes in which they were living.[9] These landscapes formed part of Indigenous identity, with Indigenous peoples referring to themselves as belonging to certain Countries or nations, which provided context for marriage and other customary lore.

Indigenous peoples used a strict skin and totemic based system for the care and connection of animals in Australia. These totemic structures, in their simplest understanding, ensured that Indigenous peoples respected aspects of the land in different ways to one another, thereby ensuring the protection of species and thereby the land.[10] This strategy ensured Country, and therefore animals and people, was cared for deeply and carefully by First Nations communities.

During the initial stages and activities of colonisation, and the nuanced practices that made up colonisation through successive activities across country, Indigenous peoples were the first impacted by the failure of One Health models and the breakdown of their lifestyles across Australia.[11] During many instances of colonisation, livestock, disease and fractured Indigenous communities were forced through neighbouring landscapes prior to non-Indigenous peoples, thinking and recording.

The commentary on the health and physique of Indigenous peoples was, however, reflected upon in early journals and subsequently noted in the place names given in the landscape. Locations, such as Manly, reflect on this viewpoint noting the physical attributes of the Indigenous people witnessed.[12] These reflections in early journals provide further context for growing scholarly discussion regarding Indigenous agricultural systems prior to colonisation and the *parklike aesthetics* of Country, synonymous to European lands, viewed by early colonisers.[13]

Importantly, the process of agriculture is one colonising action, impacting landscapes seen as 'wastelands' to cultivate soils and drive Indigenous peoples off Country.[14] As the biggest land-use category of lands across Australia,[15] the process of agriculture created tension

[9] For more detail on the 260 nations see AIATSIS. 'Map of Indigenous Australia', 1996. Available at: https://aiatsis.gov.au/explore/map-indigenous-australia. This map attempts to represent the language, social, or nation groups of Aboriginal Australia. It shows only the general locations of larger groupings of people which may include clans, dialects, or individual languages in a group. It used published resources from the eighteenth century to 1994 and is not intended to be exact, nor the boundaries fixed. It is not suitable for native title or other land claims. David R. Horton (creator), © AIATSIS, 1996. No reproduction without permission. To purchase a print version visit: https://shop.aiatsis.gov.au/.

[10] See, for example, Deadly Story. 'Totems'. Available at: https://deadlystory.com/page/culture/Life_Lore/Family/Totems#:~:text=A%20totem%20is%20a%20natural,caretaking%20responsibilities%20for%20their%20totems.

[11] See, for example, P. J. Dowling, 'A Great Deal of Sickness: Introduced diseases among the Aboriginal People of colonial Southeast Australia 1788–1900'. Available at: https://openresearch-repository.anu.edu.au/bitstream/1885/7529/2/01Front_Dowling.pdf. See also the impact of colonisation on First Nations people in relation to possum-skin cloaks: https://aiatsis.gov.au/explore/possum-skin-cloak and www.abc.net.au/news/2022-12-29/indigenous-possum-skin-cloak-culture-and-history/101739174.

[12] Hello Manly, 'Fun Facts about Manly'. Available at: https://hellomanly.com.au/2021/03/fun-facts-about-manly/#:~:text=When%20Governor%20Arthur%20Phillip%20began,cove%20was%20known%20as%20Manly.

[13] See, for example, Bill Gammage, *The Greatest Estate on Earth: How Aborigines made Australia* (Allen and Unwin 2012); Bruce Pascoe, *Dark Emu: Black Seeds: Agriculture or Accident?* (Magabala Books 2014); Charles Massy, *Call of the Reed Warbler: A New Agriculture. A New Earth* (Chelsea Green Publishing Co 2018); Peter Sutton and Kerry Walshe, *Farmers or Hunter-Gatherers? The Dark Emu Debate* (Melbourne University Press 2021).

[14] Frieda Knobloch, *The Culture of Wilderness: Agriculture as Colonization in the American West* (University of North Carolina Press, 1996).

[15] Climateworks Centre, 'Land Use Futures'. Available at: https://climateworkscentre.org/land-use-futures/australias-land-use/#:~:text=Agriculture%20covers%20over%20half%20our,of%20Australia%27s%20total%20land%20mass.

between Indigenous and non-Indigenous peoples. Importantly, this tension is still felt today as farmers compete with Indigenous Native Title rights in fear of losing land for agricultural purposes.[16]

Indigenous labour was particularly sought after during the early stages of colonisation, as farmers took over landscapes.[17] However, the result of not prioritising Indigenous Knowledges, and the subsequent colonisation through agricultural systems has resulted in, since 1940, 25 per cent of all infectious diseases and 50 per cent of zoonotic infectious diseases emerging in humans globally being associated with agricultural drivers.[18]

12.3 CURRENT STATE

While the reflection on historic experiences provides context for the current state, it is important to note the evolution of Indigenous Knowledges over this period for relevance in today's society; that Indigenous systems did not just stop with colonisation, nor was culture lost or stuck in time, but instead it transformed with society too. This is despite anthropological rhetoric that affixes Indigenous culture to time and place,[19] incapable of transformation. Actions across this landscape demonstrate adaptability of this culture to new industries and economies; for example, selling early fishing harvests to the colony for survival.[20] By exploring Indigenous Knowledges through this lens, the opportunities for unlocking Indigenous thinking and systems are demonstrated through historic and more recent Indigenous evolutions.

Importantly, this chapter is written with the key awareness that One Health systems, much alike broader healthcare frameworks, continue to fail in understanding Indigenous perspectives.[21] Current Closing the Gap targets, the Federal and State Government commitments to address social determinant discrepancies between Indigenous and non-Indigenous peoples, demonstrate some improvement in terms of Indigenous life expectancy and healthy children, though overarchingly showing a worsening rating for social and emotional wellbeing.[22] Importantly, no health outcomes, such as Indigenous children being born healthy and strong compared to non-Indigenous children, are on track for Closing the Gap between Indigenous and non-Indigenous health areas.[23]

Having experienced the challenges of health systems, in Australia, Aboriginal Community Controlled Health Organisations (ACCHOs) were established to engage better with Indigenous communities and provide a range of health support for Indigenous peoples. ACCHOs have long adopted a broader and more holistic definition of health, which provides context for Indigenous health as part of One-Health frameworks, defined in the Constitution of the National peak body as:

[16] National Farmers Federation, 'Keep Farmers Farming'. Available at: https://keepfarmersfarming.org.au.

[17] For example, Dawn May, *Aboriginal Labour and the Cattle Industry: Queensland from White Settlement to the Present* (Cambridge University Press, 1994).

[18] Jason Rohr, Christopher Barrett, David Civitello, et al., 'Emerging Human Infectious Diseases and the Links to Global Food Production' (2019) 2 *Nature Sustainability* 445–456.

[19] See, for example, WEH Stanner, *White Man Got No Dreaming. Essays*, 1938 1973, (Black Inc. 1979).

[20] See, for example, Stan Grant, 'The Australian Dream: Blood, History and Becoming' (2016) *Quarterly Essay Issue* 64; Paul Irish, *Hidden in Plain View: The Aboriginal People of Coastal Sydney* (New South Publishing 2017).

[21] Irus Braverman (ed.), *More-than-One-Health: Humans, Animals and the Environment Post-COVID* (Routledge, 2023).

[22] National Indigenous Australians Agency, Closing the Gap'. Available at: www.niaa.gov.au/sites/default/files/publications/ctg-annual-report-and-implementation-plan-hq.pdf.

[23] Ibid.

"Aboriginal health" means not just the physical well-being of an individual but refers to the social, emotional and cultural well-being of the whole Community in which each individual is able to achieve their full potential as a human being thereby bringing about the total well-being of their Community. It is a whole of life view and includes the cyclical concept of life-death-life.[24]

12.4 THE INDIGENOUS ESTATE

Indigenous land holdings represent 56 per cent of Australia's landmass[25] with government aspirations to grow the 'Indigenous Estate', in respect to both land and sea country, by 15 per cent.[26] This large representation of Indigenous interests in land cements opportunities for Indigenous inclusion in the space, practically demonstrating the connection to landscapes right across the Country for the incorporation of One Health principles, nuanced to traditional homelands.

Land use, and therefore land ownership, is integral for One Health approaches, as approximately 22 per cent of infectious diseases in Australia have been associated with land use and native vegetation change, including Hendra virus.[27] This means that future land use changes, self-determined and driven by Indigenous peoples, will have a direct impact on One Health reactionary practices but also the prevention of such events.

The World Bank recently noted that about 36 per cent of remaining intact forests are on Indigenous Peoples' lands, with First Nations communities safeguarding 80 per cent of the world's remaining biodiversity.[28] While specific data is not available regarding the comparisons between Indigenous managed landscapes and non-Indigenous lands, this international approach suggests that future land title changes will provide future protection for Australia's forests and biodiversity.[29]

However, despite this access to land, much of the country remains used by non-Indigenous peoples.[30] This is further reflected in terms of Indigenous representation across the agricultural sector, with low levels of employment, representing just 1.8 per cent of the current agricultural workforce,[31] and a pipeline of less than five Indigenous agricultural graduates across every university in Australia.[32]

24 National Aboriginal Community Controlled Health Organisation, 'Aboriginal Community Controlled Health Organisations (ACCHOs)'. Available at: www.naccho.org.au/acchos/.

25 R. Barnett, A. Normyle, B. Doran, and M. Vardon, 'Baseline Study – Agricultural Capacity of the Indigenous Estate' (2022). Available at: www.crcna.com.au/resources/publications/baseline-study-agricultural-capacity-indigenous-estate.

26 National Indigenous Australians Agency, 'Closing the Gap'. Available at: www.niaa.gov.au/sites/default/files/publications/ctg-annual-report-and-implementation-plan-hq.pdf.

27 Katie Woolaston, Zoe Nay, Michelle L. Baker, et al. 'An Argument for Pandemic Risk Management Using a Multidisciplinary One Health Approach to Governance: An Australian Case Study' (2022) 18 *Global Health* 73. Available at: https://globalizationandhealth.biomedcentral.com/articles/10.1186/s12992-022-00850-4.

28 World Bank, 'Empowering Indigenous Peoples to Protect Forests' (2023). Available at: www.worldbank.org/en/news/feature/2023/08/09/empowering-indigenous-peoples-to-protect-forests.

29 There are references that show biodiversity on Indigenous held lands is the same as, if not greater than that in legally protected areas. See I. Leiper, K. K. Zander, C. J. Robinson, J. Carwadin, B. J. Moggridge, and S. T. Garnett, 'Quantifying Current and Potential Contributions of Australian Indigenous Peoples to Threatened Species Management' (2018) 32(5) *Conservation Biology* 1038–1047. Available at: https://doi.org/10.1111/cobi.13178.

30 R. Barnett, A. Normyle, B. Doran, and M. Vardon, 'Baseline Study – Agricultural Capacity of the Indigenous Estate' (2022). Available at: www.crcna.com.au/resources/publications/baseline-study-agricultural-capacity-indigenous-estate.

31 B. Slatter, 'Snapshot of Australia's Agricultural Workforce' (2023) 3 *Department of Agriculture and Water Resources ABARES Insights* 1–16.

32 J. E. Pratley, Indigenous Students do not Choose Agriculture at University' (Proceedings of the 19th Australian Agronomy Conference, Wagga Wagga, 2019). Available at: https://acda.edu.au/resources/IndigenousStudentsDoNotChooseAgricultureAtUniversity.pdf.

12.5 AUSTRALIA, INDIGENOUS KNOWLEDGES, AND THE ONE HEALTH DOMAINS

The adoption, development, and implementation of One Health in Australia is still in its infancy, largely propelled into the spotlight by the arrival of COVID-19.[33] However, attempts to bring together Western understandings of health and Indigenous Knowledges across the three One Health domains – human, animal, and environmental health – have been underway for decades. While the narrative underpinning these efforts has typically been framed in Western narratives through a deficit-based discourse relating to the health inequalities for Indigenous peoples,[34] in recent years it has slowly been transitioning towards a more strengths-based foundation.[35]

The transitions and initiatives currently underway across the One Health domains are perhaps best conceptualised as processes of indigenisation and/or decolonisation. In a One Health context, Indigenisation centres on systems that perpetuate colonial values and privileges Western Knowledges and ways of working. It is a collaborative process that involves the transformation of colonial spaces to integrate Indigenous peoples' diverse perspectives and approaches. Indigenisation is not merely confined to projects, programs, and services; it is embedded by positioning Indigenous ways of knowing, being, and doing to the core of institutional structures and – by extension – into the principles, policies, and practices of colonial institutions. Decolonisation, on the other hand, centres on the dismantling of colonial systems and structures, deconstructing Western ideologies that privilege colonial knowledge and methods as superior, and revitalise Indigenous Knowledges and practices through a prism of sovereignty and self-determination. Both indigenisation and decolonisation play a critical role in advancing a holistic view of health, which aligns with both the concept of One Health and Indigenous ways of knowing, being, and doing.[36]

12.6 INTERSECTIONS ACROSS ONE HEALTH DOMAINS

12.6.1 *Human Health*

In relation to 'human' health – which typically dominates discussions of health in colonial spaces – it has long been established that Western biomedical approaches normalise deficit discourses upon Indigenous peoples and racism, resulting in health inequalities for

[33] Woolaston 'An Argument for Pandemic Risk Management Using a Multidisciplinary One Health Approach to Governance'.

[34] Deficit discourse refers to a mode of thinking that frames and represents Aboriginal and Torres Strait Islander people in a narrative of negativity, deficiency, and failure: C. Fforde, L. Bamblett, R. Lovett, S. Gorringe, and B. Fogarty, 'Discourse, Deficit and Identity: Aboriginality, the Race Paradigm, and the Language of Representation in Contemporary Australia' (2013) 149(1) *Media International Australia* 162–173. For further information on how this is understood in an Indigenous health context, see Lowitja Institute, 'Deficit Discourse and Indigenous Health: How Narrative Framings of Aboriginal and Torres Strait Islander People are Reproduced in Policy (2018). Available at: www.lowitja.org.au/wp-content/uploads/2023/05/deficit-discourse.pdf.

[35] Examples of this transition are explored throughout this chapter, though it should be noted this is by no means exhaustive.

[36] Tamara Riley, Neil E. Anderson, Raymond Lovett, Anna Meredith, Bonny Cumming, and Joanne Thandrayen, 'One Health in Indigenous Communities: A Critical Review of the Evidence' (2021) 18 *International Journal of Environmental Research and Public Health* 11303; Pat Dudgeon, Helen Milroy, and Roz Walker (eds.) *Walking Together: Aboriginal and Torres Strait Islander Mental Health and Wellbeing Principles and Practice* (Commonwealth of Australia 2014).

Indigenous peoples.[37] Calls for changes to the health system to both indigenise and decolonise primary care have led to a wide range of initiatives, including the ongoing leadership and advocacy of organisations such as the National Aboriginal Community Controlled Health Organisation (NACCHO) and the Gayaa Dhuwi (Proud Spirit) Australia;[38] research and programs stemming from the Poche Centres for Indigenous Health across the country and other research efforts such as the National Health and Medical Research Council (NHMRC) funded Decolonising Practice in Aboriginal and Torres Strait Islander Primary Health Care Project (2018–2023);[39] the development of culturally valid clinical testing and best practice;[40] and the establishment of Indigenous-led 'best practice' organisations such as the Lowitja Institute and the Balit Durn Durn Centre which prioritises culturally valid research,[41] knowledge exchange, and coordination and expansion of Social and Emotional Wellbeing Services to both non-Indigenous and ACCOs. While these examples represent a fraction of the initiatives that have been led by Indigenous peoples for decades, they are emblematic of the foundation pillars that drive the efforts of Indigenous peoples, communities, and organisations: a holistic conceptualisation of health and the criticality of self-determination.

12.6.2 *Animal Health*

Understanding of Indigenous Knowledges and the intersections between 'animal' health and 'human' health in a One Health context across Aboriginal and Torres Strait Islander communities has been evolving in recent years, led by Wiradjuri scholar Tamara Riley. Riley highlights that, while One Health aligns with Aboriginal and Torres Strait Islander Peoples' holistic view of health, Australia's current health systems do not 'adequately account for the impact of animal and environmental factors that contribute to human health outcomes'.[42] Riley emphasises the importance of collaborative approaches at the 'animal-human-environment interface',[43] stating that Indigenous governance and leadership is limited and argues in favour of an integrated national health system where Indigenous leadership and engagement is embedded through the development of strong networks and governance structures.[44] Such an approach, which would create space for Indigenous communities to

37 See, for example, Emma Haynes, Roz Walker, Alice G. Mitchell, Judy Katzenellenbogen, Heather D'Antoine, and Dawn Bessarab 'Decolonizing Indigenous Health: Generating a Productive Dialogue to Eliminate Rheumatic Heart Disease in Australia' (2021) 277 *Social Science and Medicine* 113829; Victorian Government, Royal Commission into Victoria's Mental Health System Interim and Final Reports.

38 Formerly the National Aboriginal and Torres Strait Islander Leadership in Mental Health. Available at: www.gayaadhuwi.org.au/our-story/.

39 University of Adelaide, 'Decolonising Practice in Aboriginal and Torres Strait Islander Primary Health Care'. Available at: www.adelaide.edu.au/stretton/our-research/stretton-health-equity/decolonising-practice-in-aboriginal-and-torres-strait-islander; https://researchdata.edu.au/decolonising-practice-aboriginal-health-care/1348216.

40 See, for example, the work of Dr Tracy Westerman.

41 The Balit Durn Durn Centre was established as a result of the Royal Commission into Victoria's Mental Health System interim and final recommendations for Social and Emotional Wellbeing in Victoria. Available at: http://rcvmhs.archive.royalcommission.vic.gov.au/.

42 Tamara Riley, Neil E. Anderson, Raymond Lovett, Anna Meredith, Bonny Cumming, and Joanne Thandrayen, 'Data Analysis of Zoonoses Notifications in Aboriginal and Torres Strait Islander Populations in Australia 1996–2021: Implications for One Health' (2023) 11 *Public Health* 1175835. Available at www.frontiersin.org/journals/public-health/articles/10.3389/fpubh.2023.1175835/full. See also I. Johnson, A. Hansen, and P. Bi 'The Challenges of Implementing an Integrated One Health Surveillance System in Australia' (2017) 65 *Zoonoses Public Health* 229.

43 Ibid.

44 Ibid.

decide what to prioritise and what steps to take, aligns with the United Nations Declaration on the Rights of Indigenous Peoples.[45]

12.6.3 *Environmental Health*

Environmental systems across Australia create fertile ground for both indigenisation and decolonisation of systems, structures, and ways of doing. The need for such approaches has never been greater; since colonisation, Australia has lost 40 per cent of its forests and nineteen ecosystems are showing signs of collapse (or near collapse).[46]

The '2021 State of the Environment Report' highlights that partnerships between Indigenous and Western approaches to biodiversity management show promise. The introduction and expansion of the Indigenous ranger programs and Protected Area programs – which combine traditional techniques with modern science approaches to protect ecosystems – create space for Indigenous communities to be directly involved and create 'locally driven, country-specific approaches into biodiversity actions'.[47] The Report noted, however, that despite their success, these 'programs and opportunities to work on Country are limited'.[48] There are many such examples where Indigenous Knowledges play a critical role in manifesting the outcomes that One Health is seeking to achieve, spanning across a wide range of fields including wildlife management,[49] fire management,[50] and so on, all of which suffer from similar resourcing constraints and practice and policy limitations.

12.7 INDIGENOUS GOVERNANCE

Governance is about who holds power, authority, and responsibility, who decides and how decisions are made.[51] Australian Indigenous governance scholarship emphasises that pre-colonisation and beyond, Indigenous peoples continue to assert sovereignty in the face of an ongoing occupation.[52] Despite sustained efforts since colonisation to deny, disrupt, and eradicate Indigenous peoples' connection to Country and relegate Indigenous peoples to the role of

[45] United Nations Declaration on the Rights of Indigenous Peoples, GA Res 61/295, UN Doc A/RES/61/295 (2 October 2007, adopted 13 September 2007); Riley, 'Data Analysis of Zoonoses Notifications in Aboriginal and Torres Strait Islander Populations in Australia 1996–2021'.

[46] Ian Cresswell, Terri Janke, and Emma L. Johnston, 'Australia State of the Environment 2021: Indigenous, Independent Report to the Australian Government Minister for the Environment' (Commonwealth of Australia 2021).

[47] Ibid.; Country Needs People. Available at: www.countryneedspeople.org.au/protecting_nature_report.

[48] Country Needs People. Available at: www.countryneedspeople.org.au/protecting_nature_report.

[49] J. Davies, R. Hill, F. J. Walsh, M. Sandford, D. Smyth, and M. C. Holmes, 'Innovation in Management Plans for Community Conserved Areas: Experiences from Australian Indigenous Protected Areas' (2013) 18(2) *Ecology and Society* 14; Emilie Ens, 'Australian Approaches for Managing 'Country' Using Indigenous and Non-Indigenous Knowledge (2012) 13(1) *Ecological Management and Restoration* 100.

[50] Grazia Borrini-Feyerabend, Nigel Dudley, Tilman Jaeger, et al. 'Governance of Protected Areas: From Understanding to Action' (Best Practice Protected Area Guidelines Series No.20, 2013). Available at: https://portals.iucn.org/library/sites/library/files/documents/PAG-020.pdf; Jeremy Russell-Smith, Garry D. Cook, Peter M. Cooke, et al., 'Managing Fire Regimes in North Australian Savannas: Applying Aboriginal Approaches to Contemporary Global Problems' (2013) 11 *Frontiers in Ecology and the Environment* e55.

[51] Grazia Borrini-Feyerabend and Rosemary Hill, 'Governance for the Conservation of Nature' in G. L Worboys et al. (eds.) *Protected Area Governance and Management* (ANU Press, 2015) 171.

[52] Suzanne von der Porten and Robert C. de Loë, 'How Collaborative Approaches to Environmental Problem Solving View Indigenous Peoples: A Systematic Review' (2014) 27(10) *Society & Natural Resources* 1040–1056.

stakeholder – rather than as sovereign nations that operate independent of colonial systems and structures – Indigenous governance endures and continues to be revitalised.[53] Indeed, governance models provide an important framework for the incorporation of Indigenous Knowledges into existing and new frameworks.

Kuku Yalanji scholar, Leah Talbot, highlights the need to distinguish between Indigenous cultural governance – where decision-making and ways of working are founded in 'social and cultural fabric and community law or lore systems that govern Indigenous People as a society or nation'[54] – and Indigenous organisational governance, which is born from the attempts of settler-colonial states, such as Australia, to establish structures that 'facilitate Indigenous People to make decisions for and on behalf of themselves'.[55] This is typically supported through policies and legislation. Both forms of governance play a critical role and co-exist with one another to facilitate positive outcomes for Indigenous peoples. Within these systems are the tools to engage in indigenisation and decolonisation efforts, as both Indigenous cultural governance and Indigenous organisational governance are underpinned by the following Indigenous governance principles: (1) sovereignty; (2) self-determination; (3) *sui generis* rights founded in 'the inherent rights of Indigenous peoples to the land they have occupied since time immemorial'; and (4) that Indigenous peoples' rightful decision-making role stems from these rights.[56] In collaborative and partnership settings, settler-colonial responses to the implementation of these principles is typically interpreted as a political act, where the assertion of sovereignty through self-determination is viewed as a threat to colonial power. This often leads to governance arrangements where settler colonial mechanisms do not adequately support these principles in practice.

Across the One Health domains, this tension is best exemplified by the evolution of Environment Protection and Biodiversity Conservation Act 1999 (Cth) ('EPBC Act'). When originally enacted, the EPBC Act – Australia's primary national environmental legislation relating to matters of national significance – was seen as a modest contribution that was (arguably unduly) narrow in scope.[57] A recent independent review of the EPBC Act was undertaken in October 2020.[58] This highlighted numerous failures of the EPBC Act in fulfilling its objectives in relation to 'the role of Indigenous Australians in protecting and conserving biodiversity, working in partnership with and promoting the respectful use of their knowledge'.[59] The Independent Review found a range of structural and systemic failures impacting on effective

[53] This includes the Colonial Frontier Massacres (1788–1930) forced removal of Aboriginal and Torres Strait Islander peoples from their country onto reserves, the prohibition of language and cultural practices, the removal of children (which continues today), issues surrounding native title and the deferment to pastoral interests, the privileging of written/colonial evidence and policy loopholes in cases such as *Cubillo v. Commonwealth* [2000] FCA 1084, *Members of the Yorta Yorta Aboriginal Community v. Victoria* [1998] FCA 1606, etc; von der Porten, 'How Collaborative Approaches to Environmental Problem Solving View Indigenous Peoples'.

[54] Leah Talbot, 'Indigenous Knowledge and Governance in Protected Areas in Australia and Sweden' (PhD Thesis, James Cook University, 2017) 2.

[55] von der Porten, 'How Collaborative Approaches to Environmental Problem Solving View Indigenous Peoples'; Talbot 'Indigenous Knowledge and Governance in Protected Areas in Australia and Sweden', 65.

[56] Talbot 'Indigenous Knowledge and Governance in Protected Areas in Australia and Sweden', 65.

[57] Lee Godden and Jacqueline Peel, 'The Environment Protection and Biodiversity Conservation Act 1999 (Cth): Dark Sides of Virtue' (2007) 31 *Melbourne University Law Review* 106–108.

[58] Under s 522A of the Act, an independent review of the Act must be undertaken at least every 10 years to examine the operation of the Act and to what extent its objectives have been achieved.

[59] Commonwealth of Australia, *Independent Review of the EPBC Act* (Final Report, October 2020). Available at: https://epbcactreview.environment.gov.au/resources/final-report.

Indigenous governance, including that the EPBC Act: (1) does not fully support the rights of Indigenous peoples in decision-making; (2) does not meet the aspiration of Traditional Owners for managing their land; and (3) is currently a barrier to holistic environmental management. The Independent Review went further, highlighting that current approaches were 'tokenistic', stating that the Act prioritises Western science and, consequently, Indigenous Knowledges and views are not 'fully valued' in decision-making. These findings are a good example of the ways in which Indigenous organisational governance systems can be undermined by the colonial structures and ways of working that necessitated their creation. In contrast, the Independent Review's recommendations go some way to demonstrating the opportunities to embed good governance through the application of the four Indigenous governance principles. There were a range of recommendations focusing on: strengthening Indigenous leadership value of Indigenous Knowledges in existing governance structures and partnerships; developing National Environment Standards on best-practice Indigenous engagement, participation, and decision-making; and the adoption of co-design and Indigenous-led processes as a core component of efforts made under the Act.

In December 2022 the Australian Government released a response to the Independent Review – the Nature Positive Plan – committing to a range of initiatives stemming from the Independent Review's recommendations.[60] This step towards national reform reflects progress already underway in Australia, such as Queensland's Biodiscovery Act 2004, which introduced protections for the use of traditional knowledge in biodiversity.[61] Consultations for the Nature Positive Plan commenced in October 2023, with a view to introducing new environment and cultural heritage laws in 2024, but this has been delayed indefinitely.[62] At the time of writing, the extent to which the Independent Review's recommendations are embedded in these reforms is unknown.

Other models for advancing Indigenous interests across the One Health spectrum also require Indigenous governance models and leadership. Initiatives include the National Indigenous Environmental Research Network (NIERN).[63] This is an Indigenous-led strategic initiative to support Indigenous leadership and participation in biodiversity conservation and environmental management,[64] which is currently underway, and a proposed Indigenous Agricultural Research and Development Corporation (IARDC).[65]

[60] Department of Climate Change, Energy, the Environment and Water, 'Nature Positive Plan: Better for the Environment, Better for Business' (December 2022). Available at: www.dcceew.gov.au/sites/default/files/documents/nature-positive-plan.pdf.

[61] Biodiscovery and Other Legislation Amendment Act 2020 (Qld); Queensland Government, Reform of the Biodiversity Act 2004 (Qld). Available at: https://environment.desi.qld.gov.au/licences-permits/plants-animals/biodiscovery/biodiscovery-act-reform.

[62] In April 2024, Federal Environment Minister Tanya Pilbersek announced that the federal government would not be introducing a full environmental reform package, electing to introduce legislation for a national Environmental Protection Agency, while continuing to consult on changes to the EPBC Act. These reforms – including the national standards – have been delayed indefinitely. See also Lisa Cox and Adam Morton, 'Labor Accused of Broken Promise after Delaying Laws to Address Australia's Extinction Crisis', *The Guardian* (16 April 2024). Available at: www.theguardian.com/environment/2024/apr/16/labor-national-environment-laws-australia-wildlife-threatened-species. See also https://theconversation.com/labors-dumping-of-australias-new-nature-laws-means-the-environment-is-shaping-as-a-key-2025-election-issue-248872.

[63] National Environmental Science Program, (2023) 'Developing a National Indigenous Environmental Research Network (NIERN)'. Available at: https://nesplandscapes.edu.au/projects/nesp-rlh/developing-niern/.

[64] Ibid.

[65] Gilbert et al., 'A call for a national First Nations agricultural representation body in Australia' (2023). Available at: www.farminstitute.org.au/product/fpj2004-gilbert-j-et-al-2023-a-call-for-a-national-first-nations-agricultural-representation-body-in-australia/ (accessed on 12 March 2024).

12.8 POTENTIAL FUTURE STATE

The introduction of One Health as part of the 'mainstream' discourse presents opportunities for a recalibration of One Health in an Australian context that embraces and centres Indigenous ways of knowing, being, and doing. In a position statement on One Health, the Australian Medical Association stated that 'Aboriginal and Torres Strait Islanders should have a central role in developing One Health policies', also acknowledging the vital expertise of Indigenous Peoples in caring for Country,[66] and the similarities between the concept of One Health and Connection to Country.[67] The lack of adequate coordination across jurisdictions and sectors across Australia to achieve a One Health approach to date also presents an opportunity to build a system that centres Indigenous Knowledges and governance structures to benefit Australia as a whole. While these examples pave the way for cautious optimism, it is important to note that, to date, the steps taken towards One Health at the federal level – such as the development of the One Health Master Action Plan for Australia's National Antimicrobial Resistance Strategy – 2020 & Beyond, and the inclusion of One Health as a core principle in the Department of Foreign Affairs and Trade's Indo-Pacific Centre for Health Security – made no mention of Indigenous Knowledges or communities at all.

It is unsurprising that initial conceptions of One Health in an Australian context privilege Western approaches; when examining the concept of One Health for Indigenous communities, Hiller et al. identified three major themes that focused on One Health: climate change, zoonosis, and social relationships between humans and animals. No significant connection between One Health and Indigenous Knowledges was established and the implications of utilising One Health towards Indigenous Peoples and culture was not explicitly addressed.[68]

To date there has been little emphasis placed on understanding and incorporating traditional Indigenous Knowledges within the One Health framework;[69] arguably, the assumption that Indigenous Knowledges are required to fit in and 'inform' yet another Western framework highlights the ongoing limitations of Western approaches. The interim Australian Centre for Disease Control (ACDC),[70] for example, which has identified One Health as key priority for the ACDC when it is established in 2025, refers to First Nations organisations as a key stakeholder.[71] While the inclusion of Indigenous peoples is an important step in the right direction in the context of One Health – one that presents opportunities to embed Indigenous Knowledges and ways of knowing, being, and doing nationally – it also raises important questions about the role of Indigenous peoples in the context of One Health. Is it appropriate to confine Indigenous peoples to the role of 'stakeholder' on one's own unceded lands, where Indigenous Knowledges are critical to the success of a holistic approach to health in Australia? As Libby Porter highlights:

> Conceptualising Indigenous peoples as 'stakeholders' in planning processes fails to appreciate their unique status as original owners of country that was wrested from them by the modern, colonial state. As Langton points out, within Indigenous law rests the notion that 'Aboriginal

[66] Australian Medical Association, 'One Health Position Statement' (2 December 2023) 1. Available at: www.ama.com.au/articles/one-health-position-statement.

[67] Ibid.

[68] Sean Hiller, Abdul Taleb, Elias Chaccour, and Cécile Aenishaenslin, 'Examining the Concept of One Health for Indigenous Communities: A Systematic Review' (2021) 12 *One Health* 1.

[69] Hiller, 'Examining the Concept of One Health for Indigenous Communities'.

[70] The ACDC is on progress to be established in early 2025.

[71] Australian Government, One Health. Available at: www.cdc.gov.au/about/what-we-do/one-health.

> people are born with an inchoate, inherited and transmissible right in a "country"' (Langton, 1997, p. 1). Indigenous peoples in Australia must occupy a position more significant than that of another stakeholder in land management questions.[72]

The answer lies in finding opportunities across the indigenisation–decolonisation spectrum to centre place-based solutions and Indigenous Knowledges to achieve One Health outcomes. Examples throughout this chapter demonstrate strides already being taken in this space; additionally, the work of civil society organisations such as Wildlife Health Australia and the Foundation for Indigenous Sustainable Health are also examples of what can be achieved. There are also opportunities to embed Indigenous Knowledges and governance at an organisational level through Reconciliation Action Plans (RAPs).[73] While RAPs are by no means a 'cure-all' for organisational change, they can play a meaningful role facilitating holistic, place-based solutions that create space for Indigenous leadership.

Additionally, there are opportunities for systemic and structural change through the ongoing treaty processes that are in train across several jurisdictions. In Victoria, for example, where treaty negotiations commenced in November 2024, the First Peoples' Assembly of Victoria – an independent and democratically elected body to represent Traditional Owners and Indigenous peoples in Victoria – has stated that 'nothing is off the table', paving the way for sovereignty and self-determination across a range of One Health domains. In South Australia, the First Nations Voice to Parliament presents an opportunity for Indigenous peoples to raise community priorities and concerns directly to decision-makers (including parliament). While not a decision-making body, it creates further opportunities for Indigenous peoples to improve outcomes for communities across South Australia. There are many other opportunities to better reorient current approaches – implementing the UNDRIP into domestic law, for example – that would create the conditions for a One Health approach that reflects Australia's existing strengths and expertise. In this way, Australia would be well placed to apply a critical lens to the existing discussions surrounding One Health, which continue to perpetuate the existing Western structural biases and power dynamics.[74] This is best exemplified by the 'human-first' approach to One Health, where animals and the environment merely become the means by which human health outcomes are achieved.[75]

12.9 CONCLUSION

This chapter has explored the need for the incorporation of Indigenous Knowledges into One Health Governance frameworks, ensuring the alignment of these models to the United Nations Declaration on the Rights of Indigenous Peoples. If One Health is to succeed as an integrated system, First Nations input is essential, not only as the proprietors of critical information and Knowledges but also given the drastic land interests and connection to Country to prevent future events.

[72] Libby Porter, 'Planning in (Post)colonial Settings: Challenges for Theory and Practice' (2006) 7(4) *Planning Theory and Practice* 383, 389.

[73] This can be seen across the public sector through the Australian government's RAP commitments across key departments and agencies, including the departments overseeing agriculture and environment, the CSIRO, and Public Health Networks (PHNs) but this is also making its way into the private and not-for-profit sectors as well.

[74] Irus Braverman, 'Introduction: More-than-One-Health, More-than-One-Governance' in Irus Braverman (ed.), *More-than-One-Health: Humans, Animals and the Environment Post-COVID* (Routledge, 2023) 2.

[75] Ibid.

The recent COVID-19 pandemic has demonstrated the importance of prioritising Indigenous Knowledges and centring our methods and approaches when dealing with pandemics, creating tools and resources to effectively engage with Indigenous people and prevent catastrophic risk to Indigenous communities at large. As Australia commits more broadly to One Health, UNDRIP, CBD, and Nagoya principles must be incorporated to effectively engage and centre Indigenous voices for success.

13

The Convention on Animal Protection

A Cathartic Resolution to a Global Pandemic Story

Rajesh K. Reddy

13.1 INTRODUCTION

A year after officially declaring COVID-19 a pandemic, the Director-General of the World Health Organization (WHO), Dr Tedros Adhanom Ghebreyesus, added his voice to those of over two dozen world leaders in calling attention to how the outbreak had 'exploited [the] weaknesses and divisions' among states and stressing the need for leaders to negotiate a 'new international treaty for pandemic preparedness and response'.[1] As is the case today,[2] the great weight of evidence at the time traced the emergence of COVID-19 to a live animal market in Wuhan, China,[3] where a vast array of wildlife was known to be held in cramped, unsanitary, stress-inducing conditions, conditions widely believed to have facilitated the spread, mutation, and subsequent spillover of the novel coronavirus into humans.[4] With SARS-CoV-2 representing yet another in a long line of zoonotic disease pathogens, or those that spill over from animals into humans and represent roughly 75 per cent of all diseases that afflict humankind,[5] it comes as little surprise that the joint letter cited the need for a One Health approach to inform how such an agreement could safeguard the health of humanity for generations to come.[6] Often conceived as a diagram featuring three distinct yet

The author would like to acknowledge the many animal law scholars, attorneys, and advocates who helped draft the Convention on Animal Protection for Public Health, Animal Well-Being, and the Environment, as well as contributed to the founding of the International Coalition for Animal Protection. In addition, he would like to express his gratitude to Nigel Blackaby, Daina Bray, Nicolas Cordoba, David Favre, Rosario Galardi, Vanessa Gischkow Garbini, Laurie Morgan, and Joan Schaffner for their longstanding support.

1 World Health Organization, 'COVID-19 Shows Why United Action is Needed for More Robust International Health Architecture' (30 March 2021), Available at www.who.int/news-room/commentaries/detail/op-ed—covid-19-shows-why-united-action-is-needed-for-more-robust-international-health-architecture.

2 Michel Worobey, 'The Huanan Seafood Wholesale Market in Wuhan was the Early Epicenter of the COVID-19 Pandemic' (2022) 377 *Science* 951–959.

3 World Health Organization, 'WHO-Convened Global Study of Origins of SARS-CoV-2: China Part' 7 8. Available at www.who.int/publications/i/item/who-convened-global-study-of-origins-of-sars-cov-2-china-part.

4 Natasha Daly, 'Chinese Citizens Push to Abolish Wildlife Trade as Coronavirus Persists: Media Coverage of China's Wildlife Markets Sends the Message that they're Hugely Popular. In Reality, Many Chinese Can't Relate' (30 January 2020) *National Geographic*. Available at www.nationalgeographic.com/animals/2020/01/china-bans-wildlife-trade-after-coronavirus-outbreak.

5 Wondwossen Gebreyes. 'The Global One Health Paradigm: Challenges and Opportunities for Tackling Infectious Diseases at the Human, Animal, and Environment Interface in Low-Resource Settings' (2014) 8 *PLOS Neglected Tropical Diseases* 1–6 at 1.

6 Ibid.

overlapping spheres,[7] the One Health model attests to the interconnectedness of human, animal, and environmental health. In this vein, what the paradigm reveals is that safeguarding the health of any one realm – whether human, animal, or environment – requires a holistic approach, as the interests of each is inextricably intertwined with those of its counterparts. Effectively blurring the conceptual boundaries that it prescribes, the One Health concept illustrates the inherent inadequacy, and even danger, of attempting to secure the health of any one sphere absent complementary efforts to buttress the health of all.

Despite the paradigm being cited as the foundation for the pandemic treaty talks that have since emerged and, as of the date of this writing, have stalled,[8] it remains to be seen whether the final form of the WHO Pandemic Agreement, if agreed upon by WHO member states, will prohibit, much less regulate the kinds of animal use, confinement, and ill-treatment believed to have given rise to the COVID-19 pandemic, not to mention several other deadly zoonotic disease outbreaks to date. Indeed, if a concluded WHO Pandemic Agreement resembles its present form, its lack of explicit obligations with regard to securing the health and well-being of animals leaves a glaring if indefensible hole in the 'robust international health architecture' that the WHO and world leaders jointly called for years before.[9] Without due regard paid to how humankind's use of and interactions with animals continues to occasion the emergence and reemergence of novel and known diseases, the world will have forfeited a critical opportunity to go beyond preparing for and responding to pandemics by preventing the conditions that lead to outbreaks at the start.

Drafted in the midst of the COVID-19 pandemic by global animal law scholars and attorneys, including the author of this chapter, the Convention on Animal Protection for Public Health, Animal Well-Being, and the Environment (CAP) was designed to fill this void by securing the braided – and inextricably intertwined – interests of humans, animals, and the environment that they share.[10] As part of its framework, the draft treaty seeks to institute binding prohibitions on and regulate interactions with and uses of animals that pose health risks within and beyond the zoonotic disease context.[11] In addition to containing protections that apply to all animals,[12] the CAP also features provisions specific to free-roaming wildlife and animals under direct human control,[13] thereby allowing for a more nuanced approach to safeguarding their interests. Owing to the oft-cited difficulty of holding states accountable to their obligations under international law,[14] the CAP advances trade-based incentives and other measures to encourage contracting parties to hold their counterparts accountable, as well as to incline non-party states to ratify the Convention.[15] By providing for the development of future protocols, or sub-agreements among contracting parties to it,[16] the CAP envisions more robust

7 Olaitan O. Omitola, 'Emerging and Re-emerging Bacterial Zoonoses in Nigeria: Current Preventive Measures and Future Approaches to Intervention' (2020) 6 *Heliyon* 1–14 at 9.

8 Elaine Ruth Fletcher, 'Breaking – WHO Member States Fail to Reach Agreement on Pandemic Accord; Way Forward in Hands of World Health Assembly' (24 May 2024) *Health Policy Watch*. Available at: https://healthpolicy-watch.news/breaking-pandemic-accord-negotiations-stall-again-with-way-forward-in-hands-of-world-health-assembly/.

9 World Health Organization, 'COVID-19 Shows Why United Action is Needed for More Robust International Health Architecture'. Available at: www.who.int/news-room/commentaries/detail/op-ed—covid-19-shows-why-united-action-is-needed-for-more-robust-international-health-architecture.

10 International Coalition for Animal Protection, 'Our Aim'. Available at www.icfap.org.

11 Ibid.

12 Convention on Animal Protection for Public Health, Animal Well-being, and the Environment 2022, Article 3.

13 Ibid., Articles 4–5.

14 Elena Katselli Proukaki, *The Problem of Enforcement in International Law: Countermeasures, the Non-Injured State and the Idea of International Community* (London and New York: Routledge, 2010) 1–2.

15 Convention on Animal Protection for Public Health, Animal Well-being, and the Environment, Articles 8, 24.

16 Ibid., Article 22.

animal protections taking root and further inuring to the benefit of the environment and humankind. Given the CAP's prospective contribution to the much-neglected sphere of animal health, this chapter explores the promise the draft treaty holds to engender a One Health-centred model, either by complementing the thrust of the WHO Pandemic Agreement or by filling in the void it would have occupied.

To this end, Section 13.2 of this Chapter interrogates how humankind's use of and interactions with animals precipitated the emergence of SARS-CoV-2 alongside other concerning zoonotic disease pathogens that garnered scant attention in the midst, or 'shadow', of the COVID-19 pandemic. Bookending this examination are reflections on the 'narratives' that the World Health Organization sought to construct upon declaring COVID-19 a pandemic in March of 2020 and in calling for a pandemic instrument to be negotiated around the One Health concept the following year. To this end, Section 13.2 captures how such narrative constructions were used to shape public sentiment and to encourage people to consider the agency that they possessed to influence the outcome of a global pandemic narrative that they may have otherwise felt they had been written into. From here, Section 13.3 takes stock of how the WHO Pandemic Agreement, if entered into force, would provide for the interests of animals as part of its recognition of the One Health concept. In doing so, Section 13.3 also highlights core issues that the WHO instrument fails to address in this vein.

In consideration of the void left by WHO Pandemic Agreement, Section 13.4 offers an overview of the origins and evolution of the CAP. In doing so, it charts the CAP's overarching framework, preamble, and fundamental principles before addressing how its substantive provisions would help achieve the promise of the One Health model given its contributions to the oft-neglected sphere of animal health. In addition, Section 13.4 highlights the CAP's noteworthy logistical and operative elements, including its trade provisions, and addresses how the treaty, if entered into force, would relate to current international frameworks and growing norms around animals. In doing so, the Chapter calls attention to potential pathways and prospects for the CAP to become a global foundation for animal protection. In conclusion, Section 13.5 returns to the grounds for world leaders' call for a pandemic treaty instrument to be negotiated around the One Health concept and observes how the CAP would not only reduce the risks of future pandemics but also provide for a more compelling, if complete, post-pandemic story by virtue of seeing animals written into international law as sentient beings as opposed to continue being written off.

13.2 COMING TO TERMS WITH THE WORLD'S PANDEMIC STORY

13.2.1 *In Medias Res*

It was near the end of his opening remarks during a virtual press conference on 11 March 2020 that Dr Ghebreyesus lamented that a single word had managed to seize the world's attention.[17] As Director-General of the WHO, Ghebreyesus had just briefed the media on the concerning rise in COVID-19 clusters.[18] Outside China, cases had increased thirteen-fold.[19] The number

[17] World Health Organization, 'WHO Director-General's Opening Remarks at the Media Briefing on COVID-19–11 March 2020' (11 March 2020). Available at www.who.int/director-general/speeches/detail/who-director-general-s-opening-remarks-at-the-media-briefing-on-covid-19---11-march-2020.

[18] Ibid.

[19] Ibid.

of affected states had tripled to well over a hundred.[20] Globally, more than 100,000 infections had been documented, with some 4,000 lives already lost.[21] It was against this meteoric rise in epidemics that Ghebreyesus disclosed the WHO's official position that COVID-19 had crossed a conceptual threshold to become a 'pandemic',[22] the one word he feared would dictate how the narrative would unfold from that moment on.

While the pronouncement was characterised by some media outlets as largely symbolic,[23] Ghebreyesus stressed it was one the WHO did not issue lightly given the gravity of its impact. Speaking to this concern, Ghebreyesus observed how the term had the power to not only incite fear but also instil a sense of resignation, if not defeatism.[24] Although Ghebreyesus did not expand upon the remark, its subtext was clear. In expressing concern that the WHO's position might incline the public to consider the 'fight [to be] over', the Director-General laid bare the distinction, at least with regard to perception, between epidemics and pandemics,[25] with the etymological root of the latter, *pan demos*, literally translating to *all people*.[26] To employ a topical metaphor in light of Ghebreyesus's repeated appeals to keep fighting,[27] the distinction between epidemics and pandemics might be conceived as one between localised battles and a world war. While the former may be beyond one's direct experience, the latter offers no retreat or safe harbour. But of course, the reality of pandemics proves far more bleak. Indeed, neither pacts of non-aggression nor declarations of neutrality can prevent a widespread disease from invading a nation's borders. Unlike epidemics, then, pandemics affect all people. And insofar as they may be considered wars, they are ones that cannot be avoided – only survived. In addition to the WHO's admission that the world had never witnessed a pandemic that could be controlled,[28] further complicating efforts to contain the disease was the unprecedented nature of the outbreak itself. Not only did SARS-CoV-2 constitute a novel pathogen, but the world, Ghebreyesus stressed, had also never been forced to confront a coronavirus-based pandemic.[29]

While the rise in both cases and number of nations affected attested to the practical difficulties that lay ahead, what Ghebreyesus nevertheless underscored was that numbers alone failed to 'tell the full story'.[30] In stating that the WHO could not say 'loudly enough, or clearly enough, or often enough [that] all countries [could] still change the course of [the] pandemic',[31] what Ghebreyesus sought to impress upon the public was how the story of the pandemic – that is, of all people – was still in the process of being written and that their leaders had the power – both the literal and figurative authority – to shape how that story would end. But just as the Director-General was calling upon leaders to take steps to mitigate the spread of COVID-19, forces were

[20] Ibid.
[21] Ibid.
[22] Ibid.
[23] Donald G. McNeil Jr., 'Coronavirus Has Become a Pandemic, W.H.O. Says', *New York Times* (11 March 2020). Available at www.nytimes.com/2020/03/11/health/coronavirus-pandemic-who.html.
[24] World Health Organization, 'WHO Director-General's opening remarks at the media briefing on COVID-19–11 March 2020'.
[25] Ibid.
[26] Sara Agnelli, 'Pandemic or Panzootic – A Reflection on Terminology for SARS-CoV-2 Infection' (2022) 28 *Emerging Infectious Diseases* 2552–2555 at 2552.
[27] World Health Organization, 'WHO Director-General's opening remarks at the media briefing on COVID-19–11 March 2020'.
[28] Ibid.
[29] Ibid.
[30] Ibid.
[31] Ibid.

already working to plot the conflict back to its origins in order to shape the dominant narrative, assign the roles of its pro- and an-tagonists, and construct the moral of the story writ large.[32]

13.2.2 *Plotting the Backstory of the Pandemic*

As fraught with consequences for public sentiment as it may have been to declare that the world was in the midst of a pandemic, the promotion of competing narratives to explain the origins of the novel virus proved concerning as well. Several accounts – some of them pure fiction – had been heavily promoted to become the dominant narrative in certain circles. One such theory asserted that SARS-CoV-2 had been leaked from the Wuhan Institute of Virology, a belief that still finds purchase given the facility's close proximity to where the first cases were catalogued, as well as the facility's multiple failures to follow through on biosecurity protocols.[33] Another widely disputed theory contended that the coronavirus had been engineered as a bioweapon by the People's Liberation Army of China.[34] Yet another asserted that it had imported into China via frozen food products,[35] the implication being that while China may have witnessed the first outbreaks, it was neither the source of, nor responsible for, the coronavirus's emergence. While a definitive answer as to the origins of the pandemic may never be established, much less agreed upon in light of the political interests involved,[36] the great weight of evidence continues to point to Wuhan's Huanan Wholesale Seafood Market as the epicentre of the outbreak, or where the novel virus spilled over from animals into humans.[37]

Serendipitously carried out between May of 2017 and November of 2019, a pre-outbreak study tracing the source of a tick-borne disease to one of Wuhan's live animal markets offered a compelling dataset for scientists to pore through.[38] Substantiated by data gleaned from monthly visits to each of Wuhan's four live animal markets, where wild animals were known to be sold as food or exotic pets, what the report illuminated was that roughly a third of the animals bore tell-tale signs of having been poached, such as leg-trap and gunshot wounds, with others likely having been bred in captivity.[39] What the overall picture revealed was that the live animal markets were host to a diverse array of species, many of which were known hosts of disease-bearing parasites and zoonoses.[40] All the more concerning was that practically all of the captive animals were stacked in cages and in poor condition, with the Huanan market featuring seven such wildlife shops.[41]

Post-outbreak reports also pointed to the Huanan Wholesale Seafood Market as the most likely source of the outbreak. For example, a joint WHO-China review of COVID-19 cases

[32] David Quammen, 'The Ongoing Mystery of Covid's Origin' *New York Times Magazine* (25 July 2023). Available at www.nytimes.com/2023/07/25/magazine/covid-start.html.

[33] Ibid; Department of Health and Human Services, 'Action Referral Memorandum for Wuhan Institute of Virology (WIV)' 6.

[34] Quammen, 'The Ongoing Mystery of Covid's Origin'

[35] Jon Cohen, 'Do Three New Studies Add Up to Proof of COVID-19's Origin in a Wuhan Animal Market?' *Science* (28 February 2022). Available at www.science.org/content/article/do-three-new-studies-add-proof-covid-19-s-origin-wuhan-animal-market.

[36] Sheryl Gay Stolberg and Benjamin Mueller, 'Lab Leak or Not? How Politics Shaped the Battle Over Covid's Origin' *New York Times* (19 March 2023). Available at www.nytimes.com/2023/03/19/us/politics/covid-origins-lab-leak-politics.html.

[37] Cohen, 'Do Three New Studies Add Up to Proof of COVID-19's Origin in a Wuhan Animal Market?'.

[38] Xiao Xiao, 'Animal Sales from Wuhan Wet Markets Immediately Prior to the COVID-19 Pandemic' (2021) 11 *Scientific Reports* 1–7 at 2.

[39] Ibid., 2–3.

[40] Ibid., 3.

[41] Ibid., 2–3.

associated 55 of the earliest 168 documented COVID-19 cases with the site.[42] In addition, the most comprehensive study to date found two lineages of the pathogen there,[43] a detail that suggests the virus had jumped not once but twice from animals into humans and undercuts the view that the market was merely a super-spreader site.[44] Furthermore, a spatial analysis conducted within the market returned numerous positive samples of the pathogen, with at least one stall returning multiple positive results and a metal cage in a back room also featuring traces.[45] Notably, the stalls in this section of the market were associated with the sale of wildlife,[46] with many of the animals, such as raccoon dogs, known to be highly susceptible to SARS-CoV-2.[47] While the authors of the report could not definitively rule out the possibility that the virus had come from another source, the cluster of cases put the odds at 1 in 10,000,000.[48] Although every outbreak proves unique, the trope that the COVID-19 outbreak fell into, however, was common; so much so that it might be described as merely a variation on a theme.

13.2.3 *Variations on a Common Theme*

In determining the Huanan Wholesale Seafood market to be the epicentre of the COVID-19 outbreak, the authors of the report buttressed their conclusion by observing how the trade and sale of captive wildlife in such markets have proven to be a 'common theme' in spillover events.[49] Indeed, it was a variation on this theme that gave rise to the first documented case of Severe Acute Respiratory Syndrome (SARS) years before.[50] Claiming roughly 1,000 lives across 29 countries,[51] the 2002 SARS epidemic was likewise caused by a coronavirus infection, with the pathogen traced to masked palm civets sold at a live market.[52] Such markets have proved hotbeds for zoonotic disease spillovers not just because they feature wildlife but also because the animals are often held in cramped, unsanitary, stress-inducing conditions. Indeed, wild animals in these settings have been documented suffering from numerous ailments, such as dehydration, open wounds, missing limbs, and so on.[53] With a diverse array of species kept in close proximity, if not stacked one on top of the other, leading to an exchange of air, faeces, and urine, the stress induced by these unhygienic conditions further compromises their immune systems, increasing chances of the spread, mutation, and emergence of novel viruses

[42] Worobey, 'The Huanan Seafood Wholesale Market in Wuhan was the Early Epicenter of the COVID-19 Pandemic', 1.

[43] Ibid., 3.

[44] Ibid., 7.

[45] Michaeleen Doucleff, 'Newly Published Evidence Points to Wuhan Seafood Market as Pandemic Origin Point' *National Public Radio* (27 July 2022). Available at www.npr.org/sections/goatsandsoda/2022/03/03/1083751272/striking-new-evidence-points-to-seafood-market-in-wuhan-as-pandemic-origin-point.

[46] Worobey, 'The Huanan Seafood Wholesale Market in Wuhan was the Early Epicenter of the COVID-19 Pandemic', 5.

[47] Doucleff, 'Newly Published Evidence Points to Wuhan Seafood Market as Pandemic Origin Point'.

[48] Ibid.

[49] Worobey, 'The Huanan Seafood Wholesale Market in Wuhan was the Early Epicenter of the COVID-19 Pandemic', 8.

[50] James D. Cherry, 'SARS: The First Pandemic of the 21st Century, 54.1 Pedriatric Research' (2004) 56 *Pediatric Research* 1–5 at 1.

[51] Ibid.

[52] Simon Denyer and Lyric Li, 'China Bans Wild Animal Trade Until Coronavirus Epidemic Is Eliminated' *Washington Post* (26 January 2020). Available at www.washingtonpost.com/world/asia_pacific/china-bans-wild-animal-trade-until-coronavirus-epidemic-eliminated/2020/01/26/0e05a964-4017-11ea-971f-4ce4f94494b4_story.html.

[53] Ibid.

and other pathogens.[54] This concerning mistreatment has seen live animal markets characterised as 'cauldron[s] of contagion'.[55]

Insofar as such spillover events represent a 'common theme' in a recurring narrative, one might be tempted to describe COVID-19 pandemic as having gone according to script, which, in many ways, it did. With its plot concerning the spread and response to a pandemic in an increasingly globalised world, the 2011 film *Contagion* prophetically – one might be tempted to say if such outbreaks were not so routine – dramatised almost this exact scenario: the transmission of a novel virus from bats to animals raised for food and ultimately into humans via live animal market-type conditions.[56] Although MEV-1, the fictional pathogen in *Contagion*, was not a coronavirus, it was based on two real-life viruses, Hendra and Nipah, which affect equines and pigs, respectively, and are likewise transmitted by bats.[57] Although the film saw its novel virus mutate in a pig as opposed to captive wildlife, the encroachment of humans into animals' habitat, whether to clear land to farm domesticated animals or otherwise, has led to numerous viral spillovers events and remains a leading theory as to how SARS-CoV-2 emerged as well. Speaking to the conditions that led to the COVID-19 outbreak, the film's director, Steven Soderbergh, stated, 'Everybody we talked to when we were preparing that film, every expert, when we asked them how will the next one start, to a person, they said, wet market, Asia, there's probably going to be a bat involved. Literally all of them.'[58] Echoing this sentiment, Scott Burns, the film's screenwriter, agreed that no crystal ball was necessary.[59] In consulting with epidemiologists as to whether the prospect of a pandemic as contemplated by their script was within the realm of possibility, their answer was that the question of a pandemic was not one of *if* but *when*.[60]

While the purpose of the film was to capture, as a sociological study, how individuals and states would respond to such a crisis,[61] what Burns did not anticipate was how real life would fail to reflect the art they had intended to reflect real life. Put differently, what proved inconceivable was just how misguided, and even dangerous, responses by governments would be.[62] Of course, *Contagion* necessitated the conditions for a pandemic in order to dramatise its impact on society. Calling attention to the ability of states to prevent such outbreaks altogether, America's top infectious disease expert, Dr Anthony Fauci, expressed incredulity as to how such markets could continue operating, stating, 'It boggles my mind how[,] when we have so many diseases that emanate out of that unusual human-animal interface, that we don't just shut it down',[63]

[54] Bing Lin, 'A Better Classification of Wet Markets Is Key to Safeguarding Human Health and Biodiversity' (2021) 5 *Lancet* 386–394 at 386–387.

[55] Daly, 'Chinese Citizens Push to Abolish Wildlife Trade as Coronavirus Persists: Media Coverage of China's Wildlife Markets Sends the Message that they're Hugely Popular'.

[56] Lane Brown, 'A Reassuring Conversation with the Writer of Contagion' *Vulture* (14 Marc 2020). Available at www.vulture.com/2020/03/contagion-writer-scott-z-burns-reassures-us-about-covid-19.html.

[57] Ibid.

[58] Mark Olsen, '"Contagion" Director Steven Soderbergh on Hollywood Reopening: "We're Going to Get Back to Work"' *Los Angeles Times* (21 May 2020). Available at www.latimes.com/entertainment-arts/movies/story/2020-05-21/steven-soderbergh-hollywood-reopening-coronavirus-contagion.

[59] Michele L. Norris, 'He Wrote "Contagion." Here's What He Had to Say about the Response to the Coronavirus' *Washington Post* (1 April 2020). Available at www.washingtonpost.com/opinions/2020/04/01/writer-contagion-imagined-all-this-except-inept-government-response.

[60] Ibid; Brown, 'A Reassuring Conversation with the Writer of Contagion'.

[61] Olsen, '"Contagion" Director Steven Soderbergh on Hollywood Reopening: "We're Going to Get Back to Work"'.

[62] Norris, 'He Wrote "Contagion." Here's What He Had to Say about the Response to the Coronavirus'.

[63] Quint Forgey, '"Shut Down Those Things Right Away": Calls to Close "Wet Markets" Ramp Up Pressure on China' *Politico* (3 April 2020). Available at www.politico.com/news/2020/04/03/anthony-fauci-foreign-wet-markets-shutdown-162975.

which, notably, China ended up doing,[64] although history suggests that the ban may only be temporary.[65]

While Dr Fauci's recommendation proves sound given the recurring if dominant theme of animal markets giving rise to novel pathogens, the world would be remiss to ignore the emergence of infectious diseases arising out of other human–animal interfaces and in other parts of the world. Indeed, multiple zoonotic disease outbreaks have been documented both in the midst, or 'shadow', of the COVID-19 pandemic,[66] as well as in its wake. In 2021, for example, the Indian state of Kerala witnessed an outbreak of Nipah virus, which features a 75 per cent mortality rate and is known to spread from fruit bats, its primary host, to pigs, as intermediate hosts, before infecting humans.[67] In 2021, severe Salmonella cases rose in the United States due to the keeping of wildlife as pets.[68] From its initial outbreak in May of 2022 to September 2022, over 60,000 cases of monkeypox, another deadly zoonotic disease, had been documented in 104 countries worldwide.[69] In that same year, the United States reported an outbreak of swine flu resulting from a child's attendance at an agricultural fair.[70] Even after the WHO's declaration that COVID-19 no longer constituted a global health emergency in May of 2023,[71] numerous outbreaks have continued to emerge. In November of that same year, Zambia reported an outbreak of anthrax, a bacterial disease that spills into humans via contact with ruminants, such as cows, goats, and sheep.[72] Yet another is an outbreak of psittacosis in late 2023 across Europe, with those who come into contact with birds, such as poultry workers, proving susceptible to contracting the deadly respiratory disease.[73] Regardless of whether these outbreaks occurred before, during, or after the COVID-19 pandemic, many continue to linger. For example, with the outbreak of a highly pathogenetic avian influenza in the United States in February of 2022, more than 1,000 flocks in 48 states have been affected, leading to the deaths of over 82 million birds and counting.[74] Having mutated to infect dairy cattle, the virus has spun off other variants and already spilled over into humans.[75]

[64] Denyer, 'China Bans Wild Animal Trade Until Coronavirus Epidemic Is Eliminated'.

[65] Of note, however, is that China previously instituted a ban on the wildlife trade following the outbreak of SARS in 2002, but ultimately lifted it. Ronald Orenstein, 'Wildlife Markets and COVID-19' *Humane Soc. Int'l* (April 2020). Available at www.hsi.org/wp-content/uploads/2020/04/Wildlife-Markets-and-COVID-19-White-Paper.pdf.

[66] Mainak Bardhan, 'Emerging Zoonotic Diseases and COVID-19 Pandemic: Global Perspective and Indian Scenario' (2023) 85 *Annals of Medicine and Surgery* 3997–4004 at 3997.

[67] Ibid., 3998; Shriyansh Srivastava, 'Recent Nipah Virus Outbreak in India: Lessons and Imperatives' (2023) 10 *Therapeutic Advances in Infectious Disease* 1–3 at 1–2.

[68] Bardhan, 'Emerging Zoonotic Diseases and COVID-19 Pandemic: Global Perspective and Indian Scenario', 4001.

[69] Irena Ilic, 'Global Outbreak of Human Monkeypox in 2022: Update of Epidemiology' (2022) 7 *Tropical Medical Infectious Disease*, 1–10, at 1.

[70] Centers for Disease Control and Prevention, 'CDC Confirms First Human Infection with Flu Virus from Pigs During 2022' (5 August 2022). Available at www.cdc.gov/flu/swineflu/spotlights/first-human-infection-2022.htm.

[71] World Health Organization, 'Statement on the Fifteenth Meeting of the IHR (2005) Emergency Committee on the COVID-19 Pandemic' (5 May 2023). Available at www.who.int/news/item/05-05-2023-statement-on-the-fifteenth-meeting-of-the-international-health-regulations-(2005)-emergency-committee-regarding-the-coronavirus-disease-(covid-19)-pandemic.

[72] World Health Organization, 'Anthrax – Zambia' (8 September 2023). Available at www.who.int/emergencies/disease-outbreak-news/item/2023-DON497.

[73] Ibid.

[74] US Department of Agriculture Animal and Plant Health Inspection Service, 2022–2024, 'Confirmations of Highly Pathogenic Avian Influenza in Commercial and Backyard Flocks' (2 January 2024). Available at www.aphis.usda.gov/aphis/ourfocus/animalhealth/animal-disease-information/avian/avian-influenza/hpai-2022/2022-hpai-commercial-backyard-flocks.

[75] Texas Health and Human Services, 'Person Had Direct Contact with Dairy Cattle' (1 April 2024). Available at www.dshs.texas.gov/news-alerts/dshs-reports-first-human-case-avian-influenza-texas.

Although they have not become widespread enough to constitute pandemics, these localised epidemics nevertheless form the substance of a collective narrative, one that offers universal lessons if world leaders wish to turn the page on a recurring story. Notably, it was a year after uttering the lone word he feared would diminish the world's resolve that Ghebreyesus echoed a dire warning in calling for a new chapter to be authored: the question of the next pandemic, he said, was not one of *if* but *when*.[76]

13.3 THE PROPOSED WHO PANDEMIC AGREEMENT

13.3.1 *A Clarion Call for Change*

Adding his voice to those of over two dozen heads of state, Ghebreyesus, the first signatory in their joint letter, issued a clarion call for the negotiation of a pandemic treaty on 30 March 2021.[77] At the time, COVID-19's death toll was nearing 3 million,[78] with roughly 130 million people having already been infected.[79] As tragic as the loss of life proved in and of itself, the pandemic had also given rise to global human rights concerns, ranging from the imprisonment of journalists and healthcare workers seeking to combat misinformation to the implementation of intrusive surveillance practices,[80] with marginalised groups bearing the brunt of harms.[81] As the joint letter attested, no one was spared. Indeed, the pandemic proved a difficult if much-needed reminder 'that nobody is safe until everyone is safe'.[82] Calling out the fractures among states that COVID-19 had laid bare, the letter framed the pandemic as the greatest challenge the world had faced since the 1940s,[83] an allusion to the devastation wrought by World War II. In observing how states at the time embraced multilateralism as a means to meet the moment, the letter articulated how state cooperation was needed yet again if global health and security, among other shared aims, were to be realised.[84]

Citing the need to protect future generations, the joint letter braided the continuing 'fight' against COVID-19 with a call for a 'more robust international health architecture', one grounded in the WHO with the purpose of serving to better 'predict, prevent, detect, assess and effectively respond to pandemics'.[85] To this end, the letter underscored that the proposed agreement would recognise the One Health model, which, in affirming the interconnectedness of human, animal, and planetary health, would guide the treaty's principle of 'health for all',[86] an echo of the

[76] World Health Organization, 'COVID-19 Shows Why United Action is Needed for More Robust International Health Architecture'.

[77] Bill Chappell, 'What We Know About the Deadliest U.S. Bird Flu Outbreak in History' *National Public Radio* (2 December 2022). Available at www.npr.org/2022/12/02/1140076426/what-we-know-about-the-deadliest-u-s-bird-flu-outbreak-in-history.

[78] Worldometer, 'Coronavirus Death Toll' (last updated 24 March 2024). Available at www.worldometers.info/coronavirus/coronavirus-death-toll.

[79] Worldometer, 'Coronavirus Worldwide Graphs' (last updated 24 March 2024). Available at www.worldometers.info/coronavirus/worldwide-graphs/#total-cases.

[80] Eric A. Friedman, Chelsea Clinton, and Lawrence O. Gostin, 'Human Rights at the Center of the COVID-19 Pandemic' *Think Global Health* (5 January 2023). Available at www.thinkglobalhealth.org/article/human-rights-center-covid-19-pandemic.

[81] Ibid.

[82] World Health Organization, 'COVID-19 Shows Why United Action is Needed for More Robust International Health Architecture'.

[83] Ibid.

[84] Ibid.

[85] Ibid.

[86] Ibid.

signatories' acknowledgement that none could be safe until all were safe. Although the letter made explicit mention of the need to contemplate the health of animals, nothing in the non-exhaustive list of provisions that a prospective accord might feature includes considerations for them.[87] This lack of detail as to what measures might buttress the sphere of animal health has created significant uncertainty as to the effectiveness of such a treaty in light of the proposition – one informed by the One Health concept – that none can be safe until all, including animals, are safe.

13.3.2 *The Draft Agreement*

It was in December of 2021 that prospects for a WHO Pandemic Agreement began to emerge.[88] It was during the second-ever special session of the World Health Assembly, comprised of all 194 WHO member states,[89] that the Intergovernmental Negotiating Body (INB) was formed.[90] With the Constitution of the WHO empowering the Assembly to adopt international agreements on matters within the WHO's sphere of competence,[91] the INB was charged with constructing an agreement on 'pandemic prevention, preparedness, and response'.[92] With the INB beginning its work in February of 2022, the prospect of an accord was heralded as a 'once-in-a-generation opportunity to strengthen the global health architecture to protect and promote the well-being of *all people*',[93] an allusion to the etymological roots of the term 'pandemic'. To date, the INB has produced multiple drafts of the proposed treaty instrument,[94] whose text was slated to be finalised by May 2024.[95] As noted above, however, the language of the proposed treaty has yet to be agreed upon by states. That said, some have expressed optimism that the instrument will eventually be agreed upon and concluded.[96]

[87] Ibid., ('The main goal of this treaty would be to foster an all-of-government and all-of-society approach, strengthening national, regional and global capacities and resilience to future pandemics. This includes greatly enhancing international cooperation to improve, for example, alert systems, data-sharing, research, and local, regional and global production and distribution of medical and public health counter measures, such as vaccines, medicines, diagnostics and personal protective equipment').

[88] World Health Organization, 'World Health Assembly Agrees to Launch Process to Develop Historic Global Accord on Pandemic Prevention, Preparedness and Response' (1 December 2021). Available at www.who.int/news/item/01-12-2021-world-health-assembly-agrees-to-launch-process-to-develop-historic-global-accord-on-pandemic-prevention-preparedness-and-response; World Health Organization, 'Intergovernmental Negotiating Body/INB process'. Available at https://inb.who.int/home/inb-process.

[89] Ibid.

[90] World Health Organization, 'World Health Assembly Agrees to Launch Process to Develop Historic Global Accord on Pandemic Prevention, Preparedness and Response'.

[91] Constitution of the World Health Organization, 22 July 1946, 14 U.N.T.S. 185, Arts. 19, 21 (Article 21 authorises the World Health Assembly to 'adopt regulations concerning: (a) sanitary and quarantine requirements and other procedures designed to prevent the international spread of disease; (b) nomenclatures with respect to diseases, causes of death and public health practices; (c) standards with respect to diagnostic procedures for international use; (d) standards with respect to the safety, purity and potency of biological, pharmaceutical and similar products moving in international commerce; and (e) advertising and labelling of biological, pharmaceutical and similar products moving in international commerce').

[92] Ibid.

[93] Ibid.

[94] World Health Organization, 'World Health Assembly Agrees to Launch Process to Develop Historic Global Accord on Pandemic Prevention, Preparedness and Response'.

[95] Ibid., ('The INB Continues to be Guided by the Timeline Set Out in Document A/INB/3/4, Notably the Submission of its Final Outcome to the Seventy-Seventh World Health Assembly, in May 2024').

[96] Fletcher, 'Breaking – WHO Member States Fail to Reach Agreement on Pandemic Accord; Way Forward in Hands of World Health Assembly'.

Although all aspects of the instrument are subject to change until that time,[97] certain provisions have already witnessed consensus.[98] For example, the preamble as currently drafted acknowledges the danger of antimicrobial resistance.[99] The instrument defines the One Health concept as an approach that seeks to 'sustainably balance and optimise the health of people, animals and ecosystems' and affirms 'that the health of humans, domestic and wild animals, plants and the wider environment (including ecosystems) is closely linked and interdependent'.[100] To be sure, the definition of the One Health model as currently constructed appears to devote appropriate attention to the health of animals, whose interests are intertwined with that of humankind. Yet the actual measures to safeguard those interests prove ambiguous at best.

Again, with many of the provisions of the current draft not yet agreed upon, with regard to One Health-related obligations, Article 5 would require parties to develop a coherent and integrated strategy into national law.[101] In addition to calling for collaboration,[102] the treaty would obligate parties to identify and address pandemic drivers, including the emergence and re-emergence of diseases at the human–animal–environmental interface, and to intervene to prevent, prepare for, and respond to zoonotic outbreaks.[103] Article 4 would require parties to, subject to their individual capacities, take measures to prevent the spread of infectious diseases between humans and animals and to combat antimicrobial resistance.[104] The actions a party would be required to take to meet these obligations is not identified in the present draft. Although the text does feature language that would commit parties to lay out the 'operational' among other dimensions of what the One Health approach would require at a later date, the provision itself is contested and its integration into the final treaty, if one is concluded, is uncertain.[105]

Assuming the WHO Pandemic Agreement is concluded and meets the requisite threshold to enter into force,[106] the qualifying language in many of the substantive provisions regarding the capabilities of parties to fulfil their obligations, in addition to the lack of specific obligations, may yield few if any gains for the interests of animals. That said, assuming that the Agreement is concluded and enters into force, its provisions may be complemented by the Convention on Animal Protection for Public Health, Animal Well-Being, and the Environment, which was designed to fill this void.

13.4 THE CONVENTION ON ANIMAL PROTECTION

13.4.1 *Overview and History*

The origins of the CAP trace back to the early stages of the COVID-19 outbreak, specifically to the efforts of international animal law scholars, attorneys, and advocates working within the

97 World Health Organization, 'Proposal for the WHO Pandemic Agreement', Annex A77/10, App. 17.
98 Ibid., Article 3.
99 Ibid., Preamble.
100 Ibid., Article 1(b). An alternative construction for the definition of One Health underscores the need to 'recognise the risk of pandemics links and interdependen[ce] with health of animals and environment and requires integrated disease surveillance, prevention and control at the animal-human interface'. INB May 2024 Draft, Article 1(ALT(b)). Notably, this arguably more robust construction emphasises the need to focus on humankind's interaction with and use of animals.
101 Ibid., Article 5(1).
102 Ibid., Article 5(3).
103 World Health Organization, 'Proposal for the WHO Pandemic Agreement', Articles 5(1)–(3) and 4(1)–(2).
104 Ibid., Article 4(1)–(2).
105 Ibid., Article 5(4).
106 As of the current draft, sixty states must ratify the agreement before it enters into force. Ibid., Article 35.

International Animal Law Committee of the American Bar Association (ABA).[107] Notably, it was just before a long-planned Committee meeting to discuss the International Convention for the Protection of Animals, which was drafted in 1988 and represents the first proposed treaty to contemplate the interests of animals as individuals, that COVID-19 was reported as having struck the United States.[108] Given the likely animal origins of the novel coronavirus and several of the Committee members' acute awareness of how the health and well-being of animals is inextricably tied to that of humans and the environment, the question that emerged was whether world leaders might, in light of the health crisis that was unfolding, finally prove receptive to the need for global standards regarding the protection of animals.

As a first step toward this goal, core members of the International Animal Law Committee authored a Resolution and Report for the ABA as a whole to consider taking a formal position on this issue.[109] To that end, the language of the Resolution, which was approved, read that the ABA 'urges all nations to negotiate an international convention for the protection of animals that establishes standards for the proper care and treatment of all animals to protect public health, the environment, and animal wellbeing' and that it likewise encouraged the US State Department to initiate and assume a leadership role with respect to its negotiation.[110] Given the ABA's general anthropocentric focus, what this development attested to was the need to embrace animal health and well-being as a means to safeguard the interests of humankind. Coming off this development, the core working group that authored the ABA Resolution and Report founded the International Coalition for Animal Protection (ICFAP), a nonprofit organisation through which they developed two drafts of the CAP treaty.[111]

13.4.2 *The Draft Convention*

Notably, both drafts of the CAP employ the One Health model to advance the interests of animals yet differ widely with regard to approaches taken. Whereas the protections advanced by the first specifically arise out of the disease prevention context,[112] those in the second are informed by the intrinsic interests of animals, with the prevention of disease, among other benefits, necessarily flowing from those safeguards. Put differently, while the second draft of the CAP is still informed by anthropocentric interests, these interests feature less prominently than the inherent interests of animals themselves. This shift is reflected by the change made to the title in the second draft of the Convention, with the term 'Welfare', which primarily focuses on reducing pain and suffering, replaced by the arguably more holistic term 'Well-Being',[113] which contemplates the need to consider, if not provide for, animals' positive affective states.[114] Although other noteworthy distinctions between the drafts exist, going forward, this chapter will focus on the second and, at present, final draft of the Convention.

107 Rajesh K. Reddy, 'The Convention on Animal Protection: The Missing Link in a One Health Global Strategy for Pandemic Prevention' (2022) 10 *Global Journal of Animal Law* 1–33 at 18.
108 Reddy, 'The Convention on Animal Protection: The Missing Link in a One Health Global Strategy for Pandemic Prevention', 19.
109 Ibid.
110 Ibid., 19–21.
111 Ibid., 21; International Coalition for Animal Protection, 'Who We Are'. Available at www.icfap.org/about.
112 Reddy, 'The Convention on Animal Protection: The Missing Link in a One Health Global Strategy for Pandemic Prevention', 1.
113 See ibid. (capturing the title of the first draft of the Convention).
114 David Fraser, 'Assessing Animal Well-Being: Common Sense, Uncommon Science' (1993) *Agriculture Canada* 37–54 at 37–39.

13.4.3 *Preamble and Fundamental Principles*

Informed by the One Health concept, the CAP foregrounds the interconnectedness of anthro-, eco-, and zoo-centric concerns in its preamble while also emphasising the intrinsic value of animals and the need to safeguard their interests for their own sake. To this end, the first preambular statement observes how protecting animals and the ecosystems that support them promotes public health, biodiversity, and economic development, among other benefits.[115] From here, the second attests to the need to secure the interests of animals outside of the species context,[116] which many international agreements concerning animals fail to go beyond.[117] By stressing that animals, as sentient beings, have intrinsic value, the CAP indicates that their individual well-being merits consideration.[118] In addition, the preamble attests to how failing to do so poses a critical risk factor with regard to the spread of infectious diseases and how an integrated approach to global health, as contemplated by the One Health approach, can mitigate such risks.[119] In a similar vein, the CAP addresses the ecosystem functions that animals provide by mitigating the effects of anthropogenic climate change, which they also suffer from.[120] It is in light of the interconnectedness of human, animal, and environmental interests, as well as the fact that animals cross geopolitical borders, that the preamble stresses the need for cooperation among states if their interests are to be secured.[121] Appreciating that doing so represents a complex, multifaceted endeavour, the CAP distinguishes itself in desiring to realise benefits to public health, the environment, and the well-being of animals through the development of binding obligations for contracting parties to it.[122]

In terms of the rationales that guide the provisions of the Convention, Article 1 of the CAP establishes five fundamental principles.[123] The first attests to humankind's evolutionary heritage and coexistence with animals within interdependent ecosystems; in doing so, it articulates how the health and well-being of animals at the group level, both species-specific and as to local populations, and individual level buttress the health of shared ecosystems, thereby supporting public health, environmental protection, and conservation efforts.[124] Beyond extrinsic value, the second affirms that animals, as sentient beings, have intrinsic value, one that creates a moral imperative to 'act responsibly' toward them.[125] Far from prescribing animal abolitionism, what the principle advances is the view that animals should not be subjected to cruelty and 'unnecessary suffering',[126] with this language mirroring many states' existing animal cruelty frameworks.[127] While this provision arguably creates a general, if ambiguous, floor with respect to limitations as to how animals should be treated, the CAP's third fundamental principle states

115 Convention on Animal Protection for Public Health, Animal Well-Being, and the Environment, Preamble.
116 Ibid.
117 Reddy, 'The Convention on Animal Protection: The Missing Link in a One Health Global Strategy for Pandemic Prevention', 11.
118 Convention on Animal Protection for Public Health, Animal Well-Being, and the Environment, Preamble.
119 Ibid.
120 Ibid.
121 Ibid.
122 Ibid.
123 Ibid., Article 1.
124 Convention on Animal Protection for Public Health, Animal Well-Being, and the Environment, Article 1 (1).
125 Ibid., Article 1 (2).
126 Ibid., Article 1 (2).
127 Darian M. Ibrahim, 'The Anticruelty Statute: A Study in Animal Welfare' (2006) 1680 *Faculty Publications at William and Mary Law School* 175–203 at 178–180.

that positive duties exist in the context of animals under human control.[128] In this regard, the CAP requires their well-being to be provided through an 'adequate, species-specific environment and care appropriate for their particular needs'.[129] In doing so, the CAP contemplates the interests of animals at both the species and individual level. In observing how psychological, physical, and environmental stressors compromise their well-being and increase their likelihood of becoming vectors of disease, the last two principles observe the need to employ a precautionary approach in regulating human interaction with animals.[130]

13.4.4 *Substantive Provisions*

While the CAP's preamble and fundamental principles do not in and of themselves establish specific obligations, they nevertheless inform the anthro-, eco-, and zoo-centric arguments for why the substantive provisions of the Convention prove critically important. Recognising that any specific obligations that arise must be attentive to differences in states' use of and interaction with animals, the CAP first creates a baseline of protections applicable to animals generally, then advances provisions specific to free-roaming wild animals and to those animals, whether domestic or wild, under human control.[131] While numerous other categorisations could certainly be conceived, the CAP appreciates that different obligations may, and arguably should, flow to animals based upon humans' use of and interaction with them. With regard to these duties, contracting parties are required to designate a competent authority to carry out all matters relating to their obligations under the CAP.[132]

With respect to protections applicable to all animals, the Convention requires contracting parties to, as far as is possible, take legislative, administrative, and other policy measures to construct a minimum baseline.[133] Captured in Article 3, these measures include ensuring animals are not subjected to cruel acts or conditions and that, if killed, the methods employed inflict the least amount of pain and suffering possible.[134] In addition to the killing of animals for food, clothing, and other commercial purposes, this provision would also apply to non-commercial activities, such as hunting and the eradication of non-native species. Furthermore, the CAP also requires contracting parties to consider the well-being of animals across all sectors, programs, and policies in order to provide for a whole-of-government approach to promoting their interests.[135] As part of this mandate, contracting parties would be required to identify the actual or likely impact of their activities upon their well-being and develop measures to mitigate such harms.[136] In addition, contracting parties must ensure that these measures are not weakened so as to undermine existing protections.[137]

Subject to their capability, contracting parties are required go further in providing for the well-being of animals under human control. As articulated in Article 4, such measures take into account differences in requirements among species and require contracting parties to ensure that animals are provided: sufficient and suitable food and water; shelter from the environment;

128 Convention on Animal Protection for Public Health, Animal Well-Being, and the Environment, Article 1 (3).
129 Ibid., Article 1 (3).
130 Ibid., Article 1(4–5).
131 Convention on Animal Protection for Public Health, Animal Well-Being, and the Environment, Article 2.
132 Ibid., Article 15.
133 Ibid., Article 4.
134 Ibid., Article 3 (1).
135 Ibid., Article 3 (2).
136 Ibid., Article 3 (3).
137 Ibid., Article 3 (4).

opportunities for exercise, movement, socialisation; an environment that allows them to engage in natural behaviours; veterinary care that contemplates not just their physical health but also their well-being and the sanitary conditions of their surroundings.[138] In addition to echoing the prohibition against cruelty and unnecessary suffering, Article 4 prohibits the overworking and abandonment of animals,[139] with the latter being attentive to the reality that animals, whether domestic or captive wildlife, may not be able to survive on their own after having been dependent upon human care. For animals in transport, contracting parties must establish maximum times for their transport and confinement, as well as develop species-specific requirements for rest, food, water, and ventilation and protections against adverse environmental conditions.[140]

With regard to wild animals not under human control, contracting parties are obligated to take measures, insofar as possible, to secure their interests as captured in Article 5. First, contracting parties must establish and maintain a system of protected areas for the express purpose of conserving and protecting them.[141] They, too, must promote non-lethal management practices, ones that result in the least suffering of both targeted and non-targeted animals.[142] Furthermore, contracting parties must develop measures to protect wild animals in their assessments of infrastructure and development projects. In addition to monitoring the impact of such projects on wild animals and their habitats, contracting parties are also required to monitor the impact of climate change and other anthropogenic stressors.[143]

As discussed in Section 13.2, the failure to provide for the interests of animals and protect their habitat has driven the emergence and reemergence of new and known pathogens. Taken together, then, Articles 3, 4, and 5 of the CAP inherently serve to mitigate the risk of such outbreaks, both zoonotic and non-zoonotic, by obligating states to secure the physical and psychological health and well-being of animals both within and beyond the direct human–animal interface.

That said, Article 6 of the CAP features provisions focused specifically on combating the emergence and spread of pathogens, as well as antimicrobial resistance.[144] To this end, the CAP requires contracting parties to develop veterinary services tailored to locally relevant pathogenic risks, to create facilities to monitor and prevent their emergence, and to detect and manage high-risk practices with respect to the wild animal, human, and animal-under-human-control interface.[145] With respect to what has been termed the 'silent pandemic', or the emergence of antibiotic-resistant bacteria through their overuse in animal-based agriculture,[146] the CAP goes beyond what is prescribed by the present draft of the WHO Pandemic Agreement by prohibiting the prophylactic use of antibiotics for purposes of promoting growth or increasing yield outside of exceptional cases.[147] Notably, this prohibition would echo what the EU requires for its domestic producers and for imported products.[148] In addition, the CAP proves attentive to the need to monitor animal-use facilities and transport chains and requires that animals be properly contained

138 Convention on Animal Protection for Public Health, Animal Well-Being, and the Environment, Article 4 (1).
139 Ibid., Article 4 (1)(f–h).
140 Ibid., Article 4 (2).
141 Ibid., Article (1)(b).
142 Ibid., Article (1)(c).
143 Ibid., Article 5 (1)(d)
144 Ibid., Article 6.
145 Ibid., Article 6.
146 Ka Wah Kelly Tang, 'Antimicrobial Resistance (AMR)' (2023) 80 *British Journal of Biomedical Science* 1–11 at 1–3.
147 Convention on Animal Protection for Public Health, Animal Well-Being, and the Environment, Article 6.
148 Alliance to Save Our Antibiotics, 'New European Union Rules on Farm Antibiotic Use' (September 2020). Available at www.saveourantibiotics.org/media/1842/2022-changes-to-european-law-farm-antibiotics.pdf.

and separated by species, with due regard needing to be paid to health and sanitation conditions.[149] The CAP also obligates contracting parties to promote alternative practices to reduce the risk of the emergence and spread of pathogens.[150] With Article 6 requiring that contracting parties exchange information regarding the link between animal well-being and the emergence and spread of disease, it inherently complements the substantive provisions from Articles 3, 4, and 5. Finally, in recognising that the emergence of pathogens cannot be eliminated outright, Article 6 obligates contracting parties to prioritise the use of non-lethal management methods so as to consider the well-being of animals, whose suffering should be minimised.[151]

Taken together, the provisions advanced through Articles 3–6 of the CAP establish a global floor for animal protection, yet the CAP also provides for the development of protocols to further elevate the interests of animals beyond it.[152] As such, the CAP holds the promise of housing critical gains for animals over time. With states being able to enter into a protocol only if a contracting party to the Convention,[153] states are further incentivised to ratify the CAP in order to help shape future animal protections, which may seek to strengthen or expand upon those already contemplated by the CAP or else result in wholly new requirements, such as prohibitions against the use of animals for cosmetic testing purposes or bans on whaling, both of which have already gained traction globally.[154]

13.4.5 *Promoting Protections through Trade*

To be sure, one of the most criticised aspects of treaties concerns their enforcement. While this issue is arguably exacerbated by the CAP's limiting language that obligates contracting parties to carry out measures 'as far as possible', the Convention contemplates the use of trade and trade agreements as a means to encourage both contracting parties and non-contracting party states to meet the thresholds envisioned by the CAP. Articulated in Article 8, contracting parties engaged in the trade of live animals or their products are expected to encourage non-contracting party states to adopt animal well-being standards that either meet or exceed those prescribed by the CAP.[155] Furthermore, when developing trade agreements concerning live animals or their products, contracting parties are required to include provisions to see that the well-being of the animals involved meets or exceeds those contemplated by the Convention.[156] Together, these provisions help to ensure that contracting parties do not suffer economic disadvantages by virtue of having advanced animal protections. In a similar vein, the CAP also prevents contracting parties from weakening their domestic animal protections for the purpose of inducing trade.[157]

Given the immensity of the trade in animals and their products globally, these provisions serve to encourage non-contracting party states to ratify the CAP, as contracting parties would be incentivised, whether for economic, health, or moral reasons, to restrict engaging in trade

149 Convention on Animal Protection for Public Health, Animal Well-Being, and the Environment, Article 6.
150 Ibid., Article 6(f–g).
151 Ibid., Article 6(2).
152 Ibid., Article 22.
153 Ibid., Article 22.
154 Jennifer Mishler, 'Whale Hunting Still Exists in 3 Countries, but It Is Declining' *Sentient Media* (1 September 2023). Available at https://sentientmedia.org/whale-hunting; Humane Society of the United States, 'Timeline: Cosmetics Testing on Animals'. Available at www.humanesociety.org/resources/timeline-cosmetics-testing-animals.
155 Convention on Animal Protection for Public Health, Animal Well-Being, and the Environment, Article 8(1).
156 Ibid., Article 8(2).
157 Ibid., Article 8(3).

with them. Critically, the CAP's framework would not provide for new forms of economic protectionism than those that already exist today. Rather, it could help formalise, if not ground, the existing use of trade barriers to prohibit the import of lower welfare and higher disease risk animal products.

Indeed, while the world's foremost regulatory trade body, the World Trade Organization (WTO),[158] is fundamentally concerned with removing obstacles to trade among states, several of its regulatory frameworks permit states to construct trade barriers for 'justifiable' reasons,[159] reasons that include safeguarding animals and their interests. For example, one such exception to the rule that prohibits discriminating against foreign products under the WTO's General Agreement on Tariffs and Trade (GATT) permits states to create barriers if deemed 'necessary to protect human, animal, or plant life or health'.[160] Another WTO framework that permits the construction of trade barriers is the Sanitary and Phytosanitary (SPS) Agreement.[161] Negotiated between the WTO and the World Organisation for Animal Health (WOAH), the SPS Agreement permits states to develop trade barriers based not just upon WOAH's animal health standards, which conceivably operate as a global floor, but also their own national regulations, thereby providing flexibility to secure the health of their citizens, as well as that of animals by extension.[162] Citing the SPS Agreement, the EU has entered into trade agreements that prohibit the import of meat products if the well-being of animals was not taken into account during stunning and slaughter.[163] In a similar vein, the EU has also prohibited prophylactics for the purpose of stimulating the growth and yield of farmed animals, an issue that, while focused on preventing antimicrobial resistance, implicates the well-being of farmed animals.[164] By banning the import of animal products developed using the prophylactic use of antibiotics, the EU measure has considerable extraterritorial reach, one that the CAP's provisions on trade would not just allow for but also encourage.

On top of this, the WTO framework also permits states to prohibit or otherwise construct welfare labelling around the import of animals and animal products based upon the moral views of its citizens. In one such case, the EU moved to ban the import of seal products for commercial purposes.[165] Referred to as the EU Seal Regime, the ban was founded upon the EU public's moral distaste for the killing of seals.[166] Although the WTO's Appellate Body found that the EU Seal Regime violated the GATT because its exception for seal products from Inuit and Indigenous community hunts provided favourable market access to Greenland's Indigenous

[158] World Trade Organisation, 'Agreement: Marrakesh Agreement Establishing the World Trade Organization' (15 April 1994) 1867 U.N.T.S. 154, 33 I.L.M. 1144 (1994).

[159] World Trade Organisation, 'WTO Rules and Environmental Policies: Key GATT Disciplines'. Available at www.wto.org/english/tratop_e/envir_e/envt_rules_gatt_e.htm. This allowance, however, is subject to the requirement that 'measures are not applied in a manner which would constitute a means of arbitrary or unjustifiable discrimination between countries where the same conditions prevail, or a disguised restriction on international trade'. GATT 1994: General Agreement on Tariffs and Trade 1994, (15 April 1994), Marrakesh Agreement Establishing the World Trade Organization, 1867 U.N.T.S. 187, 33 I.L.M. 1153 (1994).

[160] General Agreement on Tariffs and Trade, Article XX(b).

[161] Agreement on the Application of Sanitary and Phytosanitary Measures, 15 April 1994, 1867 U.N.T.S. 493.

[162] Agreement on the Application of Sanitary and Phytosanitary Measures, Annex A(3)(b).

[163] Decision No. 1/2006 of the Joint Management Committee Set Up Under the Agreement Between the European Community and the Republic of Chile on Sanitary and Phytosanitary Measures Applicable to Trade in Animals and Animal Products, Plants and Plant Products and Other Goods and Animal Welfare of 9 November 2006, amending Appendices IC, IIIA, IIIB and XI to Annex IV to the Agreement (2007/177/EC).

[164] Alliance to Save Our Antibiotics, 'New European Union Rules on Farm Antibiotic Use', 1.

[165] Appellate Body Report, European Communities – Measures Prohibiting the Importation and Marketing of Seal Products, WT/DS400/AB/R, WT/DS401/AB/R (22 May 2014) (adopted 18 June 2014).

[166] Ibid., 24.

communities compared to those of Canada, among other reasons, it nevertheless affirmed that public moral sentiment around the ethical treatment of animals could justifiably be used to restrict market access.[167] In light of this pronouncement, the WTO has effectively provided that states may leverage the strength of their domestic animal protection laws to encourage other states to follow suit if they wish to gain access to markets with higher animal welfare standards,[168] an argument that is already gaining traction in some states, like New Zealand.[169] By encouraging contracting parties to adopt such barriers, the CAP promotes the protection of animals for their own sake, to prevent the emergence and spread of pathogens, and to gain certain economic and market advantages.[170]

13.4.6 *Entry into Force, Compliance Measures, and Enforcement*

Requiring at least ten states to ratify the Convention before going into force,[171] the CAP is open indefinitely to accession.[172] Upon joining, contracting parties must furnish the Secretariat with all domestic laws, policies, and regulations related to their obligations,[173] with biennial reports regarding how they continue to fulfil them submitted every two years.[174] Similar to other conventions, the CAP features a Conference of the Parties (COP), which would meet every two years after the initial COP.[175] In addition to contracting parties adopting financial and administrative rules and procedures and contemplating the creation of new committees to carry out functions,[176] each COP would be charged with reviewing the implementation of the Convention by contracting parties and scientific data and recommendations concerning the well-being of animals and the emergence and spread of pathogens and potentially act upon recommendations and adopt resolutions, amendments, and protocols.[177] Notably, it is also at each COP that a Standing Committee comprised of representatives from contracting parties would be elected to investigate issues, consider and offer recommendations, and suggest new protocols and amendments, among other powers.[178] Notably, a Standing Committee would have the power to interrogate the legislation and enforcement efforts of contracting parties.[179] Although only contracting parties are afforded a vote at a COP, non-contracting party states, international organisations, and non-governmental organisations that work in the realm of animal protection, environmental protection and conservation, or disease would have an opportunity to attend and participate.[180]

Of course, as with any international agreement, a critical question concerns how to ensure that parties are fulfilling their obligations and how disputes between and among them will

167 Ibid., 189.
168 Gerald Piddock, 'Report Warns of Animal Welfare "Gap"' *Farmers Weekly* (27 March 2024). Available at www.farmersweekly.co.nz/news/report-warns-of-animal-welfare-gap.
169 Ibid.
170 Ibid.
171 Convention on Animal Protection for Public Health, Animal Well-Being, and the Environment, Article 29.
172 Ibid., Article 28. While the CAP does provide for specific reservations, general reservations are prohibited under Article 25.
173 Ibid., Article 17.
174 Ibid., Article 17.
175 Ibid., Article 17(1).
176 Ibid., Article 17(2–3).
177 Ibid., Article 12.
178 Ibid., Article 16.
179 Ibid., Article 16 (8).
180 Convention on Animal Protection for Public Health, Animal Well-Being, and the Environment, Article 13.

be handled. As to the former, the CAP empowers contracting parties to develop procedures and mechanisms to determine when a contracting party is in non-compliance and what measures may be taken, including: the provision of advice and assistance; an official notice of non-compliance; a suspension of rights under the Convention itself; and, in cases of repeated non-compliance, other measures as deemed appropriate by the Standing Committee.[181]

As it concerns disputes among contracting parties related to the interpretation, application, performance, or implementation of their obligations, the Convention provides three options, including: negotiations between the contracting parties involved; submission by mutual consent to the Permanent Court of Arbitration at The Hague for a binding decision; and conciliation through the creation of a commission, whose resolution is not binding yet is expected to be considered in good faith.[182] Of course, while contracting parties may withdraw from the CAP,[183] the ability of contracting parties to employ trade measures to encourage non-contracting party states to meet or exceed the provisions of the CAP offers a compelling opportunity to ensure that the interests of animals are centred on the global stage – whether for their health and well-being or for humankind's, as contemplated by the One Health concept.

13.5 DENOUEMENT

To turn back to 11 March 2020, to Ghebreyesus's briefing of the press, and the one word he expressed regret at having to say, what the pandemic he announced into existence made clear is the power that words hold. Given the power it held to cast narratives to its mould, it was that one, he lamented, that enjoyed more attention than it deserved, and in transitioning into the conclusion of his address, what Ghebreyesus expressed wanting to leave the world with were others, 'actionable' words, words that he felt mattered more.[184] The first among them was 'prevention'.[185] At that time, what the word meant was that all people, as individuals and together, could take actionable steps to mitigate the spread of the novel virus. They could rewrite the narrative that they had been cast into.

It was just one year later, in March of 2021, that the word took on new meaning, one gleaned by context and *noscitur a sociis*, or the doctrine of construction entailing that the meaning of a word may be gleaned by its relation to those around it. As expressed by the WHO Director-General and two dozen world leaders calling for more than just 'preparedness' and 'response' but also 'prevention',[186] part and parcel of the robust international health architecture was the ability to prevent outbreaks before they began. With such an accord to be informed by the One Health model, the WHO Pandemic Agreement's consideration of the human–animal interface and the emergence and spread of zoonotic diseases appropriately points out where the world should look and what it should be looking for yet fails to advance the measures necessary to regulate or eliminate the uses of or interactions with animals that the world has seen to give rise to the kinds of outbreaks that have become pandemics. Rather, its measures approach pandemics as a given.

[181] Ibid., Article 23.
[182] Ibid., Article 24.
[183] Ibid., Article 30.
[184] World Health Organization, 'WHO Director-General's Opening Remarks at the Media Briefing on COVID-19 – 11 March 2020'.
[185] Ibid.
[186] World Health Organization, 'COVID-19 Shows Why United Action is Needed for More Robust International Health Architecture'.

But even if the question of pandemics is not one of *if* but *when*, the frequency with which the world must be 'conscripted' into the next pandemic story should not go unquestioned. Given that a strong argument can be made that, given the purview of the WHO as contemplated by its constitution, the WHO Pandemic Agreement may not be the appropriate instrument to feature the animal protections necessary to reduce the occurrence of pandemics, another agreement that does must be negotiated to fill this space. As discussed, the Convention on Animal Protection for Public Health, Animal Well-Being, and the Environment advances several protections designed to safeguard the health of animals and, by extension, that of humankind as well. In its affirmation of animals' sentience and intrinsic value, the CAP seeks to not just advance their protections on the global state but also their status in eyes of the law.

Indeed, the last in the short list of important words that Ghebreyesus offered the world in declaring the pandemic was 'people'.[187] Although there may be little doubt the Director-General conceived the term as coterminous with 'humans', it bears noting that significant gains have been realised – many of them in the midst of the COVID-19 pandemic itself – in extending substantive as well as procedural rights to animals around the world, thereby helping shift their status in the eyes of the law from that of mere property, or legal objects, into legal subjects, or 'persons'.[188] Against the backdrop of this shift in the legal status of animals worldwide, insofar as pandemics may be considered to be the story of 'all people', the CAP, in complementing the WHO Pandemic Agreement's focus on animal health, provides a unique opportunity to reimagine the 'character' of animals in our collective story and, conversely, animals as 'characters' in it, with the resulting fable revealing deeper moral truths over time and with further re-visions.

[187] World Health Organization, 'WHO Director-General's Opening Remarks at the Media Briefing on COVID-19 – 11 March 2020'.

[188] Amicus Brief for International Animal Law Scholars, 2–15, *Justice v. Vercher*, Supreme Court of Oregon No. S069799 (31 August 2022).

14

Advancing One Health Legal and Policy Action for the Environment

Urias S. Goll and Catherine Machalaba

14.1 INTRODUCTION

The environmental dimensions of health for society and nature are many. With the health of humans, animals, and ecosystems all recognised as target outcomes under the inclusive definition of One Health developed by the One Health High-Level Expert Panel (OHHLEP) (which serves as an advisory group to the Food and Agriculture Organization of the United Nations (FAO), United Nations Environment Programme (UNEP), World Health Organization (WHO), and World Organisation for Animal Health (WOAH), through their 'Quadripartite' collaboration), environmental laws and policies can be examined in an expanded way to consider their relevance for health. In addition, the underlying principles accompanying the OHHLEP One Health definition reinforce many aspects of environmental protection and environmental justice initiatives,[1] particularly regarding the meaningful inclusion of marginalised voices, socio-ecological equilibrium and intrinsic values, stewardship and responsibility to future generations, and traditional forms of knowledge. These provide important entry points and implications for action, including through the law and policy lens.

This chapter examines how a One Health approach can increase the scope and effectiveness of environmental laws and policies, including in the national uptake of multilateral environmental agreements (MEAs). Opportunities for integrating environmental considerations into health and other sectors, including through One Health coordination platforms, are also explored. Solutions to embed One Health considerations in regulatory environmental and social impact assessment process, using insights from Liberia, are presented. Thinking to the future, the chapter offers ideas for the legal sector to be a key contributor to progress on One Health implementation and achieving target outcomes.

We thank USAID for their support of the Conservation Works activity in Liberia, which has informed insights in this chapter.

[1] One Health High Level Expert Panel. One Health definitions and principles. https://www.who.int/publications/m/item/one-health-definitions-and-principles.

14.2 NATIONAL IMPLEMENTATION OF INTERNATIONAL FRAMEWORKS

While some notable cases have afforded components of the environment legal standing,[2] in general, laws and policies for environmental protection remain weak and face limited monitoring and enforcement.[3] The voluntary nature of environmental commitments at the international level, particularly under the Convention on Biological Diversity (CBD) and the United Nations Framework Convention on Climate Change (UNFCCC), provide little international motivation for meeting broad commitments.[4] National action planning allows for global and regional targets to be put into the national context of priorities, local actors, and capacity. Yet, most countries, particularly developing nations, adopt and ratify international environmental commitments which, in most cases, become domestic law, but fall short of enforcing or aligning these commitments with the national priorities. A One Health lens provides several core considerations that can help to support practical implementation: finding entry points; identifying gaps; ensuring policy is evidence-based and considers possible trade-offs; promoting coordination and harmonisation; and enabling equitable prioritisation and access to capacity strengthening. While discussed section-by-section below, these dimensions often overlap in practice.

14.2.1 *Finding Entry Points*

The National Biodiversity Strategies and Action Plans (NBSAPs) are the main implementation mechanism under the CBD. In line with the Kunming-Montreal Global Biodiversity Framework (GBF), parties have been requested to revise their NBSAPs to reflect the GBF's four goals and 23 targets. Like the preceding Aichi Biodiversity Targets, the GBF has several points of relevance for One Health – in particular Targets 5, 7, 11, and 14 – and mentions 'One Health and other integrated approaches' in its introductory text. A clear One Health scope is reflected in GBF Target 5 through the focus on reducing disease risks associated with wildlife trade, calling on parties to 'Ensure that the use, harvesting and trade of wild species is sustainable, safe and legal, preventing overexploitation, minimising impacts on non-target species and ecosystems, and reducing the risk of pathogen spill-over, applying the ecosystem approach, while respecting and protecting customary sustainable use by Indigenous peoples and local communities.'[5] Target 7 examines the risks and impacts of pollution on biodiversity, opening the door for legislation on the human and wild animal health effects of chemical exposures, including 'cumulative effects'.[6] Target 11 acknowledges the value of ecosystem services,[7] many directly or indirectly contributing to health, to 'Restore, maintain and enhance nature's

[2] Mihnea Tanasescu, 'When a River Is a Person: From Ecuador to New Zealand, Nature Gets Its Day in Court' (2017) 8 *Open Rivers: Rethinking Water, Place & Community*. Available at https://openrivers.lib.umn.edu/article/when-a-river-is-a-person-from-ecuador-to-new-zealand-natur)e-gets-its-day-in-court/.

[3] United Nations Environment Programme, 'Environmental Rule of Law: Tracking Progress and Charting Future Directions Nairobi' (2023). Available at https://doi.org/10.59117/20.500.11822/43943.

[4] Liability under the loss and damage fund is likely to emerge as a legal focus in the upcoming years, particularly with worsening impact under increased warming and more precise attributions of cause and effect.

[5] See www.cbd.int/gbf/targets/5.

[6] See www.cbd.int/gbf/targets/7.

[7] 'Ecosystem services' is specifically used here given that services have a basis of quantification and use in economic analyses, including for environmental policy decisions; however, other terminology more fully captures the broader value of nature to people and intrinsically, including wording used in the target itself.

contributions to people, including ecosystem functions and services, such as regulation of air, water, and climate, soil health, pollination and reduction of disease risk, as well as protection from natural hazards and disasters, through nature-based solutions and/or ecosystem-based approaches for the benefit of all people and nature.' Finally, Target 14 refers to a suite of broad tools at the national level through which biodiversity can be mainstreamed, to

> Ensure the full integration of biodiversity and its multiple values into policies, regulations, planning and development processes, poverty eradication strategies, strategic environmental assessments, environmental impact assessments and, as appropriate, national accounting, within and across all levels of government and across all sectors, in particular those with significant impacts on biodiversity, progressively aligning all relevant public and private activities, fiscal and financial flows with the goals and targets of this framework.

Each of these targets offers entry points for implementation under a One Health approach, including for infectious and non-infectious disease risks and outcomes. For example, under a One Health frame, environmental impact assessments – a routine and typically legally required tool used in countries' project and development proposal review and permitting processes – could in theory consider outcomes for human, animal, and environmental health.[8] Multi-sectoral participation in the development of NBSAPs and monitoring of their implementation progress may also help to encourage legal action from other sectors to support environmental protection (for example, tackling the illegal trafficking of wildlife based on public health endangerment and invasive species risks in addition to conservation status, in line with GBF Target 5).

Interactions with biodiversity by local communities are based on several different cultural, spiritual, nutritional, and economic factors. Hence, a multisectoral and multi-dimensional approach to the NBSAP revision and implementation can also affect options for law and policy development or changes. For example, in Liberia, partners have requested inclusion of One Health provisions in the amended and restated wildlife law to address zoonotic disease risks related to wildlife trafficking and increase access to information appertaining to threats to local residents based on interactions with wildlife. A similar call is made to provide varying sets of legal treatment for cases involving illegal wildlife capture by local residents, where the intended use relates to the local's livelihood (for wildlife used as protein sources) compared to individuals illegally collecting wildlife for commercial benefit; however, a public health risk may be present in both situations.

14.2.2 *Identifying Gaps*

National legislation is a key channel for translating international agreements and mandates into action. Until an international agreement is ratified nationally, it does not carry the same weight as a national legislation.[9] However, even where there is a substantial body of legislation at a national level, the scope may not necessarily cover all contexts needed under a One Health lens. For example, a legislative review of 38 jurisdictions (in Africa, Asia, Australia, North America, and South America) found that despite existing global and legal responses around the management of zoonotic disease risks, legislation did not fully address risks presented by the

[8] L. E. Sanchez and P. Croal, 'Environmental Impact Assessment, from Rio-92 to Rio+20 and Beyond' (2012) 15(3) *Ambient Soc*. Available at https://doi.org/10.1590/S1414-753X2012000300004.

[9] United Nations, 'What Is the Difference between Signing, Ratification and Accession of UN Treaties?' *ASK DAG*. Available at https://ask.un.org/faq/14594.

wildlife trade.[10] The lack of harmonisation among laws, as well as the variation in risk contexts, leaves gaps among different sectors, settings, and jurisdictions. To overcome this, One Health coordination is needed in the review of proposed and existing policies to ensure coherence and coverage. In Liberia, for example, with several national outbreaks of zoonotic diseases, the One Health Coordinating platform was instrumental in recommending the restatement and amendment of the Public Health Law to include all aspects of One Health and enhanced provisions for mitigating the risk of zoonosis.[11]

Mapping the coverage of laws and policies through a One Health lens can also reveal gap areas, including where formal authority, legislation, or implementation mechanisms are lacking. For example, responsibility for environmental health is often fragmented, and a designated authority for the full scope of wildlife health and wildlife disease has been lacking at the global level and within countries.[12] Overburdening national institutions/agencies with a plethora of functions or responsibilities beyond their individual capacities tends to limit the focus on environmental and wildlife health. A case in point is the Liberian Forestry Development Authority, which has operated as an entity with extreme focus on commercial timber harvest. Lately, it veered into conservation practice, initially with no or limited focus on wildlife health.[13] Its wildlife program is skewed towards illegal trade rather than wildlife health and risk of zoonosis. For instance, the national forest policy and implementation strategy, the overarching policy for forest conservation and terrestrial wildlife in Liberia, does not mention any activity related to wildlife health. It focuses on the ban on bushmeat hunting,[14] collecting biodiversity information for the establishment of protected areas and promoting community participation in area-based conservation.[15] Disentangling and specialising the focus of these agencies to account for One Health application will require legal and policy in addition to implementation efforts being championed by the National Focal Point for Wildlife. A former USAID project, Conservation Works, supported The Forestry Development Authority is finalising the National Conservation Strategy that incorporates issues of wildlife health and the general concept of One Health.

The local, national, and transboundary threats to wildlife health from infectious and non-infectious disease and anthropogenic change reinforce the need for law and policy action and coordination on wildlife health. In light of this, in 2022 WOAH adopted a Wildlife Health Framework that formally brings biodiversity and wildlife health into their scope;[16] however, as WOAH is an international organisation with voluntary membership, this Framework, like all WOAH frameworks and policy documents, has not been paired with legally binding requirements. At the global level, WOAH's reporting obligations only extend to diseases of concern for international trade (WOAH listed diseases), which in general primarily affect domestic

[10] J. Wingard, S. Belajcic, M. Samal, et al. 'Wildlife Trade, Pandemics and the Law: Fighting This Year's Virus with Last Year's Law' (2020) *Legal Atlas, LLC*. Available at https://biodiversitylinks.org/learning-evidence/one-health-evidence/one-health-evidence-inbox/wildlife-trade-pandemics-and-the-law_fighting-this-years-virus-with-last-years-law.pdf.

[11] Food and Agriculture Organization of the United Nations, 'Public Health Law: Title 33 Liberian Code of Laws Revised' (2017). Available at www.fao.org/faolex/results/details/en/c/LEX-FAOC174510/.

[12] C. Machalaba, M. Uhart, R. Kock, F. Diaz, and W. B. Karesh, 'Urgent Needs for Global Wildlife Health. Zenodo' (2020) 1–23. Available at http://doi.org/10.5281/zenodo.4105126.

[13] Organisation des Nations Unies pour l'alimentation et l'agriculture, 'National Forest Policy and Implementation Strategy' (Liberia, 2006). Available at www.fao.org/faolex/results/details/fr/c/LEX-FAOC148345/.

[14] Ibid., Section 6.2.

[15] Ibid., Section 7.1.

[16] World Organisation for Animal Health (WOAH), 'WOAH Wildlife Health Framework' (Paris, 2020).

animals. Outside of the listed diseases, reporting is voluntary for disease in wild animals, and subsequently, limited. Member countries could potentially use national legislation to require reporting of wildlife diseases (as well as pathogens and toxins) based on conservation, public health, or other reasons. A natural extension of this is a mechanism for the reporting of findings to government from research, as demonstrated by Indonesia's reporting framework mandate on wildlife and human disease surveillance studies.[17]

14.2.3 *Ensuring Policy Is Evidence-Based and Considers Possible Trade-Offs*

Another dimension of One Health, the translation of evidence-based recommendations into practice, can also be supported by legal and policy action. For example, the Food and Agriculture Organization (FAO) Convention on the Conservation of Migratory Species of Wild Animals (CMS) Task Force on Avian Influenza and Wild Birds has repeatedly identified opportunities to reduce disease risk, including for the protection of wild animals.[18] Some of these opportunities include national-level implementation considering regulating livestock production activities around migratory areas in land planning decisions (e.g. restricting poultry production around wetlands and associated risks of highly pathogenic avian influenza). To ensure effectiveness, a suite of laws, policies, or regulations would need to be issued and adequately enforced. In Malaysia, several disease risk reduction requirements were enacted following the Nipah virus epidemic in 1999, such as distancing between orchard trees and livestock, enhanced biosecurity, and the designation of farming areas safe for pig production areas (with alterative livelihoods encouraged outside of those areas).[19]

14.2.4 *Promoting Coordination and Harmonisation*

Without sufficient coordination and harmonisation, there may also be unintended consequences of environment regulations on health. For example, Convention on International Trade in Endangered Species of Wild Fauna and Flora (CITES) listings have inadvertently affected the timely movement of emergency diagnostic specimens through restrictions on international movement.[20] While simplified procedures have been enacted under CITES in response, they do not provide automatic exceptions for Appendix I species, which are often among the most threatened with extinction, and thus would logically be considered priorities for rapid disease investigation.[21] In another example, decisions to manage health in some sectors could have consequences for others; the need for a One Health approach to the licensing of veterinary pharmaceuticals was highlighted after a mass decline in *Gyps* vulture populations in South Asia from chemical

[17] See www.cbd.int/health/onehealth-casestudies2016-final-en.pdf.

[18] FAO, 'Scientific Task Force on Avian Influenza and Wild Birds' (July 2023). Available at https://openknowledge.fao.org/server/api/core/bitstreams/9b880198-02d2-4eda-a860-d1a56299bc31/content.

[19] A. A. bin Jamaluddin and A. bin Adzhar, Case Story 2: Nipah Virus – Experience from Malaysia 1998 1999. OIE Global Conference on Wildlife: Animal Health and Biodiversty- Preparing for the Future. 2011, available at: S1_3_AzriBinAdzhar.pdf; Y. Suit-B, L. Hassan, S. E. Krauss, et al., 'Mental Model of Malaysian Pig Farmers in Implementing Disease Prevention and Control Practices' (2021) 8(8) *Frontiers in Veterinary Science* 695702.

[20] W. B. Karesh, R. Kock, and C. C. Machalaba, 'CITES: In Sickness and in Health?' (2016) 13 *EcoHealth* 441–442. Available at https://doi.org/10.1007/s10393-016-1154-4.

[21] Appendix I species require intervention by the importing country to use simplified procedures. See: CITES. Scientific Exchange Exemption and Simplified Procedures: Guidance on the Use of the Scientific Exchange Exemption and the Simplified Procedures to Issue Permits and Certificates (2021). Available at https://cites.org/sites/default/files/eng/prog/exemptions/E_SimplifiedProcedures_endorsed_SC73.pdf.

poisoning linked to the ingestion of cattle carcasses that had been treated with diclofenac for pain relief.[22] The loss of vultures has wide-ranging implications for ecosystem health given their unique and valuable role as scavengers.[23] Negative impacts to wildlife and ecosystems can also be generated from ill-informed responses to infectious disease threats; for example, the vilification and culling of bats overlooks their important ecosystem services and may actually increase zoonotic disease risk.[24] These misguided responses reinforce the importance of multi-sectoral coordination to proactively minimise trade-offs and maximise co-benefits.

14.2.5 *Enabling Equitable Prioritisation and Access to Capacity Strengthening*

In addition to the scope of international environmental agreements and their associated national legislation, implementation support may similarly influence priorities and progress. The overwhelming voluntary nature of funding of capacity building and technology transfer (CBTT) to support international environmental protection agreements results in uneven availability and access by countries and stakeholders;[25] it is also foreseeable how this could subject CBTT to potential conflicts of interest with economic investment priorities at odds with environmental protection. For example, a demand for investment and expansion of the Liberian government rent-seeking agenda from large-scale iron ore mining is potentially undermining the original intention to convert the Wologisi Proposed Protected Area into a National Park, thereby increasing the risk of environmental degradation, exacerbating climate change impact, and potentially generating health consequences from mining chemicals.[26] While the reporting of human and animal diseases is often associated with One Health initiatives, the reporting of environmental damages, environmental crime enforcement and deterrent capacity strengthening, and remediation measures should also be considered a priority to promote the same transparency prioritised by human and animal health sectors.

14.3 GOVERNANCE SYSTEMS

We briefly examine the four contexts for governance systems for One Health law and policy for environmental action: national and subnational (governmental), community, protected and conserved areas, and industry. Examples of key governance mechanisms and issues from each of these contexts are discussed in terms of implications from a One Health lens, acknowledging that a much wider scope of governance topics and contexts may be relevant.

[22] A. Margalida, G. Bogliani, C. G. Bowden, et al., 'Science and Regulation: One Health Approach to Use of Veterinary Pharmaceuticals' (2014) 346(6215) *Science* 1296–1298.

[23] A. Santangeli, S. A. Lambertucci, A. Margalida, et al., 'The Global Contribution of Vultures towards Ecosystem Services and Sustainability: An Experts' Perspective' (2024) 27(6) *iScience* 109925.

[24] D. MacFarlane and R. Rocha, 'Guidelines for Communicating about Bats to Prevent Persecution in the Time of COVID-19' (2020) 248 *Biological Conservation* 108650.

[25] Several studies, cited in the following references, have examined CBBT for marine protections; our generalization reflects our experience with the implementation of other, non-marine environmental conventions; Marjo Vierros and Harriet Harden-Davies, 'Capacity Building and Technology Transfer for Improving Governance of Marine Areas Both Beyond and within National Jurisdiction' (2020) 122 *Marine Policy* 104158; H. Harden-Davies, V. F. Lopes, L. F. Coelho, et al. 'First to Finish, What Comes Next? Putting Capacity Building and the Transfer of Marine Technology under the BBNJ Agreement into Practice' (2024) 3 *npj Ocean Sustainability* 3. Available at https://doi.org/10.1038/s44183-023-00039-1.

[26] Based on an official communication (2023) from the Liberian Minister of Mines to the head of the Forestry Development Authority expressing disapproval of the conversion of Wolegisi to a protected area. Consultation is still ongoing regarding final decision and underscores the importance of One Health coordination among agencies.

14.3.1 *National and Subnational*

The establishment of multi-sectoral coordination mechanisms, such as national One Health coordination platforms, is a major focus for advancing One Health implementation at the government level.[27] Different models have been used for governance structures, with varying form and funding mobilisation mechanisms (e.g. a lead agency, coordinator role, pooled resources).[28] These models have also been established at regional levels.[29] These mechanisms provide a foundation for the coordination and mapping of roles and responsibilities; in doing so, the clarification of mandates can reveal gaps needing attention. In most cases, the roles and responsibilities of government ministries and agencies overlap and/or are absent on the issue of wildlife health. When coordinated through the One Health platforms, the need to delineate the specific functions of wildlife health becomes apparent, from wildlife protection, public or domestic animal health protection, protected area management and environmental protection. These functions, in some cases, could be housed in a single ministry or department but the clarity, through law or policy, on the responsibility to ensure adequate protection must be stated. Additionally, in general, responsibility is fragmented for managing risks and impacts (e.g. certain agencies are responsible for watershed management and agricultural runoff, whereas water, sanitation, and hygiene (WASH) services and treatment for waterborne diseases are handled in other domains). This division and resulting dis-incentives for collaboration (and lack of jurisdiction) can hinder coherent policy decisions; the need to engage beyond the health sector is recognised in the sentiment of 'health in all policies'.[30]

A mix of assessment, planning, information sharing, and risk communication tools have been used to operationalise collaboration under national (and in some cases subnational) One Health platforms. The ongoing development of One Health Strategic Plans, intended as a national-level translation of the global One Health Joint Plan of Action developed by the Quadripartite,[31] offers an opportunity to contextualise a One Health approach to each country's unique context, including risks and policy instruments.[32] To inform decision making, a One Health economics approach has the potential to support more robust evaluation of investments, in particular to assess and weigh trade-offs and co-benefits.[33] While the value of 'societal' (versus single-sector) perspectives in economic analysis has been emphasised, the increasing integration of environmental and health economic methods provides an exciting opportunity for the field of

[27] United Nations Environment Programme and World Organisation for Animal Health, 'A Guide to Implementing the One Health Joint Plan of Action at National Level' (Geneva: World Health Organization, Food and Agriculture Organization of the United Nations 2023). Licence: CC BY-NC-SA 3.0 IGO.

[28] FAO-OIE-WHO, 'Taking a Multisectoral, One Health Approach: Tripartite Zoonoses Guide'. Available at www.woah.org/fileadmin/Home/eng/Media_Center/docs/EN_TripartiteZoonosesGuide_webversion.pdf.

[29] V. K. Lokossou, N. C. Atama, S. Nzietchueng, et al., 'Operationalizing the ECOWAS Regional One Health Coordination Mechanism (2016–2019): Scoping Review on Progress, Challenges and Way Forward' (2021) 13 *One Health* 100291.

[30] L. O. Gostin, J. T. Monahan, J. Kaldor, et al., 'The Legal Determinants of Health: Harnessing the Power of Law for Global Health and Sustainable Development' (2019) 393(10183) *Lancet* 1857–1910.

[31] See www.fao.org/one-health/background/coordination/en.

[32] World Health Organization, Food and Agriculture Organization of the United Nations, World Organisation for Animal Health United Nations Environment Programme (2022). 'One Health Joint Plan of Action (2022–2026): Working Together for the Health of Humans, Animals, Plants and the Environment' World Health Organization. Available at https://apps.who.int/iris/handle/10665/363518.

[33] OHHLEP, 'One Health Theory of Change'. Available at www.who.int/publications/m/item/one-health-theory-of-change.

economics.[34] Economic and other evaluations can also be informed by the findings from the Intergovernmental Science-Policy Platform on Biodiversity and Ecosystem Services (IPBES), in particular in terms of an increasing evidence base on the interlinkages between biodiversity and health.

14.3.2 *Community*

Community governance can play a key role in managing natural resources, including in decision making on use of proposed protected and conserved areas. These rightsholders (whether formally or informally established) often include Indigenous Peoples, who make up approximately 6 per cent of the world's human population but govern a quarter of terrestrial areas, including 39 per cent of the planet's most ecologically intact landscapes, many of which are threatened by industrial development.[35] One important element of governance centres on land tenure, including those with formal ownership as well as those with informal rights and dependence on ecosystems (e.g. for cultural, religious, economic, or other reasons). The lack of clarity on land tenure or the absence of specific rights to land by local communities can undermine conservation efforts, lead to uncontrolled and unsafe interactions with wildlife, and destruction of key habitats with the risk of increasing the probability of zoonotic disease spillover and vulnerability of these communities.

The principle of Free, Prior, and Informed Consent (FPIC) is recognised (and increasingly enforced) as a minimum standard for decisions on land tenure in/around proposed protected areas. Defined as 'a specific right granted to Indigenous Peoples recognised in the UN Declaration on the Rights of Indigenous Peoples (UNDRIP), which aligns with their universal right to self-determination', 'FPIC allows Indigenous Peoples to provide or withhold/ withdraw consent, at any point, regarding projects impacting their territories. FPIC allows Indigenous Peoples to engage in negotiations to shape the design, implementation, monitoring, and evaluation of projects'.[36] Factors such as influence, awareness, and different value systems should be considered throughout community land formalisation processes to ensure FPIC is respected. Importantly, the lack of recognition of certain rights of communities to land and natural resources in local policy and legislation can undermine the principles of FPIC and increase the likelihood of conflict, unstainable harvest of natural resources and unsafe exposure to wildlife. In Liberia, for example, the Land Rights Act 2018,[37] has vested in the community unequivocal and unconditional right to customary land and the resources thereon. This has improved bargaining power of the community to negotiate, using the FPIC principles, for sustainable utilisation of their land. In addition, the national guidelines for establishing protected areas, as a legal instrument, require land tenure clarification as condition precedent to the creation of conservation or protected areas on land.[38]

One Health understanding is particularly relevant for the 'informed' component of FPIC, given how direct and indirect impacts may affect the health and wellbeing of communities in

[34] 'The Return on Investment for One Health and One Health Investment Planning is explored in a Community of Practice'. Available at https://virtual-learning-center.fao.org/mod/page/view.php?id=14276.

[35] C. M. Kennedy, B. Fariss, J. R. Oakleaf, et al., 'Over half of Indigenous Peoples' Lands Are Threatened by Industrial Development, Global Conversion Risk Assessment Reveals Need for Greater Support of Indigenous Stewardship' (2023) 6(8) *One Earth* 1032–1049.

[36] See www.fao.org/indigenous-peoples/our-pillars/fpic/en/.

[37] Land Rights Act 2018 (Liberia) Chapter 8.

[38] Step 3 (B), National Guidelines for Gazetting Protected Ares in Liberia, No-2-2022.

diverse and potentially complex ways. For example, a timber logging concession in a primary forest area may generate jobs, revenue, and potentially improved access to health and other services, at least in the short term; whereas longer-term environmental consequences could lead to persistent pollution of waterways, change in species ecology, and other effects that may be at odds with other principles (e.g. intergenerational and multi-species rights and equity). Even formalising or increasing the protection status of a conserved area can potentially have adverse consequences for communities and rightsholders, such as loss of access to sacred sites. The use of a One Health lens in cost-benefit or cost-effectiveness analyses can explore trade-off and co-benefits and consider the distributions of monetary and non-monetary costs and benefits (e.g. to government, private industry, and local communities).[39] An extended time horizon, in some cases longer than a development project lifespan, may be needed to reflect long-term impacts on the environment and health, societal, and economic impacts (whether positive or negative) to a community.

14.3.3 *Protected and Conserved Areas*

Protected and conserved areas (PCAs) and Other Effective Area-Based Conservation Measures (OECMs) can involve a range of governance and management strategies. The IUCN has broadly defined these relevant for protected areas as governance by government, shared governance, private governance, and governance by Indigenous Peoples and local communities, with a set of management categories generally based on use purpose and restrictions.[40] In practice, PCAs often face multiple demands (some competing) from conservation management (including external management models), large-scale tourism and revenue generation (e.g. private lodging concessions, mining, and logging), as well as small-scale livelihood and cultural and space considerations (e.g. poaching, transhumance, access to medicinal plants). Activities at the periphery may also affect conditions within a protected area, such as through livestock grazing or wastewater generated via mining. As conditions are often dynamic, monitoring and decision-making processes can benefit from a One Health lens to identify and manage risks and impacts to human, animal (domestic and wild), and environmental health, requiring coordination between communities, industries, environmental scientists, the human and animal health sectors, and park managers.

International standards also provide guidance and benchmarks for the effective management of PCAs. For example, the IUCN Green List Standard for protected areas provides a voluntary certification on the basis of sites demonstrating certain criteria: 'Respect: for the local community through fair and meaningful engagement of rights-holders and stakeholders; Design: planning that identifies the needs to secure the important values of the area; Effective management: monitoring of the status of these important values; Successful conservation results: for nature and for people; clear contribution: to climate change responses, health and well-being and other challenges'. The integration of a One Health approach in the Green List Standard has been recognised, with the planned integration of disease management indicators into the revised Green List Standard,[41] and the formation of multi-sectoral Expert Assessment Groups (including veterinary expertise, for example) for the Green List at the country level.

[39] Some benefits are not readily quantified in monetary terms; a mix of monetary and non-monetary indicators may relevant. See e.g. K. A. Brauman, L. A. Garibaldi, S. Polasky, et al., 'Global Trends in Nature's Contributions to People' (2020) 117(51) *Proceedings of the National Academy of Sciences of the United States of America* 32799–32805.

[40] N. Dudley, *Guidelines for Applying Protected Area Management Categories* (Gland: IUCN, 2008).

[41] Illustrative indicators have been proposed. See: IUCN and EcoHealth Alliance 'Healthy People and Wildlife through Nature Protection: Guidelines for Prevention, Detection, Response, and Recovery from Disease Risks in and around Protected and Conserved Areas. (Gland: IUCN and New York: EcoHealth Alliance 2022).

14.3.4 *Industry*

There is precedent for voluntary sustainable industry standards, potentially to pre-empt environmental regulations, respond to public demand, and meet corporate social responsibility obligations. For example, the Forest Stewardship Council (FSC) has developed a system for voluntary accreditation to certify companies as providing services and goods in line with 'environmentally appropriate, socially beneficial and economically viable forest management'.[42] The existing FSC standard includes indicators around worker health and ecosystem services and could potentially be interpreted under a One Health lens. Parallel mechanisms could be explored for other industries; for example, an audit checklist was developed to assess emerging infectious disease risks in the extractive industries.[43] Implementation of such tools and standards in line with a One Health approach will likely require a broader scope of expertise (e.g. disease ecology and wildlife health) than commonly included in biodiversity and community health impact assessment and monitoring.

14.4 CASE STUDY: INSIGHTS FROM LIBERIA

Liberia is rich in biodiversity and plays a vital role in climate change mitigation and adaptation, with the largest remaining tract of the Upper Guinean Rainforest and important wetland and mangrove ecosystems. After two Civil Wars between 1989 and 2003, the country's institutions were left weakened, affecting the governance of environmental laws and policies. Following the cessation of hostilities in 2005, Liberia embarked on a rigorous process to improve the legal and regulatory landscape in support of sustainable natural resources management, land tenure and security, especially in the context of community ownership, access and use, and wildlife management. In 2016, Liberia adopted the National Wildlife Conservation and Protected Area Management Law of Liberia.[44] While it prohibits wildlife hunting and trade by default, the harvest, sale, and consumption of wildlife has continued, and the enforcement of the law and its penalties remain weak, with few prosecutions. In 2020, the process to amend and restate the wildlife law began. Following three years of painstaking research, consultation, and redrafting, the amended and restated wildlife law was submitted to the Office of the President, now inclusive of provisions on institutional arrangements and establishing regulation to minimise zoonotic disease risk. Application of the existing law to practice reinforces the importance of multi-sectoral planning, resourcing, and prioritisation; for example, wildlife confiscations may require the involvement of the Liberian National Police, requiring joint security initiatives. In addition, the lack of suitable facilities and caretaking requirements for rescued wildlife served as a deterrent to confiscation.[45] The availability of rescue centres in the country, through partnerships between non-governmental organisations and the Forestry Development Authority and sustainable resourcing for day-to-day operations, has helped to overcome this barrier.

[42] See https://connect.fsc.org/document-centre/documents/resource/392.C-STD-01-001 FSC Principles and Criteria for Forest Stewardship Standard (STD).

[43] USAID PREDICT, 'Preparedness & Response: Audit Checklist to Reduce Potential Exposure to Emerging Infectious Diseases' (July 2017). Available at: https://s3.amazonaws.com/one-health-app/static/docs/toolkits/Private_Sector_Engagement_Toolkit/Tools/Private_Sector_Audit_Tool.pdf.

[44] Ministry of Foreign Affairs Monrovia Liberia, 'An Act Adopting the National Wildlife Conservation and Protected Area Management Law of Liberia' Approved 5 October 2016. Available at: http://wri-sites.s3.amazonaws.com/forest-atlas.org/lbr.forest-atlas.org/resources/Documents/National%20Wildlife%20Law%20of%20Liberia.pdf.

[45] 'Liberia Chimpanzee Rescue and Protection'. Available at: www.liberiachimpanzeerescue.org/protection.html.

14.4.1 *National One Health Coordinating Platform*

Liberia has been a leader in operationalising One Health, including through the establishment of a National One Health Coordination Platform in 2016.[46] A formal governance structure set expectations and designated roles for participation, including for its Steering Committee, Technical Committee, and Technical Working Groups.[47] The Steering Committee is chaired by the Vice President; the Technical Committee is chaired by the Director General of the National Public Health Institute of Liberia; and the six Technical Working Groups have a rotational chairing format. This leadership structure is supported by a One Health Secretariat with a coordinator and officers from seven target agencies (Ministry of Health, Ministry of Agriculture, Forestry Development Authority, Environmental Protection Agency, National Disaster Management Agency, National Public Health Institute of Liberia, and Ministry of Defense). Terms of Reference have been developed in the Platform's Governance Manual to clearly define roles and responsibilities for each component of the governance structure. A standalone website managed by the One Health Platform Secretariat has been developed to provide a central place to access information, including laws and policies.[48] The development of county-level platforms is now translating this model to the subnational level to promote more localised dialogue across ministries and support information flow to and from national authorities.

14.4.2 *Revision of the National Biodiversity Strategy and Action Plan (NBSAP)*

The National Biodiversity Strategy and Action Plan (NBSAP), in theory, presents a turnkey solution for the sustainable management of biodiversity and creating a conditionality whereby humans, ecosystems, and wildlife can thrive harmoniously. NBSAPs are 'central for mainstreaming biodiversity by translating global ambition into national policies'.[49] They are also useful ways of integrating the One Health concepts and practices into national planning and decisions for managing wildlife. The first NBSAP for Liberia was designed in 2004 in an effort by the national government to centralise decisions and incorporate issues affecting biodiversity into national policies and plans. Upon the signing of the Nagoya Protocol and Aichi Targets, Liberia, again, realised the need to adjust its NBSAP to mirror and align with the international agreement.

Despite the attending value attached to sustainably managing biodiversity, certain underlying conditions, if not addressed, can lead to a complete failure of the NBSAP. 'Conflicting interests, weak financial support, and poorly integrated institutional and regulatory structures can affect implementation of NBSAP'. Thus, coordination across sectors is vital.[50]

[46] S. Agbo, L. Gbaguidi, C. Biliyar, et al., 'Establishing National Multisectoral Coordination and Collaboration Mechanisms to Prevent, Detect, and Respond to Public Health Threats in Guinea, Liberia, and Sierra Leone 2016–2018' (2019) 1 *One Health Outlook* 4. Available at: https://doi.org/10.1186/s42522-019-0004-z.

[47] 'Liberia One Health Governance Manual' 2nd ed. (2021). Available at: https://onehealthliberia.org/download/one-health-coordination-platform-governance-manual-2nd-edition/.

[48] See https://onehealthliberia.org.

[49] E. M. Cardona Santos, S. Schmid, N. Butner, et al., 'Mainstreaming Revisited: Experiences from Eight Countries on the Role of National Biodiversity Strategies in Practice' (2023) 16 *Earth System Governance* 100177. Available at: https://doi.org/10.1016/j.esg.2023.100177.

[50] Ibid.

In March 2017, a new revised NBSAP, encapsulating five goals and twenty targets, was endorsed by the Liberian Government spanning the period 2017–2025. Positioned as the overarching national strategy for managing biodiversity, neither the 2004 nor the 2017 described the concept or mentioned the word One Health. Understandably, this may be as a result of the limited exposure and understanding of One Health in the country. More so, the international community was still piecing together the inextricable link between wildlife health, environmental change, and disease spillover vis-à-vis the need to imbed these considerations into national planning for environmental decision making.

The twin devastating outbreaks of Ebola and COVID-19 impetuously shattered health systems, livelihoods, and human wellbeing. Incontrovertibly, the Ebola outbreak was a wake-up call for Liberians that highlighted the unavoidable need to integrate One Health into national policies and laws. This notion was furthered re-echoed following the global pandemic of COVID-19. In time past, global biodiversity instruments did not reference or strategically consider the importance of this concept. Notwithstanding, following the devastating impact of the Coronavirus, the Kunming-Montreal Global Biodiversity Framework moved significantly towards integrating One Health. With the vision to align its national strategy with the GBF, Liberia embarked on the revision of its NBSAP, as a standard practice and based on a request from the Convention on Biological Diversity (CBD). Interestingly, the initial call from the government was to integrate the interfaces between wildlife health, environmental changes, and human health. After a few national consultations and engagements with key national experts, the government took a bold step towards establishing a new target in the revised NBSAP relating to One Health. Submitted to the CBD Secretariat and awaiting finalization of the implementation plan and monitoring and evaluation framework, Target 1.5 of the 2024 revised NBSAP provides that it will 'by 2030, integrate the One Health approach into the assessment and management of biodiversity and establish and implement a comprehensive national program to monitor, control, and reduce the risk of chemical hazards and pathogen spillover presenting risks to human and animal health'.[51] To this target, six indicators were correspondingly developed for monitoring and evaluation purposes. When finalised and officially endorsed, this will not only highlight the importance of improving policy and legislations for One Health but will increase awareness on the subject, attract international and national support, and subsequently reduce the risk of zoonosis.

14.4.3 *Integrating One Health in Environmental and Social Impact Assessment (ESIA)*

Environmental Impact Assessments (EIA) are a tool typically used to assess the effects of a proposed project on the environment.[52] In Liberia, EIA is the primary mechanism for assessment of potential development projects, covering a wide scope ranging from commercial and artisanal extractive activities to agricultural and transportation development to protected area establishment and ecotourism. Projects classified in Annex I of the Liberia Environmental Protection and Management Law of Liberia (EPML) must undergo the EIA process prior to receiving approval by the government. Health impacts are potentially included in the scope of the EIA procedures, but there has historically been limited awareness of health aspects by the country's impact assessment workforce. The system, processes, and regulations for EIA

[51] Liberia revised NBSAP (2024).

[52] J. Glasson, R. Therivel, and A. Chadwick, *Introduction to Environmental Impact Assessment*. 4th ed. (New York: Routledge, 2012). (The Natural and Built Environment series).

significantly improved over time due, principally, to the evolution of different impacts associated with major capital projects that were not originally embedded in the EIA framework. For instance, after many years of evaluating project impacts via the EIA process, many issues still existed within these locations including those affecting residents, expropriation of land, and health-related impacts not necessarily attributed to environmental pollution. Hence, the Government of Liberia, through the Environmental Protection Agency of Liberia (EPA), published the first legal instrument, in the form of regulations in 2016 calling for the adjustment to the list of project categories that are covered under the EIA process as well as the inclusion of social impacts.[53] Essentially, this resulted in the designation from EIA to ESIA, with the 'S' representing social impacts.

Despite this seemingly progressive intervention, the evaluation of health impacts from these projects under the ESIA process did not meet the required threshold. Project proponents or developers were required to assess only the occupational health risks and hazards of their interventions and not a full health impact assessment with consideration of direct and indirect impact to wildlife, environment, or people as a result of the project. A One Health approach was proposed as an anchor for evaluating health impacts, mainly those associated with the project and directly affecting wildlife or indirectly leading to a zoonotic spillover. In 2022, the EPA launched a call for inputs to be made to the ESIA regulations. With support from national and international experts, a set of recommendations were proffered as an improvement to evaluating health impacts with emphasis on integrating the One Health concepts in the revised regulations. Unfortunately, by the time the recommendations were received, EPA had already published the new revised ESIA Regulations, 2022. Notwithstanding, the government received the draft of recommended changes and committed to integrating specific language during the next iteration of the regulations in 2026. More importantly, the new requirement for assessing health impacts under the 2022 revised regulations incorporates wildlife health impacts associated with projects earmarked for an ESIA study. This progress is not the anticipated result but it is a watershed movement for highlighting, in a legal instrument, the importance of integrating One Health as well as the immense contribution this can have on wildlife and ecosystem health with a cascading effect on human health. At the request of the EPA, to support capacity for implementation, in 2023 training on One Health in ESIA was conducted for members of the Union of Certified Environmental Professionals of Liberia.[54] The training highlighted how a One Health approach can more comprehensively assess the impacts of toxicology and infectious disease risks across a project lifespan, including direct impact at a site as well as from biodiversity offsets.

14.5 CONCLUSION

This chapter has demonstrated there are numerous needs and opportunities for integrating One Health in environmental law and policy. Future decisions and frameworks can be examined with a One Health lens to identify relevant stakeholders for monitoring and implementation. The relevance of human, animal, and environmental health risks and outcomes to legal standing and liability requires an interdisciplinary team. Academic institutions have a role to play in bridging disciplines to encourage new ways of envisioning and implementing legal frameworks.

53 See www.epa.gov.lr/sites/default/files/ESIA%20Procedural%20Guideline.pdf.

54 'USAID's Conservation Works Trains Environmental Professionals on One Health in Impact Assessment', 26 September 2023. *New Dawn* newspaper. Available at: https://thenewdawnliberia.com/usaids-conservation-works-train-environmental-professionals-on-one-health-in-impact-assessment/.

Similarly, practitioners from human, animal, and environmental health disciplines should consider the legal and policy elements of the topics they are working with to support a comprehensive understanding of the issue and viable solutions. At the national and subnational level, and university levels, the role of One Health coordination platforms could expand to deliver broadly on sustainable development objectives, including outcomes relevant for biodiversity and ecosystems, rather than only disease response as a primary objective. The practice of environmental law and legal training can encourage interaction with other sectors, including for harmonisation and more holistic interpretation of law and liability.

15

One Health and Multispecies Urban Infrastructure

Jeff Sebo, Alisa E. White, and Toni Sims[*]

15.1 INTRODUCTION

In the coming decades, cities and other local governments will need to transform their infrastructure as part of their climate change mitigation and adaptation efforts. When they do, they have the opportunity to build more resilient, sustainable, and accommodating infrastructure for humans and non-humans alike. From industrial farming practices to the wildlife trade, human interactions with animals currently pose significant threats, including infectious disease transmission, environmental degradation, and biodiversity loss. These problems are best addressed through a One Health approach, which recognises the interconnectedness of human, animal, and environmental health.

Animal welfare, in particular, is often neglected in public policy. Cities can address this gap by incorporating animal welfare into their local policymaking.[1] Some governments may consider establishing a dedicated animal welfare planning process that supports animal habitats, shelters, food, and other needs. Governments can also add proxies for wild animal welfare into their existing monitoring and evaluation efforts. They can pursue institutional reform, including appointing officials or establishing offices for animal welfare to coordinate city-wide efforts. And they can pursue infrastructural reform, by implementing co-beneficial land use and built environment policies for humans, non-humans, and the environment.

This chapter makes the general case for including animal welfare in local policymaking, with special focus on institutional and infrastructural change. We start by discussing the importance of animal welfare for the One Health framework, along with key questions about animal welfare. We then discuss general principles and policies that can guide cities in building multispecies urban infrastructure. For example, cities can implement bird-friendly building materials, improve road design and operation, provide guidance for incorporating animal shelter and habitat into green infrastructure, and shift their lawn maintenance practices. These policies benefit humans, animals, and the environment alike. By researching and adopting these and other, similar policies, cities can work towards creating environments that support all species within their boundaries.

[*] Views expressed are solely those of the authors.

[1] Alisa E. White, Jeff Sebo, Becca Franks, et al., 'Wild Animal Welfare in Local Policies on Land Use and the Built Environment' (Guarini Center on Environmental, Energy, and Land Use Law & Wild Animal Welfare Program 2024).

15.2 ONE HEALTH, ANIMAL WELFARE, AND THEORIES OF CHANGE

15.2.1 *Expanding One Health*

One Health is a policy framework that recognises that human, animal, and environmental health are linked. Accordingly, the One Health framework requires a 'collaborative, multisectoral, and transdisciplinary approach – working at the local, regional, national, and global levels'.[2] The UN Food and Agricultural Organization describes One Health as an 'integrated approach' with implications for 'food security, sustainable agriculture, food safety, antimicrobial resistance' and more.[3] Given these links between human, animal, and environmental health, governments can improve outcomes for human health and well-being in many contexts by improving outcomes for animal and environmental health as well.

To see why One Health is valuable, consider how humans interact with captive animals, particularly farmed animals. Humans breed, raise, and kill more than 100 billion vertebrates and more than one trillion invertebrates for food each year.[4] These practices not only harm and kill many animals, but also contribute to the spread of infectious diseases (particularly bird and pig farming) and to land-use and climate change (particularly cow farming).[5] By thinking about human, animal, and environmental health holistically, we can build future food systems that treat humans, animals, and the environment better at the same time.

Similarly, consider how humans interact with wild animals. Humans breed or capture tens of millions of wild land animals and hundreds of millions of wild aquatic animals for a variety of purposes each year.[6] But as with animal farming, many forms of the wildlife trade are bad for humans, animals, and the environment. They harm and kill many animals, contribute to the spread of infectious diseases (according to one study, animal farming and the wildlife trade are the two main causes of disease spread among wild animals),[7] and contribute to biodiversity loss and ecosystem collapse (particularly industrial fishing).[8] Once again, by thinking about these issues holistically, we can seek alternatives to the wildlife trade that are better for all.

However, while the One Health framework is valuable, current applications have important limitations.[9] One limitation is that current applications focus on benefiting humans, rather

[2] Centers for Disease Control and Prevention, 'One Health' (CDC 2024). Available at: https://perma.cc/3LNX-XLM3.

[3] Food and Agriculture Organization (FAO) of the United Nations, 'One Health'. Available at: https://perma.cc/2K7G-5VQP.

[4] H. Ritchie and M. Roser, 'How Many Animals are Factory-Farmed?' Our World in Data, 2023 *Available at: https://perma.cc/MJ6H-YHRN*; A. Rowe, 'Insects Raised for Food and Feed – Global Scale, Practices, and Policy' Rethink Priorities, 2020. Available at: https://perma.cc/356A-2URS.

[5] M. J. Gilchrist, C. Greko, D. B. Wallinga, G. W. Beran, D. G. Riley, and P. S. Thorne, 'The Potential Role of Concentrated Animal Feeding Operations in Infectious Disease Epidemics and Antibiotic Resistance' (2007) 115 *Environmental Health Perspectives* 313–16; H. Ritchie, P. Rosado, and M. Roser, 'Environmental Impacts of Food Production' Our World in Data, 2022; H. Ritchie, and M. Roser, 'Half of the World's Habitable Land is used for Agriculture' Our World in Data, 2019. Available at: https://perma.cc/37UT-TZ6C.

[6] A. Akhtar, *Animals and Public Health: Why Treating Animals Better Is Critical to Human Welfare* (Springer, 2012). A. Mood, E. Lara, N. K. Boyland, and P. Brooke, 'Estimating Global Numbers of Farmed Fishes Killed for Food Annually from 1990 to 2019' (2023) 32 *Animal Welfare* e12.

[7] P. Daszak, A. A. Cunningham, and A. D. Hyatt, 'Anthropogenic Environmental Change and the Emergence of Infectious Diseases in Wildlife' (2001) 78(2) *Acta Tropica* 103–116.

[8] D. Pauly, R. Watson, and J. Alder, 'Global Trends in World Fisheries: Impacts on Marine Ecosystems and Food Security' (2005) 360(1453) *Philosophical Transactions of the Royal Society B: Biological Sciences* 5–12. Available at: https://doi.org/10.1098/rstb.2004.1574.

[9] For examples of frameworks that move beyond current applications of One Health, see the One Welfare framework: R. G Pinillos (ed.), 'One Welfare: A Framework to Improve Animal Welfare and Human Well-being' *CAB International* (2018); and S. Stucki, 'One Rights Framework' *One Rights: Human and Animal Rights in the Anthropocene* (Springer Nature, 2023).

than on benefiting human and non-human animals alike.[10] One Health recognises that human, animal, and environmental health are linked, but responds to these links by treating animal health as a resource to protect for the sake of human health.[11] However, many non-human animals are living, conscious beings with sentience and agency; their health matters not only to us but also, and primarily, to them. By taking an instrumentalising approach to animal protection, we miss opportunities to improve animal health for the sake of the animals themselves.

Another limitation is that current applications of One Health focus on health in particular rather than on health and welfare in general. Of course, this focus on health makes sense, because health impacts are easier to measure than welfare impacts, and because health is a 'primary good' that makes possible the pursuit of all other goods. But for human and non-human animals alike, health is not an end in itself and protecting our health is not always sufficient for supporting our flourishing in life. By focusing narrowly on our health rather than widely on what brings meaning and value to our lives, we miss opportunities to improve not only human and animal *health* but also human and animal *lives and societies*.[12]

To see how these limitations can lead us astray, return to our treatment of captive animals. Many humans assume, rightly, that proper regard for animal and environmental health requires making changes to animal farming. However, when we assess our options without considering animals as stakeholders, and without considering animal welfare at all, we end up causing and allowing unnecessary harm to vulnerable animals. For example, many experts are proposing further intensification of animal farming to reduce the amount of land used per animal, despite the fact that further intensification risks increasing animal suffering.[13] Many experts are proposing a shift from cow to chicken farming for the same reason, despite the same trade-off.[14]

Similarly, many humans assume, rightly, that proper regard for animal and environmental health requires making changes to the wildlife trade. But once again, when we assess our options without considering animals as stakeholders, and without considering animal welfare at all, we end up causing and allowing unnecessary harm. For example, we tend to set limits on the wildlife trade when we see animals as vectors for disease (for instance, bans of live markets during COVID-19), or when we see particular practices as ecologically harmful (for instance, bans of 'unsustainable fisheries'). But as long as we see the exploitation and extermination of other animals as compatible with human health, we tend to permit them.[15]

Of course, there may be cases where human and non-human interests conflict. At least at present, many humans rely on animal use industries for food, income, and other vital needs. Additionally, many animals do pose threats to humans, and nonviolent resolutions to these conflicts are not always available. However, to say that we should consider human *and* non-human health *and* welfare is not necessarily to say that we should always avoid practices that harm

10 S. Coghlan, B. J. Coghlan, A. Capon, and P. Singer, 'A Bolder One Health: Expanding the Moral Circle to Optimize Health for All' (2021) 3 *One Health Outlook* 1–4.

11 L. Johnson, M. Syd, Hope Ferdowsian, and Jessica Pierce, 'How One Health Instrumentalizes Nonhuman Animals' (2024) 26(2) AMA *Journal of Ethics* 184–90.

12 L. Sellars, K. Bernotas, and J. Sebo, 'One Health, COVID-19, and a Right to Health for Human and Nonhuman Animals' (2021) 23(2) *Health and Human Rights* 35.

13 C. Verkuijl, J. Smit, J. M. Green, et al., 'Climate Change, Public Health, and Animal Welfare: Towards a One Health Approach to Reducing Animal Agriculture's Climate Footprint' (2024) 5 *Frontiers in Animal Science* 1281450.

14 Shifting from farming cows to chickens increases animal suffering because chickens are smaller, therefore many individual chickens are required to produce the same amount of calories as a single cow. Conditions for chickens in factory farms are at least as bad, if not worse, than for cows. See: Kelsey Piper, 'Farms Have Bred Chickens So Large That They're in Constant Pain' (2020). *Vox*. Available at: https://perma.cc/C357-9FSK.

15 J. Sebo, *Saving Animals, Saving Ourselves: Why Animals Matter for Pandemics, Climate Change, and Other Catastrophes* (Oxford University Press, 2022).

animals in cases where these practices are deemed necessary. Instead, it is merely to say that we should consider the impacts of policies on all relevant stakeholders, and we should seek ways of improving human and animal lives together where possible.

15.2.2 *Assessing Wild Animal Welfare*

Unfortunately, political will is not the only obstacle that stands in the way of legal and political consideration of wild animal welfare. A more fundamental obstacle is that we currently lack the ability to predict and control the net effects of our actions and policies on wild animal welfare. This is partly due to our limited knowledge about wild animal welfare and is partly due to our limited capacity to act on the knowledge that we have. Before we can find a way forward, we need to identify where we are and where we need to go. So, in this section, we briefly survey several basic questions about animal welfare that we need to answer before we can responsibly estimate the net effects of our actions and policies on wild animal welfare.

To the extent that animal welfare is currently measured in policy contexts (which, to be clear, is a limited extent), it is typically measured for alignment with the 'five freedoms'. These were developed in the early 1990s and were the first metrics to capture, or attempt to capture, the subjective experience of animals in addition to their health and behaviours.[16] They include: (1) freedom from hunger or thirst; (2) freedom from discomfort; (3) freedom from pain, injury, or disease; (4) freedom to express normal behaviour; and (5) freedom from fear and distress. Each freedom has corresponding provisions that are recommended; for example, to ensure that an animal has freedom from hunger or thirst, the standard recommendation is to provide the animal with access to fresh water and a healthy diet.

While the five freedoms represent an important step towards the inclusion of animal welfare in public policy, they are incomplete measures of animal welfare. One of their limitations is that they are open to interpretation, which means that a range of environments could arguably meet their criteria.[17] Another limitation is that they represent what humans believe is important for animal welfare. They are not backed by animal welfare science as the five most important freedoms *to animals*. A third limitation is that they focus only on freedom from negative states, when positive animal welfare should be considered a benefit in policy making.[18] A more complete metric of animal welfare might track positive experiences as well as negative ones and represent the balance between them.

To develop a better framework, however, we need to answer several basic questions about animal welfare. First: Which animals are welfare subjects? That is, which animals are capable of experiencing morally significant benefits and harms? Does this capacity require sentience (the ability to suffer), agency (the ability to pursue goals), or only life (the ability to survive or procreate)? And if it requires sentience or agency, which animals have these features? The empirical evidence supports at least a non-negligible chance that all vertebrates and some invertebrates have these features.[19] But to the degree that we remain uncertain about particular animals (say, insects), how, if at all, should they factor into welfare assessments?

[16] David J. Mellor, 'Updating Animal Welfare Thinking: Moving beyond the "Five Freedoms" towards "A Life Worth Living"' (2016) 6 *Animals* 21.

[17] S. P. McCulloch, 'A Critique of FAWC's Five Freedoms as a Framework for the Analysis of Animal Welfare' (2013) 26 *Journal of Agricultural and Environmental Ethics* 959–975.

[18] David J. Mellor, 'Updating Animal Welfare Thinking: Moving beyond the "Five Freedoms" towards "A Life Worth Living"' (2016) 6 *Animals* 21.

[19] K. Andrews, J. Birch, J. Sebo, and T. Sims, 'Background to the New York Declaration on Animal Consciousness' in *The New York Declaration on Animal Consciousness* (2024). Available at: www.nydeclaration.com.

Second: How do our actions and policies affect these animals? When we attempt to help wild animals, our interventions can easily reverberate across vast ecological webs. Thus, if we want to assess the net effect of our actions and policies on wild animal welfare, then we need to consider not only the *direct* and *intended* effects on *some* animals, but also the *indirect* and *unintended* effects on *all* animals. That requires improving our understanding of natural systems in general, so that we can find order in what currently appears to be chaos. This project is already difficult when we restrict welfare assessments to, say, mammals and birds. It will be much harder when we expand these assessments to include all animals who merit consideration.

Third: Which effects are good and bad for particular animals? Many humans assume that we benefit animals when we extend their lives and expand their populations, and that we harm them when we shorten their lives and contract their populations. However, if an individual animal experiences more suffering than happiness, then extending their life may not be good for them. Similarly, if a group of animals experience more suffering than happiness overall, then expanding this population may not be good for its members overall. Thus, even if we knew how our actions and policies would affect wild animals, we still might not know which actions and policies are *good* or *bad* unless we know which effects are *beneficial* or *harmful*.

Fourth: How can we compare welfare impacts across species? Suppose we agree about which impacts are good and bad for particular animals. In this case, we still need to ask *how* good and bad these impacts are for these animals. Do an elephant, a mouse, and an ant all have equally strong interests, such that we should give them all equal weight in our welfare assessments? Or is the strength of their interests a function of, say, their cognitive complexity and longevity, such that we should give more weight to the elephant than to the mouse, and more weight to the mouse than to the ant? Because smaller animals tend to have larger populations, how much weight we give these animals will end up mattering a lot.

Finally: How should we factor welfare assessments into our decisions? Ethics, law, and policy are about more than promoting welfare, at least in practice. They are also about respecting rights, honouring relationships, and working within our epistemic and practical limitations. When we consider all relevant factors, we might find that even if animals have a lot at stake in our decisions, there is a limit to how much we can, and should, support them. However, our claim in this chapter is merely that, for all we know now, we might be able to improve our treatment of animals at least *somewhat*. And insofar as we can improve our treatment of animals in a responsible, achievable, sustainable way, we owe it to them to try.

15.2.3 *Improving Animal Welfare, One Step at a Time*

Given the complexity of these issues, one might think that we should wait for more information before we attempt to improve our treatment of animal populations, particularly wild animal populations. After all, until we know more about which animals are welfare subjects, how our policies will affect them, which effects are good or bad for them, how to compare welfare across species, and how to factor welfare assessments into our policy decisions, our attempts to improve animal welfare can easily be ineffective or counterproductive. In the meantime, vulnerable human populations still need support too. Perhaps we should prioritise improving human lives while we wait for more information about how to improve non-human lives.

However, it would be a mistake to delay consideration of non-human animals for these reasons. First, these issues are urgent, and there are risks in both directions. Again, humans kill more than 100 billion captive vertebrates, more than a trillion captive invertebrates, more than a trillion wild vertebrates, and quadrillions of wild invertebrates every year. In the future, human-caused environmental changes will amplify our effects on non-human populations considerably. Thus, there is no risk-free option in this context. While considering animal welfare might lead us to mistakenly cause new harms, continuing to neglect animal welfare will lead us to amplify – and potentially lock in – current patterns of harm, exploitation, and extermination.

Second, we may never be able to *completely* answer these questions, and bad assessments can still be better than nothing at all. Determining how to treat wild animals requires addressing fundamental issues in ethics and science, including questions about the nature of other minds and the value of other lives. We will likely not be certain about these issues anytime soon. At the same time, we are not completely in the dark about these issues either, and we have sophisticated tools for making policy decisions about important and difficult issues under risk and uncertainty, such as precautionary principles and expected value principles.[20] We should do the best we can with what we have as we continue to research these issues over time.

Third, bad assessments can pave the way for better assessments. Part of how we can learn how to improve our treatment of animals is by *attempting* to improve our treatment of animals and then studying the effects. Of course, this is not to say that we should experiment with risky, costly, harmful, large-scale interventions simply to study the effects; it would be bad to destroy the environment simply to confirm that destroying the environment is bad! Instead, the idea is that experimenting with reasonably safe, low-cost, small-scale interventions can have both practical and epistemic benefits. Practically, it can help at least some animals in the short term, and epistemically, it can teach us how to help more animals in the long run.

Fourth, knowledge is not the only bottleneck; capacity and motivation are as well. We already know how to improve our treatment of animals in many ways, but we lack the ability and political will necessary to act on this knowledge. Thus, it would be naive for us to simply spend 100 years developing knowledge about animal welfare and then expect the world to be ready to act. We instead need to develop relevant knowledge, capacity, and motivation *simultaneously*. Experimenting with reasonably safe, low-cost, small-scale interventions can help in all these ways, as it can contribute not only to the development of animal welfare research, but also to the development of legal and political institutions for considering animal welfare.

Fifth, many changes can be *co-beneficial* for humans, (many) animals, and the environment. The One Health policy framework is a reminder that improving our treatment of animals and the environment can have positive effects for us as well. Of course, this is not to deny the reality of trade-offs both within and across species. Few if any policies will benefit *everyone*. Still, if we at least *consider* everyone when making decisions, then we might find that we can improve our treatment of humans and non-humans at the same time; or, at least, that we can improve our treatment of non-humans without worsening our treatment of humans. Experimenting with these kinds of seemingly co-beneficial options is a good place to start.

Finally, many decisions can involve path dependence and even a 'lock in' effect, particularly decisions regarding the built environment. In particular, governments are or, at least, will soon be spending vast amounts of money to build more resilient and sustainable infrastructure in the face of climate change. If we at least *consider* animal welfare when we build this infrastructure, then we might be able to identify relatively safe, low-cost, small-scale changes that appear to benefit humans, animals, *and* the environment. And of course, it would be cheaper and faster to change our infrastructure *once*, with both human and non-human interests in mind, than to change it once for humans and then all over again for everyone else.

[20] Jeff Sebo, 'The Moral Problem of Other Minds' (2018) 25 *The Harvard Review of Philosophy* 51–70.

In our view, these reflections support the following theory of change for wild animal welfare. As we research basic ethical and scientific issues regarding wild animal welfare, we should also experiment with relatively safe, low-cost, small-scale interventions that appear co-beneficial for humans, (many) animals, and the environment in the short term, and that will help us to build the knowledge, capacity, and motivation necessary to pursue better interventions over time. And in order to produce these further effects, we should focus on infrastructural and institutional changes that can involve path dependence, and to develop partnerships between researchers and policymakers so that we can study the effects of policy experiments.

15.3 MULTISPECIES INSTITUTIONS, PRINCIPLES, AND POLICIES

Despite its importance, animal welfare is still neglected in environmental, climate change, and sustainable development policy.[21] Wild animal welfare in particular has been overlooked by policymakers at the international, national, and subnational levels.[22] While action is needed at every level, we focus here on local government policies on land use and the built environment for several reasons. First, cities have the *opportunity* to test out innovative policies that take into account and promote wild animal welfare.[23] Second, cities have a *responsibility* to consider wild animal welfare as many wild animals already reside in cities, and many more may migrate to cities as a result of human-caused environmental changes.[24] Third, cities typically have *authority* over land use and infrastructure choices that affect humans and animals.[25] This combination of opportunity, responsibility, and authority positions cities to take action on wild animal welfare in the near term.

15.3.1 *Building Local Government Capacity to Advance Wild Animal Welfare*

Cities can begin to incorporate wild animal welfare into local *plans*, *monitoring*, *institutions*, and *policies*.[26] Through these cross-cutting actions, cities can build their capacity for promoting wild animal welfare consistently across local policy areas.[27]

[21] United Nations, 'Global Sustainable Development Report' in *The Future Is Now: Science for Achieving Sustainable Development* (2019), 117; Jeff Sebo, C. Verkuijl, and M. Hotzel, et al., 'Sustainable Development Matters for Animals Too: Governments have a Responsibility to Recognize that' (2022) *CABI One Health*, 1–2; UNEP/EA.5/Res.1 (7 March 2022).

[22] Stephen White, 'Shifting Norms in Wild Animal Protection and Effective Regulatory Design' in W. Scholtz (ed.), *Animal Welfare and International Environmental Law* (Northampton, MA: Edward Elgar Publishing, 2019) 180–206.

[23] Brian Galle and Joseph Leahy, 'Laboratories of Democracy: Policy Innovation in Decentralized Governments' (2009) 58(6) *Emory Law Journal* 1333–1400.

[24] Jeffrey D. Haight, Sharon J. Hall, Mason Fidino, et al., 'Urbanization, Climate and Species Traits Shape Mammal Communities from Local to Continental Scales' (2023) 7(10) *Nature Ecology & Evolution* 1654–1666; Erica N. Spotswood, Erin E. Beller, Robin Grossinger, et al., 'The Biological Deserts Fallacy: Cities in Their Landscapes Contribute More Than We Think to Regional Biodiversity' (2021) 71(2) *BioScience* 148–160.

[25] Patricia E. Salkin, Ryan Rowberry, and John Travis Marshall, *Land Use Planning and Development Regulation Law* (American Bar Association 2023) Subsection 3.5.

[26] White, 'Wild Animal Welfare in Local Policies on Land Use and the Built Environment'.

[27] To the extent that incorporating animal welfare considerations into local policy may increase human/animal interactions in urban settings, it may raise questions about spillover effects like the increased rate of disease spread. Further research will be required to address this issue. In the meantime, see Ferreira et al. regarding the main drivers of zoonotic disease: animal farming, the wildlife trade, and wild meat consumption: M. N. Ferreira, W. Elliott, R. G. Kroner, et al., 'Drivers and Causes of Zoonotic Diseases: An Overview' (2021) 27(27) *Parks* 15–24. Also see Combs et al. for discussion of the research and management of zoonotic disease in urban environments: M. A. Combs, P. A. Kache, M. C. VanAcker, et al. 'Socio-Ecological Drivers of Multiple Zoonotic Hazards in Highly Urbanized Cities' 2022 28(5) *Global Change Biology* 1705–1724.

15.3.1.1 *Plans*

Cities can incorporate wild animal welfare into ongoing city planning processes and consider developing a separate animal welfare planning process. Existing city plans for climate action, green infrastructure, capital investment, parks, and biodiversity, among others, are likely to impact local wild animals. Cities could shape these plans to better consider and support wild animal welfare. For example, local parks, green infrastructure, and climate action plans could require consideration of food, habitat, shelter, and shade benefits for wild animals. These considerations might affect the tree and plant species used for planting or ecosystem maintenance and restoration decisions. For example, cities could leverage urban forest assessment tools to model the effects on bird habitat from management decisions.[28] The City of Amsterdam, in The Netherlands, is a leading example of incorporating wild animal welfare into existing city planning processes. For one, their Green Infrastructure Vision planning document specifically includes 'care for the wellbeing of animals' as part of the plan.[29]

In addition, cities considering animal welfare more holistically may choose to adopt a separate animal welfare planning process. Amsterdam is again at the forefront of animal welfare planning with their Animals Agenda.[30] The Agenda coordinates city policy and planning processes to support the welfare of wild and domestic animals. It identifies important policies for animal welfare, coordinates different city departments and their plans to implement these policies, and establishes monitoring and accountability processes for implementing the Agenda. To benefit wild animals, the Agenda advances nature-inclusive construction policies, maintenance of city-owned meadows to provide optimal habitats for meadow birds, the removal of barriers to wild animal movement in the city, policies to reduce light pollution impacts on wild animals, and more.[31]

15.3.1.2 *Monitoring*

Cities can also identify opportunities for monitoring and gathering baseline data on wild animal welfare. While measuring wild animal welfare remains a challenge, cities can at least begin to take measures of environmental conditions that may affect wild animal welfare and physical health or behaviours of wild animals that may be indicative of their welfare. Measures of relevant environmental conditions include: exposure to extreme temperatures, anthropogenic noise, and artificial light at night. Measures of wild animals' health may include rates of disease and starvation among wild animals or observations of behaviours consistent with states of stress or relaxation.[32] Importantly, monitoring for wild animal welfare should focus not only on wild animals that belong to a threatened or vulnerable species, because animals who belong to vulnerable species are not the only ones who matter.

To start, cities can look for opportunities to include measurement of wild animals' environmental and health conditions in existing city monitoring efforts across all departments,

[28] Susannah B. Lerman, Keith H. Nislow, David J. Nawak, Stephen DeStefano, David I. King, and D. Todd Jones-Farrand, 'Using Urban Forest Assessment Tools to Model Bird Habitat Potential' (2014) 122 *Landscape and Urban Planning* 29–40. Available at: https://doi.org/10.1016/j.landurbplan.2013.10.006.

[29] City of Amsterdam, 'Amsterdam Green Infrastructure Vision 2050' (2020) 28. Available at: https://perma.cc/96PM-MVLQ.

[30] City of Amsterdam, 'Agenda Dieren (Animal Agenda) 2015–2018' (2016). Available at: https://perma.cc/89CT-DUM5; City of Amsterdam, 'Agenda Dieren (Animal Agenda) 2024–2026' (2023). Available at: https://perma.cc/NSF5-RMQN.

[31] City of Amsterdam, 'Agenda Dieren (Animal Agenda) 2015–2018' (2016).

[32] David J. Mellor, Ngaio J. Beausoleil, Katherine E. Littlewood, et al., 'The 2020 Five Domains Model: Including Human–Animal Interactions in Assessments of Animal Welfare' (2020) 10 *Animals* 1–24. Available at: https://doi.org/10.3390/ani10101870.

wherever possible. Some cities already monitor wildlife as part of their park management or biodiversity planning efforts. For example, Chicago, IL has a Nature and Wildlife Plan with a goal of '[m]onitoring the effects of management and conducting applied ecological research' including establishing baseline inventories of natural and restoration areas, setting up monitoring for endangered species, and researching how ecosystem restoration affects migratory birds.[33] Chicago's efforts could begin to incorporate or pilot assessments of wild animal welfare.

Similarly, the more than 100 cities globally with biodiversity plans could begin to assess wild animal welfare, including in their selection of biodiversity indices.[34] For example, the Urban Nature Index – a city self-assessment for biodiversity and ecological performance – includes measures of light and noise pollution.[35] Both of these measures would gather information on environmental conditions that may affect wild animal welfare.[36] Cities can also look for opportunities to partner with researchers and universities to pilot wild animal welfare assessments of local land use and built environment policies.

15.3.1.3 *Institutions*

Cities can build institutional capacity to support wild animal welfare by appointing an official or creating an office for animal welfare. This office would serve as a coordinating body for promoting animal welfare across city departments, planning, and policy. They could lead an animal welfare planning process in the city, develop checklists for each city agency to ensure the consideration of wild animal welfare, evaluate technical guidance for opportunities to promote wild animal welfare, propose budget items for animal welfare-related city action, and more. The office could also identify how existing wild animal monitoring and data collection in the city could better incorporate measurement of wild animal welfare. Ideally, there would be an official or part of the animal welfare office dedicated specifically to wild animals.

For example, the cities of New York, NY and Amsterdam, Netherlands have both created offices or appointed city officials for animal welfare. The New York City Mayor's Office of Animal Welfare was created to 'advise and assist the Mayor in the coordination and cooperation among City agencies that are involved in animal welfare administration, regulation, management or programs'.[37] The Office and its precursor, the animal welfare liaison, have supported a municipal non-lethal deer management program, the use of bird-friendly building materials, a city-wide ban on wild animals in circuses, and more.[38] In Amsterdam, Netherlands, there is a Councillor for Animal Welfare that coordinates the Animal Agenda planning process and policies for animal welfare across city departments.

33 City of Chicago, 'Chicago Nature & Wildlife Plan Update: A Strategy to Enhance Urban Ecosystems 2011–2016' (2011) 7, 26, 31.

34 R. McDonald, M. Colbert, M. Hamann, and R. Simkin, 'Nature in the Urban Century: A Global Assessment of Where and How to Conserve Nature for Biodiversity and Human Wellbeing' (2018) *Nature Conservancy* 54.

35 IUCN, 'The IUCN Urban Nature Indexes' (2023) 15–16. Available at: www.iucnurbannatureindexes.org/en.

36 Graeme Shannon, Megan F. McKenna, Lisa M. Angeloni, et al., 'A Synthesis of Two Decades of Research Documenting the Effects of Noise on Wildlife' (2016) 91(4) *Biological Reviews* 982–1005. Available at: https://doi.org/10.1111/brv.12207; Benjamin M. Van Doren, David E. Willard, Mary Hennen, et al., 'Drivers of Fatal Bird Collisions in an Urban Center' (2021) 118(24) *Proceedings of the National Academy of Sciences of the United States of America* 1–8. Available at: https://doi.org/10.1073/pnas.2101666118.

37 'About' NYC Mayor's Office of Animal Welfare (2024). Available at: https://perma.cc/4L9H-A4KQ.

38 Ibid.

15.3.1.4 *Policies*

Cities can implement policies that promote wild animal welfare on city-owned or city-controlled land and on private lands in the city. Cities can seek to provide environmental conditions that support wild animal welfare, including providing food, habitat, and shelter for wild animals; promoting habitat connectivity and freedom of movement for wild animals; alleviating extreme temperatures; reducing noise, light, and air pollution impacts on wild animals; and reducing harmful wild animal collisions with buildings and vehicles. Cities can shape these environmental conditions through their design of green infrastructure and road layouts, management of parks and lawns, and building materials and operations in city buildings and property, among other policy actions.

For private lands, cities can pass wildlife ordinances that incorporate multiple land use and built environment policies to promote wild animal welfare. Wildlife ordinances should be flexible and responsive to developments in scientific understanding of wild animals and the hazards they face. For example, city ordinances can define bird-friendly building materials based on the American Bird Conservancy Material Threat Factor Reference Standard, which can be updated as new information becomes available.[39] Los Angeles, CA has a wildlife ordinance that applies to private lands in a designated Wildlife District.[40] This wildlife ordinance combines multiple policies on private lands that promote animal habitat, shelter, and food sources; freedom of animal movement; and reduction of light pollution, among other environmental conditions that may support positive wild animal welfare. These policies include wildlife-friendly fencing, retaining native trees and large trees that provide greatest wildlife benefits, limiting outdoor lighting that could harm some wild animals, and using bird-friendly building materials to reduce animal–window collisions and associated mortality and harm.[41]

15.3.2 *Sample Local Policy Recommendations*

Cities can also implement specific policies that support not only wild animal welfare, but also human health and climate change mitigation or adaptation. They can begin with relatively safe, low-cost, small-scale interventions that appear to be co-beneficial for humans, (many) animals, and the environment, reflecting a One Health approach to local policy making. Such policies have low risks and many benefits. Over time, they will help us to build the knowledge, capacity, and motivation necessary to pursue more effective and widespread interventions in the future. There are a range of local policies on land use and the built environment that reflect a One Health approach, but this chapter focuses on a few illustrative examples that have the potential to benefit humans, animals, and the climate with relatively few welfare trade-offs.[42] The following examples can be implemented on private lands via local ordinance and on city-owned lands.

15.3.2.1 *Bird-Friendly Building Materials*

Cities should consider implementing bird-friendly building materials policies to not only reduce animal–window collisions but also improve building energy efficiency. Scientists estimate that

[39] NYC Buildings, 'Bird Friendly Building Design & Construction Requirements Guidance Document' (2020) Local Law 15 of 2020, 5–6. Available at: https://perma.cc/U8Y4-GMJA.

[40] Los Angeles City Planning Commission, 'Exhibit A: Proposed Wildlife District Ordinance Components as Approved by the City Planning Commission 12/08/22' (2022). Available at: https://perma.cc/MQ9C-3UGD.

[41] Ibid.; Karen Stagoll, David B. Lindenmayer, Emma Knight, Joern Fischer, and Adrian D. Manning, 'Large Trees are Keystone Structures in Urban Parks' (2012) 5(2) *Conservation Letters* 115–122. Available at: https://doi.org/10.1111/j.1755-263X.2011.00216.x.

[42] White, 'Wild Animal Welfare in Local Policies on Land Use and the Built Environment'.

bird–window collisions kill up to one billion birds annually in the United States alone, which does not include measures of pain and suffering from non-fatal window collisions.[43] Researchers have identified that building glass, exterior materials, and lighting are major contributors to bird-window collisions.[44] To respond to this, some cities have begun to pass local ordinances mandating or providing incentives for the use of bird-friendly materials, including those that also improve building energy efficiency, thus reducing greenhouse gas emissions and associated climate impacts.[45] In general, many existing local ordinances mandating bird-friendly building materials apply only to new buildings or major alterations to the building exterior, not to existing buildings.[46] Cities could move toward requirements or incentives to retrofit existing buildings with bird-friendly materials.

Local Law 15 in New York, NY is a leading example of a local bird-friendly building materials policy. Enacted in 2020, Local Law 15 requires bird-friendly material on 90 per cent of the 75 feet of building exterior above grade, 12 feet above green roof systems, and on some other hazardous structures for birds at any height. The law requires bird-friendly material on any new buildings and where there are major alterations to exterior glazing of an existing building. Importantly, this law is flexible to advances in understanding of bird-friendly materials; it defines 'bird-friendly material' where the maximum material threat factor is 25 or less, referencing the American Bird Conservancy Bird Collision Deterrence Material Threat Factor Reference Standard.[47]

This ordinance could be strengthened by requiring retrofits of existing buildings over time, even if they do not have a significant alteration to the exterior glazing, and increasing the height to 100 feet above grade, like the Washington DC Migratory Local Wildlife Protection Act passed in 2023.[48] Other cities and localities have taken an incentive-based approach, such as Arlington County, VA, which allows developers to access bonus density through the city's Green Building Incentive Program when they include bird-friendly materials.[49]

15.3.2.2 *Road Design and Operation*

Cities should consider redesigning roads and road operation to promote the health and safety of humans, animals, and the environment. Road deaths and injuries are a significant threat to both humans and wild animals, with one to two million annual collisions between motorists and wild animals in the United States alone.[50] Roads also produce levels of anthropogenic noise that may harm wild animals by impacting their communication, fitness, foraging, and movement patterns.[51] As cities redesign streets to reduce human traffic fatalities and respond

43 Scott R. Loss, Tom Will, Sara S. Loss, and Peter P. Marra, 'Bird–Building Collisions in the United States: Estimates of Annual Mortality and Species Vulnerability' (2014) 116(1) *The Condor* 8–23. Available at: https://doi.org/10.1650/CONDOR-13-090.1.

44 Meredith Barges and Viveca Morris, 'Building Safer Cities for Birds: How Cities Are Leading the Way on Bird-Friendly Building Policy' (2023). Available at: https://perma.cc/EG83-95GE; David Klem Jr., 'Preventing Bird-Window Collisions' (2009) 121(2) *The Wilson Journal of Ornithology* 314–321.

45 Meredith Barges and Viveca Morris, 'Building Safer Cities for Birds'.

46 Ibid.

47 Barges, 'Building Safer Cities for Birds'.

48 Migratory Local Wildlife Protection Act of 2022, D.C. Law 24-337.

49 Barges, 'Building Safer Cities for Birds'.

50 David Leonhardt, 'The Rise in U.S. Traffic Deaths' *New York Times* (11 December 2023); Robert Ament, Sandra Jacobson, R. Callahan, and M. Brocki, 'Highway Crossing Structures for Wildlife: Opportunities for Improving Driver and Animal Safety' (US Department of Agriculture, Forest Service 2021).

51 Christopher J. W. McClure, Heidi E. Ware, Jay Carlisle, Gregory Kaltenecker, and Jesse R. Barber, 'An Experimental Investigation into the Effects of Traffic Noise on Distributions of Birds: Avoiding the Phantom

to climate change risks like flooding and sea-level rise, they can also take wild animal welfare into account.

There are several road design policies that cities could consider implementing to benefit humans, wild animals, and the environment. As a threshold matter, cities could consider wild animal welfare in local transportation planning and adopt a modified Complete Streets Policy Framework that considers wild animals in road design.[52] For design elements, cities can construct overpasses or underpasses for wild animals to maintain habitat connectivity and reduce animal–vehicle collisions. For example, Los Angeles, CA is constructing an overpass over the 101 freeway to support the safe movement of mountain lions, bobcats, and other animals, and Concord, MA has constructed four underpasses that have reduced habitat fragmentation and are used by at least thirty-two different species of animals.[53]

In addition to road design, cities can consider creating some pedestrian-only streets or implementing seasonal, night-time, or temporary road closures to reduce traffic noise and vehicle collisions. For example, King Road in Burlington, ON, Canada is closed for a few weeks each spring to permit the safe road crossing of Jefferson salamanders in their breeding migration period.[54] Cities may consider permanent pedestrian-only streets to not only reduce impacts of vehicles on animals but also improve walkability and wellbeing for humans.

15.3.3 *Green Infrastructure Design*

Cities should consider how their green infrastructure (GI) can better support the welfare of wild animals. GI – including green roofs, rain gardens, bioswales, retention basins, and green spaces – can help cities and their residents adapt to the impacts of climate change. Many cities have begun to implement GI to address storm water run-off and flooding, combat air pollution, and reduce the urban heat island effect.[55] In addition to the climate and human health benefits, GI can take into account wild animals in GI planning, design, and implementation. GI can provide habitat, shelter, and food sources for wild animals and mitigate extreme heat which can harm wild animals.[56]

Cities can start by including wild animals in their GI planning. For example, Harford County, MD has a green infrastructure plan that lists providing high-quality wildlife habitat and wildlife corridors as an explicit goal in the GI network.[57] Beyond planning, cities can

Road' (2013) 280 *Proceedings of the Royal Society B: Biological Sciences* 1–9. Available at: https://doi.org/10.1098/rspb.2013.2290; Graeme Shannon, Lisa M. Angeloni, George Wittemyer, Kurt M. Fristrup, and Kevin R. Crooks, 'Road Traffic Noise Modifies Behaviour of a Keystone Species' (2014) 94 *Animal Behavior*, 135–141. Available at: https://doi.org/10.1016/j.anbehav.2014.06.004.

52 Smart Growth America, 'Dangerous by Design' (National Complete Streets Coalition 2022).

53 'The Wallis Annenberg Wildlife Crossing'. Available at: https://perma.cc/5VRF-68MD; Lydia Rodgers, Dan Stimson, Katie Holden, et al., 'Wildlife Tunnels Under a Busy, Suburban Boston Roadway' (2009). Available at: https://perma.cc/D9BF-SPEH.

54 City of Burlington, 'A Sure Sign of Spring: King Road Closed for Annual Migration of the Jefferson Salamander' (13 March 2023). Available at: https://perma.cc/Y9NA-UHLP.

55 US EPA, 'Reduce Urban Heat Island Effect'. Available at: https://perma.cc/6FFP-LKTX; Nathaniel R. Mattison and Kyle McKenney, 'Equity in Green Infrastructure' (2024). Lincoln Institute of Land Policy, WP24NM1.

56 Alessandro Filazzola, Namrata Shrestha, and J. Scott MacIvor, 'The Contribution of Constructed Green Infrastructure to Urban Biodiversity: A Synthesis and Meta-Analysis.' (2019) 56(9) *Journal of Applied Ecology* 2131–2143. Available at: https://doi.org/10.1111/1365-2664.13475; Dustin Partridge and J. Alan Clark, 'Urban Green Roofs Provide Habitat for Migrating and Breeding Birds and their Arthropod Prey' (2018) 13(8) *PLOS ONE* 1–23. Available at: https://doi.org/10.1371/journal.pone.0202298.

57 Harford County, 'Green Infrastructure Plan' (2019). Available at: https://perma.cc/FPG2-CAGD.

require consideration of wild animals in GI design and siting and issue technical guidance and GI design manuals that include consideration of wild animals. Guidance and design manuals can require plant selection for GI to provide habitat, shelter, and food sources to wild animals that could enhance their welfare. In Lancaster, PA, the city's GI design manual requires that GI plants are selected in part based on 'wildlife value', including habitat, food, and shelter for wild animals.[58]

15.3.4 *Lawn Maintenance Practices*

Cities should consider supporting lawn maintenance practices that benefit humans, wild animals, and the environment such as prohibiting gas lawn equipment and allowing naturalised lawns. Gas lawn equipment may harm human and wild animal welfare through exposure to high-decibel noise (especially for gas leaf blowers), increased air pollution, and exposure to carcinogenic chemicals and other pollutants.[59] Gas lawn equipment may further disrupt leaf litter habitat and cover for insects and reptiles, decrease their food availability, and reduce bird nesting material availability.[60] Over 100 cities in the United States have prohibited the use of gas leaf blowers, including Washington, DC and Maplewood, NJ.[61] Some cities have implemented electric municipal lawn care equipment or provided rebates to private individuals for switching from gas to electric lawn equipment.[62] Overall, cities should consider prohibiting or phasing out all gas lawn equipment.

Naturalised lawns may also provide benefits to humans, animals, and the environment. Naturalised lawns typically include a range of native plants of different types and heights, rather than monoculture or turf lawn.[63] Naturalised lawns can promote climate change mitigation and adaptation by reducing water use in drought conditions, greenhouse gas emissions from lawn fertiliser, and the use of gas lawn equipment.[64] The benefits of naturalised lawns for wild animal welfare are not well established, but naturalised lawns may promote habitat connectivity and provide wild animals (such as insects) with habitat and food sources.[65] This is an example where a city could partner with a research institution or otherwise study the effects of naturalised lawn policies on wild animal welfare. To start, cities can at least amend existing local laws to remove height limits for plants in lawns or exempt naturalised lawns from laws limiting plant height. As scientific understanding of wild animal welfare benefits of naturalised lawns develops, cities

58 City of Lancaster, 'Green Infrastructure Design Manual' (2019) 148. Available at: https://perma.cc/7SH7-RM5A.

59 Graeme, 'A Synthesis of Two Decades of Research Documenting the Effects of Noise on Wildlife'; 'Investigating the Welfare of Wild Animals in Urban Environments' (Animal Ethics 2021). Available at: https://perma.cc/VP7F-EXUV; Mount Sinai Institute for Climate Change, Environmental Health, and Exposomics, 'Gas Leaf Blowers are Health Hazards' (2024). Available at: https://perma.cc/M345-XCU8.

60 Animal Ethics, 'Investigating the Welfare of Wild Animals in Urban Environments' (2021). Available at: https://perma.cc/VP7F-EXUV; Elizabeth A. Johnson and Kefyn M. Catley, 'American Museum of Natural History, Life in the Leaf Litter' (2002). Available at: https://perma.cc/Q4J7-MD7A.

61 Oliver Milman, 'Tree-mendous News: Noisy Gas-Powered Leaf Blowers Banned in Washington DC' *The Guardian* (5 January 2022); Town of Maplewood, 'Ordinance' (2022) 3057–22. Available at: https://perma.cc/J6QJ-6E24.

62 Bill Glazier, 'Protecting the Environment, One Mower at a Time' *South Pasadenan* (18 December 2020); City of Yonkers, 'Electric Leaf Blower Rebate Program' (2024). Available at: https://perma.cc/HW2N-HRE9.

63 Washington State University Spokane Country Extension, 'Naturalizing a Landscape: Preparing a Grassy Area for Planting' (2017). Available at: https://perma.cc/4M7P-G8RT.

64 Pernilla Tidåker, Therese Wesström, and Thomas Kätterer, 'Energy Use and Greenhouse Gas Emissions from Turf Management of Two Swedish Golf Courses' (2017) 21 *Urban Forestry & Urban Greening* 80–87.

65 Alexander Adams, Anne Benaroya, Julia Bevacqua, Lana Marcy, Danielle Liao, and Cameron McCoy, 'Urban Biodiversity: Cultivating Support Through Municipal Codes' (2021) *Ecological Design Lab. Available at: https://perma.cc/LEB3-KJ8V.*

could go further to provide incentives for naturalised lawns on private lands (including turf grass replacement programs) and install naturalised lawns on non-functional city lawns. A number of cities have already removed plant height limits and implemented incentive programs for naturalised lawns.[66]

15.4 CONCLUSION

While the One Health framework offers a promising pathway towards creating co-beneficial policies for human, animal, and environmental health, its current applications often fall short of its potential. In particular, they remain human-centric, often overlooking the intrinsic value of non-human animals and their wellbeing. But non-human animals matter for more than just their instrumental value; they matter for their own sakes.

Moreover, current One Health applications often take a narrow emphasis on health outcomes, neglecting other aspects of wellbeing. This may be, in part, because health outcomes are easier to measure than welfare outcomes (which is not, of course, to say that they are easy to measure). But for human and non-human animals alike, health is not an end in itself; we also value human and animal *lives and societies*. Expanding the One Health approach to account for other outcomes will require building our knowledge about animal welfare. It will also require building the capacity and the political will to act on the knowledge we have.

To advance a One Health approach to local policymaking, cities should seek to incorporate wild animal welfare into their institutions, principles, and policies. Institutionally, cities should consider creating animal welfare planning processes, establishing an office or official for animal welfare, collecting data that could support assessment of wild animal welfare, and other institutional changes.

As we research basic ethical and scientific issues regarding wild animal welfare, we should experiment with relatively safe, low-cost, small-scale interventions that appear co-beneficial for humans, (many) animals, and the environment in the short term. We have outlined examples of four such policies that cities can implement in the chapter: bird-friendly building materials, improved road design and operation, green infrastructure design, and lawn maintenance practices. Implementing them, and monitoring their impact, will help us build the knowledge, capacity, and motivation necessary to pursue increasingly effective and evidence-based interventions over time. As we pursue this work, we will begin to bridge the gap between environmental policy and the wellbeing of humans and non-humans.

[66] Ibid.; Austin Water, 'Waterwise Landscape Residential Rebate' (2021). Available at: https://perma.cc/YSQ9-NGMV.

16

Achieving One Health Policy Objectives through a Legally Supported, Value-Based Health and Care Approach

Helen Yu

16.1 INTRODUCTION

Affordable access to quality healthcare is generally recognised as a basic human need and one of the grand challenges our society currently faces, especially in the wake of the COVID-19 pandemic.[1] However, according to the World Health Organization (WHO), the cost of healthcare has continually risen globally since 2000, reaching 10 per cent of global GDP in 2018.[2] Although healthcare systems are financed in different ways across the world, current global data demonstrates that the demand for healthcare generally exceeds the available resources.[3] These statistics are often reviewed and discussed in the context of the common values and principles represented by United Nations Sustainable Development Goals (SDGs), particularly SDG 3 'Global Health and Well-being' to 'healthy lives and promote well-being for all', in part by providing access to quality essential healthcare services through universal health coverage.[4] However, similar to the One Health approach, SDG 3 is not meant to be considered independent of the other SDGs, which includes animal and environmental health represented by SDG 13 Climate Action, SDG 14 Life Below Water, and SDG 15 Life on Land.[5] One Health advocates for a balanced approach to optimise the health of people, animals, and the environment.[6] At the core of the SDGs and the One Health approach is a holistic strategy and global responsibility to collaboratively achieve well-being for the planet and all beings that inhabit it.

Unfortunately, there is increasing criticism that the focus on public health is driving a predominantly human-centric approach to One Health initiatives, with a disproportionate emphasis on human health at the expense of giving adequate consideration to animal and environmental health.[7] For example, in June 2017, the European Commission adopted the EU One Health

[1] B. Toebes, 'Towards an Improved Understanding of the International Human Right to Health' (1999) 21(3) *Human Rights Quarterly* 661–679.

[2] World Health Organization, 'Global Spending on Health: Weathering the Storm' (2020). Available at: www.who.int/publications/i/item/9789240017788.

[3] Eurostat, 'Healthcare Expenditure Statistics' (2021). Available at: https://ec.europa.eu/eurostat/statistics-explained/index.php?title=Healthcare_expenditure_statistics_-_overview.

[4] United Nations Sustainable Development Goal 3: Ensure Healthy Lives and Promote Well-being for All at All Ages. Available at: https://sdgs.un.org/goals/goal3.

[5] The 17 Goals. Available at: https://sdgs.un.org/goals.

[6] World Health Organization, 'One Health' (2017).

[7] See for example L. Guardabassi, P. Butaye, D. H. Dockrell, J. R. Fitzgerald, and E. J. Kuijper, 'One Health: A Multifaceted Concept Combining Diverse Approaches to Prevent and Control Antimicrobial Resistance' (2020) 26(12) *Clinical Microbiology and Infection* 1604–1605; S. Nzietchueng, A. Kitua, T. Nyatanyi, and I. B. Rwego,

Action Plan against Antimicrobial Resistance (AMR), setting out concrete actions to combat AMR and to encourage research and innovation to develop new effective antibiotics.[8] Because bacteria naturally evolve over time and develop resistance to antibiotics, there will come a time when existing antibiotics become ineffective to treat an infection. The misuse and overuse of antibiotics in both human and veterinary medicine attributable to prioritising human health without sufficient consideration to the impact on the entire ecosystem has accelerated the development and transmission of AMR with significant consequences on the health of humans, animals, and the environment.[9] According to the WHO, the increasing global threat posed by the rapid spread of AMR requires immediate and coordinated action across multiple sectors to attain better public health outcomes.[10] Under the One Health approach, the WHO, the Food and Agriculture Organization, and the World Organization for Animal Health joined forces to promote cross-sectoral collaboration to assess, control, and prevent the spread of AMR in human and animal populations and in the environment.[11] Without effective antibiotics to prevent and treat an increasing range of infectious diseases from a holistic One Health approach, an estimated 10 million human lives per year may be lost by 2050 as a consequence of the rise in drug-resistant infections and at a cost of US$100 trillion in lost global production.[12]

However, the ongoing concerted reliance society has placed on innovation and technology-driven solutions may exacerbate the problem because innovators are primarily focused on addressing societal challenges from a human perspective without being required or incentivised to consider the broader environmental and ecological impact of their innovations. Continuing with the global AMR example, current research and data on the numerous models to incentivise and encourage the development of new antibiotics has generated mixed results, from ambivalence to cautious optimism.[13] The often-discussed disconnect between intellectual property (IP) or exclusivity-based incentives and the development of new antibiotics to address the AMR problem is well documented and discussed in the literature.[14] Other push and pull incentives to reduce barriers to market entry and to encourage investment in the later stages of development

'Facilitating Implementation of the One Health Approach: A Definition of a One Health Intervention' (2023) 16 *One Health* 100491.

8 European Commission, 'A European One Health Action Plan against Antimicrobial Resistance' (2017).

9 Ibid.

10 World Health Organization, 'Global Action Plan on Antimicrobial Resistance' (2015). Available at: www.who.int/antimicrobial-resistance/publications/global-action-plan/en/.

11 Food and Agriculture Organization of the United Nations & World Organization for Animal Health, 'Monitoring and Evaluation of the Global Action Plan on Antimicrobial Resistance: Framework and Recommended Indicators' (World Health Organization 2019).'

12 J. O'Neill, 'Tackling Drug-Resistant Infections Globally: Final Report and Recommendations' (2016) *The Review on Antimicrobial Resistance, Chaired by Jim O'Neil*. Available at: https://amrreview.org/sites/default/files/160518_Final%20paper_with%20cover.pdf.

13 European Commission, 'Progress Report 201 EU AMR Action Plan' (2021); European Commission, 'Pharmaceutical Strategy for Europe' (2020); I. A. Dutescu and S. A. Hillier, 'Encouraging the Development of New Antibiotics: Are Financial Incentives the Right Way Forward? A Systematic Review and Case Study' (2021) 14 *Infection and Drug Resistance* 415; K. H. Luepke, K. J. Suda, H. Boucher, et al., 'Past, Present, and Future of Antibacterial Economics: Increasing Bacterial Resistance, Limited Antibiotic Pipeline, and Societal Implications' (2017) 37(1) *Pharmacotherapy: The Journal of Human Pharmacology and Drug Therapy* 71–84; N. Gallini 'Do Patents Work? Thickets, Trolls and Antibiotic Resistance' (2017) 50(4) *Canadian Journal of Economics/Revue canadienne d'économique* 893–926.

14 E. Mossialos, C. M. Morel, S. Edwards, J. Berenson, M. Gemmill-Toyama, and D. Brogan, 'Policies and Incentives for Promoting Innovation in Antibiotic Research' (World Health Organization Regional Office for Europe 2010); A. Kesselheim and K. Outterson, 'Fighting Antibiotic Resistance: Marrying New Financial Incentives to Meeting Public Health Goals' (2010) 29(9) *Health Affairs* 1689–169; M. Sinha and A. Kesselheim, 'Regulatory Incentives for Antibiotic Drug Development: A Review of Recent Proposals' (2016) 24(24) *Bioorganic & Medicinal Chemistry*

and commercialisation have also been equally extensively examined in the literature, with hopeful prospects that the right combination of incentives along the entire value chain – from discovery to commercialisation – can be devised.[15] Because the responsible use of antibiotics to mitigate against AMR means limited financial returns for those developing and bringing new antibiotics to market, even if the innovation can be protected by proprietary rights, some scholars question whether IP and exclusivity-based rights are effective tools to be used as part of the solution to drive antibiotic innovation to address the AMR challenge.[16] Relying on technology to address the AMR problem by incentivising and encouraging the development of new antibiotics primarily for human use ignores the broader One Health considerations of safeguarding animal and environmental health through conservation and stewardship approaches to preserve the future effectiveness of antibiotics. The question is how can society achieve the goal of global access to quality health and well-being while recognising the economic realities of rising healthcare expenditures and safeguarding the environment and animal welfare?

To encourage and incentivise the development of new innovations that adopt a true and balanced One Health approach, there needs to be a framework that captures the social value as well as the technological value of innovations, while recognising the economic challenges of a more value-based approach, such as stewardship in the case of AMR.[17] For greater clarity, because AMR stewardship advocates for the judicious use of antibiotics, diminished commercial returns associated with prescribing less antibiotics would discourage innovation (under a traditional business model perspective) despite the societal need for developing new antibiotics. Without the appropriate legal and policy framework to incentivise and capture the social value of research and innovation, there is a risk the resulting solutions will fail to achieve the balance between animal, environment, and human health. Drawing on socio-legal theory, this chapter presents a legally supported approach to innovation, informed by the intellectual property framework and the principles of Responsible Research and Innovation (RRI) and Value-Based Health and Care (VBHC), to support the implementation of a true One Health framework. The objective is to ensure that innovation incentives are responsive to all stakeholder interests from the early stages of research and throughout the innovation process.[18] To achieve this, the

6446–6451; J. Darrow and A. Kesselheim, 'Incentivizing Antibiotic Development: Why Isn't the Generating Antibiotic Incentives Now (GAIN) Act Working?' (2020) 7(1) *Open Forum Infections Diseases* 1–3.

[15] V. L. Simpkin, M. J. Renwick, R. Kelly, and E. Mossialos, 'Incentivising Innovation in Antibiotic Drug Discovery and Development: Progress, Challenges and Next Steps' (2017) 70(12) *The Journal of Antibiotics* 1087–1096; B. Spellberg, P. Sharma, and J. H. Rex, 'The Critical Impact of Time Discounting on Economic Incentives to Overcome the Antibiotic Market Failure' (2012) 11(2) *Nature Reviews Drug Discovery* 168–168; M. Savic and C. Årdal, 'A Grant Framework as a Push Incentive to Stimulate Research and Development of New Antibiotics' (2018) 46(S1) *Journal of Law, Medicine & Ethics* 9–24; P. H. D. Batista, D. Byrski, M. Lamping, and R. Romandini, 'IP-based Incentives against Antimicrobial Crisis: A European Perspective' (2019) 50(1) *IIC-International Review of Intellectual Property and Competition Law* 30–76.

[16] Andrew Jenner, Naresh Bhagwandin, and Stanley P. Kowalski, 'Antimicrobial Resistance (AMR) and Multidrug Resistance (MDR): Overview of current approaches, consortia and intellectual property issues' (Global Challenges Report World Intellectual Property Organization 2017); Christine Årdal, Yohann Lacotte, and Marie-Cecile Ploy, 'Financing Pull Mechanisms for Antibiotic-Related Innovation: Opportunities for Europe' (2020) 71(8) *Clinical Infectious Diseases* 1994–1998.

[17] Michael R. McKellar and A. Mark Fendrick, 'Innovation of Novel Antibiotics: An Economic Perspective' (2014) 59(3) *Clinical Infectious Diseases* 104–107; John H. Rex and Kevin Outterson, 'Antibiotic Reimbursement in a Model Delinked from Sales: A Benchmark-based Worldwide Approach' (2016) 16(4) *The Lancet Infectious Diseases* 500–505.

[18] European Commission, Directorate-General for Communication, Directorate-General for Research and Innovation, 'Responsible Research and Innovation (RRI), Science and Technology: Report' (2013); H. Yu, 'Redefining Responsible Research and Innovation for the Advancement of Biobanking and Biomedical Research' (2016) 3(3) *Oxford Journal of Law and Biosciences* 611–635.

second section of this chapter will contextualise One Health in the policy landscape of RRI and VBHC. This analysis of the policy landscape will then be used in section three to inform and enable the development of legal tools that will give credibility, legitimacy, and accountability to the design, development, and implementation of a sustainable One Health framework through meaningful and inclusive societal engagement. Overall, the proposed framework described in the third section helps redefine the balance of rights and limitations of public, private, and global health interests to (1) promote innovation, (2) prevent the creation of scientific and access barriers, and (3) provide a governance structure to support a balanced and holistic approach to the EU One Health Action Plan where human, animal, and environmental considerations can be given equal consideration.

16.2 THE POLICY LANDSCAPE

16.2.1 *One Health*

The One Health Initiative, working at the local, regional, national, and global levels,[19] has the goal of achieving optimal global health outcomes through recognising the interconnection between people, animals, plants, and their shared environment.[20] However, the environment is certainly the most neglected pillar of the One Health triad, including in addressing the AMR challenge.[21] Misuse and overuse of antibiotics in humans and animal production globally needs to be understood in the context of the physical, biological, and societal drivers as pathways for AMR to find its way into the environment and subsequently to humans and animals.[22] There is growing support in the literature raising the alarm for a more integrated and holistic approach for any global One Health action plan to be effective and complete.[23] There is a need to generate innovative ideas and put them into action to ensure a more sustainable global ecosystem in the years to come, including production methods and systems with high animal welfare and health and less climate and environmental impact as ways to ensure human health. Research and innovation alone are not sufficient to achieve societal transformation. They need to be supported by policy and practice to foster inclusive participation by stakeholders (i.e. government, industry, society, academia, scientists, and special interest groups) to ensure effective societal uptake of the resulting solutions.[24] For example, because AMR surveillance requires access to data, legal questions associated with privacy, data protection, and intellectual property, as well as data security concerns relating to transparency, accountability, and responsibility can manifest as barriers.[25] By better understanding the interests and concerns of each of the relevant

[19] 'One Health Initiative'. Available at: https://onehealthinitiative.com.

[20] Nzietchueng, Kitua, Nyatanyi, and Rwego, 'Facilitating Implementation of the One Health Approach: A Definition of a One Health Intervention'.

[21] S. Fletcher, 'Understanding the Contribution of Environmental Factors in the Spread of Antimicrobial Resistance' (2015) 20(4) *Environmental Health and Preventive Medicine* 243–252; D. J. Larsson, A. Andremont, J. Bengtsson-Palme, et al., 'Critical Knowledge Gaps and Research Needs Related to the Environmental Dimensions of Antibiotic Resistance' (2018) 117 *Environment International* 132–138.

[22] A. C. Singer, H. Shaw, V. Rhodes, and A. Hart, 'Review of Antimicrobial Resistance in the Environment and its Relevance to Environmental Regulators' (2016) 7 *Frontiers in Microbiology* 1728.

[23] M. W. Parkes, B. Poland, S. Allison, et al., 'Preparing for the Future of Public Health: Ecological Determinants of Health and the Call for an Eco-Social Approach to Public Health Education' (2020) 111(1) *Canadian Journal of Public Health* 60–64.

[24] Yu, 'Redefining Responsible Research and Innovation for the Advancement of Biobanking and Biomedical Research'.

[25] World Health Organization, 'Challenges to Tackling Antimicrobial Resistance Economic and Policy Responses: Economic and Policy Responses' (OECD Publishing 2020).

stakeholders, there is an informed basis to design, develop, and implement initiatives and solutions that are responsive to stakeholders' needs. This in turn will foster greater trust and accountability, along with a change in perception to reduce societal opposition to innovative solutions.

16.2.2 *Value-Based Health and Care (VBHC)*

Globally, the cost of delivering health and care has increasingly become unsustainable, with the aging world population placing significant pressure and demand on health systems.[26] Without an integrated and holistic value-based approach to achieving a balance between human, animal, and environmental health, there is a real risk that the global health ecosystem will become unsustainable. The concept of 'one medicine' has been explored in the literature to emphasise the dangers of siloed approaches to human health without considering the social-ecological or human-environmental context.[27] The inextricable interconnectedness and interdependence between human, animals, and the environment requires an alignment in practice and framework structures to deliver comprehensive health and care solutions that do not negatively impact the planet. Sustainability of the entire health and care ecosystem therefore needs to be assured to continue to meet the current and future needs of the people and the planet through a value-based strategy that optimises human, animal, and environmental health.[28]

The core principle of VBHC is to achieve the best possible health outcomes within the resources available.[29] VBHC is currently defined by the National Health Services as '[t]he equitable, sustainable and transparent use of the available resources to achieve better outcomes and experiences for every person'.[30] In view of growing demand and limited resources, it comes as no surprise that VBHC is gaining acceptance as a model to address increasing health and care demands by including patients, public authorities, industry, and healthcare providers in a coordinated effort to collectively achieve improved outcomes for all.[31] In principle, the adoption of VBHC approaches will lead to long-term social and economic benefits from optimising the use of available resources to support a health and care system that delivers a productive and healthy population. Society as a whole stands to benefit from lower costs and improved public health by sharing risks and rewards through a system of mutual accountability. However, to achieve value, the stakeholders that make up the health and care ecosystem need to come together in a coordinated effort to collectively define what constitutes value from a One Health perspective. Most of the literature on the concept of value in VBHC focuses mainly on the relationship between value and financial cost with the aim of lowering costs without sacrificing human health outcomes.[32] There appears to be a disconnect between the concept of value as understood in the literature compared to the proposed practices aimed at

[26] H. Yeganeh, 'An Analysis of Emerging Trends and Transformations in Global Healthcare' (2019) 24(2) *International Journal of Health Governance* 169–180.

[27] J. Zinsstag, E. Schelling, D. Waltner-Toews, and M. Tanner, 'From "one medicine" to "one health" and Systemic Approaches to Health and Well-being' (2011) 101(3–4) *Preventive Veterinary Medicine* 148–156.

[28] N. Crisp, 'What Would a Sustainable Health and Care System Look Like?' (2017) 358 *BMJ* 1 3; E. Hoban, R. Haddock, and K. Woolcock, 'Transforming the Health System for Sustainability: Environmental Leadership through a Value-based Health Care Strategy' (Deeble Institute for Health Policy Research 2021).

[29] M. E. Porter, 'Value-based Health Care Delivery' (2008) 248(4) *Annals of Surgery* 503–509.

[30] L. Hurst, K. Mahtani, A. Pluddemann, et al., 'Defining Value-based Healthcare in the NHS' (CEBM Report 2019).

[31] M. E. Porter and E. O. Teisberg, *Redefining Health Care: Creating Value-based Competition on Results* (Harvard Business Press, 2006); NEJM Catalyst, 'What Is Value-based Healthcare?' (2017) 3(1) *NEJM Catalyst*.

[32] J. Tsevat and C. Moriates, 'Value-based Health Care Meets Cost-Effectiveness Analysis' (2018) 169(5) *Annals of Internal Medicine* 329–332; J. M. Bae, 'Value-based Medicine: Concepts and Application' (2015) 37 *Epidemiology and Health* 1–5; Porter, 'Value-based Health Care Delivery'.

implementing and achieving VBHC outcomes, which seem to focus predominantly on devising funding models and strategies to optimise effective resource management by lowering cost without One Health objectives in mind.[33]

One of the key challenges to successfully develop and implement VBHC practices is the lack of a common definition or shared understanding of the concept of 'value'. For example, what may be the best solution for the treatment of a particular disease from a clinician's or scientist's perspective may not be viable to industry because the value proposition from a commercial standpoint does not justify the time and costs required to bring the product on the market. Alternatively, what may be an affordable treatment from a hospital or public authority's perspective may not be the best solution for the intended user because of undesirable side effects that interfere with the patient's ability to take part in everyday life. The flip side of that example is the long-term personal health and societal benefit of expensive, potentially curative solutions that will enable patients to contribute more to society over a longer period of time as a healthy individual. Furthermore, curative solutions will also enable family members of patients to be more productive if they are relieved of care responsibilities. Similarly, the healthcare system will also be relieved of the long-term financial investment to treat patients over the course of their lifetime.

Understandably, efforts focused on cost reduction are pragmatic given the public scrutiny and accountability for the use of limited public resources to meet health and care needs. There is evidence in the literature of overuse and underuse of healthcare services and technologies, both of which contribute to waste of resources in addition to causing potential harm to patients and the planet.[34] However, if the concept of value focuses (or is even perceived to focus) too heavily on reducing expenditure without sufficient and inclusive consultation with different stakeholders and impact on environmental and ecological sustainability, there may be very little support and uptake of practices aimed at achieving VBHC outcomes due to lack of transparency and trust and insufficient consideration to achieve broader One Health goals.[35] In addition to health gains to humans, the environmental footprint and impact on animal health also need to be measured and considered as a concrete value.

Without a framework that is upheld by legally supported governance structures and informed by policy objectives such as One Health, SDGs, the principles of RRI, and the Health System Governance strategy,[36] effective implementation of VBHC practices to address global health will continue to remain elusive and challenging. Decisions driven mainly by cost containment or reduction efforts without considering the impact on environmental and animal health will likely obscure innovative opportunities to improve outcomes and lower the true cost to the system.[37] The value proposition of incentivising the development of new innovations from a

33 E. Teisberg, S. Wallace, and S. O'Hara, 'Defining and Implementing Value-based Health Care: A Strategic Framework' (2020) 95(5) *Academic Medicine* 682; S. N. Landon, J. Padikkala, and L. I. Horwitz, 'Defining Value in Health Care: A Scoping Review of the Literature' (2021) 33(4) *International Journal for Quality in Health Care* 140; B. Eggbeer, K. Sears, and K. Homer, 'Finding the 'Sweet Spot' in Value-based Contracts' (2015) 69(8) *Healthcare Financial Management* 48–57.

34 OECD, 'Health at a Glance: OECD Indicators' (2021); J. Watson, C. Salisbury, A. Jani, M. Gray, B. McKinstry, and R. Rosen, 'Better Value Primary Care Is Needed Now More than Ever' (2017) 359 *BMJ* 4944; J. W. O'Sullivan, A. Albasri, and B. D. Nicholson, 'Overtesting and Undertesting in Primary Care: A Systematic Review and Meta-analysis' (2018) 8 *BMJ Open* e018557.

35 OECD, 'Draft Report on Innovating Global Health: Collaborative Action Where Markets Fail' (2022).

36 World Health Organisation, 'Health Systems Governance'. Available at: www.who.int/health-topics/health-systems-governance.

37 Teisberg, 'Defining and Implementing Value-based Health Care: A Strategic Framework'.

VBHC perspective requires a mindset of prioritising patient-centred outcomes as well as environmental and animal health considerations.

Even if there is a sufficient level of societal readiness from patients to adopt a solution, the innovation may not be commercially viable to industry to justify the time and costs required to translate and develop the solution into a market-ready product because the value proposition does not justify the resources required. Alternatively, a patient-preferred and scientifically supported treatment may not be sustainable from an environmental and global common good perspective. Bioprospecting under the banner of sustainable drug discovery may lead to conservation, biopiracy, and cultural appropriation concerns if not governed properly. For example, natural compounds derived from bioresources such as plants are considered more sustainable than creating chemical compounds in drug discovery and development,[38] but have also attracted criticism when the resources and knowledge of Indigenous communities are exploited and appropriated through commercial activity without any benefit sharing.[39] As such, value in terms of efficacy of treatment, value in terms of financial costs, value in terms of profitability, value in terms of societal acceptance, and value in terms of patient welfare are all 'valued' differently from the perspective of different stakeholders. Despite a shared intent, because stakeholders define and perceive value very differently, there may be very divergent opinions and approaches to achieving the same goal of improving health outcomes through a One Health approach. For example, when making decisions on the allocation and use of healthcare resources from a VBHC perspective, understanding value based on a short-term assessment of efficiency at the expense of considering investments in the long-term One Health outcomes may be short-sighted and give rise to health inequities, especially for those suffering from rare or neglected diseases. Advanced therapy medical products (ATMPs) are an example of a very expensive personalised medicine treatment that has the ability to *cure* rare diseases compared to lower cost solutions that are currently being offered to *treat* the same diseases. Despite the high upfront cost of ATMPs, this investment needs to be considered in light of the financial, environmental, and well-being cost of resources required for the care and treatment of the disease over the course of the patient's lifetime, which may far exceed the cost of the curative potential of ATMPs. The long-term environmental impact, healthcare, and social outcomes of more expensive solutions do not seem to fit well with the current economic models of, and approaches to, VBHC despite recognition on a policy level of the importance of equity, One Health considerations, and value judgments.[40]

The literature therefore supports the argument that a value-based approach to capturing and incentivising the social value as well as technological value of innovations may be a viable solution to encourage the development of health- and care-related innovations. By focusing on the blended value of private and social return on investment and rewarding innovations with high social benefits by translating social value into economic value, a responsible, sustainable, and value-based innovation framework emerges to reinvigorate the innovation pipeline.[41] However, without an appropriate legal framework that takes into consideration and balances the social, political, financial, and administrative pressures associated with innovation development and

[38] N. Mateo, W. Nader, and G. Tamayo, 'Bioprospecting' (2001) 1 *Encyclopedia of Biodiversity* 471–487.

[39] T. Efferth, M. Banerjee, N. W. Paul, et al., 'Biopiracy of Natural Products and Good Bioprospecting Practice.' (2016) 23(2) *Phytomedicine* 166–173.

[40] E. Hanna, C. Rémuzat, P. Auquier, and M. Toumi, 'Advanced Therapy Medicinal Products: Current and Future Perspectives' (2016) 4(1) *Journal of Market Access & Health Policy* 31036.

[41] A. Lingane and S. Olsen, 'Guidelines for Social Return on Investment' (2004) 46(3) *California Management Review* 116–135.

procurement, there will always likely be implementation challenges and frustrations. As will be described in greater detail below, the procurement of innovative technologies is well suited to value-based procurement as a way to encourage and incentivise the development of innovations that are socially, economically, and environmentally sustainable.

For new models or framework designs to have legitimacy in the eyes of those who will implement and operationalise VBHC, as well as those that VBHC intends to benefit, there needs to be meaningful engagement to align stakeholder interests and needs through responsive dialogue to include One Health perspectives. This is where the law and the principles of RRI can play a key role in providing the necessary legal and policy framework to give credibility and accountability to ensure that stakeholder interests and concerns are reflected and taken into to account as part of the process of implementing and adopting VBHC initiatives.[42] A more nuanced and holistic approach to global health requires exploring how the principle RRI can help achieve the objectives of VBHC in a more balanced, inclusive, and equitable manner in line with a One Health approach. Existing legal tools can also be leveraged to operationalise RRI to practically align societal needs with the economic realities of healthcare systems to achieve One Health objectives and VBHC outcomes.

Through the inclusive engagement envisioned and described under RRI, a foundation for collaborative partnerships based on a system of mutual accountability and understanding of the underlying interests can be formed. Legitimacy, trust, and accountability are essential to ensure that the development of VBHC solutions that include a One Health approach is sustainable in terms of effective societal uptake.

16.2.3 *Responsible Research and Innovation (RRI)*

Research and innovation have been identified as key pillars of the EU's strategy to create sustainable growth and prosperity.[43] RRI was therefore adopted as an approach to govern research and innovation in a manner that is interactive, transparent, and responsive to public concerns to reduce the risk of societal opposition to new innovations arising from research efforts.[44] One of the main objectives of RRI is to align research with societal values through inclusive engagement to make science more responsive to societal needs and to ensure effective uptake of the resulting innovations.[45] Broadly speaking, RRI refers to efforts aimed at enhancing the accountability of research through societal engagement and societal inclusion.[46] The premise is that research done responsibly will help form the foundation for the sustainable development of resulting innovations.

There has been an increasing policy focus on meaningfully engaging different stakeholders in the process of research and innovation to ensure that research and development takes social considerations, values, and interests into account so that the outcomes of research meet

[42] Yu, 'Redefining Responsible Research and Innovation for the Advancement of Biobanking and Biomedical Research'.

[43] European Commission, 'Europe 2020, A Strategy for Smart, Sustainable and Inclusive Growth' (2020); European Commission, 'Europe 2020, Flagship Initiative. Innovation Union Brussels' (2020).

[44] Yu, 'Redefining Responsible Research and Innovation for the Advancement of Biobanking and Biomedical Research'.

[45] S. de Saille, 'Innovating Innovation Policy: The Emergence of Responsible Research and Innovation' (2015) 2(2) *Journal of Responsible Innovation* 152–168.

[46] B. C. Stahl, S. Akintoye, L. Bitsch, et al., 'From Responsible Research and Innovation to Responsibility by Design' (2021) 8(2) *Journal of Responsible Innovation* 175–198.

societal needs.[47] While there is an ongoing demand for greater reflection of responsibility, particularly on emerging science and technologies,[48] interests in responsibility need to be considered along with real-world dynamics such as economic complexities and accountability to public interests,[49] particularly in the field of healthcare.[50] Because of the uniquely high costs and sector-specific dynamics associated with innovating health-related technologies,[51] the principles of RRI can be a useful policy tool to reconcile the objective of global access to affordable and quality healthcare without stifling innovation.[52]

For example, in response to the COVID-19 pandemic, significant public funds were invested into the research and development (R&D) of innovations with the aim of securing global health for everyone everywhere. In 2020, an estimated €16 billion in pledges from governments and international donors worldwide were used to fund R&D of diagnostics, treatments, and vaccines for COVID-19.[53] In 2021, a further estimated €20 billion was provided, largely from government sources, to continue to fund the global response to COVID-19.[54] In addition to concrete funding, other public initiatives were introduced to further support international cooperation and collaborative efforts to develop health innovations. For example, the WHO and its partners launched the COVID-19 health technology access pool (C-TAP), a global initiative to facilitate access to data and open sharing of scientific knowledge by removing legal barriers such as intellectual property (IP) and other proprietary rights.[55] The express intent of C-TAP was to accelerate the discovery of innovations through open science and to ensure that 'the latest and best science benefits all of humanity … and made universally available'.[56] A second initiative launched by the WHO and its partners known as the Solidarity Trial was an international collaborative clinical trial effort to rapidly assess promising treatment options by adopting an adaptive design that significantly reduced the time needed to generate the necessary evidence on safety and efficacy.[57] Similarly, the United States Food and Drug Administration (FDA) launched its Coronavirus Treatment Acceleration Program to accelerate the development and approval of treatments by reducing the regulatory burden and increasing the efficiency of the evaluation process.[58]

47 H. Zwart, L. Landeweerd, and A. van Rooij, 'Adapt or Perish? Assessing the Recent Shift in the European Research Funding Arena from "ELSA" to "RRI"' (2014) 10(1) *Life Sciences, Society and Policy* 11.

48 S. Yearley, 'The Ethical Landscape: Identifying the Right Way to Think About the Ethical and Societal Aspects of Synthetic Biology Research and Products' (2009) 6(Suppl. 4) *Journal of The Royal Society Interface* S559–S564.

49 R. von Schomberg, 'A Vision of Responsible Innovation' in *Responsible Innovation* (eds.) M. Richard Owen, M. Heintz and J. Bessant (London: John Wiley, 2013) 51–74.

50 H. P. Silva, P. Lehoux, F. A. Miller, and J. L. Denis, 'Introducing Responsible Innovation in Health: A Policy-Oriented Framework' (2018) 16(1) *Health Research Policy and Systems* 1–13.

51 J. A. DiMasi, H. G. Grabowski, and R. A. Hansen, 'Innovation in the Pharmaceutical Industry: New Estimates of R&D Costs' (2016) 47 *Journal of Health Economics* 20–33.

52 H. Yu, 'Return of Benefit to Society of Publicly Funded Innovations to Combat COVID-19' (2021) 58 *INQUIRY: The Journal of Health Care Organization, Provision, and Financing*.

53 European Commission, 'Coronavirus Global Response: Breakdown of the Pledges Made Today in the Global Goal Summit' (2023).

54 A. E. Micah, K. Bhangdia, I. E. Cogswell, et al., 'Global Investments in Pandemic Preparedness and COVID-19: Development Assistance and Domestic Spending on Health Between 1990 and 2026' (2023) 11(3) *The Lancet Global Health* e385–e413.

55 World Health Organization, 'WHO COVID-19 Technology Access'. Available at: www.who.int/initiatives/covid-19-technology-access-pool.

56 Ibid.

57 World Health Organization, '"Solidarity" clinical trial for COVID-19 treatments'. Available at: www.who.int/emergencies/diseases/novel-coronavirus-2019/global-research-on-novel-coronavirus-2019-ncov/solidarity-clinical-trial-for-covid-19-treatments.

58 US Food & Drug Administration, 'Coronavirus Treatment Acceleration Program'. Available at: www.fda.gov/drugs/coronavirus-covid-19-drugs/coronavirus-treatment-acceleration-program-ctap#intro.

The result of these publicly funded initiatives and investments into open and collaborative R&D efforts have largely proven to be successful. However, as various innovations approached market readiness, private rights and commercial return on investment interests began to overshadow the previously shared spirit of collective action towards achieving global public health.[59] The assertion of IP and proprietary rights were used by the pharmaceutical industry to maintain market exclusivity by limiting access to the use of knowledge and know-how. Traditionally, IP rights have been justified in the pharmaceutical sector because of the time and cost associated with drug discovery and development.[60] However, if the cost of research for COVID-19-related innovations have largely been subsidised by the public through public research grants and the time and risk for development has been significantly reduced through publicly funded initiatives, should IP rights be asserted on innovations that have largely already been paid for by the public? In response to a global pandemic, there must be legally supported mechanisms to ensure the pharmaceutical industry and national interests cannot undermine the ability to rapidly distribute essential medicines worldwide at the expense of environmental considerations. While commercial interests need to be recognised to incentivise innovation, private profits should not be subsidised by the public purse that supported the development of essential medical solutions.

The proactive approach of RRI to critically assess the broader impact of innovation on society in a responsive and reflexive manner makes the RRI framework particularly relevant to the healthcare context as a way to align the values, needs, and expectations of relevant stakeholders in a holistic and balanced manner.[61] Examples of stakeholders that form a part of the healthcare ecosystem broadly include patients, healthcare providers, public health authorities, funding agencies, and industry. However, in practice, the notion of alignment is often confounded with agreement, making the challenge of imparting the core values and reasoning of RRI and social impact into traditional science and technology research practices even more difficult to implement.[62] For example, despite the trend towards collaborations between academia and industry and the shared commitment to optimise the impact of research and innovation for the benefit of society,[63] significant 'cultural' obstacles continue to hinder successful partnerships between stakeholders.[64] The translation of policy into practice requires the reassembling of policy ideas into context-specific settings.[65] To be successful, science-society policies need to recognise competing cultural norms and logics of different institutional and professional settings in order to connect the underlying reasoning of the policy objectives in a relatable way to different stakeholders.[66]

[59] E. J. Emanuel, A. Buchanan, S. Y. Chan, et al., 'What are the Obligations of Pharmaceutical Companies in a Global Health Emergency?' (2021) 398(10304) *The Lancet* 1015–1020.

[60] Yu, 'Redefining Responsible Research and Innovation for the Advancement of Biobanking and Biomedical Research'.

[61] Yu, 'Redefining Responsible Research and Innovation for the Advancement of Biobanking and Biomedical Research'; P. Lehoux, B. Williams-Jones, F. Miller, D. Urbach, and S. Tailliez, 'What Leads to Better Health Care Innovation? Arguments for an Integrated Policy-Oriented Research Agenda' (2008) 13(4) *Journal of Health Services and Research Policy* 251–254.

[62] Yu, 'Redefining Responsible Research and Innovation for the Advancement of Biobanking and Biomedical Research'.

[63] European Commission, 'University-Industry Collaboration: A Policy Brief from the Policy Learning Platform on Research and Innovation' (2020).

[64] D. S. Siegel, D. A. Waldman, L. E. Atwater, and A. N. Link, 'Commercial Knowledge Transfers from Universities to Firms: Improving the Effectiveness of University–Industry Collaboration' (2003) 14(1) *The Journal of High Technology Management Research* 111–133; V. Galán-Muros and C. Plewa, 'What Drives and Inhibits University-Business Cooperation in Europe? A Comprehensive Assessement' (2016) 46(2) *R&D Management* 369–382.

[65] S. Griggs, A. Norval, and H. Wagenaar, *Practices of Freedom. Decentred Governance, Conflict and Democratic Participation.* (Cambridge: Cambridge University, 2014).

[66] Yu, 'Redefining Responsible Research and Innovation for the Advancement of Biobanking and Biomedical Research'; H. Åm, 'Limits of Decentered Governance in Science-Society Policies' (2019) 6(2) *Journal of Responsible Innovation* 163–178.

Because RRI focuses on the interdependent relationship between science, innovation, and society,[67] the principles of RRI could be used to inform the concept of value in a One Health context to include a reflexive, inclusive, and responsive understanding of beneficial outcomes for human, animal, and environmental health. The scholarship on RRI continuously highlights that the concept of responsibility is multiple and changes its shape and meaning depending on the context of use.[68] By adopting an RRI approach to engage each of the stakeholders in the One Health ecosystem to better understand what motivates them, a holistic innovation framework that incentivises collaborative participation can be developed.[69] As recognised in the RRI literature, translating policy into practice has proven to be challenging.[70] Similarly, translating One Health goals into practice could encounter similar difficulties if steps are not proactively taken to identify and create conditions necessary to adopt One Health practices that reflect the culture of the specific healthcare setting and ecosystem. By instilling a sense of ownership, control, and self-determination of what value-based outcomes means in a One Health context, there is a greater likelihood that a VBHC model co-created by the relevant stakeholders through an inclusive dialogue to better understand the reasoning and objectives underlying VBHC initiatives will be successfully adopted. To achieve this, the generally practiced stakeholder engagement activities such as focus groups, interdisciplinary involvement, public outreach, and semi-structured interviews remain the same.

Although the literature suggests these alone do not lead to successful implementation of science society policies,[71] the background training and education leading to and in support of the engagement activities aimed at contextualising the core values and principles of VBHC will create a common basis for stakeholders to engage in meaningful and responsive dialogue. By identifying and understanding the root cause, real or perceived, underlying the reluctance to implement and adopt VBHC initiatives, there is an informed basis to design, develop, and implement policy and legal structures that are responsive to stakeholder interests and concerns. This in turn will foster greater trust, accountability, and willingness to collaborate. Furthermore, as discussed in greater detail in the next section, a legally supported governance structure to incentivise and de-risk the adoption of VBHC initiatives would encourage all participants to be active, responsible, and accountable for achieving VBHC outcomes.

16.3 LEGALLY SUPPORTED APPROACH

Although soft law plays a leading role in setting strategic agendas and guiding the interpretation and implementation of legal principles to achieve policy objectives, hard law also has a commensurate role to safeguard shared interests and ensure accountability with binding force to help build trust and legitimacy of new policy frameworks. In the context of VBHC,

[67] R. Owen, R. von Schomberg, and P. Macnaghten, 'An Unfinished Journey? Reflections on a Decade of Responsible Research and Innovation' (2021) 8(2) *Journal of Responsible Innovation* 217–233.

[68] S. R. Davies, C. Glerup, and M. Horst, 'On Being Responsible: Multiplicity in Responsible Development' in Simone Arnaldi, Arianna Ferrari, Paolo Magaudda, Francesca Marin (eds), *Responsibility in Nanotechnology Development* (Dordrecht: Springer Netherlands, 2014) 143–159.

[69] Yu, 'Redefining Responsible Research and Innovation for the Advancement of Biobanking and Biomedical Research'.

[70] Åm, 'Limits of Decentered Governance in Science-Society Policies; Z. Bajmócy and G. Pataki, 'Responsible Research and Innovation and the Challenges of Co-creation' in Arno Bammé, Günter Getzinger (eds.) *Yearbook 2018 of the Institute for Advanced Studies on Science, Technology and Society* (München: Wien Profil Verlag, 2019).

[71] S. Hartley, W. Pierce, and A. Taylor, 'Against the Tide of Depoliticisation: The Politics of Research Governance' (2017) 45(3) *Policy and Politics* 361–377.

collaboration to create value requires a closer alignment of stakeholders to collectively achieve value-based outcomes.[72] Similarly, RRI requires close cooperation between all stakeholders and a setting that supports and fosters collaboration. The reality of meaningful stakeholder engagement in both RRI and VBHC frameworks is that it is a complex collaborative process involving multiple and potentially conflicting interests, agendas, and interpretations of ways to achieve socially responsible and desirable One Health objectives.[73] This is where hard law plays a key role in creating the infrastructure necessary to support, incentivise, and hold stakeholders accountable to do their share in the collaboration to make the whole (i.e. One Health-informed VBHC outcomes) greater than the sum of its (policy) parts.

16.3.1 *Dispelling Legal Misconceptions*

One of these pressure points is the tension between 'law according to the books': what the law says according to those in the legal field; and 'law in reality': how the relevant stakeholders interpret or experience and put the law into practice in their particular setting. In the context of VBHC and One Health, and other data reliant initiatives, there is an observed reluctance by parties who have access to valuable data to allow and operationalise the use of the data to support the development of data-driven solutions by third parties.[74] By understanding and dispelling misconceptions of what are perceived as opposed to actual legal barriers, there is a greater likelihood of achieving policy objectives and realising value propositions. For example, as recognised in the VBHC literature, access to available data is essential to determine metrics by which to align health outcomes with the impact of health interventions on the environment and society as part of the assessment of any VBHC framework.[75] The inability to measure and determine what metrics demonstrate a value-based outcome, how should the metric be assessed, and over what period of time for the promised reward to be earned under the VBHC model becomes a significant barrier to adoption.[76]

The European Commission estimates that US$20 billion are spent every year to develop innovations and technologies that have already been developed elsewhere because existing knowledge is not being shared or made available.[77] The reluctance to share and operationalise the use of existing data can only be understood and solved through meaningful engagement with the relevant parties that have control over the data. Based on the principles of RRI, if there is a mutual understanding by all stakeholders of both 'law according to the books' and 'law in reality', there is an informed basis to articulate and shape legally supported data sharing

[72] D. J. Rees, V. Bates, R. A. Thomas, et al., 'Collaborating to Deliver Value in Health Care: Exploring Conditions Required for Successful Healthcare and Life Science Sector Collaboration' (2021) 15(1) *Transforming Government: People, Process and Policy* 169–190.

[73] Yu, 'Redefining Responsible Research and Innovation for the Advancement of Biobanking and Biomedical Research'.

[74] E. Pisani and C. AbouZahr, 'Sharing Health Data: Good Intentions Are Not Enough' (2010) 88 *Bulletin of the World Health Organization* 462–466; W. G. van Panhuis, P. Paul, C. Emerson, et al., 'A Systematic Review of Barriers to Data Sharing in Public Health' (2014) 14 *BMC Public Health* 1144.

[75] Rees, 'Collaborating to deliver value in health care'; NEJM Catalyst, 'Healthcare Big Data and the Promise of Value-Based Care' (2018) 4(1) *NEJM Catalyst*; Porter, 'Value-based Health Care Delivery'; J. F. Baumhauer and K. J. Bozic, 'Value-Based Healthcare: Patient-Reported Outcomes in Clinical Decision Making' (2016) 474(6) *Clinical Orthopaedics and Related Research* 1375–1378.

[76] P. J. Neumann, J. D. Chambers, F. Simon, and L. M. Meckley, 'Risk-Sharing Arrangements that Link Payment for Drugs to Health Outcomes Are Proving Hard to Implement' (2011) 30(12) *Health Affairs* 2329–2337.

[77] European Commission, 'Exploitation of IP for Industrial Innovation – Final Report' (2015) No. 213/PP/ENT/CIP/12/B/N04C03.

agreements to better align VBHC initiatives with stakeholder interests and concerns.[78] For example, stakeholders have expressed concerns related to potential liability under existing data protection laws,[79] as well as relinquishing intellectual property (IP) interests and entitlements to benefit should the use of data lead to some commercialisable success.[80] There is also the confusion between IP rights and the broadly accepted policy mandate for data sharing, open science, and open access to support the advancement of scientific research and free exchange of knowledge.[81] Many large health and innovation-related organisations adopt a data sharing policy,[82] encouraging the sharing of available data in accordance with FAIR principles (findable, accessible, interoperable, and reusable) to foster scientific progress by reducing barriers for the reuse of available knowledge. However, the 'IP status' of data is not generally well understood but it is commonly recognised as proprietary information that has significant potential value.[83] Because of this gap in knowledge and limited access to resources, guardians of valuable data are often paralysed into inaction and opt for the safest option, which is to not permit access to data under their control.[84] If proprietary information necessary to create innovations and solutions cannot be adequately protected by traditional forms of IP, stakeholders are likely to safeguard their personal interests at the expense of sharing data despite the potential advantages of open science.[85]

16.3.2 *Leveraging the Law to Safeguard Stakeholder Concerns*

By involving and consulting with stakeholders at the outset, there is an opportunity to identify and characterise the observed hindrances and opportunities from the perspective of the relevant stakeholders to have an informed understanding of how each stakeholder group perceives the role of law and regulations that impact the use and sharing of existing data. This type of engagement will allow for a better alignment of objectives with the expectations of stakeholders. Legal mechanisms can be used to support what VBHC and One Health initiatives want to achieve by defining the 'rules of engagement' to safeguard the interests and concerns underlying the reluctance to operationalise the use of available data. Like a marionette puppet, pulling on one string to address a concern of a single stakeholder might get one step closer to the desired outcome, but the rest of the stakeholders that make up the healthcare ecosystem need to readjust and have an incentive to readjust to accommodate the change to get to a new equilibrium. The law can be a useful tool to help strike a balance and define a legally protected framework where the stakeholders can reach an understanding on what conditions need to be in place to

78 H. Yu, 'Leveraging Research Failures to Accelerate Drug Discovery and Development' (2020) 54(4) *Therapeutic Innovation & Regulatory Science* 788–792.

79 van Panhuis, 'A Systematic Review of Barriers to Data Sharing in Public Health'.

80 P. Andanda, 'Managing Intellectual Property Rights over Clinical Trial Data to Promote Access and Benefit Sharing in Public Health' (2013) 44(2) *IIC-International Review of Intellectual Property and Competition Law* 140–177.

81 Yu, 'Redefining Responsible Research and Innovation for the Advancement of Biobanking and Biomedical Research'.

82 See for example World Health Organization Policy on sharing of all research data. Available at: www.who.int/news/item/16-09-2022-new-who-policy-requires-sharing-of-all-research-data; UK Medical Research Council data sharing policy. Available at: www.ukri.org/publications/mrc-data-sharing-policy/; European Medicines Agency clinical data publication. Available at: www.ema.europa.eu/en/human-regulatory/marketing-authorisation/clinical-data-publication.

83 W. A. Günther, M. H. R. Mehrizi, M. Huysman, and F. Feldberg, 'Debating Big Data: A Literature Review on Realizing Value from Big Data' (2017) 26(3) *The Journal of Strategic Information Systems* 191–209.

84 T. Hulsen, 'Sharing Is Caring – Data Sharing Initiatives in Healthcare' (2020) 17(9) *International Journal of Environmental Research and Public Health* 3046.

85 Yu, 'Leveraging Research Failures to Accelerate Drug Discovery and Development'.

continue to function within the new norm. Value-based agreements have slowly gained traction globally in the healthcare context and require a mutually shared understanding of the financial and operational impact of adopting a new model delivering healthcare.[86] Without a bespoke legal framework to alleviate real and perceived challenges, One Health-informed VBHC initiatives will encounter implementation challenges no matter how sound the model may theoretically be. The relationship between RRI and the sustainable implementation of VBHC practices requires the law to de-risk and incentivise the partners between the stakeholders. In other words, the law can be used as a tool to manage and reduce the real and perceived risk associated with achieving VBHC outcomes. For example, contractual obligations can be used as neutral arbiters to compel and capture the value of sharing data on the one hand while protecting against free-riding and unauthorised use of the data on the other through the threat of enforcement measures.

16.3.3 *Leveraging Public Procurement to Drive One Health Policy*

The public procurement framework also has a key role to play in realising the One Health objectives as part of Europe's strategy to achieve smart, sustainable, and inclusive growth through R&D.[87] For example, in 2016, new rules governing the innovation partnership procedure introduced in the EU Public Procurement Directive enabled public authorities to combine the development and purchase of successfully developed innovative products.[88] By comparison, the procedure that preceded the innovation partnership where the pre-commercial procurement of R&D services is followed by a separate procurement process for the large-scale commercial rollout of the product itself would not have been suitable to incentivise the development of One Health value-based innovations because it failed to take into account any benefits beyond the technological capabilities of new innovations.[89] With the introduction of the combined development and procurement procedure, innovations with high social, environmental, and ecological value can be strategically procured as part of a collaborative R&D process to address societal challenges such as One Health approach to human healthcare, while respecting wider socio-economic, environmental, and policy agendas.[90] The Guidance on Innovation Procurement document states that innovation partnerships can only be used to procure solutions tailored to address a specific challenge identified by the authority where the market 'does not offer a satisfactory solution or where an adaptation of existing solutions is unlikely to meet the needs'.[91] A strong argument can be made that innovation partnerships are a viable solution for a public buyer to enter into long-term partnerships with suppliers of innovation to co-develop innovative solutions that adopt a One Health perspective. Through the innovation partnership framework,

[86] Teisberg, 'Defining and Implementing Value-based Health Care: A Strategic Framework'; Landon, 'Defining Value in Health Care: A Scoping Review of the Literature'; Eggbeer, 'Finding the 'Sweet Spot' in Value-based Contracts'; A. Chatterjee, C. Dougan, B. J. Tevelow, and A. Zamani 'Innovative Pharma Contracts: When do Value-based Arrangements Work?' (2017). Available at: www.mckinsey.com/~/media/mckinsey/industries/pharmaceuticals%20and%20medical%20products/our%20insights/innovative%20pharma%20contracts%20when%20do%20value%20based%20arrangements%20work/innovative-pharma-contracts-when-do-value-based-arrangements-.

[87] European Commission, 'Europe 2020, A Strategy for Smart, Sustainable and Inclusive Growth'.

[88] Directive 2014/24/EU of the European Parliament and of the Council of 26 February 2014 on public procurement and repealing Directive 2004/18/EC (OJ L 94, of 28.3. 2014). Article 31.

[89] R. Carant and P. Gomes, 'Public Procurement and Innovation' 2021 22 *ERA Forum* 371–385. Available at: https://doi.org/10.1007/s12027-021-00674-6.

[90] Recital 47 of the Directive 2014/24/EU.

[91] European Commission, 'Commission Notice, Guidance on Innovation Procurement, C (2021) 4320 Final' (2021).

public authorities will have a legal basis to exercise decisive influence over stakeholders to achieve One Health objectives through the procurement of innovations that prioritise One Health considerations. The purchasing power of public authorities combined with the health and care decisions that naturally follow from choosing to purchase one solution over another makes public procurement an extremely influential tool that public authorities can wield to strategically steer different stakeholders towards achieving One Health objectives. Value-based procurement integrates the concept of quality health and care with environmental, societal, and ecological impact and translates them into tender criteria that can include technical merit as well as One Health characteristics to drive long-term goals beyond traditional considerations of cost, making this a useful tool, for example, with ATMPs that do not fit with the traditional cost model.

16.4 CONCLUSION

Science and technology alone are not sufficient to address issues that healthcare systems are currently facing globally. The reality is incorporating the use of available healthcare technologies into a One Health VBHC framework and translating that into practice in a healthcare setting requires the involvement of multiple stakeholders. None of the individual players have all the necessary skills and resources to achieve One Health VBHC outcomes independently. Adopting a VBHC approach needs to be supported by behaviour and attitude change to ensure the solutions society invests time, effort, and resources into developing stand a better-than-average chance of being adopted as long-term solutions. This requires leveraging people with experience and credibility from working in interdisciplinary environments to decipher and translate discipline-specific perspectives into a common language and common purpose that all stakeholders in the healthcare ecosystem can understand and support. There also needs to be a clear legal framework to support One Health VBHC initiatives, informed by policy objectives, to ensure that outcomes of publicly funded efforts can ultimately reach the intended public. While commercial interests of industry need to be recognised to incentivise innovation, private profits should not be subsidised by public funds that supported the development of essential medical solutions. Value-based procurement can be leveraged to encourage industry to proactively develop innovations with One Health objectives in mind. The incentive of a lucrative procurement contract places some onus on industry to become an active responsible player. RRI principles therefore govern the responsible participation of stakeholders, and the law can be used to provide legally supported and incentivised ways to help implement One Health VBHC practices and to give credibility and accountability to ensure that stakeholder interests and concerns are reflected and taken into to account as part of the implementation process.

17

Public Health Law

One Health's Influence on Reimagining Public Health Law for the Twenty-First Century and Beyond

Sam Roach and Fiona McDonald

17.1 INTRODUCTION

One Health challenges the foundations of public health law. Modern public health law was formulated in the nineteenth century when industrialisation and urbanisation necessitated a focus on population-level interventions.[1] These interventions largely focused on minimising the spread of infectious diseases, including through sanitation measures and vaccination, and on managing localised pollution associated with occupational and industrial activity.[2] Public health was further modernised in the twentieth century to include managing non-communicable diseases, such as obesity.[3] But at its base, we argue that current formulations of public health law are problematic due to its anthropocentric foundations and failure to acknowledge non-state actors in regulating public health.

In this chapter, we argue that One Health approaches indicate the need for a re-conceptualisation of public health law. To address public health effectively we need to attend to our interdependencies with each other, with other animals, and with the environment.[4] As Gill and Bakker have noted, there is 'a crisis in the relationship between human beings and nature'.[5] There is increasing awareness of the impact of the environment on human health, but, until recently, less recognition of the impact of the treatment of animals on human health.[6]

We argue that a failure to recognise the interdependence between humans and nature unnecessarily limits the scope of public health law, as it restricts the regulatory interventions and actors available to achieve desired public health outcomes. One Health offers an opportunity to broaden our understanding of what it means to regulate public health in a

[1] Dorothy Porter, *Health, Civilization and the State: A History of Public Health from Ancient to Modern Times* (Routledge, 1999).

[2] Ibid.

[3] Kristin Harper and George Armelagos, 'The Changing Disease-scape in the Third Epidemiological Transition' (2010) 7(2) *International Journal of Environmental Research and Public Health* 675; J. Michael Gaziano, 'Fifth Phase of the Epidemiologic Transition: The Age of Obesity and Inactivity' (2010) 303(3) *Journal of the American Medical Association* 275.

[4] Isabella Bakker and Stephen Gill, 'Towards a New Common Sense: The Need for New Paradigms of Global Health' in Solomon Benatar and Gillian Brock (eds.), *Global Health and Global Health Ethics* (Cambridge University Press, 2011) 329.

[5] Stephen Gill and Isabella Bakker, 'The Global Crisis and Global Health' in Solomon Benatar and Gillian Brock (eds.), *Global Health and Global Health Ethics* (Cambridge University Press, 2011) 221–222.

[6] David Benatar, 'Animals, the Environment and Global Health' in Solomon Benatar and Gillian Brock (eds.), *Global Health and Global Health Ethics* (Cambridge University Press, 2011) 210.

non-anthropocentric manner. It also allows us to acknowledge that non-state actors that advance animal and environmental health via standard-setting, gathering information, and influencing behaviour can mitigate risks to public health. A core function of public health is prevention and re-conceptualising the scope and actors involved in public health law to encompass the more holistic approach suggested by One Health is critical to its continued evolution as the twenty-first century progresses.

We first analyse the presumptions embedded in modern formulations of public health and public health law established during the period known as the Enlightenment. We then examine various formulations of the definitions of public health law. The next sections of the paper argue that public health law needs to reassess its roots in the Enlightenment and consider expanding its orientation away from its anthropocentric focus and recognise the multiplicity of actors that engage in the contemporary regulation of public health interventions. One Health emphasises the importance of and need for this transformation.

17.2 POSITIONING PUBLIC HEALTH AND PUBLIC HEALTH LAW

The shape of public health and public health law, as we conceptualise it today, has its roots in the period that is referred to as the Enlightenment in European history. In the nineteenth century, this thinking was the basis, in so-called western society of a social order which influenced the structure of modern public health law. In this section, we highlight some of the presumptions emerging from this period that are important when considering the scope and shape of public health law.

Starting with public health itself, public health interventions have a long pre-history but were significantly developed during the nineteenth century with a focus on sanitation and infectious disease management.[7] This was a period of industrialisation, urbanisation (expansion of population and population density), colonisation, and social and economic change. The population experienced the human costs of the expansion of industrial and economic growth. In the west the pattern of disease gradually evolved during this period, on aggregate, from epidemic to endemic.[8] However, the impact of colonisation saw epidemics cause significant, and culturally crippling, waves of mortality through colonised populations. As patterns of disease changed during the twentieth century, public health in the west expanded its focus to include chronic illness as it impacted population-level health outcomes.[9] Sanitation and prevention remained core business, especially in low and middle-income countries (LMICs), but public health increasingly focused on health promotion, for populations such as women in LMICs, and individuals so they could choose a 'healthy lifestyle'. During the nineteenth and twentieth centuries, new tools of analysis and understanding of disease and disease prevention mechanisms were developed.[10]

A core driver underlying Enlightenment thinking was a movement from the dogmas of religion as a basis for thinking to rationality. Rationality (in the sense of the use of the scientific method of inquiry) is seen as a process or mechanism for formulating new knowledge and values and using these to drive human progress. Disease impeded human progress and economic

7 Porter, 'Health, Civilization and the State'.

8 Abdel R. Omran, 'The Epidemiological Transition: A Theory of the Epidemiology of Population Change' (2014) 7(1) *Global Health Action* 23303.

9 Harper and Armelagos, 'The Changing Disease-scape in the Third Epidemiological Transition', 275; Gaziano, 'Fifth Phase of the Epidemiologic Transition', 275.

10 Porter, 'Health, Civilization and the State'.

development and therefore needed to be managed scientifically but only insofar as disease impacted *human* flourishing. The greatest good of the greatest number of people (a utilitarian approach) was part of this calculation.[11] In many accounts, public health was framed as an achievement of the rationality associated with the Enlightenment.[12] The expanded scope of public health, and accordingly, public health law, did not, we argue, change the fundamental underpinnings of public health law based on the preconceptions of the Enlightenment.

How law was conceptualised and used was also developed during the Enlightenment. There are two elements that we focus on in this chapter: centralisation of power in the state; and dominion. In this formulation of law, an approach referred to as legal positivism, the state had exclusivity over law-making powers, such as legislation and enforcement/punishment mechanisms, and was the only legitimate actor in the legal space.[13] This was important as law was, and remains to be used as a tool of social control and to give effect to the state's duties both to protect individuals and the market economy.[14] Rationalism was deeply intertwined with capitalism. In the health context, while the free market was seen as important, it was also recognised that for the system to work the state had a role to act to correct for market failure in assuring the conditions for individuals to flourish. This was complemented by a concern, emerging from philanthropy, about the welfare of the poor.[15] These factors lead to a recognition of the need to control structural factors that impact human morbidity and mortality at the population level. Centralising power with state actors positioned the state as the legitimate and only actor in the public health law space.[16]

Further, the Enlightenment developed a conceptual distinction between humans and nature. This was a departure from past beliefs derived from the Aristotelian conception that there was an integral connection between people and nature.[17] In contrast, the Enlightenment viewed nature as both an object of study and an object of control.[18] For example, Descartes wrote of making men 'masters and possessors of nature' and conceptualised human beings as outside of and separate from nature.[19] Capitalism also supported this approach to nature, enabling exploitation of nature to maximise human interests (and especially those of the 'civilised peoples', i.e. Europeans).[20] Despite the Enlightenment being an intellectual movement separate from religion, the view of the dominion of man over nature was also consistent, at least in part, with some versions of religious thought.[21] Animals and land or nature are accordingly subject to human dominion for exploitation and development. The legal norms emerging from the Enlightenment were therefore inherently anthropomorphic, albeit as many critics justly

[11] john a. powell and Stephen M. Menendian, 'Remaking Law: Moving Beyond Enlightenment Jurisprudence' (2010) 54(4) *St. Louis Law Journal* 1035.
[12] Porter, 'Health, Civilization and the State'.
[13] John Austin, *The Province of Jurisprudence Determined* (London: John Murray, 1832); H. L. A. Hart, *The Concept of Law* (Oxford: Clarendon Press, 1961); A. V. Dicey, *An Introduction to the Study of the Law of the Constitution*. 10th ed. (London: Macmillan, 1960); and Jeffrey Goldsworthy, *The Sovereignty of Parliament: History and Philosophy* (Oxford: Clarendon Press, 1999).
[14] Porter, 'Health, Civilization and the State'.
[15] Ibid.
[16] Ibid.
[17] powell, 'Remaking Law', 1035.
[18] Ibid.
[19] René Descartes, *Discourse on the Method, tr Donald A. Cress*. 3rd ed. (Hackett Publishing, 1998) 35.
[20] Carmen Gonzalez, 'Bridging the North-South Divide: International Environmental Law in the Anthropocene' (2015) 32 *Pace Environmental Law Review* 407.
[21] See a critique of this view in Peter Harrison, 'Subduing the Earth: Genesis 1, Early Modern Science and Exploitation of Nature' (1999) 1 *The Journal of Religion* 86.

conclude, in a way that was structured to ignore the interests of those humans and civilisations who were not considered by the colonising powers to meet euro-centric norms (including those living in harmony with nature), who were women, or who were othered for some reason.[22]

It can be argued that the Enlightenment influenced and influences public health law by centring the state at the centre of public health, positioning public health as focused only on protecting human health, and that animals and nature are subject to human dominion. While there are many definitions of public health law, the next section explores some of the most established.

17.3 DEFINING PUBLIC HEALTH LAW

The scope of 'public health law' has evolved through time, though its purpose remains the same: 'promoting the health of populations by scientifically proven and economically feasible means'.[23] It is worth acknowledging from the outset that even this broad aim is inconsistent with the inclusivity and approach to justice espoused by One Health, which affords weight to evidence that sits outside the scope of science.[24] There are a multiplicity of definitions of public health law and this section does not address all of them; choosing to focus on some key definitions. A traditional account of this field restricts government intervention to infectious disease and pollution.[25] Epstein reasons that public health law is only justified where private law is insufficient.[26] Free markets are built on contract law and torts law, which provide limited recourse against such issues. As Epstein observes, how would one sue for damages if they contract a communicable disease? How would they know *who* to sue?[27] Even if they could sue the person responsible, this would not prevent disease transmission. As private rights are ill-equipped to deal with such public issues, government regulation is justified. However, in matters of personal responsibility, market incentives are a more appropriate means of controlling risk.[28] Issues like obesity and smoking therefore fall outside the ambit of public health law, according to Epstein, as one chooses to assume such risks.

Gostin and Bloche adopt a broader notion of public health law that encompasses the development of 'evidence-based responses to contemporary health risks'.[29] They argue that this conception better accommodates the public's changing risk-profile, which ensures that issues like obesity and smoking are not neglected.[30] They criticise Epstein's reliance on 'market failure' as a precondition for government intervention, noting its normative underpinning. Whether the market fails to achieve an outcome depends on the outcome one

[22] Gonzalez, 'Bridging the North-South Divide', 407; Porter, 'Health, Civilization and the State'.

[23] L. O. Gostin and M. Bloche, 'The Politics of Public Health: A Response to Epstein' (2003) 46(3) *Perspectives in Biology and Medicine* S163.

[24] Ian Puppe, 'When the Bough Breaks: Balancing Heritage, Forestry, and Unsustainable Standards in Algonquin Provincial Park' in Janice Graham, Christina Holmes, Fiona McDonald and Regna Darnell (eds.), *The Social Life of Standards: Ethnographic Methods for Local Engagement* (UBC Press, 2021) 199; Dean Jacobs, Regna Darnell and Gerald P. McKinley, 'Negotiating Good Development: Standards for Consultation' in Janice Graham, Christina Holmes, Fiona McDonald and Regna Darnell (eds.), *The Social Life of Standards: Ethnographic Methods for Local Engagement* (UBC Press, 2021) 237.

[25] Richard Epstein, 'Let the Shoemaker Stick to His Last: A Defense of the "Old" Public Health' (2003) 46(3) *Perspectives in Biology and Medicine* S141.

[26] Ibid., S143.

[27] Ibid., S143–S144.

[28] Ibid., S143.

[29] Gostin, 'The Politics of Public Health', S163.

[30] Ibid.

identifies as desirable.[31] Epstein does not acknowledge the normative theory that guides his judgments, which leads him to conflicting conclusions on what constitutes market failure. For example, he criticises anti-discrimination laws for 'people living with HIV/AIDs' on the basis that discrimination promotes public health by deterring risky behaviour (e.g. unsafe sex, drug use).[32] In contrast, he simultaneously claims fast food vendors should not be held liable for selling unhealthy food. Yet, imposing liability would similarly promote public health by deterring risky behaviour (e.g. the sale of unhealthy food).[33] Gostin, Wiley, and Frieden have since identified social justice as a moral foundation for the dual aims inherent in public health: 'to advance human well-being by improving health and to do so by particularly focussing on the needs of the most disadvantaged'.[34] A focus on population health and prevention distinguishes this field from medicine, which typically centres on individual health and amelioration.[35] Public health seeks to alter the determinants of morbidity and mortality to *prevent* poor health, whereas medicine typically focuses on the *treatment* of poor health.[36] Importantly, these are themes, not unbreakable rules. Medicine plays a hand in preventing disease, just as public health may contribute to amelioration. Public health law is also grounded in social justice. As such, a central focus in this field is the disruption of systemic issues that perpetuate poor health outcomes for disadvantaged groups. These factors formed the basis of Gostin, Wiley, and Frieden's definition of public health law, which we examine further throughout this chapter:

> Public health law is the study of the legal powers and duties of *the state* to assure the conditions for *people* to be healthy (to identify, prevent, and ameliorate risks to health in the *population*) and the limitations on the power of *the state* to constrain the autonomy, privacy, liberty, proprietary, or other legally protected interests of individuals for the common good.[37]

As we can see, key definitions of public health law encompass some of the central threads from Enlightenment thinking; anthropocentric and centred approaches (states are the only regulatory actors in this space) to public health law.[38] We use a One Health lens to argue that we need to move past anthropocentric framings. A further challenge to public health law in the twenty-first century is the limitations associated with sovereignty which have traditionally (with a few exceptions) limited the scope of public health law to domestic matters. The interconnectedness of people, animals and nature is not limited by artificial geographical boundaries. We also argue that we should recognise that non-state actors are also engaging in regulation to promote public health.

17.4 THE FUTURE OF PUBLIC HEALTH LAW

In this section, we explore some key issues that public health law, in our view, will need to grapple with moving forward relating to the scope of public health law and actors in that space.

31 Ibid., S165–S167.
32 Ibid., S168–S169.
33 Gostin, 'The Politics of Public Health', S168–S169.
34 Lawrence Gostin, Lindsay Wiley, and Thomas Frieden, *Public Health Law: Power, Duty, Restraint*. 3rd ed. (University of California Press), 18.
35 Ibid., 12.
36 Ibid., 14–15.
37 Ibid., 4 (emphasis added).
38 Julia Black, 'Critical Reflections on Regulation' (2002) 27 *Australasian Journal of Legal Philosophy* 1–2.

17.4.1 *Expanding the Scope of Public Health Law*

Law has evolved to encompass, albeit incompletely, the diversity of the human condition. One of the ways in which it has done and continues to do this is through the integration of human rights norms into legal, political, and social systems, especially as related to equality. However, the question remains whether and how public health and public health law can evolve beyond its anthropocentric foundations. There are at least two ways in which public health can develop informed by One Health or similar approaches: through incorporating the moral standing of animals and the ecosystem into how we conceptualise public health and public health law; or, at the very least, acknowledging that the well-being of the ecosystem and animals has an instrumental importance.[39] An intrinsic view of ecosystems and animals suggests that they are an end in and of themselves; they have intrinsic value.[40] This has been recognised in a very limited way in some countries. For example, in Aotearoa New Zealand, the Te Urewera (a former national park) and the Whanganui River have been recognised as having intrinsic value and afforded status as, respectively, a legal entity and legal person.[41] Critics argue that this status is more about creating a mechanism to manage relationships between humans, rather than anything else (a relational view).[42] A relational view is perhaps a middle ground between intrinsic and instrumental in that it focuses on the perception of people, individually or collectively, that they have a relationship(s) with the ecosystem and responsibilities arising from that relationship. Empirical research has indicated that this view is more often seen in non-Western cultures.[43] An instrumental approach to public health law suggests that ecosystems and animals only have value in terms of being a means to the end of achieving the conditions to maximise human health or human well-being. These views can and do overlap for some people and relational is sometimes subsumed as instrumental if it is framed to confer a health benefit for the person from that relationship (i.e. mental health).[44] Currently, public health law (domestic or global), unsurprisingly considering its western Enlightenment foundations (discussed above), is fundamentally instrumental. The focus, therefore, is on the well-being of animals and the ecosystem because of its instrumental value for human health (physical or mental).[45] One Health could be characterised as an integrated approach straddling intrinsic value, relationality, and instrumentalism in emphasising the importance and inter-connectedness of the health of people, animals, and the environment. While some would, and do, emphasise the instrumental benefits of One Health, One Health creates a model that embraces relationality and intrinsic value. It has the potential, if fully realised, to move away from bio-medical reductionalism that some have argued is an issue for One Health, as much as it is for public health law.[46]

[39] Benatar, 'Animals, the Environment and Global Health', 210; Berta Martín-López, 'Plural Valuation of Nature Matters for Environmental Sustainability and Justice' *The Royal Society*. Available at https://royalsociety.org/news-resources/projects/biodiversity/plural-valuation-of-nature-matters-for-environmental-sustainability-and-justice/.

[40] Martín-López, 'Plural Valuation of Nature Matters for Environmental Sustainability and Justice'.

[41] Katherine Sanders, 'Beyond Human Ownership? Property, Power and Legal Personality for Nature in Aotearoa New Zealand' (2018) 30(2) *Journal of Environmental Law* 207.

[42] Ibid.

[43] S. C. Klain, P. Olmsted, K. M. A. Chan, and T. Satterfield, 'Relational Values Resonate Broadly and Differently Than Intrinsic or Instrumental Values, or the New Ecological Paradigm' (2017) 12(8) *PLOS ONE* e0183962. See also discussion in Chapter 12 of this volume.

[44] Martín-López, 'Plural Valuation of Nature Matters for Environmental Sustainability and Justice'.

[45] Benatar, 'Animals, the Environment and Global Health', 210.

[46] Julianne Meisner, Hilary McLeland-Wieser, Elizabeth Traylor, et al., 'Relational One Health: A More-than-biomedical Framework for More-than-human Health, and Lessons Learned from Brazil, Ethiopia, and Israel' (2024) 18 *One Health* 100676; J. Beever and N. Morar, 'The Epistemic and Ethical Onus of "One Health"' (2019) 33 *Bioethics* 185.

One Health challenges public health law to think about the limitations of an instrumentalist view of animals and the ecosystem where the balance remains focused on short-term human interests as mediated by capitalism. Contesting the Enlightenment thinking that permeates public health and public health law is critical for ecosystems, animals, and human interests. It is also an important step in de-colonising public health as a field and how public health law is conceptualised and employed.

Public health law has, in addition to being anthropocentric, also been primarily domestic in its orientation,[47] despite its overlap with imperialist colonisation practices.[48] This too reflects the limitations of existing legal structures with the primacy accorded to the sovereignty of nation states. Public health law has increasingly acknowledged this global context.[49] Gostin et al., as part of the Lancet Commissions, have recently argued: 'Health risks in the twenty-first century are beyond the control of any government in any country. In an era of globalisation, promoting public health and equity requires cooperation and coordination both within and among states.'[50] The pandemic context led to the introduction, and post-SARS pandemic revision, of the International Health Regulations (IHR). The IHR imposes obligations on signatory states to undertake surveillance, investigation, reporting, and coordination of emerging pathogens.[51] The expansion of the scope of public health law to include non-communicable diseases has led to international legal instruments such as the Framework Convention for Tobacco Control 2003.[52] While the impacts of global infectious pathogens on human health are clear and have been experienced through epidemics and pandemics across the centuries, environmental degradation, until recently, had only localised impacts. This is changing: the impact of climate change and widespread environmental degradation have global impacts on human health that cross national boundaries. The centred definition of public health law with powers resting with the state has resulted in public health law being slow to recognise and respond to these changes. There has been some limited recognition of the transboundary impact of climate change and environmental degradation on human health; for example, the Association of Southeast Asian Nations – ASEAN Agreement on Transboundary Haze Pollution.[53] Gostin et al., conclude:

> Globalisation has heightened risks to our health, but it also presents unprecedented opportunities to confront global health threats collaboratively, drawing on expertise and lessons learned within and among nation states. No government acting alone can achieve health with justice. Instead, we need laws and policies at every level – local, national, and global – to achieve a world that is healthier and safer.[54]

In keeping with the positivist limitations on public health law, the discussion in this report predominantly focuses on how states can use law, singularly or in collaboration with other nations to achieve global public health ends, including through coordinating with non-state actors. However, it does not recognise non-state actors as potential regulators of public health practice.

[47] Lawrence Gostin, Hilary McLeland-Wieser, Elizabeth Traylor, et al., 'The Legal Determinants of Health: Harnessing the Power of Law for Global Health and Sustainable Development' (2019) 393(10183) *Lancet* 1857.

[48] Gonzalez, 'Bridging the North-South Divide'.

[49] Gostin, 'The Legal Determinants of Health', 1857.

[50] Ibid.

[51] World Health Organization, *International Health Regulations*. 2nd ed. (World Health Organization, 2005).

[52] WHO Framework Convention on Tobacco Control 2003, opened for signature 21 May 2003, 2302 UNTS 166 (entered into force 27 February 2005).

[53] Association of Southeast Asian Nations, *ASEAN Agreement on Transboundary Haze Pollution*, signed 10 June 2002.

[54] Gostin, 'The Legal Determinants of Health', 1857.

17.4.2 *Decentred Approaches to Public Health Law*

One Health practices draw on interdisciplinary expertise in recognition of 'the interdependence between human, animal and environmental health'.[55] Gostin and Bloche acknowledge the importance of these non-state actors as a source of information.[56] Nevertheless, they identify the state as the sole-regulator.[57] We challenge the view that One Health practitioners merely inform the state, and instead argue that their actions are a form of regulation. Decentring our understanding of this field better reflects their contributions. This section begins by examining the themes that underpin Gostin et al.'s centred definition of public health law and then Black's decentred conceptualisation of regulation. We argue that Black's work applies to public health law. Indigenous Land Management (ILM) in Australia is used as a case study to explore the legitimacy of a decentred conception of public health law.

17.4.2.1 *A Decentred Definition of Public Health Law*

Gostin et al.'s definition establishes several themes that demarcate public health law from related disciplines: a focus on population health, an orientation toward prevention, a social justice foundation, and the state's exclusive role in regulating risk.[58] Most relevant for our purposes is Gostin et al.'s final theme: the regulation of public health risk. Gostin et al. contend that the state is the only legitimate body that can engage in regulation of this kind. They offer two reasons to support this position. Gostin et al. first observe that as an elected entity, the government is *primarily* responsible for the health of the population.[59] However, it seems clear that non-state actors play an increasingly important role in promoting population health. For example, non-governmental bodies, such as the Bill and Melinda Gates Foundation, often lead public health initiatives and in so doing regulate public health in the nations in which their initiatives are implemented.[60]

Gostin et al.'s second justification rests on one of the tenets of public health law: prioritise the common good over liberty. The 'common good' refers to communal values in maintaining 'healthy and secure communities'.[61] Public health is a common good because its promotion benefits the population. It is frequently necessary to restrict liberty to promote the common good because it is often advantageous for an individual to undermine a common good. For example, it is more convenient to dump hazardous waste at a local park than it is to pay for it to be processed at an appropriate facility. At its core, risk regulation involves balancing liberty and the common good. Gostin et al. observe that coercion is needed to restrict liberty to promote the common good. Hence, they limit public health law to government intervention, as only the government is capable of regulating risk via coercion.[62] This highlights that risk regulation is central to our conception of public health law, whereas the regulator is only a means of achieving that end. Altering the identity of the regulator does not undermine the aim of public health law. It follows that a decentred conception of this field is viable, provided non-state actors are engaging in risk regulation.

[55] Katie Woolaston, Zoe Nay, Michelle Baker, et al., 'An Argument for Pandemic Risk Management Using a Multidisciplinary One Health Approach to Governance: An Australian Case Study' (2022) 18(1) *Globalization and Health* 73–74.
[56] Gostin, 'The Politics of Public Health', S 163.
[57] Gostin, 'Public Health Law', 5–6.
[58] Ibid., 4, 39.
[59] Ibid., 6.
[60] 'Our Work', Bill and Melinda Gates Foundation. Available at www.gatesfoundation.org/our-work.
[61] Gostin, 'Public Health Law', 6.
[62] Ibid., 9.

Before considering whether non-state actors regulate risk, we must first ask: what does it mean to regulate? Regulation refers to an interference with some form of activity.[63] Selznick defined the concept as a tool that governments use to exercise 'command and control'.[64] However, contemporary lines of regulatory theory recognise that regulation is not synonymous with coercion. As Parker and Braithwaite observe, '[e]arly empirical studies of how regulatory officials actually enforce the law found that they often prefer in the first instance to use strategies of education, persuasion, and cooperation'.[65] This highlights that one can regulate risk without coercion. Selznick also employs a centred definition of regulation, which is problematic because non-state actors frequently engage in regulation. Industry self-regulation is a clear example. As Black observes 'whatever "self"-regulation is, it is not state regulation'.[66] In recognition of non-state regulators, Black advocates for a decentred definition of regulation: 'the sustained and focused attempt to alter the behaviour of others according to defined standards or purposes with the intention of producing a broadly identified outcome or outcomes, which may involve mechanisms of standard-setting, information-gathering and behaviour-modification'.[67] Four criteria underpin Black's definition. She first includes 'intention' as a criterion to distinguish regulation from other forms of 'social control and ordering', such as market forces.[68] However, her definition remains decentred as it does not limit regulation to intentional state action.[69] Black next recognises that regulation is an ongoing activity through her use of the words 'sustained and focussed'.[70] She then observes that regulation is orientated toward problem-solving.[71] Finally, Black specifies three regulatory outcomes (standard setting, information gathering, and behaviour modification) to distinguish regulation from other forms of problem solving (e.g. mathematics).[72] Black's conceptualisation of regulation is a framework that can be used to decentre Gostin et al.'s definition. However, to be considered a form of public health law, non-state regulation must satisfy the themes embodied in Gostin et al.'s definition: it must reflect a focus on population health; a preventative orientation; a social justice foundation; and a balancing of liberty against the common good (i.e. *risk* regulation).

17.4.2.2 *Case Study: ILM*

Here, we use ILM to test the legitimacy of decentring our understanding of this field by applying Black's definition. ILM encompasses Indigenous resource management, settlement improvements and threat abatement,[73] which involve leveraging the interconnectedness of the

[63] B. Mitnick, *The Political Economy of Regulation* (Columbia University Press) 2 cited in Christel Koop and Martin Lodge, 'What Is Regulation? An Interdisciplinary Concept Analysis' (2017) 11(1) *Regulation & Governance* 95, 97.

[64] Robert Baldwin, Martin Cave, and Martin Lodge, 'Introduction: Regulation – the Field and the Developing Agenda' in Robert Baldwin, Martin Cave and Martin Lodge (eds.), *The Oxford Handbook of Regulation* (Oxford University Press, 2010), 2, 6 citing Philip Selznick, 'Focusing Organizational Research on Regulation' in Roger Noll (ed.), *Regulatory Policy and the Social Sciences* (University of California Press, 1985), 363.

[65] Christine Parker and John Braithwaite, 'Regulation' in Mark Tushnet and Peter Cane (eds.), *The Oxford Handbook of Legal Studies* (Oxford University Press, 2005), 10.

[66] Julia Black, 'Decentring Regulation: Understanding the Role of Regulation and Self-Regulation in a "Post-Regulatory" World' (2001) 54(1) *Current Legal Problems* 103, 113.

[67] Black, 'Critical Reflections on Regulation', 1–2.

[68] Ibid.

[69] Ibid.

[70] Ibid.

[71] Ibid.

[72] Ibid.

[73] Rosemary Hill, Petina Pert, Jocelyn Davies, Cathy Robinson, Fiona Walsh, and Fay Falco-Mammone, *Indigenous Land Management in Australia: Extent, Scope, Diversity, Barriers and Success Factors* (Report, CSIRO Ecosystem Sciences, May 2013), 6.

environment, animals, and humans to promote the health of each. This form of relating to Country aligns with the objectives of One Health, although the practices should not be conflated. As Jacobs, Darnell, and McKinley observe: 'if good development is to take place, the local knowledge surrounding the origins of relationships must be included as valid and important rather than simply as a different way of describing a One Health concept'.[74]

First Nations people improve environmental health through various activities, such as restoring natural habitats.[75] This exemplifies the interconnectedness of environmental and animal health, as improving the land's habitability directly impacts animal health. ILM also improves the health of First Nations people. Davies et al. observe that ILM creates a 'sense of control', which is a psychosocial factor that improves health by moderating sustained stress. Sustained stress refers to the helplessness a person experiences upon learning an outcome is outside of their control. Moderating this factor is meaningful, as sustained stress 'is a significant cause of illness and disease among Aboriginal people'.[76] While ILM can positively impact human health, it does not prioritise humans. Instead, an equilibrium exists, wherein human health is improved by promoting animal and environmental health. Without engaging in conservation practices, First Nations people would not derive the sense of control attached to this work, and so human health would suffer alongside animal and environmental health. Such practices are an example of relating to Country, which First Nations people have engaged in for millennia. One Health shares the same aims as relating to Country because it is the western form of this practice. ILM highlights how equal weight can be afforded to human, animal, and environmental health. This is uncommon even amongst One Health initiatives. While non-anthropocentric framing is employed at a conceptual level, in practice One Health initiatives are often criticised for prioritising humans. As Woolaston notes, existing One Health practices reflect a hierarchy wherein 'humans [are] at the top and environment and individual non-human animals [are] at the bottom'.[77]

The themes of public health law are reflected in this approach to relating to Country, which shares the same aims as western One Health practices. Consider the field's emphasis on population health and prevention. The preceding discussion makes clear that ILM improves the health of First Nations people.[78] However, health benefits also flow to the broader population. In particular, ILM is integral to Australia's pandemic prevention strategies, as Indigenous rangers undertake a large proportion of 'on-the-ground biosecurity work'.[79] These interventions align with the preventative orientation that is characteristic of public health law.[80] In particular, Gostin et al. emphasise the importance of protecting public health by addressing environmental determinants of poor health.[81]

74 Jacobs, 'Negotiating Good Development', 240–241.

75 Woolaston, 'An Argument for Pandemic Risk Management Using a Multidisciplinary One Health Approach to Governance', citing Ian Leiper, Petina Pert, Jocelyn Davies, Cathy Robinson, Fiona Walsh, and Fay Falco-Mammone, 'Quantifying Current and Potential Contributions of Australian Indigenous Peoples to Threatened Species Management', 1040.

76 Jocelyn Davies, David Campbell, Matt Campbell, et al., 'Attention to Four Key Principles Can Promote Health Outcomes from Desert Aboriginal Land Management' (2011) 33(4) *The Rangeland Journal* 417, 420.

77 Katie Woolaston, *Ecological Vulnerability: The Law and Governance of Human-Wildlife Relationships* (Cambridge University Press, 2022) 212.

78 See also Rosalie Schultz, Tammy Abbott, Jessica Yamaguchi, and Sheree Cairney, 'Indigenous Land Management as Primary Health Care: Qualitative Analysis from the Interplay Research Project in Remote Australia' (2018) 18(1) *BMC Health Services Research* 960.

79 Katie Woolaston, *Working Together to Protect Australia in the Age of Pandemics: Managing the Environmental Drivers of Zoonotic Disease Risks* (Queensland University of Technology, 2022) 16–17.

80 Gostin, 'Public Health Law', 13–17.

81 Ibid., 16.

ILM similarly promotes social justice, consistent with the moral foundation of public health law. As Woolaston et al. observe, 'First Nations Australians are disproportionately affected by pandemics',[82] which has the potential to exacerbate existing social inequalities.[83] Implementing ILM to address the ecological determinants of pandemics is therefore central to empowering First Nations people to overcome disadvantage. Nevertheless, on Gostin et al.'s account, ILM is not an example of public health law. This initiative sits outside the ambit of his definition, as Gostin et al. contends that the government is solely responsible for regulating risk.[84] ILM is not a government initiative, as these practices are undertaken by non-state actors, including First Nations people, groups, and organisations.[85] This raises two questions: does ILM fall within Black's conception of *regulation*? And if so, is ILM a method of regulating *risk*?

Returning first to Black's criteria for regulation: intention, the temporal dimension, the problem-solving orientation, and specificity. ILM satisfies the first of these criteria, as it is a deliberate practice that First Nations people engage in, distinct from unintentional forces like weather. Similarly, it reflects the ongoing nature of regulation, due to its longevity. Such practices are deeply rooted in Indigenous culture, having evolved over 50,000 years.[86] ILM is also orientated toward a variety of distinct problems, such as controlling invasive species and habitat restoration. Taken together, these issues are representative of an overarching problem: ecological damage. While ILM encompasses numerous practices, they are unified in their orientation toward this problem.

As Black observes, three outcomes distinguish regulation from other forms of problem-solving: standard setting, information gathering and behaviour modification. Beginning with standard setting, ILM involves altering the environment with reference to standards. For example, fire management is undertaken with reference to 'Indigenous customary patterns and science'.[87] These customary practices are linked to a reduction in greenhouse gases and wildfires.[88] ILM similarly encompasses information gathering. In a survey of 153 ILM projects, Leiper et al. found that monitoring and surveying animals, plants, and ecosystems was the most common activity. These practices centre on recording information about ecological changes to inform conservation management.[89] Finally, ILM includes practices that modify human behaviour to promote One Health. For example, the Yolnga people control access to regions in north-east Arnhem Land using an access permit system. The permits were introduced to combat ecological damage that stemmed from unfettered access.[90]

As ILM satisfies Black's criteria, we contend that it is a form of regulation. We can turn then to our final question: is ILM a method of regulating *risk*? As Gostin et al. observe, balancing the common good against liberty is a defining aspect of public health law.[91] Thus, if ILM is to be a form of public health law, it must balance these competing interests. The Yolnga people

[82] Woolaston, 'An Argument for Pandemic Risk Management Using a Multidisciplinary One Health Approach to Governance'.
[83] Woolaston, 'Ecological Vulnerability', 6.
[84] Gostin, 'Public Health Law', 4–12.
[85] Hill, 'Indigenous Land Management in Australia', 6.
[86] Ibid.
[87] Ibid., 39.
[88] Ibid., 39; Leiper, 'Quantifying Current and Potential Contributions of Australian Indigenous Peoples to Threatened Species Management'.
[89] Leiper, 'Quantifying Current and Potential Contributions of Australian Indigenous Peoples to Threatened Species Management', 1043–1044.
[90] Hill, 'Indigenous Land Management in Australia', 37.
[91] Gostin, 'Public Health Law'.

showcase how ILM regulates risk. Restricting access to land infringes on the liberty of those who would otherwise travel unimpeded. Yet this infringement is justified, as it protects a common good (ecology). Prioritising conservation efforts ultimately benefits public health also, given its interconnectedness with ecology. It follows that ILM embodies the themes that define public health law. We argue that One Health practitioners do more than inform the state's regulation of public health; at least in some cases, their practices are a form of public health law. As such, a decentred conception of public health law is important to the ongoing development of public health law.

17.5 CONCLUSION

In this chapter, we have argued that One Health approaches indicate the need for a re-conceptualisation of public health law. One Health offers an opportunity to move away from Enlightenment presumptions and broaden our understanding of what it means to regulate public health in a non-anthropocentric and de-centred manner. We have argued that a failure to recognise the interdependence between humans and nature unnecessarily limits the scope of public health law and creates barriers to achieving desired public health outcomes. Additionally, the focus on the state as being the only legitimate regulatory actor in the public health space limits the impact of effective, more integrated public health interventions led by non-state actors, particularly in the context of First Nations land management and in a globalised world. What does this mean for the reframing of public health law into the twenty-first century?

We need to begin by reconceptualising the definition of public health law. Returning to Gostin, Wiley, and Frieden's definition of public health law:

> Public health law is the study of the legal powers and duties of *the state* to assure the conditions for *people* to be healthy (to identify, prevent, and ameliorate risks to health in the *population*) and the limitations on the power of *the state* to constrain the autonomy, privacy, liberty, proprietary, or other legally protected interests of individuals for the common good.[92]

The implications of our argument in this chapter are that the definition of public health law needs to move away from its roots in the Enlightenment by addressing its anthropocentric and positivist foundations. The core of public health remains prevention. But effective prevention can only occur by, the evidence, understood broadly, tells us, acknowledging, understanding, and addressing the interconnectedness of people, animals, and the environment. Prevention is also the role of everyone; there are a variety of actors with formal and informal regulatory functions in this space. Building on Gostin, Wiley, and Frieden's definition, a new definition of public health law that moves on from its Enlightenment roots could be:

> Public health law is the study of the formal and informal regulatory tools used by state and non-state actors to assure the conditions for health (to identify, prevent, and ameliorate risks to health in the populations of humans and animals and in the environment).[93]

If we reformulate the definition of public health law in this way, what may some of the practical implications of this be? Currently, actors, government or non-governmental, are often both highly siloed and give pre-eminence to the concerns and needs of humans. A major

[92] Gostin, 'Public Health Law', 4.
[93] Ibid.

reconsideration of the structure and scope of organisational actors would need to occur to enable a One Health-influenced definition of public health law. Decentring public health law from government recognises the broader range of actors in the public health space. It also acknowledges that the impact of capitalism and other political trends sees many governments continue to retreat from comprehensive engagement in the business of prevention, leaving that space open to non-state actors, particularly at the global level. This reformulation has the potential for the employment of and valuing of a wider range of evidence in public health law; important given that what we have traditionally considered evidence is also impacted and constrained by Enlightenment thinking.[94] To address public health effectively, One Health reminds us that we need to attend to our interdependencies with each other, with other animals, and with the environment.[95] The more holistic approach suggested by One Health is critical to the continued evolution of public health law as the twenty-first century progresses.

94 Puppe, 'When the Bough Breaks'.
95 Bakker, 'Towards a New Common Sense'.

18

One Health in South Africa

Tony Gerrans

18.1 INTRODUCTION

Many nature conservation and animal protection advocates argue that thirty years of 'sustainable use' has failed to deliver meaningful ecological sustainability or improved protections for animals from most avoidable harms.[1] This observation is informed by the ongoing decimation of natural abundance and vitality in the pursuit of infinite economic growth within a finite system of resources. Instead, the idea of sustainable use and the sustainable development paradigm have legitimised ever more rapacious forms of exploitation of both animals specifically and the environment more generally. It was recognised as long ago as 2001 that, 'More people are using more resources with more intensity that at any time in human history.'[2] Lavinge argues that, 'The only thing we have managed to sustain, it seems, are the economies of developed nations, and – despite all the evidence to the contrary – the idea that "sustainable development" is the solution to the world's ills. In short, sustainable development … has failed to achieve its objective.'[3]

The One Health policy framework offers an appealing model to policy advocates disillusioned with the sustainable use narrative, because it seeks to expressly align considerations of human, non-human, and environmental health in a single conceptual framework. South Africa has endorsed the One Health Approach, manifesting support for the concept through a National One Health Forum with diverse membership drawn from the national Department of Agriculture, Land Reform and Rural Development (DALRRD), the Department of Health (DOH), the Department of Forestry, Fisheries and the Environment (DFFE), and supported by research institutions, academia, the veterinary industry, environmental health officials, NGOs, and international organisations like the World Health Organization (WHO). Yet

[1] See for example D. Lavigne, 'Wildlife Conservation and the Pursuit of Economic Sustainability: A Brief Introduction' in *Gaining Ground. In Pursuit of Economic Sustainability* (IFAW, Guelph, 2006) 9. In the South African context, the tension between sustainable use and the protection of the environment (and animals in particular) has been highlighted by the Constitutional Court (*Fuel Retailers Association of Southern Africa v. Director-General: Environmental Management, Department of Agriculture, Conservation and Environment, Mpumalanga Province and Others* (CCT67/06) [2007] ZACC 13; 2007 (10) BCLR 1059 (CC); 2007 (6) SA 4 (CC) (7 June 2007)), and in legal opinion interpreting the environmental right in s24 of the Bill of Rights – see Cullinan and Associates, *The Legal Basis for the 'Sustainable Use of Wildlife in South Africa*, 29 September 2016.

[2] This quotation comes from *The Globe and Mail* (Canada), reporting on the Publication of the United Nations Population Division, *World Population Prospects: The 2020 Revision*, Department of Economic and Social Affairs, United Nations (New York, 28 February 2021).

[3] Lavigne, 'Wildlife Conservation and the Pursuit of Economic Sustainability: A Brief Introduction'.

commercial interests continue to expand the exploitation of the environment generally and animals more particularly, often in ways overtly at odds with the ethos of One Health. This is often abetted both in practice and policy by government, with this abetment justified in South Africa by the pressing need for poverty alleviation, which in turn is usually premised on economic growth.

This work will argue that the theoretical appeal of acknowledging the overlapping dependencies that unpin the framework is of itself entirely inadequate to arrest and reverse the destruction of the environment and the institutionalised suffering of animals in practice. It will explore the practical application of One Health in two South African contexts – the commercial ranching of wildlife species and intensive animal agriculture – and examine whether the One Health framework is impacting policy design and implementation in these two contexts. It will close by exploring what might be done to operationalise the philosophy of One Health more fully, and the implications of such progress for the relationship between humans, non-human animals, and the environment.

18.2 UNDERSTANDING THE ONE HEALTH POLICY FRAMEWORK

The rationale of the One Health framework is not new, with the origins of an integrated approach to human and non-human health sciences dating back to the 1800s.[4] The idea of 'one medicine' reflected the intuitive understanding that better health could best be pursued by understanding both the human- and non-human animal condition. In practice, however, veterinary and human medicine have long been institutionally distinct, perhaps reflecting the anthropocentric bias that underpins much western thought on the relationships between human beings and the rest of nature. More recently, growing concerns with zoonotic disease have re-highlighted the interrelationships between human and animal health, and the greater environment as a whole. The One Health concept has been widely promoted by the Food and Agriculture Organization of the United Nations (FAO), the WHO, and the World Organisation of Animal Health (WOAH, known formerly as the OIE) as a tool to address these issues of growing concern.[5]

One Health has many definitions, most of which convey the general idea of converging interests and correspondingly co-operative policy responses across three different spheres of concern: non-human animals, human animals, and the broader environment. Yet few definitions offer any tangible direction as to what form this co-operation should take. This general framing may allow different stakeholders to all embrace common terminology and facilitate dialogue about health concerns at the interface between the three component branches of the concept. Yet, such a broad definition does little to highlight tensions inherent in realising desired outcomes with respect to the interests of humans, good health for animals and a protected environment as a whole. Indeed, as the pressures on animal and environmental health continue to grow under the relentless expansion of human consumption, the concept presents a fresh lens to identify health issues at the human–animal interface (for example, food security and safety, disease management), and perhaps also a deeper look into environmental health (conservation of biodiversity and climate change), but little by way of direction as to how all three issues could be addressed simultaneously.

4 M. Bresalier, A. Cassidy, and A. Woods, *One Health in History. One Health: The Theory and Practice of Integrated Health Approaches.* (Oxfordshire: CABI, 2015) 1–15.

5 P. Gibbs, 'The Evolution of One Health: A Decade of Progress and Challenges for the Future' (2014) 174(4) *Veterinary Record* 85–91.

A further complication arises within our understanding of the term 'health' itself. Human health is generally understood as encompassing both physical and mental well-being, but animal health is still largely considered simply as the absence of physical disease.[6] As the science of animal cognition and subjective experience advances, the mental experiences of animals are becoming better understood, and fulfilment of mental health standards should accordingly be a valid enquiry into the determination of animal health. Giving due regard to the consideration of non-human mental health will have massive implications for industries that currently exploit animals in ways that ignore animals' own interests so as to satisfy human ends, and especially for those who currently measure animal health merely as the absence of disease. Nicks and Vandeheede argue that until such time that mental wellbeing forms a valid part of the enquiry into animal health, considerations of animal welfare should be included within the determination of factors in assessing animal health.[7] Arguments for defining animal health in this way, and the importance of broader welfare concerns as an element of animal health, will be returned to in sections on the use of wildlife and farmed animals below.

18.2.1 *South Africa's Endorsement of One Health in Theory*

The South African National Department of Health (DOH) established the National One Health Forum (NOHF) in 2014 to detect, respond and prevent zoonoses, to comply with the International Health Regulations with respect to the detection and response to zoonotic events in South Africa through improved sectoral collaboration to secure optimal animal, human and environmental health.[8] Local participation mirrored the international tripartite arrangements of the WHO, the FAO and the WOAH; membership of the NOHF includes DALRRD, DOH and DFFE, supplemented by research institutions, academia, vet industry, environmental health officials, and NGOs. The expressed purpose of the forum is to pursue optimal health for people, animals, and the environment, with terms of reference addressing the following priority areas: surveillance programs, gaps and challenges, training needs, to ensure safe food supply, communication, outbreak and disaster preparedness, and identify research gaps.

18.2.2 *The Department of Forestry, Fisheries and the Environment*

In May 2016 a zoonoses prioritisation exercise was attended by an expert group and work is underway in 2024 to develop a One Health Framework and Implementation Plan Adoption of One Health by the DFFE. The DFFE formally recognises One Heath as a significant tool in environmental management, claiming it as an integrating unifying approach that aims to sustainably balance and optimise the health of people, animals, and ecosystems.[9] That department has recognised four focus areas for One Health implementation: Chemicals and Waste Management, Biodiversity and Conservation, Fisheries Management, and Air Quality

[6] B. Nicks and M. Vandenheede, 'Animal Health and Welfare: Equivalent or Complementary' (2014) 33(1) *Revue scientifique et technique / Office international des épizooties* 97.

[7] Ibid., 99.

[8] J. Weyer, webinar on 'The Status of One Health in South Africa, hosted by the National One Health Steering Committee' (19 January 2024). Available at: www.youtube.com/playlist?list=PLtwuO3ftwuo7rLtlLYMey9XFQfrY64JVx.

[9] A. Baker, webinar on 'The Status of One Health in South Africa, hosted by the National One Health Steering Committee' (19 January 2024). Available at: www.youtube.com/playlist?list=PLtwuO3ftwuo7rLtlLYMey9XFQfrY64JVx.

Management.[10] However, despite this program framework, and although the DFFE recognises increased risk of diseases transmission through climate change, negative impacts to biodiversity through land-use change, over-exploitation, pollution, and invasive species impacts, One Health as a management tool barely warrants a mention in a whole raft of recent conservation policy documents made public by the Department. The 2020 'High Level Panel Report of Experts for the Review of Policies, Legislation and Practices on Matters of Elephant, Lion, Leopard and Rhinoceros Management, Breeding, Hunting, Trade and Handling',[11] for example, mentions One Health once in 582 pages of wildlife policy analysis (and only in reporting a stakeholder proposal that it be adapted as a management tool).[12] The 'White Paper on the Conservation and Sustainable Use of South Africa's Biodiversity' does not make a single reference to the concept.[13] Similarly, the 'Policy Position on the Conservation And Ecologically Sustainable Use of Elephant, Lion, Leopard and Rhinoceros', finalised in April 2024, makes no mention of One Health whatsoever.[14] It is clear that the concept is far from being the 'significant tool in environmental management' claimed by the DFFE, much less that it is providing 'an integrating unifying approach that aims to sustainably balance and optimise health of people, animals and ecosystems' as asserted by the DFFE.[15]

18.2.3 *The Department of Agriculture, Land Reform and Rural Development*

The agricultural policy ambitions of DALRRD are set out in the Integrated Growth and Development Policy for Agriculture, Forestry and Fisheries.[16] The Agricultural Policy Action Plan (APAP) seeks to operationalise the policy framework into concrete steps. There is no mention of One Health in the APAP, probably reflecting a pre-Covid, pre-SARS era when zoonotic diseases were not recognised as significant public health concerns.

The DALRRD Ministerial Representative on the South African Veterinary Council has since recognised that, 'We have a common goal of optimal health for humans and animals, and to ensure a sustainable environment for our future existence. The One Health approach brings together expertise and resources to achieve this goal.' However, there is no explanation evident of how this is to be achieved in practice. Notably, DALRRD did not present at the 2024 National One Health Forum Workshop, and there is not a single mention of One Health as an operational tool or performance measure in the DALRRD Annual Performance Plan 2023/24.[17]

10 Ibid.

11 See www.environment.gov.za/sites/default/files/reports/2020-12-22_high-levelpanel_report.pdf.

12 Department of Forestry, Fisheries and the Environment, 'High Level Panel Report of Experts for the Review of Policies, Legislation and Practices on Matters of Elephant, Lion, Leopard and Rhinoceros Management, Breeding, Hunting, Trade and Handling' (December 2020). Available at: www.environment.gov.za/sites/default/files/reports/2020-12-22_high-levelpanel_report.pdf.

13 Department of Forestry, Fisheries and the Environment, 'White Paper on the Conservation and Sustainable Use of South Africa's Biodiversity' (14 June 2023) 48785 *Government Gazette*.

14 Department of Forestry, Fisheries and the Environment, 'Position on the Conservation and Ecologically Sustainable Use of Elephant, Lion, Leopard and Rhinoceros' (24 April 2024) 4750 *Government Gazette*.

15 Baker, 'The Status of One Health in South Africa'.

16 This policy framework was developed when the mandate for forestry and fisheries still vested with the Department of Agriculture (then Department of Agriculture Forestry and Fisheries, now DALRRD) and before it was transferred to DFFE.

17 See www.dalrrd.gov.za/index.php/publications/14-annual-performance-plans?download=1667:annual-performance-plan-2023-to-2024.

18.3 ONE HEALTH AND SUSTAINABLE USE IN PRACTICE

18.3.1 *Sustainable Use as Government Policy*

In 2011, the National Planning Commission published the National Development Plan, a comprehensive analysis document that sought to map out a poly-centric policy framework to reduce poverty in South Africa. It recognised nine central socio-economic challenges requiring integrated solutions.[18] It also recognised that threats to the environment 'are real and growing',[19] and that, '[a]lthough climate change is the chief ecological challenge, others closely linked also pose serious risks such as water scarcity, pollution, food production and safety and depleted fishing stocks'.[20]

The Bill of Rights of the South African Constitution sets out a right to a safe environment, protected for benefit of present and future generations,[21] to be achieved, inter alia, through the fulfilment of positive duties by the state to effect reasonable legislative and other measures directed at the achievement of the specific rights and the general principles of the Constitution. The right to environment in Chapter 2 of the Constitution sets out:

Environment

24. Everyone has the right –

(a) to an environment that is not harmful to their health or wellbeing; and
(b) to have the environment protected, for the benefit of present and future generations, through reasonable legislative and other measures that –
  (i) prevent pollution and ecological degradation;
  (ii) promote conservation; and
  (iii) secure ecologically sustainable development and use of natural resources while promoting justifiable economic and social development.

Clearly the quest for economic growth as a foundation of poverty alleviation exists in tension with protecting and restoring a degraded environment, and this tension is evident in the wording of Section 24(b)(iii). Yet the government did not formalise a definition of the sustainable use of natural resources until June 2023.[22] In the interim, South Africa developed a substantial and diverse range of mature and sophisticated businesses that exploit the environment in new ways, most importantly in this context through the increasing domestication and commodification of wildlife. Such exploitation, which now constitutes a material component of the 'biodiversity economy' and is recognised as such in the National Biodiversity Framework, is premised on the

[18] National Planning Commission, *National Development Plan*, 2011, 3.

[19] Ibid., 73.

[20] Ibid., 69.

[21] The Constitution of the Republic of South Africa 1966 (entered into force on 4 February 1997) Section 24. Available at: www.justice.gov.za/constitution/chp02.html.

[22] Department of Forestry, Fisheries and the Environment, 'White Paper on the Conservation and Sustainable Use of South Africa's Biodiversity', 20; The South African Constitutional Court noted in the *Fuel Retailers* case, that the '[C]onstitution … recognises the need for the protection of the environment while at the same time it recognizes the need for social and economic development … Sustainable development and sustainable use and exploitation of natural resources are at the core of the protection of the environment'. This judgement arguably recognises that economic and environmental interests must be harmonised, but provides no guidance as to how this is to be achieved, given that the former are typically more immediate, more measurable and more aggressively pursued than the latter. See *Fuel Retailers Association of Southern Africa v. Director-General: Environmental Management, Department of Agriculture, Conservation and Environment, Mpumalanga Province and Others* (CCT67/06) [2007] ZACC 13; 2007 (10) BCLR 1059 (CC); 2007 (6) SA 4 (CC) (7 June 2007).

notion of private ownership of wild animals originally established by the Game Theft Act 105 of 1991.[23] South Africa's controversial captive lion breeding industry, with the associated revenue generators of lion cub petting, human interactions with sub-adult animals, canned hunting and lion bone export is an example of this extreme form of private ownership of wild animals. 'Put and take' trophy hunting of managed wildlife species, and the ranching of wildlife for sport hunting, trade, and game meat are further examples.

These activities are premised on an extractivist interpretation of sustainable use, which relies on a reading of Section 24(b)(iii) of the Constitution which favours the 'use of natural resources' wording over the provisions requiring the promotion of conservation, the protection of the environment for the benefit of future generations, *ecologically* sustainable use and *justifiable* economic social and economic *development* (own emphasis). Such views presuppose that the benefits of income-generating activities which are demonstrably harmful to animals and the environment transcend other considerations in the Bill of Rights, such as genuine conservation,[24] the right to live free from violence,[25] and the right to dignity.[26] Many of the activities which intensify the production and exploitation of wildlife come with other policy risks, and they arguably fail to accord with established court jurisprudence recognising that,

> [c]onstitutional values dictate a more caring attitude towards fellow humans, animals and the environment in general, and that the law has recognised that it relates (a)nimal welfare to questions of biodiversity. Animal welfare is connected with the constitutional right to have the "environment protected … through legislative and other means". This integrative approach correctly links the suffering of individual animals to conservation, and illustrates the extent to which showing respect and concern for individual animals reinforces broader environmental protection efforts. Animal welfare and animal conservation together reflect two intertwined values.[27]

Despite this clear statement of the law by the nation's highest court which explicitly rejects an instrumental view of wild animals as commodities, government support for sustainable use of 'faunal resources' remains resolute.[28] In 2023, the Minister of Forestry, Fisheries and the Environment promulgated the Game Meat Strategy of South Africa.[29] This strategy seeks to, inter alia, 'unlock the full potential of the natural game meat industry', with product that is 'ethically produced with less or no impact on the environment or biodiversity', and which is 'safe, traceable and produced within the regulatory framework governing the wildlife sector and food safety protocols'.[30] This sounds good in practice, but South Africa's wildlife ranching industry does not materially fulfil the requirements above. The DFFE's own 2018 'Report on Intensive and Selective Game Breeding' noted that, 'intensive management and selective

23 Section 2(1) of the Game Theft Act 105 of 1991 holds that, 'Notwithstanding the provisions of any other law or the common law – (a) a person who keeps or holds game or on behalf of whom game is kept or held on land that is sufficiently enclosed as contemplated in subsection (2), or who keeps game in a pen or kraal or in or on a vehicle, shall not lose ownership of that game if the game escapes from such enclosed land or from such pen, kraal or vehicle'.

24 *Game Theft Act* 105 of 1991, section 24(b)(ii).

25 Ibid., Section 12(1)(c).

26 Ibid., Section 10.

27 *National Society for the Prevention of Cruelty to Animals v. Minister of Justice and Constitutional Development and Another* [2016] ZACC 46.

28 This way of describing animals as 'faunal resources' is inconsistent with recognising that they are living beings whose health and welfare are a matter of public interest. The National Environmental Management Act of 1998, for example sets out in Section 45(2) that, 'The Minister may, by notice in the Gazette, specify the species and the circumstances under which the State remains the custodian of *faunal biological resources* that escape from land under its control'. (Own emphasis).

29 'Game Meat Strategy' (8 November 2023) 701 *Government Gazette*.

30 'Game Meat Strategy', 5.

breeding of game poses a number of significant risks to biodiversity at the ecosystem and species levels … and may compromise the current and future contribution of the wildlife industry to biodiversity conservation'.[31] The harms inherent in intensive wildlife production include landscape fragmentation, hazardous chemicals, concentration of desired species, killing and/or removal of conflict species, the disruption of normal predation, biological invasion, pest control resistance, rare wild species removal, deleterious gene expression, reduction of genetic material and associated diversity, outbreeding depression, physiological stress, species domestication, the disruption of natural selection and reduced meat for human consumption.[32] Given this extensive list of identified harms, it is not surprising that a central recommendation of the 'Report on Intensive and Selective Game Breeding' was to phase out intensive wildlife production, a recommendation entirely inconsistent with the sustainable use business model of much of the wildlife ranching industry in South Africa.

Here we see then a practical demonstration that the pursuit of the human leg of the One Health triad, in this illustrative case of the sustainable use doctrine manifesting in the DFFE's Game Meat Strategy, has very real and apparent detriment to the other two legs. Given that the Game Meat Strategy also proposes self-regulation of the industry, it is apparent that the pursuit of this form of sustainable use can hardly be understood to fulfil the One Health Framework at all. Indeed, this is arguably the case for many elements of the biodiversity economy: the intensification practices on which wildlife ranching, captive breeding, and 'put-and-take' trophy hunting depend often pose significant risks not only for animals but also for human and environmental health.

18.3.2 *One Health in Practice and Intensive Animal Agriculture*

We know now that the intensification of production of wild animal species, in systems that increasingly mirror methods of agricultural production, can lead to practices inconsistent with the sound management of biodiversity.[33] Habitat fragmentation, intolerance for predators, selective breeding for unnatural traits, and overstocking of preferred species have negative impact on both biodiversity and animal health. The transport of animals, intensive confinement, poor genetics, and inappropriate diet can also escalate disease risk. These issues are not confined to wildlife ranching. They manifest most significantly in the context of intensive animal production for food. Furthermore, the looming public health challenges of zoonotic disease and anti-microbial resistance are most obviously illustrated in the context of intensive animal agriculture. Concentrated animal feeding organisations are now comprehensively recognised as potential reservoirs for both animal and human disease, posing a substantial and immediate risk to public health.[34] They are also the largest sectoral contributors to both terrestrial and marine

[31] Department of Forestry, Fisheries and the Environment, 'High Level Panel Report of Experts for the Review of Policies, Legislation and Practices on Matters of Elephant, Lion, Leopard and Rhinoceros Management, Breeding, Hunting, Trade and Handling' (December 2020) 97. Last accessed on 25 February 2024. Available at: www.environment.gov.za/sites/default/files/reports/2020-12-22_high-levelpanel_report.pdf.

[32] Department of Forestry, Fisheries and the Environment, 'High Level Panel Report of Experts for the Review of Policies, Legislation and Practices on Matters of Elephant, Lion, Leopard and Rhinoceros Management, Breeding, Hunting, Trade and Handling', 98.

[33] N. Banasiak, J. Shaw, L. Rall, and N. Vundla, *Connecting South Africa's Wildlife, Landscapes And People* (WWF-SA: Cape Town, South Africa, 2019) 11.

[34] G.Rambozzi, L. Bonizzi, E. Crespi, et al., 'Emerging Zoonoses: The "One Health Approach"' (2012) 3 *Safety and Health Work* 77–83. Available at: http://dx.doi.org/10.5491/SHAW.2012.3.1.77.

pollution,[35] as well as a significant driver of both biodiversity loss,[36] as well as climate change.[37] There are increasing calls for specific preventative interventions to address diseases like Highly Pathogenic Avian Influenza (HPAI) and Severe Acute Respiratory Syndrome (SARS). Indeed the revival of One Health as a relevant policy framework owes much to the challenges posed by these diseases.

Yet, little is being done to address the root causes of these zoonoses. The numbers of animals raised and killed for food globally continues to rise, now at 83.3 billion terrestrial animals per year at the last count.[38] Most of these animals are raised in intensive confinement facilities. The UN forecasts that demand for meat will continue to rise, and growing calls for transitions to plant-based food systems are yet to yield meaningful change in practice.[39] The animals used in these systems cannot be understood to enjoy even the narrow definition of health (freedom from disease), much less the broader definition that gives regard to their mental wellbeing. Indeed, these facilities are typically the antitheses of healthy, high-welfare animal husbandry. To the extent it is being applied to this massive and unsustainable industry, the One Health framework is used to motivate not for structural reform (reduction in intensive animal production) but for symptomatic technology solutions (new vaccines to counter disease and new genetics for improved 'natural' resistance).[40] Yet there is no escaping the environmental costs: the pollution impacts and reduction in the food balance by growing feed for animals instead of food for people simply cannot be ignored.

In 2023, the South African animal production sector battled a range of farmed animal diseases including blue tongue, African swine fever, highly pathogenic avian influenza (HPAI) and African Horse Sickness.[41] DALRRD has active programs to manage HPAI, yet despite these programs in 2023 the poultry industry lost 8.5 million birds due to disease and or pre-emptive culling.[42] There has been a prolonged national shortage of vaccines, leading to material animal health issues, further highlighting the vulnerability of this sector to animal disease. Yet, the DALRRD website continues to promote the production of pigs, sheep, goats, and cattle as part of that organisation's development agenda. The stated aim of the Animal Production directorate is

> to make sure that the livestock industry performs at its optimum capacity, with emphasis on providing support to emerging black farmers to be able to participate in the mainstream activities (e.g. marketing, value-add etc.), through introduction of programmes such as the Kaonafatso ya Dikgomo (Cattle Improvement), Provincial Aquaculture, Milk Recording, and Livestock

35 United Nations Food and Agriculture Organization, 'Livestock's Long Shadow' (2006) *The Livestock Environment and Development Initiative*.

36 Ibid.

37 IPCC, 'Summary for Policymakers. In: Climate Change And Land: An IPCC Special Report on Climate Change, Desertification, Land Degradation, Sustainable Land Management, Food Security, And Greenhouse Gas Fluxes In Terrestrial Ecosystems' (2019) 13. P.R. Shukla, J. Skea, E. Calvo Buendia, et al. (eds.). Available at: https://doi.org/10.1017/9781009157988.001.

38 See www.fao.org/faostat/en/#home.

39 United Nations Food and Agriculture Organization, 'The State of Food Insecurity in the World' (2013); United Nations General Assembly, 'Critical Perspective on Food Systems, Food Crises and the Future Right to Food: Report of the Special Rapporteur' (21 January 2020). Available at: https://documents-dds-ny.un.org/doc/UNDOC/GEN/G20/015/74/PDF/G2001574.pdf?OpenElement.

40 See 'SA and Poultry Sector Mull the Use of Vaccinations'. Available at: www.iol.co.za/business-report/economy/sa-and-poultry-sector-mull-the-use-of-vaccinations-bef65ef3-fe1e-4db4-8cd1-11edd1e5db3f.

41 The Department of Agriculture Land Reform and Rural Development, *Annual Performance Action Plan 2023/24* catalogues at p. 38 the extensive list of farmed animal diseases currently affecting livestock production. The report is available at www.dalrrd.gov.za/images/Docs/annual-performance-plan-2023-to-2024.pdf.

42 See also www.sapoultry.co.za/hpai-and-the-poultry-industrys-recovery-status/.

and Poultry support within rural development nodes. Other key programmes include the Goat Productivity Improvement and the Development of Feedlot/Grasslot facilities within the rural development nodes[43]

In 2021 DALRRD proposed further amendments to Meat Safety and Animal Improvement Acts which would have facilitated the intensification of wildlife production. This initiative is entirely contrary to the DFFE policy of reversing the intensification of wildlife ranching. There is no acknowledgement within the agricultural policy framework of the environmental and human health harms implicit in these strategies, much less an effort to align policy within a multicentric framework such as One Health.

18.4 CRITIQUE OF ONE HEALTH FRAMEWORK IN PRACTICE

It is clear that the One Health model has brought a positive impact at a global policy level. In March 2022, the United Nations Environment Program joined the so-called global Tripartite – the FAO of the United Nations, the WHO, and the WOAH – to form the Quadripartite. In the year that followed, the Kunming-Montreal Global Diversity Framework was agreed, and the UN General Assembly resolved that a clean, healthy, and sustainable environment is a basic human right. Inger Andersen, the Under-Secretary General of the United Nations and Executive Director of the United Nations Environment Program claims that the One Health Joint Plan of Action and the associated One Health High-level Panel have been instrumental in this progress.[44]

Yet even Ms Andersen recognises that operationalising One Health will be a key challenge. She argues that, 'We must ensure that the world fully understands and acts on the overarching drivers of health risk, including climate change, land-use change, and environmental degradation',[45] noting that the One Health approach must be integrated into national biodiversity strategies and action plans, and must support sustainable food systems transitions. But there is precious little by way of practical steps on how this might be achieved. So although we are seeing movement in terms of global policy, One Health remains a challenging concept to implement in practice at a national level. There are two salient reasons for this, explored in more detail in the South African context.

18.4.1 *One Health Not Applied in South Africa's Policy Framework*

Although both the DFFE and to a lesser extent DALRRD profess to embrace the One Health framework in principle, we see in practice that it is not employed in any meaningful way to inform policy. It is virtually invisible in both the wildlife and agricultural policy frameworks. Unless it is actively adopted in the policy frameworks of environmental conservation, agriculture, and health, it is difficult to imagine how it can have any impact whatsoever. One other alternative might offer more prospects for adoption, and that is to embed One Health in the poly-centric policy framework of a 'just transition'. This will be explained further in the final sections of this chapter.

[43] See www.dalrrd.gov.za/index.php/core-business/agricultural-production/animal-production.

[44] I. Andersen, 'The Quadripartite Alliance and One Health'. Speech delivered for the 1st Quadripartite Executive Annual Meeting, Geneva (27 March 2023). Available at: https://unep.org/resources/filter/type=article/story_type=408.

[45] Speech delivered by Inger Anderson, 'The Quadripartite Alliance and One Health', 27 March 2023, accessed at: www.unep.org/news-and-stories/speech/quadripartite-alliance-and-one-health.

18.4.2 *Anthropocentric Bias in Implementation*

The One Health framework aspires to frame a dialogue about balancing different requirements which manifest harm and benefit over different time scales. It seeks to reconcile short-term easily quantifiable commercial benefits to humans (human food supply, for example) with externalised harms to non-humans (animal health, which in the broader sense includes welfare) and negative impacts on the greater environment (eliminating pollution and promoting conservation). It is an attractive idea that these three outcomes can and should be aligned, but at an implementation level, we find they often exist in tension. The pursuit of low-cost food derived from animal sources continues to come at significant cost to animal health and the broader environment. These costs are now so severe, ironically, that they are starting to feed back and impact human health, through poor diet, zoonotic disease, degraded water and air, destruction of biodiversity, and climate change. Far from balancing the needs of the One Health triad, our modern global economy continues to externalise costs onto vulnerable groups, animals and the environment, and the calls for reform find their origins not in a One Health analysis, but principally in anthropocentric concerns about human needs.

18.5 CONCLUSIONS

Proper fulfilment of the One Health framework will require not just the symbolic adoption of an ethos of One Health, but a deliberate conscious effort to make significant practical changes to the way political and economic systems currently interact with animals and the broader environment. If the concept is to yield meaningful practical impact, the second and third legs of the One Health triad cannot continue to be subordinated to short-term anthropocentric interests. The underlying assumption of human exceptionalism will have to yield to an eco-centric consciousness which in turn informs new ways of organising human society that give due regard to the protection of animal health (in the broader sense) and the health of the environment. We already know that free-market forces need to be tempered to protect vulnerable groups – women, children, minorities, animals – from the logic of neo-liberal capitalist wealth accumulation, and to sustain the ecological systems on which all life ultimately depends. Giving proper effect to the One Health framework will require a greater deference to our common interests of protecting the environment and all beings that live within it.

In agriculture, a meaningful adoption of One Health would require a transition away from intensive high-volume animal production as a cornerstone of contemporary food systems. To do so we would need radical changes: true-cost accounting food production, and major policy and legislative shifts to recognise externalised costs and restrict relevant industries accordingly. We would need to end subsidies for harmful agricultural and environmental practices and materially support environmentally friendly food production systems. We would need to challenge corporate power in the food systems, addressing the practical immunity of vertically integrated food companies for harms currently externalised with transparent mechanisms addressing direct corporate, shareholder, and director liability for harms caused to animals and the environment.

In the conservation space, we would similarly need to transition management frameworks away from limited protected areas and the sustainable use of natural resources by the wealthy towards an ecosystem approach to health and conservation policy. Such a transition would recognise the public interest in protected ecosystem services and limit the private harvesting of such benefits by giving due regard to animal (in the broader sense) and environmental health.

At a minimum, this would require reframing the sustainable use/development narrative to incorporate human and animal health risks and genuine environmental conservation concerns.

The Wild Law Institute has proposed a new conceptual framework of harmonious co-existence to regulate our interactions with nature.[46] Building from the 2022 Conference of the Parties to the Convention on Biodiversity, and the 2050 Vision for Biodiversity of the Kunming-Montreal Global Biodiversity Framework, harmonious coexistence seeks to displace the assumption that economic growth will increase social wellbeing with a new narrative that puts ecological sustainability at the centre of governance. Such a framework takes an eco-centric management approach, replacing the human-centric ethos which prevails currently, one which gives due regard to the inter-connectedness, and inter-dependency of all life on earth. As such, it provides a conceptual foundation for frameworks such as One Health and provides clear direction that economic expediency should no longer crowd out valid considerations of animal and ecosystem health.

Implementing changes such as those proposed above will require the unseating of multiple powerful groups with interests vested in the status quo. This seems unlikely without legislative intervention. Current struggles to agree on and implement climate change mitigation strategies, and to restrict only a few of the more egregious harms suffered by animals in food production and wildlife ranching demonstrate the enormity of this challenge.

Murcott has argued that the concept of 'transformative constitutionalism' can facilitate a more eco-centric approach to law and policy in South Africa.[47] She recognises that the environmental right in the South African Constitution imposes a positive duty on the state to take reasonable measures to protect the environment for present and future generations. She argues further that the implementation of the National Environmental Management Act is to be informed by principles that require the avoidance or at least the minimisation of harm to the environment,[48] and that social justice, 'is dependent on well-functioning ecological systems'. In other words, the Constitution requires not only fulfilling the specific rights in the Bill of Rights, but more generally, the fulfilment of the social justice outcomes set out in the Preamble requires good environmental health. Protecting the environment therefore becomes a necessary condition of constitutional fulfilment and social justice, not a trade-off to be considered when considering short-term human expediency. By recognising both the immediate and future requirement of a protected environment as an element of social justice, the environmental health leg of the One Health triad is emphasised, and may not be dismissed in subordination to short-term human interests.

Similarly, in South Africa's response to the climate change crisis, the Presidential Climate Change Commission has adopted a 'Just Transition' framework.[49] Clearly the required transition to a low-carbon economy will adversely affect some people and advantage others. Understood in the narrow sense, the notion of a just transition requires the protection of those persons who lose livelihoods; for example, those in the thermal coal power generation value chain. But in the broader sense, a just transition must also consider those who suffer the impacts of climate change, for whom urgent mitigation is no longer sufficient and urgent assistance in adapting to a new climate reality is a priority. Of course, climate change affects more than just the climate. Biodiversity is materially impacted as well, and climate change can be understood

[46] From an unpublished report by the Wild Law Institute, 'Harmonious Coexistence within Nature: Re-envisioning our Relationship with Nature' (26 March 2023).

[47] M. Murcott, *Transformative Environmental Constitutionalism* (Brill Bijhoff, 2020), XI.

[48] National Environmental Management Act 107 of 1998, South African Government, Section 2.

[49] See www.climatecommission.org.za/just-transition-framework.

as a major driver undermining ecological sustainability. A just transition therefore *requires* due regard be given to environmental health as a whole and the health of the animals with whom we share that environment more specifically. Framing the One Health Triad this way mitigates against the subordination of environmental and animal health; it provides a more engaged and nuanced argument that all three elements need to be sustained simultaneously.

Our current reality of inter-related poly-centric socio-ecological crises requires an urgent response from all governance stakeholders. The One Health framework offers a useful tool to re-frame current human exceptionalism, perhaps by replacing narratives of human exceptionalism and sustainable use and development. But to be effective, it will have to be adopted in practice, not just in principle and implemented by skilled and committed stakeholders capable of driving real change within and beyond current economic and governance practices. Even if this is the case, it is unlikely that the One Health Framework alone will yield the type of systemic change required to secure human, environmental, and animal health. It will need to be supported by 'roadmaps' or workplans with clear policy outcomes, which expressly and systematically target all practices that undermine human and environmental health if it is to be effective. By linking poor animal and environmental health back to detriment to human health, the One Health framework may be one tool to start this urgent and critical process. Building the model from a framework into a practical transparent model of change could be an important first step.

Index

For EU product safety concerns, contact us at Calle de José Abascal, 56–1°,
28003 Madrid, Spain or eugpsr@cambridge.org.

www.ingramcontent.com/pod-product-compliance
Ingram Content Group UK Ltd.
Pitfield, Milton Keynes, MK11 3LW, UK
UKHW050955290926
15470UKWH00006B/1829

* 9 7 8 1 0 0 9 6 5 3 7 1 8 *